DOUGLAS FLAMMING

CREATING

THE MODERN

SOUTH

THE UNIVERSITY OF
MILLHANDS AND

NORTH CAROLINA PRESS
MANAGERS IN

CHAPEL HILL
DALTON, GEORGIA,

AND LONDON
1884-1984

96   95   94   93   92   5   4   3   2   1

Library of Congress Cataloging-in-Publication Data

Flamming, Douglas.
    Creating the modern South : millhands and managers in
Dalton, Georgia, 1884–1984 / Douglas Flamming.
      p.   cm. — (The Fred W. Morrison series in Southern
studies)
    Includes bibliographical references and index.
    ISBN 0-8078-2056-3 (alk. paper)
    1. Crown Cotton Mills Co. (Dalton, Ga.)—History.
2. Cotton textile industry—Georgia—Dalton—History.
3. Dalton (Ga.)—Economic conditions.   4. Southern States—
Industries—Case studies. I. Title. II. Series.
HD9884.U64C764   1992
338.7'67721'09758324—dc20

                                          92-53624
                                            CIP

For Dave

WHOM WE LOST

AND FOR

BETSY, ANNA, CATHEY, AND SARAH

WHOM WE LOVE

CONTENTS

ILLUSTRATIONS

TABLES, FIGURES, & MAPS

FIGURES

Maps

ACKNOWLEDGMENTS

It is with great pleasure that I recognize those who helped me create this book. Without the help of fellow historians, librarians, academic institutions, and historical foundations, I might not have made it. Without the fine people of Dalton, Georgia, and the inspiration of friends and family, I know I never would have.

My interest in southern industrialization began when I was a doctoral student at Vanderbilt University, where it was my good fortune to work with many fine historians who were actively reinterpreting the region's past. My mentor, Don H. Doyle, deserves much of the credit for whatever merit this book possesses. He embodies the best qualities of both a fine academic and a decent human being, and I am more grateful for his influence than he could possibly know. David L. Carlton brought his remarkable knowledge of southern history to the topic and generously offered encouragement, challenging critiques, and sound advice. Paul K. Conkin, Donald L. Winters, and sociologist Barratt A. Lee also deserve a hearty thanks for all of their advice and support. The Southern Social History Group at Vanderbilt offered helpful criticism of my work in its initial stages. I want especially to thank Mary Ann DeCredico,

Robert Tracy McKenzie, and Henry M. McKiven, Jr., for their thoughtful suggestions and their enduring friendship. Robert Hall encouraged me to look beyond
the United States and shared his wide-ranging knowledge of European labor history. John M. Glen lent me his expertise on southern Appalachia and labor radicalism. Charles S. Thomas III, a native Daltonian and fellow historian out of Vanderbilt, generously read every chapter I sent his way and remained unfailingly
enthusiastic to the end.

At the Virginia Polytechnic Institute and State University in 1987–88, I was
encouraged by many gracious and insightful colleagues. Special thanks to Kathleen
Hilton, Richard Hirsh, Tom Howe, Mary Neth, Crandall A. Shifflett, and Peter
Wallenstein, all of whom took time to discuss my work.

In my current position at the California Institute of Technology, it has been my
privilege to work with some remarkable scholars. Many thanks go to J. Morgan
Kousser, a critic of no meager intensity, who has always pushed me to improve the
depth and rigor of my work. His careful, insightful readings of this manuscript
were most rewarding. Beyond academic matters, he has befriended me and my
family in countless immeasurable ways. Daniel J. Kevles has been a steady source of
worthy advice, needed encouragement, and intellectual inspiration. He is a fine
friend and a scholar of the highest caliber. Will T. Jones, James Z. Lee, Martin
Ridge, and the late David Smith all sounded out my ideas and forced me to
sharpen my arguments. Lance E. Davis offered indispensable advice on analyzing
wages. Laird Boswell, Glen Bugos, and Leonard J. Moore lent me their expertise in
related fields and helped me consider the broader implications of my own story.
William Deverell carefully critiqued drafts of the first ten chapters and helped me
view the complexities of paternalism through a larger lens, all the while providing
an abundance of camaraderie.

The many scholars around the country who took the time to read and think
about my work convinced me that the "community of scholars" is alive and well.
At various conferences over the years, commentators have accepted and rejected
my arguments and contributed significantly to the overall work. I have always
appreciated, if not always appropriated, every bit of advice. In this regard, thanks
to Bess Beatty, Richard Boyden, Ronald D Eller, Barbara S. Griffith, Jacquelyn
Dowd Hall, J. Kenneth Morland, Steve Rosswurm, and Nan Woodruff. James A.
Hodges has been one of my most valued intellectual confidants, ever ready with
good humor and a good eye for arguments that cannot hold water. My friends in
the Los Angeles Social History Group have commented on versions of several key
chapters, and their insights have been of inestimable value. Many thanks to Hal S.
Barron, Sanford M. Jacoby, John H. M. Laslett, Jackie Greenberg, Nancy Fitch,
Leila Zenderland, Dorothee Schneider, Robert A. Slayton, Frank Stricker, and
Devera Weber. Steven J. Ross, also part of this group, deserves a very special word
of appreciation. He braved the entire manuscript twice and never failed to offer
encouragement, friendship, and wise counsel. He is a superb critic.

Many thanks to Edward L. Ayers, a reader for the University of North Carolina Press, whose gracious support for this book helped spur me on and whose helpful suggestions on two separate versions of the manuscript greatly improved the final product. An anonymous reader for the Press made beneficial comments on an early draft of this book. None of these scholars, of course, should be held accountable for what I did—or did not do—with their suggestions.

I want to express my appreciation to everyone at the University of North Carolina Press who supported this project. Special thanks to Lewis Bateman, who provided timely encouragement and who handled this book with skill and patience. It was also a sincere pleasure to work with Pamela Upton, whose conscientious and helpful editing saved the day.

A variety of institutions supported the research and writing of this book, including the Museum of American Textile History and Vanderbilt University. Very special thanks to David Grether and Susan Davis of the Division of Humanities and Social Sciences at Caltech for coming through with generous and much-needed funding for new research and for giving me time to expand and enhance the manuscript. At Caltech I also had the invaluable assistance of Gina Morea and Helga Galvan, who shouldered more tasks for me than they should have and who worked hard to make this book a reality. Eric Fung and Craig Volden, former Caltech students, contributed important research assistance.

Library and archive staffs around the country deserve recognition for jobs well done. The interlibrary loan staff of the Vanderbilt University Library dutifully hauled in loads of material during my graduate days. The Georgia Department of Archives and History rendered needed assistance. The fine scholars at the Southern Labor Archives at Georgia State University finally tracked down the records of the Crown workers' union (TWUA Local 185), and they dug up important material on the Dalton Red Scare of 1955. Special thanks go to Robert Dinwiddie, Les Hough, and Cliff Kuhn and to their colleagues at Georgia State University, Gary Fink and Merl Reed, who took an interest in my work and made me welcome in Atlanta. The State Historical Society of Wisconsin at the University of Wisconsin, Madison, was a delightful place to work, and the staff there helped me go through the national TWUA records for the 1930s. The Appalachian Collection at the Virginia Polytechnic Institute and State University Library made copies of my oral history tapes and accepted them as a part of the collection. The Caltech librarians deserve a medal for putting up with my unending requests for new materials. Thanks especially to Tess Legaspi and the staff of interlibrary loan for being my lifeline to southern sources, and to Nancy Brown, Alma Feuerabendt, Barbara Huff-Duff, Janet Jenks, Judy Nollar, and Kathleen Potter for their indispensable assistance.

My greatest archival debt is to Polly Boggess and the Crown Gardens and Archives in Dalton, Georgia. Polly, the director of Crown Gardens, did everything possible to facilitate my use of the Crown Mill records. She also introduced me to dozens of Crown's former millhands; without her, my Crown Cotton Mill oral history project might never have gotten rolling. She is a true gem. Many thanks as well to Jean Breeden, Mary Gene Dykes, and Jean Manly, all of whom offered hospitality and assistance. Eugenia Cavender and Marsha Hoole of the Dalton Regional Library, with its nice collection of microfilm newspapers and Dalton memorabilia, were also a great help to me.

The people of Dalton helped me in every conceivable way. I cannot possibly mention everyone who showed me kindness or extended a helping hand during my stays there, for the list would be far too long to print. James R. Litterdale was an always reliable source of hospitality. The Whitfield-Murray County Historical Society allowed me to stay in Dalton's historic Blunt House during the summer of 1985. Archie Gallman and the good folks at H&S Office Supply let me use their machines to make extra-large photocopies of Crown's massive payroll ledgers. The staff of the Whitfield County Superior Court Clerk's Office helped me navigate through county records and court case documents. Historian Tom Deaton of Dalton College shared his knowledge of the carpet industry's early years. Dean Smith, Jr., gave me a tour of CrownAmerica's Phelps plant and helped me understand the present state of southern textiles. Charles S. Thomas, Jr., father of the aforementioned historian, deserves a special commendation for making it possible for me to take an inside look at Dalton's modern carpet industry.

The officers of CrownAmerica, Inc., successor of the Crown Cotton Mills, went out of their way to assist my research. Before I had ever heard of Dalton, they had saved the old Crown Mill records from destruction and, much to their credit, had made those records available to the public. Moreover, they gave me access to documents preserved in the company office, including the first board of directors minutes book and the more recent stockholders reports of CrownAmerica. David D. Hamilton, the last president of Crown Mills and currently head of Crown-America, took time for a formal interview and offered insightful perspectives on the development of southern industry. Harmon Conner, Crown Mill's last personnel director, organized the annual company reunions, where I learned a great deal from returning millhands.

A profound expression of thanks goes to those former Crown Mill workers and their children, who let me intrude on their time and their memories. Some people shared their stories with me informally, at reunions and picnics and on front porches. Others, to whom I am most indebted, gave formal oral history interviews. They included John Bramblett, Sarah Bunch, Bishop Caylor, J. W. Crow, Hazel Cruce, Willie Mae Defore, Desmond Ellis, the late Ed Felker, Anna Nell Garren, Lucile Hall, Earl Hardin, the late Lillie Ann Hill, Juanita Hughes, Patricia Lowrance, Thelma Parker, Sibyl Queen, the late Nancy Rogers, Marselle Thompson, and Henry Wade. I cannot possibly convey to these fine people and their families the importance of their contributions to this book. I will forever be grateful to all of them. Special thanks go to Lucile Hall, who introduced me to many other former millhands and fed me one of the most amazing dinners ever; to Sarah Bunch, who assisted in my interview with Hazel Cruce; to Pat Lowrance for a personal tour of the old mill village; to Lillie Hill, who let me borrow her remarkable social security notebook and gave me access to her photo collection; to Thelma Parker, who shared her photo collection; and to Earl Hardin, who invited me to the annual Crown Mill "oldtimers" baseball picnic, where I heard many wonderful tales, a few of which were actually true and many more that should have been.

For the people of Dalton, I need to add that the story told herein is not without controversy; some of it is downright explosive. And I am keenly aware that many of the people and families represented in this story are still residents of Dalton and still feel deeply about these events. For the record, I should say that I struggled to be fair to everyone involved: to explain conflicts not in terms of good versus evil but in terms of differing viewpoints; to understand behavior, not condemn it. My biases doubtless show through, however, and some Daltonians may feel I have misrepresented them or their families. In the end, though, historians have to tell it like they see it. I have made mistakes, no doubt, but I hope the people of Dalton will understand that they were honest ones.

It has long been customary for authors to save their final acknowledgments for family. I used to think this was simply a matter of convention, but now I realize it is because those who are closest to us give our work a deeper meaning than it otherwise would have. My family could not have been more supportive during the many years I spent researching and writing this book, and I wish to thank them one and all. Warmest appreciation to my grandfather, Dr. Jesse J. Northcutt, who bought my books through college and who always kept the faith; to Jim, who taught me the meaning of work; to Shirley, who showed me the importance of creativity; and to my brother, J. Dee, who taught me how to fight and how to laugh. Mere words cannot express how thankful I am for my wife, Judith Crothers, whose career inspires my own and whose life I am so lucky to share; and for our newborn son, Peter, who is my joy.

This work is dedicated to the memory of Peter Dave Flamming, my brother and best friend. We lost him to cancer, but not before he showed us how to live. And it is dedicated to his wife, Betsy, and his daughters, Anna, Cathey, and Sarah, whom he so dearly loved, and in whom his spirit of courage and grace so clearly abides.

Nothing so clearly dominated the landscape of the post–Civil War South as the region's cotton textile mills. They were new and imposing—bulky, red-brick factories with towering smokestacks and belfries—and many southerners viewed them in light of the struggle to rebuild their war-torn economy. Beginning in the 1880s and with increasing speed thereafter, cotton mills sprang up in towns and small cities throughout the hilly upcountry, a section of the South previously known for its self-sufficient yeoman farmers and its economic isolation. As the textile industry boomed, the South's economic core shifted from the Plantation Belt to the emerging urban centers of the upcountry, and by the mid-1920s the productive capacity of Dixie's cotton mills exceeded even that of New England. The rise of the mills marked the advent of large-scale manufacturing in an overwhelmingly rural and agricultural world and reflected a fundamental transformation in southern life—a transformation as much social as economic. The owners and managers of the early mills were mostly local merchants and financiers who had no previous experience running factories or employing large numbers of workers. The millhands were country-bred southern whites, most of whom had never worked for cash wages, much less in a factory. When the traditional farm economy began to collapse after the war, entire families went to work in the mills, eventually settling in company-owned mill villages that represented a new way of life for the region's poor whites. Within this setting, a small group of industrialists and a large population of millhands gradually, sometimes painfully, worked out the terms of industrial order in the New South.

One of those new southern mills was the Crown Cotton Mills Company, established in 1884 by local entrepreneurs in Dalton, Georgia, a small but growing agricultural depot in the northwest part of the state. Crown struggled during its early years but grew rapidly between the mid-1890s and the end of World War I, expanding its payroll to nearly one thousand workers and enlarging the size of its mill village to accommodate hundreds of families. By the 1920s an elaborate system of corporate paternalism had developed that included an assortment of nonwage economic benefits as well as a variety of programs intended to create a thriving corporate culture, such as mill-sponsored athletic teams and a company band. As it happened, this paternalistic system could not withstand the economic pressures of the Great Depression, which slashed company profits and pushed hard-hit millhands to the wall. For complex reasons rooted in paternalism, the millhands organized a union in the 1930s, a labor organization that, despite considerable opposition, became a permanent part of the Crown Mill community. World War II ended the depression and ensured paternalism's demise, as war production opened new labor markets and granted workers a time of economic progress and union growth. But the postwar decades proved chaotic for the Crown Mill community when textile-market volatility, postwar anticommunism, and regional economic changes placed both management and labor in precarious positions. Even as the South made substantial gains within the American economy during the 1960s, traditional cotton textiles plunged toward disaster, and as the decade drew to a close, Crown's corporate directors shut down their aging Dalton mills and moved into a new line of manufacturing. Crown was the last old-line cotton mill in town to close shop. Its demise signaled the end of an era for Dalton and, in a larger sense, for the South.

This book is about the people of Crown—about the business leaders who built and managed the mill and the thousands of mill-worker families who made it run. It is the story of how millhands and managers brought the industrial revolution to the American South. Although I hope the people of Dalton and Crown Mill recognize their past in this rendition of it, my larger purpose is to explore the social consequences of industrialization and to determine how the southern experience fits into the larger pattern of American development. The book's title, *Creating the Modern South*, is intended to emphasize that the industrial revolution was not an invisible and mysterious economic force that rolled across the South. Modern industrial society is better understood as the end result of a dynamic process of exchange between groups of corporate managers and workers. The interaction between mill officials and wage earners at Crown sometimes led to conflict and occasionally to violent confrontations. But efforts at compromise and consensus were equally important. The workers had only limited power to control their own lives, but they were never slaves to the industrial system, and they worked hard, sometimes collectively, to shape that system to their advantage. Not all decisions worked out as planned. Both managers and millhands saw schemes go awry; both confronted the ironies of unintended consequences. But, as the story of Crown makes clear, failure and ambiguity were as much a part of the industrializing process as success and predictability.

Creation, as I use the term here, is intended to mean an ongoing process, not a single event. The behavior of Dixie's mill officials and wage earners hinged on a variety of factors—the condition of the southern economy, the availability of factory labor, the power of unions, the flow of world events, the influence of state and national labor legislation—all of which changed over time. The landscape of southern industrial relations was mapped and remapped on a regular basis, and when we analyze the entire course of Crown's history, the details of that process become much clearer. By *industrialization* I mean not simply the arrival of large-scale manufacturing enterprises, but also the entire constellation of events that accompanied factory building: rapid improvements in transportation and communication; an expanding dependence on distant markets; the decline of self-sufficient agriculture and traditional crafts; the growing importance of corporations and corporate power; the development of a permanent wage-earning population; the advent of retail consumerism; the emergence of permanent bureaucratic organizations for solving socioeconomic problems; in short, all of the interrelated developments that, for want of a better term, we call economic modernization. I use the term *modern* to mean this larger process of industrialization. Modernization did not happen suddenly or mechanistically; nor were the outcomes inevitable. But all of these interrelated phenomena became part of the historical reality of the Western world, and my task here is to understand how common, everyday southerners reacted to and shaped that reality.

Less than a decade ago, southern labor history was a largely underdeveloped and isolated area of study.[1] But in recent years this trend has changed dramatically, as a spate of books, articles, and dissertations on southern workers has lifted the field to new levels of richness and significance.[2] Far from remaining an intellectual backwash, southern labor history has emerged as one of the most vibrant fields in American historiography. The story of Dixie's cotton-mill workers has been at the heart of this resurgence. In the past six years alone, three major works on southern millhands have appeared, each of which has deepened our knowledge of southern industrialization and enriched our understanding of the people who were part of that process.[3]

Yet there is more to be said. These recent works are regional surveys of mill workers, and as such they lack the detail and focus necessary for an adequate representation of mill-village life and how it changed over time. To understand any community of workers we must first gather a good deal of information about individuals within that group. This book, for example, traces individual workers as they moved into and out of the mill during the early twentieth century, thereby illuminating previously undetermined patterns of labor migration and clarifying the way in which mill workers and sharecroppers confronted the emerging industrial system. Such microanalysis is possible only through a detailed community study. Local-level research also makes it possible to blend quantitative methods with oral histories and other traditional sources. Despite a long precedent of sophisticated quantification among historians of southern politics and agriculture, southern labor historians have been slow to use statistical methods of analysis.[4] In this book, I have drawn on census data and company records to provide an empirically grounded view of mill-village society as it evolved in the century after 1880. As I trust my version of the Crown Mill story will show, statistics need not detract from the narrative, and without them the story itself would lack the rich detail it demands.

Another advantage of local-level history is that it allows us to draw upon many different points of view—those of town builders, industrial managers, rural folk, newspaper editors, government officials, union representatives, and the workers themselves—without losing contextual specificity. *Creating the Modern South* thus avoids one of the central difficulties faced by regional surveys. Finally, most recent studies of southern textiles have been chronologically limited, focusing primarily on the late nineteenth and early twentieth centuries. Very few historians have explored the fate of Dixie's millhands beyond the New Deal period, and virtually no previous work has offered a thorough investigation of a single cotton-mill community from the 1880s into the Sunbelt era. The benefits of widening the scope of study can, I hope, be seen in this book.

The story of Crown allows us to grapple with critical questions in the history of labor and of the South. Most of these are addressed in the narrative itself, but it might be worthwhile at this juncture to lay out three of the larger issues at stake and my basic approach to them. The nature of southern industry—and particularly of southern textiles—is a matter of considerable controversy. Some scholars and journalists have seen the development of Dixie's cotton mills as distinctively skewed from "American" norms, arguing that southern planters built and controlled the industry to create a stunted pattern of growth that would safeguard their own preeminence within the region. From this perspective, the rise of the mills in the South marked a continuation of the antebellum economy and power structure.[5] Other historians, following C. Vann Woodward's lead, have countered that the Civil War fundamentally altered Dixie's economic path and created new opportunities for entrepreneurial capitalism within the towns and cities of the Piedmont and Appalachian regions.[6] The crux of this debate is the question of who controlled the New South, as well as when and why the former Confederate states began to converge with the rest of the nation. More than likely, champions of both the Woodwardian and continuity schools will find evidence in Dalton's past to support their respective causes. But in viewing the Crown Mill community over the course of a century, it is the relentless onslaught of change that seems most remarkable.

A second critical issue concerns the nature of southern workers, who have consistently been the least-unionized employees in the nation. New South boosters always insisted that Dixie's millhands were both passive and content, happy to have abandoned their wretched farms and to have found security in the mills. Writing in the early twentieth century, historian Broadus Mitchell cemented this idea into southern historiography by describing mill workers as peasantlike people, incapable of jealousy toward capital and grateful for whatever the benevolent managers offered them.[7] This view has received a spirited thumping by critics of the southern mill-village system and, more recently, by practitioners of the new social history. The evidence is clear that, throughout the late nineteenth and twentieth centuries, southern millhands proved willing to organize and protest. They were never as compliant or satisfied as booster rhetoric suggested. But if southern millhands were prone to rebel, why did they so seldom organize successful unions? A familiar answer is that poor whites came to the mills so imbued with a culture of rural individualism that they could not embrace the idea of collective solutions. They were too stiff-necked to harness themselves to a union; eager to improve their situation and open to temporary associations for problem solving, they were nonetheless disinclined to embrace permanent labor organizations that might inhibit individual freedom of action.[8] This interpretation has recently come under attack from scholars who argue that an ethic of cooperation characterized pre-industrial rural life and naturally found its way into the mill villages. In time, those traditions of mutuality became the seedbed of unionization, but unions failed because corporations and state governments effectively undermined the power of organized labor.[9]

In studying the rural "plain folk" of north Georgia and the cotton-mill workers of Crown, I have found considerable evidence of mutuality and collective action. And in the 1930s, this heritage of cooperative effort fed a strong union movement in Dalton. Unlike most cities in the textile South, Dalton actually became a strong union town, at least for a while, and the rise and fall of unions there is an important part of my story. But the Crown Mill operated for nearly half a century before any union, or even any significant union movement, materialized. An implicit point throughout the book is that the absence of unions should not necessarily be viewed as evidence of the workers' passivity or individualism any more than the presence of a cooperative tradition should be seen as a guarantee of prounion sentiment. Southern millhands assessed their own interests carefully, and they were often willing to fight—individually and collectively—to secure those interests. They were steeped in traditions of collective effort, but they did not always agree on where their interests lay. Nor did they automatically perceive unionization as the key to improving their lot in life. My approach to the issue has been to analyze the workers in relation to the company over time, during periods of labor stability as well as during times of labor crisis. The key, as I see it, is to pay close attention to the ways in which wage earners defined their interests and sought to achieve their goals, with or without unions.

The third central issue—company paternalism—has been at the heart of important historical debates and demands a more extended discussion at the outset.[10] By concentrating my research on the local level and observing the changes over a period of one hundred years, I have become convinced that the central theme in the history of the textile South is the rise and fall of mill-village paternalism. This belief sets my work apart from one important study, *Like a Family: The Making of a Southern Cotton Mill World*, a collective effort authored by Jacquelyn Dowd Hall, James Leloudis, Robert Korstad, Mary Murphy, Lu Ann Jones, and Christopher B. Daly. This artfully crafted study offers a rich description of workers' lives but virtually ignores the issue of paternalism. The authors were trying to dislodge southern labor studies from an old historiographical quagmire in which notions of distinctive southern paternalism seemed to inhibit any advance in methods or ideas. By shunting mill-village paternalism to the background and focusing on the workers' responses to industrialization, they did indeed advance the field and succeeded in placing the history of southern labor squarely within the realm of American labor historiography. But there was a danger in this strategy.

The workers described in *Like a Family* drew upon preindustrial customs of mutual cooperation to form closely knit communities that perceived themselves and their interests as separate from, and largely in opposition to, company management. In a subtle but important way, this interpretation misrepresents the worldview and the behavior of southern millhands. To the people of Crown Mill, *community* meant kinship, neighborliness, mutual interests, common values, a sense of place. That was what mill workers meant when they said the mill village was like "one big family." Such notions, as *Like a Family* suggests, were common to the southern countryside and were largely imported to the industrial world. But the factory community was different from the preindustrial rural community in at least one critical respect: without the existence of the mill, there was no community, no family. To identify with the Crown Mill "family" was to link oneself and one's household to the corporation itself. This is not to infer, as some recent studies have, that workers embraced traditional notions of deference to wealthy patrons.[11] Nor is it to suggest that workers were responsible for their own oppression. Millhands had good reason to see themselves as partners, not servants, within the paternalistic system. Any attempt by either the workers or mill officials to alter that system resulted in conflicts of enormous complexity, for every battle was fought within a community structure that inextricably bound millhands with managers. By studying this process of entanglement, *Creating the Modern South* seeks to reposition corporate paternalism at the center of southern labor history (indeed, of American labor history), and to do so without reverting to older notions of southern exceptionalism.

The origins of mill-village paternalism have been a matter of wide-ranging speculation and debate. To oversimplify a bit, historians of the southern-continuity school naturally point to the Old South plantation and master-slave paternalism. From this vantage point, the theory goes, the elite transferred their paternalistic inclinations from black slaves to poor white mill workers, thereby maintaining control of the work force and justifying their continued control over the southern economy. An alternative and more recent argument is that mill-village paternalism was not an echo of master-slave relations but a manifestation of upcountry cultural traditions, including a widespread devotion to patriarchy and a tendency among poor whites to look to wealthy whites as benefactors.[12] Both arguments, it seems to me, rest on a type of cultural determinism and fail to determine exactly how values and traditions were translated into company policies. Both also point toward mill-village paternalism as evidence of southern distinctiveness, thereby ignoring national and international trends.[13] One important finding presented in this book is that corporate paternalism scarcely existed at Crown during the mill's first twenty years of operation. Rather, it emerged as a definite response to labor market trends that developed during the first two decades of the twentieth century. Paternalism at Crown stemmed neither from planter ideals nor from upcountry culture. It was driven by a regional labor crisis even as it reflected larger trends in welfare capitalism throughout industrial America. Ironically, cotton-mill paternalism in Dixie was not a throwback to the past but a manifestation of regional modernization.

But pinpointing the origins of corporate paternalism does not necessarily enable us to predict its subsequent evolution or its consequences. One critical question concerns the extent to which workers accepted corporate paternalism: Did workers in the early twentieth century embrace it as a viable approach to industrial relations, or did they resent it and long for better opportunities to organize unions?[14] In grappling with this issue, I have tried to avoid two common, misleading assumptions. The first is that corporate paternalism was something imposed from above, to which workers could only respond. If we view workers as agents of history in their own right—as collaborative architects of the industrial system—we are free to examine their own role in shaping the paternalistic system. Having been there at the creation, they had a definite stake in the operation of that system. They neither blindly accepted it nor continually chafed under it; rather, they sought to use it to their advantage. The millhands demanded of the company their due. Working within the system required loyalty to the company, but, to borrow the apt phrase of historian Gerald Zahavi, it was "negotiated loyalty."[15]

Second, I have rejected the prevailing assumption that paternalism naturally undermined possibilities for unionization. In its origins, paternalism at Crown Mill was intended to create a settled community of working families. From management's point of view the system worked very well, perhaps too well, for it created a cohesive community of permanent wage earners who had clear expectations about the proper arrangement of life and work in the Crown Mill village. When the Great Depression made it difficult for Crown to hold up its end of the paternalistic bargain, the workers felt a profound sense of betrayal and formed a union partly as a new means of reestablishing older community norms. But not all workers supported the union, and some openly fought it. At Crown, paternalism cut both ways and ultimately provoked an unprecedented crisis among the mill workers of Dalton. To delve into that crisis is to gain a deeper understanding of working people and industrial unionism during the New Deal era.

I have organized this study into four parts, each constituting a cohesive period in the history of Dalton and the Crown Mill. The emphasis in Part 1 is on the rise of Dalton as a cotton-mill town and on the larger patterns of economic development in the post–Civil War decades. Parts 2 and 3 focus more closely on the Crown Mill community, with an eye toward regional and national events. By the end of the 1930s, the foundations of corporate paternalism at Crown had crumbled, and the federal government had become a powerful force in the everyday workings of the mill. These trends became even more evident over the next three decades, which are covered in Part 4. The four phases reflect distinct periods in the history of southern industrialization. The story is more tightly focused on the South in the early chapters and becomes gradually more national in scope, a narrative strategy that flowed naturally from the sources and that offers some indication of my views on the overall evolution of southern society.

Part 4 breaks new ground, because almost no studies of the South have analyzed a single community over a continuous span from the late nineteenth through the late twentieth century. Southern millhands, so central to the history of the New South, all but drop out of the historical literature after the 1930s.[16] We know surprisingly little about the full effect of World War II on the South, even though that global conflict reshuffled the region in ways not seen since the Civil War. One debate just emerging is whether the 1940s offered workers a window of opportunity for remaking their region and, if so, why that opportunity was lost.[17] Another important question is why southern textiles remained largely nonunion after the war, despite vigorous efforts to organize the mills. The few scholars who have grappled with this issue have suggested a variety of answers, the most frequent of which is that Dixie's millhands maintained an enduring antiunionism deeply embedded in southern society and mill-village culture.[18] But the world of southern millhands changed in important ways after 1945. To be sure, the region maintained some of its cultural mores in the postwar decades, but mill villages were being sold, southern industry was moving in new directions, and the mill-family economy was undergoing a fundamental transformation. Under such circumstances mill-village traditions, however antiunion, could not remain undisturbed. And because national trends were having an ever greater impact on southern society, it is equally appropriate to seek the sources of postwar antiunionism in the federal arena, especially in changing union policies, antiunion legislation, and the cold war Red Scare.

Finally, Part 4 deals with plant closures in an industrial society, a topic of growing importance in labor history since the manufacturing heartland of the North has become a "Rustbelt." The postwar urban South—emerging as part of the Sunbelt in the 1960s and often blamed for the demise of northern industry—had its own Rustbelt equivalent in textiles. Following regional trends, all of Dalton's old-line textile mills shut down during the 1950s and 1960s. That Dixie's traditional industrial base declined just as the region reached new levels of prosperity within the national economy was a matter of no small irony, and the collapse of the Crown Mill community offers fresh insights into the changing nature of southern industry and working-class life in the post–New South era.

A few caveats are in order lest my basic arguments and assumptions be misconstrued. First, I have not lost sight of the fact that the South was more than just cotton mills in upcountry towns. Fortunately, the social history of the New South is now being written more broadly, and studies of southern workers outside of textiles are now appearing steadily.[19] But it is no accident that cotton mills have demanded such attention; no other industry had a more powerful impact on the region, and no other created such a large population of wage-earning factory hands. Textiles are not the whole story, but to understand the origins, evolution, and demise of southern cotton mills is to go a long way toward comprehending the larger process of modernization in Dixie and the complex human dimensions of that process.

Second, important groups of southerners are largely missing from my story. Middle-class townspeople, and even Dalton's industrial elite, are underrepresented here, even though they provided an important backdrop against which the Crown Mill community acted out its history. More important, although issues of race wind through the narrative, black Daltonians make few appearances in this book. African Americans comprised nearly 30 percent of the town's population in 1890, but increasingly less thereafter, making up little more than 10 percent by 1930. The relative decline in black population was linked directly to Dalton's emergence as a textile town in which the mills used white labor exclusively. The city's African

Americans nonetheless had their own vibrant community, and the small size of that community is no reason for leaving it out of the story. Indeed, a better understanding of small black communities in upcountry towns would add immeasurably to our understanding of southern race relations.[20] Dalton's black population is not much in evidence here because my focus is on the Crown Mill, a company that never hired a black person for any kind of job. Ever. Nor, so far as I can tell, did any of the other cotton mills in Dalton. In an important sense, the absence of African Americans in this book reflects the racial reality experienced by Crown's millhands, who, on a daily basis, had very little interaction with black people. Race played an overpowering role in southern life, and it is important to acknowledge that the millhands and managers of Dalton shared racist assumptions; but for the town's white mill-village families, blacks existed mainly in the background and served essentially as a negative reference group.

Finally, a word about romanticizing the history of working people. A good deal of historical writing during the 1960s and 1970s stressed the hardships of workers in order to counter lingering notions that industrialization had been an unqualified benefit to wage earners. Such analyses, the heirs to a long line of sociological studies sympathetic to the plight of workers, had the unintended effect of dehumanizing the very workers they studied, making them appear simply as victims of a vicious process. In recent years, however, a countertrend has stressed the historical agency of ordinary working people and highlighted ways in which they carved out lives of dignity and purpose within the industrial capitalist system. Now there have arisen new concerns that such studies gloss over the hardships of working-class existence and that they uncritically accept the oral histories of workers whose stories suggest connections between personal hardship and a satisfying community life.

The issue of romanticization is a legitimate one, and although I think my basic views should be clear by the end of the book, some explicit statements now may prevent misunderstandings along the way. I do not view "community" as something intrinsically good. Any closely knit body of people provides its members with a sense of place and belonging, a benefit of extraordinary importance, but communities also have exclusionary and coercive tendencies, and I have not hesitated to reveal the underside of the Crown Mill community in telling its story. At some point, any clear-eyed historian of the southern textile industry has to grapple with feelings of outrage over the poverty and depredations suffered by the working people of the South. But like most social historians, I believe we must view working people as more than victims, and that we must accept the mounting body of evidence—presented in a broad array of recent studies of American workers— which demonstrates that working families saw their lives and their work as worthwhile and meaningful. We should not have expected less, but the evidence is complicated by the fact that workers sometimes linked their sense of worth and meaning with the company they worked for, even as they were toiling as poor wage earners within the industrial capitalist system. My basic challenge in writing this book, then, was to present an analysis that would reflect the ambiguity of the workers' world, avoiding the pitfalls of both victimization and romanticization. That is what I have tried to accomplish in *Creating the Modern South*—whether adequately, time will tell.

We understand the past experience of American workers and the process of industrialization much better today because social historians have studied a wide array of communities, mostly in the North but increasingly now in the South and West as well. The diversity of experience apparent in all these studies makes it clear that no community at any time can be labeled "typical." The remarkable thing, though, is that common themes and patterns of behavior have emerged from these disparate analyses. The persistence of preindustrial traditions within industrial environments; the reluctance of first-generation workers to accept industrial time discipline; the importance of family labor for working-class households; the ongoing efforts of industrialists to recruit and control a stable labor force; the gradual development of a self-conscious and permanent community of industrial wage earners; the powerful sense of "family" and mutual interdependence that reinforced industrial communities; the tendency of workers ultimately to attempt unionization and their equally apparent inclination to divide over organized labor—all of these patterns seem to have been followed, in a rough and general way, throughout the nineteenth and twentieth centuries, as Americans everywhere became an increasingly industrial people.

In their own particular place and time, the people of Dalton and northwest Georgia experienced the advent of industrialization in their own unique way. Yet the broad similarities linking their lives with those of other Americans indicate that the gradual transition from an agricultural to an industrial society involved a common set of circumstances and impinged upon a familiar set of expectations. Such similarities suggest that the story of Dalton is of more than local importance, and that it can serve as a window through which to view the process of industrialization in a region, indeed a nation, caught up in the dynamics of social and economic change.

CREATING THE MODERN SOUTH

BEGINNINGS: THE CROWN

COTTON MILL OF DALTON, 1884

Hamilton's Spring, a serene stretch of land in north Dalton, was an unlikely setting for an industrial revolution. But in 1884 the place came alive when a group of business leaders in Dalton decided to build a textile mill there. Without public fanfare, they pooled their capital with business associates from Tennessee and proceeded to form a corporation. Exactly how and when they were lured into textile manufacturing will probably always remain a mystery. None of them were industrialists. Nor were they well-known southern businessmen. Their fortunes were hardly remarkable in Gilded Age America, but as merchants and financiers in Dixie's expanding commercial economy, they had grown rich and were looking for smart investments. In time they would sink their money into a wide variety of industrial concerns in Dalton, but the Crown Mill was their initial venture. It was the first large-scale manufacturing plant in their north Georgia town, and for many north Georgians, it was the first factory they would ever see.

The plan was to build a spinning and weaving operation, in which cotton would be transformed into plain heavy cloth for the national textile market. Or, as the mill's officials originally phrased it, the business of Crown was "the ginning and conversion of cotton into yarns and any other manufactured articles thought proper." And, they added, "to sell the same for gain." At the outset, Crown was not overwhelmingly large or expensive; the mill was established with a capital stock of $55,000. It did not need to be bigger. In small towns and cities throughout the southern upcountry, nascent industrialists were successfully producing varieties of "coarse" textiles in modest-sized mills and, if the glowing reports were true, reaping substantial profits. Not that any of Crown's leaders knew anything about industrial management. Indeed, the day after they organized the mill, company directors sent a contingent to visit other southern cotton mills to obtain information on how to run one.[1]

The location for the new mill, the Hamilton's Spring area, was a sweep of flat land tucked between the rolling hills of north Dalton. It lay just inside the city limits, which extended in a one-mile radius from the railroad depot, the official center of town. Although it provided a useful supply of water for the mill, the spring itself, which flowed clear and strong (and does so to this day) was largely incidental to the factory's location, since the mill was powered by steam, not water. The main attraction was the level terrain and, equally important, the close proximity of the Western and Atlantic Railroad (W&A), which ran immediately west of Hamilton's Spring. There was also plenty of undeveloped land around the site on which the company could build what the first mill directors called "tenement houses," a half-dozen rental homes intended for Crown's employees. The houses were perched on a hill overlooking Hamilton's Spring—"Factory Hill," the townsfolk called it—about two hundred yards southeast of the mill itself. That these small dwellings would become the center of a large company-owned village consisting of three hundred homes could hardly have occurred to observers watching the first tenements being built.

Before the Civil War, this land had been owned by John Hamilton, a wealthy slaveowner. But the transformation of Hamilton's Spring in 1884 was not a shift from cotton fields to cotton mills. The history of the spring and of the Hamilton family was not that of an Old South steeped in tradition. Indeed, it suggested that the late antebellum period was a curiously fluid time for people in the southern upcountry. Before white people conquered northwest Georgia, Chief Redbird of the Cherokee Nation controlled the land surrounding the spring; but Redbird's death and the forceful removal of the Cherokees from Georgia in the late 1830s opened the land to white ownership. The man who bought that land was not then a slaveowner or even a southerner; John Hamilton was, in fact, a Yankee and a structural engineer who had come south to do some work for the proposed W&A Railroad. Hamilton never returned to the North. He soon married a southern woman and built a sturdy brick house—the Hamilton Homestead—on a knoll east of the spring. He also bought more than a dozen slaves to tend his farm, which grew no cash crops worth noting. When Hamilton died in the 1850s, his wife, Rachel, kept the land and managed the homestead until the Civil War.

During the war, the Hamilton land became home to thousands of Confederate soldiers, who camped there during the bitter winter of 1863–64 and soon thereafter fled southward as Sherman advanced toward Atlanta. In less than thirty years, this land had been stripped from the Cherokee Nation and cultivated by a northerner with southern ambitions, only to become a battleground upon which white southerners were willing to die for a traditional way of life. After fighting for the Confederacy, two of Hamilton's sons, George and Henry, returned to Dalton, became successful merchants, and sold Hamilton's Spring to the Crown Cotton Mills Company. Taken as a whole, it was an odd prelude to southern industry, but in 1884 the ironies embedded in the soil of the Hamilton Homestead were of little concern to Dalton's developers, who divided the town's history into two periods—before Crown and after Crown.[2]

The anticipation engendered by Dalton's new industrial venture was offset by frustrating delays in construction. Materials were obtained easily enough, particularly bricks, which were made on location at Hamilton's Spring. But the weather did not cooperate, and corporate directors watched with exasperation as torrential rains made a mudhole of the place. Equally disturbing were disputes with the construction crews, which offered these managers-in-the-making their first taste of labor troubles. When stockholders gathered in September 1884, mill officials explained that the delays were attributable to "weather most unfavorable and combinations of labor antagonistic to your interests." But as 1884 drew to a close the pace of construction quickened, and the mill building took shape. Taking in the scene, local boosters could hardly restrain themselves.[3]

"Dalton's Grandest Enterprise, All Ready for Motion," crowed the *Dalton Argus* in January 1885. A three-story edifice with a lofty belfry, Crown resembled an enormous church save for the smokestack, which stretched upward one hundred feet. The Crown Cotton Mill was easily the most impressive building in northwest Georgia. Bordered by both the W&A and the main road through town, the mill signaled to all passersby that Dalton had joined the New South's industrial crusade. According to the *Argus*, Crown represented the dawning of a new era in the town's history. It stood on the old Hamilton Homestead, whose "grove of great forest trees and . . . grassy meadow" had long served as a pastoral picnic ground where children romped and lovers strolled. This "long stretch of park" had been "an integral part of Dalton's identity" since the town was founded in the late 1840s. But now the Hamilton place had a new look, and Dalton was taking on a new identity. The "halcyon groves" of Dalton's "primitive days" had given way to the factory, which "shut out the romance of ages past." The *Argus* was content to let the misty memories fade, choosing instead to cast its lot with the new age of industrial development.[4]

Everyone in town knew the *Argus* was exaggerating the magnitude of change. In 1885 Dalton seemed an unlikely place for an industrial boom, editorial exultations notwithstanding. The town's population was a mere 2,780, and even after Crown

The newly built Crown Cotton Mill, 1885. (*Courtesy of Crown Gardens and Archives*)

began production, only a small percentage of people were employed in large-scale manufacturing. Since the Civil War, which had left much of the town in ruins, Dalton had rebuilt steadily as a commercial center serviced by the W&A and Southern railroad lines. Local business leaders looked to agricultural trade, not industry, for prosperity, and there were naysayers who questioned whether anything profitable could come of the Crown Mill venture. To be sure, some southern cities were hailing the benefits of urban growth and industrial development, but it was not altogether clear that a town lacking experienced factory workers and trained industrial managers could be home to a successful cotton mill. From an economic point of view, Dalton seemed more an overgrown hamlet than a nascent manufacturing center.[5]

In retrospect, though, the *Argus* proved prophetic. Crown Mill ultimately came to symbolize the larger economic transformation wrought by industrialization in Dalton and north Georgia. By the mid-1880s, the local economy showed signs of change. More factories began to appear in Dalton, and as Crown prospered in the late 1880s, a new enthusiasm for industrial development arose among the city's economic leaders. When the mill expanded during the late nineteenth and early twentieth centuries, it inspired the establishment of other textile mills and manufacturing plants. By the end of World War I, Crown was one of the largest cotton mills in Georgia, boasting 50,000 spindles and a full complement of looms. Although few would have believed it in 1885, Dalton by the end of the 1920s had become known as "the city of smiles and smokestacks."[6] Cotton mills had become the backbone of the local economy and would remain so for many years.

But the story of Crown was more than a tale of economic development and business success. Equally significant was the impact the mill had on the social order of Dalton and north Georgia, an impact duplicated in other parts of the southern upcountry as small-town cotton mills formed the economic core of the New South. Most important, the mills created something new in the region: a permanent population of wage-earning factory workers, whose lives were increasingly tied to corporations and the vicissitudes of industrial capitalism. But the millhands—poor whites from the southern upcountry—were not simply spectators in this process; they placed their own stamp on the southern industrial system. Cotton-mill villages such as Crown became arenas of conflict, compromise, and collaboration, as textile managers and ordinary working people gradually created the modern South. The history of Crown, in its own small way, would tell the story of that creation. But as the new mill arose near Hamilton's Spring, such considerations were distant at best. In 1884, no one could as yet foresee the social consequences of industrialization in Dixie.

PART I

THE ORIGINS

OF INDUSTRY,

1865–1900

1

AN ECONOMIC

RECONSTRUCTION

In 1886 a roving journalist stepped off the train at Dalton and surveyed the town. What he saw took him by surprise. "I well remember my first glimpse of this place a few years after the war," he reminisced. "The dilapidated houses that had long since cut the acquaintance of paint, the broken down fences and the woe-begone appearance of people and things in general, were pathetic reminders of the fearful combats that had been fought in and around this then, almost depopulated town." But now, some twenty years later, he was thrilled to discover a Dalton that "contrasted pleasantly with that gloomy day." The sounds of progress, he marveled, could be heard all around. The "clatter of machinery," the whistling of the trains, and the ringing of school bells blended in a sweet harmony that convinced him Daltonians were "as wide awake to their moral and educational interests as to their pecuniary growth." However attentive the people of Dalton were to money and morals, their town seemed to have made a remarkable recovery from the economic setbacks of the Civil War. General William T. Sherman's Atlanta campaign in 1865 had

ravaged the small railroad town and the surrounding countryside, but a generation later Dalton was back on its feet. Or, as the *Atlanta Constitution* put it in 1887,
"Dalton has at last awakened from its Rip Van Winkle slumber, and now steps to
the front with the martial music of the great southern boom."[1]

In the generation following the Civil War—between the "woe-begone" years
and the awakening of Old Rip—the modern South began to take shape. Railroad
companies spun webs of steel across Dixie, widening southern tracks to meet
northern standards and linking the war-torn region to a rapidly expanding national railway network. Cities and small railroad towns emerged along the tracks,
particularly in the hilly Piedmont (or "upcountry") region, which cut a crescent-
shaped swathe above the old plantation belt from western Virginia across the
Carolinas and Georgia and into northern Alabama. The Confederacy's demise and
the emancipation of southern slaves decimated the antebellum system of credit
and human capital upon which the plantation regime had rested. Gradually a free-
labor economy took shape, and Dixie's upcountry towns and cities became the
economic core of the New South. Small farmers in the region shifted from self-
sufficiency to cash-crop agriculture and developed a new dependence on consumer credit and store-bought goods. This trend enriched a new cadre of small-
town merchants, who soon had both the money and the incentive to invest in local
manufacturing plants, particularly cotton textile mills. In these mills, merchants
learned to be corporate leaders and poor white families learned to be what most
working people in America were becoming: wage earners in an industrial economy. Nothing in Dixie signaled the shift toward modernization more clearly than
cotton mills.

Yet to many observers—then and since—the cotton mills of the New South
seemed more medieval than modern, a perverse distortion of capitalist economic
development. Critics charged that Dixie's mill villages, scattered at the edges of
backwash towns and overlorded by paternalistic mill owners who exercised complete control over "their people," represented a new type of feudalism. New South
boosters, feverish with notions of urban growth and industrialization, glibly countered that mill work offered poor whites a new lease on life and represented a
triumph of the southern spirit. A few early historians of the industry heartily
seconded these conclusions, ignoring the obvious hardships and inequities of
cotton-mill life. Other observers were more honest and less gracious. Some were
so disturbed by mill-village conditions that they condemned southern textiles as a
form of slavery that firmly enshackled poor white "lintheads." This view endured
well into the twentieth century and eventually found a powerful voice in southern
journalist W. J. Cash, whose classic *The Mind of the South*, published in 1941,
dubbed Dixie's mill villages "industrial plantations," a concept still embraced by
some historians.[2]

For all its ethical sensibilities, this perception fails to explain the complex dynamics of southern modernization and ignores the role that the workers themselves played in shaping the region's economic development. Southern mill villages were not modeled after plantations, and southern mill workers were not slaves. One need not accept the cheerful assurances of New South boosters to reject the "industrial plantation" thesis and to see the cotton mills for what they were: a fundamental departure from the past and part of a larger process that changed America from a rural, agricultural nation to an urban, industrial one.[3]

The people of the Crown Cotton Mill took part in this larger process. While constantly reacting to national and regional developments, the managers and millhands of Crown created an industrial community, struggled to make it work, and finally destroyed it. Although Crown was established in 1884, the evolution of the Crown Mill community was largely a twentieth-century occurrence. But the earlier decades deserve attention, for the people of Crown played out their lives in the twentieth century on a stage erected during the final four decades of the nineteenth. That stage itself forced upon the actors certain restrictions. These first chapters therefore focus less on the Crown Mill than on the tapestry of southern economic change and the rise of Dalton as a cotton-mill town. At the heart of these developments was the economic reconstruction of the South after 1865, which involved the expansion of commercial capitalism and then, beginning in the 1880s, the tentative beginnings of industrialization. Dalton and dozens of other obscure railroad towns in the southern upcountry formed the vanguard of this process. Dixie's absorption into the national economy, the ascension of small-town merchants, and the deepening poverty and dislocation of poor white farmers and artisans were interconnected developments that created a foundation for large-scale industry in the New South.

Before Dalton ever graced the map, there was the land, and few elements would have a greater impact on the city than the countryside surrounding it. The history of Dalton began in the late 1830s, when several white families formed the village of Cross Plains in the Cherokee Nation. The Cherokees held all the land in Georgia north of the Chattahoochee River, including the upper Piedmont and mountain areas. But whites wanted the land, and they would have it. Anticipating the Indians' removal, the state legislature in 1831 surveyed "Cherokee County" in preparation for a land lottery held the following year, at which time the state established the boundaries of Murray County in the northwest part of the region. By the time federal authorities forced the Cherokees out in 1838–39, Cross Plains already existed as a tiny hamlet in the western half of Murray County (which later became Whitfield County). After the Cherokees were gone, whites poured into the region from southern Georgia and the surrounding states. But Cross Plains was not their preferred destination. By 1845 only ten families lived there. Towns were of little importance to the first wave of land-hungry whites moving to north Georgia.[4]

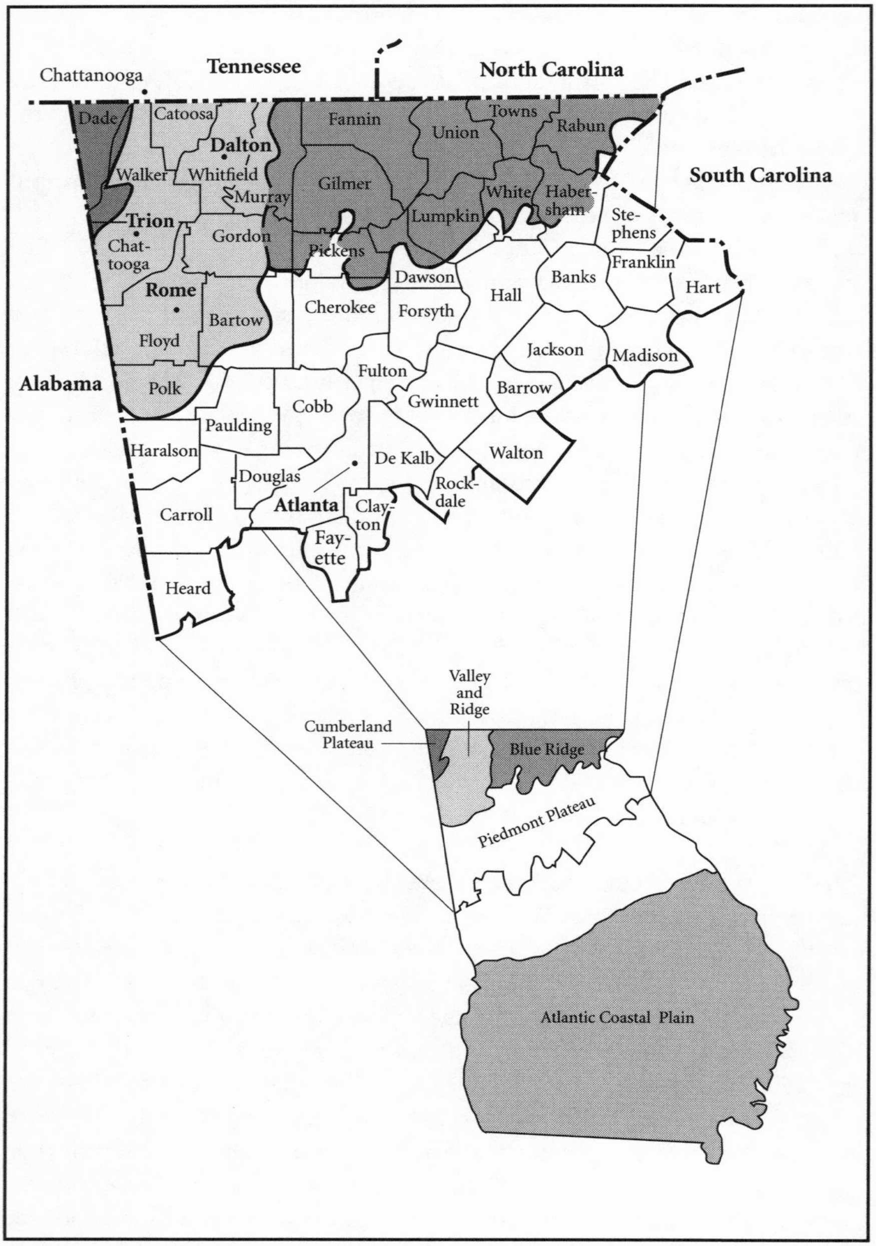

Chattanooga
Tennessee

North Carolina

Dade · Catoosa · Fannin · Union · Towns · Rabun

South Carolina

Walker · Whitfield · **Dalton** · Gilmer · White · Haber-sham

Trion · Murray · Lumpkin · Ste-phens

Chat-tooga · Gordon · Pickens · Franklin

Rome · Dawson · Hall · Banks · Hart

Bartow · Cherokee · Forsyth · Floyd

Polk · Fulton · Jackson · Madison

Alabama · Cobb · Gwinnett · Barrow

Paulding · De Kalb · Walton

Haralson · Douglas · Rock-dale

Carroll · **Atlanta** · Clay-ton

Fay-ette

Heard

Valley
and
Ridge

Cumberland
Plateau

Blue Ridge

Piedmont Plateau

Atlantic Coastal Plain

MAP 1.1. The Georgia Upcountry

The land was good, even beautiful—well timbered, fertile, and fed by innumerable springs. Northwest Georgia was part of the Great Appalachian Valley that swept southward west of the Blue Ridge Mountains down through east Tennessee, across northwest Georgia, and into northeast Alabama. The Georgia Valley offered southern yeomen rolling vales of durable clay soil, rich farmlands that lay between sharp ridges running roughly parallel, northeast to southwest. "The great variety of soils," wrote one government agent, "together with a diversity of climate, due to the varying altitudes of this country, render it suitable for the successful culture of perhaps every agricultural product of the temperate climate." East of Murray County, the Blue Ridge loomed above the Great Valley. Rugged and rocky, northeast Georgia proved less hospitable to farmers and was more sparsely populated than the valley. As it turned out, both valley and Blue Ridge were seedbeds for southern textile workers. But in the antebellum era, such a possibility seemed very remote.[5]

Before the Indians were displaced, white people in Georgia sang a popular ditty: "All I want in this creation / Is a pretty little wife and a big plantation / Way up yonder in the Cherokee Nation." But the song lyrics did not reflect reality. North Georgia was not a place for plantations. In the mountainous northeast, the terrain and the short growing season—not to mention the difficulties of transportation—rendered cotton cultivation nearly impossible. Even in the more fertile areas of the northwest, the climate usually precluded cotton production without the use of commercial fertilizers (which did not become readily available in the upcountry until after 1870). Contrary to common assumptions about yeoman areas, however, some whites in the Georgia Valley owned a considerable number of slaves. One in five residents of Murray County in 1860 were slaves, and 17 percent of Whitfield County's population lived in bondage, a telling indication that affluent whites used slave labor for general farm work and household chores even where there was no plantation agriculture. This was, after all, the South, where slave property reflected wealth and influence. But the cotton plantations of the Black Belt found no parallel in Cherokee Georgia. Most farmers did not own slaves and grew no cotton. It was the ordinary white yeoman families, the proud and sturdy "plain folk" of legend, who commanded the valleys and ridges of the Georgia upcountry.[6]

Families migrating to the area settled in small farming communities that were largely self-sufficient. Early patterns of settlement in the 1830s and 1840s reflected an undeveloped region and the traditions of community interdependence common among the yeomanry. As a young boy in the 1830s, J. C. Head moved with his family into a farming community in an area that later became part of Whitfield County. "Neighbors were not crowded together very closely," he recalled later in life, "but they were neighbors indeed." Rural folk, he said, "were drawn together in the strongest ties of friendship, and assisted each other as a band of brothers. When one had a cabin to raise, or logs to roll, all in the same neighborhood, extending four or five miles around, cheerfully met at his place and helped him do his work." Head's romantic memories of cheerful communal effort did not obscure completely his recollection that local camaraderie was born of mutual need. Clearing and repairing new roads required cooperation. "When supplies were needed," he added, "two or three teams and wagons were banded together and sent to the landing [later Chattanooga] for such things as were needed by anyone in the same community." In a land of inadequate roads and unbridged streams, "this was sort of a necessity." Rural communities were founded upon shared interests among local households; reciprocal obligations among community members were economically essential. Or, to use Head's words, "this was a time when men felt their dependence, one upon another, and they were ready to combine together to assist and protect each other."[7]

Rather than scatter haphazardly across the countryside, the yeomanry settled in loosely clustered farming communities. Kin groups often migrated together, and though each family established a separate farmstead, they built homes reasonably close to one another to ensure that reliable neighbors would be available in this rough-hewn, largely isolated land. Frontier settlements required a certain population concentration to survive. The three fundamental institutions of farming communities—church, gristmill, and country store—demanded a steady clientele to function properly. The boundaries of each rural community could basically be defined by locating the families who patronized a particular gristmill or church house. North Georgia's farming communities soon took on names, usually inspired by a distinctive natural feature—Dug Gap, Red Clay, Five Springs—or in acknowledgment of a particularly influential family—Redwine's Cove, Houston Valley. These names, as much as anything, signified that the families who remained in such communities developed a clear sense of place, a sense of belonging to an identifiable group of people.[8]

Each rural settlement became almost an economic system within itself. Households utilized the labor of all able family members in raising and processing foodstuffs, and they produced most of what they needed through extensive home manufacturing. But every neighborhood also needed millers, merchants, blacksmiths, and other artisans to provide the goods and services ordinary farm families could not obtain by themselves. Moreover, because individual families alone normally could not muster an adequate number of hands to build a house or even harvest a corn crop, a system of community labor exchange developed that proved mutually beneficial to all. The farming *community*, not the individual household, was self-sufficient. In northern Georgia's early years of white settlement, economic relations—that is, the personal relationships involved in raising crops and livestock, in processing and trading agricultural goods, and in purchasing land—were characterized by household production and community interdependence. In this environment, almost no one was a wage earner in the modern sense. No one worked for a company. No one toiled by the clock. Children worked for their parents, and some families were indebted to others in the community, but no one answered to a "boss."

These farm families practiced what Georgians called "mixed farming"—referred to by economic historians as "safety first" agriculture. They grew most of what they ate and made most of what they wore. During the antebellum era, small farmers throughout America had shown reluctance to plunge headlong into cash-crop agriculture, despite the emergence of growing urban markets. Commercial production might mean riches, but it might also mean ruin. In Georgia, cotton production entailed clear risks for petty producers, because it took up space that would otherwise be used for corn, the basic food crop of the plain folk. It also encouraged economic dependence on merchants, creditors, middlemen, and shippers, a dependence yeomen were loath to accept.

Poor transportation further reinforced self-sufficiency. One man sorrowfully described the roads in his section as "dim and doubtful, rough and narrow." In the first ten years of white settlement, no railroad tracks ran within one hundred miles of farmers in the Georgia Valley. Connections to the outside world did exist, to be sure. Steamboats traveled as far north as Carter's Quarters, a landing on the Coosa River near the southern intersection of Murray and Gilmer counties. But there was no railroad, and without one the upcountry remained largely isolated from both the modernizing North and the plantation South. The climate and the absence of an adequate marketing system made staple cultivation in the region a doubtful enterprise. The first settlers played it safe, focusing their energies on subsistence rather than potential profits from cotton.[9]

Yet the Georgia upcountry experienced only a decade of isolated agriculture, for the Western and Atlantic Railroad (W&A) began to reshape the region as it reached northward from Atlanta in the late 1840s. As a state-owned, state-operated railroad, the W&A was a rarity in the antebellum South. Its central purpose was to create nontax revenue for the state, providing money for expanded social services while simultaneously lowering taxes for the state's white citizenry. Black Belt planters also hoped to tap into the Midwest's wheat boom in order to devote less of their own land to foodstuffs and more to cotton. As planned, the road stretched northward from a point called Terminus (later Atlanta) across northwest Georgia and straight through Cross Plains to Chattanooga, Tennessee. When the railroad finally reached Cross Plains in 1847, it sparked an immediate economic boom. Because completion of the line to Chattanooga was delayed three years, the north Georgia town remained the road's northern terminus—and a very prosperous one.[10]

The W&A transformed sleepy Cross Plains into the bustling town of Dalton. Knowing the proposed railroad would run through Cross Plains, a company from Massachusetts with its eye on southern real estate investments bought most of the land in and around the hamlet. Captain Edward White, the leader behind the purchase, was thinking big. He moved to the north Georgia village where, in true New England style, he laid out wide streets, donated plots for churches and schools, and set aside land for a city park. He anticipated urban greatness, and for a time he seemed to have planned correctly. Cross Plains became incorporated as the town of Dalton in December 1847, only five months after the railroad reached it. During the next two years, the population of Dalton swelled from a few hundred to about fifteen hundred. Drovers herded cattle and hogs to Dalton. Farmers hauled in bushels of wheat. Dalton quickly became the commercial center for much of north Georgia and east Tennessee. In 1851 the boom town became the seat of newly formed Whitfield County, which was carved from the western half of Murray.[11]

The most immediate change in agriculture—the one that most aided Dalton's growth and established the town as an important commercial center—was the rise of commercial wheat production. Farmers in the valley shipped their produce out of Dalton to be sold in Georgia's plantation belt. Unlike cotton, winter wheat was a relatively safe commercial crop. It could be used as a source of food, and it did not compete directly with corn or potatoes for use of the land. Between the coming of the railroad and the outbreak of the Civil War, north Georgia's farmers began to produce a noticeably higher level of wheat.

Ironically, at the same time that farmers began to grow wheat for the plantation belt, the W&A started offering discount shipping rates to out-of-state grain producers. In order to make the W&A profitable for the state, Georgia's railroad managers sought the trade of farmers in the border South and Midwest, who consequently undercut their competitors in Georgia. Wheat producers in northwest Georgia were furious about these discounts, but W&A leaders remained unmoved. One manager scoffed at naive upcountry farmers who believed "the Road was constructed for the purpose of promoting the agricultural and industrial interests of one peculiarly favored section of the state," when in fact its founders "undertook its construction because they were convinced it would offer the best and easiest connection between the Ocean and the West." Such a response may have convinced north Georgia farmers that "safety first" agriculture was still the best policy. Per capita corn production remained above the state average through 1860, and there was no major surge into cotton production. Overall, self-sufficiency did not seem to be on the decline, and, in any case, Dalton's influence over the countryside had begun to wane.[12]

Dalton's growth spurt ended when the W&A reached Chattanooga in 1850, making the Tennessee city the leading commercial center in the lower Appalachian Valley. Dalton remained an important agricultural depot between Chattanooga and Atlanta and staked its claim as one of the few upcountry towns with a viable economic base, but its second-class status mocked Edward White's dreams of grandeur. Dalton's development-minded crowd nonetheless took heart from the ongoing efforts of Duff Green, one of the town's early leaders and a prominent advocate of industrial development in Dixie. Green worked successfully to make Dalton the southern terminus of the East Tennessee and Georgia Railroad, which linked his town with Knoxville—and by extension with Virginia—by the mid-1850s. Such endeavors expanded Dalton's economic foundations, and by 1860 the town even boasted a smattering of manufacturing enterprises, including a carriage factory, two furniture shops, two leather mills, a machinery manufacturer, and an ironworks. It ought not be supposed, however, that such enterprises marked the origins of modern industry in the region. Dalton's manufacturing establishments were on a very small scale. Along with some lumber and flour mills in Whitfield County, they had an average capitalization of $7,083 per enterprise (actually above the state average, which was only $5,762) at a time when a modest cotton mill would have cost $50,000. In 1860 all of Whitfield County's manufacturing plants employed a total of only eighty-three men and, in stark contrast to postbellum patterns, no women or children. Antebellum Dalton was a town of traditional workshops, not of factories in the making.[13]

The antebellum upcountry simply could not become what Edward White and Duff Green had hoped. Most southern transportation networks were geared toward plantation stability, and the principal goal of the W&A was not urban growth but state revenue. North of the Mason-Dixon line, the transportation revolution of the early nineteenth century sparked the rise of bustling cities and an aggressive commercial society. In the South, that revolution was delayed until after the Civil War, and the delay had enormous consequences for southern industry. The small farmers who still dominated the southern upcountry did not need town services to survive. In one way, Dalton's antebellum legacy did contribute to its postbellum growth. The town's position on the W&A line put it on the map before the war and gave the town something of an economic head start after 1865. As in the case of other upcountry railroad towns, this advantage was no small contribution to the subsequent development of small-town commerce and the rise of cotton mills in the New South. But as long as plantation slavery dominated the southern economy, and as long as the upcountry yeomanry remained on the periphery of national and international markets, economic modernization could not take place in Dixie.[14]

The Civil War cleared the way for southern industry by abolishing slavery and by destroying the economic independence of most upcountry yeomen. The Confederacy's defeat, in effect, forced modernization upon the South. Initially, too, the war effort itself infused the regional economy with a new dynamism, because military commanders needed entrepreneurs like Duff Green to supply armies in the field. Green opposed secession, but he profited from the war, using the conflict as a means to implement various industrial schemes. In response to the Confederate need for manufactured goods, he established an ironworks near Dalton and was instrumental in turning a deserted hotel into a munitions plant. A Confederate "pork packing" factory arose outside the town as well. But soon the war turned against Dalton and crushed its rising prosperity. The Army of Tennessee, ragged and retreating, camped in the town during the winter of 1863–64, awaiting a Union onslaught that spring. The W&A, which had brought life to Dalton in 1847, served as General Sherman's avenue of war in his Atlanta campaign. His main army swerved around Dalton, but destructive skirmishes within the town continued for some time afterward. At conflict's end, most of the local trees had been felled, and many buildings lay in rubble. Dalton was a spectacle of desolation.[15]

The countryside was also in utter disarray. As in most upcountry areas of the South, north Georgia's farmers were divided in their loyalties during the war, and vicious guerrilla warfare between Confederate "home guards" and Union sympathizers devastated many farming communities. Virtually all healthy males fought on one side or the other. Many of the area's farmers and most of its farm capital were obliterated in the process. Whichever side families chose to fight on, normal farm operations were abruptly interrupted if not completely wrecked. Total warfare cut a path from Chattanooga to Atlanta, resulting in the widespread destruction of farm property and the virtual annihilation of all existing produce and livestock. The war also destroyed most of the W&A. Even after the railroad underwent repairs in late 1865, one observer described the road as "a rough patchwork of damaged and crooked rails, laid on rotten cross-ties and on rough poles and other makeshifts; eight miles of track at the upper end were entirely missing, while the rolling stock was more nearly fit for the scrap heap than for traffic." North Georgia's economy was a shambles. Whitfield County's Inferior Court mourned that "the public buildings, bridges and roads . . . [are] all in a dilapidated condition, requiring large expenditures to repair."[16]

Ironically, southern defeat and economic devastation actually facilitated industrialization. The loss of so many men and so much farm capital left most plain folk in dire straits—and in desperate need of credit to get their farms back into operation. Crossroads stores and neighborly support were not adequate to the enormous task of rebuilding. In the upcountry, people with money to lend resided in railroad towns such as Dalton. The demand for credit was high, and so therefore were interest rates. The town-based merchants and financiers soon found themselves with tremendous leverage over ordinary farm families. Unlike White and Green, postbellum business leaders found it possible to break through regional trade barriers and to become part of a larger process of economic growth that was sweeping the North and West. Confederate defeat and emancipation paved the way for an integrated national economy, symbolized most clearly by the expanding railroad network that finally linked northern and southern railways and laid the groundwork for an increasingly urban-industrial America.

Railroads were the key to the South's economic reconstruction. Almost immediately after the war, Georgia legislators allocated large sums—nearly one million dollars—to repair the W&A and thereafter launched numerous schemes to promote privately owned railroad companies. A new line connected Dalton to Rome in the early 1870s, and a road from Atlanta reached even mountainous Ellijay, the Gilmer County seat, in the eighties. By 1890 every county in northwest Georgia (except Murray) was served by one or more lines; five of the ten Blue Ridge counties also had railroad connections. Overall, railroad mileage in Georgia expanded from 1,404 miles in 1860 to 2,433 miles in 1880, an increase of 73 percent. (This figure actually understates the degree of postwar growth, as the figure in 1860 was far greater than it was after Sherman's march.) The trend was by no means limited to Georgia. North Carolina's railroads expanded by 62 percent, South Carolina's by 41 percent. Northern tracks also expanded rapidly—mileage in New York and Indiana, for example, more than doubled between 1860 and 1880. Transcontinental lines connected East with West. Southern lines finally widened their tracks in accordance with northern standards (before the war track gauges north and south of the Mason-Dixon line were different, thereby preventing continuous railroad lines across regional lines). Railroad companies divided the nation into time zones, which were adopted as the standard by business leaders and governments everywhere. The iron horse exposed rural America to the machinery of modern capitalism. It fostered a new concern for time. Most important, it created an integrated system of national markets—markets of finance, trade, and culture— and by the 1880s the South was rapidly becoming part of that national system.[17]

Villages popped up in abundance along the South's expanding railroads, and the larger of these—generally towns like Dalton that had gained some commercial advantages before the war—became centers of agricultural trade. The national economic depression of the 1870s hindered rapid growth in the South, as did the fiscal turmoil wrought by regional political upheavals, but railroad expansion and small-town growth continued apace. A new commercial orientation was reshaping the southern upcountry. In the 1870s this trend manifested itself in a growing commitment to cash-crop agriculture and monetary interactions. The number of general stores and groceries in the Georgia Valley increased almost 60 percent. Although most of these businesses were small concerns—with less than $5,000 in assets—they were not merely the reincarnations of antebellum country stores. Before the war, general stores stood at the crossroads of rural communities; store owners went to the farmers. By 1880 farmers in need of credit and goods from merchants came to town. As railroads spread throughout the upcountry, the number of communities in the valley that could boast five to ten retail stores increased; the number of isolated country stores actually declined. The rise of upcountry railroad towns and the farmers' shift to cash-crop agriculture were mutually reinforcing trends.[18]

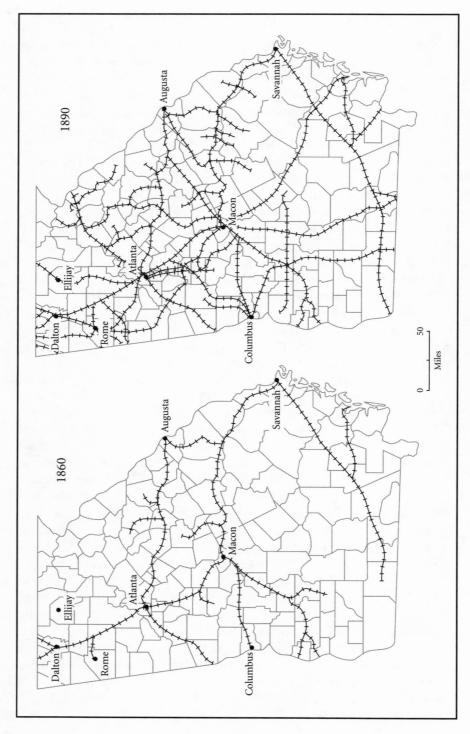

MAP 1.2. Railroad Expansion in Georgia, 1860–1890. *Source:* Flynn, *White Land, Black Labor,* pp. 138–39.

Commercial capitalism manifested itself most clearly in the cotton economy, and bat dung, strange to say, was the key to cotton production in the Georgia Valley. In the immediate postwar years, farmers did not plunge directly into the cotton market, even though prices for the staple were startlingly high in the late 1860s. Whether they wanted (or needed) to adopt a cash-crop system, the lack of an adequate commercial network would not allow it. But railroad expansion changed that. Beginning in the 1870s, north Georgia's farmers could move into staple production as guano—commercially packaged bat manure from South America—found its way into the general stores of Dalton and other railroad towns. Commercial fertilizer enabled farmers in the Georgia Valley to produce high-grade cotton within a shorter time period. Up to 1870, Georgia farmers had used almost no commercial fertilizers, but as Dixie's commercial networks burgeoned, guano spread, literally, across the upcountry. By the mid-1870s, Georgians were importing 55,316 tons of fertilizer annually. By the end of the decade, that figure had more than doubled, to 119,583 tons.[19]

Thus fertilized, cotton bloomed throughout the Georgia Valley. As one agricultural consultant for the federal census of 1880 observed, "There is a marked increase in cotton production in all of these [valley] counties in the last ten years." Counties in the southern part of the valley made the transition to cotton more rapidly than northern counties, but the trend was nearly universal. Although the average increase in cotton production between 1860 and 1880 was only 16 percent statewide, the number of cotton bales produced by farmers in Whitfield and Murray counties increased 112 percent and 177 percent respectively. In Gordon County, just south of Whitfield, cotton production jumped an eye-popping 664 percent. During the same twenty-year period, per capita corn production in the Georgia Valley declined more than 30 percent. There was little doubt that cash-crop agriculture was the wave of the future for north Georgia.[20]

Subsistence farmers did not surrender their self-sufficiency overnight, of course. As census officials from the valley counties reported in 1880, mixed farming still prevailed in many areas. But the census representative from Walker County (just west of Whitfield) caught the fundamental trend: "Because the cotton area is increasing, the tendency toward [producing one's own] home supplies is decreasing." Nor was cotton the only cash crop. Wheat was still a going concern, especially after railroad towns began to build flour mills. Fruit production represented still another route to commercial agriculture. In the Blue Ridge, apples were the principal product of the orchards. Poorer mountain farmers also found that railroad connections to Atlanta created an urban market for vegetables and herbs such as ginseng. In the valley, some farmers grew apples, but peaches were the fruit of choice. Particularly after the advent of refrigerated railroad cars, farmers in Whitfield, Murray, and Gordon counties shipped tons of peaches to northern cities. After growing almost no commercial fruit in the antebellum era, farmers in

Whitfield County produced 4.33 bushels per capita in 1880, well above the state average (.91 bushels). The per capita production figure for Gilmer was an impressive 2.58 bushels. Like the spreading cotton economy, commercial fruit production boosted trade in Dalton, thereby deepening the wealth of the town's merchants, who financed the crops, outfitted the farmers, and grew increasingly influential in upcountry society.[21]

Because staple-crop agriculture necessitated the services of merchants and middlemen, the channels of trade in northwest Georgia began to flow toward the towns, whose influence over the countryside expanded far beyond what it had been in antebellum years. Railroad towns became marketing, service, and financial centers for farmers who grew cotton and commercial food crops. When a Murray County observer remarked, "cotton is ginned as fast as picked, and is sent to Dalton by wagon," he touched on a critical shift in upcountry society: commercial towns were replacing isolated farming communities as the centers of economic activity. In the Georgia Valley, Dalton and Rome emerged as the two leading centers of trade. Just as the South's large interior cities—Atlanta and Nashville, for instance—serviced and dominated huge agricultural hinterlands, smaller southern towns extended their influence over hinterlands of more modest breadth. Dalton served as the cotton market for Whitfield, Murray, some sections of Gordon and Walker counties, and some counties along the Tennessee border. Rome serviced cotton farmers in Floyd and parts of Chattooga, Gordon, and Polk counties, along with some areas of neighboring Alabama. The merchants of each city also had connections in nearby mountain areas. Many Gilmer County farmers, despite accessible rail connections to Atlanta, brought their crops by wagon to Dalton, where they settled accounts and acquired supplies. Rome became the commercial center for Sand Mountain farmers, who hauled sorghum syrup, among other things, to town. Significantly, the areas over which Dalton and Rome exerted their commercial influence matched, almost exactly, the rural districts from which they later recruited cotton-mill workers.[22]

During the 1880s, Dalton's role as a center of agricultural commerce expanded. The city's development paralleled that of small railroad towns throughout the cotton South, most of which encircled major urban centers such as Atlanta and specialized in the processing and marketing of cotton. The Dalton Compress Company, established in the early 1880s, typified the kind of enterprise that both accompanied and promoted the new industrial expansion. Compresses reduced the size of cotton bales by half, which in turn enabled the cotton to be marketed and shipped more quickly and in greater volume, thereby facilitating trade for both farmers and merchants. As a result, a compress attracted trade to its city and fostered commercial development.

By the latter part of the decade, the *Dalton Argus* reported that the local Compress Company was processing twelve thousand bales a year and that almost half a million dollars' worth of the staple was marketed in the city. Cotton farmers hit Dalton like a whirlwind each fall after picking began in late August or early September. Wagons crowded the dusty, sometimes muddy streets. Some farmers brought their cotton to town already ginned and baled, and others utilized one of the two gins in town. They fanned out across Hamilton Street, Dalton's major business thoroughfare, selling their cotton and produce in exchange for foodstuffs and other necessities. Normally their crops fetched a price below that of the store-bought goods they needed, and so the local supply merchants usually extended them credit, taking a mortgage on the farmers' crops and land in return. Business remained strong through late November, after which Dalton assumed a more sleepy posture, its dozen daily passenger trains and growing local population notwithstanding. In the spring another round of town-country transactions would stir Dalton as the farmers prepared for planting.[23]

The commercial successes of Dalton's postbellum merchants illustrate how agricultural trade—particularly the cotton economy—created a substantial pool of wealth in upcountry towns. In 1867 J. F. Denton and A. W. Lynn established a firm for the purpose of selling provisions to farmers and shipping agricultural produce, especially grain. Before long they began buying cotton, and by the 1880s they were taking in three thousand bales per season. An expansive two-story warehouse in town reflected their growing success. Sam E. Berry and T. A. Berry, brothers born and reared in Whitfield County, also made fortunes as merchants. They took over a local hardware store in the late 1870s and built it into a large three-story opera-tion on Hamilton Street. Berry Hardware sold farmers a broad line of basic goods, most of which, before the 1870s, had been made by independent artisans in rural communities. Emblematic of the New South cotton economy was the Berrys' large supply of guano for sale. The brothers sold goods for affluent Daltonians and wealthy farmers as well, including northern-made carriages and buggies.

The Cartwright Brothers dry-goods firm also carried merchandise for the local elite—silks and cigars, for instance—but focused primarily on basic staples and necessities for small farmers. Tennesseans-turned-Georgians A. J. and I. F. Cart-wright opened a small general store in the village of Dawnville, ten miles northeast of Dalton. After three successful years, they left that store in the hands of a hired clerk and opened a large second store on Hamilton Street, where they not only prospered from local trade but also, according to one observer, did "considerable jobbing business to country stores" in the "territory dependent on this market." George W. Oglesby and J. W. Barrett tapped into the valley's expanding wheat production by establishing a local flour mill in 1876. Oglesby then went into the supply business in the mid-eighties and, according to one source, soon developed "a very nice trade among the farmers in Whitfield and surrounding counties, . . . giving credit on all goods sold on the coming season's crop." Barrett, meanwhile, joined with Denton and Lynn to establish the Dalton Roller Mills, which found a large market for processed flour in the Southeast. With Barrett as a partner, Denton and Lynn were able to expand their agricultural trade, and the three became leading cotton buyers, produce shippers, and supply merchants. New men of enterprise were becoming increasingly interconnected within Dalton's business circles. The town's growing cadre of merchants and financiers accumulated small fortunes as the avenues of trade were remapped in the southern upcountry.[24]

Despite their affluence, Dalton's new business leaders were neither satisfied nor secure. Cotton service towns faced natural limits to commercial growth. Because numerous smaller agricultural boroughs encircled Dixie's major urban centers, the area of each cotton town's hinterland was limited. The population of these small cities normally spurted upward after 1880 only to level off somewhere under ten thousand. Dalton's growth was steadier than most, but its population was smaller than that of many commercial hubs, expanding from 1,809 in 1870 to just over 3,000 in 1890 (see population figures in table A.1). Equally troubling to business leaders was the instability and general decline of the cotton market. To bet exclusively on the cotton and agricultural trade was risky business. Local merchants and creditors, themselves often in debt to northern financiers, therefore came to view economic diversification in a positive light. To forestall their financial ruin in an agricultural crisis and to boost Dalton's population, affluent commercial leaders began to contemplate the city's future as an industrial center.[25]

But why cotton mills? At the time, southern developers claimed it was natural to "bring the cotton mills to the cotton fields." This was a catchphrase more conducive to booster rhetoric than to industrial success. As British and New England textile enterprises had demonstrated in earlier eras, nearby cotton fields were hardly necessary prerequisites for profitable mills. There was, nevertheless, a connection between cotton mills and upcountry staple production. The small-town merchants who were pushing for local industrial development already controlled the cotton crop. By building cotton textile mills they could protect themselves from financial disaster—could, in the words of one local editor, "cover the decline in price." Whereas a decline in staple prices might hurt mercantile enterprises, it would work to the advantage of cotton-mill managers, who could then purchase their raw materials at a very low cost.[26]

Ultimately, though, the decision to invest in cotton mills instead of other industries had less to do with the availability of cotton than with the very nature of the American textile industry. Cotton mills had already served as the entry wedge of large-scale manufacturing in Great Britain and New England, and they would do the same in the American South (as well as in Japan, India, and other newly industrializing countries). By the 1880s, textiles were the most mature and highly developed industry in the American North—and also the most transportable. By themselves, southerners had virtually no way of making sophisticated textile machinery or putting a large factory into operation. Industrial dreamers in Dixie would have to import their machinery and expertise, and textiles offered the least painful, most reliable acquisition. America's urban boom generated an enormous demand for factory-made cotton cloth, and northern machine makers and shipping agents saw in southern textile development the opportunity to expand their own operations. This made Dixie's manufacturers dependent on Yankees for outfitting their mills and marketing their product, but there was not much choice. In any case, start-up costs for modest-sized cotton mills were not prohibitive; a cotton mill was a relatively low-risk endeavor that could pay big dividends and possibly provide an economic boost for a small town.[27]

An equally important consideration was the South's labor force. Dixie had no adequate pool of skilled industrial workers; no economically underdeveloped area would. And, with the exception of immigrant ironworkers who moved to Birmingham, Alabama, in the late nineteenth century, southern industrialists had little success in luring talented labor from outside the region. Nascent southern industry would have to rely almost exclusively on the labor of rural-bred folk, most of whom had no experience whatsoever in wage work, to say nothing of factory labor. This labor force "in the making" did not have to be impoverished, merely displaced from traditional patterns of family production and consumption. Economic historians have demonstrated the importance of surplus family labor in fueling the rise of New England textiles during the early nineteenth century, a surplus created largely by the increasing dominance of commercial agriculture in the northeastern states. In the postbellum South, the advent of a consumer economy undermined traditions of home production and created a similar pool of rural surplus labor.[28]

It was not the labor of failing artisans or farmers but the labor of their children that actually formed the basis for early southern textile development. As self-sufficiency declined in the countryside and traditional crafts suffered in competition with readily available, mass-produced goods, the conventional economic contributions of children and single women, who were no longer needed for the production of clothing and the processing of foodstuffs, became less vital. Farmers who were losing money in the cotton market—or watching their old clientele for handmade goods disappear—needed alternative outlets for their families' surplus labor power, and upcountry industrialists needed laborers from the towns and countryside who were willing to take on mill work. What southern manufacturers got, due to sagging commodity prices (which were beyond their control) and abusive credit arrangements and land laws (which were of their own making), was an impoverished work force for whom even meager wages were a significant contribution to the family budget. Precisely because the available workers lacked industrial experience, cotton mills made sense. The skilled adult labor needed for any successful iron mill or machine works, for example, was not to be found in the South of the 1880s. With minimal training, though, cotton textile machinery could be run by children and young adults, as demonstrated in New England half a century earlier.

Even though cotton mills were an obvious choice for New South developers, the prospect of successful industrialization in Dixie at first seemed remote. In 1880 Dalton had virtually no significant manufacturing plants—fewer, in fact, than it had before and during the Civil War. The census for that year listed twenty-two "manufacturing establishments" for all of Whitfield County, none of which were particularly important to Dalton's economy. About three-fourths were small gristmills, scattered throughout the county, that serviced the needs of farming communities. Some of these, like Henry Yaeger's mill in the Dug Gap community south of Dalton, dated from antebellum times. There were seven small sawmills, which had an unimpressive average capitalization of $1,000. Only a few individuals were needed to run these grist and lumber mills, which produced for local markets and were more geared to an agricultural than a diversified economy. Such establishments gave no indication that large-scale manufacturing for national markets would soon develop in Dalton. Merchants were the main beneficiaries of economic change, but by 1880 they may have harbored doubts about Dalton's economic future. From their point of view, the town needed safer investments—it needed prosperous local industry. But, as one local editor complained, some wealthy Daltonians still questioned their town's "adaptability to factory enterprise."[29]

Dalton's leading merchants nonetheless began to channel their wealth into local industry and, in doing so, led their town into the world of large-scale manufacturing. The Berry brothers became major investors in a host of nonagricultural ventures, as did Denton, Lynn, and Barrett. George Oglesby became one of Dalton's foremost industrialists, owning stock and serving as a director in numerous enterprises. Frank T. Hardwick used profits from his grocery business to establish Dalton's first bank and became the city's leading investor in local industries. George W. Hamilton and his brother, Henry C. Hamilton, the heirs of wealthy slaveowners, prospered in the postwar era through retail sales and the extension of farm credit. They also became major investors in and directors of a variety of local industries. Upon this foundation of local investment, factories began to appear in Dalton. By 1882 the city boasted a variety of small-to-middling manufacturing interests, including several lumbering and woodworking establishments, two cotton gins, the cotton press, and a slaughterhouse. In 1885 Anthony Johnson Showalter established in Dalton one of the largest publishing houses in the Southeast. And in that same year, the Crown Cotton Mill began operations. It represented the city's first textile concern and was easily its most important enterprise.[30]

Dalton's leading merchants played fundamental roles in financing and directing the Crown Mill. All of the businessmen mentioned above served as directors or officials of the company. J. F. Denton and A. W. Lynn invested heavily in the enterprise and served as corporate directors. J. W. Barrett also contributed money to Crown and was the company's vice president for three years. Frank Hardwick became the town's leading textile magnate. He was a director for Crown until his death in 1921 and was also largely responsible for building Dalton's second cotton mill, the Elk Mill, in 1907. George W. Hamilton, whose family land provided the site for Crown Mill, became virtually synonymous with the enterprise. He served as secretary-treasurer at Crown for nearly a decade and then, in 1894, assumed the position of president, a post he held until his death in 1919. Some merchants from Sweetwater, Tennessee, who had kinship ties to some of Dalton's leading business leaders were instrumental in getting the mill started, but local business leaders and their families held nearly 60 percent of Crown Cotton Mill stock in 1885 (see table 1.1). There was virtually no northern money involved and, in the beginning, very little southern money from outside Dalton and Sweetwater. Most of the money to build Crown sprang from Dalton's agricultural trade of the 1870s and early 1880s.[31]

It was no accident that the Crown Mill was founded at the very time poor farmers in the Georgia Valley were becoming less self-sufficient and more en-tangled by poverty, tenancy, and a declining cotton market. Conventional wisdom holds that the process by which this took place was clear enough. The crisis of the cotton economy plunged farm families into deep and abiding poverty and pushed many into the ranks of landlessness. The same turn of events enriched upcountry merchants, who sought to boost their towns as well as their own fortunes by building cotton mills and filling them with workers drawn from the vast pool of desperate labor in the countryside. There is truth to this scenario in its broadest outlines, but the rise of the cotton mills was neither so simple nor so sudden. The decade of the 1880s, during which Dixie made its first major industrial advances, was not a period of complete agricultural disaster or of industrial triumph. It was a decade of flux for the South's economic system. When cotton mills first began to materialize in the upcountry, it was not yet readily apparent that ordinary farmers were losing their hold on the land.

As plain folk planted their cotton in the spring of 1880, there was still hope for recovery in the countryside. Only a decade earlier, the price of cotton had been twenty-nine cents per pound. Prices had fallen steadily since then, and by 1879 the staple earned only eleven cents per pound. But cotton prices could rise in any given year, and for those who risked planting a good-sized cotton crop, the gamble was not as fearful in 1880 as it would be later. The dreaded sharecropping system, so central to the economic woes of the New South, was not yet fully in place in the Georgia Valley. In the standard sharecropping arrangement, tenants farmed some-one else's land and, by contract, gave a share of the crop (usually one-third to one-half) to the landlord, who in return sometimes provided tools and stock, and who also provided a shack on the land in which the tenant family lived. Tenant farmers

TABLE 1.1. Crown Cotton Mill Capitalization, 1885–1910

Crown Mill Stockholders by Location (percentage)

	1885	1901	1910
Dalton	66	49	48
Tenn. Valley	28	27	22
Other South[a]	4	20	22
Non-South[b]	2	4	8
Total	100	100	100
	(n=50)	(n=94)	(n=124)

Distribution of Shares by Location (percentage)

	1885	1901	1910
Dalton	57	45	44
Tenn. Valley	41	35	36
Other South[a]	1	17	15
Non-South[b]	1	4	5
Total	100	100	100
	(n=668)	(n=3,006)	(n=5,981)

Source: Crown Cotton Mills Stockbook, 1885–1910, CGA.
[a]Includes all former Confederate states, excluding Dalton and the Tennessee Valley counties.
[b]Includes all non-Confederate states and foreign countries.

sold their shares of the crops, but years of bad prices and high interest rates created a deepening cycle of dependency and debt. At the outset of the 1880s, however, tenancy rates in north Georgia were still low. More than 80 percent of the farmers in Gilmer County owned their land, and in Murray County the tenancy rate was only 16 percent. Slightly more than one-third of all Whitfield County farmers were tenants, but 64 percent still owned their land at the beginning of the decade. In Gordon County, 60 percent of the farmers were landowners. Tenancy rates in northwest Georgia were considerably lower than the state average, which was 45 percent, and the larger regional average, which was 39 percent. The sharecropper system was more in evidence in the old Plantation Belt than in the new cotton lands of the upcountry. Tenancy arrangements in north Georgia were still flexible, and some were perhaps even attractive to young, up-and-coming farmers. For example, in some less-developed rural areas, tenants were allowed to keep all profits from their crops for a period of three to four years, in exchange for timbering the land and enclosing it with a sturdy fence. Census agents in Gordon and Catoosa counties even reported that credit advances for cotton crops were not much in evidence in 1879.[32]

At the same time, the potential for increasing dependency and debt was clear. One observer noted that Murray County farmers, virtually all of whom owned their farms, were dependent on credit "to a very great extent." A census official in Bartow County averred, "Since the late war the great majority of the people have been in debt, and hence the system of credits and advances." Advances led to more debt, and the only way out was to raise a cash crop. In 1880 that meant cotton and more of it. One observer from Polk County described at length the plain folk's path to cotton agriculture and dependency: "Before the war the poorer whites owned and occupied small, poor places and produced nearly all they used of both food and clothing; but they produced very little cotton. . . . Now the poorer whites have abandoned their poor farms and work for shares on the larger and better farms, under the general direction of land owners. As cotton is the profitable crop, these poor people produce cotton almost exclusively, and with it buy everything they need, except bread, and some buy even that." The thought of producing only cotton and buying one's bread would have seemed mind-boggling to antebellum yeomen. In 1880 such practices were still exceptional in northwest Georgia. But farmers involved in the cotton economy were heading in that direction, and the danger remained that staple prices would fall even further and that economic dependency, the age-old dread of petty producers everywhere, would become widespread, even permanent.[33]

By the end of the 1880s, these fears had become reality for many poor upcountry farmers. During the decade, real cotton prices had fallen, and they would dip lower in the 1890s, not returning to the level of the early 1880s until after 1904 (see table 5.4). State legislators created laws that gave merchants increasing leverage over their debt-ridden clientele. Slowly, new state and county legislation rendered illegal the plain folk's tradition of open-range grazing. Tax exemptions for poor farmers were abolished. Young farmers found it difficult to attain land; old farmers struggled and sometimes failed just to hold on to it. By 1890 Georgia's tenancy rate had jumped to 54 percent, and, in contrast to 1880, northern county rates paralleled, and sometimes even surpassed, the state average. Tenants, mostly sharecroppers, worked 46 percent of Whitfield's farms in 1890. Gordon County tenancy figures for that year were nearly the reverse of what they had been a decade earlier, as 57 percent of the farmers were now landless. In Murray County, where renting a farm was a rarity in 1880, the tenancy rate soared to 54 percent. Even in the Blue Ridge area, debt and dependency plagued ordinary farmers. "Everybody is pushing to collect what is due," moaned a Pickens County editor in 1885, "and nobody is able to pay what he owes." No wonder hard-pressed farm families began to view factory work—which they called "public work"—as a means of family survival.[34]

Crown's first millhands left no diaries or letters to explain why they moved to the mill, but census materials make it possible to partially reconstruct their lives and the paths they took to Dalton's new textile factory. The oldest surviving payroll books for the Crown Mill date from 1888 and 1890. It is possible to locate some of these millhands and their families in the manuscript census for 1880—eight to ten years before they took jobs at Crown. This process allows us to step back in time and examine the families who, several years hence, would send some household members to work in the mill. In all, I was able to trace fifty-seven of Crown's early employees to the Georgia manuscript census schedules. These fifty-seven workers comprised over 40 percent of the combined work force listed in the payrolls of 1888 and 1890, not an insignificant proportion of Crown's first cohort of workers. The resulting information on migration to Crown clearly demonstrates that the move to mill work was a family affair; the fifty-seven employees were drawn from only sixteen households. An analysis of those households in 1880 offers a better understanding of early labor market trends and a penetrating look at the social and economic backgrounds of Crown's initial work force.[35]

Many myths have surrounded the first generation of cotton-mill workers in the New South, but almost no empirical work has been done to trace their origins. Decades ago, historian Broadus Mitchell portrayed them as hopeless, impoverished peasants, torn from the land. They were a submissive people, their docility stemming from feelings of gratitude toward the mill owners for steady wages and solid mill-village homes. Less romantic scholars soon came to view the workers as less grateful and less docile, but the image of a trapped and defeated lot persisted, at least until recently. The latest works on southern millhands have been keenly attuned to the integrity of plain folk culture. Mercifully, the "defeated lot" view has all but disappeared. And yet the notion still remains that mill workers were suddenly wrenched from the land by the forces of the market economy and that the mill village immediately emerged as the central institution in their lives. The evidence from Crown presented here and in later chapters cautions against such a view. During the 1880s, the workers who labored for Crown Mill came from diverse backgrounds and were only marginally committed to the mill. As late as 1900, only about one-third of Crown's employees lived in mill-village housing. The eighties and nineties were decades of transition. In Dalton at least, the full-blown cotton-mill village as we have come to know it did not take shape until the early twentieth century.[36]

Most of Crown's first mill families hailed from north Georgia and boasted substantial numbers of children. In 1880, before the Crown Mill began operation, these households squeezed an average of eight people into their modest dwellings, and in most homes several children worked to support the family. By the end of the decade, the same households were sending an average of 3.6 family members to work in the Crown Mill. Family labor was the order of the day for poor whites in the mills, just as it had been on the farms. Although all of these findings might be expected, my analysis did yield some surprises. Despite talk by Dixie's mill officials about hiring war widows and their children, fewer than 20 percent of the house-

Crown Mill spinning department workers, ca. 1886. (*Courtesy of Crown Gardens and Archives*)

holds that I located in the 1880 census were headed by women. A large majority of the male household heads worked in agriculture, but the occupations of their children were more diverse. In these households in 1880, the children were as likely to be employed in cotton mills as they were to be working on farms. For some families, or at least for some individuals within them, the move to Crown did not represent a complete break from past work habits.[37]

This migration analysis also speaks to the issue of the textile labor market in the early New South. Reflecting labor supply trends often noted in the history of southern mills, Crown drew the bulk of its early laborers from a limited geographical area. Over half the workers listed in the payroll records in 1888 or 1890 had been residing in Whitfield County a decade earlier, and the majority of these lived in farming areas just outside the Dalton city limits (see map 1.3). Of the workers found in the 1880 census, 65 percent were located within Whitfield and the counties immediately surrounding it. The Crown Mill "labor shed" bore a striking resemblance to Dalton's agricultural hinterland.[38]

The first workers at Crown Mill were not necessarily strangers in a strange place. Nearly four of every ten workers traced to the 1880 census were located in the Dalton District of Whitfield County, and many of these hands came from families who lived very near each other in the same rural neighborhoods surrounding the town. Early on, community-based migration chains were developing. In the 1880s, much of the land within Dalton's city limits was still undeveloped, and there were

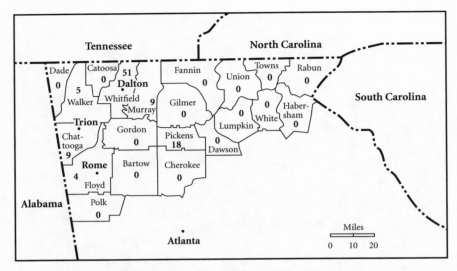

MAP 1.3. Counties from which Crown Mill Workers Migrated during the 1880s.

Source: U.S. census manuscripts, Georgia, 1880.

Note: Numbers indicate the percentage of migrants (from a total of 57) located in each county in 1880. Percentages are rounded off.

farming communities located on the outskirts of town. One such neighborhood lay just west of Dalton; at least four of Crown's earliest working families—the Eskews, Hamiltons, Loners, and Springfields—lived there in 1880 and sent family members to work at Crown sometime before 1888. According to the census schedules, these families lived just down the road from one another, which meant that when one family took on mill work, the others knew it.[39]

These households offer a revealing picture of the early mill families and their lives before Crown. Two of the families were supported not through agriculture per se, but rather by artisanal work. In 1880 W. J. Eskew was a bricklayer, age forty-five, whose thirty-two-year-old wife, Amanda, had been through seven childbirths. Their oldest son, age nineteen, worked as a day laborer, but the oldest daughter, four years younger, went to school. It was not these older children but the ones too young to work in 1880 who ultimately found employment at Crown. In 1888 both Emma and Burt Eskew, ages fifteen and twelve respectively, worked regularly for the mill. Even for artisans, family labor was essential—more so, as Emma and Burt could attest—as commercial capitalism advanced. The Hamilton family (apparently not related to the merchant-industrialists) was also supported through artisanal work in 1880, but not by the head of the house, who was a forty-four-year-old widow. Frank Hamilton, who at nineteen was the oldest son, worked ⁔ver to put food on the table for his mother and two younger brothers. But sawyering was a losing proposition in an age of increasingly larger lumber mills. The family took in boarders to help make ends meet. By 1888 both Frank and his brother Rufus had taken employment at Crown. Frank, because of his experience with machines and his gifted mechanical mind, was in demand around Dalton, and by the early twentieth century the city had hired him as the municipal super-intendent of water, light, and gas. Crown later rehired him as a "master me-chanic."[40]

Not far from the Hamiltons in 1880 lived a poor farm family by the name of Loner. William, who had been born in South Carolina, and his wife, Crayton, were both thirty-five years old, and they had four children ranging from one to eight years of age. Before the next decade dawned, most of the family had gone to work for Crown, including William, two sons, and one daughter. William and Patty Springfield's family lived down the way from the Loners. The Springfields were a large farming family with eight children, who, unlike the Hamiltons' and Eskews', could neither read nor write. William was listed as a farmer but also as a disabled person, which doubtless made it difficult for the family to earn a living. Perhaps that is why three of his sons went to work for Crown after it opened. In one case the relationship with the company would be a long one. Hugh Springfield, who was working for Crown in 1888 at age seventeen, was still earning wages as a weaver there in 1910.[41]

Beyond this local labor market composed of families with little or no industrial experience, a more far-reaching channel of labor migration provided hands who did boast textile skills. One-third of the millhands traced to 1880 came from the second tier of counties surrounding Whitfield, and these people often had work experiences that made them valuable to Dixie's early mill officials. William P. Fallis is one example. In 1890 Fallis was the only person by that name working for Crown, but he was not new to cotton mills. Indeed, he came from a family with a tradition in southern textile work. A decade earlier, at age fourteen, William was one of four children in Thomas A. Fallis's household who worked for the cotton mill in Trion, Georgia. Apparently he was either recruited by Crown or saw oppor-tunities for himself when the mill opened, for he moved to Dalton by the time he was twenty-two and stayed on with the mill through 1900. By that time he was a foreman and owned his home free of mortgage.[42] The Trion mill produced an-other of Crown's early foremen in Jesse Jackson, who, in 1880, lived several blocks from the Fallis household. Jackson apparently was a new arrival in northwest Georgia at the time of the census, as his entire family, including a one-month-old infant, was born in South Carolina. Evidently Jackson knew cotton mills, for not long after starting work at Trion he moved his family to Dalton, where he took a leading position in the Crown Mill.[43]

Similar examples were found among Blue Ridge households. It was no easy trip from mountainous Pickens County to Dalton, but two large families made the journey to Crown during the late 1880s. Neither were primarily farm families, although both allotted some of their household labor to agriculture. Frank M. Pearce was a farmer, but two of his children worked in a small, rural cotton mill that stood amid a sea of farms in the Talking Rock District of the county. By 1888 five of his family members earned wages from Crown.[44] Rash Roe of the Persimmon Tree District was a miller for a farming community in 1880. The eighties were not a good time to be a traditional miller, given Pickens County's railroad connections to Atlanta, and perhaps commercial competition proved too much. By 1890 Roe's family had made its way to Dalton, where five of his children (ages nine to seventeen) worked in the Crown Mill.[45]

The diverse backgrounds of these early millhands is instructive. It has been suggested that southern plain folk who took up work in the cotton mills thought of themselves (and were thought of by their neighbors) as failures. One study argued, for example, that "to leave the farm for the factory was to sink so low in social status that often families were severed by the transition."[46] It is difficult to square such statements with the evidence that early mill families were making careful economic decisions and doing so in collaboration with other people in their rural communities. The Crown Mill example suggests that friends and family were not severed by farm-to-mill migration but instead were bound together by increasingly complicated networks of labor. Even in 1880, before the southern mill boom, poor whites were engaged in diverse occupations; the family economy already demanded flexible strategies for survival.

Family labor was the key to making a living, and households did not hesitate to parcel their labor power into a variety of jobs. Moreover, rural people were accustomed to working within tightly knit communities. A family who moved to the mill or sent some family members to work there was not an outcast but a potential source of information about what the mills were like and how one could get a job there. The South's ordinary white farmers were pragmatic realists. Some might have talked down the mills, but most families behaved as if mill work was just one economic option that might work to their advantage or might be necessary. Like the merchants who became industrialists, poor farmers and struggling artisans tried to hedge their bets against economic disaster. In their case, however, disaster might mean starvation, not just a bad investment.

By the mid-1880s, enduring postwar poverty and the modernization of the upcountry economy had begun to create a pool of needy and discontented white families who were willing to become factory wage earners. Most were poor farmers—probably sharecroppers—but others were artisans whose traditional roles in the agricultural economy were being undermined by the availability of mass-produced goods and by the farmers' increasing dependence on town merchants. Widespread agricultural disaster was not a necessary condition for mill building. Textile mills arose and succeeded in the South even before conditions in the countryside reached a severe crisis point in the 1890s. Willing workers were easy enough to find, because the process of rural dislocation had already begun and because the mills did not yet need large work forces. During the 1880s, southern cotton mills remained relatively small. Two dozen families could supply enough workers to run most mills. The sprawling textile complexes of the twentieth-century South could not yet be envisioned, nor could the labor problems that would arise out of such explosive growth.

A generation after the Civil War, it could hardly be argued that the South was an industrial region or that Dalton was a "modern" town. To suggest as much would have been almost laughable. But the power of the American economy was no joke, and by the 1890s Dalton, along with the rest of the southern upcountry, had become part of an expanding industrial capitalist system. At a very basic level, the economic reconstruction of the South was complete. New England textile moguls did not lose any sleep over their small-time southern competitors, and southern plain folk did not suddenly leave their farms for the factories. But the foundation for large-scale manufacturing in the New South had been laid, and a wealthy group of small-town merchants and financiers was building on it. As with any capitalist venture, success was uncertain. And because of Dixie's late arrival on the industrial scene, New South manufacturers had fewer options for economic development available to them than had their counterparts in the North, which was already the well-established center of American industry and finance. The South's new economic leaders nonetheless looked toward the future with an almost ludicrous optimism. Profits were their principal concern, and by the late 1880s they were reaping ample rewards for their efforts. Having succeeded in making money, Dalton's budding industrialists fashioned for themselves a larger vision of who they were and what their town should be. With a boldness that belied their small-town status, they launched a remarkable campaign to turn Dalton into a thriving New South city.

2

DALTON'S INDUSTRIAL RESOLUTION

There was more to the modernization of Dixie than economic change. The new order also required a new way of thinking about local prosperity, an ideological adaptation to the economic realities of the postbellum world. It was one thing for small-town business leaders to finance a mill, but quite another for them to embrace a larger vision of urban-industrial progress. To a degree largely unappreciated by historians, that vision followed rather than preceded the rise of the mills. In Dalton the 1880s were less a decade of frenzied mill building than one of careful, modest investment. The city's would-be industrialists watched the Crown Mill carefully to see if it would succeed. When it faltered early on, enthusiasm for local industry waned. A little success went a long way, however. Once Crown began to pay substantial dividends, Dalton's business leaders endorsed the New South creed of industrial development as if they had never believed anything else. They went even further, placing responsibility for Dalton's prosperity squarely on their own shoulders and demanding control of local affairs. At one point, they even orchestrated the passage of a formal civic resolution in which the people of Dalton pledged to work for an industrial future. Overwhelming the town with aggressive enthusiasm and political prowess, Dalton's rising business class built new factories, passed local reform measures, and gained considerable authority. In so doing, its leaders emerged as a type of southern bourgeoisie and pushed their small town further into the modern age.

The 1880s, it has often been said, marked Dixie's industrial "takeoff," the point at which widespread and lasting industrial development began. The cotton-mill "boom" of the eighties was the key to this regional economic expansion, and the boom was fueled not only by spindles and looms but also by unending booster rhetoric of near-Pentecostal intensity. One less emotional way to evaluate the rise of mills in the South is to examine the number of spindles available for production in the major textile states. Figure 2.1 shows that Georgia and the Carolinas witnessed impressive growth during the 1880s, with spindleage increases ranging from 124 percent in Georgia to over 300 percent in South Carolina. But if southern textiles took off during the 1880s, the trajectory was hardly spectacular. The legend of the southern textile boom has some basis in fact, but, from a strictly quantitative standpoint, promotional bluster seems to have outweighed actual development. Taking a long-term view of cotton-mill expansion, the growth of textiles in the eighties appears unimpressive compared to the astonishing development that followed. As state spindleage levels reached the half-million mark sometime during the 1890s, textiles truly exploded. Nonetheless, the cotton mills of the 1880s were extremely important, for they allowed potential southern investors to evaluate the viability of large-scale manufacturing in Dixie. Each success story inspired a more aggressive approach to small-town industrialization.[1]

In 1885, Dalton's Crown Mill was an impressive sight for small-town Georgians. It dwarfed all other buildings in town. Its steam-powered engine (250 horsepower, as boosters were quick to point out) drove three floors of heavy machinery and billowed impressive plumes of black smoke out of a one-hundred-foot chimney. Its main entrance was topped by a stately belfry that made the mill resemble a very large and imposing church. Anyone entering the plant for the first time must have been overawed by its size, the speed and noise of the machines, the lint-filled air, and the sheer efficiency with which raw cotton was turned into cloth. From a small picker room on the mill's east side, where bales were opened and the unruly staple was given a preliminary cleaning and straightening, the cotton was taken to the carding room, which occupied the first floor of the main building. There the cotton was further straightened and prepared for the spinning room, which was on the third floor. Finished thread was taken to the second-floor weaving room, where high-speed automatic looms turned the warp and woof (or warpin' and

FIGURE 2.1. Southern Textile Growth, 1840–1920

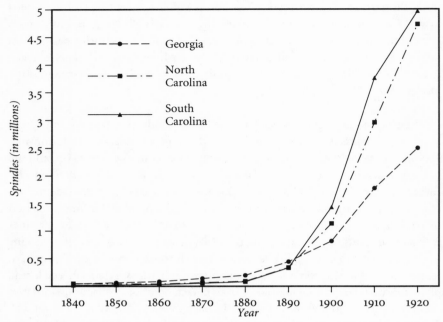

Source: U.S. Bureau of the Census, *Twelfth Census, 1900: Manufactures*, 9(3): 57; ibid., *Fourteenth Census, 1920: Manufactures*, 10:152.

fillin', as the workers put it) into cloth. Crown's finished product was then put onto northbound trains to be sold by Yankee agents. Compared with Crown's size and scale of operations in later decades, the first mill was actually a small affair. But in 1885 it was a remarkable addition to the town.[2]

The problem was, it was not yet a profitable one. Had Dalton's business leaders been able to foresee the spectacular textile growth that lay in the future, they might not have been so worried about the viability of the Crown Cotton Mill. But for a time in 1885 and 1886, they appeared quite concerned. Perhaps many thought—as some openly stated—that Dalton was not quite capable of large-scale industry. Part of the problem, apparently, was management skills—or more precisely the lack thereof.

Crown's initial managers were wealthy and notable figures chosen for their reputations rather than for their ability or desire to manage the mill. J. H. Patton of Sweetwater, Tennessee, the first stock subscriber and a prime mover of the mill, was elected by stockholders as the first president. He was a director of the Sweetwater Valley Bank and a Presbyterian elder—the latter a qualification that became almost a prerequisite for mill management at Crown. Patton's brother Wiley, also from Sweetwater, was the company's first superintendent and oversaw the initial phases of mill construction, which did not go well. The Pattons did not remain in office long. Wiley served only eight months. J. H., already an older man when he assumed the presidency, stepped down after a year and a half and later served briefly as vice president in 1887 before resigning. David Persons Bass became the next president. Bass, who moved to Dalton from Summerville, a small town in Chattooga County, was a Methodist minister and a successful merchant in both Summerville and Dalton. Like Patton, he served only a short term as company chief. Both men were probably elected for symbolic reasons: they were aging and respected individuals who lent credibility to the enterprise. It was not unusual in the 1880s for the directors of upcountry mills to elect such men to top positions. But experience soon demonstrated that younger, more aggressive leadership would be needed.[3]

Before 1887 it was not clear that the Crown Mill would survive, much less prosper. Construction of the plant had moved slowly in 1884, exasperating directors and stockholders alike. The mill's completion in January 1885 only marked a continuation of the company's difficulties. That spring, Crown ran short of working capital and offered new stock subscriptions to local investors. From the company's inception, Dalton had been the mill's main source of capital, but now local people proved reluctant to purchase more stock. The *Dalton Argus* lamented that Crown's offer "excited some croaking comment" among Daltonians who had little faith in the enterprise. In response to this rebuff, the company's directors, most of whom were Daltonians themselves, "stepped to the front, filled the gap, and closed the books." These industrialists, boasted the *Argus*, "are nervy men." Perhaps they were desperate. In either case, croaking seemed the better part of valor in 1885, as Crown suffered a net loss of over $800 (a 2 percent loss on capital) for that fiscal year. During the next twelve months, the company managed a 7 percent return on capital, but considering the hype that had promised huge returns from southern cotton mills, local investors were something less than jubilant.[4]

A lingering uncertainty about local industry began to manifest itself in Dalton during the mid-1880s. Small-town editors could carry the banner of New South urban-industrialism as well as any Atlanta journalist, but through 1886 Dalton's newspaper editors were still considering alternative visions of local well-being. Henry A. Wrench, editor of the *Argus* for most of the late nineteenth century, was one of Dalton's most enthusiastic boosters, and his weekly paper served as a barometer of entrepreneurial sentiment. In 1884, even as the Crown Mill corporation was being organized, Wrench maintained that Dalton would "never be a brisk manufacturing town." Instead, he envisioned the city as an "all the year round mart" for agricultural goods, a "suburban retreat from the dust, confusion and miasmatic poison of the larger cities." He hoped Dalton could become a prosperous commercial center while still retaining its pastoral qualities. Factories did not make his list of "What Dalton Needs" in the spring of that year. Hoping to lure new citizens to the town in 1885, Wrench saw no need to promote the Crown Mill or a coming industrial boom. Of Dalton, he said that there was "no better place in the world for a home and the legitimate accumulation of moderate wealth." Chattanooga, with its burgeoning population and heavy industry located thirty miles northwest, provided a point of comparison. Dalton might not be a "great town" industrially, acknowledged Wrench, but it was a marvelous place to live. Although Chattanooga had become a "big town" with a "great future," it was too dirty and hectic. Dalton, he concluded, was the perfect answer for the Chattanoogan entrepreneur who wanted to retreat from the grimy city by commuter train after work.[5]

Along similar lines, Wrench hoped to facilitate New South prosperity by maintaining north Georgia's antebellum reputation as a summer resort area. Whereas by the late 1880s the *Argus* would thrill to the sound of factory whistles, in 1885 it still described Dalton as "a pleasant little city of 3,000 inhabitants, cozily reposing in a picturesque valley," in which lush foliage fanned by gentle breezes resembled "the fluttering of angels' wings." The vision of Dalton as a health and recreation resort did not necessarily exclude industry altogether. Such booster rhetoric may have been a strategy to attract industrialists to the area. Town leaders throughout Appalachia knew that tourism not only brought an influx of trade for local merchants but also introduced wealthy outside capitalists to their city. Perhaps these Yankee entrepreneurs might fall to the temptations of the region's vast lumber and mineral resources. No doubt one booster's dream came true when George W. Vanderbilt sought to regain his health at a western North Carolina resort in 1888. Immensely impressed by the area's beauty and economic possibilities, the multimillionaire bought vast tracts of land, constructed his famous Biltmore House, and established a large forestry enterprise.[6]

But for a time the *Argus* seemed to view tourism more as an end than as a means to achieve industrial prominence. Henry Wrench, at least, did not deem large-scale manufacturing essential to Dalton's economic success. His emphasis on a nonindustrial future stemmed from his perception of small-town limitations. The economic downturn of the mid-eighties had a dampening effect on industrial spirit in the city. Several local firms collapsed or moved away in 1885–86. To some degree, too, the regional and national market shaped Wrench's vision of Dalton's future. He was skeptical of the city's industrial potential in 1884 because "the source of supply and demand is already nearly settled, at least for many years, [and we cannot] hope for any very great improvement over our present out-put." Until after the middle of the decade, he continued to downplay industrial growth, preaching instead the benefits of agricultural advancement and resort trade, which would improve local commercial strength.[7]

What an about-face, then, when in March 1887 the front page of the *Argus* cried, "We must have factories. We must have big factories and little factories. We must have factories that will pay stockholders reasonable dividends and the workmen good wages." The old emphasis on agriculture took a new twist: "We must have factories—the ever growing crops which carry with them a harvest with each day's beginning." The *Argus*'s message had begun to change in late 1886, when reports from rural correspondents and stories on agricultural trends dropped sharply. By early 1887 the local news focused almost exclusively on Dalton, and a push toward urban-industrial development was the central theme. Wrench urged his readers to "boom" the town, which involved throwing off the shackles of "old fogyism" and investing in local factories. Increased population and prosperity would naturally follow. Wrench's change in attitude probably reflected, in part, his growing real estate investments. Virtually every issue of the paper in 1887 advertised his own business: "Special Attention Given to Investment for Outside Parties, and *Information Furnished to Parties Wishing Factory Locations*." But factories were not necessarily essential to boost land values. Local newspapers had long predicted that resort trade and increased agricultural commerce would have the same effect. Moreover, if Wrench sought to shape local opinion, he also reflected it. No doubt his ideas jelled during conversations with local businessmen over dinners at Dalton's Lewis House hotel or on the elite verandas overlooking Thornton Avenue. The vision of a booming industrial Dalton, as presented in the *Argus*, reflected an emerging consensus among the city's commercial and professional leaders, a consensus that hailed industrial development as the key to local prosperity and well-being.[8]

The *Argus*'s change of heart coincided with the beginnings of prosperity at Crown Mill. By early 1887, Crown's fortunes had improved dramatically under the leadership of well-known civic and business leaders. The mill earned 27 percent on capital stock in 1887 and paid a handsome 25 percent dividend from net profits of $19,123 (see Crown's profit figures in table A.2 and figure A.1). Several leading merchants from Dalton had taken control of the company, and they were able to make the mill pay. In September 1886, Dalton's Thomas R. Jones, who had been vice president for two years, assumed the helm. Almost a year before that, George W. Hamilton had taken the job of secretary-treasurer, and in the fall of 1887, J. W. Barrett assumed the position of vice president. These changes placed three of Dalton's foremost economic leaders and industrial boosters in Crown's top managerial positions.[9]

In August 1887, Crown president Thomas Jones stood proudly before company stockholders and announced, "I see nothing in the future to dim the hope that a greater financial conquest awaits us." Little more needed to be said; word was already out among potential investors. As early as March, the *Argus* reported that "Dalton cotton mill stock" was selling high. The struggling company had clearly stabilized, and the *Argus* flung Crown's success in the face of local naysayers who had questioned "Dalton's adaptability to factory enterprise." That the paper referred to the "Dalton" rather than the "Crown" mill revealed a growing appreciation of the factory's importance to the city and the editor's desire to identify his town with a prosperous industrial operation. When Crown fared poorly during the mid-1880s, Daltonians appeared reluctant to embrace the industrial faith. By 1887, however, citizens could point to a large and successful manufacturing plant financed primarily with local money and operated by local businessmen.[10]

But translating enthusiasm into new factories proved difficult. Dalton's boosters quickly learned that building an urban-industrial society demanded more than purple prose. Obstacles loomed at every turn. Many people in Dalton had little or no money to invest, and some of those who did evidently were not disposed to risk losing it in local industrial ventures. The *Argus* constantly railed against the "fogy element," a local group of affluent citizens whose passive resistance to industrial development exasperated Wrench. "All we ask is that our people may look upon the outside, restless, ever moving world, and then consider whether or not our sleepy way is the best way." Some locals apparently opposed rapid urban growth and factory expansion for religious reasons. One Reverend Johnson warned that a boom in Dalton might weaken the town's moral fiber. In "the impulsive energy of secular affairs," he told his congregation, "one sins in the forgetfulness or neglect of religious duties." The energetic leadership of "secular affairs" was, in fact, exactly what the boosters were about, but many of them were also extremely zealous in their "religious duties." Industrial crusaders throughout America often became religious crusaders as well, for they were not simply acting from profit motives; they were also guided by a worldview that emphasized the sobriety, orderliness, dependability, and social stewardship so vital to religious commitment. For the emerging business class, industrial growth, urban progress, and social control were so tightly woven together as to be inseparable.[11]

To overcome "fogyism" and capital scarcity, Dalton's industrial boosters launched an organized campaign to convert (and loosen the purse strings of) local unbelievers and to attract outside capital. In March 1887, the *Argus* pointed to a new spirit of cooperation among local business leaders: "Under the electric impulse" of Dalton's rising New South spirit, "men combine in common effort to do as they have never done before." This was not all fluff, for less than a month later the new business leaders held a mass meeting designed to organize local forces for the coming economic battle. On the night of April 5, an assembly was held at the courthouse in the middle of town. Enthusiastic citizens crammed into the main room for what was advertised as an open forum on how to facilitate "an active growth of the town." According to the *Argus*, many of the fogy element attended. But in reality the evening was less an open forum for development strategies than a well-planned organizational meeting led by the industrial boosters.[12]

An anxious crowd soon outgrew standing room in the courthouse chamber and overflowed into the corridors. Frank T. Hardwick, founder and president of Dalton's leading bank, was elected to preside. This was fitting, for Hardwick would soon become the city's leading textile entrepreneur and a major figure in the development of Crown Mill. He asked a succession of men to speak, all of whom represented the proindustry camp and waxed eloquent on its behalf. One of the speakers was Thomas Jones, Crown's president, who blended evidence of the mill's success with recitals of Dalton's educational and religious advances, thereby linking—in a vague but effective way—the city's social advances to its industrial growth. Following numerous other speeches, a group was appointed to draw up "resolutions embodying the sense of the meeting." Henry Wrench was on this committee, which soon emerged with a recommendation worthy of any New South booster standard. The *Argus* reported that a "hearty and spontaneous" affirmation filled the room "when the fact was stated that manufacturing industries were the essential element of growth." Rising to their feet with a hearty "aye," the crowd approved Dalton's industrial resolution: "We, as citizens of Dalton, will do all in our power to aid and encourage emigration [of capital], and if necessary donate sites for industrial enterprises, and that we will, so far as we are able, take stock in any and all such enterprises as will locate with us, and that we will work to make permanent the results of this meeting by cultivating a cooperative spirit and work to the accomplishment of permanent good to the town."

As the crowd spilled out into the city park across from the courthouse, where a black band entertained the ecstatic white throng, it seemed the industrial crusaders had won the day. Virtually all of Dalton's leading citizens publicly agreed that industrial development was crucial to the city's future and pledged to support it. In anticipation of the coming boom, the Dalton Land and Improvement Company was organized immediately following the meeting. The ideal of cooperation found tangible expression in the formation of local streetcar and telephone companies in which each citizen could own only a single share, "thus rendering them cooperative entirely." Two days after the town meeting, a correspondent for the *Atlanta Constitution* reported that Dalton "is full of strangers daily and the hotels cannot accommodate the crowds . . . [for] the boom is fully upon us."[13]

The weeks following passage of the industrial resolution witnessed a stunning display of small-town entrepreneurial bravado. By mid-April, local businessmen had established seven new companies and applied for corporate charters from the state. The new firms included mining, manufacturing, and real estate ventures as well as the Dalton Electric and Gas Light Company and the Dalton Hotel Company. The total capital stock of these associations amounted to $160,000, of which $35,000 had already been paid. Some months later the Manly Manufacturing Company, destined to become the city's leading producer of iron and steel products, applied for a charter. Most striking about these eight corporations was that a surprisingly small group of men, virtually all Daltonians, organized and provided the original capital for all of them. Of these entrepreneurs, eleven could be positively identified as local business leaders, and they were generally the same men who orchestrated the industrial resolution. Each man in this group of eleven was personally involved with the organization and capitalization of two or more of the eight new companies.[14]

The enthusiasm continued for some time. By May 1887, another cotton factory seemed imminent. "It appears needless to urge Dalton people to take stock in a [new] cotton factory with the result of Crown Mill's three years existence before them," stated the *Argus*. Actually, Daltonians would not build another mill until 1907, despite occasional fits of cotton-mill fever during the remainder of the 1880s and 1890s.[15] But the absence of new cotton mills did not mean that local industrial development had halted. By 1900 the city showed signs of significant growth in large-scale factory production. Economic historians often gauge the extent of industrial development in an area by calculating the monetary value added to raw materials by the manufacturing process. Rising "value added" figures reflect an increase in the size and number of industrial enterprises. In 1880, when the value added by manufacturing for Georgia (per capita) was a meager eight dollars, the figure for Whitfield County languished at three dollars (see table 2.1). The state's value-added index rose by nearly 200 percent during the next two decades, indicating substantial industrial development in Georgia as a whole. But the state figure did not come close to that for Whitfield County, which skyrocketed by nearly 1,000 percent between 1880 and the turn of the century. Most of this county growth was attributable to the startling rate of development in Dalton. By 1900, valued added per capita in the city stood at nearly ninety dollars, some 300 percent higher than the state figure. The key to Dalton's growth, of course, was the Crown Mill.

The industrial leaders who played prominent roles in Crown's development were mostly young and aggressive businessmen from diverse backgrounds. Frank Hardwick was born in Cleveland, Tennessee, in 1852, to parents affluent enough to give him a college education after the Civil War. In 1871 he returned to Cleveland and prospered in the grocery business. The young merchant turned to banking in 1873 when he moved to Dalton and established the C. L. Hardwick and Company Bank (named in honor of his father). A Methodist and a Mason, Hardwick served as director and officer for numerous companies and, by the early 1890s, was one of the ten wealthiest men in Dalton. Thomas Jones hailed from less affluent surroundings in Chattooga County, northwest from Whitfield, where he received only a rudimentary education. But he was ambitious. After moving to Dalton in 1863 at age sixteen, he was fortunate enough to read law with William Moore, Sr., a highly successful attorney and one of Dalton's leading citizens. Jones passed the bar in 1872 and thereafter rose rapidly in wealth and status, serving in the state senate in the early 1880s. Aggressive in business and devoted to evangelical Christianity, he served numerous directorships in local enterprises and maintained a leadership role in both the Whitfield County Sunday School Association and the Dalton Bible Association. At the time he was president of Crown Mill (1886–94),

TABLE 2.1. Value Added by Manufacturing in Northwest Georgia, 1880–1900 (per capita, in dollars)

	1880	1900	% Change
Georgia	7.97	21.85	174.15
Dalton	n.a.	88.81	—
Counties:			
Catoosa	5.75	4.95	−13.94
Chattooga	14.58	26.39	81.00
Dade	28.95	9.99	−65.49
Gordon	3.05	4.23	38.69
Murray	n.a.	1.76	—
Walker	1.88	26.06	1,286.17
Whitfield	3.10	32.32	942.58

Sources: U.S. Bureau of the Census, *Tenth Census, 1880: Manufactures*, 2: 207–10; ibid., *Population*, 1(2); ibid., *Twelfth Census, 1900: Manufactures*, 8(2): 131, 136–47; ibid., *Population*, 1(1).
Note: In 1900 the Census Bureau explained that meaningful comparisons could be made between "value of materials" as listed in the returns for 1880 and 1900. In both years, the value of materials meant raw materials, factory supplies, and fuel costs. The 1900 returns included a "miscellaneous expenses" category that had not been part of the 1880 statistics. Although this did not alter the returns much, the Census Bureau noted that "it is probable that some of the items included in the cost of materials at the census of 1880 were included in 'Miscellaneous Expenses' at the inquiry of 1890 and 1900" (*Manufactures*, p. ix).

he was also the secretary of a local ironworks and the Dalton Hotel Company (of which Hardwick was president).[16]

Unlike Hardwick and Jones, George W. Hamilton came from a wealthy slave-owning family and fought for the Confederacy. Born to John and Rachel Hamilton in 1847, George grew up in luxury, with twenty slaves working the family plantation. When his father died in 1853, he inherited part of the $40,000 estate. The family moved temporarily to Butts County, Georgia, during the Civil War, leaving the Hamilton homestead to Confederate troops in 1863. The following year, at age seventeen, George and his twin brother, Henry C. Hamilton, joined the Third Georgia Reserves, Company G. They fought in South Carolina during 1864, and Henry lost an arm in the hostilities. After the war, George made his home in Dalton and took a position as clerk for the W&A railroad. Later, after working as an express manager for the East Tennessee and Georgia Railroad, he entered the grocery business and became a successful merchant. Although not an original stockholder in Crown, he worked his way to the top of the company by the mid-1890s and thereafter devoted the rest of his life to the mill.[17]

Despite their varied backgrounds, these industrialists had much in common. Like Henry Wrench, whose editorial campaigns to boost land values accompanied his own real estate advertisements, they were driven by a quest for wealth, epito-mized by the elegant mansion that George Hamilton acquired on Thornton Ave-nue in the 1890s. Of Thomas Jones, one observer noted, "He has made quite a fortune by his [law] practice, and has been very successful in his business ven-tures." Will N. Harben, a native Daltonian who wrote novels set in the town of "Darley," described these New South men in his work. Himself an investor in Crown Mill and other local ventures, Harben knew such men well, and his novels about Darley are meant to reveal their character. His main protagonists are men on the rise, men from the middling ranks of society who shoved aside the old economic ways (but never the genteel manner) to amass fortunes. They were cunning speculators and nervy investors. They understood, as Harben wrote in *The Georgians*, that in Darley "money earned money easily." Harben knew the language of modern capitalism, and that was the language of the New South.[18]

Historians have engaged in brutal debates over whether Dixie's postbellum business leaders were in fact a different breed—both genetically and ideologi-cally—from the antebellum planter crowd. The family backgrounds of New South elites appear to have been a mixed lot, in Dalton and elsewhere. And New South ideology was fundamentally different from that of slaveholding planters, if only because it embraced a free-labor economy and focused on urban development. But the key to business in the New South was neither family background nor ideological persuasion. What mattered most was that the world in which wealthy southerners operated had changed, and changed dramatically, since 1860. Old South planters could not have worked within a national capitalist economy be-cause no such economy existed at the time, and, equally important, their commit-ment to plantation slavery gave them little inclination to create or be a part of such an economy.

Nor will it do to argue, as one historian recently has, that the southern elite was always essentially capitalist—during slavery as well as after emancipation—and that its acceptance of the New South creed required only a simple ideological sleight of hand, a change in rhetoric, an "alteration of forms and means." Forms and means counted for something in the Old South as well as in the New. Wealthy postbellum southerners had to behave differently in the economic arena than their antebellum counterparts, and new forms of behavior required new ways of think-ing. Whatever their physical or ideological genealogy, New South boosters were true believers in the system they championed. Their faith in retrospect may appear foolish and crass, sometimes utterly destructive. But to deny its existence is to purge from the historical record an important ingredient in southern develop-ment. Those southerners who capitalized, literally, on the new economic realities of the postwar world fashioned in their own minds a vision of the future that wove together personal and regional progress with industrial capitalism in powerful ways. To recognize that vision and the grip it had over the faithful is to understand more clearly why, when threatened, the New South business elite fought so viciously to preserve it.[19]

Although the worldview of Dalton's entrepreneurs rested on the quest for wealth, their motives were more complex than that. The men who promoted an industrial city and took control of Crown Mill acted on their faith in two fundamental ideas that fostered among them a strong desire to control local events. Their first crucial belief was that urban growth and large-scale industrial development would benefit everyone in Dalton.[20] This view had been espoused by urban boosters throughout the North during the early part of the century.[21] Factories would create wealth for local investors, of course. But, in the minds of the industrialists, they would also attract a large population of laborers, who would reap the material benefits of urban civilization while providing a ready market for local merchants. As Dalton's booster sheet explained in 1890:

> It is not that men may make dollars that the *Argus* has stuck, with frenzied sameness, to the single text [of city building]. It is that people of the present generation may enjoy for themselves the things which are sure to come; that our children may find paths of usefulness, and places of profit, without leaving home; that thrift and prosperity may freshen and beautify our farms and country homes; that churches and schools may dot the roadsides and give brilliance to our civilization; that loveliness and natural splendor shall mark the whole country, [and] that we may all be happy in our well-doing.

This hyperbolical barrage should not disguise the serious point of view presented here. Expressed in countless other New South sermons, this fusion of self-interest and social uplift was no mere rationalization. When the *Argus* concluded the same article by claiming that "with a recognized part in the accomplishment of this grand scheme one's life may not be rated a failure," it underscored the cultural meaning inherent in the postbellum industrial crusades.[22]

The industrial ethos had its defensive side as well. Local boosters believed that manufacturing enterprises and the growth they would create would mitigate the unrest associated with economic stagnation and unemployment. "Where a people are idle," warned Dalton's *North Georgia Citizen* during the economic depression of the 1870s, "they do not only fail to prosper, but they are sure to get into trouble with each other, and then follow backbitings, quarreling, fighting and murder." In support of Dalton's 1886 waterworks campaign, the *Argus* warned opponents that the proposition's defeat would crush local development and therefore prompt an uprising among Dalton's "wage-workers." Laborers needed employment and were "in a humor to pull at the purse strings in another way . . . sometimes a very effective one." To drive home the point, the paper raised the ominous specter of class warfare: "The communistic spirit of the human family is very much of kin the world over, and the only reason that it does not everywhere develop into harsh and aggressive phazes [sic], is because in some sections that cause of conflict is re-moved." Economic development and steady paychecks presumably would remove the point of conflict. By such reasoning, Dalton's industrial leaders saw the pros-perity and well-being—not to mention the safety—of the city as inseparable from their own.[23]

The second fundamental belief of Dalton's industrial elite was that civic leaders control the destiny of cities. Implicit in the rhetoric and behavior of the city's boosters throughout the late nineteenth century, this idea occasionally found explicit expression. "Natural advantages, as a sole theme of a country's attractions, are a humbug," wrote Henry Wrench. He valued instead the human attributes of "law, system, obedience, effort, ambition, energy."[24] An article that graced the *Atlanta Constitution* in 1887 demonstrated the importance of this idea to Dalton's emerging group of industrialists. "DALTON! North Georgia's Little City Enjoying a Season of Progress," read the headline. In many ways, this was merely another puffed-up panorama of a small southern city. As predictable as rebel yells at Confederate reunions, such articles heralded a city's major industries, exaggerated its minor ones, stressed the healthful climate and outstanding educational facilities (accuracy not required), and, if at all possible, reenacted the city's wartime de-struction to provide ashes aplenty for the small-town phoenix. But this particular article provides some significant material for the historian, because the journalist interviewed Frank Hardwick, Henry Hamilton, and Henry Wrench, whose re-marks revealed their own interpretation of Dalton's history and their place in it. "The law of progress or the rules of destiny appear to have no set principles to guide mankind on his onward career," began the article, "save on the basis that the gods help those who help themselves." In the author's view, the city of Dalton represented "an exemplification of the above assertion." Dalton's history, as related by its industrial leaders, demonstrated that urban prosperity resulted less from the fortuitous advantages of location and bountiful resources than from the efforts of aggressive civic leaders who were willing to capitalize on their city's positive at-tributes, overcome its liabilities, and create new avenues of progress.[25]

As related to the *Constitution* by Hamilton, Hardwick, and Wrench, Dalton's history began during the late 1840s and early 1850s, when the city "was more prosperous and enjoyed a greater share of this world's blessings than at any period since." The W&A linked Dalton with Atlanta in 1847, turning the struggling moun-tain hamlet into the commercial trading center for an extensive agricultural hin-terland. For a few years, Dalton enjoyed a period of unprecedented prosperity. But, the story went, good fortune proved fleeting. When the track stretched north to Chattanooga in 1851, making that city the new northern terminus for the region, "Dalton could only cross her hands and say 'such is life.' " The town became a shell of its former self, lapsing into "a state of indifference and painful lassitude." While other towns continued to strive forward, Dalton "got the 'dry rot' and was slowly losing its substance, its spirit, its purpose." It mattered not that valuable natural resources—thick forests, abundant streams, vast mineral deposits—lay "at the very threshold of the city's gates." According to Dalton's New South leaders, the local citizenry had long recognized these potential sources of wealth but failed to develop them. Instead of rowing their ship of fortune confidently toward the future, the people of Dalton "rested silently on their oars, floating down the sluggish stream of inactivity, content to eke out a pittance of a living."[26]

Such lassitude apparently persisted after the Civil War. "Dead Dalton," as people called it, was a place where "two railroads crossed each other and left nothing in their track but . . . the curling smoke of the engines, which hung like a great black pall over a sleeping people." Fortunately, the story continued, "New South" winds eventually blew into Dalton (presumably sometime during the 1880s). Invigorating breezes whisked away the spell of sluggardliness from those whose "buoyant young blood" had not been dried up by the "decay of years." Fully revived, a group of local businessmen (the narrators themselves) pledged to pull the city "out of the rut of despondency." This seemed no small task, because old fogyism ran deep in Dalton. Undeterred, these wide-awake men of the New South grasped the clubs of rhetoric and organization and, symbolically speaking, proceeded to beat the local naysayers into submission. "There is not a croaker left in Dalton," boasted Hardwick. "We can do anything." Along similar lines, Henry Hamilton explained the recent sharp rise in Dalton's real estate values by reasoning, "The most prominent cause, probably, is the *awakening of the people* to the fact that Dalton possesses advantages not often possessed by the average Georgia town."[27]

This New South version of Dalton's past was not entirely faithful to the historical record, but its accuracy is less important than what the history reveals about Crown's managers and the ideals of Dalton's industrialists. By the late 1880s, these men had accepted full responsibility for the city's well-being. Believing that Dalton's destiny lay in their hands, they confidently sought to promote urban expansion and industrial development through their own entrepreneurial efforts and through an organization in which they wielded considerable clout—the Democratic party. By the late 1880s, they were committed to shaping Dalton according to their own image of a "progressive" social order, and as they gained increasingly more economic and political power in local affairs, they gained the authority with which to carry out their plans.

It was not merely economic power that set Dalton's industrialists apart from the plain folk of Crown and the countryside. The business class also helped shape an "uptown" culture—bourgeois culture, if you will. In Dalton, "uptown" actually referred to both a place and a lifestyle. Geographically, it meant the central business district and the town's affluent neighborhoods (which were south of the Crown mill village and west of the railroad tracks). More important, "uptown" came to mean a lifestyle conspicuously adopted by wealthy Daltonians. The industrialists and their families took the lead in establishing uptown standards, but they were followed and assisted by an eager group of people from the middle ranks of Dalton society. Uptown values were reflected in elaborate church buildings, ornate houses, elite clubs, and a variety of local reform efforts. Uptown people were also defined by who they were *not*—namely, poor farmers, cotton-mill workers, and blacks. They deliberately set new social standards for the local elite, at the same time remapping their own relationship with north Georgia's common folk.

Uptown church buildings, erected by the city's three mainline Protestant denominations, afforded one of the most visible signs of an emerging elite culture in late-nineteenth-century Dalton. Members of the First Presbyterian Church, their comfortable but hardly elaborate antebellum church house having been destroyed by Union soldiers, built a large replacement complete with towering steeple and pipe organ. Virtually all of Crown's leaders worshiped in this sanctuary. The First Baptist Church forsook its modest prewar facility for a grand brick edifice that boasted a steeple as lofty as the Presbyterians'. The Southern Methodists, who built their first church in 1851 for $500, spent $3,000 for a parsonage alone in 1883 and thoroughly remodeled their house of worship three years later. By the turn of the century, the three churches had constructed houses for their full-time pastors, all well-educated men of the cloth.[28]

The industrialists' wives and children were often leaders of the city's cultural transformation. Gertrude Manly Jones, the sister of one local industrialist and the wife of Crown's Thomas Jones, diligently sought to advance the fine arts in Dalton. Besides writing poetry of more than local repute, she played the harp and actively encouraged the young, affluent women of the city to reach the heights of their artistic and intellectual powers. A photograph of Jones sitting in a parlor dressed in fine Victorian raiment, her imposing and elegant instrument resting on her shoulder, reflected the cultural leadership role she envisioned for Dalton's New South women. Her primary vehicle of influence was the Lesche Club, which she established in 1890. The Lesche was attended by many of the city's leading women and their daughters. The name of the association, Greek for "where the literati meet," bespoke the aspirations of Jones and her followers, as well as how far apart they were from women and girls on north Georgia's small farms and in Dalton's mill village. The Lesche met regularly for a variety of activities. At some sessions, women read formally prepared papers—on ancient history, for instance—which were followed by discussion. In other meetings focusing on artistic development, participants learned how to paint fine china or make jewelry.[29]

The Dalton Opera House reflected the larger contours of the cultural transformation. Established by Frank Hardwick and several other business leaders in 1885, the Opera House attracted a wide variety of entertainment to the city and became a major social center for affluent Daltonians. It was a two-story brick building with a conspicuous sign on top and a seating capacity of nearly six hundred. Because Dalton was situated on the railroad between Nashville and Atlanta, it became a common overnight stop for national entertainers, who performed at the Opera House and sometimes in the homes of the local elite. Atlanta, with its genteel cultural amenities and its impassioned booster spirit, served as elite Dalton's model for a proper urban environment more than New York or any other Yankee city. But there was more to the ornate churches, the Lesche, and the Opera House than just a desire for local refinement. The town's affluent families, with the rising industrialists in the vanguard, were striving to create meaningful social roles for elite men and women and to establish the proper boundaries of status in the "new" Dalton, boundaries that set them apart from ordinary working people.[30]

But the emerging elite culture did not rely simply on social segregation. It also demanded active involvement in a variety of civic and religious organizations, as well as reform efforts that, in some ways, increased the elite's interaction with people of lower economic standing. Throughout the late 1880s and the 1890s, the Whitfield County Sunday School Association was run primarily by men who were officials or directors at Crown Mill—Thomas Jones, William Moore, Sr., Sam E. Berry, and R. J. McCamy. Berry and Moore also served as presidents of the Dalton Bible Association. Shortly before becoming president of Crown, David Bass served as a delegate of Dalton's "Friends of Temperance" group at the Georgia prohibition convention. Moore and other members of the local elite worked vigorously and successfully to enact (and maintain) prohibition laws in Dalton and Whitfield County during the 1880s and 1890s.[31] Through such efforts, business leaders and professionals established themselves as guardians of moral integrity who were leading north Georgia toward what they perceived as a better social order. Many affluent Daltonians saw prohibition as a necessary ingredient of that new order. Many plain folk also were in favor of a "dry" county, but the elite took charge of the movement and made it a badge of uptown respectability. The industrialists' active participation in such organizations as the Sunday School Association and in the prohibition campaigns helped legitimize their control over local affairs. Their involvement also comprised part of their effort to uplift (or at least reduce the threat of) what they increasingly perceived as the disruptive natures of poor whites and of blacks. This seems to have been what one man meant when he noted with relief the effects of Dalton's prohibition law: "The hoodlum element is eliminated, the police courts idle, the prisons empty. . . . Quiet and good order prevails."[32]

The hog law of 1888 represented another way in which local economic leaders sought to reform their town. Tradition dictated that hogs be allowed to roam free in town, feasting upon the garbage. This practice eliminated fencing and feeding costs for less affluent townspeople and reduced the problem of waste disposal. But New South boosters viewed the street hogs as symbols of backwardness and, worse, as impediments to commercial traffic and Dalton's newly proposed street-

Gertrude Manly Jones and her husband, Thomas R. Jones, president of Crown Mill (photographs ca. 1885), set new standards of boosterism and cultural refinement for Dalton's
emerging business class. (*Photo of Gertrude Jones courtesy of the Georgia Department of Archives and History; photo of Thomas Jones courtesy of Crown Gardens and Archives*)

car line. Civic leaders therefore proposed an ordinance requiring that pigs be penned. Some Daltonians protested on the grounds that the law would undermine the economic security of the town's less affluent residents. In a letter to the *Dalton Citizen*, "A Tax Payer" complained that unfettered hogs provided a vital service in waste disposal, a service that otherwise would need to be replaced by a full-time garbage collector and supported by a tax increase. John Q. Lewis, proprietor of the Lewis House hotel, thought penning the pigs would be "unfair, unjust, and . . . detrimental to the poor." Others interviewed by the *Argus* following passage of the law agreed with Lewis, one condemning the new ordinance as "an outrage." But the vast majority of businessmen and professionals hailed the law as a progressive step for Dalton. The directors and officers of Crown Mill enthusiastically endorsed the new regulation. Company president Thomas Jones best captured their enthusiasm when he pronounced the hog law "a thing of beauty and a joy forever."[33]

The ascendance of Dalton's industrialists climaxed in the summer of 1888, when a spontaneous celebration greeted the completion of the city's new waterworks plant. Anticipation had been building for some time. During 1886 the waterworks issue had dominated local politics, with budding industrialists insisting on a new facility. Whitfield County had abundant springs, but Dalton always had a water shortage. Postwar growth had exacerbated the problem and intensified efforts to find a solution. Hamilton's Spring, the Crown Mill's water supply, represented the best source for the city to tap. According to one observer, the spring gushed a million gallons per day. The *Argus* encouraged local officials to "meet the company with business intent" and draw up a contract for dual use of the spring. Lengthy and complex negotiations resulted in a proposal whereby Crown would allow the city "free" use of its water in return for a ten-year tax exemption. The city also agreed to build and maintain the waterworks and a large reservoir, which Crown could use for industrial purposes. The problem was that the waterworks involved a major tax increase, and the proposal met some strong resistance on this account.[34]

As election day neared, an anxious *Argus* blasted opponents of the proposal. "Whenever anything is suggested in Dalton," complained Wrench in a revealing editorial, "there are those who rise up in perfect bewilderment and want to know what's the use of it?" The use, he fumed, was clear (if somewhat multifarious): "It is, O sluggard, to increase values. . . . It is the law of God working through man. . . . It is the law of duty to our children who are coming up in our places. . . . It is everything that life is worth living for." On a more practical level, Wrench also suggested that the W&A would subsequently purchase its water from Dalton rather than from Tilton, a small railroad town in the southern part of Whitfield County. This would add to the city coffers and reduce local taxes. Eventually, local voters sided with the waterworks plan by a margin of 260 to 90, with Wrench hailing the election as a great victory over the "fogy element." For Dalton's new cadre of city builders, it was symbolically appropriate for the waterworks to be constructed near the Crown Mill. Both were part of the same vision developing in the minds of the city's economic leaders. The waterworks building was con-structed beside Hamilton's Spring, one hundred yards south of the Crown Mill belfry. The city marked the new facility with a large sign proclaiming "Dalton Water Works," which was clearly visible from the W&A tracks to the west and Chattanooga Avenue to the east. Will Harben used the scene in his novel *The Georgians* to describe the growth mentality of the town: "Darley was a growing place. It was gradually recovering from the serious back-set given it by the Civil War. A big cotton factory had been built in the suburbs of town, . . . and a system of water-works supplied the place with water from a big, clear spring which gushed from the rocky side of a hill and advertised to all prospective settlers that Darley was in favor of progress."[35]

With the works finally completed in August 1888, city officials turned on the water, letting it spray out over Hamilton Street to spatter, as it were, the dust of fogyism with the refreshing water of progress. The leaders of the waterworks campaign then hosted an impromptu banquet at the Lewis House. Many a speech and toast rang out as these wealthy Daltonians celebrated what they perceived to be the advent of a new era in the city's history. The completion of the waterworks provided a nice occasion for camaraderie and backslapping, but the larger cause for celebration was the process of industrial development taking place in their town. Always the practical, no-nonsense booster, Thomas Jones calculated prog-ress by the numbers at hand. Only a year earlier, he had examined the state of affairs at the Crown Mill and predicted that "financial conquest awaits us." Subse-quent events had proved him right. Now, heeding calls to take the floor, the Crown Mill president proudly announced that "one-third of the population of Dalton is now deriving a direct support from factories built or newly equipped within the last five years." William Moore, Sr., whose son would serve as president of Crown Mill from 1919 to 1935, struck a more eloquent note when he announced that the city's recent progress amounted to nothing less than the "new birth of Dalton."[36]

New birth. Financial conquest. The law of God working through man. These were weighty concepts to hoist upon an economic foundation that was still re-markably fragile by the end of the 1880s. Dalton's city builders seemed to expect the urban-industrial millennium to burst upon their small town at any moment. It took a little success at the Crown Mill to convert doubters, but a more enthusiastic group of disciples could hardly be found. Firmly tied to the national economy and to their own local enterprises, southern business leaders sought to ensure for themselves and their towns a continued season of urban growth and industrial productivity. They pictured themselves leading the South into a new era of pros-perity and well-being. They thought the common people were following grate-fully. They were in for quite a shock.

3

PATTERNS OF PROTEST

As prophets of the New South, Dalton's business elite
foretold a harmonious relationship between management and labor. "The success of the man who pays
the wages, means the success of the man who works
for wages," the *Dalton Argus* had asserted in 1886.
Boosters assumed that everyone would benefit from
and support industrial development. They should
have known better. During the antebellum era, many
southerners had pointed toward New England as an
example of what their society should not become,
claiming that the emerging factory system turned
working people into "wage slaves." Dixie's postbellum boosters tried to bury such concerns under a pile
of upbeat rhetoric that emphasized the positive aspects of economic modernization. They insisted that
industrial relations in southern textiles would remain
cordial because the unity of southern whites would
undermine the potential for class conflict. These notions of white supremacy and worker docility endured as mainstays of regional discourse for decades
to come, but in reality the harmony between wealthy
whites and poor whites in the New South broke down
almost at the start. In the late 1880s and the 1890s,
uprisings among factory workers and small farmers

rocked the South and the nation, calling into question the economic and ethical foundations of the new order. North Georgia did not escape this turmoil.

The ways in which Dixie's poor whites fought against modern capitalism shed light on their own culture of protest, a culture rooted in rural community and one that would have a profound impact on the evolution of the southern cotton-mill village. In and around Dalton, the most severe threats to the new order came not from factory workers but from small farmers in the countryside. This was cold comfort to textile managers, however, because their growing mills needed an increasing supply of workers, almost all of whom would be poor whites from these very areas of rural protest. One of the most tenacious myths in the history of southern textiles is that the early workers, fresh from the farm, were too individualistic to mount any organized protest against the system. A look at traditional rural culture and the protests of the late nineteenth century suggests a different view. Far from being political pushovers, Dixie's poor whites had surprisingly strong traditions of collective action. As their own economic crisis deepened, southern plain folk channeled conventional forms of rural protest into modern engines of political insurgency.

It is not clear, however, that the cultural norms of the countryside formed the nucleus of class identification or class conflict. Even though rural poor whites viewed themselves and their families as part of cohesive farming communities, those communities sometimes divided over controversial issues. Moreover, the economy was changing so fast that it became increasingly difficult for poor southerners to determine exactly what their interests were and how to achieve them. Modernization pressed hard on all plain folk, but it did not always push them in the same direction. In very important ways, the new order fragmented traditional collectivism. So although ordinary southern whites were accustomed to band together, the labor unions and political coalitions that they formed during the late nineteenth century were decidedly short lived.

The last thing Dalton's industrialists expected was trouble from their millhands or from the plain folk in the countryside, or so they said. When the Baltimore *Manufacturers' Record*, Dixie's most enthusiastic industrial advocate, interviewed Henry C. Hamilton in 1886, the Crown Mill director made his views perfectly clear. The article noted that Crown's "employees are all home people and understand their work; they are industrious and satisfied." Although merely poor farm folk before the Civil War, they had "developed into steady and industrious [factory] hands" whose "tastes are simple and wants [are] few." Crown's operatives, the *Record* stated, "work with satisfaction and make but few demands." Hamilton reported that "strikes are unknown in this locality." As a reflection of what Dalton's industrial managers wanted in a millhand, Hamilton's words speak volumes. The workers were "home people"—that is, not European immigrants, the firebrands of working-class radicalism in the North. Native white southerners, by contrast, came from "simple" rural or small-town backgrounds and were easily satisfied. They accepted low wages without grumbling, much less striking. Yet despite their "primitive" heritage, Dixie's country folk readily adapted to steady factory labor. According to Dalton's industrialists, the ideal cotton-mill hand was dependable and docile, hard working and grateful for the work, satisfied with little and incapable of jealousy toward capitalists.[1]

Hamilton was right about one thing: the workers were "home people," upcountry whites from Dalton and the surrounding countryside. Nothing distinguished the southern textile industry from the rest of the country more than the ethnic makeup of its work force. A flood of immigrant labor poured into northern and western cities during the late nineteenth century, profoundly altering the composition of America's population and fueling the national industrial explosion. During the 1880s and 1890s alone, nearly nine million immigrants entered America— mainly from Europe, Asia, and Canada. Almost none of them chose to live in the American South. Why should they? No other region paid lower wages, and southern agriculture was something less than an economic lure. Even southerners were leaving the South in droves. Industrialists viewed this trend in contradictory ways, one being that the South's low number of immigrants robbed the region of potential labor power. But because the horde of immigrant ethnic workers threw fear into the hearts of many native-born Americans, who saw them as a major source of social disruption and labor agitation, southern mill owners also found it comforting that their own mills would be run by southern-born whites who, rich and poor, had been through the fires of defeat together.[2]

But although the workers were "home people," they were hardly as complacent as Hamilton suggested. Upcountry whites did not bring a heritage of passivity with them to the mills, and labor relations at the Crown Mill were sometimes troubled. The first generation of millhands did not form a union, but in 1888 they pressed for housing improvements and the addition of water hydrants near the mill houses. Whether the millhands went on strike to achieve their goals remains unclear; historical evidence is very scant. President Thomas R. Jones made a rare mention of the workers at the stockholders' meeting that year, explaining that the ceilings had been replaced on all of the original houses and water pipes run throughout the housing areas. Perhaps some workers had quit because of poor housing and water facilities, for Jones assured stockholders "that our operatives seem contented and located since the added comforts to their homes and the convenience of good water at their doors."[3]

In 1890 Henry Wrench continued to promote the image of the happy southern mill worker. "While the labor centers of the North are in a state of violent revolution," he wrote, "it is a beautiful picture to look upon the prosperous South, all classes joining heartily in contented effort, and the promise of abundance unifying the golden compact." But such rhetoric may have been more an effort to calm local fears of class conflict and to attract outside capital than a sincere evaluation, for by the 1890s many laborers in the South were clearly rejecting the "golden compact." In 1891 the *Argus* itself reported that Thomas Jones traveled to Atlanta to borrow $5,000 because "he was having some trouble with the employees of the mill . . . and needs [more] money." During a decade when Dalton's newspapers virtually ignored the millhands at Crown, this terse reference to labor problems provides rare evidence that the tensions of the 1890s were manifest in Dalton's cotton mill. There is no way of knowing what kind of "trouble" Jones had with the millhands. Perhaps a large number of them quit during a short time, leaving the mill without an adequate supply of operatives. In any case, it was clear that industrial relations between Crown's directors and their millhands had yet to be worked out satisfactorily.[4]

Elsewhere in the industrial South, labor turmoil was more intense, and the reaction of business leaders was often remarkably hostile. Workers throughout the region rebelled against long hours and low wages. In the late 1880s the Knights of Labor, a national labor group, found millhands eager for organization in several key textile communities in Georgia and the South. In mid-1886, for example, organized textile workers in the Augusta area squared off against local employers in a strike that lasted months. Knights in other basic industries struck as well. During the final years of the 1880s, southern miners, ironworkers, and lumber millers from Virginia to Mississippi walked off the job in startling numbers. These efforts at collective action by Dixie's industrial workers proved largely ineffective, in part because the Knights of Labor maintained an official no-strike policy and therefore offered little support for workers who went on strike. Equally important, textile manufacturers in Augusta set a significant precedent by aggressively attacking the Knights with a broad range of antiunion tactics that successfully crushed the protest.[5]

In east Tennessee, not far north of Dalton, labor violence of a different sort erupted in 1891. Miners in that area organized a virtual army when the Tennessee Coal, Iron, and Railroad Company attempted to replace them with convict labor. The governor of Tennessee responded by sending in the state militia to restore order. "The South has heretofore escaped the confusion of open labor riot by a tendency of public sympathy to the laboring class," commented the *Argus*, but "the wild scenes at the Coal Creek mines, the past week, show that the beginning of such troubles are upon us." Initially the paper ascribed blame to Tennessee's state officials for not dealing adequately with the convict labor problem. But as the violence of the strike increased and sparked labor demonstrations throughout Dixie, the *Argus*'s "public sympathy" chilled rapidly. "Men have lost their reason in upholding the act of the coal miners of Tennessee—in expressing sympathy with armed mobs of the strikers—in expressing the possibilities whereby riot . . . may force terms of adjudication." Later, when Thomas Jones and Anthony Showalter took over the *Dalton Citizen*, they editorialized that the shooting of sixty miners who threatened mill property in Pennsylvania was "thoroughly justified." For Dalton's uptown people, the "laboring class" was becoming a dangerous class.[6]

But these labor protests reflected more than spontaneous explosions by plain folk sensitive to insult or injury; they also continued a rural upcountry tradition of mutuality and collective protest. That southern millhands maintained many of their rural customs is beyond dispute. One early analyst of southern textiles correctly observed that "the factory population was born upon the farms, or is only one generation removed. The operatives have come to the mill with generations of fixed rural habits behind them, and necessarily are greatly influenced by their past."[7] But scholars have often misunderstood rural culture, viewing poor farmers as either passive peasants or staunch individualists, unable or unwilling to join in cooperative efforts to improve their lot in life. Historian I. A. Newby, for example, has recently written that "the folk brought no sense of group identity to the mills," and that "mill workers did not think in collective terms or recognize a common interest with other workers." The notion that Dixie's plain folk were backwoods individualists dies hard. The evidence, however, greatly favors the view that rural people throughout the nineteenth century were guided by notions of community cooperation. Individual households were closely tied together through extensive kinship connections and economic necessity. An ethos of mutual aid and group effort permeated the southern upcountry before the coming of industry and, to a significant degree, long afterward.[8]

In the farming communities from which Crown's workers migrated, powerful traditions of family loyalty and local cooperation characterized daily life. One overriding goal of every rural family was to acquire enough land for the children's inheritance. But each family understood that this goal could only be achieved through cooperation with other local producers—farmers, millers, and artisans— in the community. Farm households could prosper and expand their land holdings, but not without the collective labor and mutual assistance that were the bedrock of economic security in rural society. This understanding was clearly manifest in the communal "workings" that were a familiar way of life for people in the upcountry. Although corn shuckings, log rollings, and house raisings were social gatherings, they also revealed how economic necessity worked to shape local relationships. But "swapping work" was just one way in which the local economy engendered a community outlook. Customs of cooperation among white families extended into other areas of life as well. Local welfare provides an excellent example. In an age of minimal public social services and an area lacking in philanthropic organizations, families in the north Georgia countryside who faced a crisis had no source of aid save that offered by other households in the community. Plain folk therefore developed voluntary systems of mutual aid. The community assumed responsibility for families stricken by illness or tragedy. "If anyone got into trouble," recalled one old-timer from north Georgia, "everyone went. I mean the whole neighborhood." A woman from the Blue Ridge remembered that her father "went around doing work on neighbor's farms when they all took sick. He was gone from sun up to sun down and came home exhausted." One need not romanticize this state of affairs to appreciate its significance in shaping expectations of and responses to the new economic order.[9]

In some instances, the rise of the market economy actually enhanced customs of mutual aid. Wheat production offers a case in point. The horse-drawn (and later steam-powered) wheat threshers that rolled onto upcountry farms beginning in the 1880s represented an advance in farm technology, a form of rural modernization. But threshers also provided new opportunities for old-style cooperative effort. In one north Georgia community, the man who owned the only thresher let each farmer in the vicinity use it in return for a payment in kind. But such work could not be accomplished alone, so all the farmers in the threshing circuit—in this case fifteen—contributed their labor at each farm. In keeping with custom, the farmers' wives prepared meals for the visiting laborers. In one Gilmer County settlement, tradition dictated that all boys leave school to work a threshing. The expanding urban market for foodstuffs also created greater demand for mountain syrup. To meet that demand, farm families in the Blue Ridge responded by preparing sorghum for the syrup mill at "cane strippin' " parties. Wheat threshers and sorghum strippers grafted cultural traditions to commercial capitalism, offering evidence that plain folk were gradually adapting older notions of community cooperation to new economic circumstances.[10]

In times of crisis, the cooperative ethic of the countryside could also be channeled into forms of collective protest that imposed policies on others or resisted intrusions from outsiders. By the late nineteenth century, rural people in north Georgia had plenty of precedents to follow. Vigilante gangs had assisted federal forces in removing reluctant Cherokees during the late 1830s. Unofficial military units had roamed the area during the Civil War, representing both sides and fighting guerrilla skirmishes in communities that never witnessed formal battles. Reconstruction had witnessed the rise of a strong Ku Klux Klan, which originated in Murray County and became the standard for later vigilante organizations. When it came to banding together to fight, north Georgia's plain folk had plenty of experience, and, as the new economy turned against them, they did not passively accept their fate. As the crisis deepened, they banded together and fought against whomever they perceived as the foe. Their cultural heritage ensured that they would be formidable opponents.[11]

By the late 1880s, many struggling farm families had good reason to be angry. The Civil War had ravaged their lives; whichever side they supported, they had lost. Afterward, cash-crop agriculture seemed to offer a way to rebuild, but it only undermined their economic independence and boosted the fortunes of merchants, who were getting rich on the labor of poor farmers. New laws, supported largely by merchant-creditors, found their way onto the books and further undermined the independence of many rural people by abolishing tax exemptions for poor farmers and outlawing the open range. Tenancy rates were on the rise as cotton prices continued to fall, and sharecropping arrangements had become ruinous. Cotton mills offered alternative employment for some, but the wages were pitifully low and the hours very long. The New South seemed to be emerging as a society of wealthy "haves" and bitterly impoverished "have nots."[12]

The Crown Mill itself represented this severe economic imbalance. Crown's directors were some of the wealthiest and most influential men in northwest Georgia. Their doings filled the pages of Dalton's weeklies. Socially prestigious, economically and politically active, they self-consciously left their mark on the town's history. By north Georgia standards they were rich. In 1892 the *Argus* published a list of taxable wealth possessed by some of Dalton's most affluent citizens, and, not surprisingly, many of Crown's officials were on it. Overall, the mill's managers owned an average of about $13,000 worth of taxable property each, not counting income from salaries or stock dividends and not counting properties owned outside of Whitfield County. J. W. Barrett and George W. Oglesby had $25,000 worth each, which was considerably more taxable property than most Dalton businesses possessed. Crown leaders R. J. McCamy, Sam E. Berry, Frank Hardwick, and Thomas Jones also served as directors for numerous local firms, such as the Dalton Hotel Company, the First National Bank, the Dalton Street Railroad Company, and various insurance and real estate companies.[13]

Compared with these men, the working people employed by Crown were very poor and were largely ignored by the press. In 1890 Crown's millhands earned an average wage of $3.13 for a sixty-six-hour work week, which meant a yearly income of about $150 barring sickness and downturns in the business cycle, both of which were common. For the entire year of 1888 the company's gross annual payroll was $15,637, a sum nearly $10,000 shy of Oglesby's taxable property in Whitfield County.[14]

With the economic depression of the 1890s came even greater hardship for the poor. The depression, which was at its worst from about 1893 to 1897, was national and catastrophic in scope, the worst economic crisis Americans had ever seen. Unemployment in the cities skyrocketed and businesses closed. The decade was marked by protests and violent confrontations between capital and labor. Poor whites in the southern upcountry watched in despair as cotton prices plunged to all-time lows and conditions in the countryside grew desperate. In the cotton mills, wages were pitifully low. At Crown, average weekly earnings declined about 6 percent from 1890 to 1896 (see table 5.5), and the millhands had no leverage whatever to improve their situation. Because of the farm crisis, there were plenty of southern whites willing to work in the mills for a pittance.

Yet for southern textile managers it was a curious depression indeed, because Dixie's cotton mills experienced very impressive growth during the decade. Spindleage in the South's three leading textile states increased 84 percent in Georgia, 236 percent in North Carolina, and a shocking 330 percent in South Carolina (see figure 2.1). In Georgia, more new mills arose and succeeded during the 1890s than in the "boom" decade of the eighties. During the depression decade, the number of millhands employed in Georgia increased 78 percent, compared to 62 percent in the previous decade. Crown Mill managers enjoyed healthy profits during the 1890s, averaging a 27 percent return on capital for the ten-year period. At the very time many desperate Americans were launching protests against industrial capitalism, southern textile leaders were striking it rich.[15]

Upcountry plain folk—in the mills and on the farms—felt their lives thrown off balance. The railroads, cities, and factories of the New South announced to everyone that the southern economy was growing, but poor whites realized that they were not the beneficiaries of the new order. Something was wrong in Dixie, and they were not the type of people to accept this state of affairs with a passive shrug. Their initial response was unsurprising. They organized gangs and lashed out in anger. A wave of collective violence rolled across north Georgia during the late 1880s and early 1890s, as white vigilante groups whipped, burned, and lynched with great ferocity. Generally known as "white caps," north Georgia's night riders consisted primarily of landless tenants and small landowners. Seeking to gain a "just price" for their crops, hard-pressed farmers in the 1890s gathered for night rides against local cotton ginners, who were warned not to accept any staple until prices rose to ten cents per pound. Some merchants (who were also creditors) received visits from the mobs, and others simply found notes advising them not to foreclose against area farms.[16]

Whitecappers also sought to enforce adherence to certain moral standards—including, ironically, keeping the peace. In 1885 a gang of fifty masked riders from the Owl Hollow community descended on Dalton. After raiding five brothels, assaulting the perpetrators of sin, and gunning down one black man in the process, they delivered a message to the mayor, who prudently had it published in the local papers. The self-proclaimed purpose of the "Owl Hollow Brotherhood" was to abolish prostitution and racial mixing and to "terrorize the congregation of boot blacks and loafers, white and black," who had been destroying the moral fiber of the city. The "town dudes," according to the brotherhood, had "no discretion in this matter" and therefore could no longer be counted on to "protect the good people of Dalton, especially the widows and orphans." Organized vigilante mobs policed moral behavior in rural settlements with equal vigilance. In 1889 the *Argus* reported: "The 'White Caps' waited on Tom Rogers in Gilmer county, . . . strapping him and his wife because they failed to live peaceable together, and [for] abandoning their child on a neighbor's doorstep. They will take care of the child. About the same time they visited a Mr. Wilson on Blue Ridge, a saloon keeper, and tried to persuade him to quit business. It is surmised that he'll quit." Moral intolerance also led to organized attacks against outsiders who tried to promote new doctrines or values in the countryside. Mormon missionaries, for example, fell prey to vicious attacks in east Tennessee and north Georgia, including a murder in Whitfield County.[17]

Poor farmers and mill workers were also bitter about the growing behavioral gap between them and the townspeople. The elegant new Protestant sanctuaries in Dalton could not have offered a more stark contrast to the small, austere churches of the plain folk, most of which contained little more than a pulpit and some rough pews (which, in many cases, still kept male and female worshipers carefully segregated). Unlike the staid, mainstream church services, rural worship and mill-village worship often involved shouting, leaping, and exuberant manifestations of joy and praise. Country churches also "turned out" members for inappropriate conduct, a practice abandoned by wealthy urban denominations. The records from one north Georgia congregation in the 1890s, for example, stated: "Excluded four sisters, two brothers. Reasons: Intoxication, [failure to pay] debts; church non-attendance, adultery, fornication and immoral conduct." In the world of these upcountry farmers, private lives were still public property, and public behavior was still supposed to be austere. It was not the world of the South's urban bourgeoisie.[18]

Dalton's new elite made no effort to hide its pretensions, and ordinary whites often resented both the haughty attitudes and the cultural tastes of the uptown crowd. Beyond the churches, nothing so clearly displayed the cultural values of town leaders as the Dalton Opera House. Established by industrialist Frank Hardwick and other local businessmen in 1885, the Opera House attracted a wide variety of entertainment to the city and became a major social center for the elite. But to some rural observers the theater seemed a step in the wrong direction. Dalton novelist Will Harben humorously portrayed rural sentiment on this subject in *The Georgians*. In a descriptive passage, Tom P. Smith, an imposing evangelist holding forth at a rustic Methodist meetinghouse, roars that folks in Darley have "taken on city ways and left the Lord in the backwoods." Amidst a searing indictment of high society in the city, he announces that "the leadin' men o' that Sodom and Gomorrah have chipped in an' build 'em an' up-to-date opra-house." From a pious and distraught man in town, he has learned that the "old, half-blind" churchgoing men pack the front row of seats ("ball-head row") to "see what keeps the gals' stockin's up." The opera house, moreover, is a place for the evils of poker playing and "swarees." In such a setting, courtship loses all sense of decency. "It means," Brother Smith booms, "a man an' woman up before a gapin' crowd with

Mary Goforth (ca. 1910), an upcountry farm woman whose family later moved to Crown Mill, embodied the plain folk's traditional values of hard work and simplicity. (*Courtesy of Lillie Ann Goforth Hill, Dalton, Ga.*)

the'r chest wadded together, spinnin' round in each other's arms, with the'r heels on a level with the'r backs." As the sermon builds to a crescendo, Smith pounds the pulpit and cries, "They say Paris, France, is the devil's pride, but I'm here to say that, fer its age an' opportunities in wickedness, Darley is certainly in the procession."[19]

Harben wrote with playful intent, but the Owl Hollow gang that taught the "town dudes" a lesson in morality was not kidding. The economic growth that alienated small farmers from the new order found a curious parallel in Dalton's cultural development. To the business class, the merchants' stores, the Crown Mill, the ornate churches, and the opera house all betokened a seamless vision of progress. With considerable foreboding, poor whites also viewed these develop-ments as interconnected parts of a single process. To be sure, economic inequality and cultural dissension were apparent to all in the antebellum period. But during the late 1880s and the 1890s, the gap that separated rich and poor in the Georgia upcountry became a widening chasm—at least from the viewpoint of the plain folk—and it was increasingly difficult to disentangle the cultural tension from the economic turmoil.

On matters of race, however, culture brought whites together across class lines. The one societal norm about which poor whites and wealthy whites readily agreed was that blacks should be subordinate to all whites, economic status notwithstand-ing. As the Owl Hollow Brotherhood demonstrated, some rural whites clearly viewed Dalton as a cauldron of racial depravity. But uptown Daltonians were themselves racists and strict segregationists. When a group of Whitfield County blacks met to consider moving to Liberia in 1885, one local editor wished them a speedy departure, for, he said, "there is no hope for any reasonable advancement of the negro in the land of the whites. He may reach a decent thrift, but there his progress must end." Blacks who tried to advance were thwarted in various ways. In 1887 a black man who gave a public speech in favor of temperance reforms was, the papers said, "given emphatic assurances of displeasure." The *Argus* insisted that no black should talk to whites in such a manner: "There are very few communities in this county who will take moral training from the fifteenth amendment end of the line." One local black who made good "in the land of whites" was Ben Jones, a business leader for whom Dalton's African American community named their public hall, which was built by Jones himself. He even had a barn outside town devoted to nothing other than a massive wine collection (1,500 gallons in all). The wine cellar must have exceeded "a decent thrift," for an arsonist torched the building, and the white fire department made no effort to save it, despite Jones's pleas.[20]

North Georgia whites—rich and poor alike—would have endorsed the Murray County history book, used in public schools during the early twentieth century, which stated that many blacks during Reconstruction "became idle, insolent, and eventually dangerous members of society. The young negroes, no longer under strict control, became troublesome. To make matters worse, certain misguided white men chose to put false notions of civil rights and social equality into their heads. So unbearable did the situation become that a band of citizens known as the Ku Klux Klan was organized to deal with the offenders." Dealing with offenders was something the plain folk, in particular, were eager and able to do.[21]

The upcountry had always been a violent area, but it was particularly unsafe for blacks during the 1880s and 1890s. Before the late nineteenth century, lynchings of whites by whites outnumbered reported black lynchings in the South. But after the 1880s, lynchings of freedmen—probably by groups such as the Owl Hollow crowd—became all too common. Small-town editors were often ambivalent about the doings of night riders, but they almost never questioned race-related lynchings. Indeed, the Dalton papers reported black lynchings with perverse enthusiasm, sometimes describing in detail the suffering of the victims and offering unambiguous warnings to all African Americans, especially black men, that a similar fate awaited them for even the most minor offenses.

The story of Lee McDaniel's swift demise was not unusual. In late July 1892 Clemmie Woods, a teenage white girl living near Tilton, a railroad junction in western Whitfield County, awoke one night to find a man in her room. When she screamed, he fled into the night. The *Argus* reported that "he was, in general outline, recognized as McDaniel," a black man employed by the Woods as a household servant. Apprehended the following day, McDaniel was tried, imprisoned, and then, when it was "nearly night," taken on the road to Dalton by lawmen. The procession was "met by masked men, who ordered a return march" to the Tilton area. The gang placed a noose around McDaniel's neck and asked for a confession, whereupon the black man "denied any purpose, 'only to feel of the girl a little.' " No white person in Whitfield County would have dared to question these proceedings or the newspaper's account of them. And few would have cringed at the story's conclusion: "Lee McDaniel, with a broken neck swung into eternity, paying the inevitable forfeit, which, in this county, is sure to follow the transaction with which he was charged." Dalton's editors hailed lynching as the only deterrent and proper punishment for what they termed the "frightful frequency" of "Negro assaults upon white women." On matters of racial control, most whites were united much of the time.[22]

But on other issues, whites were not always united, not even poor whites. North Georgia's moonshine wars bore witness to both the inherent solidarity of rural communities and their potential polarization. Most whitecapping incidents involved the protection of local moonshiners from federal revenue agents and their local spies. Whiskey had been distilled in north Georgia since before the Civil War. Conditions there were optimal for making corn "likker," and poor roads made it easier and more profitable for farmers to sell their surplus corn in liquid form. Problems arose during Reconstruction when the federal government began to enforce a "luxury tax" on whiskey and demanded that producers purchase a license. Mountain moonshiners considered the new laws an abomination and tried to get around them by producing whiskey in secret. The federal government's intrusion into traditional patterns of production offended their localistic sensibilities, and besides, the new taxes and license fees made it impossible for small-scale whiskey makers to gain any profit. Once it became clear that rural distillers were circumventing the law by producing liquor in well-hidden stills, the federal government sent in revenue agents, armed with broadly defined powers of enforcement, to destroy stills and arrest offenders. To protect the interests of local moonshine producers, secret whitecap societies organized throughout Gilmer, Gordon, Murray, and Whitfield counties. This issue provided clear evidence of traditional mutuality appropriated for community service. But it was also one over which the white community divided.[23]

The major problem for whitecappers was not so much the federal revenue agents as it was local residents who supported those agents by serving as spies and leading them to the illegal stills. White caps swore blood oaths to drive revenue informants from their communities. According to the oath, threats and physical abuse would be used to persuade traitors to leave the neighborhood. If these methods proved unsuccessful, the proper solution was murder. This was serious business, and it exposed severe cleavages within the community of poor whites. Grisly fighting erupted between white caps and revenue gangs, both of whom organized for the conflict. In 1884 the *Argus* reported that a married woman in Gilmer County "was killed by a mob, who put out both her eyes, pierced her through the body with a sharpened pole, and then hung her lifeless and terribly mutilated body up in a tree to dry." The paper speculated that it was "the work of revenue informers" but admitted that "there are no clews [sic] as to the guilty perpetrators." Groups of poor whites were at war with one another. Battles between revenuers and moonshiners reached a climax during the early 1890s when the federal government sent in swarms of agents at the precise time that the agricultural depression was pushing many small farmers into whiskey production. Whitecappers in north Georgia killed some 15 to 20 people and assaulted 150 others during the first four years of the decade.[24]

The whitecap turmoil of the late 1880s and early 1890s showed both the strong point and the fatal flaw of plain folk protest. Vigilante societies normally had semiformal organizations similar to that of the Ku Klux Klan. In Whitfield, Murray, Gordon, and Gilmer counties, antirevenuer bands had a combined membership of about one thousand. This movement marked a considerable degree of collective action among the region's poor whites and clearly revealed the cooperative ethic that existed in the countryside. Yet, as organizations go, the secret societies were fundamentally different from the business and labor coalitions that were forming in late-nineteenth-century America. The modern interest-group organizations that came to characterize the urban-industrial world were officially chartered, bureaucratically structured institutions. They were intended to be permanent agents of influence within the national economy. Night riders, even those who joined a gang and swore a blood oath, envisioned their efforts as short-term solutions to temporary difficulties. Their focus on the problem and its solution remained essentially local and personal. Moreover, although the whitecap move-ment pointed up the strong legacy of cooperative effort that existed in Dixie's upcountry regions, it also demonstrated how polarized rural communities could become when divided by controversial cultural or economic issues. Historian Edward L. Ayers hit the mark when he described north Georgians as "an agreeable and violent people." They would remain so for many years to come, and in time both mutuality and polarization would reappear in Dixie's cotton-mill villages.[25]

As the traditional rural economy deteriorated, plain folk protest took new forms and became more focused politically. It was not that poor whites suddenly became interested in politics. They had demonstrated a deep and abiding interest in affairs of state since the settlement of north Georgia. One historian recently missed the point by arguing that small farmers and cotton-mill workers in the early New South era had little interest in larger political affairs: "Before the first decade of the twentieth century what governments did was of little concern to them." To accept this view is to misrepresent the historical record and to underesti-mate the importance of early labor protests and the agrarian revolt in establishing the context of southern industrial relations. Subsistence farmers were never apolit-ical. During the antebellum era, ordinary white families supported a powerful and activist government's attempts to remove the Cherokees from north Georgia and to keep blacks in bondage. The Western and Atlantic Railroad was a state-owned, government-run enterprise in which they would hardly have been disinterested. And hundreds of men in the upcountry had allowed themselves to be slaughtered for the Confederacy, offering proof enough that political matters were of some concern to them. For those who never went to battle, state-funded emergency food relief in north Georgia during and after the war was critical. In the postbellum decades, the moonshine wars were a direct result of state intervention. The point should be clear: plain folk understood very well that state power could make a critical difference in their lives. What changed in the late nineteenth century was not their level of interest but their political goals and their means of trying to influence policy.[26]

As the economic plight of poor white families worsened and they saw around them an expanding array of national and regional organizations that claimed to be working for the "producing element," they channeled traditional cooperative net-works into new forms of collective protest. Some joined the Knights of Labor, which had rural organizations for farmers as well as industrial unions.[27] Many more flocked to the Southern Farmers' Alliance, a social club and political organi-zation that flourished during the late 1880s. The Alliance was an important transi-tional organization for poor farmers. The club's neighborhood meetings included singing and scripture reading and family entertainment, all emanating from the wellsprings of plain-folk culture. But the organization also championed innovative methods for controlling the market economy so that farmers would not be controlled by it. The Alliance attempted, for example, to improve the lot of small farmers through the creation of producer-controlled cooperatives, which sought to eliminate middlemen and curtail the power of servicing merchants. Many within the organization also began to advocate federal government intervention in the form of a "subtreasury plan," a marketing system intended to give southern farmers greater control over the sale of their crops in order to push staple prices higher.[28]

The Alliance's advocacy of the subtreasury plan and other reform measures turned it into a political lobbying group that began to endorse pro-Alliance candidates within the Democratic party. The organization had an economically diverse membership, however, and not everyone was pleased with the Alliance's drift into agrarian politics. Members of considerable wealth who were boosters of the New South and staunch supporters of laissez-faire economics were particularly concerned, especially when Alliance-backed candidates swept the state elections of 1890. To many it seemed that the farmers' organization had taken control of Georgia's Democratic party. But it soon became apparent that the old party leaders retained control and that most Alliance-backed representatives in the statehouse were only mildly committed to the cause. Georgia's "Alliance legislature" of 1890 proved dedicated instead to the status quo.

Many small farmers, pressed by hard times and outraged by what they perceived as a legislative sellout, soon pushed their protests one step further by throwing their support to the newly created Populist (or People's) party. The Populist movement was a national phenomenon, one rendered inordinately complex by the economic peculiarities and political circumstances of each state and region. In Georgia, it gave angry white farmers a chance to fight the Democratic party and to alter the economic system to their own advantage. No longer relying on voluntary cooperatives or political lobbying, the farmers directed their energies toward third-party politics. The Populists endorsed a platform that called for fundamental and permanent government intervention into the capitalist economy. This type of protest was a long way from whitecapping, although the third party's rhetoric of producerism, as well as its clientele, reflected traditional rural society. In this way the Populist revolt exemplified the modernization of plain-folk protest.[29]

Georgia's Democrats had a decided advantage over any third party because many potential recruits for political insurgency had already been disfranchised. The state constitution of 1877 mandated that everyone pay a poll tax in order to vote. The tax was just one dollar, but for poor people that amount was hardly trivial. Worse, the tax was cumulative. If left unpaid, the amount a person owed the state would build up over time, and the complete bill had to be paid in full in order for that person to vote again. As historian J. Morgan Kousser has demonstrated, the poll tax quickly undermined the potential electoral power of blacks and many poor whites, thereby striking a critical blow to Georgia's Republican party. Some poor whites and even some blacks continued to vote, as evidenced by the independent political movements that flared in northwest Georgia during the 1870s and 1880s. And as the Populist challenge emerged, Democratic election officials found it within themselves to overlook the poll tax debts of those poor men who seemed inclined to vote for the Democratic party. Whether the Populists could overcome the poll tax barrier and successfully tap rural discontent was anybody's guess. But as the state elections of 1892 approached, it was clear that the People's party represented the plain folk's most aggressive assault on the new economic order.[30]

In northwest Georgia, leaders of the Democratic party—including the directors of the Crown Cotton Mill—fought skillfully and vigorously to defeat the Populists. Crown's managers had been pivotal Democrats in Whitfield County throughout the 1880s, and they viewed their party as the necessary political vehicle for a new Dalton and a New South. Before his tenure as Crown Mill president, Thomas Jones had even served as a Democratic state senator. Dalton's new economic leaders correctly saw populism as an affront to their social and economic authority. Their vision of the New South and their place in it had committed them to an unflinching defense of modernization, but above all, these industrialists cherished and demanded the public control now sought by the Populists.

Having shouldered the responsibility for the region's welfare, they demanded in return jurisdiction over its political and economic institutions. As a result, Dalton's New South elite expected to fill key positions in political and civic organizations, and they did so. When in 1892 Thomas Jones chided a friend for not accepting a political nomination, saying, "Why didn't you take it, always take all that is given you," he voiced the creed of Dalton's industrialists. Because populism sought, in part, to strip the economic elite of their newfound authority and economic power, town leaders perceived the movement as a threat and acted accordingly. In 1892, when the People's party first emerged as a political force, several of Crown's directors and stockholders, with Jones at the forefront, helped establish the Central Democratic Club to battle populism in Whitfield County. Jones himself personally hit the stump for "true-blue" Democracy, giving speeches for the cause throughout north Georgia. Before three thousand people who had massed for a Democratic "cue" in Dalton during the state campaign, the man who introduced incumbent governor William J. Northern (who strongly opposed the Populists) was none other than the president of Crown Cotton Mills.[31]

But Whitfield County farmers showed noticeably little respect for Jones and his kind, and the Populists gave the Democrats a tough fight in the elections of 1892 and 1894. The *Argus* excoriated the People's party and gave it virtually no coverage save that of derisive remarks, but in the spring of 1892 one rural correspondent had to admit that "third party men are as thick as grasshoppers in August." In the gubernatorial contest, the Democrats carried the county, winning a comfortable 57 percent of the vote. Had the Dalton vote been excluded, however, the Populists would have won in Whitfield. The Dalton district represented half of the voters in the county, and 70 percent of them voted Democrat. In Whitfield's five poorest districts—all strictly rural—three out of every four voters dropped in a Populist ticket. The election results two years later, in the state contests of 1894, were roughly the same, with the Populist percentage slightly lower overall and another strong Democratic showing in Dalton (75 percent). Nevertheless, the combined 1894 returns for Whitfield, Murray, and Gordon counties (in the senatorial race) showed that 45 percent voted for the People's party, a figure that matched the state's overall third-party returns.[32]

For a recently born third party, the Populists had made an impressive showing, widespread ballot fraud by the Democrats notwithstanding. Ironically, within two years the national Populist party would be subsumed and essentially destroyed by the Democratic party as the two organizations united behind William Jennings Bryan in his ill-fated bid for the presidency in 1896. That election was an unmitigated disaster for the People's party, and it ensured that southern Populists would never again threaten their Democratic rivals.[33] But even without the calamity in 1896, it is questionable whether Georgia's third party could have conquered the Democrats or even emerged as an enduring party of opposition. At the very least, it might be said that matters of race and questions of third-party economic policy guaranteed the Democrats a prominent and lasting place in southern politics.

Every major protest organization of the late nineteenth century—the Knights of Labor, the Farmers' Alliance, and the Populist party—suggested that producer-oriented labor unions or political coalitions should transcend racial barriers. In some ways these groups did seek biracial alliances. The Farmers' Alliance of Murray County held mass meetings to protest the lynching of Hosey Jones, a member of the Colored Alliance, and these meetings actually led to the arrest and conviction of several white men in the area. The *Argus* blasted Populist leader Tom Watson for preaching social equality between the races. Perhaps the *Argus* was putting the point too strongly, but Watson and other third-party leaders did speak out boldly in favor of a legitimate biracial political alliance.[34]

But what Watson said and what rank-and-file Populists did were two different things, and the race issue mingled with class and politics in enormously complex ways, as the night riders' raid on Dalton after the 1892 state elections attests. Shortly after the Populists' defeat, a gang of 150 white caps stormed the town, shot down one black man, and beat a black couple almost to death. The following day, when anxious citizens gathered at a town meeting to condemn the raiders, accusations flew between Democrats and Populists. Local Democrats, the majority group, charged that the mob had consisted of Populists seeking to avenge the Democratic loyalty demonstrated by local blacks. They took up a collection for reward money with which to apprehend the perpetrators. But a group of local Populists contended that the mob was led by Democrats who assaulted Republican party regulars who had made pro-Populist speeches. In Dalton, as elsewhere, white Democrats and white Populists both laid claim to the black vote and were willing to go to extremes to get it or keep it from going to the opposition. After elections, white Populists often blamed their defeats on black voters, and some third-party leaders, who early on had been firm advocates of biracial politics, later became bitter racists.[35]

But there was more to third-party defeat than race-baiting Democrats or even ballot fraud. The ultimate problem for the Populists was more complex and painfully ironic. The consequences of economic modernization in the South caused plain folk to channel their traditional patterns of collective dissent into modern engines of political protest, but those same economic changes made it especially difficult for ordinary whites to maintain their collective sensibilities. The rhetoric of producerism touched deep impulses among poor farmers, but it was not always easy for a family or a community to ascertain its own practical economic interests. Theoretically, for example, both modest landholders and poor farm laborers were part of the broadly defined "producing element." In a cash-crop economy, however, the wishes of these two groups did not always run parallel. Small farm owners sought high commodity prices and inexpensive labor; farm laborers required just the opposite. Sharecroppers, depending on whether they considered themselves on the way up the agricultural ladder or on the way down, might feel a bond with either group. No political party could very well address the immediate economic needs of all these plain folk.

It is especially difficult to assess how mill workers might have voted. In the North and the larger urban areas of the South, the Populists courted the vote of industrial workers but had difficulty winning it.[36] The basic reason was simple enough: populism sought higher prices for farm produce, an inflationary trend that would only harm the pocketbooks of urban consumers. But in the mill towns of the southern upcountry, no sharp line divided mill workers from rural folk—certainly not during the time of the Populist revolt or for many years to come. Some tenant farmers had children in the mill; some people in mill households hired out as farm laborers. Dalton went solidly and persistently Democratic, but not because of the mill-worker vote. At the time, Crown did not employ enough workers for there to be a concentrated labor bloc and, to state the more obvious point, most of the millhands at the time were women or children and were therefore ineligible to vote. Presumably the poll tax kept some of the mill-working men from casting ballots, but even those who did vote faced a difficult choice. If an adult male had long-range plans to save enough from mill work to buy a small farm and return to the land, he might vote Populist to ensure long-term improvements for petty producers in the countryside. But because Populist policies were inflationary, they would, in the short run, work to the economic disadvantage of any mill family, making it harder to save enough to purchase a farm.

As economic modernization advanced, the plain folk seemed to become less and less of a coherent socioeconomic group. It was not that they carried a culture of individualism into a modern world in which collective action was needed; rather, their culture of informal collectivism was stripped of its economic logic in the new capitalist order. Before the Civil War, subsistence farmers in the upcountry could still view their own family interests as roughly synonymous with the interests of the community, at least most of the time. In the New South, these same people clung to many of their cultural norms and maintained many of their social and economic expectations, but the economic interests of ordinary white producers no longer coincided so neatly with those of the larger community. The manifold political considerations of millhands, sharecroppers, farm laborers, and small farm owners testified to interest-group fragmentation. In time, though, and under different circumstances, the plain folk's traditions of community cooperation would reemerge in Dixie's mill villages.

From the labor protests and political insurgency of the late 1880s and 1890s, upcountry whites drew contradictory lessons. These conflicts forced rural people to reconstruct their traditional forms of collective protest and taught them much about power and privilege in the new economic order. But those who fought to change the system had lost, and those who did not fight had witnessed the defeat. In Dixie's larger textile centers, unionization efforts surged once again between roughly 1898 and 1902, but these workers' organizations were crushed as completely as the Populists had been. Poor whites who chose to stay in the South would have to make peace with the new order, shuttling between tenant farms and cotton mills, neither of which, in 1900, offered much hope for a better life.[37]

But poor whites had one unchangeable advantage: their race. It was a cruel advantage, but poor whites embraced it all the more closely because it was one of the few things that could not be taken from them. Once populism had failed, the question of a biracial political coalition was moot, because poor whites saw no more political or economic incentives to form such an alliance with blacks. Jim Crow laws soon came into being, and disfranchised blacks had no political leverage by which to change the system of segregation. For their part, white sharecroppers and millhands tried to make the most of this situation.

In the cotton mills especially, where mill owners stressed the importance of reserving mill jobs for fellow "Anglo-Saxons," poor white families seized their racial advantage as a right. During the labor glut of the 1890s, mill owners could hardly have foreseen the profound long-term implications of this labor policy. When threatened with insurgency from below, southern business leaders, like their northern counterparts, demonstrated a cold capacity for political and economic brutality. But Dixie's elite also tried to defuse class antagonisms with the rhetoric of "Anglo-Saxon" unity and the notion that, at some basic level, southern whites were equals. This idea made for good political guff. It also carried enormous weight among poor whites, and it became an important and enduring undercurrent within the world of southern textiles.[38]

So the stage was set for the formation of Dixie's cotton-mill communities. Southern-born poor whites would tend the machines. They were people whose lives had been upended, who were willing to try alternative ways of making a living. They would operate from the perspective of a family economy, utilizing the labor of their children to full advantage. Their culture of cooperative effort had undergirded the unsuccessful rural protest movements of the late nineteenth century and had been damaged by the dictates of the new order. But there was more to rural culture than protest, and much of it survived, although at the turn of the century it was not yet clear how cultural persistence would affect the industrial environment.

Southern-born business leaders would own the machines and manage the corporations. They were part of an ascendant core of new industrialists who controlled not only the mills but almost everything else in their small-town world. They had fashioned a vision of elite stewardship, economic growth, and political power that future generations of boosters would act upon and protect. The vigor and brutality with which they crushed all efforts to alter the new order reflected the depth of their faith in that vision. As long as the mill owners were in control of the upcountry, and as long as their cotton mills churned out huge dividends, southern industrialists could afford to compromise a little with their workers, to appear magnanimous without losing any money or control. Ironically, their mills were so successful that they were forced to compromise, as southern mill expansion created a regional labor shortage and demanded that management work harder to recruit an adequate supply of workers.

By the turn of the century, upcountry plain folk had been defeated at every turn and had been rendered politically powerless. But they were not quite helpless in the economic arena. Poor whites had one final piece of leverage—their labor power—and when the opportunity presented itself, they employed that power selectively and forced fundamental changes in southern textiles. In doing so, the workers themselves played a crucial role in the creation of cohesive mill-village communities in the modernizing South.

PART II

CREATING THE

CROWN MILL

COMMUNITY,

1900–1919

4

MANAGING GROWTH

During the first two decades of the twentieth century, a cohesive industrial community took shape at Crown Mill. Working families slowly began to sink roots into the mill village as wages increased and company officials implemented new labor policies that encouraged workers to remain with the mill. An identifiable company culture emerged, one that served to bridge the cultural and economic gap separating managers and millhands and that built upon their heritage of racial unity. Both workers and mill officials played a part in the rise of a paternalistic mill-village system, and both eventually embraced the notion that they were part of a corporate "family." The necessary condition underlying this process of community development was Crown's success as a business enterprise. Not only did the mill prosper, it expanded significantly during the late nineteenth and early twentieth centuries. Its managers displayed an insatiable desire for growth. They saw factory expansion as an essential ingredient for profits. With each new facility the company erected, a host of new working families made their way to Dalton. The number of millhands working for Crown increased from 110 in 1890 to more than 640 by the end of

World War I. As the mill-village population grew, company officials used corporate paternalism to stabilize the community. Business strategy and corporate success therefore had a powerful impact on the evolution of mill-village society. The development of an industrial community in Dalton would not have occurred when and how it did had Crown not been a profitable and expanding enterprise.

During these years Crown's leaders reached maturity as industrial managers. Although they were savvy businessmen, the mill officials knew virtually nothing about running a large manufacturing plant when they first began. As a result they relied heavily on northern (they always said "eastern") textile expertise. Crown bought its machinery from the North, sold its products through Yankee sales agents, and solicited basic advice on how to manage a profitable mill. In time, however, Crown's managers developed considerable expertise in their own right. Company records reveal an increasingly hard-boiled, efficiency-minded management that shrewdly kept an eye toward plant modernization and expansion. Crown's growth sparked unanticipated problems, however. Early in the new century, local critics began to insist that the mill was too powerful for Dalton's own good. But this hometown opposition proved no match for Crown's leaders, who managed local discontent as skillfully as they ran their mill.

Through the early 1890s, Crown experienced moderate growth. During Thomas R. Jones's eight-year tenure as company chief (1887–94), the mill expanded from about 2,000 spindles and 50 looms to some 5,000 spindles and 130 looms, more than doubling its modest production and filling the factory building to capacity. During those years, Crown's profits averaged an impressive 22.4 percent return on capital. (See table A.2 and figure A.1 for Crown's earnings.) But these commendable results satisfied neither Jones nor the other company directors, for they sought to double the size of the factory itself. Although rumors to this effect surfaced in the local press throughout the early 1890s, the proposed expansion had not occurred by the time Jones quietly resigned the presidency in spring 1894.[1]

Soon thereafter Crown entered a new era of growth, culminating in the construction of an expansive factory complex that dwarfed the original mill. In 1895 the original mill doubled in size, and new company offices were built near Hamilton's Spring, south of the factory entrance. Before the end of the decade, the company constructed both a weave shed and a warehouse north of the enlarged factory, as well as a new picker room just east of the main mill. In late 1908 the officials added an entirely new spinning and weaving plant, which became known as Mill No. 2, or simply the New Mill. This factory arose just north of a sharp curve in Chattanooga Avenue, about one hundred yards north of the original factory complex, which everyone subsequently called the Old Mill (or, more formally, Mill No. 1). Eight years later, during the World War I textile boom, Crown built expansive additions to the New Mill, which brought the total spindleage of the company to 50,000 and the number of looms to about 1,200. By 1916 the Crown Cotton Mill complex stretched a quarter-mile north of the original mill, a remarkable symbol of small-town industrial success.[2]

The individual most responsible for this growth was George W. Hamilton, who became president in late 1894 and held that position for the next quarter-century. It was appropriate that Hamilton, whom everyone at the mill knew as "Mr. George," became the company's leading statesman, for the mill was built on Hamilton family land, where he was born in 1847. Though not an original stockholder, George Hamilton quickly worked his way into a position of prominence in the Crown organization during its first decade of operation. In September 1885, the directors hired him as secretary-treasurer, and he assumed primary responsibility for purchasing cotton, selling finished goods, keeping company records, and generally handling almost all daily financial and bookkeeping matters. Four years later, the stockholders elected him a director, which meant that he owned at least five hundred shares of stock, the minimum requirement for that position. The first decade of Crown's history provided Hamilton with an extended apprenticeship, during which he developed astute managerial skills in the textile business.

Hamilton's leadership meant mill expansion. In the interim between Jones's departure in April 1894 and the annual stockholders' meeting that September, the directors authorized Hamilton (who was himself on the board) to purchase material for an addition nearly equal in size to the existing plant. After the September meeting, the directors elected Hamilton to succeed Jones. Thereafter the expansion of the original mill, as well as construction of the new office building south of it, proceeded rapidly. In virtually every department—picking, carding, spinning, spooling, and weaving—productive capabilities nearly doubled. Crown now had 9,680 spindles and 256 looms. The main building measured 260 by 50 feet, most of it three stories.[3]

This first major expansion demonstrated Hamilton's consistent goal of efficient production. The new wing was attached to the old building in a straight line, so that only three new walls were needed; the fundamental design of the original facility was merely expanded. This method of mill development was common among successful enterprises because it allowed the basic arrangement of the factory and its machinery to remain intact, ensuring a smoother transition period.[4] Hamilton's report to the stockholders at the end of the year clearly revealed his business strategy. "All machinery put in is of the latest improved pattern," he boasted. "Our new cards are doing today 225 lbs per day of much superior work than our old ones, which are only doing 100 lbs per day. Our new spindles have a capacity of 10,000 revolutions per minute while our old ones have only 7,000 per minute. All of which put us in condition to manufacture fine goods on our fine [machinery] as cheaply as anyone."[5] The company's return on capital in 1895

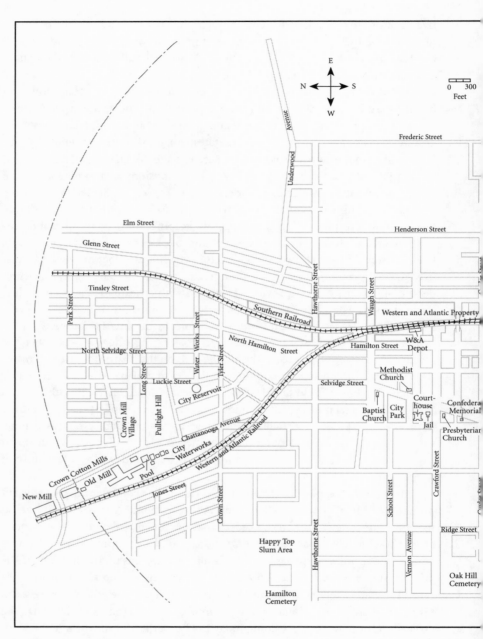

MAP 4.1.
Dalton, Georgia, 1910

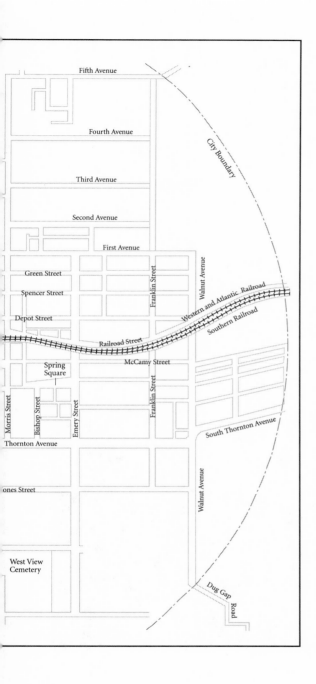

George W. Hamilton, Sr. (known by the millhands as "Mr. George"), president of Crown Cotton Mills from 1894 to 1919, ca. 1900. (*Courtesy of Crown Gardens and Archives*)

reached a remarkable 41 percent. Stockholders pocketed a lucrative 10 percent cash dividend from $50,786 net profit. By all accounts, Hamilton's first year as president and secretary was an astounding success.

These results inspired the confidence to undertake even greater expansion. The annual meeting in September 1895 evoked a resounding call from directors and stockholders for an $80,000 increase in the building and machinery. For two years it was difficult to carry out these plans, because returns on capital fell to 16 percent in 1896 and remained there for the next twelve months. Still, as most industries considered 10 percent profits good, these returns were hardly setbacks. Plans for a massive new weave shed were discussed at the annual meeting in 1897, and in the following summer Crown's directors authorized Hamilton to make the necessary purchases. He still had not done so by the time the stockholders convened that fall; three years of planning and boisterous talk of new additions had so far resulted in nothing. But a bottom line showing the best profits ever in 1898—net profits of $73,391 and a stunning 45 percent return on capital—inspired Hamilton to follow through on the proposed expansion. The plan called for a weave shed that would nearly double the mill's productive capacity. Directors hoped to run carding and spinning shifts day and night, thus providing enough material for a full day's run of weaving in the new facility. A wide, flat-roofed, single-story building, the weave room represented, in both form and function, Hamilton's goal of creating an economically efficient factory environment.[6]

The drive for efficiency that characterized Crown's expansion in the late 1890s was nothing new to the company. The directors had always pursued an explicit policy of purchasing the best available spinning and weaving machines in order to produce high-quality goods. Machinery considerations were crucial and could make a major difference in the quality of goods. As early as 1884, the company sent its first secretary, J. K. Brunner, to visit numerous mills in New England and the Midwest before making any purchasing decisions. The directors instructed Brunner to determine the "latest and most improved pattern" of machinery. From the beginning, management made it clear that the major consideration should be "quality rather than price." The original mill rumbled with machines that were remarkably swift and labor efficient for the 1880s. High-speed Sawyer spinning frames, built and installed by Rhode Islanders, whirled at 7,500 revolutions per minute, and looms capable of producing 4,000 yards of quality sheeting a day shook the building. The entire mill ran on steam, the directors having purchased an excellent two-hundred-horsepower engine that, the local press boasted, "stands like a giant." Even as the mill lost money its first year, one manager crowed, "There is not a fixture but that is of the very best and latest patent, of recognized superiority, enabling the largest yield of any mill in the South at a lower cost."[7]

The inaugural commitment to high-quality machinery persisted after the mill was firmly established. In 1890 Thomas Jones traveled to the Northeast to examine machinery, and in 1892 Crown purchased new equipment from a firm in Lowell, Massachusetts. Six years later directors approved an "experiment" with humidifiers in the mill. The impulse toward mechanical efficiency was clearly evident after "a conflagration caused by lightning" visited the mill's main warehouse and adjacent weave shed in July 1890. The blaze destroyed hundreds of cotton bales and damaged nearly forty looms. Even after insurance benefits had been paid, the mill suffered a $10,000 loss of property. Rather than try to make up the balance with increased production on old machines, the directors shut down the mill for a full six weeks to install superior equipment and train the workers to use it. At the annual stockholders' meeting two months later, Jones reported the decision with pride and predicted that the current demand for cotton duck, coupled with Crown's exceptional machinery, would bring substantial profits. "The Mill," he stated, "is now in a much finer condition to give results in an increased product than at any time since its inception. . . . No known addition can be suggested to increase its efficiency." George Hamilton continued to uphold this policy throughout his years as company chief. Significant investments to replace existing machinery in 1903, 1905, 1911, and 1914 attested to the consistency of this entrepreneurial strategy.[8]

Crown's insatiable desire for better machinery was part of a larger trend among southern textile mills. Dixie's mill managers believed that using the newest labor-saving machines would give them a competitive advantage over northern mills in the coarse textile market.[9] Ironically, Crown and other southern mills had to purchase their machinery from Yankee firms, because no machine shops in Dixie could produce such equipment. Superintendent Brunner's 1884 tour through northern plants and Thomas Jones's purchases from Lowell in 1892 were not isolated events in Crown's history. All of the expansions led by George Hamilton demonstrated the mill's enduring dependence on northern textile expertise and equipment. Southern textile leaders developed strong ties to Yankee machine works even as they competed with northern manufacturers for shares of the national textile market.[10]

Dixie's textile manufacturers also largely depended on northern commission houses to sell their goods. Hamilton had been in charge of sales since taking the secretary-treasurer's position in 1885. More accurately, he dealt with northern agents who marketed Crown's cloth. Occasionally he also worked with British commission houses, which sold Dalton-made textiles in Europe, Latin America, and the Far East.[11] Foreign trade was not critical to Crown's success, but it appealed to the romantic in local boosters. "It makes a Dalton man feel proud to see the car loads of goods going out to the four corners of the earth," boasted the *North Georgia Citizen*, "and when we consider that the web and woof of the white duck pantaloons of the German army are spun and woven right here in Dalton, it stirs our latent military feelings."[12] Despite such bluster, Crown's basic avenues of trade led to the North and the Midwest, where it sold goods through agents based primarily in New York (the major American cloth market), Boston, Philadelphia, Cincinnati, and Chicago.[13]

Necessary ties between southern mill managers and northern machine shops and commission houses fostered close relationships across regional lines, but they also led to conflicts. The commission system had ample room for abuse, and some southern firms found themselves in dire straits due to underhanded dealings in the national market. Moreover, Hamilton's background as a loyal Confederate sometimes made it difficult for him to deal with insolent northerners. In 1895 Crown broke off relations with Turner Brothers and Company, a commission house in Chicago, shortly after "Mr. George" was insulted by Turner's representative. Hamilton and Crown's directors officially recorded their indignation, tersely stating that "after hearing [the representative's] contentions and noting his hostile attitude toward and want of confidence in Company's president, decided not to allow Turner Bros. and Co. to handle our goods in future." To set matters straight, the directors demanded the return of 275 bales of duck already sent to Chicago. One early adviser to southern industrialists suggested that "great care should be exercised in the selection of a commission house, and having found a good one, it is well to stay with it." Crown did just that with J. H. Lane and Company, which operated mills in New England and also served as a commission house. Lane was Crown's primary agent from the 1890s throughout the twentieth century. The company's relationship with Lane reflected the close interconnections between southern mills and northern businesses, but it did not prevent Hamilton from trying to maintain home control of his plant.[14]

Hamilton's decision to send his sons to the Georgia School of Technology's new textile engineering program showed his desire to make southern industrialists more independent. Southern manufacturers had long been obliged to send their sons or prospective supervisors to northern schools or mills to learn industrial skills; or they had to recruit knowledgeable northerners. Georgia Tech, consciously patterned after northern textile schools and equipped with machines donated by Yankee firms, dedicated itself to providing a southern alternative for hands-on training in textile manufacturing and management. George W. Hamilton, Jr. ("Little George"), who joined Crown as superintendent in 1904 at age twenty-three, was one of the first graduates of the textile engineering program. Another of Mr. George's sons, Cornelius ("Neil"), also studied at Tech for three years before going to work in the Crown office. In time, Little George and Neil would see the day when J. H. Lane and Company sought *their* help, and Crown ultimately bought out the northern firm altogether—events that indicated Dixie's industrial maturation during the twentieth century and the North's corresponding decline in the textile industry. But as Mr. George brought Crown into a new age of expansion, such a shift in manufacturing dominance remained well in the future.[15]

Crown's penchants for expansion and high-quality machinery and its dependence on northern machine companies were both manifest in the new factory
built in 1908. The idea of a second mill complex developed in the directors' minds
almost as soon as the Old Mill reached its full capacity with the weave shed
addition in 1899. Anticipating future expansion, the corporation revised its charter
in 1900 to allow capitalization of up to $1 million. Two years later the directors
purchased forty acres of land north of their existing property, just east of the
W&A. This was the future site of Mill No. 2, but several years passed before any
further action was taken. When the return on capital reached 36 percent in 1905
and 41 percent the next year, the directors unanimously resolved to build the new
mill just north of the sharp bend in Chattanooga Avenue (see map 4.1). They
envisioned a facility with 12,500 spindles and some 300 looms, and, not surprisingly, they demanded "modern plans with [the] latest improved equipment." The
Lowell Machine Shop of Massachusetts furnished the equipment. (David D. Hamilton, grandson of Mr. George and current president of CrownAmerica, recently
reviewed Crown's contract with the Lowell firm and quipped, "Apparently those
astute Yankee manufacturers had little confidence in Southern mill managements
of that day, for the proposal was in minute detail everything necessary to start
production, down to hammers, files, and of all things, toilet paper.") Despite calls
for rapid implementation of the building plans, construction had not begun by the
end of 1907. A gap in the directors' minutes during the 1908 fiscal year obscures the
precise time of the expansion, but the New Mill arose sometime during those
twelve months, for the company's annual report in September 1908 shows that the
company's holdings in both real estate and machinery had nearly doubled. Some
months passed before the New Mill actually began production. Mill No. 2 consisted of a one-story weave shed, a large two-story building for carding and spinning operations, and another two-story multipurpose building.[16]

The architecture of Crown's new buildings reflected an increasing awareness
and appreciation of practical design and economic rationalization. Each new
structure from the late 1890s on utilized the latest innovations in industrial construction. The new buildings forsook the grandeur of the Old Mill, taking on a
more practical, if more mundane, appearance. High, narrow rooms and vaulted
roofs gave way to broad, spacious buildings with flatter roofs and lower ceilings.
Never again would Crown build a lofty belfry. As one architectural analyst noted,
the New Mill manifested "the tendency towards larger, lower, and wider industrial
buildings, and features a more highly rationalized framing system."[17]

George Hamilton, Sr., had reason to feel successful as the first decade of the new
century came to a close. Since 1900 Crown had doubled in size and had averaged
an impressive 24 percent return on capital. The mill had found an extremely
capable "master mechanic" in Frank A. Hamilton, whose skill with machinery
proved a great asset. Moreover, Mr. George could now rest comfortably with the

knowledge that the company possessed substantial managerial experience. At the end of 1910, Crown's directors averaged nearly twelve years of continuous service on the board, and by the end of World War I that average had reached almost sixteen years (see figure 4.1). Remarkable stability was displayed by company officials as well. By 1910 Hamilton had been president more than fifteen years, and during that time he had also been serving as secretary. In 1910 he relinquished the latter position to his thirty-four-year-old nephew, William K. ("Will") Moore, Jr., who had been working in the company office for thirteen years. Frank Hardwick had served (without salary) as Crown's treasurer since Hamilton gained the presidency in 1894. R. J. McCamy, who acted as vice president for seventeen years, resigned in 1907 and was replaced by W. M. Patton (from the Sweetwater group), who had been a director for ten years by that time. Having served as superintendent since 1886, J. W. Brown resigned in 1904, but he was replaced by none other than "Little George" Hamilton. Experience helped southern cotton-mill managers to safely navigate the textile market, and by the early twentieth century, Crown's officials and directors had accumulated a wealth of such experience. Crown's managers were a firmly established group of mostly local men who had known each other for years and who upheld consistent strategies of productive expansion and efficiency. The harmony among them, combined with their proven ability to earn profits, provided a solid foundation for a successful manufacturing enterprise.[18]

Despite such clear evidence of monetary success and managerial stability, however, all was not well at Crown. Indications of wretched, unhealthy living conditions in the mill village surfaced occasionally from the beginning. Daltonians expressed particular concern about disease among the millhands. The *Dalton Argus*'s first mention of the workers at Crown dealt with a possible epidemic of scarlet fever in the mill village. Sometime after the company built the New Mill, Dalton's *North Georgia Citizen* lamented the loss of "another victim to Great White Plague" (tuberculosis) at Crown Mill. Epidemics often threatened southern mill villages during the late nineteenth and early twentieth centuries. Plain folk in rural settlements also faced epidemics and disease, but country life afforded a natural segregation that normally prevented the rapid spread of crippling ailments. In the mill village, this natural barrier to epidemics broke down, for residents dwelled comparatively near to one another and worked in close quarters in the mill. In other ways, life in the mill village was much the same as in the country: flies buzzed through unscreened windows in warm weather; privies accumulated human waste; snuff and saliva flew everywhere. Among closely congregated mill families and within a factory building, these conditions created serious health hazards.[19]

Company managers could not be held fully accountable for the problems, but neither could they be fully absolved. An incident in the late 1890s vividly illustrated not only the unhealthy conditions in the village, but also the increasing power that

FIGURE 4.1. Experience of Members on Crown's Board of Directors, 1885–1919

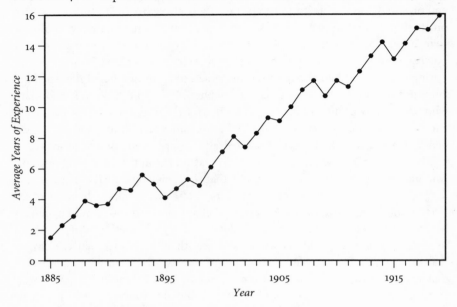

Source: Crown Cotton Mills Board of Directors Minutes, Book 1, CGA.

Crown's leaders exercised over local affairs and the mill's working families. In 1896 Dalton's mayor, J. G. McAfee, investigated a pollution problem on the Mill Creek branch some fifty yards north of Hamilton's Spring, where a bridge crossed the stream. Millhands walking to and from the mill along Chattanooga Avenue had to cross this bridge. The creek at that point served as an outlet for factory sewage, but the area had become clogged and stagnant, exuding a horrific stench. McAfee received assurances from Crown's superintendent, J. W. Brown, that the creek would be cleaned up immediately. But Brown did nothing to remedy the situation, and one year later he himself summoned H. P. Colvard, chairman of the Nuisance Committee of Dalton's city council, with his own complaint that "some of his tenants were keeping nuisances on their premises and [he] wanted the city to have them removed." Crown's workers complied with the city official's request, but they told Colvard that Brown's own place was even worse and demanded that his premises be cleaned as well. Moreover, they revived the issue of the Mill Creek stench. Colvard found the creek filled with "the excrements from the Crown Cotton Mills" and noted that not only did the workers pass over the reeking cesspool "three or four times every day," but "their cows drank" from the same water. The young city official demanded that Brown clean his basement and fix the sewerage system. Once again Brown refused to act upon these requests.

Undaunted, Colvard served the Crown superintendent with legal papers commanding him to solve both problems. Because proper repairs to the sewer evidently would cost more than most of the requests made by the Nuisance Committee, Colvard explained the case to other council members at the next meeting. To his surprise and dismay, the other men, who included Henry Hamilton and another Crown director, "all voted to drop it." Colvard understood this to mean "for me to let the Crown Cotton Mill nuisance alone." "In other words," he continued, "you can make his employees move the nuisances about their premises, but you must not bother Mr. Brown." Publishing his letter of resignation in the local papers, an outraged Colvard stated his conviction that the city should be willing to make Brown "move a nuisance as quickly as . . . his most humble employee." Because the rest of the council disagreed, Colvard quit his post in protest.[20]

At the same time that Daltonians such as Colvard were voicing concern over Crown's sanitation problems and the mill management's unwillingness to deal fairly with the millhands, child labor became a significant issue of debate in Georgia. Plain folk had always worked their children hard on the farm, but many southerners found it deeply disturbing that youngsters eight and nine years old toiled inside factories sixty-five to seventy hours a week. During the late 1890s and the early years of the new century, Georgia's textile leaders staved off a threat to implement a state child labor law like the one passed in 1903 in North Carolina, which made it illegal for children under twelve to do mill work and set the maximum number of hours for all millhands at sixty per week.[21] Georgia's manufacturers wielded substantial influence in the legislature, and they argued that poor mill families demanded that their children be allowed to work in the factory to help support the household, among other reasons. The reformers disagreed. "Making every allowance for any possible element of exaggeration," wrote Alabamian Edgar Gardner Murphy in 1904, "can so profitable an industry for one moment present the plea that it must fix its adult wage at so low a point as to force the family, in the mere struggle for existence, to throw the burdens of employment upon its children under twelve?"[22]

Novelist Will Harben, his ear always tuned to Dalton's affairs, clearly reflected the growing debate in *The Georgians*. It seems no coincidence that this work, written at the height of the child-labor-law campaign, deals more directly with industrialization in "Darley" than do Harben's other books. Although his novels mostly trumpet New South development, *The Georgians* reveals an underside to the southern cotton mills. One mountaineer tells "about havin' a job . . . at Darley in the cotton-mill, [where] he got lint in his lungs an' was down at death's door." When the doctor tells the sick man to go back to the mountains or perish, the millhand despairs: "He didn't have a cent, an' was thinkin' about drowndin' hisse'f in the creek." Fortunately, a wealthy citizen (himself an outcast among local elites due to his father's pro-Union stance during the Civil War and support for Negro education afterward) discovers the man's plight and lends him the money for the life-saving journey.[23]

A revealing look at the child labor debate is provided when Carlton Blaithwait, a "young capitalist" well known in Darley circles and widely sought after throughout the South for his mill-building and management skills, encounters a reform-minded belle, one "Miss Winston," at an uptown reception. "The cotton industry is a good thing for the poor people who have no employment," she says, "but the pity of it is that it too often furnishes work only for the weak women and little children, and not for the strong, able-bodied men. . . . I saw strong men who were actually living in idleness on the earnings of their wives and children." Blaithwait agrees that this situation is a "ticklish problem," but adds that "we cannot build and equip [the mills] and run them at a profit with any other labor." Insisting that "we mill-owners are almost as deep in the mud as the operators are in the mire," Blaithwait tries to win Winston to the cause by adding, "The poor white people here in the South are in such desperate straits to earn a living that the employment women and children can get under our factory roofs and in our well warmed buildings is so much better than their ill-paid work in the fields, that they are fortunate to swap one for the other." Not convinced, Winston reminds him of "the paltry wages paid them for close work from dawn to dark." "You buy them, body and soul, for a few pennies," she continues, "when the product of their hands, their eyes, and their brains enables you stockholders to live in luxury." Blaithwait contends that "we can't, at this stage of the game . . . pay any more for labor than we do . . . that is, and meet competition." To this Winston blurts out, "Competition! That's it! . . . Hundreds of moneyed men are competing with one another to grind the labor of women and children down to the very lowest mark in order that big dividends may be declared." "What a change there would be," she concludes, "if all you manufacturers were to begin to compete with one another on raising wages and bettering the conditions of labor in the South!" At this point her father interrupts good-naturedly, quickly dismissing her remark as "illogical" with paternal condescension.[24]

Regardless of whether Blaithwait or Winston was more logical, the former laid forth basic assumptions embraced by Dalton's manufacturers, whereas the latter voiced criticisms of Dixie's industrial capitalism, which, although still a minority view, were becoming increasingly common. A long string of local editors took it upon themselves to undermine the sentiment in favor of child labor laws. A common tactic was to insist that the mill people themselves sought no such law and often opposed it. "We made a thorough study of the Crown Cotton Mills here," wrote the editor of the North Georgia Citizen, "and we found no opposition whatsoever [by the parents] to children working in the mill." This article ascribed such attitudes to the "princely sum" mill families earned each month compared with their counterparts on the farm. A more accurate assessment might have been that mill parents were desperate for any family income they could get and had to sacrifice their children accordingly. Whatever Daltonians thought of these issues, it could not have been comforting when the local press reported in 1899 that "Lillie Staten, a 12-year-old employee at the Crown Cotton Mill, got her hair caught in a steel spinning frame yesterday and her scalp was literally torn from her head. . . . President Hamilton had to take the machine apart to get the scalp from the rollers around which it had become tightly wound."[25]

Crown faced conflicts with some local businessmen as well. Foremost among these were disputes over local taxation and the city's water supply. Crown's expansion in the 1890s and early twentieth century exacerbated tensions between Crown and the city that had been building for a decade. The company's water contract with Dalton proved a continual source of dissension, because the original 1888 settlement weighed heavily in Crown's favor. Desperate for adequate water and cognizant that Hamilton's Spring represented the best available source, the city gained "free" access to Crown's water by giving the company a ten-year tax exemption. Moreover, Dalton authorities agreed to provide the standpipe reservoir on Pulltight Hill and run water lines to any part of the mill specified by Crown officials. By the time that contract expired in 1898, the mill was well established financially, but it had never dropped one cent of tax money into the city coffer. To make matters worse, Dalton's water supply languished during dry spells. Negotiations for a new contract began in early 1897 and continued through the fall, with some civic leaders calling for terms more advantageous to the city. The *North Georgia Citizen* warned frustrated townspeople not to antagonize Crown, which remained "a very component part of Dalton." The mill received another good contract in 1898, although this one bent toward some city needs. Crown officials, for example, offered company land for the construction of a large reservoir that would be owned by the city. But Dalton still had to furnish the factory and the mill village with water.[26]

More important, the contract included a "maximum taxation" clause, which stipulated that Dalton could only assess Crown $850 per year, regardless of the value of mill property. This contract was to be valid for twenty-five years. When a new editor took over the *North Georgia Citizen* in 1903, he openly criticized the company for enjoying lucrative tax advantages while the city was burdened with an expensive and inadequate waterworks facility. If some businessmen complained of an unnecessary drought of both water and tax money, Crown's officials grew increasingly frustrated because the pipeline laid at Dalton's expense proved inadequate to supply the condenser of the mill's new engine, causing shutdowns and mounting losses. To raise the water level high enough to alleviate the problem, Crown had to construct a dam on Mill Creek, which involved, among other things, paying a nearby resident $200 for the privilege. But the crux of the matter was taxation more than water. Crown paid substantial county taxes and viewed additional city tolls as an insufferable burden. Rumors circulated in 1903—probably in response to editorial attacks on Crown—that "North Dalton" would secede from the city and become an independent suburb.[27]

This game of boundaries and taxation was nothing new. Crown had delayed its expansion in 1899 until the exact location of the city limits north of the Old Mill could be determined. Not surprisingly, the new weave shed was built just beyond the Dalton line, and Crown subsequently constructed Mill No. 2 north of the city line. In 1909 a local attorney, angry at Crown's evasion of local taxes, independently brought suit against the city for negligence in its duties to serve Dalton's interests, and the tax dispute soon came to a head. The writ demanded that the city nullify its 1898 water contract, reassess Crown's property, and collect back taxes from the mill. Such action was by no means unprecedented. As small towns throughout the nation industrialized during the nineteenth century, citizens in both town and country sought to curb the growing power of the mills, usually with only limited success. One observer of southern textiles in 1906 noted that, although tax exemptions were readily granted by towns during the late nineteenth century, "this attitude of friendliness is changing in some sections . . . and suits are more frequent." In the case against Crown, the Whitfield County Superior Court ruled in favor of the mill, but the case was appealed and ultimately reached the Georgia Supreme Court, which overturned the first ruling and forced Crown to pay Dalton $18,000 in back taxes.[28]

Almost immediately Crown's directors began to regain the support of local business leaders and officials. The company's main strategy was to threaten to move away from Dalton. At the annual stockholders' meeting, four months after the court decision, a committee was appointed to "investigate [a] site for additional mill plants," ostensibly to obtain "cheap power." The company sent scouts to examine property some fifteen miles south of Dalton near the village of Phelps, thereby attracting enough attention to warrant notice in the local newspaper. By 1912 Crown had bought a large piece of land at the new location, and at the September meeting stockholders approved a resolution "that the mills be ultimately removed to Phelps." This turn of events put pressure on Dalton officials, some of whom apparently had hoped to annex Crown's New Mill, but Crown did not act immediately, and the situation remained uncertain. Then, in April 1915, Crown quietly entered negotiations with the Saco-Lowell Company to furnish machinery for an expansion of Mill No. 2, after which the directors met on May 11 and formally disclosed plans to expand their existing mill if the city promised by May 19 not to annex the New Mill. If no such assurances were forthcoming, the implicit threat was that Crown would leave the city entirely.[29]

In response, the chamber of commerce hustled up a petition, "signed by about 500 representative men of Dalton," which pledged their "full moral and political support" against any further annexation of Crown property. These city boosters sought to "encourage the building of manufacturing plants contiguous to Dalton and especially to encourage the Crown Cotton Mills to build additions to their plants in the near future." With these assurances in hand, Crown carried out the expansion of Mill No. 2 that it apparently had envisioned all along. The directors sent a letter to chamber of commerce members expressing their "appreciation of the efforts they have put forward toward a solution of the problem of possible extension to the city limits." Whether the idle land near Phelps represented a grand bluff by the directors, it demonstrated the leverage a large mill could exert over a small-town chamber of commerce. Well into the twentieth century, Dixie's lesser cities heralded manufacturing plants as harbingers of growth and offered tax benefits as an incentive to potential investors. The chamber's 1915 petition essentially reaffirmed Dalton's commitment to the "industrial resolution" made in 1887. After 1915, criticism from local business people and professionals virtually ceased. Crown was king of Dalton.[30]

The aftershocks of industrial development took many southerners by surprise. When Dalton's leading citizens supported the "industrial resolution," they could not have envisioned a local enterprise large enough to create unprecedented problems and powerful enough to thwart all efforts to solve those problems. Much like today's "Rustbelt" cities of the North, the New South's small industrial cities lived on the brink of economic disaster. Most townspeople relied on the mill in some way or another. Dalton was never a single-mill city, but a handful of textile plants remained its bread and butter for over half a century. In a region plagued with grinding poverty, mill survival meant town survival. Angry citizens usually had to swallow their discontent or leave town. Those options mirrored the basic alternatives available to workers who were dissatisfied with their jobs at the Crown Cotton Mill.

The chamber of commerce's pledge against annexation, combined with huge profits fostered by World War I, allowed the expansion of the New Mill during 1916. A major carding and spinning addition was added north of the existing plant, while the weave shed was extended eastward. Together the two new buildings added almost 45,000 square feet of productive space to Crown—over 38,000 more than the entire original mill built in 1884. In all, Crown's machinery increased by 46 percent, the goal being to add 15,000 spindles and a "full complement of looms and preparatory machinery." The vast factory complex doubtless exceeded even the most optimistic expectations of the company's original investors.[31] By the late 1910s, Crown stood as a symbol of stability in the often chaotic—and highly profitable—world of southern textiles. Its officials and directors were experienced; its productive capacity was impressive for a small-town mill; its return on capital remained consistently high; and its power in local affairs was unchallenged.

But the company's very success carried seeds of instability. Factory expansion necessitated a vast influx of new operatives and their families. The number of millhands working for Crown increased nearly fivefold between 1890 and 1920. The larger work force strained Crown's small-scale managerial system. This predicament plagued industrial managers throughout America as the nation's "factory system" expanded in the late nineteenth and early twentieth centuries. More bosses, better communication, tighter administration—bigger mills required all of these. Most important of all, expanding factories demanded a stable, predictable work force. But during the early years of the new century, Crown's millhands were anything but settled. A constant stream of plain folk flowed in and out of the factory and mill village. As the mill grew and its need for a larger pool of adequate labor became greater, rapid worker turnover created serious managerial problems. From the beginning, Crown's directors and officials relied on company housing and the family labor system to recruit and retain a well-trained work force. But as Crown expanded, this system of labor management did not function as intended. Even while the company's fortunes soared and the mill reasserted its power over Dalton's economic affairs, Crown's working families appeared unconvinced that mill work and company housing represented their best option for economic security in the New South.

5

LABOR IN SHORT SUPPLY

At the turn of the century, Dalton's cotton-mill families had not yet coalesced into a stable community of
workers. Although the Crown Mill had been in operation for fifteen years, its mill-village boundaries
were not yet well defined, and most workers did not
live in mill-village housing. Few millhands in 1900
had a long association with the company. In that year,
less than 4 percent of Crown's employees had worked
for the mill ten years or more.[1]

Just as the mill entered a new era of expansion,
many workers were abandoning factory life for upcountry tenant farms or alternative wage-earning
jobs. Southern-born whites were the only available
labor supply for the mills; it was risky to hire blacks in
a race-conscious region where cotton mills themselves symbolized white supremacy, and the low
southern wages were no inducement for Yankee or
immigrant workers. The southern economy was not
stagnant, but in terms of wages and industrial diversification it lagged behind the rest of the nation. As
a result, a regionally distinctive labor market took
shape in Dixie. Within this isolated and restrictive
market, poor whites did have some options available
to them. That none of those options were very good

did not prevent mill workers from exploring better ways to make a living within the new economic order. Rapid labor turnover, coupled with the mill's increasing need for good workers, created an employment problem throughout the textile South during the first two decades of the twentieth century. The labor shortage that beset Crown and other mills forced managers to raise wages and to provide better job opportunities for adult household heads in an attempt to attract and retain an adequate supply of well-trained hands. The workers' willingness to turn their backs on the emerging industrial system and the managers' ongoing need for good workers facilitated changes that laid the foundations for a stable mill-village community.

Historians have underestimated the importance of labor shortages in shaping industrial capitalism. The industrial revolution was not a mechanical force that swept unchecked across the nation, forcing agrarian people everywhere to adopt modern ways. It was instead a human creation that evolved over time. The power of workers within the emerging system was circumscribed by their economic dependence on employers and by the power of the state, which usually supported the interests of the capitalists at the expense of the workers. But viewing workers as passive victims of industrialization is a grievous mistake, as much of the new labor history has demonstrated. Poor families always had their labor power, and when industrialists were desperate to get it, the system changed in favor of the workers, usually in the form of better wages, working conditions, and nonwage benefits. Such alterations in the world of large-scale manufacturing were not necessarily permanent, but even minor deviations from the status quo could alter the course of industrial relations for decades to come. Not all changes worked as planned, of course, because managerial policies and workers' responses often had unintended consequences. But industrial capitalism was nothing if not flexible. When southern mill officials faced their first severe labor shortage, they raised wages and created systems of corporate paternalism to lure poor whites away from the farms. Over time, as workers responded favorably to these policies, cohesive mill-village communities developed. Whether or not the advent of company paternalism marked a long-term improvement for workers, it demonstrated how ordinary millhands—through careful occupational choices—forced a renegotiation of industrial relationships in the modernizing South.

In 1900 Crown Mill's work force was extremely young—startlingly so compared to present-day standards. One-third of the millhands who entered the factory for sixty-six-hour work weeks were children less than sixteen years old. The normal starting age was ten, but many children began working as young as eight. One child reported in the census as six years old was listed on Crown's payroll. Many aging millhands recall seeing young girls in the mill who were too short to reach their spinning frames and so stood on boxes while they worked. Lewis Hine's

TABLE 5.1. Age of the Crown Mill Work Force, 1900 and 1910 (percentages)

	1900	1910
Under 16	33	24
16 to 21	37	30
22 to 27	18	17
28 to 33	7	11
34 and over	5	18
Total	100	100
	(n=430)	(n=571)

Source: U.S. census manuscripts, Georgia, Whitfield County, 1900, 1910. These figures do not reflect the record linkage to Crown Mill payrolls; they are census figures only.

photographs of child laborers in Dixie during the early twentieth century offer a poignant vision of children in the mills. Such scenes were not simply a reformer's fancy, as the Crown Mill statistics demonstrate. Not all millhands in 1900 were children, but the average age for male workers was only twenty-two, and female workers averaged a mere nineteen years. Fully 80 percent of Crown's employees at the turn of the century had yet to reach their twenty-fifth birthday.[2]

Although the majority of Crown's early workers had been female, by the turn of the century the work force was divided equally between the sexes. The carding department, where people and machines prepared raw cotton for spinning, was worked almost exclusively by young adult males, who had the physical strength necessary for this task. The youngest workers of both sexes toiled in the spinning department. More than six of ten operatives in the spinning room were girls who averaged sixteen years of age. Males constituted less than 40 percent of this department, and most of these were doffer boys whose average age was fourteen. Workers in the weave room were older, that job being the most prestigious, demanding, and well-paying job below the level of fixer. In 1900, female hands still predominated here as well, their average age being seven years above that of spinning-room girls. Males in the weave room, although slightly older on average than the women, comprised less than 45 percent of that department's employees, a figure that would soon increase dramatically.[3]

Crown's young employees, in general, came from large households steeped in traditions of family labor. In 1900 there were 131 cotton-mill families in Dalton and the surrounding county.[4] Each of these had an average of more than seven household members (including immediate family, kin, and boarders) and sent an average of three workers to Crown Mill. Household heads made up only 15 percent of Crown's work force in 1900. Mill managers in Dalton and elsewhere liked to enhance their public image by telling how they helped local widows by employing their children. There was some truth to this, for in 1900 over 25 percent of all cotton-mill families were headed by widows. Even so, seven of every ten mill-worker households were headed by married men, and few of them had jobs in the mill.[5] Uptown people voiced considerable consternation over "cotton mill drones," the unemployed mill fathers who undertook no useful work save that of hauling dinners to their children, who were toiling in the mill twelve hours a day. "Able-bodied vampire fathers," one observer moaned, "living upon the earnings of minor children."[6] Stories passed down to the present day by Dalton's cotton-mill families indicate that there were indeed some "drones" who lounged while their children worked. A leader for the Georgia Federation of Labor actually argued that child labor in the cotton mills turned hard-working adult farmers into mill-village idlers, and he pointed to Dalton's Crown Mill as evidence that fathers sometimes "put all their children in the mill" and thereafter refused to hit "a lick of work" themselves.[7]

In 1900 the reality of the situation in Dalton was not so simple. Although less than 50 percent of male household heads worked in the mill, only slightly more than one in ten had no jobs at all. About 10 percent were listed in the census as "day laborers" but were not found on Crown's payrolls, and some of these may have been drones. An equal number continued to work in agriculture, including some who lived in the mill village but hired on as farm laborers in and around the city, which still had plenty of large, open plots on which modest cotton crops could be grown. However many drones there were in Dalton, their situation was not entirely of their own making. Some scholars have suggested that the textile industry had no place for older, thick-fingered farmers, except in a few menial positions such as sweeper or yard hand. But it was more likely, as Carlton Blaithwait explained to Miss Winston in *The Georgians*, that the mills simply did not pay enough to attract many adult males.[8]

If the occupational situation for Dalton's cotton-mill fathers was more complex than is often assumed, the mill village itself, normally envisioned as a readily identifiable section of any textile town, was not clearly defined by 1900. At the turn of the century, Dalton's cotton-mill families did not constitute a very coherent social group, in part because they were not concentrated geographically in the mill village and because they were diverse in their occupational composition. To be sure, "factory hill" stood on the northern edge of town, and Crown had been steadily expanding its factory complex and mill-village housing. But even factory hill, at least as its boundaries could be defined by the census taker in 1900, included dwellings that were not owned by the company and housed no cotton millers. Because mill-village housing was a fundamental part of Dixie's textile industry from its beginnings, it is frequently assumed that all workers lived in the village. It is therefore surprising that only 38 percent of Crown's cotton-mill families actually lived in company-owned housing in 1900. Most families did rent their homes, but many of their dwellings were scattered loosely around the perimeter of the mill village. Moreover, nearly 15 percent of Crown's millhands in 1900 lived in houses owned by the family. Some cotton-mill households were actually farm families, located well outside the city limits, who sent a few children to work in the mill during the week. Several household heads were lower-level service workers, such as traveling salesmen, ministers, or grocers, and some gainfully employed children worked for companies other than Crown.[9]

The textile industry required workers who were accustomed to a mill environment, who could cope with large and complicated machines, and who lived and worked by the clock. But Dalton's mill managers found themselves searching for skilled millhands among highly mobile families, most of whom had only a brief association with Crown and were not obliged to the company for housing. Although, as in textile mills throughout Dixie, Crown's work force in the late nineteenth century was remarkably young and mostly female, this state of affairs began to change during the first decade of the twentieth century. Gradually the work force became substantially older and predominantly male as officials recruited male household heads and encouraged them to stay by offering employment and wage incentives. Substantial outmigration continued into the early 1900s and after, but by World War I a solid core of families had tied their hopes for economic stability, as well as a measure of comfort and dignity, to the Crown Cotton Mill.

In 1900, males already comprised half of Crown's work force, but ten years later two-thirds of all workers were men and boys. The increase in male workers resulted less from an influx of young boys than of adult household heads. Among Crown's cotton-mill families, the number of male household heads working in the mill increased from less than 50 percent to 65 percent. By 1912, three of every ten workers at Crown were household heads, compared with just one in ten in 1900. The number of children in Crown's work force during this period fell from 66 percent to 48 percent. The changing composition of the spinning and weaving departments in the decade after 1900 clearly reflected the growing number of adult men in the mill. The proportion of males in the spinning department increased from nearly 37 percent to 45 percent. More significantly, men were no longer a minority in the higher-paying weave room, where women had long predominated. By 1912, men—most of them married—filled 68 percent of the weave-room jobs. The proportion of household heads among males in the weaving department jumped from 45 percent in 1900 to 62 percent in 1912.[10]

The emerging dominance of adult males was also evident in the changing age distributions among operatives. Taken as a whole, Crown's millhands in 1912 were an average of five-and-a-half years older than they had been at the turn of the century. But here again the key change occurred among males, whose average age jumped from less than 22 to more than 28, a six-and-a-half-year increase. The average age of Crown's female workers increased by less than three years, from 18.6 to 21.3. Within different departments, the ages of male and female workers diverged strikingly. In the spinning department, the average age among males rose from about 14 in 1900 to 24 twelve years later, while the average age of female spinners increased only half that much. Among weavers, the men's average age increased by more than six years, while the women's remained essentially unchanged. Adult women had never made up a substantial proportion of the work force, and, because cultural and economic customs dictated that young women marry and quit full-time mill work for household labor and childrearing, they did not enter the mill in substantial numbers after the turn of the century. Among males, however, a permanent shift toward adult workers occurred.

This change reflected, in part, the logical evolution of the family labor system. Hypothetically, family labor offered management a convenient means of securing a stable, well-trained work force. Mills could lure poor farm families to the factory and leave the parents to other tasks, hiring instead their poorly paid and malleable children, who would later come of age as well-trained, disciplined millhands. Having developed a working knowledge of the mill, and lacking adequate experience on the farm, young adults would tie their hopes for the future to the mill; they would marry and settle down in the village and then raise a household of new millhands, who would repeat the process. As it happened, young women and children were indeed central to the success of Dixie's early mills, but as the industry matured and expanded it became clear that cheap labor was not necessarily the most productive and cost efficient. As one analyst of southern textiles noted in 1906, "An operative who gets from a machine a large percentage of its theoretically possible productivity may be cheaper at a high wage than one who gets much less per machine for similar work." Simply put, a well-trained adult was a better investment.[11]

This was especially true for married adult men, who usually were the ones to determine whether a family would leave or stay in the mill village. Young children as millhands were problematic, and single women usually married and left the work force. Married men not only offered the promise of their own long-term productivity, but also the labor of their children and, in a pinch, their wives. In order for Crown's managers to stem the tide of outmigration, they had to create an effective family labor system, and in order to do that, they had to convince young men and newlyweds to stick with the mill. But at Crown during the early twentieth century, young people—men and women alike—still proved remarkably willing to look beyond the textile industry for their opportunities.

An analysis of labor turnover at Crown from 1890 through the 1920s indicates how difficult it was for management to retain a stable work force during the first two decades of the century. Table 5.2, which is drawn from surviving Crown Mill payrolls, offers two different but complementary turnover statistics. The persistence figures for Crown's millhands remained relatively low from 1902 until World War I, after which more workers began to stay with the company for longer

TABLE 5.2. The Crown Mill Labor Supply, 1890–1927

	Average Number of Workers on Payroll[a]	Persistence Rate (percentage)[b]	Annual Turnover (percentage)[c]
1890	109	—	91.6
1896	264	24.5	85.2
1902	508	20.4	103.0
1908	513	21.6	120.6
1915	559	23.6	91.1
1922	623	26.1	55.5
1927[d]	846	33.2	70.6

Source: Crown Cotton Mills Payroll Records, CGA. See appendix B for a further elaboration on methods.

[a]Calculated from four quarterly payrolls for each year.

[b]Defined as the percentage of workers in any one year who were still on the payroll in the next year studied (e.g., 24.5 percent of the mill's workers in 1890 were still with the company in 1896, and 20.4 percent of all workers on the 1896 payroll were still at the mill six years later). These figures are crude persistence rates, not adjusted for deaths or female name changes.

[c]Calculated from four quarterly payrolls for each year. The formula was: all newcomers plus all outmigrants, divided by the average payroll size for that particular year.

[d]Figures do not include workers from the Boylston-Crown Mill, which was established in 1924.

periods of time. The annual turnover rates, which measure how transient the work force was within each particular payroll year, also substantiate the notion that southern textiles experienced a dramatic labor problem in the first fifteen years of the century. The higher the annual turnover rate, the more footloose the workers. So, for example, mill officials could relax in 1896, because their labor supply during that year remained relatively stable. They must have been troubled in 1902, when workers were much more likely to come and go, and they might have panicked when the turnover rate jumped to nearly 121 percent in 1908. During World War I, Crown's annual turnover rate dropped noticeably and remained low thereafter. Taken together, then, the persistence and annual turnover rates demonstrate that a labor problem developed at Crown during the late 1890s and continued through the first decade of the century. The figures for 1915 suggest that the company began to solve its difficulties by the mid-1910s (despite disruptions caused by World War I) and continued to enjoy a stable work force through the 1920s. But in the first decade of the century, these years of stability were only a dream. Crown's managers did not need to undertake a statistical analysis of worker turnover to recognize their labor problems. The shortage of millhands plagued cotton mills throughout the region and forced southern industrialists to formulate new labor-recruitment strategies.[12]

For the family labor system to work to management's advantage, young male cotton millers had to be induced to stay with the company. If a substantial group of them settled down in the mill village and raised families, additional labor recruitment was largely unnecessary for the present—and for the future, assuming their children would stay and marry within the village. But keeping these workers was not easy, because Crown had traditionally offered few jobs to adult men. The best rank-and-file jobs were in the weave room, but from 1885 to 1900, young women held most of the better-paying weaving jobs. A more significant factor in depleting Crown's supply of young men was the lure of the land. Beginning with the earliest studies of southern cotton mills, observers noted the prevalent desire among millhands to return to farming. But none of these studies have systematically traced outmigrants to their destinations to determine whether they abandoned the factory for the countryside. The prevailing assumption is that few actually returned to farm life. As one recent study stated, "Typically neither the parents nor the children returned to the agricultural sector."[13]

Where did the workers who left Crown Mill go? Using the Soundex indexes to Georgia's census schedules, I have managed to trace a substantial number of millhands who left the mill between 1900 and 1910 to their new homes. Sixty-two adult males from Crown's working families in 1900, who were not in the mill a decade later, were registered in Georgia's 1910 census.[14] The average age of these men before their outmigration was twenty-two years, and 63 percent of them held jobs in Crown Cotton Mill at that time. They were young men in 1900, over half of them still living with their parents.

One might expect that outmigrants from cotton-mill families ventured to other cotton mills, but this was not the case. Stories about labor recruiters luring millhands away from one company to another surfaced during the early twentieth century and have often been repeated by historians. A corollary to the view that most millhands never returned to farming is that the southern mills created a "floating proletariat" of disenchanted workers whose ties to the land had been cut and whose hopes in the mills had been crushed. This desolate class supposedly roamed aimlessly from one mill town to another. My outmigration analysis suggests that these two arguments do not adequately reflect the reality of the southern labor market in the early twentieth century. Evidence derived from Crown Mill payrolls and census data indicates that outmigrants from cotton-mill families seldom left one textile firm only to cast their lot with another. Of the male outmigrants traced here, only 6.5 percent were employed as textile workers in 1910. When men quit Crown Mill, they were not searching for a better mill village but hoping instead to leave the industry behind altogether.

There were exceptions. Stiff competition developed among mills to attract and maintain supervisory workers. Men who could work skillfully with both textile machines and the laborers who ran them were in high demand in Dixie's cotton-mill towns, as the experience of two Crown overseers demonstrated. In 1900, both

William P. Fallis and Henry A. Powell were foremen at Crown. Although their families lived on factory hill, according to the census they owned their own homes. But by 1910 both were gone. Apparently they were recruited by another company and left Crown together, for they both became foremen for the ATCO textile mill in Cartersville, Georgia, some forty miles south of Dalton—and it could hardly have been coincidence that they lived next door to each other in the ATCO village. Mills made life relatively comfortable for supervisory personnel, and these men probably moved because the Cartersville plant offered them better pay, and perhaps better living and working conditions.[15]

But most men who left Crown avoided other mills. A tiny minority experienced upward mobility in either occupational status or property acquisition. Joseph Nichols, for example, lived with his family on Dalton's North Depot Street in 1900. Nichols, a middle-aged minister, had two children working in Crown's weaving department and one employed at the A. J. Showalter Company. The Nichols family fared well according to uptown standards. By 1910 the minister owned a mortgage-free farm north of Dalton in the Varnell District of Whitfield County, and none of his children who still lived at home had to toil in "public works" as their older siblings had. During this same decade, Howard Farley advanced from being a boarder who worked as a card grinder at Crown to the post of Whitfield County constable, which clearly marked a rise in local status.[16] But such examples were exceptions among Crown's outmigrants. Even other lower-white-collar workers rarely did as well as Reverend Nichols, as another minister's experience indicates. In 1900 Reverend Harris Singleton lived on factory hill in a company house packed with thirteen people, four of whom were mill-working children and three of whom were boarders who also worked in the mill. Ten years later he had left both the ministry and factory hill and was tilling the land as a tenant farmer near Tunnel Hill.[17]

Most outmigrants followed Singleton's path to tenant farms in northwest Georgia. Nearly 55 percent of all outmigrants lived and worked on farms in 1910, and fewer than two in ten of them owned their land. Younger men were particularly prone to leave mill families for the countryside. Of the outmigrants between sixteen and twenty-four years old in 1900, 63 percent lived on farms by 1910. During their young adult years, men in mill families faced the critical decision of whether to try a new occupation or remain in the cotton mill. The parents' occupations apparently had little influence on a young man's choice to return to the countryside, for children with parents from a variety of occupational backgrounds still chose farming over other vocations. Among outmigrants whose parents worked for Crown at the beginning of the century, 44 percent became farmers by 1910. Even without the benefit of statistics available to us today, mill officials—certainly the superintendents and foremen who did the hiring—understood the basic conclusion: Crown was not able to hold on to its young men, most of whom preferred farming, even tenancy, over mill work.

Those who left the mill for the farm were not necessarily breaking family ties. Indeed, kinship connections frequently seemed to facilitate the move. When Frank Elrod abandoned Crown to work a farm in Hall County, several counties away from Whitfield in Georgia's upper Piedmont, his neighbor in 1910 also bore the Elrod name, as did another farmer down the road.[18] The James Pope family offers further evidence of kinship migration patterns. In 1900 the Popes lived among other working families on North Depot Street in Dalton. James was a day laborer who did no mill work, but his son John was a weaver at Crown. A decade later, James Pope and his wife, Caroline, lived in a rural district of Gordon County, where they rented a farm. John no longer lived with them—he lived next door with a wife, Sallie, and five young children. Father and son evidently abandoned city life together, choosing instead the lives of tenant farmers in the north Georgia country-side.[19] Common destinations among men who had been neighbors and fellow workers indicate that community friendships also facilitated movement from one place to another and helped mitigate the pain of severed relationships. William Fallis's and Henry Powell's move to the ATCO mill in Cartersville provides one example. Walter Stone and George Williamson, both weavers for Crown in 1900, moved to within several houses of each other in rural Whitfield County sometime before 1910. Doyle Huckabee was a young hand who worked in the spinning department, but several members of his household worked in the weaving department with Stone and Williamson, and Huckabee later joined the two men in the countryside. By 1910 these three former millhands headed their own households, and all were tenant farmers in the same rural community. Perhaps they sometimes met to reminisce about their younger days at Crown or to discuss the possibility of returning to the mill.[20]

For outmigrants who did not end up on farms, the most likely occupational choice was "public works" other than cotton mills. Twenty percent of the male outmigrants were listed in the 1910 census as being employed in nontextile industrial jobs. A significant minority of young men from cotton-mill families, it seems, found wage-earning work a more reasonable, or more familiar, alternative than agriculture. This trend indicated the increasing importance and variety of industrial labor in north Georgia in the early twentieth century. Mill officials imbued with the booster ethic might cheer this regional development in the abstract, but the expansion and slow diversification of industry in their corner of Georgia meant that young men from local working families were being siphoned off to other areas of employment—whether to other cotton mills, copper mines, or marble quarries made little practical difference to them. In the years following World War I, a critic of southern cotton-mill villages insisted, "once a mill-worker, always a mill-worker. Not only you, but your children and children's children forever and ever." By the 1920s there was much evidence to support this view, but as Crown first entered the twentieth century, the labor supply was not so settled. Cotton milling had not yet become a hereditary occupation.[21]

An analysis of female outmigrants further substantiates this view. It is much more difficult to trace women through the censuses than men. Both the census manuscripts and Soundex indexes listed most individuals under the names of the household heads (usually men or widows), thereby decreasing the chances of tracing a woman independently from her family. But it has been possible to trace some female outmigrants across census years: specifically, women who married and left Crown could sometimes be traced through the census by way of their husbands' names. Of seventy such women, only seventeen appeared in the 1910 census within a three-state area.[22] According to that year's listings, none of these women held wage-earning jobs outside their homes. This finding should not be surprising, because at the time most white married women in the United States (especially those with children) did not work for wages outside the home on a regular basis.

Nonetheless, the census did list the occupations of the outmigrants' husbands, and those are very revealing. Of the seventeen men, only two were working in textile mills in 1910. Three held other types of industrial jobs. Eight husbands were farmers, none of them landowners, and four others were engaged in service-sector jobs as grocers and traveling salesmen. Assuming the women involved knew of their beaux's ambitions before they married, these figures cast light on a heretofore neglected topic and suggest that southern cotton-mill women in the first decades of the century were not yet locked inalterably into the mill-village system. Even though we should view such a small sample with caution, it is nonetheless striking that 88 percent of these men worked outside textiles and that nearly half tilled the soil as tenants. If cotton-mill women chose prospective husbands partly for the types of lives they envisioned for their families, then some women, by choosing men likely to return to the countryside, were clearly expressing their dissatisfaction with the world of southern textiles. As table 5.3 shows, poor whites in the early twentieth-century upcountry—women and men alike—largely preferred farming to the cotton mills.

From one perspective, quitting the mill for the farm simply reflected one person's (or family's) preference or, at most, an independent gesture of protest. But the patterns of factory-to-farm migration in north Georgia suggest another interpretation. As indicated by the behavior of the Elrods, Popes, and the three Crown Mill companions, decisions to leave the mill were sometimes collective in nature. Collaborative decisions involving family and friends clearly influenced the behavior of outmigrants and, doubtless, of inmigrants as well. As farmers and millhands swapped stories, compared their lives, and experimented with alternative occupations, informal networks of information developed in north Georgia, linking rural neighborhoods to mill villages and ultimately governing the amount of labor to which Crown and other mills had access.[23]

The tradition of family farming clearly remained strong among the South's poor whites, even though tenancy came to be the best most poor farmers could

TABLE 5.3. Occupations of Outmigrants, 1910

Occupations	Percentage Employed
Cotton Mills	10.1
Farming	53.2
Industry (nontextile)	19.0
Other	17.7
Total	100.0
	(n=79)

Source: U.S. census manuscripts, Georgia, 1900, 1910.

Notes: The number of outmigrants includes the husbands of female outmigrants from Crown Mill. "Other" includes a variety of nonindustrial, nonfarm jobs, including clerk, grocer, salesman, and minister, as well as those who were unemployed. See appendix B for a further elaboration of the methods used.

hope for. Early in the twentieth century, however, millhands who wanted to return to the land saw encouraging signs in the rise of staple prices. Table 5.4 examines one of the fundamental contributors to the labor shortage in southern textiles— rising cotton prices. A careful consideration of "real" cotton prices ("real" prices take into consideration changes in the cost of living) provides a picture of rural resurgence. Real staple prices sagged in the late 1880s, sank abysmally during the early 1890s, and remained low the rest of the decade. The early years of this century clearly reversed these depressing trends; real cotton prices in the period 1900–1904 rebounded nearly to the level of the early 1880s. During the next ten years—1905 to 1914—the real price of cotton topped 10 cents per pound. Not incidentally, these were also the years of the severest labor shortage in the southern textile industry before World War I.

Rising cotton prices would not have so affected mill recruitment efforts if southern textiles had been in a slump. But to the contrary, Dixie's cotton mills were expanding with remarkable speed. Crown's own growth mirrored regional trends. The mill had grown rapidly during the 1890s, increasing its payroll from an average of 109 workers to 264 workers by 1896. During the following twelve years, the number of workers employed by Crown nearly doubled, reaching an average of 513 by 1908. The need for new textile hands in Dixie had never been stronger. In 1900 the cotton mills of Georgia and the Carolinas needed about 83,000 workers to operate. Five years later they needed over 106,000 millhands. Recruiting more than twenty thousand new workers from the southern upcountry was no simple matter. The renewed appeal of cotton farming and the mills' initial reluctance to improve real wages made the task all the more difficult.[24]

Given the upward shift in cotton prices and the continuing expansion of cotton mills, the textile industry was bound to suffer a labor shortage. Indeed, by about

TABLE 5.4. Average Real Cotton Prices, 1880–1929

	Average Real Price (in 1890 cents per pound)
1880–84	9.11
1885–89	8.41
1890–94	7.18
1895–99	7.26
1900–04	8.96
1905–09	10.57
1910–14	10.27
1915–19	15.80
1920–24	11.04
1925–29	9.04

Source: Nominal cotton prices and consumer price indexes, Bureau of Labor Statistics figures for "all items," in U.S. Bureau of the Census, *Historical Statistics*, pp. 211, 517–18.

1905 the need for more millhands was a widely discussed phenomenon and a matter of no little angst to mill managers. Reports of Piedmont mills sending labor recruiters into remote Appalachian communities date from these years. Irate mill officials lashed out at competitors who were "stealing" workers by surreptitiously sending sweet-talking labor recruiters into mill villages. Some exasperated industrialists actually formed gentlemen's agreements to stop labor pirating, but these compacts quickly broke apart under the competitive demand for millhands. During the rapid mill expansion of the 1890s, an agricultural depression had mitigated the difficulties of finding adequate "help." But as industrial development continued unabated in the new century and as prices for cash crops began to rise, managers faced a situation that would drastically alter their labor recruitment policies.[25]

By the early twentieth century, southern textile managers had few options when it came to labor supply. Even in the late antebellum era, most southern cotton mills had operated exclusively with white labor. In the early days of postbellum textile development, industrial boosters had promised skeptical southern whites that mill jobs would be reserved for poor white families who needed an economic lift. Many mill managers were themselves racists who thought black workers inferior to whites, but some (not at Crown) had hired blacks to do "menial" nonproduction work, and as the regional labor shortage deepened, more textile leaders grew eager to tap the South's enormous supply of poor black labor. From a strictly economic viewpoint, it made sense to hire blacks, but those managers who tried it quickly learned that such efforts were counterproductive. In every case from the late 1890s through the 1910s, white millhands reacted violently to the introduction of black workers: they staged walkouts, organized unions to maintain white supremacy in the mills, and took political action against industrialists who dared to breach racial mores. And, in every case, management conceded. By 1915 the South Carolina legislature had even passed a segregation act that legally barred blacks from all but the worst mill jobs. From 1900 to 1920, blacks filled less than 2 percent of Dixie's rank-and-file operative jobs in textiles. Historian I. A. Newby rightly argues that the white millhands' fight against black labor "shows quite clearly that mill officials had little or no room to maneuver in racial matters." It was no accident that most clashes over a biracial work force occurred during these years of labor shortage and that white workers, seeing the advantages of that shortage, vigorously sought to maintain their advantage by keeping blacks out of the mills. Over time, southern mill managers found it not only culturally prudent but also economically rational to maintain a white-only work force, because the region's upcountry whites soon developed considerable expertise in textile production and therefore were more productive than novice black workers would have been.[26]

It was considerably easier for poor whites to keep immigrants out of Dixie's mills. The Europeans who flocked to northern factories avoided the South, as did the Asian newcomers who landed on the West Coast, the French Canadians who moved into New England textile plants, and the Latin Americans who crossed the border into the Southwest. The reason was simple. "The South," as economic historian Gavin Wright has written, "was a low-wage region in a high-wage country." Aside from a very few uncommon jobs, immigrant workers had no interest in Dixie's low-wage industrial opportunities. A single example from textiles helps illustrate the larger pattern of regional wage differences. In 1907 the average male weaver in Georgia earned 12 cents per hour, while his counterparts in Massachusetts commanded 18 cents. This 50 percent wage differential was by no means exceptional. No wonder a government survey around 1910 found that 89 percent of northern textile workers were foreign born, compared with less than 1 percent of southern cotton millers. Cheap labor allowed southern plants to dominate America's coarse-cloth textile market, and it made mill owners very rich. But coupled with the region's racially segregated hiring policies, that same cheap labor locked southern managers into a curious sort of labor dependency. By 1900 mill managers in Dixie had only one possible labor pool—the white plain folk of the southern upcountry.[27]

Crown continued to recruit new workers to replace outmigrants, but the evidence suggests that many of those newly hired in 1910 were not experienced textile workers who were roving from one village to another. Most were inexperienced farm folk. Even as some cotton-mill workers were leaving the mill for the farm, a stream of new families flowed in the opposite direction. By tracing the adult males who were new to Crown in 1910 back to the 1900 census, it has been possible to establish the origins of the people filling the spaces left vacant by outmigrants.[28] Of Crown's millhands in 1910 who could be positively identified in the earlier census, fully two-thirds had been living and working on farms, primarily on land in the northwest Georgia counties surrounding Crown Mill. On the whole, these men were unlike their counterparts who were leaving Crown for the countryside. Almost all the inmigrants from farms married and had families before moving to Crown. At an average age of thirty-five in 1900, they usually had teenage children who also could be employed in the mill. Perhaps these families viewed their move to the mill as temporary. During the nineteenth and early twentieth centuries, this was a common tactic among America's farmers-turned-industrial workers, many of whom took on factory work in an effort to save money with which to purchase a farm of their own. John C. Kinsey of Walker County, Georgia, may have had such a plan when he moved to Crown. In 1900 Kinsey was thirty-three and, with his family of four, worked as a tenant farmer. He had come of age during an era when the odds of any tenant's becoming a landowner in Dixie were extremely poor. But the family farm ideal was part of his heritage, for his next-door neighbor in Walker County, also a Kinsey (probably his father), owned a farm free of mortgage. Whatever drew John Kinsey and family men like him to Crown Mill, they usually entered the factory with little or no experience in large-scale manufacturing.[29]

Picture, then, the bewildering migration patterns that crisscrossed the upcountry South during the first decade of the century. Many young men and women from cotton-mill families were abandoning the industry; at the same time, hard-pressed tenant families were drifting toward the cotton-mill villages, whether with the intention of returning to the land or with the full knowledge that they were turning their backs on the farm. Clearly the population flow was steady both from mill to farm and vice versa, and this trend affected the stability of Crown's work force in diverse ways. Apparently a substantial number of rural folk saw in Crown the possibility of improving their situation, a view that worked to the company's advantage, because each new wave of families brought a new generation of young people who could be trained in industrial skills. But at the same time, the superintendent watched in frustration as many well-trained cotton millers chose the farm over the factory.

Despite these fluctuations, many working families began to put down roots at Crown, and one logical reason was the better earning power millhands acquired after 1900. Table 5.5 outlines, in broad strokes, the trends in "real" earnings at Crown over a span of nearly forty years. The numbers tell four stories, each of which adds to our understanding of southern textiles and mill-village development. Between 1890 and 1902, average weekly earnings at Crown remained basically stagnant. "Nominal" wages (that is, the amount workers actually received in their pay envelopes) actually declined slightly, but the cost of living also declined at about the same rate. As a result, the "real" earning power of weekly wages changed very little for more than a decade, with an average yearly increase of only .11 percent. The average millhand at Crown made $3.13 per week in 1890; in 1902 the average real earnings (in 1890 dollars) were $3.17 per week. The story of this period is one of very inexpensive labor for the mills, despite their growing demand for workers. Over the entire twelve-year period, the maximum annual amount that Crown's millhands could earn, on average, was about $164. Textile labor was cheap, and agricultural depression was the key to depressed wages. When cotton rebounded and mills expanded rapidly after the turn of the century, it was a different story.

Most historians probably assume that southern textile wages remained pitifully low until World War I gave them a temporary boost. This assumption contains an important grain of truth. During the early years of the twentieth century, cotton-mill wages in Dixie were much lower than the national average; southern mill-hands labored long hours for practically nothing; families lived hard and went hungry. In many ways this situation hardly changed before World War II, and some might say it still exists. Among America's industrial workers, few were so poor for so long as southern cotton millers. But from their own perspective, millhands at Crown witnessed impressive gains in their earning power between the turn of the century and World War I. For more than a decade, they saw their real wages increase by an average of almost 6 percent per year. Between 1902 and 1908 alone, real average weekly earnings at Crown rose 52 percent. By the outbreak of war in Europe in 1914, average workers at Crown were earning nearly 73 percent more than they had in 1902. Rising cotton prices, the lure of the farm, the continued expansion of southern textiles—these elements combined to push wages upward during the prewar decade.[30]

To move beyond World War I here is to get ahead of the story, but it is worth briefly placing the prewar years in a larger context. Wartime military production (first for European nations and later for the United States) prompted an explosive growth in southern textiles and an intense labor shortage that caused wages to skyrocket. But the critical story of the period 1915–22 is not so much wartime gains as postwar wage maintenance. Wages everywhere fell sharply after the war ended, but in southern textiles they did not drop below prewar levels. Indeed, real earnings for workers at Crown in 1922 were, on average, 38 percent higher than they had been in 1915. The fourth story in table 5.5 is that of the mid-1920s, during which twenty years of steady wage increases came to an end. As in the 1890s, the wage stagnation of the mid-1920s was largely the result of a textile labor glut created by a slump in upcountry agriculture. The oversupply of millhands came about because, unlike cotton prices, mill wages held steady after the war. Consequently, Crown's annual turnover rates dropped substantially during the 1920s, and its persistence rate between 1922 and 1927 was an impressive 33 percent (see table 5.2). Such trends had a profound impact on southern mill villages during the

TABLE 5.5. Average Earnings at Crown Mill, 1890–1927

Nominal versus Real Earnings

	Average Weekly Nominal Earnings[a]	Average Weekly Real Earnings[b] (in 1890 dollars)
1890	$3.13	$3.13
1896	2.73	2.95
1902	3.05	3.17
1908	4.81	4.81
1915	6.18	5.49
1922	14.07	7.57
1927	14.99	7.78

Average Yearly Change in Real Earnings, Selected Periods

Time Period	Average Yearly Change (percentage)
1890–1902	0.11
1902–1915	5.63
1915–1922	5.41
1922–1927	0.55

Source: Crown Cotton Mills Payroll Records, CGA; consumer price indexes, Bureau of Labor Statistics figures for "all items," in U.S. Bureau of the Census, Historical Statistics, p. 211.
[a]"Nominal" earnings indicate the amount of money the workers actually received on payday.
[b]"Real" earnings reflect changes in the cost of living, the figures for which were taken from the national consumer price index cited above.

postwar era. But in the first decade of the century, foreknowledge of future trends was not needed to convince Crown's working families that textile jobs were becoming more worth their while. The 1890s had been terrible, and after 1902 earnings had improved noticeably. This was reason enough to take a more favorable view of mill work, but the dynamics of mill-village stability ran even deeper.

Wage increases at Crown were not distributed evenly throughout the work force. Some workers commanded higher pay than others, and discovering who earned more and why provides us with a fuller understanding of mill-village development and labor-force stabilization. Gender appeared to have been one important determinant of weekly earnings. As table 5.6 illustrates, between 1900 and 1912 men were able to improve their earning power much more than women. In 1900 males earned about 31 percent more each week than females in the weave room, but by 1912 the men's wage advantage had increased to 63 percent. Men in the spinning department earned almost exactly what women did in 1900, but

TABLE 5.6. Wage Differentials between Male and Female Employees of Crown Mill, by Age, 1900 and 1912

	1900	1912
All workers	37.2	46.1
Old Mill weaving department		
All ages	30.5	63.1
Below 16	5.4	106.8
16–24	28.8	38.1
25–33	50.5	37.8
34–42	26.6	64.4
43 and above	−6.3	15.6
Old Mill spinning department		
All ages	2.8	24.6
Below 16	−9.5	−20.7
16–24	40.3	13.5
25–33	26.2	42.6
34–42	n.a.	331.1
43 and above	n.a.	−7.2
New Mill		
All workers	n.a.	44.0

Sources: U.S. census manuscripts, Georgia, Whitfield County, 1900, 1910; Crown Cotton Mills Payroll Records, 2 June–14 July 1900, 13 Jan.–24 Feb. 1912, CGA.
Notes: Figures in the table indicate the percentage by which average male earnings exceeded average female earnings. The New Mill employed workers in all departments, but the payroll records for 1912 do not separate them by department.

twelve years later their weekly wages were almost 25 percent higher. Age also appeared to influence wage rates and tended to complicate the role played by gender. For example, in the spinning department, although male employees as a whole increased their earning advantage over females after 1900, in the sixteen to twenty-four age group that advantage decreased. In 1900, girls under sixteen actually earned more than boys of the same age, and they had increased the margin by 1912. Yet at the same time, men in the spinning room who were between the ages of twenty-five and thirty-three extended their earnings advantage over women in the same category to more than 40 percent. In the weave shed, among workers aged thirty-four to forty-two, the male earning differential increased dramatically, as it also did for boys under sixteen. But among weavers aged twenty-five to thirty-three, the male earning advantage actually declined. In most age categories, men did earn more than women, but the size of the differential varied greatly.

Figures based on age and gender are actually only crude measures of wage determination. Multiple regression analysis offers a much more powerful and

TABLE 5.7. Earnings Functions for Full-time, Nonsupervisory Workers at Crown Mill, 1900 and 1912

	1900		1912	
	i	ii	i	ii
Age	.013[a]	.009	.004[a]	.000
Gender (male)	.053[a]	.014	.083[a]	.025
Married household head		.092[a]		.082[a]
Literacy		.096[a]		.138[a]
Experience		.076		.103[a]
Boarder		.089[a]		.068[a]
Native Georgian		−.052		−.009
Deductions		.087[a]		.057[a]
Persistence		.079[a]		−.007
R^2	.28	.39	.17	.35

Sources: U.S. census manuscripts, Georgia, Whitfield County, 1900, 1910; Crown Cotton Mills Payroll Records, 2 June–14 July 1900, 13 Jan.–24 Feb. 1912, CGA.

Notes: The dependent variable for all four equations is a logarithmic transformation of weekly earnings. The equation is: Log earnings = $a_o + b_i X_i$ ($i = 1, \ldots,$ n). Dummy variables are as follows: gender, 1 = male, 0 = female; married household head, 1 = married, 0 = not married; literacy, 1 = literate/semiliterate, 0 = illiterate; experience (indicates whether a worker was listed in a Crown payroll ten years or more before regression date), 1 = yes, 0 = no; boarder (boarder in a household), 1 = yes, 0 = no; native Georgian, 1 = born in Georgia, 0 = born outside Georgia; deductions (whether workers had a portion of their gross earnings deducted for rent, coal, or cash advances), 1 = yes, 0 = no; persistence (whether a worker's family was in the mill ten years or more before regression date), 1 = yes, 0 = no.

[a]Indicates statistical significance at the .05 level.

sophisticated means by which to determine the relationship between the mill-hands' personal characteristics and their wage-earning capabilities at Crown Mill.[31] When only the workers' age and gender are tested as potential determinants of wages, the regression equation reveals that these variables were significant in influencing weekly earnings in both 1900 and 1912 (table 5.7, equation i).[32] In other words, older males commanded higher wages and steadier work. But this was not the whole story. When other variables are added to the original equation (table 5.7, equation ii), sex and age lose some of their explanatory power and, more important, lose their statistical significance, suggesting that individual characteristics other than gender or age exerted a significant influence on wages. The regression results indicate, for example, that workers who were married household heads earned higher wages than those who were not.[33] Being a boarder also had a significant positive impact on individual earnings in both years, indicating perhaps that the labor market was different for boarders than for family units.

Boarders may well have been more skilled workers who had been recruited by the mill, or who were serving as advance scouts for families looking to change mills, or who were simply trying to find a better mill for their own advancement. Reflecting the mill's increasing need to retain good workers, a person's experience at Crown, though not a determinant of earnings in 1900, exerted a statistically significant influence on average weekly wages by 1912.[34]

In both years, workers tied to the company through payroll deductions for various services—rent, coal, or cash advances—actually commanded higher earnings than those who did not. This may have indicated that the best-paid members of each household were shouldering the deductions on behalf of the other family members, or perhaps that the company provided such services more readily to its most productive hands. Whatever the reason for this correlation between payroll deductions and weekly earnings, it seems clear that the company did not possess monopsonistic control over its work force in the early twentieth century. If mill-hands had truly been slaves to the system, as some scholars have suggested, the relationship between deductions and wages would have been a negative one, for the company could have paid lower wages to those tied to the mill village.

One interesting result of the regression analysis was the positive relationship between literacy and earnings. A similar study on North Carolina millhands did not show this characteristic to have a significant influence on earning capabilities, and it is logical to assume that mechanical dexterity would have been more important for a cotton-mill worker than literacy.[35] Intelligence, after all, comes in many forms, and industrialists in the early twentieth century did not seem overly concerned with the educational attainments of their employees. But perhaps literacy meant something more than simply the ability to read and write. Schoolwork and factory labor did require a similar sort of work discipline, as educational reformers in the United States had been suggesting since the early industrial revolution. Having learned to read and write, a millhand had already become accustomed to long-term repetitive tasks and had learned to work successfully alone and unsupervised.[36] Apparently, too, literate workers were more productive at Crown. A regression equation for 1912 shows that for weave room employees, who were paid by the "cut" instead of by the day and whose wages therefore reflected individual productivity, literacy had a significant positive effect on earnings.[37] This finding suggests that mill officials were acting on more than philanthropic instincts when they built Crown Point School in 1910.

By the early 1910s, it is clear, certain millhands held a decided advantage in weekly earnings—particularly household heads who had developed textile skills and factory discipline. This helps explain the increase in the average age of the work force early in the century. Company records do not reveal an explicit policy of recruiting more productive adult hands in order to stabilize Crown's work force. But rising wages, the increasing number of male household heads in the mill, and the earning trends among Crown's millhands all point in that direction.

Long-term earnings, as opposed to daily wages or piece rates, were particularly critical in maintaining a steady work force. For cotton-mill workers, they were more important than average weekly earnings. Textile plants often ran regularly for long periods of time (always steadily from the standpoint of farm folk), but work could be erratic. Mechanical problems or the installation of new machinery could shut a mill down for days or even weeks at a time. More important, the company's production needs rose and fell, which meant that even when the factory was operating, it might employ a reduced work force.[38] Crown employed both full-time hands, who worked whenever the mill was running, and "spare hands," who worked part time as needed—often only one or two weeks each month. When the mill ran at full capacity, the wages of the spare hands were not substantially less than those of regular hands, but when work ran slack and spare hands stayed home, being a full-time millhand made a major difference in long-term earnings. The earnings advantages enjoyed by mill-worker fathers after 1900 revealed themselves most clearly in these long-term earnings: When we compare the total wages for males and females over an eight-week period, the differences in favor of the men are much more apparent than when only average weekly wages are considered. One reason for the differential was that Crown gave work preference to men over women when the mill ran slack. The company's efforts to retain skilled adult males apparently hinged on changes in the weaving department, for it was there that men began to be concentrated after 1900 and there that they began to enjoy a very substantial difference in long-term earnings. In 1900 male weavers already brought home about $7.50 more than female weavers during a two-month period. By 1912 the wage gap had widened to $20.95.[39]

Demographic changes among mill families outside the factory also reflected a trend toward stabilization. As table 5.8 shows, the proportion of working families living in company housing rose sharply from 38 percent in 1900 to 76 percent in 1912. During the same period, the proportion of mill families who owned their homes declined slightly, and the number of households renting outside the Crown village fell dramatically. Living in the mill village entailed certain social costs; families suffered a lack of privacy and had to abide by company rules, such as the prohibition of alcohol in the village. At the same time, the village provided an increasingly strong sense of community as the company expanded, built new houses, and drew a growing number of cotton-mill families within its boundaries. However millhands perceived the social liabilities and benefits of mill-village life, they clearly understood its economic advantages. In 1900 families from the mill village earned only about one dollar more per month than families residing outside the village. But by 1912, mill-village households were pulling in over ten dollars per month more than nonvillage families. Clearly, the mill was beginning to privilege workers who were willing to settle down in company housing.[40]

Moreover, as wages slowly rose, the rent for a company house remained the same. During the first decade of the century, the portion of a mill-village family's

TABLE 5.8. Residences of Crown Mill Families, 1900 and 1912 (in percentages)

	1900	1912
Company housing	38.2	76.1
Rented outside mill village	46.6	13.9
Owned home	15.3	10.0
Total	100.1	100.0
	(n=131)	(n=180)

Sources: Crown Cotton Mills Payroll Records, CGA; U.S. census manuscripts, Georgia, Whitfield County, 1900, 1910.

income that was used for rent steadily declined. Compared to conditions in the countryside, where tenant families paid roughly half the value of their production for rent, cotton-mill workers who lived in the mill village had a clear advantage (see table 5.9). In 1900, six in ten mill-village families paid 10 percent or less of their combined family earnings for a company house. Another quarter of the village households used between 10 and 20 percent of their earnings for rent, and about one family in ten paid more than 20 percent. By 1912 a downward trend in rent costs was evident. In that year, nearly eight of ten mill-village families spent 10 percent or less of their income for company housing, and of the 137 households in Crown Mill tenements, only 3 percent saw more than 20 percent of their earnings go for rent.[41]

A stable core of working families was settling in at Crown Mill, forming the nucleus of a cohesive mill-village community. At the beginning of the twentieth century, it was by no means clear that the family labor system and mill-village housing would adequately provide for Crown's labor needs. By the early 1910s, though, the system appeared to be moving in the direction mill officials desired. In part, workers were responding to changes in the company's hiring practices and wage rates. But, by themselves, better opportunities for adult males and greater family earnings were not enough to hold families at Crown. For one thing, the wages that Crown offered in the 1910s, though better than they had been ten years earlier, were still low even by southern standards. Nor were wages the only concern of the plain folk who became permanent cotton millers. These poor white families had seen enough of economic conditions in the New South to know that home ownership or the acquisition of a small farm—not to mention the rapid accumulation of wealth or social status—was highly unlikely for them. They sought the more realistic goal of economic stability. Whether they toiled for landlords in the countryside or industrialists in the cotton mills, poor whites worked hard and received little in return. But for all their hardships, millhands were not a defeated lot, nor were they peasants helplessly out of place in an industrializing world. They could, they did, make demands on their employers. They voted with their feet, leaving the factory behind when circumstances warranted.

TABLE 5.9. Rent Expenditures on Company Housing, 1900 and 1912

Percentage of Family Earnings Used for Rent[a]	Percentage of Families in Each Category	
	1900	1912
More than 50	2.0	0.0
21 to 50	12.0	2.9
16 to 20	4.0	7.3
11 to 15	22.0	11.0
6 to 10	52.0	37.2
1 to 5	8.0	41.6
Total	100.0	100.0
	(n=50)	(n=137)

Sources: Crown Cotton Mills Payroll Records, CGA; U.S. census manuscripts, Georgia, Whitfield County, 1900, 1910.
[a]Crown Mill earnings only.

Both millhands and managers in Dalton worked for economic and social stability. And although they viewed such stability from different perspectives, desired it for different reasons, and used different tactics to attain it, southern mill officials and cotton-mill families nonetheless were able to find a middle ground on which both could stand with a modicum of comfort and feel their basic needs were being met. Wages were fundamental to labor relations at Crown, but because they were so low, they provided a weak foundation for mutual compatibility between managers and millhands. Instead, the common ground was negotiated through relationships between the two groups that went beyond the wage contract. These relationships stemmed from a series of compromises between mill officials and working families that took shape during the early twentieth century and, combined with changes in wages and work-force composition, fostered the development of a stable working community. Reflecting larger trends taking place throughout industrial America, but stemming principally from regional circumstances, these relationships formed the essence of the industrial system known as mill-village paternalism.

6

THE CREATION OF MILL-

VILLAGE PATERNALISM

The maturation of Crown's labor force after 1900 was partly due to the natural evolution of the family labor system in an agriculturally depressed part of the country. As parents recognized the increasing opportunities for stable employment and better wages, they began to tie their hopes for the family's economic stability to factory work and mill-village life. But the development of a permanent core of working families in the company village also stemmed from managerial policies aimed at attracting such families and fostering their loyalty to the company. These policies involved employee provisions that were not part of the basic wages-for-labor contract. Apart from low-rent housing, the company had offered little in the way of nonwage compensation during its first fifteen years of operations. But company policy changed during the first two decades of the twentieth century, when Crown built two schools and established an employee life insurance policy, a savings plan, and a burial association. Mill officials also encouraged a flourishing company culture that included, among other things, baseball teams and a concert band. It was no accident that the development of a stable mill-village community at Crown paralleled the implementation of such programs.

The new corporate policies constituted what is usually referred to as mill-village paternalism. To deal with corporate paternalism (also called welfare capitalism) is difficult, in part because the term *paternalism* has been so frequently and carelessly employed that it has all but ceased to have any specific meaning.[1] Yet if we restrict the term to mean official company policies, which provided nonwage benefits to workers, sought to create a distinctive corporate culture, and regulated the living environment of the millhands and their families, then something called paternalism did exist—not only at Crown, but throughout the South and in countless manufacturing firms throughout the United States and Europe. Southern culture may well have embodied traditions of patriarchy, elite beneficence, and a highly personal style of business management, but corporate paternalism, narrowly defined, did not depend on any of these cultural mores. Instead, southern social customs worked through institutionalized company policies. Welfare capitalism originated essentially as a labor market phenomenon, but, once established, its programs served as conduits through which conventional values and patterns of behavior flowed. As a result, paternalism emerged as both a modern industrial system and a powerful cultural force.

As a historical concept, paternalism is worth salvaging, for insofar as labor history and southern history are concerned, the stakes are high. The relationship between factory owners and factory workers was central to the evolution of industrial capitalism throughout the nineteenth century and much of the twentieth. From the beginning, that relationship hinged on interactions between managers and workers that went beyond the basic exchange of wages for labor. By exploring those interactions, we can comprehend many of the fundamental dynamics of modern society and see how they changed over time. This quest ought to engage the best efforts of southern historians, many of whom view mill-village paternalism as a central ingredient of regional distinctiveness. But to view industrial paternalism as somehow "southern" is curious indeed, for a cursory study of other regions will reveal the importance of corporate paternalism to Yankee industrialists, even to European manufacturers. Taking welfare capitalism as the national norm during the early twentieth century, it might well be argued that southern textile firms were actually less devoted to paternalistic programs than northern manufacturing companies.[2]

Misconceptions persist partly because few historians have carefully examined the origins and evolution of mill-village paternalism in the New South. The workers' response to welfare capitalism at Crown Mill and the larger consequences of that response are the underlying themes of Part 3 of this book. The current chapter focuses on the beginnings of mill-village paternalism, which were largely related to changes in the southern textile labor market after the turn of the century. Cotton-mill paternalism was a system of industrial relations created by dynamic interaction between managers and millhands in an expanding free-labor economy. Recent arguments that mill-village paternalism was a throwback to slave plantations or to traditional upcountry culture have it wrong. Instead, the rise of industrial paternalism in the early twentieth-century South marked a distinct break with the past and exemplified regional modernization.

The fundamental misconception about mill-village paternalism in the New South is that it stemmed naturally from regional culture.[3] One recent school of historiography, for example, maintains that mill-village paternalism had its origins in Old South master-slave relations. According to this view, many of Dixie's early textile leaders were (or had been) planters themselves, and their aristocratic ideals were deeply rooted in the Old South. It was natural, therefore, for these planter-industrialists to transfer their paternalism from black slaves to poor whites. Southern manufacturers ensured their control over their operatives by establishing paternalistic mill villages, which were in reality "industrial plantations."[4] That this argument has been widely accepted is evident in a recent survey of American labor history, which states that, after the Civil War, paternalism "blossomed in the mill villages of the South" and that, as servants of the planterlike industrialists, southern workers "experienced paternalism at its most pathetic. The Southern textile millhand was at the total mercy of the mill-village overlord and his retinue of preachers, foremen, and retailers."[5]

This "industrial plantation" argument is inappropriate for several reasons. It assumes too much, for one thing, taking for granted that a coherent planter ethic existed in the antebellum period, that this ethic persisted among Dixie's elite even after dramatic changes in the economy, and that the planter ideal could easily be fitted to the structure of industrial capitalism. It also views paternalism as something that was simply imposed on the millhands from above, even though evidence suggests that labor market pressures were the fundamental catalyst for institutional paternalism. Certainly no white mill workers viewed themselves as slaves in any literal sense; they would have been deeply offended, perhaps to the point of violence, by any suggestion to the contrary. They knew that mill work, even though they themselves sometimes called it "slave labor," was not the same thing as chattel slavery, and their relation to wealthy whites did not parallel that of slave to master. The industrial plantation view also fails to pay careful attention to the ongoing dynamics of the mill-village system or to the timing involved in the development of mill-village paternalism. Finally, it presents a regionally myopic argument, which fails to acknowledge that the advent of an industrial paternalism, much of it remarkably similar to its southern manifestation, paralleled the growth of industry throughout the Western world.

Another culturally oriented explanation is that upcountry Piedmont culture, not the Old South plantation, provided the fertile ground in which industrial paternalism took root. Allen Tullos, in *Habits of Industry*, offers a variation of this argument. He sees mill-village paternalism as an extension of traditional Piedmont Protestantism and the "deferential patterns and customs of the region's eighteenth-century Scotch-Irish, German, and English settlers." According to Tullos, such cultural traditions sprang from an unquestioning acceptance of "fatherly sovereignty," which had its origins in a stern Protestant God. "Paternalism or fatherly authority," he writes, "ranging from the despotic to the well-intentioned, in relations both familial and societal, constituted a deep legitimizing force within white Piedmont society from the time of backwoods settlement through the era of capitalist industrialization." Most historians would agree that cultural traditions played an important role in the lives of upcountry whites, but the critical question left unanswered here is one of connections. How, specifically, did patriarchal Protestantism become manifest as corporate policy? And if cotton-mill paternalism increased markedly after most southern mills had already been operating for ten to twenty years, how could traditional culture alone explain such a shift? The view that industrial paternalism grew out of socially legitimized notions of fatherly dominance amounts to a form of cultural determinism that fails to clarify the origins of specific corporate policies.[6]

An examination of the Crown Mill community reveals the inadequacy of both the industrial-plantation and the Piedmont culture approaches to explaining the origins of mill-village paternalism in the New South. A confluence of events just after the turn of the century—regional textile expansion, the maturation of Dixie's textile managers, the resurgence of cotton prices, southern labor market trends, and the national boom in welfare-capitalism approaches to labor relations—created a situation in which industrial paternalism made sense in the textile South. The economic structure of Dixie's textile towns also influenced industrial relations in a paradoxical way. Because Crown was the major employer in a small city, it was one of the few places poor whites could earn wages. But the labor shortage of the early twentieth century turned the tables on the small-town mill, which then had to scramble to find enough help. As a result, the rise of industrial paternalism in Dalton was a process mediated simultaneously from the top down and from the bottom up. Timing was the critical factor.

At Crown, personalism—a highly personal style of management that involved informal interactions between company officials and their millhands—developed before formal paternalism. Small favors, personal demonstrations of concern, and outward acknowledgments of Anglo-Saxon unity characterized personalism, which in many ways reflected the landlord-tenant relationship in the countryside. The institutionalized paternalism of welfare capitalism, which involved formal managerial policies bearing directly on the entire community of workers, provided an environment within which personalism could flourish. At Crown, informal interactions between managers and millhands seemed to increase considerably after formal policies were established to facilitate such interactions. And because these formal policies were played out through face-to-face interactions, personalism assumed an importance within the community that it had not previously possessed. Corporate paternalism was everywhere apparent throughout industrializing America, but personalities and local social customs mattered because, in the end, it was individuals who administered policy. Thus the line between personalism and official corporate paternalism was blurred—with important long-term consequences for industrial relations at the Crown Cotton Mills.

Company personalism alone could make lasting and powerful impressions on workers. One of Crown's longtime workers, Sibyl Queen, revealed George Hamilton's personal style of labor relations. Sibyl, who was one of fourteen children, went to work in the mill during the 1910s when her father became too ill for factory labor. Mr. George secured a mill house for the Queens and visited Sibyl's father when he was bedridden, saying, "If there's anything you need, don't hurt to call." Grateful to this day for such kindness, Sibyl recalled, "That done something to me about the Hamiltons that I'll never get away from." Queen also viewed mill superintendent Frank Springer as a father figure. Sometimes, when visitors came through the plant, "Mr. Springer" affectionately introduced Queen to them, adding, "I've just about raised you in the mill, haven't I?" Queen proudly recalled how Springer enlisted her help to aid a badly impoverished family who came to the mill in the 1920s. "They wanted to help you, you see, 'cause they wanted nice, decent people." This comment revealed how Queen's own self-image was based partly on her association with company leaders and company policies. And though her words reflect a deference to the mill leaders, she clearly understood that the company had its own needs—including the need for "nice, decent people."[7]

Frank Springer came to embody both the individual and the corporate aspects of Crown's paternalism. He was himself a beneficiary of George Hamilton's personalism, having moved up through the ranks in the company. He began work at Crown Mill as an ordinary bobbin boy in 1887, and by the 1920s he was superintendent of the spinning and carding departments and had charge of all mill-village housing. He received support from Hamilton along the way. One day in February 1909, for example, when Springer was a foreman at Crown, Hamilton purchased two adjacent land lots on Thornton Avenue, not far from the mill, for $450. The very next day, he sold the land to Springer for the same price, on credit, at no interest.[8] Through small acts of kindness—visiting sick employees, acting courteously toward children "raised in the mill," elevating local hands to front-line management positions—Crown's mill officials slowly ingratiated themselves with the working people.

So although corporate paternalism was a general phenomenon everywhere apparent in the developing nations of the Western world, it operated on a daily basis through individual representatives of each separate company. When people like Springer and Hamilton carried out the policies of welfare capitalism, personalism and paternalism became inextricably intertwined. But personalism hinged on arbitrary decisions and on favoritism, which meant that it could engender jealousy and hard feelings as well as camaraderie. Superintendent J. W. Brown's clash with the workers over mill-village sanitation in 1897 reflected the tension inherent in highly personal relations within an industrial hierarchy. Henry Wade's experience at Crown exemplified both the gratitude and the resentment that company personalism could inspire. After Wade's father died suddenly in the 1920s, leaving a widow and a large number of children, "Little George" Hamilton personally guaranteed the Wades a company house and mill jobs for all the children. The family remained indebted to Hamilton for his concern and his promise of employment; as Henry put it, "They was real good to us." Yet later, when one of Springer's favored millhands complained about the Wade family's dog, the superintendent forced Henry's sister to get rid of her beloved pet, thereby creating permanent resentment against him and arbitrary company decisions. By doing one family a favor, Springer alienated another. In a community of conflicting needs and desires, personalism cut both ways.[9]

Compared with individual personalism, corporate paternalism was more visible, more important to the company's image, and more significant for labor recruitment. The public face of paternalism made mill managers the idols of uptown citizens, who viewed schools and baseball parks as resulting from benevolent sacrifices to uplift the "downtrodden" poor whites. But corporate paternalism also inspired harsh criticism. Many contemporary observers, especially sociologists and reformers from outside the South, condemned welfare capitalism as a coercive system that crushed the workers' independence and ambition while mitigating the possibility of organized protest. Not surprisingly, company paternalism did embody aspects of both genuine benevolence and hard-nosed social control. But to view the issue so narrowly is to miss its larger significance to American industry and the textile South.

During Crown's first generation, company housing was virtually the only tangible nonwage benefit offered to employees, and at the time neither the managers nor the millhands viewed the tenements as part of a paternalistic program. When Crown was built in the mid-1880s, mill housing for workers was already an established pattern in Dixie's new upcountry textile towns. Such dwellings were essential for mills in small towns and rural areas, where housing facilities for prospective working families were inadequate. The directors planned the first houses two months before the mill began operations in 1885 and gave no indication that the rental properties would be a special benefit to their future millhands. Reflecting Crown's productive capacity at that time, only six houses were originally built on Pulltight Hill.[10]

Crown's directors intended the mill-village neighborhoods to be spacious but

Spartan. The standard lot for each home consisted of a quarter-acre with the house in the center. Normally the houses were built at least sixty feet apart. This arrangement provided enough space for each family to raise a garden, which was an important part of the mill workers' economy. "The whole matter of providing attractive and comfortable habitations for cotton mill operatives in the South may be summarized in the statement that they are essentially a rural people," wrote one early industrialist. "They have been accustomed to farm life, where there is plenty of room. . . . The ideal arrangement is to preserve the general conditions of rural life and add some of the comforts of city life." Crown's officials tried to maintain low building costs. They paid $350 each for the original houses and spent only $250 on some of the later additions. Initially, the directors provided no facilities for running water near the homes, a situation the workers were loath to accept and one that was remedied in 1888. The homes were single-story wood frame or clapboard structures perched on brick pillars, with tin—later shingle—roofs. The early homes were single-family dwellings, but in later years Crown sometimes built duplexes. Every house had a coal-burning fireplace, a porch, and an outhouse in back. Often, a centrally located privy (an "eight holer") served four households. There was nothing fancy about these houses, but they were fairly similar to poor rural homes and were clearly superior to those in the Happy Top slum area that was less than a mile southwest of the mill.[11]

Crown's mill-village neighborhoods expanded as the factory complex grew. The original 6 dwellings on Pulltight Hill were surrounded by nearly 70 new homes when Crown enlarged the mill in the 1890s. As clusters of new tenements were built in the early twentieth century, distinctive neighborhoods developed within the mill village (see map 6.1). After the company built Mill No. 2 in 1908, the Frog Town subdivision arose north of Pulltight, bordering the baseball field and stretching to the foot of Mount Rachel. By this time, Crown furnished over 100 homes for its workers. With the expansion of Mill No. 2 in 1916, the company constructed additional housing developments. New Town grew up north of the ballpark, at the base of Mount Rachel's western slope. The largest new neighborhood was located west of the Western and Atlantic Railroad on Jones Street. Originally, over 100 homes were built in this Westside area, and in subsequent years more followed. Eventually the Crown Mill village consisted of about 350 houses. Throughout this entire period, rents remained the same—a dollar per room, per month—encouraging a higher proportion of the work force to move into village housing. By the 1920s, the mill neighborhoods were an important aspect of Crown's corporate culture, and later still, when the company houses were sold in the 1950s, managers and mill families alike saw them as one of the last remnants of traditional cotton-mill paternalism.[12]

But it is important to emphasize that the people of Crown came to view mill-village housing as a central manifestation of paternalism only *after* the company

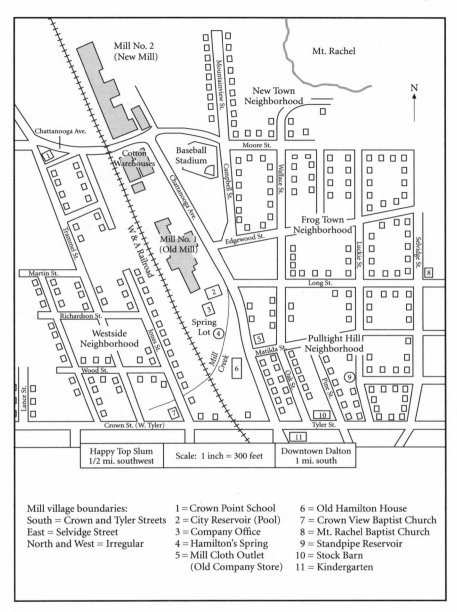

Mill No. 2
(New Mill)

Mt. Rachel

Mountainview St.

Chattanooga Ave.

New Town
Neighborhood

N

Cotton
Warehouses

Baseball
Stadium

Chattanooga Ave.

Campbell St.

Moore St.

Wallace St.

Frog Town
Neighborhood

W. & A. Railroad

Mill No. 1
(Old Mill)

Edgewood St.

Luckie St.

Selvidge St.

8

Martin St.

Trammel St.

Long St.

2

Richardson St.

3

Spring
Lot (4)

Jones St.

Westside
Neighborhood

5

Matilda St.

Oak St.

Pulltight Hill
Neighborhood

Mill Creek

6

Wood St.

7

Pine St.

9

Lance St.

Crown St. (W. Tyler)

10

Tyler St.

11

Happy Top Slum 1/2 mi. southwest	Scale: 1 inch = 300 feet	Downtown Dalton 1 mi. south

Mill village boundaries:
South = Crown and Tyler Streets
East = Selvidge Street
North and West = Irregular

1 = Crown Point School
2 = City Reservoir (Pool)
3 = Company Office
4 = Hamilton's Spring
5 = Mill Cloth Outlet
 (Old Company Store)

6 = Old Hamilton House
7 = Crown View Baptist Church
8 = Mt. Rachel Baptist Church
9 = Standpipe Reservoir
10 = Stock Barn
11 = Kindergarten

MAP 6.1.   The Crown Mill Village, ca. 1919

developed an extensive system of nonwage benefits for the workers and their families. At the turn of the century, company housing at Crown was just rental property, and less than 40 percent of the mill families actually lived in it (see table 5.8). Two decades later, it had evolved into an important symbol of the corporate community. Village housing was not the foundation of cotton-mill paternalism. Rather, the advent of welfare capitalism created a stable community of workers, for whom company housing and mill-village neighborhoods subsequently became a hallmark of the Crown Mill "family."

To chart the rise of Crown's paternalistic programs is to reveal the importance of the labor market crisis in facilitating major changes in southern textile labor relations (see fig. 6.1). The timing of paternalism's advance was no coincidence. First in 1899, and rapidly after 1905, Crown began to introduce a variety of non-wage benefits for its employees. The minutes from Crown's board of directors meetings offer no explanation for this flurry of activity, but the connection with high labor turnover is very suggestive. The rise of corporate paternalism at Crown corresponded neatly with the company's growing desire for a more stable work force, an imperative shared by other labor-hungry textile managers throughout Dixie. By 1920 Crown's paternalistic program included a kindergarten, grade school, night school for adults, life insurance policies, and recreational facilities, as well as opportunities to join a burial association and to earn interest in a company savings account.

Other factors worked in conjunction with management's labor market predicament to foster welfare capitalism in southern textiles. For many Americans, in the North and the South, the early twentieth century was a time of reflection on, and reaction to, the tumultuous era of the 1880s and 1890s. Throughout the nation, "progressive" reformers worked to stabilize society and temper the worst ills of industrial capitalism through the creation of enlightened institutions. Some industrial reformers saw nonwage benefits and visible manifestations of company interest in employees as positive ways to ameliorate the darker aspects of factory life and thereby to curtail the possibility of social disruption. Crown's move toward paternalism also no doubt reflected a broader trend among America's industrial leaders toward welfare capitalism. The last three decades of the nineteenth century witnessed the explosive rise of organized labor and of radical groups aiming at a thorough restructuring of the economic system. Industrial leaders in the early twentieth century were eager to avoid a resurgence of aggressive labor organization. One solution was to institute a variety of corporate programs that would smooth over the most prominent sources of worker discontent. Equally important, northern industrialists were faced with a labor crisis of their own, and they were actively exploring new policies for recruiting and retaining a stable, well-trained supply of workers. In both regions, the surge in corporate paternalism reflected a national trend toward a system of welfare capitalism that was intended

FIGURE 6.1. Labor Turnover and Paternalism at Crown, 1884–1927

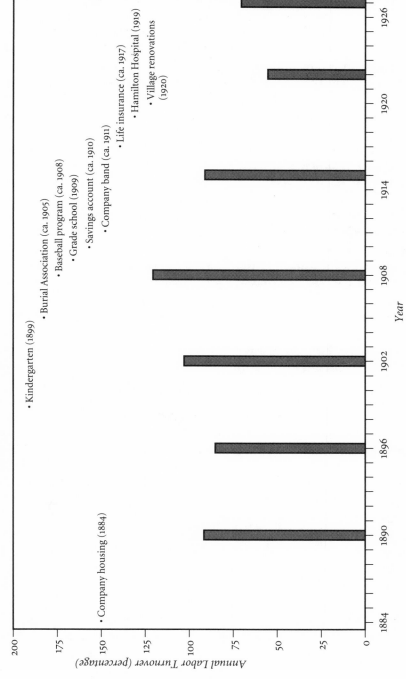

Source: Turnover calculated from Crown Cotton Mills Payroll Records, 1890–1927, CGA; on programs, see chap. 6 notes.

to secure a large quantity of high-quality factory hands and to forestall working-class dissent.[13]

Educational facilities for workers were an important component of welfare capitalism. Southern industrialists often pointed to company schools as manifestations of their commitment both to the progress of the town and to the uplift of the local mill workers. Northern corporations did the same, often stressing the advantages of educating and Americanizing immigrant workers. Because schools were such a highly visible part of company paternalism, it is significant that Crown built no school at all during its first fifteen years. The mill's first school was established in 1899, the same year in which, not incidentally, Crown added its expansive weave shed to the Old Mill and in which farmers saw cotton prices rise sharply. A one-room wooden building south of Pulltight Hill, the school was used not as a grade school but as a kindergarten. It served essentially as a day care center for children younger than seven or eight. Night classes for employees were also offered, although no records indicate how many workers attended or how long the evening school continued.[14]

Crown made no further provisions for mill-village education until after it built the New Mill in 1908. This factory expansion occurred during the most widespread labor shortage in southern textiles before World War I. Crown's expansion and the labor market contraction perhaps underlay the directors' decision in late 1909 to build a grade school. At the time, the only educational facility in the mill village was the old company store, which was serving temporarily as a school. Local newspaper editors, apparently alarmed that so many school-age children had no appropriate schoolhouse, also pressured the company to construct the new building with utmost dispatch. By late 1910, Crown Point School stood complete north of the new Jones Street neighborhood, just outside the city limits. A two-story wooden structure, the school fell under the joint authority of the Whitfield County school system, which paid expenses for five months, and the mill, which assumed the cost of four more. This was a common arrangement for southern mill schools, which found it useful to run for nine months rather than five (the standard in most rural, county-level public schools), because their mill children did not take time off to work harvests. Crown Point went through seven grades, the maximum number before high school. But most mill children began work at about age ten or twelve, so that few actually graduated from grade school until the mid-1920s, when Georgia finally passed an effective child labor law.[15]

Some families in rural communities and mill villages actively sought out good educational facilities, which were very often lacking in north Georgia. Sarah Bunch and Anna Nell Garren, whose family (the Travillians) migrated to Crown from a Walker County farm after World War I, recalled that their father made the decision to move primarily because the mill offered better educational facilities for his children than the county school in their district. Mill officials viewed families like these as the type that would become stable, hard-working cotton millers, and the company school reflected management's effort to attract higher-quality working families. The school therefore served a variety of functions. It lured better recruits and inculcated work discipline in mill-village youngsters. It deflected local criticism of the mill (which was growing over the tax and water issues at the time the school was built) and boosted the company's image as a benevolent institution. Finally, Crown Point became an integral part of an emerging company culture by integrating newcomers into the mill-village community and providing a common link between the mill and the different generations of workers.[16]

The school was merely one of the many tools Crown's mill officials used to create a company culture in which working families could take pride and to which they would feel a sense of loyalty. Special holiday occasions were a small but influential aspect of this strategy. During the late nineteenth century, the mill occasionally offered train excursions and picnics for the workers on the Fourth of July, and in the twentieth century, the hands received several days off for the holiday. At Christmas the company gave every mill child a gift sack full of candy, fruit, and nuts, a tradition that endured throughout Crown's history. Almost every worker interviewed for this study fondly recalled the Christmas sacks. In 1920, these holiday treats cost the company about $516 total, or roughly 25 cents per child—not a bad business proposition. During the early 1910s, the company began to sponsor the Crown Mill Concert Band, which featured a big bass drum sporting the company name. Evidence suggests that the workers themselves were influential in getting the band started. The group, consisting of some fifteen members, played at various Dalton celebrations and mill-village events. In the late 1910s, the mill sponsored yard-beautification contests and took photographs of the winning families. The managers also installed playground equipment for children (and benches for the more relaxed crowd) in the "Spring Lot," the casually landscaped, comfortably shaded area surrounding Hamilton's Spring. The Spring Lot became the focal point of the community, where millhands gathered every Sunday to visit, play, and court.[17]

The most visible symbol of company culture was Crown's baseball park, which was built during the early years of the twentieth century and later expanded. The management supplied uniforms (gray with blue trim) emblazoned with the company name. Although only about a dozen young men actually made the mill's "first nine," which played highly competitive ball with other textile teams from north Georgia and Tennessee, millhands by the hundreds packed the company stadium for Saturday games. The local papers, which usually ignored Crown's millhands, were faithfully reporting the company games by the mid-1910s. A dramatic example of personalism occurred on the ballfield during the early years of mill competition. George Hamilton's son Neil was a fine ballplayer, and when he returned from college to work for the company, he played on the team himself. This fortuitous

Crown Mill band, ca. 1915. Sam Hardin (*bottom left*), later a supervisor in the mill, is said
to have been influential in organizing the band. (*Courtesy of Crown Gardens and Archives*)

circumstance provided management with a direct, interactive link with the millhands.[18]

Beneath the flare of home runs and bass drums, some less visible but highly
significant policies were put into place to enhance the workers' security, particularly if they remained with the company. The Crown Cotton Mills Burial
Association was established around 1905. Workers could become members by
paying 25 cents, whereupon they received a handsome certificate, printed by the
company. When a member died, a previously specified relative would receive the
equivalent of 25 cents from each remaining member of the association to pay for
an adequate burial. Funerals were important to poor southerners, but funds for
even a simple service were hard to come by, and burial associations offered a
collective solution. The burial association offered an excellent way to draw on the
millhands' heritage of community cooperation, provide a symbol of corporate
compassion, and engender feelings of loyalty to the company. Frank A. Hamilton,
Crown's master mechanic, was president of the association, which meant that it
was an organization established by the company but run by the workers themselves.[19]

A decade later, during the World War I labor shortage, the company took
paternalism to a higher level when it inaugurated the employee life insurance

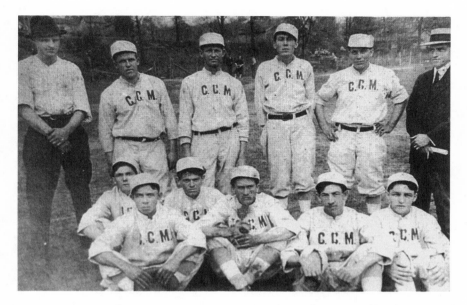

Crown Mill baseball team, ca. 1915. Cornelius L. "Neil" Hamilton, son of Crown Mill president George W. Hamilton, Sr., and himself later president of the mill, is the player at top left. (*Courtesy of Crown Gardens and Archives*)

policy. Beginning in 1917, workers were automatically covered by AEtna Life Insurance Company at the Crown Mill's expense. Managers explained the policy to the millhands in a pamphlet that read: "Insurance means something for loved ones after we are gone. Any man or woman having dependents should carry some insurance. Realizing this and how difficult it is for all of our employees to carry insurance, we take this method of giving each employee a policy in the AEtna Life Insurance Company. In case of permanent total disability, through sickness or accident, the amount of the policy will be paid to you. We trust that it will help keep you free from worry over the future." The rates of coverage clearly reveal the company's intention of using the life insurance benefits as a means of securing a stable work force. In their first year of employment, Crown's millhands were insured for $300; in their second year, $350. The coverage increased by $50 each successive year that a worker remained with the company up to the fifth year, when the policy reached a maximum $500. This insurance provided mill families with a modicum of economic security they could not have otherwise afforded and also created a strong incentive for remaining with the company. During an era in which workers' compensation, pension plans, and government welfare programs were unknown in southern textiles, this nonwage benefit may have helped temper any desire to move away from Crown.[20]

A company savings policy, inaugurated by Mr. George, illustrated another aspect of corporate paternalism. Mill managers sought not only to attract an adequate number of workers but also to mold them into thrifty citizens. Workers with their minds on accumulating cash, it was assumed, would be good, dependable millhands who caused little trouble and produced quality cloth under minimal supervision. Such was the idea behind the employee savings program. The savings account also reflected the officials' desire to hold on to families who exhibited thrifty tendencies. Crown paid its workers higher interest rates than local banks, which encouraged those with savings in mind to remain with the company. Most mill families saved little because they earned so little, but some workers adopted the habit of systematic savings. Lillie Hill, looking back on her life as a cotton miller, described the Crown Cotton Mill as "a school, an alma mater" and credited the company with teaching her to manage money. In the early 1920s, the mill added a "bonus" program that dovetailed with the ideal of thrift while spurring workers to greater production. The plan set workers' wages by the piece, but all their output after they "made production" (that is, after they reached a production goal established by management) accrued to "bonus" earnings.[21]

The company also exerted significant control over the workers' lives outside the factory. Mill-village regulations were not so strict as long as Crown remained small, but as the company expanded and new families flooded the village, the need for orderliness increased. Mill-village discipline therefore may be viewed as part and parcel of the emerging paternalistic system. This facet of paternalism often smacked of patriarchal authoritarianism to the workers. Millhands knew the social implications of living in a company-owned home. Crown maintained its own special police force, and drunkenness—even drinking in public—was cause for dismissal and eviction from company housing. Management maintained exacting standards of behavior in both mill housing and the mill itself; for example, it outlawed chickens in the village and snuff in the factory. Such corporate discipline irked some household heads, who normally maintained firm control over their own families and who had reason to resent managerial intrusion into their personal affairs. Although company paternalism offered cotton-mill families a degree of economic security rare in their deeply impoverished region, that security, for adults in particular, cost dearly in terms of individual liberty.[22]

The workers responded to corporate discipline in diverse ways. Many families were firm supporters of temperance and looked favorably upon the company's antidrinking policies. Cotton millers who were strong on discipline themselves expected as much from their mill. Some people—particularly mill women—demonstrated a near obsession for cleanliness. They ostracized wives and mothers who did not clean constantly and supported the mill's efforts to keep "trash" out of the village. But some workers who enjoyed drinking and a less stringent lifestyle, or others who simply did not appreciate the mill's telling them how to live, chafed under company rules. As far as the mill officials were concerned, company rules created a mechanism for selective recruitment. Workers who could abide—even support—the regulations were the people managers hoped would stay with the mill. Supervisors might have eagerly disposed of mill families who found the rules intolerable—except for the nagging problem of labor shortages. As part of the emerging paternalistic system, Crown's mill-village regulations came into being just at a time when experienced workers were hard to find. As a result, the company had to exercise some restraint in the enforcement of its own rules. Outlandish displays of drunkenness would certainly mean banishment. But management was reluctant to fire good workers who went on occasional binges, especially if they were part of large mill-working families. As longtime millhand Des Ellis wryly remarked, "They tried to have rules." The unspoken policy of lenience, a result primarily of the tight labor market of the early twentieth century, became a tradition within the mill's paternalistic system. Personal, informal negotiations over policies helped define the boundaries of power within the formal system of discipline. The arbitrary enforcement of paternalistic regulations demonstrated that workers understood their value to the company and were able to use that knowledge to gain certain concessions from the managers.[23]

Corporate discipline nonetheless reminded workers that the drive for profits lay behind mill-village paternalism. The limits of corporate benevolence were evident in the mill's insurance policy for workers injured on the job. By the terms of this policy, Crown was liable only if the accident resulted from negligence on the part of the mill, and when the company was at fault, the managers tried hard to work out a less expensive private settlement rather than submit the claim to the insurance agent. For example, in March 1914 an elevator at Crown fell with Clarence Grant in it, fracturing the millhand's right foot and making it impossible for him to work for the next two months. "As there was almost a clear case of liability we have kept in touch with the case and made several efforts to adjust it," one Crown manager wrote to the Maryland Casualty Company, which served as Crown's insurer:

> About six months ago we made him an offer of one hundred dollars. He thought that in addition to this amount he should be paid for his lost time which we believe amounted to something over fifty dollars. We let the matter drift along but had it in mind and the other day when opportunity offered we suggested to him that it would be best to settle the matter for our last offer and he agreed to do so. We have accordingly made him the payment and enclose herewith release in this case. Under the circumstances we are sure that the Maryland Casualty Co. will be willing to refund us this amount.

Business, in short, was business. Corporate paternalism was not the antithesis of hard-nosed management but an integral part of Crown's aggressive corporate strategies. Profits and paternalism went hand in hand, and the Clarence Grant settlement only hinted at what might happen when welfare capitalism and corporate profits clashed.[24]

Corporate paternalism at Crown reached maturity during the World War I years. The long, costly conflict into which Europe plunged in 1914 had a dramatic impact on the southern textile industry. Long before the United States entered the war in 1917, the European demand for cotton goods sparked an unparalleled boom in textile production. Mills expanded rapidly to meet the military's demands. "All the manufacturing industries of Georgia made very gratifying progress during the year," the Georgia commissioner of commerce and labor announced in 1917. "The textile mills did splendid work, especially on such articles as are most essential to the war work of the Government." The report also noted "a large increase in the production of the heavier kinds of cloth, such as would be the most serviceable for army use." Crown's cotton duck was this type of product, and the mill prospered with government contracts (as it would again in World War II). Wages rose accordingly, along with the workers' tendency to search for better employment elsewhere. Wealthy landholders in need of farm labor were hard pressed, the commissioner warned, because industry paid better wages than farmers could. Given the southern labor shortage during the war, Crown's persistence figures from 1915 to 1922 were surprisingly high, and the company's aggregate turnover rate was unusually low (see table 5.2), suggesting that rising wages and Crown's new system of paternalistic benefits helped stem the tide of outmigration.[25]

World War I was a lucrative time for mill managers and, to a lesser extent, for workers as well. The major expansion of Crown Mill No. 2 in 1916 was a direct product of the war. Despite the substantial expenses incurred for the expansion, Crown averaged a hefty 40 percent return on capital from 1915 to 1919, including an eye-popping 59 percent during the final year of the war (see table A.2). As labor became scarce, workers throughout the southern textile belt saw their real wages rise significantly. Crown pleaded with the government to excuse certain employees from the draft. "We are in full sympathy with the conscription measure and are prepared to stand the hardships imposed by the loss of ordinary labor," the company wrote to one government official, "but there are places difficult to fill and if it be possible we should like to have protection in these special cases." The war's impact on wages can be gleaned from the only surviving Crown Mill payroll from these years, which is from the New Mill spinning department in 1917–18 (see table 6.1). From August 1917 to June 1918, average two-week earnings for workers in the spinning department increased 38 percent, with the largest jump occurring as America's military involvement deepened during the spring of 1918. During the same one-year period, the national inflation rate was only 6.7 percent. For workers who had endured decades of poverty, such gains were not trivial.[26]

But the war boom also caused mill-village disruption and ravaging epidemics,

TABLE 6.1. Earnings in New Mill Spinning Department, 1917–1918

Payroll Date	Number of Workers	Average Weekly Earnings
August 18, 1917	151	$5.98
October 27, 1917	147	6.27
January 19, 1918	146	6.27
April 27, 1918	100	6.54
June 22, 1918	125	8.26

Source: Crown Cotton Mill Time Book, Mill No. 2, Spinning Department, 1917–18, CGA.

creating the need for more corporate welfare. The rapid influx of new mill families created serious sanitation problems. When Georgia's board of health inspector visited Dalton in summer 1917, he issued an alarming report that a major typhoid or malaria epidemic was imminent. He may have been referring to conditions in Crown Mill and Elk Mill villages when he described the "miserable condition and surroundings" in poor homes, where flies and mosquitoes flourished in the filth and swarmed around fever-wracked patients. But this report did not prevent Crown's working families from suffering a terrible influenza epidemic.[27]

Disease had plagued southern millhands from the start of industrial development. Hookworm, tuberculosis, and pellagra constantly threatened the health of poor southerners on farms and in mill villages. Inadequate sanitation and dietary deficiencies were the principal causes of these maladies, and the mill-village environment only exacerbated the problem. Village outhouses and stockpens, and the worms and insects that swarmed in and about them, created almost perfect conditions for the spread of contagious diseases among a growing population that was poorly fed, inadequately clothed, and often barefoot. The almost universal use of snuff inside and outside the factory ensured that infectious germs would be spread around as mill folk spit out their juice. Early in the twentieth century, campaigns led by medical reformers had often been viewed suspiciously by the workers and attacked as unwarranted Yankee interference by Dixie's New South boosters. But World War I elevated southern consciousness about epidemics, and because wartime emergency production demanded a healthy work force, southerners everywhere became more receptive to measures aimed at alleviating mill-village health problems.[28]

There were solid economic motivations for Crown's directors to confront the problems of sanitation and disease. Having carefully recruited a dependable core of working families, the company needed to protect its investment. Faced with a regional labor shortage, management wanted to avoid an epidemic that might decimate their workers or at least send them packing. Like most other southern mills of the day, Crown sought to upgrade its village through landscaping and improved housing and by adding a sewerage system. When the U.S. surgeon general warned of rampant plagues in 1919, Crown's directors began to investigate the possibilities of building an employee hospital and refurbishing the village's older sections.[29]

Just as Crown's officials were contemplating the establishment of a company medical facility, George Hamilton, Sr., died following an extended illness. As president of the mill for a quarter-century, Mr. George had been the person most closely associated with Crown Mill's growth and its system of corporate paternalism. The workers turned out en masse for his funeral and offered moving expressions of gratitude for his services and sorrow at his passing. As both Hamilton and the workers well knew, however, the mill-village community at Crown was not held together by any individual, no matter how prominent. Mr. George and the men like him who headed Dixie's textile mills may have been symbols of cotton-mill paternalism, but the system was less patriarchal than corporate, and the workers were part of the system. A good deal more than the impulses of any one person was involved in the creation of company paternalism, and it would take far more than the passing of one individual to destroy it.

The development of Hamilton Memorial Hospital later that year marked a further extension of paternalism. It also reflected management's sharp-eyed concern for Crown's business interests, a concern fostered by Mr. George and now carried on by his successors. Plans for the hospital took shape in late 1919. At the time, no hospital existed anywhere in Whitfield County, and mill workers had long relied on home remedies and the powers of a few local "healers." On September 17, Crown's board of directors met to discuss the possible "establishment of a modernly arranged and equipped Hospital House." They were concerned about "the danger of the impending recurrence of the 'flu,' as outlined in the U.S. Surgeon General's late warning, and the always dangerous epidemics of spreadable diseases." They realized "the need for methods of prevention, etc, for not only this mill community but for this section." The directors appointed an investigative committee consisting of Will K. Moore (who became Crown's new president at the same meeting), "Little George" Hamilton, Neil Hamilton, and two other leading stockholders. In December the committee reported that corporate health-care facilities had been developed successfully throughout the country, but that a hospital built by Crown and operated solely for the company would prove too expensive. Fortunately for the city, local physicians provided an alternative plan whereby Elk Mill, Crown Mill, and the physicians themselves would all take stock in a hospital that would serve all of Whitfield County. Crown's managers found this suggestion acceptable, and they pledged $25,000 for the new facility. The mill's investment was substantial, partly because the directors saw that a community hospital promised to save Crown both money and managerial effort in the long run. The new facility would be self-supporting and would offer the services of Whitfield's best medical professionals. Ultimately Crown took $50,000 worth of stock in the thirty-bed enterprise, which, largely through Frank Hardwick's efforts, was named in memory of Mr. George. Crown's employees received treatment at a discount at Hamilton Memorial, paying 50 percent of the bill themselves and letting the company absorb the other half. The board of directors also made provisions for "an auxiliary unit, preferably near the mill, for the care and treatment of contagious diseases . . . when the stressful occasion arises."[30]

In conjunction with the hospital development, Crown hired a "landscape architect and city planner" from North Carolina to prepare blueprints for a company park and recreation center as well as for a renovation of the Pulltight Hill neighborhood. In 1920 the popular southern mill-village consultant, E. S. Draper, laid out a model recreation facility to be located south of the Old Mill on the land surrounding the city reservoir, Hamilton's Spring, and the company offices. Draper suggested turning the old Hamilton house into a community center and proposed the construction of a swimming pool, playground area, and tennis courts. The facilities would be surrounded by landscaped flower gardens and walking paths. Only a small part of Draper's plan actually became reality. Frank Hamilton's family continued to live in the old house, which was never made into a community center. Children continued to swim in the city reservoir or in various watering holes in and around Dalton. Crown did build a tennis court, but not until several years later, at the request of several young workers. The directors allocated funds for new playground equipment, swings, and benches, which were spread throughout the Spring Lot, and they had weeping willow trees planted around the reservoir.[31]

Draper's plans for Pulltight Hill focused on sanitation improvements and beautification. He suggested abolishing a large "cow paddocks" and two smaller stables, which were to be replaced by ten new houses. Draper also recommended the construction of an underground sewerage tank. This would allow the company to install indoor toilets and baths in the company houses. Again, the directors delayed carrying out these plans. Toilets were finally added to the houses during the 1920s, as were electric lights, but metal tubs remained the only way of taking a bath. Draper's beautification plan for the old mill neighborhood probably made a few jaws drop when the directors first viewed the blueprints. The architect envisioned 135 new trees (varieties of oak and maple) around the houses and along the streets. He called for the planting of nearly 2,000 flowering plants and shrubs (twenty-one varieties) within the three-block area, including 122 *rosa rugosa* rose bushes. The company did plant the roses, and during the 1920s, superintendent Frank Springer tried to persuade the millhands to call the old neighborhood Rose Hill rather than the less poetic Pulltight. But the new name never took, perhaps because the company did not follow through on much of Draper's beautification proposal. An aerial photograph of Dalton, taken about a decade later, shows a Pulltight Hill strangely barren of trees and foliage, a testimony to managerial frugality.[32]

The Rose Hill failure notwithstanding, Crown's efforts to improve village life worked in harmony with rising wage rates to attract an ever greater number of families to the Crown Mill village—and to keep them there through subsequent generations. Of the 845 teenagers who applied for work in the mill between 1926 and 1934, fully 25 percent had been born in the Crown Mill village during the 1910s. As Will Moore and the Hamiltons looked back from 1920, they could reflect upon a generation of success and growth. The mill had expanded greatly since the mid-1890s, thanks in part to healthy profits and aggressive management. The work force, also growing rapidly, was clearly becoming less transient. North Georgia's poor whites had begun to commit themselves to mill-village life as a means of attaining family security. Their decision to become permanent industrial workers hinged partly on the nonwage benefits Crown began to offer during the first two decades of the twentieth century. In this sense, company paternalism at Crown was highly successful.

Labor historians often argue that corporate paternalism undermined class conflict and unionization efforts by inhibiting the workers' sense of class consciousness. Although partly true, this view misses an important function of welfare capitalism. The fundamental goal of company paternalism—in the North and the South—was to secure a well-trained and reasonably content work force. In an era of weak industrial unions, limited government welfare, and general economic growth, corporate paternalism succeeded. During the first two decades of the twentieth century, workers gradually settled down in mill-village communities and company towns. The growth of paternalistic programs communicated to these workers that they were indispensable to the corporate enterprise. As a result, they viewed themselves not as victims but as participants. Paternalism created not a "false consciousness" but rather a "community consciousness." Managers must have been pleased by this turn of events, but they would ultimately learn that company paternalism worked too well—indeed, it carried the seeds of its own demise. If the mill families had not come to see themselves as a permanent group of working people whose economic security depended on the industrial system, they would never have looked to unionization to ensure that their needs would be met within that system.

However harsh mill work and village life seem in retrospect, millhands in the early twentieth century believed they had a stake in cotton-mill paternalism. Their reliance on the system was not due to an irrational assessment of possible alternatives; nor was it naive. During the early years of the century, north Georgia's plain folk had demonstrated an unwillingness to accept mill-village life. They were quick to leave the company's employ and return to the countryside, even if tenant farming seemed economically hopeless. By so doing, they gradually put pressure on textile managers to raise wages and, more important, forced the mills to offer a larger compensation package in order to retain good millhands. The entire process promoted notions of racial unity, which in turn loaded southern paternalism with an explosive emotional burden not found outside the South. North Georgians of quite ordinary origins thus had a profound impact on the process of industrialization in Dalton and ought to be seen alongside the company's managers as the instigators of Crown's paternalistic policies. The mill-village system and company paternalism at Crown represented a compromise—an unequal one, to be sure, but a compromise nonetheless—between managers and millhands.

Viewed from this perspective, mill-village paternalism was not emblematic of either the Old South plantation or the deeply embedded social traditions of the southern upcountry. It was not the offspring of a culture stuck in time. Rather, it marked a fundamental shift toward modern capitalist relations and an increasingly sophisticated free-labor outlook among the southern plain folk. Because paternalistic policies were intended to lure workers to the mill, those policies reflected aspects of the millhands' rural-based culture. But because industrial paternalism also sought to reshape its work force in the image of industry, it channeled traditional patterns of behavior into new molds and created a new culture in which the workers' lives were inextricably entwined with the corporation. The workers, in short, were encouraged to commit themselves to permanent wage-earning employment in the mills. This was a dangerous step to take, as poor white southerners well knew. But as World War I gave way to the 1920s, it was clear that workers throughout America and the South were taking that step and not looking back. They had helped to shape the system of welfare capitalism. Whether that system would work to their long-term advantage was not the least bit clear.

PART III

THE FAMILY

AND THE FEUD,

1920–1939

7

THE CROWN MILL FAMILY

The two decades following World War I witnessed both the climax and the demise of a way of life that had slowly been developing at Crown since the turn of the century. At the beginning of the 1920s, the Crown Mill community was more stable than it had ever been. During the decade that followed, the general prosperity of Dalton and Crown provided a foundation upon which a thriving workers' community emerged in the mill village. It was not a community that defined itself as separate from and antagonistic toward Crown and its managers, but one that was so closely linked to the mill itself that it was scarcely distinguishable from the larger company culture. This reconciliation of interests between the millhands and managers of Crown was based on the paternalism that emerged in the early twentieth century and was further facilitated by the agricultural decline and comparative mill-village prosperity of the 1920s. Critics charged that southern mill villages enslaved impoverished whites and robbed them of individuality and initiative. Apologists countered that southern textile paternalism marked the highest form of harmonious labor relations. Despite their different views, both groups perceptively recognized the importance of mill-village paternalism in shaping the textile South. But both also overestimated the strength of the paternalistic system, which appeared sturdy but had serious internal flaws and rested upon an unexpectedly brittle foundation. When the Great Depression undermined Crown's profitability, the system fell apart with surprising suddenness. Until that time, though, the community enjoyed a period of remarkable cohesiveness.

In the 1920s it became common for workers to think of themselves and their mill as a "family." Lucile Hall, looking back on her many years at Crown, recalled that "it was more or less a family thing, you know. The whole family worked . . . and it was more or less like a family in the mill. They cared for one another." The family metaphor of mill-village culture was one the workers themselves used. Virtually every person interviewed for this study described Crown's mill community as "one big family," just as textile workers throughout the South used the same phrase to explain the patterns of mill-village life. The extensive kinship ties among mill families and their heritage of community cooperation imported from the countryside provided a solid basis for the "family" ideal that developed in an industrial setting. The racial and cultural homogeneity of the cotton-mill people, as well as their social isolation in Dalton, further enhanced a group identity. Mill-village culture embodied a complex mixture of rural traditions and new forms of behavior endemic to an industrial environment, both of which helped strengthen the workers' sense of belonging.[1]

When interviewed about her life at Crown Mill, Lillie Ann Hill said, "Now I've got a love story, but nobody'd be interested in listening to my love story." On the contrary, her tale of romance amply illustrates the makeup of the Crown Mill family and how it functioned. Lillie Goforth moved to Crown with her family in the 1920s and began working in 1927. She had a boyfriend in the country up near Cleveland, Tennessee, not far north of the Georgia line. Cletus Hill had already asked Lillie to marry him and return to farm life, but she liked the mill village and answered, "No way, I've come to Canaan land." Cletus then wrote Lillie to see if she could get him a job at Crown. His request came in the early 1930s, but it did not matter to Lillie that "times were sorta hard and maybe work slowed up." As she recalled, "I come in and said to my mother, I said, 'Mama, I'm going down and get my man a job.' Mama said, 'Lillie Ann, I'd be ashamed of myself.'" Undaunted, Lillie intercepted superintendent Frank Springer at the mill door.

I said, "Hey, Mr. Springer, I'd like to ask you something." He said, "All right, Lillie, what is it?" I said, "Well, I've got a friend here and I'd like for you to give him a job. I'll show you his picture." He looked at it. He said, "Well, Lillie, he's got the job if he's here in the morning at 6:30." I said, "Why, Mr. Springer, he lives away out in the country in Cleveland, Tennessee, and I'd have to send him a telegram. And he couldn't get here in the morning at 6:30." Mr. Springer said, "You could go get him, can't you?" Well I didn't have a car, I didn't have anything, [but] I said, "Oh, yes, I can."

Upon hearing this news, Lillie's mother said, "Lillie Ann, your daddy'll kill you." But the daughter retorted, "Why, he might kill me but he can't eat me."[2]

Lillie Goforth was more concerned with how to get her "sweetheart" to the mill by 6:30 the next morning, and the way she did so revealed how closely knit the Crown Mill community was and how informal labor relations there could be, even in the early 1930s. Without a plan, she walked through the mill community: "Up there is Henry Sneedly, and he's a little kin to us, and I said—of course they all knew one another way back, the families—I said, 'Henry, I've got Cletus a job and I wondered would you go and get him?' He said, 'Lillie, I'd be glad to,' but says, 'I've got the flu. But I'll tell you what I will do. You can have my car' [an old Model T]." This offer was a good start, except that Lillie could not drive. So Sneedly said, "You can go get your Uncle Homer and he'll drive you." Lillie responded, "Oh, that's fine," but then she confessed, "Henry, I don't know the way." As it turned out, Henry's young son, James—age ten—knew the road, so Henry offered to let James serve as guide. Lillie then went up to the Old Mill, where Uncle Homer "was working away." She said, " 'Hey, Uncle Homer, will you do me a favor?' He said, 'What is it?' I said, 'Will you get off and take me up to Tennessee to get Cletus? He's got a job if he'll be here by early in the morning.' Uncle Homer says yes. So he goes and gets off and I told him what were the arrangements. He went right on and he went and got his wife, and they had a little baby." The entire bunch picked up James Sneedly and set out for the Hills' farmhouse.

The journey itself was a struggle. The tires suffered numerous "punctures," but these were graciously repaired by country folks along the way. Finally, around 9:00 P.M., the crew reached the farm, and Lillie Goforth knocked on the door. "Mr. Hill was an old-timer. So, [he booms], 'Who is it?' Said, 'It's Lillie Goforth from Dalton, Georgia, and I come up here to see Cletus.' Well, Cletus was at the door before Mr. Hill could turn around, says, 'Come in, Lillie.' And I said, 'Cletus, you've got a job down yonder if you want it, if you're there in the morning by 6:30.' He said, 'Good,' [and then] he had to go over to the neighbors to borrow a suitcase." Mr. Hill, a farm owner and, in Lillie's words, "an old-timer," was against his son's leaving. As Cletus packed he said, "Good God, son, we don't have much around here, but we're fixing to build a new house. I think you ought to stay here and help build it." Unmoved, Cletus said, "Dad, I know God's good, but I've got an opportunity to go to work now and I'm going to work." Several flats and quite a few dusty miles later, the very crowded Model T arrived in Dalton just before daylight. Uncle Homer, fearing Lillie's father, who "was just as strict as he could be," let the couple off down the street from the Goforth house. "We went in. It's about 5 o'clock in the morning. Well, my parents, they were good, and treated Cletus very nice. They was very nice to me. So I went on to work. Cletus, he goes up and sees Mr. Springer. So of course he gets his job."

"So from there," Lillie concluded, "Cletus and I spent our lives together with the Crown Cotton Mill. When we encountered a problem, we went to the company. And they were so good to help us. . . . And of course we realized that they had to have us, and we had to have them. But with good cooperation, we have all done quite well."

The principal attributes of mill-village paternalism and company personalism, as well as some new social trends of the 1920s, are illustrated in this story. Kinship connections and community support made Lillie's journey possible. A friend who was "a little kin" loaned his car without hesitation and sent his young son to navigate on an all-night trip. An uncle took off work (and evidently the mill let him off without any trouble) to drive Lillie, and he naturally brought along his wife and baby. People along the way helped out when the car broke down— apparently without question and asking nothing in return. The carpool brought Cletus (with a suitcase borrowed from the neighbors) back to Dalton, where he started work immediately. Frank Springer—representing the company—played a critical role. Springer was notorious for making people wait long periods of time for jobs and for having applicants form a line outside his office. And yet, at a time when Crown was having difficulty keeping its workers fully employed, he gave Lillie Goforth's boyfriend a job without hesitation, basing his decision on a photograph and, apparently, on the Goforths' reputation in the mill village. Critics claimed that Springer would not let his enemies off work even when they needed to attend a family funeral. And yet Lillie and Uncle Homer left work without any trouble.

Springer's action was favoritism, pure and simple; for those who could benefit from it, company personalism could be fruitful. No wonder Lillie Hill later claimed that she and Cletus spent their lives together "with" the Crown Cotton Mill. Yet their attitude was not simply one of blind loyalty to the company. As Lillie's story made clear, the young couple demonstrated little deference for old-fashioned values or notions of propriety. Their flippant remarks to the "old-timer" parents who opposed their plans reflected a widespread change in attitude among young southern millhands in the 1920s. They had little patience with out-of-date conservatism. They took chances. They wanted wage-earning jobs, not a life on the farm. They could accept a paternalistic system, even thrive in it, but they were not naive. They expected their due from the company. Perhaps that is why, when Crown's paternalistic system collapsed, both Lillie and Cletus became leaders in the union.

The necessary condition for the family ideal to flourish at Crown Mill was a stable mill-village community. During the 1920s, this requirement was fulfilled largely because Crown remained prosperous while the countryside suffered economic stagnation. The resulting labor glut ensured that Crown would have no shortage of eager applicants, that the lure of returning to the farm would subside, and that mill families would probably remain with the company. The final years of the 1910s had been exhilarating times for Dixie's cotton farmers, as wartime demand and industrial expansion boosted staple prices dramatically. Between 1915 and 1919, real cotton prices averaged nearly sixteen cents per pound (see table 5.4). In 1919 Whitfield County farmers grew more than twice as much cotton as they had produced ten years earlier. Gordon and Murray counties also witnessed an impressive rise in staple production. But in 1920, a confluence of events sent real cotton prices spiraling downward to eleven cents per pound, and thereafter during the 1920s cotton farmers continued to despair as staple prices sagged. To make matters worse, the cotton-destroying boll weevil arrived in northwest Georgia in the late teens, with the infestation reaching epidemic proportions at the very time prices plummeted. Marauding insects and low staple prices turned the gaze of poor farmers toward factory work. In the five years following the agricultural crisis of 1920, the total number of farms in Crown's labor-pool area declined nearly 20 percent, whereas Dalton's population rose rapidly. As the city's industrial capacity expanded during the early 1920s, struggling tenant farmers often packed it in and opted for a new start in the mills.[3]

Shortly after the war, it became clear that Crown's labor-supply problems of the early twentieth century had vanished. In a report to the Georgia Department of Commerce and Labor in 1921, Crown's mill officials noted that "labor conditions [were] good." Indeed, the company was inundated with applicants for work. A stack of hand-scrawled letters from job seekers in 1921 offers a revealing look at the sluggish market for mill employment. Sam Tibbs of Dalton wrote asking for a job and added, "I never did work in a mill. But maby I could learn. . . . I sure will appreciate it and I will return the favor by making you a good man." Most letters came from out of town, and many applicants already had textile-mill experience. One man who worked in the mill at New Holland, Georgia, asked for work at Crown because he needed to move to Dalton to care for his aging parents, who relied on him for support. "Now I am not looking for a gravy train or a soft job, you are at liberty to write my Supt. here," he added. Parents looking for work often stressed the working potential of their families. W. O. Hall from Aragon, Georgia, wrote, "we have 4 Darffirs 2 girls that can work where every you need them . . . & I can weave ar Doe any thing in the mill. So if you need our help let Me no Real soon if we can get a job and 5 or 6 Room House all my Hands can work full time." Roy Helton from Shelbyville, Tennessee, asked for an overseer or section-hand position and added, "My wife [is] a 12 Side Semmer."[4]

Some applicants had worked at Crown before. "Mr. George" Hamilton had died in 1919, but in 1921 he received a letter from Nettie and Sarah Stover. From

Diamond, Georgia, the Stovers wrote, "Dear friend a few lines in regard to no if you can give me and my sister ar wark Back to us after christmas we made you good hands when we was thir and will make you stedie hans a gin if you will give us wark after Christmas and will Be ever so much er Blige." Willie Collier imaginatively suggested, "I am considered a good weaver but had rather let my work do the talking." These letters and others like them are rare written testimony from southern millhands during the early twenties, and they divulge a rising concern over dwindling employment opportunities in the textile mills, a condition up-country whites had faced infrequently in the previous twenty years. Mill management obviously was pleased by this glutted labor market, which caused workers to think twice before moving on. "Labor plentiful," wrote Crown's officials in 1923, "business good."[5]

Thanks to such good business conditions, Crown not only profited but also expanded during the twenties. The company's growth was part of Dalton's general economic upswing and the widespread boosterism of the post–World War I era. Throughout the South, small towns embarked upon new development plans that drew from and extended the industrial campaigns of the 1880s. The agricultural depression that followed the war, with the accompanying tendency of young country people to abandon the farms, had a stabilizing influence on Crown's working community. So too did local economic development.

Dalton strode into the 1920s with a noticeable swagger. Despite a national economic downturn from 1920 to 1922, local boosters proudly advertised the biggest and brightest Dalton ever. The business class still viewed population growth and industrial expansion as the key indicators of progress, and on both scores their city was faring well. Along with Dixie's other small towns, Dalton expanded significantly during the postwar decade. After suffering a decline in population during the 1910s, Whitfield County's chief city grew nearly 60 percent between 1920 and 1930, boasting 8,160 residents by the end of the decade (see table A.1). A number of manufacturing establishments stimulated the town's economy, including Crown Mill, Manly Manufacturing Company, Farrar Lumber, Cherokee Manufacturing, A. J. Showalter Company, the Real Silk Hosiery Mill, Duane Chair Factory, the Chero-Cola and Coca-Cola bottling companies, and several bedspread companies. Crown also joined with its longtime northern selling agent, J. H. Lane, to buy and enlarge the old Elk Mill, renaming it Boylston-Crown. The American Thread Mill, a New York–based, British-owned company, built a large village in south Dalton and ultimately employed nearly as many workers as Crown. Between 1920 and 1930, the number of industrial workers in Whitfield County increased more than 60 percent. The county's value-added-by-manufacturing figure rose from $104 per capita to $188, an impressive 81 percent increase that placed Whitfield County far above Georgia's average of $101. Compared with 1887, when the struggling town had passed its "industrial resolution," Dalton looked impressive. Viewing the local scene in 1924, a journalist from Atlanta waxed enthusiastic: "Dalton is destined to be one of the principal industrial cities of Georgia, and that at no distant day. Already it has taken its place in the forefront of the small industrial centers of the state and is making such strides that one can very easily visualize it as a city of 25,000 within the next twenty years." Fifty years earlier, skeptics had called it Dead Dalton. Now it was the City of Smiles and Smoke-stacks.[6]

An aggressive group of local business men and women engineered Dalton's growth during the 1920s, building on a foundation laid during the late nineteenth century by Dalton's early entrepreneurs. Firmly committed to an urban-industrial ethos, this new generation of business leaders proudly carried the torch of the New South into the 1920s. Dalton's Babbitts initiated new town-building techniques. Like those before them, the business leaders of the twenties saw organization as the key to urban-industrial development, but the newcomers took organization to a higher plane by launching a plethora of business and civic clubs. The Dalton Civitan Club, organized in 1922 and dedicated to "civic progression" and business prosperity through "co-operative force," took the lead. Four years later, the Junior Chamber of Commerce organized. With an eye toward new trends in the economy, the "Jaycees" used radio to advertise Dalton and placed signs along the Dixie Highway to direct tourists to local merchants. An earlier generation of boosters had secured Dalton's place on the Dixie Highway in 1915, and business leaders of the twenties made full use of the road's potential for tourism and trade when it officially opened in 1925.

Following earlier trends, the new town builders vigorously sought outside capital investment in Dalton. During the early 1920s, textile towns throughout Dixie launched cotton-mill campaigns that rivaled in enthusiasm those of the late nineteenth century. As soon as Georgia's voters amended the state constitution in 1924 to legalize local tax exemptions for new manufacturing plants, Dalton's business leaders inaugurated an aggressive advertising scheme to lure northern capital. The people of Dalton, one publication insisted, "believe in inviting and locating new industries here. They believe in those they already have. They believe in pay rolls."[7]

By the 1920s, the idea that the South contained a limitless supply of cheap and docile labor had become an article of faith among small-town boosters seeking infusions of Yankee wealth. Dalton's business class had always been strong on this line, despite the contradictions it posed for industrialists who also claimed to be helping the local working people. In 1924 the city advertised that its 2,500 factory hands were "all American," which was intended to mean that, as sturdy "Anglo-Saxons," they would not be given to the labor unionization and agitation often associated with ethnically diverse cities of the North. In case readers missed the point, conspicuous capital letters spelled it out: "DALTON NEVER HAD A STRIKE."[8]

Crown Mill remained the hub of the local economy—the "backbone," as longtime residents called it. "If they had gone under," recalled one man, "so goes Dalton." But far from going under, Crown earned impressive profits throughout most of the 1920s. At the outset of the decade, the mill's directors assured stockholders of "the fine physical condition of the mills." Results were not disappointing. After peaking at an astonishing 67 percent in 1920, Crown's return on capital dropped to 10 percent the following year. But from 1921 through 1929, the company's returns averaged a noteworthy 38 percent. By the mid-1920s, the South had clearly replaced New England as the leading textile center of the nation, a fact that would hardly have seemed possible when Crown was founded four decades earlier. In early 1926, Crown Mills 1 and 2, together with the new Boylston-Crown Mill, employed nearly 1,000 millhands, and stockholders received a 23 percent cash dividend for that fiscal year. Beneath the gleaming surface of Dixie's textile industry, dwindling markets and rising labor costs had begun to corrode the foundation of prosperity by the mid-twenties, and many mills faced an economic downturn by the latter part of the decade. But in Dalton, where the textile economy remained generally healthy until the end of the decade, pessimists were hard to find.[9]

Crown Mill's prosperity was due in part to a new generation of managers who assumed the mantle of leadership after George W. Hamilton, Sr., and Frank T. Hardwick died. The new managerial triumvirate consisted of William K. ("Will") Moore, Jr., president from 1919 to 1935; George W. ("Little George") Hamilton, Jr., vice president, 1919–35, and president, 1935–50; and Cornelius L. ("Neil") Hamilton, treasurer, 1921–51. Unlike Mr. George and Hardwick, who had begun their business careers as merchants, the new managers spent their careers in the Crown Mill office. The sons of Dalton's earlier generation of industrial crusaders, they came of age just when Dalton was emerging as a significant New South town, and they helped engineer Crown's post–World War I boom. Young, well trained, confident, they embodied the spirit of the 1920s urban South, and their business acumen was widely recognized—as revealed by Will Moore's election as president of the Georgia Manufacturers' Association in 1934.[10]

The new managers' boldest move occurred in 1924, when they purchased the old Elk Mill and created the Boylston-Crown Mill in southeast Dalton. With an eye toward the burgeoning automobile industry, they planned to produce cotton fabrics for tires and interiors. The triumvirate also knew that many northern firms had been looking to invest in southern mills since the New England textile belt had begun its historic decline in the early 1920s. Crown therefore opted for a partnership in the new plant, going halves with J. H. Lane and Company. When they presented the plan to stockholders at the annual meeting, Crown's managers encountered some skepticism from those who disliked the idea of yoking their company with a northern firm. After all, Crown was a symbol of local and southern industrial success. But the new company officials knew how important northern contacts had been in establishing the southern textile industry. As Little

George explained, Lane had been a loyal and indispensable agent for Crown, and a partnership would be advantageous to both firms. By 1925 the Boylston-Crown plant housed 14,000 spindles.[11]

The Boylston venture built upon a strategy of expansion inaugurated decades earlier, but, in the area of labor relations, Crown's new leaders diverged significantly from the old guard. Mr. George had maintained an open-door policy in his office and spent time associating with the millhands—occasionally even eating supper with a mill-village family and visiting those who were ill. Whatever motivated such behavior, it evidently appealed to the workers. After World War I, though, personal interaction between mill officials and workers became increasingly rare. Crown's size partly accounted for this trend. Between 1915 and 1925 the company's work force had nearly doubled in size, making it more difficult for management to know all the employees personally. But equally important were the personalities of the new managers. Although Will Moore was one of the most influential industrialists in the state and was much beloved by friends and associates, the millhands who worked at Crown during the twenties and early thirties have virtually no recollection of him. When the workers interviewed for this study were asked about the Hamiltons, some responded by talking about the family of Frank Hamilton, Crown's longtime master mechanic, who was no relation to Mr. George or his sons. Such mistakes were not common, and many workers commented on the ongoing open-door policy, whereby any millhand with a problem could go to the office and see "Little George." But whereas Mr. George had earned a reputation for gregariousness, neither of his sons shared that trait. Little George was an expert with machines, and some claimed he knew what kind of thread or cloth every machine in the mill was running. Neil was a numbers man who could add several columns of figures at a glance. But both men possessed a certain shyness—perhaps an aloofness—and preferred the details of work to fraternizing with visitors or workers.[12]

During the 1920s and 1930s, the daily routine of labor relations fell primarily to Frank Springer, the man who hired Cletus Hill. The workers knew him as Mr. Springer, never as Frank. Springer moved to Dalton as a young boy with his parents and went to work as a bobbin boy for Crown in 1887. By 1900 he was a foreman and held that position for two decades until, shortly after World War I, company officials appointed him superintendent of Crown's spinning and carding departments and placed him in charge of company housing. After Boylston started production, he took charge of the entire mill as well as the company housing surrounding it. Loved and hated, respected and feared, Springer was the company representative with whom working families dealt most closely between the world wars. To most cotton millers at Crown, he *was* management, regardless of who sat in the "big office." Those whom Springer liked, he rewarded with favors. Others could find dealing with the company difficult. Disgruntled workers often swal-

Frank Springer, longtime superintendent of Crown's carding and spinning departments and director of mill-village housing, ca. 1927. "Mr. Springer" was a former millhand who had made it nearly to the top, but although some mill workers revered him, others chafed under his rule and organized a union partly to curb his authority. (*Courtesy of Crown Gardens and Archives*)

lowed their complaints, however, for the economic conditions of the interwar years did not make a return to the country very appealing. Nor was changing jobs easy, for a serious labor glut had developed.[13]

Springer was in charge of almost all of the hiring at Crown and therefore had a direct role in shaping the mill-village community. He generally hired the family and friends of people who were already firmly entrenched mill-village residents. "If you didn't have somebody pulling for you," recalled Bishop Caylor, "you didn't get a job here back then." As a result, newcomers to the mill village during the 1920s usually had connections in the community before their arrival. The Travillian family exemplified this trend. The parents and their six children lived as sharecroppers in Walker County. In the mid-1920s, two of the children, Hershel and Dorothy, left the farm and went to Crown Mill. As their younger siblings Sarah

Bunch and Anna Nell Garren recalled, the two had grown up and they "just wanted off the farm." They already had connections at Crown: "We had uncles, well, they all worked in the mill, Will Travillian and his family. And of course we lived in the country and they liked to visit us." Hershel and Dorothy stayed with their uncle in the mill village. A few years later, in 1927, the rest of the Walker County Travillians moved to the mill in "an old '22 T-Model." They did not travel alone. As the sisters remembered, their family picked up Ora Groves, a neighboring friend, who went with them to the Crown Mill village. "She lived with us for several years," Bunch recalled, "and [then] her family moved to Dalton." Similar kinship and neighbor chains ran through the mill village and bound the community together.[14]

As the Travillians' story suggests, migrants to Crown often came from farms in surrounding counties. This pattern of labor migration had been evident from Crown's earliest days (see map 1.3), and it remained essentially unchanged. As map 7.1 demonstrates, 71 percent of the applicants for jobs at Crown Mill from 1926 to 1934 had been born in Whitfield, Murray, Gilmer, and Gordon counties. Most of these people were the children of parents who had moved to Crown from the countryside in an earlier era and already worked in the mill. The connections between upcountry farms and cotton-mill villages, between farm folk and mill folk, were no less strong in the 1920s than they had been in the late nineteenth century. The labor market itself therefore enhanced the workers' sense of stability and kinship within the Crown Mill community.

Mill-village culture, therefore, was partly an import from the countryside. The interconnections between farm and factory ensured that rural traditions remained central to life at Crown. Mill workers were visited by rural friends and occasionally journeyed to the country themselves on weekends. Some households split their family labor between mill and farm. For example, the Gazzaway family of Redwine's Cove (a rural community ten miles south of Dalton) sent several children to Crown while the parents and older sons maintained the family farm. During the week, the children boarded with cousins in the mill village, only to return home on Saturday afternoons. Kinship ties among Crown's operatives were a fundamental ingredient of the workers' community. Almost every family that moved to Crown between the world wars joined kin who were already there, and marriages between millhands created more extensive kinship connections. The "family" ideal thus developed naturally out of community relationships that were, quite literally, of family. The interweaving of kinship and community was a fundamental part of life in the surrounding countryside and, given the persistence of the family labor system at Crown, proved easily adaptable to the mill environment. Continuing exchanges between farm and factory, along with the vegetable gardens, cows, and hogs that formed an integral part of the mill-village scene, gave the village a rural aura, despite the imposing factory that loomed nearby. One woman recalled, "The

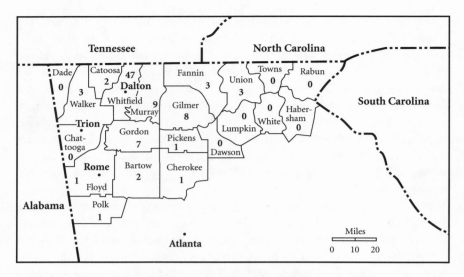

MAP 7.1. Birthplaces of Workers Applying for Jobs at Crown Mill, 1926–1934.

Source: Crown Cotton Mills Work Certificates, 1926–34, CGA.

Notes: Numbers indicate percentage of applicants (from a total of 845) born in each county. Percentages are rounded off. The total does not equal 100 because some applicants were born outside the state.

way that they operated when I was little on Jones Street, I don't think, was that much different than being on a farm."[15]

The rural tradition of cooperative welfare also played an important role in shaping the Crown Mill family. The millhands' commitment to their own families meshed with a community consciousness among village folk. Although the company helped out when necessary, most of the welfare cotton millers received came from other workers. "In the mill village . . . you were not number one," Pat Lowrance recalled. "It didn't matter if you didn't quite have enough for yourself or your family, if someone else needed it they got part of it." In the winter of 1928, Lucile Hall's entire family "got down with the flu" as soon as they moved to the mill village. When neighbors discovered "that we were sick, they were real good," said Hall. "One neighbor, Mrs. Weaver, let her son come and stay with us while we were sick to give us medicine and build us fires." When someone died, friends and kin sat up through the night with the corpse in a customary show of support for bereaved neighbors. Child care for working parents, as well as care for invalids and aging kin, were other examples of community social services provided through cooperative effort. To the mill people, this was just good neighboring, a fundamental and familiar way of life for the region's plain folk.[16]

In the mill village, as in rural settlements, the church was the heart of the community. *Church* meant more than Sunday worship, for the congregations gathered several days each week for social and religious activities, and periodic "singing conventions" and ice-cream socials drew enthusiastic crowds. The basic moral values by which all cotton millers were judged within the community issued from local pulpits and churchgoers—one reason that some workers viewed the company's policy against drinking in a positive light rather than as a manifestation of corporate coercion. The village had its share of nonbelievers and backsliders, but these people never fully escaped the gaze of the faithful, and they faced a general public consensus on proper behavior that was based on Protestant mores.[17]

The social and spiritual power of mill-village churches became manifest each summer during revival season. The rural custom of holding protracted meetings between planting and harvest times still held sway in Dalton's industrial community. Revivals attracted overflow crowds each evening, among whom were many a soul who had not polished a pew during the year. On occasion, Crown View Baptist placed loudspeakers in the windows so those who could not get in the building—or who did not want in—could hear the sermon outside. Services were enthusiastic, and the fire of the spirit sometimes inspired joyous pew jumping and hollering among the devout. Nancy Rogers fondly recalled, "I've seen times when all were shouting." Nor was such spiritual fervor confined to the church. During a particularly successful revival season, workers in the Old Mill spinning room brought their excitement to the job and struck up an impromptu meeting in the mill, shouting and leaping with abandon and causing such a commotion that superintendent Frank Springer was called in to handle the situation. A staid Presbyterian, Springer probably viewed the scene with astonishment and perhaps a certain disdain, but he was never one to squelch Christian sentiment. In any case, there was little he could have done to get those fervent millhands back to work. Prudently, he simply ordered the machines shut down until the shouting was done, after which everyone returned to their jobs.[18]

Revival preaching focused on human sinfulness and the threat of hell, on the need for repentance and God's grace. "There was much pressure to go to the mourners' bench," explained Pat Lowrance. "Church could go on all night . . . until someone was saved, . . . until someone converted." Whether through mysterious ways of the spirit or pressure from the anxious crowd, conversions often numbered in the dozens, especially when a popular preacher such as the Reverend Charlie P. Maples stood in the pulpit. Revivals climaxed in large baptismal services. Charles Kenemer, a mill-village resident from 1917 to 1933, remembered a Mr. Morgan who "always jumped the pews and shouted in the church," and who also "climbed in the tree at the baptisms and did his shouting from there."[19]

Baptisms, which were held in the large reservoir pool at Crown, reflected the importance of Christianity for the working community and pointed to a fundamental characteristic of mill-village life and the Crown Mill family. The mill

Postrevival baptism in the Crown Mill pool (city reservoir), summer 1917. The minister at the far right is Charlie Maples, a popular north Georgia evangelist billed as "the sinner's friend." (*Courtesy of Crown Gardens and Archives*)

workers' churches were autonomous; management did not pay for the buildings or hire the ministers. There was scarcely any interaction between mill churches and uptown churches, especially the Presbyterian congregation to which a large majority of Crown's managers belonged. Yet the leading church in the village was named Crown View, and the annual revival baptisms took place in the company pool, in the shadow of the mill. Those baptismal services symbolized one central difference between rural communities and the Crown Mill family: In the mill village, community life was inextricably tied to the company, even in those areas over which the millhands themselves exercised control.

So while mill-village culture incorporated many traditions of the countryside, it was something more than rural wine in industrial skins. Cotton millers thought of themselves as a family not just because the rural customs they brought to the mill encouraged a community outlook, but also because they shared experiences in their industrial environment. Where rural families resided on scattered farms, millhands lived in tightly grouped neighborhoods. Farm folk came together as a community on a seasonal basis or in times of crisis, but the cotton-mill community interacted daily, both at work and at leisure. Rural people trafficked in the market economy only a few times each year, whereas families at Crown engaged fully in the emerging consumer culture of the era. Despite the countrified appearance of the mill village, the living environment at Crown differed significantly from that in the hinterland. One major difference was living space—or rather, the lack of it at Crown. Compared with settlements in the countryside, mill families lived in much closer proximity to one another and, by necessity, came into more frequent contact.

Living in mill-village housing forced millhands to adapt to a complex bureau-cratic residential system. The mill village encompassed about one square mile of land in north Dalton and had four distinct housing sections: Pulltight Hill, Frog Town, and New Town, all east of the mill; and Westside, an area in which residents sometimes distinguished between different neighborhoods, such as Lance Street and Jones Street. There was also a smaller mill village near the Boylston plant in south Dalton. Crown continued to rent its houses cheaply—one dollar per month per room, the same amount the mill charged at the turn of the century—and as a result, there was always a waiting list of workers who wanted the next vacant house. Ed Felker, for example, waited nearly two years before getting his first mill house. Families already in a company house were often on the list as well, hoping for a better location or a more spacious dwelling. Some cotton millers moved several times within the village, and over time, compatible families tended to gravitate toward the same sections of the mill village, creating strong neighbor-hood bonds of friendship. Marselle Thompson remembered her Lance Street neighborhood, consisting of six to eight families on a rather isolated street in the far western part of the village, as "a church family," in which households visited nightly and went on weekend excursions. On Jones Street, Hugh Cheek, a popular worker in Crown's woodshop and the self-appointed children's activity director for that part of the village, became famous for hauling kids from the neighbor-hood to swimming parties and cookouts in the country. Helping neighbors was a traditional ideal, but doing so within an institutionalized housing system required some adjustments.[20]

Mill-village housing improved slightly during the twenties and thirties, when the company added electric lights and other amenities. The lights consisted of a single bulb hanging from the ceiling of each room. This in itself elevated company housing over most rural dwellings. "We had a friend in from the country one time," laughed Anna Nell Garren, "and she tried to blow out the light bulb!" (Not all residents were enamored of the change, however. One millhand recalled a woman who "was afraid of electricity. Wouldn't allow it to be put in her house even when everybody else was getting it.") There were limits to the improvements. Although the company put in electric lights, there were no electric outlets. The windows lacked screens, and there were no indoor baths. The houses were plain and were all painted white, but some residents planted flowers and shrubs, thereby lending some color and attractiveness to the village. The mill management had plans for indoor toilets drawn up in 1920 but was slow in carrying out the project. Most households continued to use the outhouses until the mid-1930s. To Gover-

Crown Mill family in front of their mill-village house. This household was one of the win-ners in a yard-beautification contest, ca. 1919. (*Courtesy of the Georgia Department of Ar-chives and History*)

nor Beasley, a man who had long done odd jobs for the mill, fell the unenviable task of cleaning the privies. "You could smell him coming," the millhands joked. That mill people so frequently told stories about their countrified cousins and universally found humor in Beasley's work indicated that living arrangements in the village helped them forge a new group identity.[21]

Among children, common educational experiences reinforced the camaraderie fostered by housing conditions and neighborhood bonds. Until the late 1930s, high school remained beyond the reach of mill-village families. "Education was not pushed then like now," Ed Felker recalled. "Now you have to have a diploma to dig a ditch." The important thing about Crown Point School, in terms of community, was that it separated the mill children from uptown children and promoted a familiarity and common outlook among the young people of Crown. The school provided a sense of generational continuity among the mill families. (This was partly because some teachers seemed ageless. Hazel Cruce, who became the princi-pal of Crown Point School, and Vera Deck both taught three generations of mill children.) Every Crown Point student knew where school would lead—to the mill.

So even as the school taught mill children the fundamentals of reading, writing, and arithmetic, it began to shape village children into cotton-mill people at an early age.[22]

But school was only part of the process whereby Crown's youth took on a distinctive social identity. Recreation also played a major role, as children banded together during leisure hours to entertain themselves. Boys and girls had little money to spend on recreation, save perhaps a movie on Saturdays, so they had to create their own fun. As Lillie Hill recalled, "We had amazing entertainment that today wouldn't be thought of as entertainment." "Peg," a universal pastime for children, was played by knocking a stick (which was stuck into the ground at an angle) into the air with a "bat" (a larger piece of wood) and then hitting the stick as far as possible before it fell to the ground. The company set up some playground equipment at the Spring Lot and near the foot of Mount Rachel on the northeastern border of New Town. In summer the children swam in the reservoir pool outside the Old Mill or at other swimming holes in and around Dalton.[23]

By the time they reached their mid-teens, mill-village children were part of a sharply demarcated youth culture within Dalton. Not only did they work in the mill together, but they spent their leisure time together as well. Every Saturday they went to town to stroll the streets or catch a "picture show" at the Crescent Theater. They "sat on the bank" (a high embankment north of the mill), watching the traffic pass on the Dixie Highway. Teenagers often spent time in gender-specific groups and drifted into conventional male-female roles. Boys often gathered at Crown's ballpark, while girls looked over new clothes at Cannon's, McLellan's, or other local department stores. Older boys might be found at the Palace Billiard Parlor. Teenage girls and boys did get together at organized gatherings such as the "singing schools," melon cuttings, and ice-cream suppers sponsored by the Baptist Young People's Union. Mill-village parents also offered a variety of activities for teens, including "Jump Joe" dances, masquerades, and Halloween parties. These events provided opportunities for courtship, thereby encouraging the tendency toward intermarriage among young people in the village. In fact, cotton-mill boys could be territorial when it came to mill girls. According to Charles Kenemer, young men from Crown called town people "muckety-mucks," and they "sure didn't like the guys from there dating our girls." Although some mill girls may have resented such attitudes, Kenemer's comment illuminates the one area in which mill boys clearly dominated the town boys: they could always intimidate the "muckety-mucks" and did not hesitate to do so. Young people from the mill village thus partook of a youth culture endemic to their industrial community, a culture that set them apart from both their rural counterparts and uptown teenagers.[24]

One of the fundamental differences between rural and mill-village life was the notion of leisure time as a measurable quantity. For farm families, work proceeded erratically, and the line between production and play blurred when it came to fishing, hunting, quilting, and berry picking. Industrial people viewed time differently. For those toiling in the mill, being "at work" was easily distinguished from being "off work." Of course, leisure time in the mill village did not necessarily mean relaxation or recreation. Millhands—adults and children alike—usually had chores to do after quitting time. And women with children, who rarely worked regularly at Crown before World War II, may have viewed their endless cycle of cooking, cleaning, sewing, and childrearing as similar to rural ways of life. But even mill-village homeworkers had their days divided by the factory whistle. Crown's manufacturing schedule determined when they had to have food on the table and when their mill-working husbands and children might be available at home to help with the chores. For most people in the village, leisure entailed a fair amount of work at home. There was nonetheless some free time for other activities, which ranged from honky-tonking to churchgoing. On weekday evenings, most adults simply "went visiting," which meant dropping in on neighbors and kin after dinner for some porch sitting and story swapping, with no particular goal but to relax and be with friends.

The notion of leisure time made weekends special occasions for cotton-mill people. Between Saturday at noon, when the work week ended, and Monday morning, when it started once again, their time was not controlled by the company. Ironically, though, many people spent their weekends engaged in what were, in effect, company-sponsored activities. This was true for those who played for, or watched, any of the Crown Mill athletic teams. And it was evident every Sunday afternoon, when families by the dozen gathered at the Crown Mill Spring Lot. With its towering shade trees, benches, and playground equipment, the Spring Lot was, as one longtime resident recalled, "a good cool place to gather . . . for courting, swinging, playing, and family gatherings." Even at ease, even on their own time, the people of Crown remained closely associated with their mill.[25]

During the 1920s and 1930s, Crown's mill officials were seldom personally involved in the lives of the millhands, but they sponsored a variety of recreational programs that promoted higher morale and personal identification with the company. Crown supported a girls' basketball team during the twenties and added a men's team during the early thirties. The mill foreman who organized the men's team recruited workers who were also talented players, and although Frank Springer frowned on this practice, he allowed it to continue, apparently believing that the millhands expected Crown to have successful teams. The company also started a women's softball team and built a tennis court at the request of some young workers. Some millhands played tennis and badminton, and for a while the company actually sponsored a tennis team.[26]

The most important company-sponsored activity was, of course, baseball, for which Crown had built a large stadium within the mill village. During the 1920s, baseball truly gained its position as a sport of the masses. The origins of baseball fervor were not necessarily industrial, for loosely organized teams flourished in rural communities throughout north Georgia and southeast Tennessee. But cotton-mill baseball built on this enthusiasm and channeled it into organized leagues that became fiercely competitive. Coach B. L. "Crook" Smith of South Georgia Teachers College in Collegeboro (a "suburb of Statesboro") took advantage of mill-village athletics to give his teams experience and to earn some money (apparently for his athletic program). In 1931, for example, he asked Neil Hamilton to schedule two baseball games with the Crown team, for which Coach Crook hoped to earn sixty dollars. "You can place us in homes as we once did," he added. A letter to Crown's baseball manager from the Tubize Chatillon Athletic Association (a worker-management organization established by the Tubize Chatillon Corporation in Rome, Georgia) suggests both the intensity and the importance of baseball in the mill villages. "Dalton is a good drawing card in Rome," wrote the Tubize baseball "commissioner" in response to Crown's suggestion for a two-game series. But he was worried about fights: "We would like to mention here that both Rome teams and Rockmart teams have had some unhappy experiences with Dalton teams in several branches of sports, though I don't believe your teams have been involved. . . . Baseball was then not very well organized. . . . But the employees here have bought season tickets to build a nice park and we would not want a recurrence of that happening." The association agreed to pay Crown's team ten dollars for expenses and added, "If the public likes the game [we] will pay you fifteen dollars . . . for later games." At Crown's home games on Saturday afternoons, fans packed the mill-village stadium, two to three hundred strong.[27]

Everyone knew that a talented ball player had a job waiting in any mill town. At Crown, as elsewhere in the textile South, such recruiting operated through informal channels and was usually kept confidential. But many of Crown's best players were homegrown, so to speak. Every spring, the team manager would post a notice calling for all interested males eighteen years and older to try out for the team. (The team manager, an old joke ran, was the guy who had enough courage to go into the big office and ask for new equipment each year.) Those who did not make the main team could play on a "second nine," which competed with other second nines in the area. It was difficult to make the first team. During the 1920s, legends grew up around Crown's famous Caldwell boys, whose proclivity for both baseball and brawling seemed limitless. The Caldwell boys hailed from a large clan, and at one point they filled nearly every starting position on the company team—hence, the famous "Caldwell Nine" of the twenties. A group of local boys who grew up watching the Caldwell Nine came of age in the 1930s and, building on a winning tradition, led Crown to the Tennessee–North Georgia Industrial League championship in 1939.[28]

Organized sport was a product of modernization, and the growth of industrial baseball leagues in the New South reflected an increasingly developed industrial society. Criticized as an agent of social control utilized by the company and praised as a sign of paternal benevolence, company-sponsored baseball had more of the workers in it than outsiders usually recognized. Still, the team uniforms sported the Crown logo, and the players competed in a company-built stadium. The baseball team was yet another indicator of how tightly interconnected the mill and its working people had become.

Another factor contributing to the development of the family ideal among mill-village residents was the workers' social isolation within Dalton. By the 1920s, cotton millers throughout the South had become a people set apart. The mill village itself fostered a type of geographic segregation. More important, though, was the condescending attitude of Dalton's uptown families toward the textile workers of their city, as revealed in one man's frank assessment of middle-class sentiment: "We wouldn't associate with mill workers and we wouldn't let our children play with their children. We hated to go into their homes, even on charity missions—they were that dirty. The people were ignorant, lazy, never paid their debts, and they used to fight a lot among themselves. At least that's what we thought."[29]

Millhands would have been highly insulted, but probably not surprised, by these troubling words. "I heard 'linthead' all my life," recalled John Bramblett, a longtime Crown employee; "as a child it didn't bother me none." When mill-village children first began to attend high school during the late 1930s, the chasm between social groups became more visible. Uptown boys in their coats and ties looked askance at overall-clad mill boys. Elite girls attended debutante functions and brandished their social rank in front of mill girls. "You resented it," remembered one mill resident; "you had to." "It made you feel like the underdog, kinda inferior," said another. Adult cotton millers faced a mixed reception from uptown people. Local judges deemed Crown's employees to be good, honest jury members, and local merchants treated the millhands with respect. But aside from professional and commercial courtesies, the line between textile workers and town people remained unbroken. Association between the two groups was minimal, and they viewed each other distantly, from different social worlds. "We considered them 'big wigs,'" recalled Marselle Thompson. "They considered us 'little wigs,' I guess."[30]

Yet even as uptown Daltonians shunned cotton millers, Crown's families also avoided other social groups they deemed undesirable. In particular, the mill people did not associate with blacks. A small African American community lived in a segregated neighborhood in Dalton, known by cotton millers simply as Negro Hollow. From the day it opened in 1885 until it shut down in 1969, Crown never employed a black person, partly because of the racial biases of the managers and partly because, had a black person been hired, the white millhands probably would have revolted, as they had in Rome and Atlanta during earlier decades. For their part, local blacks had seen too many of their own people lynched by the region's poor whites to desire any close association with the millhands. Dalton's African American community generally avoided the mill-village area altogether; as one village resident recalled, the idea of a black family living there would have been "literally unspeakable."[31]

But blacks were not the only people excluded from the mill-village community. Crown's employees also eschewed any association with poor whites they deemed "trash." The idea of "poor white trash" had a long history in Dixie, and by the 1920s the label was bestowed without much precision on a variety of poor whites. Uptown families considered cotton millers "trash," but millhands had different views. Crown's workers were fond of saying their company "didn't hire trash," and they pointed to impoverished whites in the nearby Happy Top slum (who lived alongside poor blacks) as examples of such undesirables. Just as uptown parents warned their children about the mill village, cotton-mill people told their children to stay away from Happy Top. Mill-village children were also told harrowing stories about traveling bands of "gypsies" (actually a transient group of poor whites who occasionally camped northwest of the Crown Mill village) who, they were warned, would steal children who ventured too near. Such stories were part of a larger effort among cotton millers to separate themselves from anyone considered "trash" and to define their own place in society by pointing out those who were "beneath" them on the social scale.[32] Because Dalton's affluent families excluded the "lintheads" from their social world and the cotton millers excluded blacks and "white trash" from theirs, the mill workers were set apart as a distinctive group in the city. This social isolation helped solidify the collective identity already fostered by kinship networks and the shared experiences of mill-village life.

Historians have become so enamored with the idea of "community" that they have often lost sight of its darker implications. The underside of community was coercion, for although accepted standards of conduct—imposed formally by the mill or informally by the working families themselves—helped create an orderly mill-village environment, they also squelched individual freedom. Social insulation made mill people feel at ease within the village, but it also exacerbated their racism. Indeed, it could be argued that white racist codes of behavior formed the heart of the Crown Mill community. Close-knit communities offered a sense of belonging, but they also divided society into separate, often antagonistic, groups. Moreover, because of their seclusion, cotton millers channeled most of their hostility into conflicts, not with blacks or rich whites, but with other cotton-mill workers in the village community.

The Crown Mill community was no stranger to tension, even in its heyday. Some conflicts pitted workers against managers, as in the case of layoffs or the company's mill-village regulations. But many others arose among the workers themselves. This should not be surprising given the traditions of unity and divi-

sion that characterized upcountry farming communities. In the mill village, disputes among the working families were disruptive, to be sure, but they did not
necessarily connote the absence of community feeling. Conflicts were still defined
by the corporate culture and resolved within it. They helped create status distinctions and offered various groups within the village the chance to feel superior over
the others. Under normal circumstances, mill-village disputes did not threaten the
"family" system, but throughout the 1920s, foreboding tensions occasionally surfaced between workers and managers and among the workers themselves.

One of the latter tensions, reflecting new divisions among Christian workers,
was manifested in the rise of Holiness churches in the 1920s. Organized during the
late nineteenth century in the Tennessee counties just north of Whitfield, the
Church of God embraced the Pentecostal movement during an explosive revival in
1908 and began to spread through lower Appalachia and the southern Piedmont.
With its emphasis on the literal interpretation of Scripture, its rejection of worldly
affairs, and its mission to restore the first-century church, this Holiness-Pentecostal
movement explicitly sought to reaffirm the "old-time religion" of rural Protestantism. But by celebrating the gifts of speaking in tongues and spiritual healing, the
Church of God opened new avenues of faith for poor whites in the southern
upcountry. Perhaps this blend of tradition and innovation made the Church of God
especially appealing to millhands who were holding tenaciously to rural norms
while struggling to work out their salvation in a new industrial environment.[33]

Holiness religion was, in any case, an outright rejection of the mainline Baptist
and Methodist churches. During the 1920s and 1930s, the Church of God became a
significant denomination among Dalton's working families. Three small congregations were organized in the early twenties, and, not surprisingly, one of these was
on Pulltight Hill. All of the new churches survived, and by the mid-1930s a fourth
Church of God was established in town. Most likely these churches were filled
entirely with millhands. It is impossible to know precisely why certain cotton
millers left the mainline mill-village churches for Holiness congregations, or even
how many did so, but a growing minority found fulfillment in congregations the
townspeople condescendingly called Holy Rollers. Perhaps these economically
impoverished spiritual seekers found, as historian Robert Mapes Anderson has
written, that "in the unrestrained atmosphere of Pentecostal worship, the distinctions and prejudices encountered in the larger culture were often swept away,
giving birth to a new sense of community and a new sense of status." Whatever
Holiness churches meant to the millhands who took comfort in them, the Church
of God was a significant new institution in the workers' world. The most important of Dalton's Holiness congregations was the Church of God of the Union
Assembly, which embraced powerful notions of collective social justice and which
would play a major role in Dalton's future labor disputes.[34]

The Crown community demanded a certain adherence to behavioral norms. Company regulations against drinking, as well as the workers' own values, created an environment of enforced conformity in the mill village. Problems arose when different groups of workers disagreed as to what the proper behavioral norms should be. Mill-village churches, the hub of moral values among the working families, demanded chastity for singles, fidelity for married couples, and sobriety for all. By no means did all mill people accept these norms or even pretend to live up to them, but everyone fell under the purview of these basic guidelines regardless of whether they ever darkened the church door. Various cultural issues nonetheless remained open for debate: whether it was sinful to dance or go to movies; whether it was acceptable to drink "not unto drunkenness" or for medicinal purposes; whether it was better to be Missionary Baptist, Hard-Shell Baptist, or Holiness; and whether the company should try to enforce rules on the mill-village residents.[35]

Conflicts among the mill workers were often similar to disputes in rural settlements. Cleanliness, for example, proved a divisive issue in the mill village. In the countryside, one Blue Ridge woman recalled, "one of the ways that people judged if you were 'good people' was how well you kept your yard." The same held true among Crown's more fastidious families, who viewed cleanliness (not merely of yard, but of home and children as well) as a manifestation of sturdy moral fiber. When one mill-village mother abandoned her children, everyone was indignant, but some women showed no surprise; after all, they said, that woman "never cleaned." Housewives who did not clean constantly were outcasts in many mill circles. They "could only bake and have babies," the local insult went. But there was more at stake here than simply the adherence to traditional values and behaviors. In the mill village, with its concentrated population and its undercurrent of economic competition, conflicts among neighbors took on a special urgency. No wonder disputes flared when Crown began to sponsor yard-beautification contests after World War I. Women who paid strict attention to sweeping their yards and took pains to plant flower gardens and shrubs usually won. After a select group of women took the prizes several years in a row, bitterness against them and the judges forced the mill to abandon the annual contest altogether.[36]

Tensions were inherent in mill-village paternalism because the system engendered competition within the community for the elevated status that came with a yard-beautification award, a place on the baseball team, a bigger and better mill house. In a larger, more important sense, there was competition for economic security, for better jobs and job stability. But at the same time, corporate paternalism helped to create a system of shared benefits and values. And because kinship ties within the village were strengthened by traditional rural norms, competitive tensions were usually circumscribed by the community ideal. Within limits, social conflict actually served an important function in fostering notions of "family." It helped households define their place in the industrial environment and offered a means by which they could demonstrate their allegiance to the corporate community. Most of all, it indicated that cotton millers considered the company-owned village their home, and that they were intent on working within it to build meaningful lives for themselves and their children.

8

MAKIN' DO: SURVIVAL

ON COTTON-MILL TIME

Cotton-mill people shared a common economic outlook. Some families were better off than others, but
virtually all households were involved in a similar
struggle to earn a living. To make ends meet, Crown's
families combined mill work with home production
and petty-cash jobs. They called this "makin' do"—
getting by on what little they had. Makin' do involved
hard work, stern frugality, and ingenuity. Most of all,
it demanded the resourceful use of family labor. Individuals sacrificed themselves for family, and each
family made a further commitment to the economic
welfare of the larger community of cotton millers.
Because commitments to kin and community were a
familiar part of plain-folk culture, the millhands had
a familiar cultural foothold as they confronted the
hardships and challenges of industrial life. But survival on cotton-mill time was not quite the same as
making a living on the farm. Makin' do may have
reinforced traditional customs of mutuality, but it
also encouraged among the millhands a modern consumer culture that deepened their economic dependence. The strategies of household survival that de-

manded allegiance to the company as well as to kin and community strengthened the bonds of the Crown Mill family even as they set the stage for conflict.[1]

The most basic rule of makin' do was that families sent as many members as possible to work in the mill. The family labor system remained central to southern textiles after World War I, and historians have noted that, in general, mill parents opposed child labor laws. Most parents relied heavily on the wages of their off-spring, and as a result children left school for the mill as soon as possible. Even young people who wished to continue their education gave up their books for spindles, because the exigencies of poverty demanded personal sacrifices for the sake of kin. Lillie Hill, for example, had to leave school before she wanted to because her brother fell ill, and the family needed her wages to compensate. Henry Wade recalled how important it was that he and his siblings "had four checks coming in" to support the family—especially because the household consisted of a widow and her nine children. In the countryside, parents had always viewed children as a natural and necessary labor force, and mill-village parents saw things no differently.[2]

Ironically, although households still needed the wages of their children, southern mill managers had grown steadily less reliant on child labor. In the decade before 1920, the number of children under age sixteen working in Georgia's manufacturing plants had fallen 50 percent (from 8,771 to 4,384). This trend resulted partly from Georgia's 1914 child labor law and from compulsory education legislation passed in 1916 and 1919. But these laws were largely ineffectual, as they offered numerous loopholes and virtually no means for enforcement. The decline in child labor resulted more from a growing surplus of older textile workers in the mill villages of the South. After 1920 this trend continued, in part because Georgia's industrialists feared that a strong federal child labor law or Constitutional amendment might soon be passed. By supporting a state child labor law, industrialists could deflect criticism from the press and stave off federal action. They could also reduce pressure from mill-village parents who sought employment for their children even though the mills already had a labor pool brimming with well-trained adult workers. In the mid-1920s the Georgia Manufacturers' Association, after years of battling child labor laws, suddenly did an about-face and joined concerned social groups and political leaders in support of more effective legislation. Georgia's child labor law of 1925 stipulated that no one below the age of fourteen and a half could work in manufacturing, and it created a system of certificates by which to verify the ages of young applicants.[3]

The figures presented in table 8.1 offer another explanation of why mill officials supported a state-level child labor law and why parents might have opposed it. Wages for all millhands at Crown peaked during 1920 but then quickly fell 35 to 40 percent by the following year. Not surprisingly, wages for teenagers were less than

Working girls on the job in the spooling room, 1927. (*Courtesy of Crown Gardens and Archives*)

those for adults both before and after these postwar wage cuts. But in 1923 children's wages suddenly shot upward dramatically. Instead of bringing home half of what adult workers earned, children less than sixteen years old could suddenly command almost the same wages as older millhands. This shift is difficult to explain, but it may have been related to the advent of night work, for which children were used extensively. Night work itself resulted from a glut of family labor in southern cotton-mill villages and from cutthroat competition among mills. In any event, if Crown's wage increase for children in 1923 reflected a widespread pattern among Georgia's mills, it helps explain the owners' support of the state child labor law. Once child labor was no longer substantially cheaper than adult labor, it made economic sense that industrialists would advocate new legislation and that working families would oppose it. Parents' continued reliance on family labor is revealed in the child labor certificates kept by Crown Mill from 1926 to 1934, which show that virtually all young applicants began working for Crown exactly six months after their fourteenth birthdays—as soon as they could legally engage in factory work.[4]

For those who did not already live in the mill village, getting hired was often a difficult job in itself. During the late 1920s and the 1930s, Crown had little need to hire new workers, because it had plenty of "spare hands" in the village. Whether a person was employed at Crown normally rested in the hands of Frank Springer, and after World War I he could afford to be selective about whom he hired.

TABLE 8.1. Crown Mill Wages, by Age and Gender, 1920–1923

	Average Weekly Wage for Children		Average Weekly Wage for Adults	
	Female	Male	Female	Male
1920	12.00	12.00	22.40	24.00
1921	7.50	7.50	14.00	15.00
1922	7.75	7.75	14.00	15.00
1923	14.00	15.00	15.00	17.00

Source: Georgia Department of Commerce and Labor, "Statements of Labor Conditions, Crown Cotton Mills," 1921–23, copies at CGA.

Notes: "Children" were any workers under seventeen years of age. No reports from other years were located in company records. Figures represent "nominal" earnings.

Figures for 1920 are estimates based on [Crown Cotton Mills] to Munds, Rogers, and Stackpole, 23 Jan. 1922, MDB, which states that "wages have been cut from 35 to 40 percent" from 1920 to 1921. All estimates are based on a 37.5 percent cut.

Springer screened applicants carefully. "I'll tell you one thing about him," recalled John Bramblett. "You had to see him ten times before he'd give you a job." Long-time employee Ed Felker understood that Crown "usually kept a pretty good supply of qualified people" among the families that occupied mill houses. Springer could send for or lay off these excess workers as the situation demanded, thereby reducing the need for new hands.[5]

Parents who lived in mill housing did not have to lobby for their children; Springer hired them as soon as they came of age. This guarantee of employment— at least as spare hands—was one of the main incentives for mill-worker stability. For village children, going to work in the mill was, according to Marselle Thompson, the "natural thing to do." Some children made a gradual transition to work. Those who "hauled dinners" to adults in the mill at noon often tended machines while the millhands ate, and some, from either their own sense of adventure or their parents' demands, learned to tend frames by working free of charge before they reached the legal age. But for many the mill was an entirely new experience, and the huge, thundering, lint-filled building elicited responses ranging from wide-eyed ecstasy to outright terror. But however the children responded to their first day in the factory, stepping into the mill meant crossing a major threshold in their lives. Crown was not the only employer in town, but other opportunities were limited, and because children were expected to quit school and go to work as soon as possible, few mill children seriously considered alternative employment. The notion of "one big family" stemmed partly from the most basic reality of the industrial system—the hiring process.[6]

Opportunities at Crown depended largely on an employee's age and gender.

Workers from the spinning and twisting department of Boylston-Crown Mill, 1927. (*Courtesy of the Georgia Department of Archives and History*)

Distinctions were evident even during job training. Young boys were first employed as bobbin boys or sweepers. Adult males were trained in a higher position, such as battery filler in the weaving department. Girls and young women learned mill work in groups, and they all learned the same basic skill of spinning. Under the guidance of an older woman, five to ten girls would undergo a period of on-the-job training, during which they would be paid "learners' wages" for about six weeks or however long it took them to be able to handle a full job. That males learned mill work as individuals while females learned in groups symbolized the different opportunities for upward mobility and higher wages in the mill. Young men with energy and mechanical aptitude could rise to the position of loom fixer, perhaps even to lower-level management. But no matter how adept a female hand was, she had no chance of ever rising above the level of a rank-and-file operative.[7]

Through the first half of the twentieth century, all of Crown's lower-level managers (foremen and supervisors) were recruited from within the company's work force. In this way, Crown's upper-level mill officials created examples of upward mobility that encouraged the millhands' loyalty to the company. By the 1920s, several men had risen from bobbin boys to supervisory personnel. Frank Springer was the most obvious example; Samuel Hardin was another. Born into a poor family in 1896, Hardin was the seventh of eight children. By 1900 four of his older siblings (aged eleven to seventeen) worked for Crown, and the family lived in a company house. A decade later, the four children who had first gone to work in the mill had moved out on their own, but Sam and two other brothers still lived at home and had taken on wage-earning jobs. Hardin began working as a doffer at Crown in his early teens, just like countless other mill-village boys. But the supervisors must have seen something in him they liked, for they began to groom him for a position of authority. When still a young man, he was instrumental in founding the Crown Mill Band in the late 1910s. During the 1920s, he became supervisor of the spinning department and ultimately purchased his own home not far from the mill village. His children only worked at the mill during summers and were part of the first generation of Crown children to attend high school. Hardin's rise from rags to respectability served as a reminder that Crown offered some men a chance for advancement.[8]

Not every man wanted to be a supervisor. Many considered the best position in the mill to be that of fixer, because fixers gained higher status and earned better pay than ordinary millhands while avoiding the pressures of being a boss. A fixer "didn't have all the headaches of a supervisor," recalled Ed Felker, who had worked as both. "Supervisor—that's a hard life. He's got everybody's problems plus his own." On paper the step from fixer to overseer was just a simple change of category, but in reality it was a jump "into a whole different world." Unlike a fixer, a supervisor could not just work with his tools and go home at the end of his shift. "It was an awful responsibility," said Felker. "You took the pressure home with you. You're representing millions of dollars worth of those people's money." Other men voiced similar concerns over supervisory positions. Some even refused offers to become supervisors, demonstrating that attitudes toward work and upward mobility in the mill-village community involved complex considerations that were not necessarily compatible with uptown notions about "getting ahead."[9]

Women never faced the dilemmas of promotion, because management denied them any chance for advancement regardless of their age, experience, or skill. The process of weeding adult women out of the weave shop and off the full-time payroll, begun earlier in the century, continued after 1920. Hundreds of women still worked in the mill, but none of them could ever expect to become a fixer, much less a supervisor. This situation prevailed in southern cotton mills despite the contributions of female workers to the success of the industry in the region. In 1921 an agent for the Women's Bureau of the U.S. Department of Labor surveyed a mill in South Carolina and noted, "All the supervisory positions are held by men, Why Not Some Women?" Whether or not women at Crown were asking the same question, they clearly faced a different occupational reality than men.[10]

But to discuss issues of opportunity, advancement, and mobility is to distort the meaning of mill work as the workers themselves viewed it. Mill work was essen-

Weave room workers from Mill No. 2, 1927. Note the preponderance of adult men in this department. (*Courtesy of the Georgia Department of Archives and History*)

tially a *family* endeavor, not a means of individual advancement. Once a household put down stakes in the mill village, once the farms had lost their attraction, family survival very likely required mill jobs for life. Makin' do therefore involved a fundamental dependence on steady wages from the company. A family had to have these wages, and there was pressure on everyone to work. Illness and injury could spell disaster for the family economy. The psychological pressures of being poor wage earners must have been almost crippling at times. No wonder some cotton millers nearly drank themselves to death. No wonder their families maintained a communal mentality, insisted on family unity, and tended to think in terms of economic stability rather than upward mobility. For those who wanted out, who wanted to "get ahead" in the classic middle-class sense of the phrase, a community focused on simply holding the line could be stifling. Others found such an environment comforting. For everyone, though, it was difficult enough just to make a living.

Labor at Crown also involved dangers that rural work did not. Conditions inside the mill were unhealthy, to say the least. The noise was "deafening, just deafening . . . and the lint was just flying everywhere," recalled one woman. "It was almost like eating cotton," said another. Conscientious workers constantly cleaned the lint from their frames, but they could not keep it from covering their bodies. "We'd just be white-headed" after work, Nancy Rogers remembered. The lint that covered both machines and people also settled unseen into the workers' lungs and created serious, sometimes fatal, health problems for many. In addition to the lint that hung in the air like a great fog, incessant noise from the machines slowly destroyed the workers' hearing and made them inclined to speak loudly, even outside the factory. Longtime employee Charles Kenemer pointed out also that "it was hot. When the afternoon sun hit the windows, you would almost die. It was a time of no breaks. There were no seats to sit down on. When you got caught up on one frame, you just had to go to another."[11]

Not all family members showed equal dedication to the household income and the factory system. One worker from a firmly entrenched Crown family recalled that his brother was hired and fired by the company four different times during the twenties and thirties because he never could learn to take orders. Henry Wade disliked his job because "they laid it on." He reasoned that "if I'd been management, I'd have seen different," but instead he thought "it was slave labor back then." J. W. Crow's brother had a stable position in the weave shop but was discontented. One day during a break he went outside for a smoke and had a "revelation that he was wasting his life" in the cotton mill. Rather than return to work, he walked to the Dixie Highway, thumbed a ride to Texas, and never returned. More often, dissatisfied hands worked out their futures without completely abandoning the mill. If they wanted to switch jobs when there were no alternative openings at Crown, workers sometimes left Dalton temporarily and went to work for other mills in Chattanooga, Tennessee, or LaFayette, Georgia, fully intending to return to Crown when a position opened in their preferred department.[12]

For every worker who dreaded entering the mill, there was a millhand who genuinely enjoyed factory work. A good example was Willie Mae Defore, who "always enjoyed working" for Crown and insisted that, were the mill still running, "I'd still be there today." Thelma Parker also thrived on work. She was "eager to make money" and went to work for Crown as soon as possible. In time, she came to view the spinning frames she worked on as her own, and she took pride in keeping them clean and running smoothly. "I worked to please the company," she recalled. "I kept my job up." The friendships formed in the mill made work more meaningful for some. Nancy Rogers recalled that "I loved my work at the mill. So many precious memories." She enjoyed working with bosses who were "good Christian men," and she worked to the best of her ability because "I wanted my company to prosper."[13]

Whatever their disposition toward mill work, all workers eagerly looked forward to payday. Before World War II, Crown always paid every two weeks, in cash or, beginning in the fall of 1930, with checks. Payday was a revelation for recent arrivals from the countryside. Poor farmers had only one or two paydays per year, if they made anything at all. On her first payday at Crown, Nancy Rogers made sixteen dollars, which, she recalled, was the "most money I [had] ever handled. . . . I don't remember seeing a dollar bill before." Especially for young girls, who were the least likely to share in any ready cash on the farm, mill wages encouraged a new commercial outlook. Willie Mae Defore still remembers her first payday and the clothes she immediately bought that Saturday. It was also a tradition for mill girls who had just earned their first factory wages to buy a dress and shoes for their younger sisters, who could not otherwise afford them. Payday became a ritual in mill-village life. Every Saturday about noon, the "Gold Dust Twins" would arrive in a truck, carrying the small manila envelopes in which a few dollars and some change waited for each worker. The Gold Dust boys were Charlie and Berry Woods, whose father ran a store in the village. Armed with shotguns and loaded with money, they drove two miles from Hardwick Bank to Crown, where they distributed the envelopes. That afternoon much of the money went into family coffers, from which it found its way to the local grocers who granted credit to workers between paydays. Some money went into Crown Mill savings accounts, and a little jingled in pockets and purses on the way uptown for picture shows, popcorn, and pool games.[14]

But payday was a double-edged sword. The excitement it brought could not disguise the fact that earnings were pitifully low. "I don't recall any person getting rich off their wages," said Pat Lowrance, in an understatement. "Better than nothing," shrugged Henry Wade. A few supervisors earned comparatively good money, but most mill families lived on the margins of subsistence. Although real wages for southern millhands remained higher than before World War I (see table 5.5), it is misleading to think that workers made a comfortable living. In 1927, when Crown's millhands were averaging $14.99 per week, the national average for industrial production workers was $24.47 per week. Mill people at Crown, as John Bramblett put it, lived "week to week, payday to payday." Marselle Thompson recalled that her father simply handed over his unopened pay envelope to the local grocer each payday. The coming of the Gold Dust Twins every other Saturday thus embodied both the stability and the deep anxiety that characterized mill-village life.[15]

Children normally gave their wages to their parents, a common practice among working families throughout the nation before World War II. Willie Mae Defore always gave a major portion of her earnings to her parents, though she was allowed to keep some for her own use. Sibyl Queen proudly handed her pay envelope to her mother and chastised a fellow worker who would not do the same. Children had always labored long and hard on family farms, but that their wages were so fundamental to family survival made their efforts much more important for mill-village households. This dependence on the earning power of adolescents created the potential of increasingly strained relations between parents and children, but there is surprisingly little evidence that many households experienced such crises. Apparently, the conviction that makin' do was a family affair was firmly implanted early in a mill child's life.[16]

Children too young to work for Crown could earn petty cash in several ways. Girls baby-sat, and boys shagged foul balls for small change at the Crown baseball diamond. More commonly, children made money by "hauling dinners" to the mill at noontime. Before the advent of the eight-hour day, many hands had their meals brought to them by village children, usually kin and neighbors. The standard fee was a quarter per week. Haulers often brought several dinners at once, which meant that a child who hauled meals to three workers could make seventy-five cents per week. Some of this pocket change went toward a picture show on Saturday afternoon, but that should not obscure its importance in lightening the pressure on the family economy. Mill-village parents expected their children to do this type of work, just as rural parents expected their children to pick peas or "scrap" cotton for a bit of extra cash. Children's economic responsibility was taken seriously. "I charged some candy to my daddy [at Rackley's store] one time," one millhand recalled, "and my daddy liked to have beat the devil out of me." Petty cash was significant to working families, and parents demanded that their children help stretch scarce resources even before they became millhands.[17]

For mill-village adults, Crown Mill did not offer the only means of earning wages. The managers wanted as many millhands as possible in each company house, and it was generally understood that a family living in company housing should supply one worker per room, but there was no official rule demanding that a family maintain a certain number of millhands per house. Nor was it against company policy for village residents to be employed elsewhere. Some children of legal working age took jobs in other local textile factories, lumber companies, or the bedspread industry. Some fathers and sons continued to work as laborers on farms outside the city, even though they lived in the Crown village. In fact, one mill-village father worked as a tenant farmer for Crown, which contracted with him to grow cotton on some open acreage north of the mill. A few young women worked in Dalton's dime stores, and some young men found employment as truck drivers. Simply being in the village offered one way of earning nonmill income, for there were always workers who needed room and board before a house became available for them. Widows were especially hospitable to boarders, who helped pay the rent and provided extra income. Pat Lowrance's grandmother traded furniture pieces for profit and "made money selling her dahlias . . . to local florists."[18]

The most important form of nonmill wage work in the village was the production of hand-tufted "chenille" bedspreads. The bedspread industry was the most important economic development in north Georgia during the interwar decades, and as it evolved after World War II, it came to have an enormous impact on the mill-village community and the economics of working-class life in Dalton. It was middle-class women—unlikely entrepreneurs in a small southern town—who transformed the tufted textile industry from a local hobby into a thriving national business. Around the turn of the century, Catherine Evans, a young farm girl from Whitfield County, revived the lost art of making candlewick bedspreads. Her tufted spreads became the envy of the local community, and she sold her first one for $2.50 in 1900. Eventually orders for Evans's chenilles exceeded her capacity to produce them. She trained some nearby farm women to tuft, and thus was born a cottage industry in which Evans supplied the materials and paid the tufters a certain amount for every spread they produced. The idea caught on remarkably fast among middle-class women in and around Dalton, and by the 1920s a growing industry had spread throughout northwest Georgia.[19]

There were few female industrialists in north Georgia before the 1920s, but bedspread manufacturing began to change that. In Gertrude Manly Jones's day, female boosterism had consisted of writing prodevelopment poems for local papers and working hard to enhance the cultural amenities of the town in order to lure wealthy investors. In contrast, the bedspread makers were marketwise entrepreneurs. Regardless of whether it was intended for them, the New South message of capital investment and profit, of industry and local uplift, had been ringing in the ears of middle-class town women for over a generation. Now it stirred them to action despite enduring cultural taboos. Tufted spreads originated as a product for local markets and then grew to include the tourist trade fostered by the Dixie Highway. But Dalton's newest entrepreneurs had a larger vision, and they were soon doing business with leading department stores in Atlanta and New York. "Cabin craft" bedspreads from north Georgia unexpectedly became the rage among elites in northern cities and even some places in Europe. Suddenly chenilles meant big money, and Dalton's male professionals and entrepreneurs, having scoffed at the idea that women could be successful in business, now scrambled to get into the market, in some cases taking over their wives' burgeoning enterprises.

As orders from outside merchants poured in, Dalton's bedspread entrepreneurs extended the scope of their businesses. They built centralized "spread houses," from which raw materials were sent to tufters and finished products were shipped. The materials consisted of white sheeting, purchased from local mills, and heavy thread (originally all white, later in colors). The sheeting was marked with the desired pattern before it left the spread house. Low overhead was central to the operation. Spreads were marked by rubbing a piece of hog fat over an inverted pie pan that had the design punched into the bottom. To reach an ever larger labor force, spread houses hired "haulers" who drove into the countryside each week to deliver new materials and collect the completed spreads. Alternatively, a spread house might hire one woman within a rural community to "run a line"—that is, to act as a go-between for the company. Under such an arrangement, the woman would receive material for between twenty-five and fifty spreads, some of which her family tufted but most of which she distributed to other families.

Crown's mill-village families took in tufting work to earn extra cash. Virtually every household at Crown worked spreads, and all family members took part. Married women and young children did most of the spread work, which was "put out" to families from nearby spread houses. A better-paying job, one to which mill women increasingly turned, was that of sewing "fringing" (a decorative border) for the bedspreads. The chenille boom seemed to be a curiously belated cabin-craft revolution within a region already dedicated to the factory system, but the irony mattered little to the people at Crown. For hard-pressed mill families, tufting was just another means of makin' do.[20]

The mill-family economy involved more than wage labor, of course. House-wives, even if they never earned a dime tufting spreads, were critical to family subsistence, their contributions far outweighing those of children. Without their efforts, makin' do would have been an impossibility. At the most basic level, the family labor system required reproduction; childbirth and childrearing were therefore fundamental to mill-village survival. Mothers also acted as home man-agers who shouldered the burden of putting food on the table and clothes on backs with the meager resources brought in by the family's other wage earners. "Keeping house" involved a constant round of chores that included, at the very least, cook-ing, cleaning, washing, ironing, sewing, ordering food from the grocery, and caring for children. Lucile Hall offered the reminder, "The women always worked. They worked alright, sometimes harder than the men." The few married women who worked in the mill during the 1920s also had to do their housework after they got home. It was a lot of labor not to get paid for.[21]

Mill-village gardens and home production provided indispensable resources for makin' do. Homegrown vegetables made up a large part of the mill-family diet and helped offset low earnings. Women spent a good deal of time sweating over summer stoves, canning fruits and vegetables for future consumption. Family roles in working the gardens were flexible. Some housewives took full respon-sibility for their gardens from sowing to harvesting. In contrast, Marselle Thomp-son's mother did not work in the garden because her husband believed she toiled hard enough as it was. He did most of the work himself, with the help of his children. Often he would rise at 4:00 A.M. to put in two hours of gardening before going to the mill. More typically, all family members shared responsibility for the gardens, which were as necessary to the livelihood of Dalton's industrial workers as they were to the farm folk of Whitfield County. Home production patterns were evident in other areas as well. Each year the mill workers received several days off for the Fourth of July. During this unpaid vacation, women and children often picked berries in Loner Field north of town. Enduring the chiggers, they reveled in a social event akin to a corn shucking or apple peeling as they gathered enough fruit for nearly a year's worth of preserves. Homespun cloth by this time was nonexistent, but women sewed many of their own dresses from store-bought cloth, and when poverty demanded cheaper material, they made do by purchasing flour in large cotton sacks and subsequently bleaching the coarse material for use in making shirts and blouses. This creative use of store-bought goods revealed the persistence of a self-sufficiency mentality among southern cotton millers, a way of thinking born in the countryside and reinforced by mill-village poverty.[22]

The raising of livestock for consumption was another aspect of the rural economy that endured in the mill village. In several areas throughout the village, company-owned stock pens corralled the hogs and cows belonging to Crown's mill families, enabling many workers to have an adequate supply of pork and, less frequently, milk. Before World War I, some mill families kept livestock under their houses, which were perched on brick pillars. Hugh Cheek had been in the meat-selling business before coming to Crown from a Murray County farm, and he continued to raise both pork and beef for the local market while working in the mill's woodworking shop. Some families who raised hogs hired someone else to "salt down" their pork, giving millhands with butchering skills another way of earning extra cash. Fewer people had milk cows, but those who did supported an informal milk market among mill-village residents. From mill work to milking cows, from hauling dinners to household production, work in all its various forms was geared toward providing at least a subsistence living for one's family. But makin' do was more than an individual family enterprise.[23]

The mill village ensured that the ethic of family survival was extended to the entire community of cotton millers. Although cotton-mill people primarily acted from a need for family security, they also recognized that individual household stability required a general commitment to community welfare. Notions of mutual assistance among cotton millers had deep roots in rural traditions of interdependence, and the millhands adapted these traditional economic customs to the industrial environment. The ethic of community welfare was pervasive. It helped alleviate the suffering of hard-pressed mill families and served to spread around what little wealth there was. "Poundings" for newlyweds and ice-cream suppers for neighborhood children represented the more lighthearted manifestations of this ethic, but more serious considerations drew more significant responses. When an adult worker fell ill for an extended period, the family's economic situation quickly grew critical. In these instances, Crown's millhands invoked rural traditions of community aid. If a worker "had to be out sick or anything," recalled one resident, "then the department they worked in, when payday came, everybody put in a quarter. So the one that was out sick, you know, had about as much as they would have if they had worked." Sarah Bunch recounted the example of a man who had tuberculosis and also had five young daughters to feed. "And you know they took up for him every week until he got over it and got back to work."[24]

Hugh Cheek embodied the best aspects of the community ethic. As a leading worker in the woodshop, a skilled butcher, and the father of several children who worked in the mill, he was better off than most. But he "never lost sight of a common bond with his neighborhood," recalled Pat Lowrance. "During the '30s, when folding money was in short supply, Mr. Cheek seemed to carry an endless supply of two one-dollar bills neatly folded together. He passed them along to those in need. They were slipped into the hand of an elderly, sick person or unemployed father; a young mother-to-be or to anyone who needed food or fire wood. He was known to leave as quickly as he came—never waiting for an expression of thanks." Cheek also gave away meat he cured during "hog-killing time." Not all mill workers were so committed to good neighboring, yet the overwhelming impression of mill-village life during the 1920s and 1930s is one of a people dedicated to upholding the economic welfare of both family and community. "It may not sound as if we were a much monied people but money is only worth its weight in charity," Lowrance wrote. "That being the case, we were the last of the big spenders."[25]

Makin' do not only shaped the way cotton millers worked and the way they related to other people in the community, it also altered the way they spent their money. Although there were exceptions, few mill families built up substantial savings in the years before World War II. Because many families were constantly in debt or needed help to make it until the next payday, purchasing both necessities and luxuries usually entailed buying "on time," that is, on credit. In some ways, the millhands' dependence on credit paralleled that of north Georgia's poor farmers, who were bound by a web of credit and debt to merchants and landlords. Other similarities with the rural consumer economy included the presence of peddlers who sold or traded goods in both the countryside and the mill village. But in the countryside, such commercial transactions occurred only several times a year; in the mill village they were a part of daily life. Cotton millers became much more consumer-oriented than farm folk, and mill-village survival entailed new retail strategies.

Obtaining food for the family was the first priority, and this task involved complex interactions with mill-village grocers. Money was scarce, but credit for food was easy to find. By the 1920s, the Crown company store had long since ceased to function as a village commissary; it merely served as a retail outlet for mill-made cloth and thread. Privately run general stores were scattered about the village, and the mill families knew the owners well. "Old man Cox" had a store in Frog Town, and Tom Pierce ran one just outside the village on North Hamilton Street. Many Boylston residents bought at Albertson's. Not merely retail outlets, these mill-village stores and their owners became a central part of the cotton millers' lives and their emerging consumer culture. Local stores were both a blessing and a curse for the millhands. Because workers were only paid every other week, and because the company paid them so little, they usually had to get an advance from the nearby grocer until payday. Getting an advance was easy, but paying it back was often problematic, as any unexpected expense made repaying the grocer impossible. Thus many millhands found themselves constantly in debt, often to more than one grocer. This situation made millhands easy prey for loan sharks, who pulled workers out of the frying pan through quick loans, only to toss them into the fire by charging extremely high interest rates. Workers could also get limited cash advances from the company, but as this money was taken out of the next paycheck, it often left the millhand deeper in the same cycle of debt.[26]

From another perspective, though, grocers provided housewives with exceptional service. The stores sent order boys around to their regular customers each morning, and deliveries were made that afternoon. There were few choices and no bargains, but for hard-working women the convenience was very helpful. Ice for the icebox was also delivered to the door; customers flipped color-coded cards that hung on nails in front of their houses to signal the delivery truck if they needed a new ice block. The commercialization of family food services advanced over the years, despite the continued reliance on home production. Eventually housewives could obtain everything necessary for a complete holiday dinner simply by ordering a "Thanksgiving dinner" or "Christmas dinner" package from the local grocer. Their grandmothers in the countryside might have frowned, but mill women were marching steadily into the age of consumerism. Most orders were inexpensive and mundane. Mill-village diets remained limited largely to fatback pork, beans, and cornbread, with an occasional chicken or dessert. But families did not have to be extravagant to be dedicated consumers.[27]

Grocery stores were not the only places where one could buy "on time." Department stores were gaining prominence with Dalton's consumers, millhands included. By the mid-1920s, the working families of Crown, Boylston, American Thread, and the Real Silk Hosiery Mill represented the nucleus of buying power in Dalton, which was one reason local department stores eagerly extended credit to them. Buying on credit became a way of life for southern cotton-mill people. Women could even get perms that way at the beauty parlor. Mill-village children learned the system and its pitfalls early—sometimes the hard way, as illustrated in a story told by Thelma Parker. When she was a young girl, Thelma and her sister asked their father, Hugh Cheek, for new swimsuits. When he refused, they went to town anyway and charged two suits to his account. The department store owner knew Hugh and sent him word of the purchase. Cheek told his daughters they could keep the suits, but they would have to pay for them in installments—one quarter per week. Thelma embarked on a series of baby-sitting and dinner-hauling jobs until she finally paid off her debt. When the last quarter crossed the counter, the store owner unexpectedly returned the entire five dollars she had dutifully paid. Secretly, her father had already paid the bill in full, but, as he later explained to the girls, he wanted them to experience firsthand the difficulties of buying on time.[28]

The most substantial—and risky—purchase to make on time was an automobile. Before World War II, few millhands owned cars. An automobile was a major status symbol in the village, but more important than that, in a closely knit community one automobile could provide transportation for a large number of people. The 1920s saw the beginnings of commuter mill workers who lived in the country surrounding Dalton, traveled to Crown every morning in carpools, and returned home each evening. Cars also generated greater personal freedom, especially for young people eager to escape mill-village surveillance. Weekend trips to visit kin in the countryside, to Chattanooga, or even to roadside honky-tonks outside town were possible if one had access to an automobile. Cars also helped break the village dwellers' dependence on nearby grocery stores. Once Nancy Rogers and her husband bought a car, for instance, they avoided the Boylston village stores and drove elsewhere to hunt for retail bargains throughout the Dalton area. Like everything else, cars could be bought on credit, and because they cost several hundred dollars, virtually no cotton miller ever paid for one outright. Des Ellis, for instance, bought his first car in 1932, on the eve of his marriage, by paying $100 down and the rest on time. Such purchases entailed clear risks. For people living on the margin of poverty, payments often proved impossible and repossessions were common, resulting not only in the loss of transportation and status, but also of whatever money had already been spent on the car. Repossessions represented only one of many economic pressures that slowly began to squeeze the millhands of Crown.[29]

At its best, the "family" culture at Crown softened the harsher aspects of industrial life, but it could not completely disguise the stern realities of debilitating mill work, low wages, and indebtedness. Makin' do ought not be viewed as a romantic endeavor, in which families—always loving and virtuous—good-naturedly endured their plight. The millhands who found goodness in their lives did so in spite of, not because of, their circumstances. For everyone, getting by became increasingly more difficult as the 1920s came to a close. Changes in mill work had been taking place steadily throughout the decade, making jobs more difficult to do and harder to hold.

Families who rooted themselves in the Crown Mill village or any other mill village during the 1920s had to learn to deal with night work. The night shift was a product of the post–World War I era, during which most companies had surplus labor at their disposal. Once a few mills started the practice, thereby boosting their production, other firms also adopted the system in order to compete. The southern textile industry was highly imitative, and Crown was no exception. What is surprising is that mill management was actively opposed to night work, even though Crown maintained a night shift. In 1928 Georgia textile leader William D.

Anderson blasted "the evils resulting from night running" in a speech before the American Cotton Manufacturers Association (ACMA). Crown's president, Will Moore, who served on the Textile Research Council of the ACMA, was equally opposed to the practice. When a bill to abolish night work for women came before the Georgia legislature in 1929, Moore apparently tried to persuade the Cotton Manufacturers Association of Georgia (CMAG) to endorse it. The only surviving evidence of this is the reply he received from T. M. Forbes, secretary for the CMAG. Referring to a letter from Moore, Forbes wrote, "There is no doubt but that the far thinking leaders of the Southern textile industry are beginning to share your opinion in regard to the elimination of night work for women between the hours of 7:00 P.M. and 6:00 A.M. Even though some of the mill men may try to dodge the issue there is no doubt but that a moral issue is involved and that we should look at the matter from that standpoint." Nonetheless he conceded that the bill had not been supported strongly and that it likely would not come up for a vote.[30]

The ACMA, which was a southern organization, found a surprising amount of dissatisfaction with night work among its membership. "Quite a number of members," wrote president H. R. Fitzgerald of Danville, Georgia, in 1928, "who . . . have for years operated their machinery both day and night, gave their opinion that the night running was an economic fallacy as well as a social evil and that it should be stopped." He estimated that "one-third of the spindles of the industry are run at night." This trend, he feared, created unstable market conditions, and besides, he added, the trend was unnecessary because most mills wanted to stop the practice. When completing an ACMA survey on the night work issue in 1928, Crown's managers answered "yes" to the question, "Do you favor discontinuing night work?" even though they ran night shifts at both the Boylston and Crown Mill plants full time (fifty-five hours a week). They opposed a federal law against night work, however, "because we think it a state problem." Mostly, though, it was the workers' problem, because it greatly disrupted their households. Like the managers, the workers may have been reluctant to see the system discontinued even if they opposed it. Night shifts provided steady work for more family members and greater family earnings. They also offered a bleary-eyed reminder that industrial capitalism and mill-village life demanded difficult sacrifices.[31]

The pace of work in the mill was still slow compared with later years, but changes were already evident, and the pace and scope of work were beginning to increase. In the 1920s, Crown implemented its "bonus" system, which offered workers economic incentives—in the form of bonus coins redeemable for cash—to exert more effort on the job. All employees had to "make production," but anything they produced beyond that accrued to the bonus. The bonus system could be profitable for skilled millhands, but as the decade wore on and the mill purchased machinery that ran faster, the standard quotas were raised, making it more difficult to make production. Technological efficiency, always a priority for Crown's managers, put increased pressures on the workers. In 1922 mill officials estimated that "production costs are down about 40%" and concluded, "a portion of this is due to more efficient labor." Efficiency stemmed from mechanical innovations like the Barber-Coleman spoolers and warpers, which Crown's officials installed at the Boylston plant in the late 1920s. Such machines were notorious among millhands because they eliminated jobs and made work much more grueling for the remaining workers.[32]

The maturation of the labor force also had unexpected and adverse consequences for young men in the mill village. The paternalistic system that emerged in the early twentieth century had attracted workers by offering men better-paying jobs and the understanding that loyal employees would have the opportunity to become fixers, the highest-ranking nonsupervisory position. A limited number of fixers could also become foremen. But by the late 1920s, the sluggish industry had idled many workers, and the mill village was full of young men whose chances to become fixers—not to mention foremen—were slim indeed. The mill was already glutted with experienced fixers, and no new positions were likely to open. This was not simply a barrier to individual advancement but a larger problem for young families trying to make do in the Crown Mill village.[33]

Crown suffered no meaningful drop in profits until 1930, but employment declined throughout the latter years of the twenties. At the outset of 1926, Mills 1 and 2 had a total of 730 workers on their payrolls, but by the end of the year, the number of millhands employed in those two plants fell to about 650—an 11 percent reduction in the work force. The following year saw no employment surge to reverse this trend; the payroll listed only 640 workers. Layoffs and erratic employment hit Crown's Boylston plant even harder. The south Dalton mill, which employed 225 hands in early 1926, cut its payroll 38 percent by the end of that year. Late in the decade, many workers at Crown were experiencing disturbing cycles of inactivity. It was an unsettling indication of industrial vulnerability and an ominous reminder of the risks involved in mill-village dependence.[34]

By the 1920s, a highly cohesive industrial community had developed at Crown Mill. Over a period of two generations, the company's managers and millhands had worked out a set of compromises that allowed both groups to work toward different but mutually reinforcing goals. In countless small ways, the working families accommodated themselves to the demands of the mill, and management, in turn, met some of the workers' basic needs. Mill-village society was a peculiar hybrid of industrial capitalism and traditional culture. Although the cotton millers drew on a powerful rural heritage to create a strong mill-worker community, they also committed themselves and their families to lifelong wage-earning employment and consumer dependence. The mill established an environment in which a community culture—the Crown Mill "family"—could flourish. Once the mill families put down roots in the company-owned village and began to view themselves as an entrenched group of industrial laborers, their lives became inextricably linked to the corporation itself.

In the decade after World War I, mill-village society at Crown reached a point of equilibrium. But the pressures involved in "makin' do" reflected larger tensions and inequities within the mill-village system, and the mill people's payday-to-payday existence, coupled with an increasing reliance on credit, burdened their lives with an overriding need for steady wages. Cotton-mill paternalism in the New South was born of a labor shortage, and it flourished for nearly a generation because workers settled down and the southern textile economy remained sound. As the 1920s drew to a close and the industry began to falter, the price that would be paid for mill-village paternalism could already be dimly and ominously perceived.

9 THE GREAT

DEPRESSION

AND THE UNION

Cotton-mill paternalism ultimately rested on a false promise. To those families who remained loyal, the corporation offered an implicit guarantee that steady employment would be available and that mill-village regulations would be enforced with some flexibility. Common southern nativity and deeply held notions of white supremacy lent credence to the idea of shared interests between millhands and managers. But corporate profits, not shared interests, were the bedrock of industrial capitalism, and the southern textile industry could hardly be expected to remain prosperous indefinitely. The Great Depression of the 1930s revealed clearly what southern managers and millhands had failed to recognize or refused to acknowledge—that corporate paternalism could not withstand a sustained economic downturn.

In any case, paternalism had never completely obscured the inequities in the mill-village system. Management always held ultimate power in mill-village society, and dissatisfied employees had few options open to them. In the late nineteenth and early twentieth centuries, Crown's workers normally protested with their feet, by leaving the industrial community. But with the rise of paternalism, the mill population stabilized and the workers established themselves as permanent industrial employees. This generation would not protest by quitting but rather by working within the mill-village system and trying to assert greater control over the community in which they had chosen to live their lives. Corporate paternalism raised the workers' expectations of the company and helped establish a cohesive community of workers. In doing so, it created the possibility of labor solidarity.

The economic depression of the 1930s sparked a series of local and national events that began to sever the bonds between the mill and its workers. Layoffs, evictions, and changes in the nature of work infuriated the millhands, who felt management had abandoned its commitment to earlier traditions of mill work and village life. Acting on this sense of betrayal, they joined their protests to the rising tide of organized labor during the early New Deal era. In establishing a union at Crown Mill—ultimately a strong one—the millhands were rejecting the informal and arbitrary features of the paternalistic system and calling into question the family ideal. But because the mill and its people were so closely bound together in the industrial community, the lines of conflict that emerged were remarkably complex. The struggle for economic survival and unionization that marked the Crown Mill community during the 1930s pitted workers not only against the mill but also against one another.[1]

The depth of the national economic crisis that began in 1929 was not immediately clear. In April 1930, Neil Hamilton's friend, J. S. Hall of Chattanooga, suggested a fishing trip. "Business as you know I presume is like the old maid's dream there is nothing in it and has not been so why not work a little fat off and wait until Hoover fixes things or they just grow better." In retrospect Hall's invitation for a jaunt in the country shows great insensitivity to those who had already suffered much. Of course, Hoover did not fix things, and the economic situation only grew worse. But in early 1930 the extent of the crisis at hand could not be foreseen. That April, unemployment had not yet reached alarming heights in Georgia. The rate of joblessness among the state's industrial workers that year was 3.4 percent, which was higher than Whitfield County's overall unemployment rate of 2.6 percent. There were already signs, though, that textiles were in for a debilitating season. In Georgia, 4,140 millhands—7.6 percent of the state total—had already lost their jobs or had been laid off for an indefinite period. Nationwide, the figures were more alarming, as the unemployment rate among cotton-mill workers had already topped 11 percent.[2]

Ultimately, the Great Depression devastated the textile industry and nearly overwhelmed both the Crown Mill and the economy of north Georgia. Several of

Dalton's manufacturing plants collapsed in the economic crisis and never re-opened. The city's major textile factories survived, but they ran sporadically at best. Orders for automobile fabrics from Ford Motor Company and for tufting thread and sheeting from Dalton's bedspread companies kept Crown alive through the toughest times, although in some weeks the mill ran only two or three days, and for an extended period in the mid-1930s the Old Mill shut down altogether. Before 1930, through more than forty years of production, Crown had suffered a net loss only in its first year and had earned less than a 10 percent return on capital only a handful of times. But in 1930 the company lost 12 percent on capital, and it remained in the red the following two years (see table A.2 and fig. A.1). The latter years of the 1930s brought some relief, but during the depression decade the company's average return on capital was essentially zero.[3]

For Crown's working families, the depression greatly exacerbated the difficulties that had begun in the late 1920s. The millhands "weren't making anything," remembered Hazel Cruce, longtime teacher and principal of Crown Point School, "and then came the depression." Along with other factory workers throughout the country, Dalton's cotton millers found humorous ways to express their distress. "I lost everything in the stock market," quipped Des Ellis. Other mill folk said they were so poor they hardly noticed the depression. A common joke circulated—with many variations—about the unemployed worker who saw an unfortunate man fall out of a third-story window at Crown Mill. The millhand immediately rushed into the supervisor's office and asked for the dead man's position. "Sorry," the super replied. "The one who threw him out gets the job." Like many jokes, this one reflected a bitter truth. The mill sought to keep as many hands on the payroll as possible, even if doing so meant allocating just a little work to each family. This official company policy helped the millhands survive and allowed Crown to maintain its well-trained, stable labor supply. But, given the millhands' reliance on family labor, even selective layoffs could be devastating, and "dividing time" meant smaller paychecks for those fortunate enough to have work. There were no easy solutions for either the company or the mill families. "People were really up against it and hurting," one longtime employee recalled. "It was tough. Lots of people had their backs to the wall."[4]

In the early years of the depression, both the company and the millhands tried to adapt customary welfare tactics to deal with unprecedented unemployment and poverty. The millhands turned to a new form of mutuality called the Community Chest, a local philanthropic organization created and largely run by middle-class townspeople to raise funds "for the relief of unemployed and needy people of our community." It might be imagined that Community Chest funds would be distributed to Crown's impoverished working families, and doubtless some were. But Crown's workers also *gave* the Chest a total of $283 in 1932—nearly 40 percent of the amount that Crown Mill gave to the organization that year. Their contributions reflected older traditions of mill-village welfare, but the Chest was a more formal, less personal, much larger endeavor. As such it embodied the attributes that would characterize the workers' ultimate response to the depression.[5]

The company responded to the curtailment of jobs by implementing a Share the Work plan. Share the Work was an organized, statewide effort to keep as many people employed as possible, and to Crown's management, which adopted the plan in late 1930, it represented a formal and systematic version of their long-standing paternalistic policy of making work available to mill-village families. As expressed by Robert Maddox, Share the Work chairman for the north Georgia district, the plan sought "the good that shall naturally come from more people at work which means more contentment, more happiness, and a sounder social structure." In a report to Maddox in October 1932, Crown president Will Moore stated that the mill's strategy had been to run its plants at full capacity several days per week rather than with a reduced force every day of the week. "Applying the principles of this plan [we] were able to retain a total of about 150 employees who otherwise would have been without employment."[6]

The managers' sincere efforts to maintain employment clashed with their concurrent policies of modernizing the Crown plants. These policies were designed to make the mill and its workers operate more efficiently and thereby keep the company in business. Because mill officials saw labor costs as one of the major culprits in the mill's dwindling profits, they began putting in faster, labor-saving machines. Modernization, which recalled an older company tradition of purchasing high-quality machinery, was now geared toward increasing the mill's output while cutting its labor costs. This strategy was first implemented in the late 1920s with the addition of the Barber-Coleman spoolers, but it had a larger impact after 1931, when the directors agreed to "make the proposed changes in machinery to modernize the present carding and spinning equipment." These changes would allow the company to increase the millhands' work loads and productive capabilities without increasing their earnings. Managers understood the potential labor problems associated with such tactics and therefore moved cautiously. George Hamilton questioned other textile leaders in the South before he employed the services of the Textile Development Company, a consulting firm for mill modernization. H. R. Fitzgerald, president of the Riverside and Dan River cotton mills in Danville, Virginia, gave the consulting firm his endorsement. Hamilton confided to Fitzgerald, "My fear was that [bringing in the development company] might be construed as an application of the 'stretch-out system' which has caused a good deal of friction but from the conversation of their representative it appears that their work is in great part mechanical and practical rather than along the line of labor efficiency." That Hamilton did not perceive mechanical modernization as a form of stretchout seems odd. Perhaps the distinction was a necessary fiction that allowed him in good conscience to impose new labor efficiency measures on the mill family. But as subsequent events revealed, the workers knew a stretchout when they saw one.[7]

Another way to cut labor costs was simply to lay off a substantial portion of the work force, the share plan notwithstanding. As the depression deepened and orders slowed, Crown was faced with a vast oversupply of workers, most of whom lived in the mill village and needed jobs. The company's Share the Work commitment mitigated against mass layoffs and would continue to do so throughout the 1930s. But just as the Great Depression soon overloaded relief efforts like the Community Chest, it also overwhelmed the share plan. Initially the company laid off younger workers, boarders, and mill-working mothers. Mill officials restricted work for each family to fathers and older children, and they tried to limit each family to one worker in the mill. Between 1930 and 1933, the average number of workers on Crown's payrolls fell from 650 to 430, with a particularly sharp drop in the summer and fall of 1933. Since the mid-1920s, the number of pay envelopes distributed by the company had decreased by nearly 50 percent.[8]

The Share the Work plan, despite its good intentions, created opportunities for abuse. Like all of Crown's economic policies, "dividing time" intersected with mill-village culture and filtered through the informal networks of favoritism that characterized the paternalistic system. Several months after the layoffs in 1933, the company shut down the Old Mill indefinitely. This action created an unprecedented employment problem at Crown. In keeping with Share the Work goals, superintendent Frank Springer sent the help from the Old Mill to certain departments in the New Mill. For example, he sent forty-eight hands to John A. Spurgeon, supervisor of the carding department, and instructed him to "furnish them all the extra work" he could. According to Springer's plan, the Old Mill employees would not receive regular jobs, but they would be offered part-time hours in the carding department until Mill No. 1 resumed operations. The opportunities for favoritism in this situation were readily apparent. So long as workers were being selectively laid off or integrated into different departments as part-time hands, any millhands at odds with the company's supervisory personnel were vulnerable to discrimination in the name of benevolence and expediency.[9]

By mid-1933 Springer had embarked on a series of firings that provoked the ire of many workers. Millhands (and their families) who were evicted from the village for breaking company rules became ineligible to take part in the Share the Work plan. Springer used Crown's policy against insobriety as a reason for discharging a number of families. Crown's managers had long supported the notion that "the man who drinks to excess eventually makes serious trouble." The demand for sobriety, one company memorandum noted, "has been so well known as to constitute a condition of employment." Despite such official notices, everyone knew the policy had been laxly enforced. As long as the millhands did not create too much trouble for the community and remained reasonably discreet, weekend drinking sprees had not resulted in firings or evictions. But now Springer had both the incentive and the leeway to enforce the policy more stringently. Apparently the superintendent used a variety of other mill regulations as a pretense for firing millhands. "In the mill village," one woman recalled, "if anybody didn't act like he wanted them to on weekends or when they were off from work, why, he fired them." "He fired one man," chuckled Sarah Bunch, "who called him an old codger." Jack Gregg, who became a union leader at Crown, recalled that one of his neighbors "was fired just because one of the mill officials saw two chickens in his front yard. We were not allowed to keep chickens. And those [chickens] that caused the firing did not even belong to the man who was fired." Here was a prime example of how company power and favoritism could breed discontent. "The mill managements ran our private lives," Gregg complained. "If we did anything—and I mean anything—on a weekend or any other time we were off that the company didn't like, they would call us down to the office when we got back and give us our time." The economic depression made it difficult to contest company policies. "Many a time," said Gregg, "I have had a supervisor tell me, 'Do you see that hole in the wall [the door]? Well, if you don't do as I say, get through that hole. There are men outside the front door waiting for this job.' "[10]

Although some cotton millers praised Springer's actions as a noble effort to eliminate troublemakers from the Crown mill village, others saw them as an unwarranted attack on personal liberty and, more important, as a clear symbol of the favoritism and discrimination that characterized mill-village life. Many believed that Springer used allegations of insobriety to fire anyone he did not like. They felt he abused his responsibilities and did not treat all workers fairly. The superintendent's use (some said abuse) of authority during hard times disturbed many mill people. "They say this is the only place they ever heard of where the help come in and call the boss, the president of the company, by his first name," recalled Anna Nell Garren. "They called Mr. George Hamilton 'Little George.' And one of my neighbors said that he told her when they started organizing, he said, he never did think he would see the day when his help would join the union. And she told him, you wouldn't have if it hadn't been for Frank Springer." Perhaps it is too easy, in retrospect, to single out Springer as a villain. It was not unusual for top-level officials to strike a benevolent pose while their superintendents played the role of the heavy, and even the Hamiltons ultimately had to question the efficacy of their frontline management. But although Springer was a major cause of discontent, he also represented the darker side of paternalism, for which he was not solely responsible. Company paternalism left no recourse for workers who were on the "outs" with management.[11]

Crown's millhands had always protested against perceived injustices, but their protests changed over time. In the late 1880s, workers had pushed for better housing and a better water supply in the mill village. During the early twentieth century, workers registered individual and family protests against low wages and the industrial system by leaving the mill for upcountry farms. After the mill village stabilized and a core of working families put down roots at Crown, resistance to company policies sometimes took the form of individual and small-group defiance.

Petty protests against the mill regulations served as informal assertions of individual liberty and sometimes helped enliven a dreary work day. In the mill, some workers dipped snuff on the sly. A community joke ran that one day Frank Springer warned the women in the Old Mill spinning room against dipping snuff and then stormed out of the mill; as he walked back to his office a substantial glob of spit flew out of the third-floor window and hit him squarely on the head. This event probably did take place in some form or another, but even if the story was more apocryphal than factual, it gave disgruntled millhands the chance to hold Springer up to ridicule, to feel that there were limits to corporate control. Sarah Bunch recalled similar efforts to sidestep company rules: "Back then they wasn't allowed to take a Coca-Cola or candy or anything in the mill, so the boys'd go to the store and get Coca-Colas for the people in the mill and the people in the mill would let a rope down out of the window, you know, and they'd tie a Coca-Cola to it and they'd pull it up [laughs]." Management required women workers to wear cotton hose beneath their dresses, and by all accounts the hose were hot and uncomfortable. One woman, at least, liked to test the boundaries of this rule. As a friend of hers recalled, she "like to get fired one time for going in without her hose. Mr. Springer come through and she said she got 'em on before Mr. Springer got there, and he didn't get to fire her because she had her hose on." Off the job, some workers guzzled moonshine and frequented roadside honky-tonks—risky affronts to mill authority and community mores.[12]

These informal demonstrations of autonomy were one form of protest, but mill workers also had a heritage of semiformal collective action. The whitecapping incidents of the late nineteenth century bore witness to this legacy. And the Knights of Labor, the Farmers' Alliance, and the Populist party were all emblematic of how traditional patterns of dissent could evolve into formalized collective protest. After the turn of the century, organized protest waned among poor upcountry whites, but when the economic crisis and new corporate policies of the 1930s pushed industrial workers to the wall, collective action reemerged with surprising speed.

The Great Depression changed many people's attitudes, expectations, and behavior. Before the economic catastrophe, most Americans could neither accept nor even imagine massive federal intervention in the economy. By the end of the decade, they accepted it as the status quo. A similar change took place within the realm of organized labor. Before the depression, national labor unions were decentralized organizations oriented toward skilled craftsmen and reluctant to engage in politics. By the time World War II eradicated the economic depression, highly centralized industrial unions had gained a firm foothold in most of America's basic industries and had become an integral part of the Democratic party's New Deal coalition. Industrial workers throughout the country became fervent advocates of systematized job security and vigorous opponents of the arbitrary employment systems that enhanced corporate power. Many wage earners in the 1930s felt that welfare capitalism had failed them. To these and other people, organized labor offered new hope for job security and worker empowerment.[13]

Crown's millhands became a part of this larger process when they successfully organized a union in the fall of 1933. Local 1893 of the United Textile Workers Union of America (UTW) represented a remarkable change in the Crown Mill community, where no union had ever existed and no concerted effort had ever been made to organize one. Union organizing in any southern cotton-mill village called for courageous and intelligent leadership. In this instance, two workers at Crown who had extensive labor experience outside the textile industry took command of the unionization effort. Tom Crow, the first president of Local 1893, had worked for Crown before joining the navy in World War I; after his stint in the service he labored as a dock worker and gained experience in the powerful longshoremen's union. Another early union leader was Herman Floyd, a member of the railroad workers' union before he came to work for Crown. Organizing a textile mill was risky business. Crown had fired a number of would-be organizers in the early 1930s, and in September 1933 the Real Silk Hosiery Mill laid off a group of workers who were advocating unionization. Crow and the other union organizers worked as secretly as possible to gain new recruits. One union supporter remembered that, in 1933, "they was still kinda working undercover, and had secret meetings and things." Sometimes in the dark of night, employees wishing to join the organization would walk to Crow's home on Trammel Street in the Westside section, sign pledge cards, and silently slip home again.[14]

What inspired these millhands to put their jobs, perhaps their physical safety, on the line in order to organize a union? In many ways, the ideals espoused by the union meshed with the workers' traditional community ethic. The millhands' rural-based culture accustomed them to banding together in crisis, to making sacrifices on behalf of the community. Their worldview was based on mutuality among working families; their well-being—sometimes their very survival—depended on customs of communal welfare. Yet if traditional culture helped feed the union movement, it certainly was not enough, in and of itself, to spur militant organization. Crown's cotton millers had been guided by rural customs and had adapted those customs to their industrial environment for decades without showing any interest in unionization. Their more usual forms of cooperation depended on informal organization, on customary commitments to family and community that did not necessitate a formally chartered, bureaucratic institution like the union. The mill-village system they knew and understood was itself built largely on informal relationships. Only when that system began to unravel during the Great Depression did the millhands channel their cooperative ethic into a structured organization. The frustrations engendered by layoffs, dividing time, and the intensified enforcement of mill-village rules fired a cauldron of worker discontent. The "stretchout," in which management assigned workers more machines to tend, and the "speedup," in which those machines were made to run faster, kept the pot boiling. Crown's millhands reacted strongly against the changes taking place in their mill-village world. The paternalistic system to which they had grown accustomed seemed to be falling apart. It seemed that management was abandoning paternalism just when millhands most needed the security it offered. In short, the mill people felt betrayed by their company. In many ways, the formation of a union at Crown was a reaction against change and, as such, was profoundly conservative even as it represented a significant new departure from previous custom.[15]

But there was more to the origins of Local 1893 than just local concerns. Events on the national level helped bring the movement at Crown to fruition. Inspired by Franklin D. Roosevelt's leadership, Congress passed the National Industrial Recovery Act (NIRA) in 1933. This legislation sought to bolster American manufacturing, thereby sending unemployed factory hands back to work. To stabilize industry, the new law created the National Recovery Administration (NRA), a federal agency that tried to work out production codes for troubled industries. The NRA had a direct impact on workers and foreshadowed the increasing role that federal legislation would play in the lives of southern millhands. Industrialists generally took charge of the code-drafting process and often used the federal guidelines to their advantage, but the codes dealt with hours and wages, and the NIRA offered ambiguous assurances that unions would have the right to organize. Some hard-pressed millhands throughout America and the South seized upon the law as a mandate for unionization. "Roosevelt, he told 'em to organize," recalled one of Crown's workers, voicing a common attitude in the mill village. President Roosevelt did no such thing, but many millhands believed it and acted accordingly.[16]

Company officials were caught off guard when Tom Crow informed them that a workers' union desired a meeting with mill representatives. No records survive to indicate how many of Crown's workers actually joined the union or whether Crow had assistance from labor leaders outside Dalton. How Crow was able to keep the organization a secret remains a mystery. And it is puzzling that Will Moore and the Hamiltons were apparently unaware of the organizational effort, for they were no strangers to organized labor or the conflicts enveloping mill villages throughout the South. Crown had already fired several workers simply for talking up unionization in the early 1930s, and the local hosiery mill was already embroiled in a struggle against the union.

The mill management had long relied on a well-developed information network to remain abreast of labor developments. In the early 1920s, for example, the Atlanta office of Pinkerton's National Detective Agency warned Will Moore of a roving labor organizer. "Look out for a Labor Organizer using the name of J. L. Jones and accompanied by a woman said to be his wife," advised Pinkerton spies, who were trailing the couple closely. "They left Cartersville, Ga., for Atlanta Wednesday afternoon in a Ford touring car bearing North Carolina license #123-695. They stopped in Marietta, Ga., Wednesday night at Cox's Boarding House. Jones sold the Ford car to a livery stable man named Tom Jackson, in Marietta, for $35.00, but removed the North Carolina license tag from the car and took it with him." The report continued at length and contained a remarkably precise description of the couple. "They may seek employment at your mill and endeavor to organize your employees, so we are advising you of their activities." Several days later the Pinkerton superintendent relayed news from H. F. Jones, manager of the Echota Cotton Mills in Calhoun, Georgia, not far south of Dalton. Jones had informed the Pinkerton office that the labor organizers had come to Calhoun and tried unsuccessfully to get employment. "We will certainly watch this party very close," he added.[17]

Dixie's mill managers were undoubtedly on the alert after the violent southern textile strikes of 1929, when sporadic conflicts between angry workers and intransigent management erupted in east Tennessee and throughout the Carolinas. Most of these strikes were provoked by changes on the shop floor, especially the speedup and stretchout, and most were accompanied by unionization efforts. There were no unionization activities or strikes in the Crown mill village that year. But the southern textile strikes of 1929 gained national attention and would not have been ignored by mill officials in Dalton. And after the passage of the NIRA in mid-1933, all southern textile managers must have been keeping close watch on their plants. It is a wonder, then, that Crown's millhands were able to organize so secretly and so successfully. My oral history interviews yielded no specific details on the initial organization of the union. In the absence of documentary or firsthand evidence, though, it is nevertheless safe to say that the union-building venture was essentially a local effort, as outside organizers would have been spotted immediately. That the union remained concealed until Crow confronted the mill officials testified to the willingness of most workers to give the organization a chance.[18]

Surprisingly, perhaps, Crown's managers accepted Tom Crow's offer for a meeting, and on October 11, 1933, Will Moore and the Hamiltons met for the first time with a group of organized millhands. Both groups hoped to use the meeting to their advantage. Mill officials proclaimed the meeting the inaugural session of Crown's new "industrial relations committee." As they saw it, the committee would function as a company union, that is, as a formal labor relations system that was strictly in-house, with no ties to national unions. Mill managers throughout the United States employed the same tactic, trying to convince workers that labor unions were not necessary to gain a voice in company affairs. Crow had a different agenda. Realizing the union had only a tenuous hold as yet, he hoped to use this inaugural meeting as evidence of its power to force management to address the workers' complaints.[19]

Crow and two other workers presented grievances similar to those voiced by angry millhands throughout the South. The speedup and stretchout were first on Crow's agenda, because these measures upset the traditional pace of work to which the millhands had become accustomed. Crown's officials countered that no deliberate speedups or stretchouts had occurred, but that the mill's new, technologically advanced machines simply ran faster. Crow continued by presenting a substantial list of workers who had been unfairly discharged or laid off while hands with less seniority retained their jobs in the mill. Rather than confronting this charge directly, the officials promised an investigation into the charges of discrimination. The meeting ended with Will Moore asking Tom Crow what organization he represented. The union leader remained noncommittal, saying only, "We represent a legally chartered workers' organization."[20]

No extant records reveal the number of workers who joined UTW Local 1893, but the list of union members must have been a lengthy one by early 1934, for by mid-August the local press considered organized labor in Dalton an important factor in upcoming state elections. Tom Crow and Local 1893 sent questionnaires to all candidates running for Whitfield County representative, asking, for instance, whether they supported "labor's right to collective bargaining through representatives of its own choosing," whether they would favor a state law opposing "yellow dog" labor contracts, and whether they were in favor of free textbooks in Georgia's public schools. Because all of the candidates answered yes to these questions, Crow pronounced Dalton's organized labor "neutral" on the legislative race.[21]

If county politics reflected the union's influence in local affairs, events on the national level also pulled Crown's organized workers into a larger stream of activity. The UTW, which was supposed to be represented on the NRA textile committee, received short shrift from the beginning; despite initial gains in wages and employment, union leaders quickly realized the NRA and the textile industry's board would offer them little support. Many employers stoutly refused to recognize their workers' unions, fired and evicted all suspected unionists, and eventually cut back on hours so that the NRA minimum-wage quotas no longer applied. In short, individual industrialists in Dixie were not living up to either the letter or the spirit of the NRA's textile code, and workers throughout the South suffered accordingly. National UTW leaders appeared indecisive about taking action, but angry millhands throughout Dixie—first in northern Alabama and then elsewhere—inaugurated a series of strikes that ultimately turned violent. These southern wildcat strikes prompted the top UTW leaders to threaten a nationwide strike if textile workers did not receive their due under the NRA. This threat prompted no change in the situation, and when a direct union appeal to President Roosevelt fell on deaf ears, the UTW called for a general textile strike to begin Saturday, September 1, 1934.[22]

On the first day of the strike, Dalton's millhands gathered downtown for a mass meeting. All of the town's major mills—Crown, Boylston, American Thread, and Real Silk Hosiery—actually ran until noon (the usual Saturday shift), after which the workers thronged to an open meeting, where George Logan Gooch, southern representative of the American Federation of Labor (AFL), was scheduled to explain "the textile strike situation." Young and clean-cut, Gooch was a native Georgian who, as the *Dalton Citizen* pointed out with relief, belonged "to the more conservative element of the federation." Gooch made certain "that Dalton's businessmen and the general public were cordially invited and urged to attend." Before September 1, the *Citizen* heralded the open-meeting approach, hoping it might avert the strike. Public dialogue, the paper argued, could help "settle the differences that had arisen amicably and keep our mills humming, our people working and the channels of trade busy." But by the time Gooch spoke, the UTW national office had already called the strike, and some 1,200 millhands in Dalton subsequently voted to support the walkout. Thus Dalton's cotton millers joined the largest general strike in American history up to that time. The secret union of 1933 had evolved into something much larger.[23]

Labor Day 1934 witnessed a startling display of worker solidarity in the City of Smiles and Smokestacks. Even before the UTW called the strike, Tom Crow announced plans in the *Citizen* "for an old fashioned 'non-political' Labor Day rally and parade." All of Dalton's organized laborers would be included. An *Atlanta Constitution* headline mourned that a "SPECTER OF VIOLENCE . . . CASTS SHADOW ON U.S. AS LABOR DAY DAWNS," but in Dalton, peace prevailed on Monday, September 3, as the largest labor celebration ever held in the city took place. The local press estimated that "1,500 union workers, representing every trade organization here, took part in the Labor Day parade" that afternoon. The procession first gathered at the city park where, a half-century earlier, local boosters had celebrated the now forgotten "industrial resolution." In a double-file line, they marched east on Wall Street and turned south on Hamilton, Dalton's main business thoroughfare. The impressive line of organized labor, stretching over eight city blocks, eventually turned west on Morris until it reached Thornton, the tree-lined avenue on which merchants and industrialists built their mansions, then marched northward back to city park. There, before an exuberant crowd, T. R. Cuthbert, secretary of the Chattanooga Labor and Trades Council, "stressed the rights of organized labor."[24]

In towns throughout the South, textile managers were resisting the union movement by effectively mobilizing antiunion workers to fight against the strikers.

But Crown's leaders appeared surprisingly nonchalant about the turn of events in their city. Although all of the local textile mills were shut down and over a thousand local millhands were supporting a massive industrial strike, the only comment made by Crown's officials reflected both their distance from the workers and their attitude that the strikers did not represent a severe crisis. "We know no more about the strike than what we read in the papers," said Will Moore, "and will be closed until further notice." In an economic sense, the strike worked to the managers' advantage, for they already had warehouses full of goods they could not sell, and the strike provided a decrease in labor and production costs for which they bore no responsibility. The Hamiltons redeemed the time by taking a fishing trip.[25]

Tom Crow did all he could to foster this sense of harmony, carefully working to prevent an antilabor backlash. He assured the local press that "labor wanted a peaceful strike" and reported happily that "we are receiving the cooperation of mill officials to this end." Crow published a statement in the *Citizen* thanking local officials and the Dalton citizenry for their cooperation during the Labor Day parade. He explained that the strike "is not a strike against the NRA, but to the contrary is to force compliance with some of the labor provisions of the cotton textile code." Local mill officials, he offered, were better than most in upholding federal codes, but given "unfair competition" from other southern textile firms, they could not make a profit and still maintain "decent wages and working conditions for the workers." Crow thus presented the union as an agent of industrial stability, the strike as a collective action that would benefit employee and employer alike. He also showed an awareness of national and regional market trends and their impact on the local workers' situation. With the cooperation of management, he concluded, the union hoped to make this "one of the most orderly and peaceful strikes of all time."[26]

For Crown's workers, the 1934 General Strike was largely a picnic. "We had a ball," recalled Sarah Bunch, echoing the basic sentiments of most Dalton millhands. Because none of the local mills attempted to reopen until the national strike was settled, picketing was largely a symbolic gesture. About 450 men and women, grouped in squads of 20, were assigned picket duty at Crown. Three shifts "guarded" the mill for twenty-four hours a day. Picket areas soon became points for community gatherings and recreation. Several buoyant squads called out a local photographer and joined together for a picture, revealing the pride and satisfaction Crown's millhands took in their union and the strike.[27] Every town and mill village had a different experience, the national scope of the strike notwithstanding. In some towns, the strike provoked almost no response. In others, a virtual war broke out— sometimes between opposing groups of workers, sometimes between union hands and National Guard troops brought in by management. The localistic responses to a nationally controlled labor protest suggests that 1934 was not a climax of labor strife in the South, as has often been suggested, but rather a period of transition during

Crown workers on the picket line during the General Textile Strike of 1934. (*Courtesy of Lillie Ann Goforth Hill, Dalton, Georgia*)

which the workers' village-level focus, which characterized the paternalistic system, was shifting slowly toward a regional and national perspective. Tom Crow spoke of national labor guidelines, and Crown's workers understood that unionization meant major changes, not just for themselves but for workers throughout the South.

Beneath the carnival atmosphere in Dalton, the fear of violence and community disruption grew. By mid-September accusations about company spies were flying among hosiery mill workers. A more serious cause for alarm was the bloodshed at the mill village at Trion, Georgia, some thirty miles southwest of Dalton. There, on September 5, the same day on which Tom Crow cheered the peaceful nature of Dalton's strike, gunfire between union pickets and "armed deputies" recruited from among nonunion workers took the lives of two men and wounded nearly twenty others. Strike-related violence and murders also struck the mill villages of Augusta and Macon that same day. Although the most dramatic confrontations involved the National Guard, millhands understood that a majority of the bloodshed and violence resulted from disputes among the workers themselves. Although labor historians have been reluctant to acknowledge conflict between millhands who differed over unionization, an AFL press release about violence at Honea Path, South Carolina, recognized the troubling reality when it noted that six UTW strikers "were murdered in cold blood at the Chiquola Mill here when deputy sheriffs and *nonunion men* opened fire on a flying squadron of pickets." The Great Depression and its consequences not only mocked the idea that southern whites stood on a foundation of equality, but also revealed that Dixie's white cotton millers were not solidly allied against the mill managers.[28]

"Flying squadrons" were the most controversial tactic employed by the UTW during the General Strike. These squads consisted of carloads of mill workers who rode in caravans from one mill town to another, encouraging workers to join the strike and helping those who encountered company resistance. Paradoxically, the flying squadrons represented both worker unity and intraworker divisions. Like north Georgia's white caps of old, the flying squadrons could be seen either as manifestations of community solidarity or as evidence of severe cleavages among poor whites. Many workers hailed the squadrons as evidence of cooperative attempts to help workers in nonunion mills break free from the shackles of "slave labor." Marselle Thompson recalled how her father, Herman Floyd, and other Crown Mill workers organized squads and sped across north Georgia to aid workers in mills that had not closed. Other workers, as the Honea Path incident suggested, perceived the squadrons as coercive agents illegally forcing other plants to shut down. In fact the violence at Trion was partly due to the arrival of flying squadrons from Rome, and one of the men killed was actually a Rome worker. Crown's flying squadrons were also at Trion, which brought home the threat of union-related violence to the members of Local 1893.[29]

Apparently some workers found it difficult to decide where they stood on the union, the strike, and the flying squadrons. At Crown no immediate crisis forced indecisive millhands to choose sides. After President Roosevelt intervened, the UTW called off the national strike on September 21, and Dalton's mills quietly resumed operation. Crown employees returned to their jobs, apparently without retaliation from the company. Local 1893 survived, and although it did not win a contract from Crown, the managers accepted it as a "union committee" and allowed the organization to bring workers' grievances to the attention of the company.

The response of Crown's top officials to the union seemed out of place in the New South, where stories of ruthless managerial suppression of organized labor in Dixie's mill villages were legion. During the shutdown in 1934, the *Citizen* succumbed to alarmist journalism, proclaiming that "the hand of Moscow" was directing the strike and that communist agitators were bent on the racial integration of Dixie's cotton mills. This kind of ranting was more typical of the textile South than were the bland responses of Crown's managers, but once the strike was settled, even the press let the issue rest for the time being.[30] Will Moore and the Hamiltons were level-headed pragmatists who did not feel particularly threatened by the union. In no way did they favor organized labor, but while mill officials in nearby textile towns were mounting machine guns on factory roofs to resist unionization, Crown's top managers demonstrated considerable restraint. Nationally, the

UTW emerged from the General Strike in sorry shape, and the union had made very little headway in southern mills. Moreover, economic problems threatened Crown's officials far more than a weak union that, given the state of the economy, had little leverage over the company. Will Moore voiced official company policy in a memo to the workers explaining that the NIRA made it legal to join (or refuse to join) a union. He urged them to respect each individual's decision in the matter. His admonition was, "Let's give the New Deal a fair shake."[31]

Despite the company's official policy of nondiscrimination, however, charges of favoritism began to fly soon after the strike. Managers in the big office were not personally involved in this turmoil, although they remained closely attuned to it and ultimately had to render decisions in some of the more heated disputes. Most of the conflict erupted on the shop floor, where millhands interacted constantly with foremen, supervisors, and Frank Springer. It was here that workers—union and nonunion alike—began to perceive discrimination and hurl charges against one another and against management. These conflicts in the mill reflected economic desperation within mill-village households and long-standing grudges against fellow millhands or bosses. At Crown, the General Textile Strike of 1934 was not a pivotal event that shaped local labor relations for subsequent generations. Indeed, the union had its major impact on the Crown Mill family *after* the 1934 strike.

Dividing work among hard-pressed employees proved a major catalyst for disputes. Given the depth of the textile depression and the sheer number of mill-hands firmly entrenched in the Crown Mill village, the division of work would have prompted charges of favoritism regardless of whether the union existed. But with the introduction of the union as a new source of authority on the shop floor, dividing time became linked to UTW membership in the minds of Crown's workers. Union millhands who felt abused quickly charged discrimination; non-union workers who felt wronged claimed the company was giving better treatment to union hands to avoid unnecessary grievances. A poststrike file kept by managers in 1934–35 contains numerous complaints from workers who claimed that other hands had been given an unfair advantage. Some grievance letters were from union representatives; others were not. A typical example read, "It is charged that Bob Skates has had more than a fair share of work to the hurt of John McCoy." The mill's overseers responded to each letter of grievance. In this case, T. F. Lockridge explained that Skates's extra work was performed on machines that McCoy could not run. So it went through 1934 and 1935: worker accusations and managerial explanations. The connection between accusations and union membership made these grievances extremely volatile.[32]

Disruptions among the workers exasperated management. Crown's officials posted several notices in the mill in an attempt to relieve tensions. "Many of you are disturbed. Friends are at outs," began one announcement, which promised that "it is the intention of the management of this mill to treat everyone fairly regardless of membership and non-membership in any union." The officials regretted the existing "unpleasantness" and wished "all happiness and contentment" for their employees. But they worried about more than employee happiness, as demonstrated by a later notice that pointed out "the complaints we have had from customers over quality and the losses we have sustained through production of seconds." The main reason for this problem, the announcement noted, was that whenever a foreman or other lower-level manager spoke to an operative about his or her work, agitated employees would leave their jobs unattended to gather in groups "and talk over what has been said." This practice violated company policy, and hereafter management would "take action" against workers who broke the rule. Officials carefully noted, "We do not want you to think later on that any action in this connection is intended as any discrimination against any employee for union activities."[33]

Turmoil in the card room of Mill No. 2 revealed dissension that ran so deep, no managerial plea for worker reconciliation could have been effective. These problems began before the General Strike, when Springer relocated workers from the Old Mill. He made John A. Spurgeon, supervisor of the New Mill carding department, integrate these hands into the department (but without giving them regular jobs) until the Old Mill resumed operation at some undetermined date in the future. This required Spurgeon to divide only 88 regular jobs among 136 hands, placing him, his foreman, and their section hands under great strain and ensuring that few, if any, workers in Mill No. 2's carding room would be satisfied with their working conditions.[34] An incident involving Edith Kyle, a drawing hand transferred from the Old Mill, reflected the growing tensions. In mid-August, Kyle charged that her section boss, James Ratcliff, had discriminated against her by giving her regular job to another hand and putting her on a harder job. "There has been times," she wrote, "when I was too tired to eat when I went home." Moreover, she complained, Ratcliff yelled at her "as if I were a servant."[35]

The strike in September temporarily halted the conflict but did not end it. When trouble resumed, John Spurgeon countered Kyle's grievance by saying that, as one of the displaced millhands from the Old Mill, she had been given no regular job for James Ratcliff to give away. Changes were made "to more equally divide the time between all the help, and that because the help was fussing continually about that very thing." But there was more to the dispute. Spurgeon alleged that Kyle had spread "scandalous" rumors against Ratcliff and that she "was one of the worst troublemakers I have ever known." "Her own kindred by marriage," he continued, "volunteers to tell me that he would not believe her on oath, and adds that she is mentally deranged."[36]

Spurgeon's remarks hardly settled the issue. In early October, twenty-eight union employees signed a petition demanding that Ratcliff be removed, or at least that "his authority be taken from him." In eight specific charges, the workers stated that Ratcliff openly harassed and discriminated against union millhands, making union women cry, giving nonunion workers better jobs, and heaping abuse on union president Tom Crow. "We are fully convinced," the petition stated, "that he will continue to agitate and try to stir up trouble, rather than cooperate by treating the union and non-union worker alike. . . . The workers are entitled to a square deal." In reply, Spurgeon claimed the situation was difficult to assess. He believed that the real motive behind the petition was a union plot to replace James Ratcliff as section hand with a UTW leader, J. B. Searcey, and that Edith Kyle was the instigator of the petition. Ratcliff and Spurgeon responded to all eight charges, presenting a picture of the situation entirely at odds with the UTW petition. The hands had been ganging up and talking down Ratcliff and "sometimes are very insulting when asked to do their work in accordance to the rules." Ratcliff pleaded ignorance of the millhands' union status and claimed he treated all the same, saying, "I am not responsible for this fussing." The following day, Spurgeon circulated a petition in support of Ratcliff. It was signed by thirty-seven hands, one of whom reported a union man as saying that her signature would "be held against you if you ever want to join the union."[37]

The tumult in the card room continued. Attempting to settle a dispute between Ratcliff and Lizzie Patterson, Spurgeon called in the millhand and told her firmly that he had never given her a regular job in the new mill. Then, according to Spurgeon's account, Patterson "began to cry and accused me of talking to her like a dog." He tried to persuade her otherwise, but "the madder she got . . . the worser she went on, referring to her religion and the like. She told me she was going to put a stop to James Ratcliff telling lies on her and that she had a way of stopping him." Spurgeon recommended that she talk to Springer about her job, but when she "continued to rave," he "got up and left her standing there, and stayed away until she left."[38]

Beneath the heated words, the petitions, and the ill feelings lay the bedrock of poverty and economic depression. Hard-hit mill families were fighting for survival, and community welfare among the workers could only go so far. The pressure for work and the pressures at work pushed many to the breaking point. By mid-October 1934, less than a month after the strike, Spurgeon was ready for relief. He suggested to Springer that thirty-five to forty hands be laid off. "I insist that trying to work the crew and a half of help is largely responsible for most of the so-called trouble we are having to contend with on the job." Spurgeon clearly laid out the difficulty of the situation from his point of view: "It is impossible to work all the employees the exact amount of time, unless they were all skilled at every kind of work that we have. Most all of them can only do one kind of work, and to place them on work that they cannot run only means loss of production, and lots of bad work, and more trouble and expense, caused from the practice of laying off learned help in order to work unlearned help, in order to furnish them part-time. I insist that the mill is actually losing production and making more bad work at a higher cost daily, because of this practice." Given the situation, neither managers nor workers could win. The Share the Work plan, like many depression-era programs, worked better on paper than in practice.[39]

Problems with discrimination of a different sort also arose in the wake of the strike. In late November 1934, authorities in Chatsworth, Georgia, the county seat of Murray County, threw Crown Mill employee Sim Craig in jail for being drunk in public and throwing rocks at automobiles along the highway. John R. Craig, a Crown Mill yard hand and Sim's father, was also reported drunk. Acting on the company policy against public drunkenness, Frank Springer fired Sim. John kept his job because the witness to his insobriety could not be found to sign a written statement. But two months later, on a Saturday night in January 1935, Dalton police arrested the elder Craig on charges of intoxication in public. The company terminated his services on Monday, although the chief of police pleaded his cause, saying Craig "made apologies for his behavior and was agreeable as could be." Shortly thereafter, Eulysses Kinnamon was fired for a similar offense. All three men carried union cards, and Local 1893 came to their defense.[40]

Initially the union argued that the company had no jurisdiction over the help outside working hours. This charge reflected the attitude of many millhands, but, as union leaders probably realized, it was a hopeless argument. Company policy against excessive drinking, as mill managers pointed out in a counterargument, was a long-standing tradition. The goal of this rule, according to the management, was to raise the standard of employees, to keep peace in the village, and to maintain a good reputation within the Dalton community. Revoking the rule for the sake of these three men, officials argued, would seem "to put a premium on drinking to the excess" and might create hard feelings among some families who had experienced layoffs for similar reasons in the past. "We believe," the company concluded, "that the union committee would make a mistake to place themselves on record in opposition to this rule."[41]

The management's intractability on the drinking rule caused the union to rethink its goal. Since greater personal liberty for millhands was not, for the present, a realistic possibility, union leaders sought the more attainable objective of reinstating the fired workers. They charged discrimination, producing a list of five nonunion men who had recently been arrested for public drunkenness but had not been fired. This was precisely the type of grievance that had sparked the unionization drive in the first place. A group of workers who saw themselves on the "outs" with the corporate system had seen no way to advance their interests save through organized effort—through the introduction of a new source of authority within the mill. The union represented, in part, a practical effort to champion the interests of workers who remained outside the circles of favoritism in the

Crown Mill. Its theoretical roots were shallow; it was more firmly grounded in emotional outrage and practical necessity. Mill officials seemed to recognize this, and they countered union charges with pragmatic statements aimed at soothing the workers' angst. Publicly, Crown's managers spoke of the union not as an evil but as an unnecessary organization. Instead of proclaiming their legal rights to control their property, they stressed instead their efforts to be fair. In response to the charges of discrimination, therefore, the company claimed to have discharged both union and nonunion employees for drunkenness, without presenting any evidence as proof.[42]

Meanwhile, the bosses who had been in charge of Sim and John Craig heaped abuse upon them. They presented a portrait of Sim as a young, rebellious, and undisciplined tough. Sometime before his arrest for "throwing rocks at cars on the public highway," he had been hospitalized for serious wounds incurred in a knife fight with another mill boy. Spurgeon said that Craig had disregarded basic mill rules, such as wandering the factory without a working permit, sometimes with a "strike anywhere" match in his mouth. John Craig, the bosses claimed, was known as a grumbling type who shunned hard work and suffered from kidney trouble. Worse, relatives informed Spurgeon "that John has a bad whisky making and whisky drinking record" and that he "had it in for" two other workers in the mill. Whether or not these characterizations proved true, company officials made no effort to reinstate the Craigs or Eulysses Kinnamon.[43]

Nevertheless, the union pursued the case tenaciously, perhaps because it provided such a fundamental reason for the union's being. Not that drinking privileges per se were important, but the right to be treated fairly, without discrimination, was essential to a square deal. In late March, the union secured the intervention of B. P. Williams, field representative of the federal Textile Labor Relations Board, who met with Crown officials in Dalton to discuss the case. Williams suggested that the company should reemploy the three men or else go through the unpleasant business of firing the other five workers identified by the union, if they indeed were guilty of violating the "understood rule." Writing to Will Moore, who at the time was critically ill in Washington, D.C., George Hamilton, Jr., summed up management's attitude: "It all looks rather trivial compared to the other problems facing both employee and employer, all of which we tried to impress on Mr. Williams."[44]

The amount of effort UTW Local 1893 put into this case bewildered Crown's managers, and for good reason. Why would the union try so diligently to place Sim and John Craig, evidently two less-than-upstanding millhands, back on the job? Plenty of union members were dedicated teetotalers, and many a nonunion worker spent the weekend in an amber haze. Perhaps the union pressed the case because it offered solid evidence of discriminatory practices, and the organization was desperately in need of a victory. Crown's UTW local was one of the few active in Georgia by the mid-1930s. Any victory, no matter what the issue, would have helped the union's cause and its image. But the Craig case involved more than a test of union clout. To hundreds of Crown workers, it symbolized an attack on the arbitrary authority of mill management, an attack against unjustified favoritism and the darker aspects of paternalism. Intermingled were the desires for greater job security and personal liberty. In one sense, "Little George" was right: given the severity of the textile depression, the Craigs' case did seem trivial. Yet in other ways it was not trivial in the least. By a strange turn of events, the fate of two ne'er-do-wells came to symbolize a much larger issue. Because the union represented an alternative source of power in the local community, it had a way of intersecting conflicts that normally dissipated without much turmoil and investing them with an importance and urgency far beyond their usual scope.

In the wake of the 1934 strike, conflicts among the millhands began to polarize the mill-village community. But to view the millhands simply as staunch individualists who disagreed over the union is to ignore the deeper change in relationships that took place. Discrimination and unionization split the community of workers in two. Outsiders would not have perceived any differences between the two groups: everyone in the village was poor, white, and nominally Protestant; and almost all had roots in the north Georgia countryside. But the millhands drew distinctions among themselves that outsiders could not easily discern. "They was 'bad people,'" one union supporter said of antiunion workers. "We didn't associate with any such." Nonunion folk, meanwhile, avoided the "hotheads" who supported UTW Local 1893. "My biggest problem with the union," recalled one man, "was the people they had in charge of it." The union thus became an intensely personal issue, not just an economic one. The result, Marselle Thompson recalled, was "a lot of confusion and heartaches." The pressures that ripped apart the Crown Mill family were only partly the result of outside influences—economic disaster, the New Deal, and the rise of big labor. For the most part, they developed from the very core of mill-village paternalism, which promised security to all but could not possibly deliver on that promise. Company paternalism ironically created the potential for class-based protest, and management's perceived betrayal of the system sparked what appeared to be a united movement against an antagonistic foe. But the paradox of paternalism went deeper still, for although the system sought to create a stable, homogeneous village culture, it also hinged on subtle distinctions among the mill families, linking some workers more tightly to the company than others. As a result, the working community at Crown Mill was bitterly polarized over the advent of new company policies and the rise of the union. Or, as one man who worked all his life at Crown said, "Something like that can tear up a family—just like the Hatfields and McCoys."[45]

10

TORN ASUNDER: THE
STRIKE OF 1939

Disputes within the Crown Mill community continued to simmer as the Great Depression dragged on. Those conflicts finally erupted with full force during the Crown Mill strike of 1939, a four-month struggle that polarized the workers and the mill village. Spurred by both national events and local concerns, Crown's managers and union hands headed toward a showdown, which officially began on May 30 when contract negotiations broke down and the local union voted to strike. Pickets successfully shut down all three of Crown's plants for over a month, but in mid-July the union lines began to crack, and the mill was able to resume partial production. Management did not import strikebreakers; those who crossed the picket lines were members of the Crown Mill community. The strike was therefore a family affair, and it forced workers to choose sides—for or against the union. For ten weeks, "scabs" and "hotheads" remained locked in a standoff, the two groups being nearly equal in size, with the union side enjoying a slight advantage. In late September, the exhausted union finally gave in and signed a contract favorable to the company. Management could not claim a sweeping victory, how-ever. Not only had the local union survived, but the mill's nonunion workers—insisting that loyalty carried a price—subsequently sued the company for back wages lost during the strike. When the turmoil finally subsided, it was clear that the paternalistic system had suffered a mortal blow.

National developments laid the foundation for the 1939 strike. The Wagner Act, passed by Congress in 1935, clearly guaranteed what the National Industrial Recov-ery Act of 1933 had only ambiguously suggested—that the federal government stood behind the principle of collective bargaining. Southern textile leaders at first ignored the law, certain that the Supreme Court would rule it unconstitutional. But in the spring of 1937, the court upheld the Wagner Act, finally giving organized labor the Magna Carta it had hoped for in earlier legislation.[1] Meanwhile, the moribund UTW gained new life from an unexpected source—John L. Lewis's Congress of Industrial Organizations (CIO). In the mid-1930s, Lewis and other labor leaders had bolted from the American Federation of Labor (AFL), rejecting its decentralized structure and its focus on skilled labor. The union insurgents favored a centralized organization comprised of rank-and-file industrial workers. In March 1937, the CIO virtually subsumed the UTW in a larger organization called the Textile Workers Organizing Committee (TWOC). The leaders of the TWOC resolved to concentrate their efforts on the South, where the vast majority of millhands remained unorganized. The new organization vowed to be more aggressive in enforcing the statutes of the Wagner Act and launched a general organizing drive in Dixie. Whereas the AFL had always seemed reluctant to mount a forceful attack on the nonunion South, the CIO seemed eager to tap the discon-tent evident in mill villages throughout the region. Reflecting the initial optimism, the *Textile Workers Song Sheet* sought to fuse regional culture and modern union-ism in such tunes as "The C.I.O.'s in Dixie," which began: "Away down South where we weave that cotton / Union men are not forgotten / Look ahead, look ahead, look ahead, union man."[2]

The TWOC campaign made immediate headway in Dalton. On July 8, 1937, UTW workers at Crown Mill and American Thread affiliated themselves with the CIO. Initially the two groups merged as TWOC Local 134, but Crown's workers soon formed a separate group, TWOC Local 185. Millhands at American Thread succeeded in becoming only the second group of textile workers in Georgia to sign a union contract with their company. On May 29, 1938, members of Local 185 were able to do the same and a new era began at Crown. Will Moore had passed away shortly after the General Strike of 1934, but the Hamiltons maintained the old policy of moderation toward the union. The one-year contract included a "check-off" system by which the company office simply deducted union members' dues from their paychecks. Not all workers at Crown embraced the union, and because the mill was an open shop, they did not have to join. (No records survive to indicate what percentage of the workers were members during the union's early years.) But although the Hamiltons may have signed a contract without a fight in 1938, they were hardly thrilled about the workers' organization, and they proved formidable opponents the following year, when the time came to renegotiate.[3]

In 1939 Crown's managers took the offensive in an effort to reduce the company's labor costs and weaken the union. That January the company hired an industrial engineering firm to examine Crown's labor costs. According to "Little George" Hamilton, who had become president after Will Moore's death in 1935, the study was intended to let management know "exactly where we stood" in relation to other southern mills. Crown officials believed their financial losses and dwindling orders for goods had resulted from labor costs that exceeded those of other mills, and they attributed this burden to the union. Commissioning the study did not in itself consitute a breach of contract, but Local 185 perceived the company's action as a sign of aggression. The union agreement stipulated that Crown's wage rates could be adjusted in cooperation with the workers so long as wages matched "the average wages of comparable, competitive mills in the South." In April the engineers reported that Crown's labor costs averaged "30 percent higher" than those of its competitors, and management immediately contacted the CIO to arrange a meeting for the purpose of adjusting wages.[4]

Whether or not it was deliberately planned to do so, the meeting request placed the union in an unenviable position. Most textile plants were on an economic upswing during the late 1930s, but the millhands had as yet seen little benefit from the upsurge, and Crown's operatives were anticipating a pay raise in their upcoming contract. Instead the company proposed a 10 to 12 percent wage cut, as well as an adjustment of work loads, which translated as another stretchout. If the union agreed to discussions with the company, informally or through arbitration, the workers would probably lose ground just before the old contract expired. This would set a precedent that would be difficult for union leaders to overcome when they met with company officials in late May to negotiate a new contract.

As the leaders of Local 185 pondered these circumstances, national trends once again influenced their outlook. AFL leaders, outraged that so many of their UTW members had defected to the CIO's textile organizing committee, had expelled the UTW from the AFL in April 1938. At a national convention of organized textile workers in early May 1939, TWOC and UTW locals throughout the country merged dramatically to form the Textile Workers Union of America (TWUA), a CIO affiliate. At Crown Mill, the existing TWOC union became TWUA Local 185. Just before the convention that created the TWUA, a TWOC press release had emphasized the importance of the "southern phase" of its organizational drive. Local 185's contract with Crown was one of only twenty-seven such agreements throughout Dixie. National TWUA officials understandably hoped to avoid a setback in Dalton and therefore sought to forestall an arbitration meeting with Crown's officials until after the old contract expired on May 29. When company officials appointed an arbitrator on May 13, the union followed suit, but the TWUA arbitrator delayed another week before meeting with Crown's representative. By that time it was late May and the union representative claimed, in what legally amounted to a breach of the 1938 contract, that the union would not arbitrate because the present contract was due to expire in about a week. He informed Crown's lawyer that the local union would demand a new and improved agreement as soon as the old one expired.[5]

The union's truculence frustrated Crown's managers, but it also played into their hands. Throughout the conflict that followed, they continued to claim that a reduction in labor costs would actually work to the employees' benefit, for it would allow the company to produce cheaper goods, which would lead to larger orders, steadier work, and, in the long run, healthier payrolls. The union's evasive tactics at the last moment gave the Hamiltons added ammunition. They accused the union of a breach of contract, and in doing so they were technically correct. Any ill that befell the workers could therefore be laid at the feet of the CIO. The company claimed that the union millhands had "canceled the contract" and that "there was nothing for us to do except notify them that competitive wage rates and work standards would go into effect on May 30, 1939, upon their termination of the contract." This strategy allowed mill officials to cast the union in the worst possible light, and it prompted several last-minute conferences between Crown and the union officials in late May. When the two sides remained deadlocked and Local 185 voted to strike, mill officials stated (with conscious irony) that whereas the Wagner Act sought to prevent "strikes, picketing, industrial disputes and violence," the CIO, "instead of bargaining . . . preferred to strike—to keep people who wished to work away from their places of work."[6]

Union members, who were a majority of Crown's workers, viewed events in a rather different light. Under the best possible scenario, Local 185 had hoped the new contract would provide for a pay raise and a closed shop. The company's demands therefore infuriated the union. Millhands throughout the South had always fought tenaciously against wage cuts, and, given the workers' overwhelming poverty during the 1930s, a 10 to 12 percent reduction in pay was not something to be accepted passively. On top of this, the company proposed to stretch out work loads and cut back on its work force. Layoffs, stretchouts, and pay cuts made sense to mill officials looking to reduce labor costs after a decade of virtually no profits and plenty of labor unrest. But many workers questioned whether high labor costs were the root of Crown's problems. At a late-night union meeting on May 29, after a last-minute conference with Crown's officials failed to resolve the conflict, members of the TWUA local voted to strike.[7]

Initially the strike went well for the union. Daybreak on May 30, 1939, found hundreds of pickets massed around both the Crown and Boylston mills, blocking the entrances. At the upper mills (Mills 1 and 2), a solid phalanx of picketers stretched northward from the company office on both sides of the mills, forming a human barricade across all of the entryways. As one nonunion woman later testified in court, "They just wouldn't let you in at all. They were stopping the cars out in the road." When asked what the roads were blocked with, she answered, "Men." Confronted with the picket lines, most nonunion workers who had walked to the mill that morning simply stood around or returned home; workers commuting to the plant in automobiles turned around and drove back to the country. No one entered the mill; neither gear nor spindle turned. C. E. Earnhardt, director of the TWUA in Georgia, optimistically predicted "a speedy settlement," and most union folk hoped for the same. Ice-cream parties and other traditional social events recalled the successful strike of 1934 and enhanced the celebratory mood of the picket line. It was "fun for a while," remembered one woman millhand. The mill baseball team, fielding its best nine in years, played on and continued to defeat opponents en route to winning the North Georgia–East Tennessee Industrial League championship. A week passed without any disorders. The majority of workers apparently supported the strike.[8]

Citywide labor solidarity also boded well for the strikers. All of the major textile plants in town had unions, and other local industries such as the Dalton Brick and Tile Company were organized as well. Moreover, three weeks after Local 185 went on strike, five hundred employees at American Thread walked out and shut down their plant to protest the stretchout system. The Thread Mill workers had already been through the fire once, having lasted out a long strike in 1937. Their walkout in June 1939 gave Crown's workers a boost and added a sense of legitimacy to the efforts of Local 185. A strong wave of labor camaraderie rolled over the city.[9]

But the union should have foreseen trouble. On the first morning of the strike, it was clear that some workers vigorously opposed the influence of Local 185 in the community. As one nonunion worker, the Reverend George Fletcher, later stated in court: "The morning after the strike was called, . . . we returned to work and on arriving at the mill we met mass pickets. They seemed to be very hostile and told us we couldn't go on to the mill and we tried to go on to the mill. And some of the employees on attempting to go on to the mill were dragged down. They said, the picketers, we couldn't go in and if we did there would be blood shed." James S. Lochridge remembered, "We tried to get in twice. It caused trouble. . . . They had a fight twice, they pulled part of them out and they didn't allow them to go in." It was therefore immediately clear that the unanimity of 1934 was a thing of the past, and that union millhands would have to struggle not only against the company, but also against many of their fellow workers.[10]

Serious employee opposition to the strike (and, more generally, to the CIO) quickly surfaced. John T. Cronic, a Crown Mill worker and devout Baptist who lived on Jones Street, proved the most outspoken critic of the union. With the strike barely a week old, he sent the *Dalton Citizen* an antiunion editorial that included a takeoff on the Twenty-third Psalm:

> The CIO is my enemy. I am always in want.
>
> It makes me to lie down in hog wallows, it leads me beside the still factory.
>
> It troubles my soul. It leads me in the paths of destruction for its own sake.
>
> It makes me walk in the valley of starvation, and I fear all evil for it has it with it.
>
> Their rods and brickbats trouble me; they prepare an empty table for me in the presence of my friends.
>
> They anoint me with embarrassment; my cup runs empty, and surely starvation will follow me all the days of my life and I will dwell in the poorhouse forever.[11]

Cronic's sarcasm turned to powerful condemnation a week later as he blasted "dictator" John Lewis and the CIO's "Red tactics." According to Cronic, the CIO had shunned the AFL's "democratic and self governing features" for a tyrannical form of labor organization ruled by radical outsiders. In a criticism that bespoke a tenacious defense of localism, Cronic claimed that the CIO "is the same everywhere." "Lewis," he continued, "employs and uses as his organizers red communists, who . . . carry on the fight for a Soviet America." On a more practical level, he noted, "Our pastor at Crown View Baptist did not think it best to try to have a revival on account of a strike called by the CIO. Now who is to blame?"[12]

Such verbal assaults underlay the sporadic outbreaks of violence that began to occur between union and antiunion workers. A group of pickets at Crown Mill assaulted John McClelland, the company's personnel manager, dealing him numerous blows to the face and head and breaking one rib. Three men were arrested for the attack and all made a bond of one hundred dollars, apparently paid by the union.[13] Nonunion baseball players clashed with a group of strikers who attended the game to jeer at players wearing the company uniform. The ball team at the Real Silk Hosiery Mill had exchanged the company logo for letters proclaiming their union affiliation, but Crown's team (which actually included both union and nonunion men) still wore the word "Crown" on its jerseys. On another occasion, a brick was thrown through the window of a house on Matilda Street. "The law" came to investigate and prematurely arrested three union men, who were later acquitted.[14]

But physical violence ultimately proved less destructive to the mill-worker community than the psychological havoc wreaked by severed relationships. The strike polarized the community. Two similar yet competing groups had faced off to fight for what both believed was right. Ironically, each group embraced the same basic values and goals, but they differed on the tactics they used to uphold those values and achieve those goals. As the strike wore on, the chasm between union and antiunion groups widened.

Throughout late June and early July, picket lines at Crown and Boylston stood firm, the mills remained silent, and weeks passed without serious incident. But the lines were about to break. In the first week of July, antiunion millhands at American Thread filed for a court injunction to prevent pickets from blocking the mill. At the hearing that followed, an animated crowd packed the Whitfield County Courthouse for five tension-filled days. Superior court judge John C. Mitchell struggled to maintain order until he finally granted the injunction on Saturday, July 7. This legal order limited the number of pickets at the Thread Mill to a token few, thereby dealing a serious blow to Local 134—and, as it turned out, to Local 185 as well. American Thread resumed partial operations the following Monday, when one-quarter of the millhands returned to work.[15] Judge Mitchell's injunction against the union at American Thread hit Crown's strikers hard. It compelled pickets to be less threatening so as not to bring down a similar injunction on themselves. It also served to mobilize Crown's antiunion workers, who knew that fights at the picket lines were now less likely and would, in any case, lead to an injunction that would make it easier to cross the lines.

On July 10, sixteen Crown workers finally made it through the pickets. Seven millhands entered Boylston, and nine got through at Mill No. 2, while the Old Mill remained shut tight. (See table A.3 for figures on strike support.) Obviously so few workers could not produce any thread or cloth, but that they made it through at all testified to the impact of the American Thread injunction and the growing confidence of Crown's antiunion workers. These strikebreakers received wages for that day's work, so apparently they spent the time getting their mills ready to resume production. Most, but not all, were lower-level managers. How these employees made it past the pickets remains unclear, and there is no evidence to reveal whether the company helped mobilize them. A few more strikebreakers crossed the pickets the following day, setting the stage for a large-scale assault on the union lines.[16]

On Wednesday, July 12, Boylston resumed partial operations. The *Citizen* reported that sixty workers entered the plant, providing enough labor for a single shift. Actually, only thirty-two crossed the lines at Boylston, and it is difficult to see how the mill could have run a shift with this truncated work force. The upper mills basically remained closed. By Friday a few more workers had entered the New Mill, and two millhands finally breached the picket lines at Mill No. 1, but the union's first crisis was clearly emerging at Boylston. On the same Friday that two workers squeezed into the Old Mill, sixty-two Boylston millhands were already back at work. Fully 51 percent of Boylston's hands had abandoned the strike. Suddenly pickets at the south Dalton plant were in the minority. The strikers were losing momentum, and negotiations between management and union officials had still borne no fruit.[17]

A new crisis erupted at Crown on Monday, July 17, as more than 80 millhands from the New Mill banded together and crossed the picket lines. Embittered union loyalists joined in a chorus of "Oh, When the Scabs Go Marching In." Thirty-nine days into the strike, 226 millhands (one-third of the company's work force) had returned to work. By Friday it seemed the strike was collapsing. To be sure, only one-third of the workers had crossed the lines at the New Mill, but in sheer numbers, this group of 139 millhands was larger than the entire Boylston work force. Only the strikers at the Old Mill seemed to be holding the line, and even there 16 percent of the millhands crossed the lines.

After having shut Crown Mills down completely for a month, Local 185 now had to watch as its picket lines were bested and two plants resumed partial production. Between July 10 and July 21—ten working days—the strikers lost considerable ground and faced some difficult dilemmas. Only an all-out war could have kept the strikebreakers out, and even the workers most loyal to the strike were neither willing nor able to wage such a battle. Given the number of workers who returned to the mill, there was little chance for Local 185 to win a favorable contract, and the odds for a bitter loss were increasing daily. There was still some hope, however, because overall a strong majority of workers continued to hold out, and the company was not importing strikebreakers from other towns. The Old Mill still did not have enough hands to run a full shift. A large textile company simply could not operate profitably with such a reduced work force; production was made even more difficult because, given the dearth of hands, strikebreakers often had to operate machines they did not normally run.

National and regional developments had initially helped to fuel the strike, but once Crown resumed partial operation, the conflict, so far as the workers were concerned, became decidedly local and intensely personal. The company did not bring in outsiders to take over the positions left vacant by strikers, and Local 185 refrained from bringing fellow union members from American Thread and Real Silk Hosiery into the fray. Virtually every union loyalist knew every strikebreaker. The workers who glared, hollered, and lashed out at one another across the picket lines were all part of the same community. They were "family"—or at least they had been. Corporate paternalism had forged a coherent community of workers capable of organizing a union, but it had also created different needs and divergent interests among families who were otherwise remarkably similar. To some the union represented a threat to community. To others it offered hope for the community's salvation. The paradox of industrial paternalism was that it could simultaneously inspire and undermine working-class protest.

The partial resumption of work in the mill during July split Crown's cotton-mill families into two bitter factions. Rocks shattered windows in several mill-village homes—windows of families who had crossed the picket lines. When police arrived, they found a substantial crowd of both union and nonunion hands gathered at the scene. On the basis of loose accusations, they arrested several union people for the disturbance, and that evening Judge John Ray fined Will Travillian (who had been the union's second president), Frank Carswell, and Margaret Carswell for disorderly conduct. An outraged union leader, C. E. Earnhardt, accused "company stooges of throwing rocks through their windows in order to point to us as responsible for the damage." At the same time, strikebreakers brought charges against union pickets for "addressing them with abusive language and calling them 'yellow rats' and 'yellow scabs.'" They complained as well that strikers held "toy yellow rats" high in the air "as they went to and from their jobs."[18]

A speech delivered by Judge Mitchell to the Whitfield County grand jury exacerbated this tense situation. Mitchell charged that the CIO was obtaining free food from the Whitfield County welfare warehouse, distributing it to strikers as if the supplies had been provided by the union, and then charging the workers for it. He asked the jury to investigate the validity of this rumor. If it was true, he said, "a monumental fraud is being practiced upon the union members in Dalton." In a passage obviously intended for the ears of ill-fed strikers, Mitchell claimed that Earnhardt and other TWUA officials had been soaking up union dues in order to live "in swank hotels in Chattanooga, eating T-bone steaks, [and] washing it down with burgundy and champagne . . . while furnishing you with relief rations furnished by the government." Mitchell also claimed to "believe in organized labor, and believe in collective bargaining," but he insisted that local unionists were being duped by the CIO and suggested they consider rejecting the union. Nearly one month later, the grand jury found the union innocent of Judge Mitchell's charges, but by then his speech had already stirred up bitter feelings among the millhands.[19]

Why did some within the community support the strike and others oppose it? The people I interviewed for this study offered a variety of explanations. For many, the union converged with deeply held values—particularly religious values, as John Cronic's letters to the *Citizen* attested. One antiunion hand said of the strikers, "When they get God in their hearts, they'll see a different way." Another woman tried to convince her brother to quit the union, telling him that if he "would give his dues money over to the Lord, he would prosper." One faithful Baptist man went a step further when he drew an analogy to the Old Testament book of Malachi. "You see the men there [in the Bible story] were cheating God, and that's just what the union was doing to the mill. They were cheating the Hamiltons and them." But Christianity could also carry the seeds of rebellion, and many workers were loyal to both their churches and the union. Some millhands associated with the Holiness churches viewed the union movement as an arm of Christian justice. One local editor ridiculed what he perceived as the superstition and radicalism of Holiness believers in a satirical story about a Church of God brother who watched a spider on his porch weave a web that spelled out "UNION MILL."[20]

Apart from these larger ethical considerations, union workers normally viewed the issue from a practical standpoint. "If the company treats you right," claimed one of Crown's former millhands, "you don't need a union. If they don't, you need a union." "My view of the union," recalled one woman who supported the strike in 1939, "was always job security and better working conditions." Another man said he supported the union because workers needed "the rights to . . . if something was wrong, to be able to stand up and say that 'you're not doing me right.'" Most agreed with the man who claimed the union was an attempt to "better ourselves," by which the millhands generally meant secure jobs, decent wages, reasonable work assignments, and more autonomy over their private lives.[21]

Antiunion hands opposed the organization for equally pragmatic reasons. Personality clashes kept some workers out of the union. More important, workers who were in the good graces of Crown's lower-level supervisors felt they had much to lose from a union, for the same reason those "at outs" with overseers had much to gain from it. "In" workers had more job flexibility and security as long as the semiformal paternalistic system endured, but "out" hands could never expect job security (particularly during an economic depression) unless the union attained it for them. The problem was that such security could only be gained at the expense of traditional patterns of favoritism and patronage. Those comfortable with the old system viewed union influence as a threat to their job flexibility and to former prerogatives. With the coming of the union, the hiring process was systematized, and any new job opening had to be bid for by the workers. The qualified bidder with the most seniority received the job. As a corollary to this system, jobs left vacant for a certain time were opened up to new bidders. One woman, for example, always loved her work and took great pride in how she "kept her frames." Some years after the 1939 strike, she fell ill for some time—long enough for her job to be put up for bids and, from her point of view, taken from her. Under the old system, her frames would have been given back to her; without them, she felt alienated at work and quit the mill. In 1939 this woman already perceived what the union might mean for her own work, and she opposed the strike.[22]

Another important consideration was how one's family stood on the union. Such determinations were by no means simple. A family's response to the strike was usually mandated by the household head, who was usually a male. Decisions were based primarily on a practical determination of whether the family was in a position to lose or gain from the imposition of union authority in the mill. Housewives apparently had little say in the matter, even though unionization affected their lives and mill-village relationships in vital ways. (A small number of married women did hold regular jobs in the mill in 1939, and incomplete evidence suggests they were dedicated strikers.) Younger children living at home simply took their cues from their parents. Within each household, sentiment was almost always united, but parents and their older children did not always agree. Children who had moved out on their own in the mill village decided their own fate. And because so many families in the village had intermarried over the years, it was impossible to take sides without offending some kinfolk. Individual decisions, therefore, sometimes hinged on conflicting considerations. Thinking back on the 1939 strike, John Bramblett remembered, "My daddy wasn't [in the union]. All the time he worked, he never did belong. But when they struck, he didn't come in. Some of 'em came in and went to work. My dad wouldn't come in. He said he had a son out there on the picket line, and he would not cross that line." This decision to honor a son's commitment was made easier, Bramblett said, by the fact that "at the time we lived on a farm and we had plenty to eat—raised our own stuff. Some people had to work, you can understand. A person was going to work before they'd starve." Or as Des Ellis, who crossed the lines, explained, "I made a lot of enemies, I guess, but my enemies didn't buy my groceries." What constituted the family interest and household loyalty was not always easily determined, but for that very reason family decisions—once made—were usually final.[23]

To say that practical economic considerations and family loyalties affected strike decisions only raises larger questions. Any mill family's economic security had long rested on its relationship to the company and the paternalistic system. With that system now crumbling, how could mill-village households assess their interests? Did paternalism ultimately do more to inhibit or facilitate prounion sentiment? Were Crown's longtime millhands more likely to break the strike or to support it? When making their decisions about the strike, did workers place more emphasis on their pocketbooks than on cultural factors or commitments to either the union or the company? Because male household heads apparently dominated the discussion of unionization, what role, if any, did gender play in shaping decisions to support or oppose the union? To answer these questions is to discern more clearly the dynamics of organized labor in southern cotton mills during the late New Deal period. Ultimately, however, oral histories only reveal general sentiments about the union and the Crown Mill strike of 1939, sentiments expressed nearly fifty years after the event occurred. A more precise understanding of the conflict at Crown requires more detailed information about individual decisions made at the time of the strike.

Fortunately, the company payrolls for 1939 have survived, and they have allowed me to determine exactly which workers stayed out on strike and for how long. This data on individual strike support, when combined with other information gathered about each worker (from city directories and company records), constitutes a remarkable body of evidence with which to analyze the millhands' decision-making processes during the critical period of the strike. (For more on this data and how I analyzed it, see appendix B.) The "critical period" was the two-month span during which strikebreakers returned to work and union supporters stayed on the picket lines. Statistical information may not reveal the innermost deliberations of the workers as they confronted this crisis within their community, but the choice of whether to cross the lines or stay on strike was a vitally important

FIGURE 10.1.   Strike Support in Crown's Three Mills, 1939

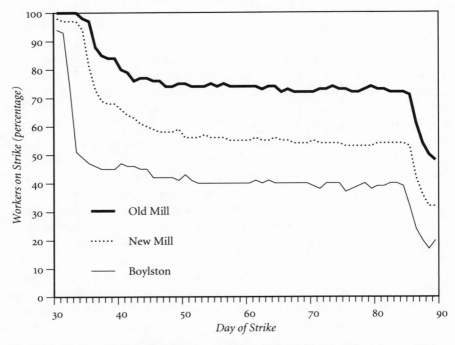

Source: Crown Cotton Mills Payroll Records and Boylston-Crown Mills Payroll Records, 1939, CGA.

decision that each millhand had to make, and the data on strike behavior offers a means of charting those decisions and pinpointing some of the factors that under-lay them.

The picture that emerges from the data is one of a sharply polarized community. Whatever the millhands' attitudes toward the union, their behavior at the mill gates during the critical period of the strike offered irrefutable evidence that here were two cohesive groups of workers locked in combat. As figure 10.1 illustrates, the initial break in the union lines was followed by a brief period of decision making, after which the community simply gridlocked. All but a few workers make their choices by August 1, and few changed their minds over the next two months. The standoff between union and antiunion workers was evident at each of Crown's three mills, but equally apparent were the different levels of strike support demonstrated at each plant.

The obvious imbalance of union support in the three plants is extraordinary. Workers at the Old Mill proved more strongly committed to the strike than those at the New Mill, whereas those at the Boylston plant were least likely to support the union. Was there something noticeably different about the workers at Boylston? It

TABLE 10.1. Persistent Core of Workers at Crown Mills, 1939

	Number of Workers in 1939	Percentage on 1927 Payroll	Percentage Hired after 1927
Old Mill	121	40	60
New Mill	431	39	61
Boylston	121	19	81
All mills	673	36	64

Source: Crown Cotton Mills Payroll Records, 1927, 1939, CGA.

might be argued that, because Boylston was the newest of the three plants and longtime residents usually preferred to live in the upper village, Boylston's mill-hands were more likely to be newer employees at Crown and hence less committed to a union that arose out of long-standing community concerns. One recent study makes an argument along these lines, suggesting that "newcomers" and "green hands" were instrumental in breaking the General Textile Strike of 1934.[24] Statistical evidence indicates that there were, in fact, more newly employed millhands in the Boylston plant (see table 10.1). Of Crown's three mills, Boylston had the smallest percentage of workers who had been with the company since 1927. On average, then, the millhands there tended to be relative newcomers to the corporate community.

But the apparent correlation between newcomers and strikebreakers does not hold up under closer scrutiny. The best way to test such propositions is through the use of multiple regression analysis, which allows us to compare the relative effects of various personal characteristics on strike support. In this case, I relied on a form of regression called logit analysis (for more on logit analysis and why it was used, see appendix B). The logit results indicate the personal traits, among the five that were available for examination, that characterized diehard strike behavior (see table 10.2). The estimated coefficients in the table reflect the strength and direction of the relationship between each variable and strike support, with the other four statistical relationships also taken into consideration. Only those coefficients that have a "t-score" of two or more can be said to have a statistically significant relationship with strike support.[25]

The logit results indicate, for one thing, that the figures in table 10.1 are misleading. Neither old-timers nor newcomers were responsible for breaking the strike; both groups were internally divided over the conflict. Working in the Old Mill was indeed significantly related to strike support, just as working in Boylston was statistically associated with strikebreaking. But the reason for this variance was not the higher proportion of newcomers at Boylston. The variable *length of employment* (the same measure of employee persistence used in table 10.1) is not signifi-

cantly related to strike support. When a number of variables are examined simultaneously, long-term employment with Crown no longer appears as a determinant
of prounion activism. Because a worker's tenure with the mill did not have any
meaningful association with strike support, it may be argued that paternalism did
indeed cut both ways when it came to the union. For some, the perception that
Crown's officials had forsaken conventional paternalistic policies created a crisis
that could only be overcome through unionization. For others, the union had
begun to impinge on formerly held prerogatives; it was not a solution but an
additional problem. Strong ties to the community did not make the workers'
decisions easier.[26]

It is also important to realize the the workers' assessments of the strike did not
rest simply on the wages they were able to earn in the mill. Many economists
would assume that pocketbook issues were always the dominant factor in shaping
a worker's decision to strike or not. They might argue, for instance, that millhands
who earned more in the mill would oppose the strike because they had more
money to lose by staying away from the job. Alternatively, such scholars might
argue that workers who normally earned more were generally better off and, as a
consequence, would be *more* likely to strike because they had a larger savings
buffer to carry them through a prolonged season of unemployment; they could
afford to risk going on strike. But as the logit results show, the workers' regular
earning power did not affect their commitment to the strike. The insignificant
coefficient for *earnings* (see table 10.2) suggests that millhands who commanded
higher wages on a regular basis were just as likely to hold the line as those whose
paychecks were meager. To be sure, economic considerations did matter. As John
Bramblett pointed out, workers were going to cross the picket lines before they
starved. The logit nonetheless demonstrates that millhands did not calculate the
cost of the strike merely in terms of their normal earnings. In the Crown Mill strike
of 1939, there was more to strike commitment than dollars and cents.

The most surprising result of the logit analysis is what it reveals about the
relationship between gender and strike support: males at Crown were more likely
to be zealous strikers than were females. This conclusion was not suggested either
by my oral history interviews or by the testimony in the poststrike court case. Both
of these sources indicated that women were vocal and active on both sides of the
issue. Although data on marriages is incomplete for 1939, what there is suggests
that *married* women in general supported the strike. Single women, on the other
hand, were least supportive of the strike, whereas single males were the most
unified in backing the union. One speculative explanation for the lack of support
from single female workers lies in the ongoing traditions of family economy and
women's wage work. Although some married women worked regularly at Crown
during the 1930s, most female millhands still left the mill upon marriage or the
birth of children, and they viewed mill work as a stage in their lives, not as a

TABLE 10.2. Logit Estimates of Strike Support, 1939

Explanatory Variable	Estimated Coefficient	T-Score
Earnings	.21	.34
Length of employment	−.11	.57
Gender (male)	.41	2.30
Worker in Old Mill	.80	3.42
Worker in Boylston	−.72	3.15
(Constant)	−.55	.42

Sources: Crown Cotton Mills Payroll Records, 1927, 1939; U.S. Internal Revenue Service, "Schedule A —Employer's Report of Taxable Wages Paid to Each Employee," ending date 31 Mar. 1939; both at CGA.

Notes: The dependent variable indicating strong support (*diehard*) was a dummy variable: 54 days or more on strike = 1; otherwise = 0.

The explanatory variables were as follows: *earnings* = log of an individual's total earnings during Crown's first quarter, 1939; *length* = 1 for those workers listed on the Crown Mill payroll in 1927, 0 otherwise; *gender* = 1 for males, 0 for females; *Old Mill* = 1 for workers on the Old Mill payroll, 0 otherwise; *Boylston* = 1 for workers on the Boylston payroll, 0 otherwise.

For more information on logit analysis and the data used here, see appendix B.

lifetime occupation. During the strike, these women might have viewed short-term earnings as more important than long-range union goals. Or perhaps families who generally supported the strike nevertheless sent a daughter or two to the mill as a means of guarding against outright destitution. In this scenario, single females who crossed the picket lines would actually have been acting as agents of family survival for strike supporters.

Beyond these considerations, however, lies the larger issue of gender and unionization. Instead of saying women failed to support the union, it might well be argued that the union failed to support women. Local 185 did not, for example, lodge any protest against the Crown Mill dress code (particularly the mandatory hose rule) that many women resented. Nor did it seek the creation of child-care facilities that would have simplified wage work for many mill-village women. And although the union did not bar women from leadership positions (in fact, several women were later elected to lower-level offices), Local 185 nonetheless was run almost exclusively by men. To male cotton millers, the union offered an alternative means of elevating their status in the community, but women—especially young, single female workers—could not look to the union for advancement. Without better data on marital status and age, it is risky to speculate further, but the logit estimates suggest at the very least that more research on this issue is needed.

Whatever the workers' gender, their propensity to strike was strongly related to their particular place of employment. The logit confirms that workers at the three different mills demonstrated significantly different levels of strike support. Regardless of their earnings, length of employment with the company, or gender, workers in the Old Mill were most likely to be diehard strikers, whereas millhands at Boylston were most likely to cross the picket lines. One reasonable explanation for this trend might be the different work environments of the three mills. But because the textile goods produced by the Old Mill and Mill No. 2 were nearly identical, it is difficult to explain why support was so much stronger at the Old Mill. The types of jobs workers held and the machinery they used were similar in both mills. It is suggestive, though, that Boylston lacked a weave room, a work area traditionally viewed as a hotbed of unionization and strikes. To explain the mill-to-mill discrepancies in strike behavior, however, would require better information on the particulars of each plant and the departments within those plants. Even these rudimentary findings do seem to indicate that each mill had a unique work environment that colored the workers' view of the union and the strike. In a court case that followed the strike, workers who took the stand were asked which department of the mill they worked in; having answered, they invariably added that they had "never worked anyplace else." During the Great Depression, workers and bosses tended to stay put in their jobs, creating distinctive subcommunities within the workplace, each of which seems to have engendered or hindered prounion sentiments in its members to varying degrees.

A related explanation may be found in the kinship and neighborhood clusters that characterized the different work areas within the mill. Although by the late 1930s a millhand's ability to move from one mill job to another was governed partly by union rules, the company still made all the hiring decisions. Attitudes toward the strike in any one plant may well have been rooted in a much older Crown Mill tradition of hiring family and kin together. The impact of familial hiring trends would have been especially great in the smaller plants such as Boylston and the Old Mill, which each employed only about 120 workers at the time of the strike. By 1939, national forces regularly influenced the daily lives of southern millhands, and the Crown Mill strike was clearly something more than a local conflict; but in the face of uncertainty, family associations and small-scale collaborations still had a powerful impact on the millhands' behavior.

The social complexity reflected in the logit results helps explain why many workers felt bewildered by the union conflict and why they did not view themselves as a working class united by common interests. Females may have been less supportive of the strike than males generally, but women themselves differed in their behavior from mill to mill; women at the Old Mill were, on average, much stronger in backing the union than were women at Boylston. Some might assume the workers' decisions were linked to their earning capacities, but this clearly was not the case. Company officials, union leaders, and antiunion workers all found it convenient to blame their problems on outsiders, but the realities of the situation were never so clear-cut, and all sides found themselves frustrated.

Tempers already on edge exploded as the strike dragged on through the steamy August heat. A young woman became infuriated by the insults hurled at her each day by the pickets. One man in particular annoyed her each morning by calling out in a loud voice, "Here comes the prettiest little scab in the mill." The woman decided to tell her brother about these incidents, but friends convinced her not to for fear he would kill the insulting striker. The company had instructed returning workers to remain silent in the face of verbal intimidation, but one morning she snapped back, "I'd rather be a scab than that what's under it!" Strikebreaker Sibyl Queen confronted a heckling woman on the picket line with the words, "There'll be a meetin' at Crown View next fall and you'll be wantin' to shout." Here was a blistering insult that would have baffled outsiders. Queen was referring to the fact that the heckler in question "went to church a lot" but "every time they had a [revival] meeting she'd have to get saved again"—something, in Queen's view, a good Christian should not have to do and which, also in her view, characterized union people. Verbal assaults from both sides inflicted deep wounds, slashing the bonds of community that had for generations helped smooth the millhands' adaptation to a very difficult life.[27]

In mid-August mill officials took action to minimize the potential of serious violence as well as to undermine the strike. They did so by filing a lawsuit against several union leaders for intimidating millhands who wanted to return to work. Soon thereafter the Whitfield County Superior Court granted Crown an injunction that severely limited the number of pickets and placed new restrictions on their behavior. Judge John C. Mitchell enjoined local unionists "against acts of violence, intimidation and coercion directed toward any person or employees" related to Crown. In particular Mitchell pronounced illegal the "use of profane, abusive or scurrilous language, including the use of such words as 'scabs' or any sign or gesture indicating such meanings." The ruling limited pickets to five per post, except near the coal trestle, where strikers had been gathering to block the traffic of commuting millhands, making it difficult for them to park and get to work on time. Here the court limited pickets to three. The injunction was not entirely adverse to the union, however. Mitchell warned the company and its working employees against violence and intimidation toward the strikers, and he allowed the union to maintain its strike headquarters on the east side of Chattanooga Avenue. More important, he declared it illegal for the company to import "strike-breakers, that is to say, persons employed temporarily for the purpose of breaking the strike." Crown could hire "bona fide (permanent) workers in place of the strikers," but the company had to notify the union in writing a week before taking such action, and it could not begin new hiring until two weeks from the day of the injunction, which was handed down on August 19. For all Mitchell's attempts to render a balanced judgment, the injunction effectively undercut the union's tactic of mass intimidation, which was the only viable tactic it had left once the mills resumed partial operation. Even so, the strikers held out tenaciously for another hot, poverty-stricken month, gamely awaiting a favorable settlement.[28]

To the union workers who recall the strike, Judge Mitchell's injunction against Local 185 remains a bitter pill, and understandably so. But in reality his ruling did little to alter the workers' behavior. Mitchell handed down his injunction two-and-a-half months into the strike. But by that time the millhands' choices were already set and did not change much afterward. The judge's ruling against the importation of strikebreakers was unusual for an antiunion injunction and was probably a political move, as Mitchell was up for reelection soon and did not want to alienate the labor vote completely. Whatever his motivations, Mitchell's restriction on the importation of new workers cemented more deeply the decisions workers had already made. Pickets could no longer intimidate the strikebreakers as they entered and left the mill, but the strikers themselves were assured that the company could not simply bring in truckloads of temporary workers. The injunction ironically reinforced the gridlock—but not indefinitely.

The union effort broke apart with startling suddenness (see fig. 10.1). On Friday, September 22, the proportion of Crown's millhands who were on strike was the same as it had been for the previous month and a half. But on the following Monday, a few loyalists at each mill defected. In total only 15 strikers trickled back into the mill that day, but this number marked the largest one-day defection since mid-July. Maybe word of a settlement was in the wind, or maybe the mill announced that it would begin hiring outsiders as permanent workers. Maybe the strikers were just getting very hungry. The union did its best to support members who were in need, furnishing money for food, medicine, and fuel. But resources were already scarce, and Local 185 could not count on a windfall from outside sources. On Tuesday, September 26, union commitment snapped as 69 staunch prounionists finally gave in, crossed the lines, and returned to work. The overall proportion of workers on strike now fell below 50 percent for the first time. By Wednesday, eight in ten workers were on the job at Boylston, and over 60 percent were crossing the lines at Mill No. 2. Even at the Old Mill—the bastion of strike support for Local 185—barely half of the millhands remained on strike. The strikers were going to lose. Nonetheless, 218 millhands (one-third of the company's total work force) held out until the very last day.

On September 28, mill officials and union representatives finally reached an agreement, and the longest strike in Dalton's history came to an end. For eighteen weeks, loyal union members had fought against wage cuts and stretchouts, but ultimately the managers got the better end of the deal. The new contract, set to be in effect until early 1941, incorporated the very work load adjustments mill officials had originally sought in May. In fact management had already put the new system of wages and work loads into effect with the workers who crossed the picket lines. The union did score a victory of sorts by having the proposed wage reduction cut by 5 percent. But as this meant that the returning workers' wages would now be 7 percent less than when they were last paid, no celebrations took place.[29]

Having sacrificed much to oppose the stretchout, many union hands found it difficult to accept the new working conditions. Henry Wade recalled returning to "the awfulest load you ever saw." He and a fellow worker could not keep up their jobs, and before two days elapsed, both walked away and never hired on with Crown again. Jobs were hard to come by, but the local bedspread industry was developing steadily, and both men found employment in a local spread house (an employment shift indicative of Crown's future). No surviving records indicate how many union hands followed Wade's example, but without doubt many found their return to the mill a frustrating experience. They could not help but think that workers who had crossed the picket lines were largely responsible for allowing the stretchout to happen, and that the nonunion hands were earning 5 percent more than they would have without the strike, even though they had sacrificed nothing, indeed had undercut the strikers' cause. For their part, nonunion hands believed that the strike had been doomed from the outset, that the company was doing the best it could under difficult circumstances, and that the union hands had ruined the mill village by stirring up unnecessary trouble.[30]

After the strike, an atmosphere of bitterness pervaded the mill. Vicious words exchanged in the summer swelter could not be forgotten. Neighbors who had chosen the opposing side could not be forgiven. After four months of outright enmity, the reintegration of the two groups in the mill demanded more grace than the exhausted hands could muster. Some from opposite camps made amends, but others, recalled one who was there, "never got over it." Some people have held grudges, said another, "even until yet." One woman's experience exemplified the deep antagonism prounion and antiunion hands felt toward each other after the strike. This woman had crossed the picket lines; the woman on the next set of frames had held out until the end. For years thereafter, the first woman recalled, they "worked right side by side, just like dummies," never speaking to one another. The cotton-mill family had been torn asunder.[31]

Corporate paternalism had created a mill-village world in which all loyal families could count on economic security, even though some families received better treatment from the company than others. All workers had a stake in preserving the system—but not an equal stake. When the managers appeared to betray the traditional codes of mill-village paternalism in the early 1930s, the workers did not coalesce into a united group with shared "class" interests antagonistic to the concerns of the company. Working-class unity in Dalton during the 1934 General Strike was more apparent than real, as subsequent conflicts in the mill demonstrated. The strike of 1939 revealed how mill-village paternalism had sowed the seeds of working-class conflict but ultimately reaped a peculiar harvest of loyalty among those millhands who believed their own interests could best be served by the old system. But it would be a grievous error to view Crown's antiunion workers in 1939 as either preindustrial individualists or naive company loyalists.

While the union exhausted itself, another group of Crown employees—composed exclusively of antiunion hands—staged a different kind of protest. Shortly before the strike ended, thirteen nonunion workers appealed to Georgia's commissioner of labor, Ben T. Huiet, to receive back wages for the weeks they were shut out of the mill. Their case hinged on Georgia's unemployment compensation law, which stated that employees were eligible to receive compensation for time lost during a labor dispute if they were of "a grade or class of workers" who were not "directly interested" in the dispute. Huiet ruled against these workers' case, stating that "interested" did not mean personal concern or "state of mind," but whether the strike would have affected their wages in the same way it did those of the people who stood on the picket line. In his view, the Bureau of Unemployment Compensation should not view industrial workers as being of a different "class" simply because they viewed a labor dispute differently from their fellow laborers. To do so would stigmatize union members and "put a premium on non-participation." The nonunion millhands, not to be denied, spread word of their case and recruited another 150 hands to join them in an appeal. But in late 1939, and again in early 1940, agencies of the Georgia Department of Labor ruled against them. In response to these losses, the antiunion workers brought suit against both Crown Mill and Ben Huiet in the Whitfield County Superior Court. During the courtroom proceedings that followed, even "Little George" Hamilton took the stand, but this time the company and the state lost. The county court ruled in the workers' favor in July 1940. Their victory was short lived, however, for the Georgia Court of Appeals soon nullified the superior court decision and placed its stamp of approval on Huiet's original decision.[32]

The suit became a symbol for a community divided. Adopting the legal terminology necessary to win their case, the nonunion hands argued that they did constitute a "separate class" of millhands, a class diametrically opposed to the union workers and the strike. As they stated in their original brief: "There were only two grades or classes of workers at the mill immediately before the commencement of the stoppage of work, . . . (1) those who called or consented to the strike or the stoppage of work and (2) those who discouraged the strike and who wanted to continue their work."[33] This was legalistic and opportunistic language, but it succinctly summarized the division among Crown's millhands in 1939. The strike demonstrated that the workers were not a single class of industrial laborers unified by their antagonistic relationship with capital. By the late 1930s, the Crown community had two basic choices. Either the company could continue to make all the rules (within new federal guidelines), or the union could have a say. In either case, some workers and their families stood to lose. The millhands' own culture was geared more toward mutual interdependence than individualism, but the tradition of unity could cut two ways. It could nourish a vibrant community of workers and contribute to successful unionization, but it could also lead to severe polarization within the mill village.

At a deeper level, the court case shed light on antiunionism itself. Antiunion sentiment did not stem simply from a sense of loyalty to the company. Neither did it reflect an aversion to modern forms of collective protest, or merely an ethic of individualism. The nonunion hands who sued their company did not have the mentality of "temporary" industrial workers. Viewed as a protest, the antiunion hands' suit actually resembled Local 185's strike, for it represented an organized struggle against what one group of workers perceived as unfair company (and state) policy. Antiunion millhands chided union members about the dues they handed to the organization each month, but the workers who brought suit against the company proved equally willing to sacrifice their hard-earned pay to a central source of authority (their lawyers) in order to exert greater control over their industrial community. The Crown Mill "family," it seemed, had fragmented into competing interest groups. Union workers fought antiunion workers, and both groups sometimes fought the company. But running through it all was a common insistence on locally controlled solutions and collective action, two older norms within the Crown Mill community that were now being channeled in new directions.

Despite the conflicts and severed relationships that marked the strike of 1939, all of Crown's millhands demonstrated a willingness to participate in modern forms of protest. Both prounion and antiunion workers behaved as cohesive interest groups, fully engaged in legal, organized—even bureaucratic—forms of protest. The Great Depression, the New Deal, and the rise of Big Labor gradually transformed life in the Crown Mill village and, indeed, throughout all of industrial America. By the end of the 1930s, even those southern mill villages that had never seen a union campaign operated within a national economic and political context markedly different from that of the early twentieth century. The demise of child labor and the advent of free high school education; Social Security and unemployment compensation; laws ordaining minimum wages, eight-hour work days, and overtime pay; federally sanctioned unions and politicized labor—all of these signaled the rise of America's welfare state, and together they chipped away at the foundations of welfare capitalism in the North and in the South. The 1930s dealt mill-village paternalism a mortal blow, but the system's final passing came slowly and fitfully, in a manner befitting its chaotic origins and erratic development. And it came painfully, in a manner consistent with the more brutal contradictions that had always been at the heart of cotton-mill paternalism in the New South.

PART IV

BEYOND

PATERNALISM,

1940–1969

11

LABORS OF WAR,

WARS OF LABOR

The Crown Mill strike of 1939 pummeled mill-village paternalism, left it in shambles, and demanded the creation of a new order. But what sort of order, and on whose terms? The strike itself had been an effort to redefine the boundaries of authority within the mill, but its ambiguous outcome failed to resolve the issue. What lay beyond paternalism could not yet be foreseen. National trends—most notably the outbreak of World War II—soon intervened to complicate matters further. Industrial relations no longer hinged on provincial struggles between millhands and managers. Daily affairs in the small-town South were increasingly shaped by developments in Washington and across the globe. National unions and social welfare legislation had played a significant role in altering mill-village life during the 1930s, but the enormous impact of World War II made earlier changes seem relatively unimpressive. When Adolf Hitler's Germany invaded Poland in September 1939 (even as the Crown Mill strike continued), the conflict that erupted set in motion forces that would transform virtually every part of the globe—including the American South.

The war had a phenomenal effect on Dixie's cotton-mill families. It banished the Great Depression and boosted the income of southern workers dramatically, as it raised American industry in general to new heights of production and power in the global economy. It brought thousands of married women into the textile work force, a trend that proved permanent and altered significantly the nature of the family economy. The war also facilitated the growth of organized labor, North and South, because the federal government enforced an armistice between managers and unions for the duration of the war. The workers paid a price: exhausting work regimens, rising accident rates in defense plants, and national union agreements that banned strikes, to say nothing of community disruption, high anxiety levels, and the deaths of loved ones overseas. The war nonetheless infused southern millhands with an unprecedented sense of pride and purpose. It raised the expectations they had for themselves and for their children. It propelled them into a larger world of politics and civic affairs. Newspapers trumpeted the patriotism and accomplishments of ordinary southern workers, and the millhands added their own voices—clearly and powerfully—to the new rhetoric of working-class respectability. Dalton's union workers presented themselves as the backbone of the local citizenry and made known their intention to become influential players in local affairs.

But given the labor unrest of the 1930s, the rhetoric of wartime patriotism and industrial harmony did not necessarily indicate permanent social change. For the millhands and managers of Dalton, the ending of the war overseas would mean the beginning of a war at home. World War II raised the stakes of the power game in the small-town South and made labor a legitimate contender in shaping the postwar order. As long as the war raged, mill owners and millhands in Dalton cooperated to produce vital textile goods for the war effort. But this patriotic task created only a temporary, tension-filled alliance that held little promise for a permanent reconciliation of interests. At the war's end, capital and labor squared off in a power struggle that, for a brief but critically important time, escalated into an all-out battle for control of the mills, the town, and, in a larger sense, the South.

Long before Japan attacked Pearl Harbor on December 7, 1941, the Second World War began to revive Dalton's textile industry. In early October 1939, the first signs of Crown's impending economic recovery were evident in a brief, casual letter sent to Neil Hamilton by F. H. Babcock, an agent of J. H. Lane and Company, Crown's longtime selling agent in New York. After congratulating Hamilton "on being in the black after months of strike trouble," Babcock expressed guarded optimism that a war-induced textile boom might prove profitable to Crown. Given the dual forces of British resolve and German aggression, he said, "It looks as though no immediate peace is in sight unless the Nazi regime collapses which seems most unlikely at the moment." The importance of this situation for Crown and the textile South was unmistakable. As Babcock remarked: "Barring an unexpected cessation of hostilities, the demand for cotton materials might be maintained [for a long time]." War in Europe not only meant increased export trade to neutral countries, he added, it also meant that "sooner or later, England and France will of course have to buy cotton materials in this market."[1] The following year was a lucrative one for the company. The mill ran two shifts, usually at full time, throughout most of 1940. For only the second time since 1929, Crown earned a 10 percent return on capital.[2]

The National Defense Act of June 1940 boosted the demand for cotton goods even more. This legislation gave the federal government the power to establish a peacetime draft. The mere possibility of conscription lured War Department officials and textile industry leaders to the conference table, where they planned a coordinated effort to supply the Quartermaster Corps with the enormous amount of cotton material it would take to supply an army.[3] In early August, F. C. Denning, an agent for J. H. Lane, monitored the meetings of the "textile advisory committee for the defense program." His subsequent report to Crown's officials spelled out the prospects for unprecedented cotton duck production. Denning noted that "with compulsory military service coming into the picture the army has got to secure a lot of tents quickly." Unlike World War I, during which the army housed soldiers in wooden barracks, the military now needed tents because "military tactics have changed . . . [and] men must be trained to move around."[4]

The "duck situation" became a quartermaster's nightmare in August 1940. War Department officials demanded two million yards of duck immediately and some four million more in the near future. One item of crucial importance was "tent shelter duck," a difficult material to make but one that would be in great demand. "Just how soon they are going to need shelter tents is [uncertain]," Denning admitted, "but if, as we expect, compulsory military service goes into effect, the first quota will probably go into training around October first, and another batch the first of the year."[5] Pondering the difficulties of making tent shelter duck, George Hamilton, Jr., responded, "We want to and of course will cooperate with this program to the fullest of our ability. We only wish though that it was on some construction which is not so difficult to make and which we had not done so well with [in the past]. . . . [We] do not want to promise a delivery on which we might fall down."[6] As Hamilton made this profession of duty to a business partner, and not for the government or for public consumption, his sincerity can hardly be questioned. Yet as Hamilton and all southern industrialists knew, wartime production, however difficult, meant full production, big profits, and, in addition, an end to labor problems caused by layoffs and dividing time. From 1940 through 1945, Crown averaged nearly $220,000 net profit per year.[7] Such an economic boon was only a dream in 1940, but, as a representative of J. H. Lane reminded Crown's managers in early August, "The present defense requirements of cotton goods are based upon peacetime training. If this country should get into the war, the quantities required would be substantially larger."[8]

When defense production quickened, the demand for labor escalated in Dalton and every other textile town nationwide. One year before Pearl Harbor, *Textile Labor*, the official newspaper of the Textile Workers Union of America (TWUA), announced that "textile employment is reaching new peaks. Most every branch of the textile industry is feeling the effects of government business." Virtually all mills were running two full shifts, many had started a third, and more government contracts were clearly on the horizon.[9] At Crown, overall employment continued to expand, reaching an average of about 1,000 workers in 1941.[10] Dixie's cotton mills began to confront their first labor shortage since the First World War. Workers not only had greater opportunities for textile work, but they could also consider a rapidly expanding array of higher-paying industrial employment. In Georgia the number of manufacturing jobs jumped from 26,900 in 1939 to 50,200 in late 1941, an increase of 87 percent in just two years. Unemployment compensation claims in the state fell from 4,886 in 1940 to 2,340 two years later; in 1943 unemployment claims filed by Georgia's manufacturing workers numbered only 270. The war had virtually abolished joblessness.[11]

As the profitability of Dalton's cotton mills increased and the purchasing power of Dalton's workers bolstered local retailers, a new cycle of boosterism swept the ranks of uptown business leaders. In the first half of 1940, local entrepreneurs launched a campaign to promote their town that seemed remarkably similar to Dalton's industrial crusades of the 1880s and 1920s. An "inter-civic club" composed of leading Civitans, Lions, Jaycees, and Rotarians organized an "industrial committee" to attract new manufacturers. The Dalton Merchant Association agitated for the creation of a new chamber of commerce (the old one having gone under), whose first priority would be to "bring in new industries and conserve existing industries."[12] As if to confirm the worthiness of such an effort, the *Dalton Citizen* soon announced that, "with most all manufacturing plants running full," the town's retail trade was brisk, and editors proudly pointed to evidence of "a small boom in construction."[13]

This entrepreneurial enthusiasm reflected more than renewed prosperity at Crown, Boylston, American Thread, and Real Silk Hosiery, the traditional mainstays of local industry. It also bespoke a growing excitement about the money to be made in tufted textile ("chenille") enterprises, which were now almost completely mechanized and were expanding rapidly. "What makes Dalton great?" asked the *Citizen*, doubling as a local puff sheet. The answer: Dalton was the "bedspread center of the universe."[14] Rhetorical flourishes aside, this claim was hard to deny. During the 1920s and early 1930s, as the small spread shops gradually expanded their operations further into the countryside of northwest Georgia, Dalton had emerged as the undisputed center of this cabin craft industry. Spurred partly by local technological innovations and partly by minimum wage laws, bedspread manufacturers in the late 1930s rapidly mechanized their operations and abandoned the put-out system in favor of centralized factory production in Dalton. The burgeoning chenille industry also branched out into new products such as bath mats, rugs, and robes. By 1940 the Tufted Bedspread Manufacturers' Association represented some 125 businesses. Log Cabin, San-Rog, Ken-Rau, Bates, Cabin Crafts, Rauschenberg, Latex, Dixie Belle—these were new and important players in Dalton's industrial game,.and they grew by leaps and bounds between 1939 and Pearl Harbor.[15]

The industrial growth of Dalton and the South created better employment opportunities and higher wages for southern factory hands. In late 1939, when many workers were still unemployed or were working part time, local cotton-mill and chenille plant managers adamantly resisted the government's imposition of a new 32 ½ cent minimum hourly wage.[16] But by late the next year, as available labor became increasingly scarce, the industrialists' resolve began to weaken. By October 1940, the local office of the State Employment Service was looking for workers to fill numerous manufacturing jobs in Dalton and across the state, in both defense and non–defense industries. Opportunities for weavers and loom fixers were especially promising.[17] By early 1941, the Whitfield County branch of the National Youth Administration (a New Deal public works program) had experienced a mass exodus of its young wards, who were leaving for jobs in industry.[18] At the same time, Dalton became a center for "Defense Course Classes," through which several hundred young white men could gain free training as welders, auto and airplane mechanics, metalworkers, and radio repairmen. Courses that taught blueprint reading and auto mechanics were also available for black workers—a significant departure for public programs in Dalton and an indication that authorities anticipated a critical shortage of skilled white labor in the region.[19]

By early 1941, the local cotton mills had voluntarily increased their minimum wage to 40 cents per hour. Spread plant managers followed suit. A spokesman for G. H. Rauschenberg's chenille plant, which employed seven hundred workers, said the new wage scale represented an effort to adhere to the national policy of "speeding up production and defense work." The most obvious and immediate benefit to Crown's millhands came in the form of more generous—and more frequent—paychecks. Beginning in late August 1940, Crown began production for the military. Federal contracts essentially put the mill on the government payroll, and the mill began to pay its workers every week, abandoning the biweekly remuneration policy that had been in place since 1885. Lillie Hill's paychecks reflected the impact of full-time earnings. Her hourly wages were only slightly higher in 1940 than in 1938, but because of the steady work available, her yearly earnings in 1940 ($666.47) exceeded those of 1938 ($348.51) by a remarkable 91 percent. The labor market was getting tight, and America was not even in the war yet.[20]

Workers who had suffered through the Great Depression made use of their newfound bargaining power; throughout the state they went on strike in unprecedented numbers. During the 1930s they had had no real economic leverage with which to win concessions from employers, but now they sought to redeem the previous decade by taking full advantage of the opportunities at hand. The Georgia Department of Labor hurriedly hired extra conciliators to help settle strikes and keep defense industries running. Workers not only sought better pay, but also a variety of improvements in their work environments. The department's annual report for 1941 noted that many disputes "revolved around jurisdictional questions" and "the improvement of working conditions." The war gave organized labor an unprecedented opportunity to expand its membership—especially in the South, where stable unions in major industries were still rare. This state of affairs was not lost on the CIO International (the union's national office), which tried to nurture and consolidate good relations with Big Government and to ensure that workers got their share of benefits from the wartime economic boom. In late 1941, shortly before Pearl Harbor, *Textile Labor* announced, "TWUA will play a major part in the great 1942 objective of CIO—the unionization of the South." In the final days of American peace, the possibility that the TWUA would sweep over the textile South was a possibility few industrialists could comfortably deny.[21]

The world of Dixie's textile workers had already changed greatly by the time Japan attacked Pearl Harbor. Like most Americans, Daltonians were shocked largely because they had grown accustomed to thinking of "the war" as a European affair. No one knew exactly where Pearl Harbor was, nor did they expect a sudden assault from the Far East. Most people later remembered the war as bursting upon America with great suddenness, but in reality the preparations for World War II had already left an indelible stamp on small-town life. National defense, the draft, home defense units, blackouts to conserve power for defense plants, defense education, the USO, defense stamps—all of these had become an everyday part of life in Dalton before December 7. America's entry into the global conflict only intensified trends that were already apparent. Military production boomed, industrial corporations grew fat on federal contracts, factory labor grew scarce, wages rose, and union influence expanded. The government became an increasingly pervasive force in people's lives, and ordinary Americans left home by the millions and scattered, literally, across the globe.

America's entry into the war infused organized labor with high hopes. In the spring of 1942, CIO president Philip Murray launched the "great Southern drive" at a rally in Charlotte, North Carolina, and by July, the massive Riverside and Dan River textile complex in Danville, Virginia, had voted in the TWUA, with 60 percent of some 12,000 employees casting ballots for the union. *Textile Labor* called it "the greatest election victory of the textile labor movement," because it doubled the number of southern millhands under TWUA contract. Organized labor's future had never looked brighter in Dixie. To union supporters, the labors of war seemed to offer golden opportunities for obtaining better paychecks, safer working conditions, and greater job security. At Crown, where the union already had a stable organization, the successful unionization of millhands across Dixie could only enhance the bargaining power and security of Local 185.[22]

The wartime protection of organized labor enabled aggressive local unions to press for new demands with greater confidence, and the leaders of Local 185 did just that. In July 1943 seven Crown workers, flanked by federal and state officials, stared proudly from a picture in *Textile Labor*, which announced that the Dalton millhands had pushed through a new contract that included "one week's vacation with pay." Workers who had struggled through the long Crown Mill strike in 1939 must have viewed this peaceful victory with a certain amount of amazement. The agreement also provided "for improvements in the hours and overtime section, a new seniority clause including [a] system for promotions, reporting time pay, [and] check off of union dues." Clearly the union was growing in power, and as the mill hired more workers and added extra shifts, Local 185 needed an increasing number of shop stewards, the union's own version of middle management. In this way, the union itself offered workers opportunities for upward mobility.[23]

Even without the union successes, America's entry into the war brought Dalton's textile workers a variety of tangible benefits. Opportunities for promotion within the mill increased—at least for men. As war demands skyrocketed and government contracts rolled in, the mill thundered into a furious three-shift, twenty-four-hour production regimen. Sometimes the machinery ran seven days a week. This work schedule forced Crown's managers to recruit new foremen and supervisors from among their crew of loom fixers and other longtime male employees. Many men who had found all avenues of advancement blocked during the Great Depression suddenly found themselves elevated in the company's managerial hierarchy. Ed Felker, for example, had been with the mill since the mid-1920s and, by the late 1930s, had worked his way up to loom fixer. Advancement beyond that point was not possible given the economic depression and the glut of experienced adult men in the mills. But when World War II created an instant need for new supervisors—not just in Dalton but throughout the nation—Ed Felker's working life changed suddenly and permanently as the mill filed for his military exemption and promoted him almost overnight to the position of supervisor in the New Mill carding department, a job he held for the rest of his career. Providing another example of sudden advancement was Bishop Caylor, who had scarcely come to Crown from the farm in 1940 when war production accelerated his promotion, first to fixer and then to foreman.[24]

Job opportunities and pay also improved for Dalton's wage-earning women. A large and not unusual advertisement in 1942, which called for women to be trained for the aerospace industry, exemplified this trend. "We Want 100 Girls," read the an-

Wartime victories for Crown's union workers. The new agreement negotiated by TWUA Local 185 included vacations with pay. Pictured, left to right, are: (*seated*) S. P. Brewer (U.S. conciliator), Homer Craig, Otis M. Weaver (president of Local 185), and R. C. Thomas (Georgia director); (*standing*) Marvin Scoggins, Lane Lowman, C. C. Forrester, Eunith D. Painter (financial secretary), and Luther Broom. (*Photo from* Textile Labor, *July 1943*)

nouncement in the *Citizen*, "Ages 17 to 40, Physically Fit—Mechanically Minded." The jobs were available immediately, and wages were "exceptionally good, $35 a week to start"—which was remarkable, given that an experienced female worker at Crown earned $10 less per week and would not earn as much as $35 until the postwar era. If the wages were not incentive enough, the ad insisted, "It is your Duty to get into (Patriotic) Defense Work whether you need to work or not." Gender was also less of a barrier to mobility in Dalton's bedspread plants, which hired mostly women, than it was in cotton mills. There were no unions in the chenille factories, but there at least women could become "foreladies."[25]

New factory jobs drew many young, single women into the labor market for the first time, but a more significant and lasting trend was the return of working-class wives and mothers to the mills. For them World War II offered, not the upward mobility it offered men in the factory, but instead the opportunity (or family responsibility) to work a full-time job. Many mills in Dalton, including Crown, traditionally had not provided steady employment for married women, particularly those with children, except in the event of a family economic emergency. But hiring policies affecting married women changed dramatically as war production increased and the size of the military swelled. By late 1944, American Thread had a company nursery and Crown was working to establish one. Fifteen other manufacturing firms, according to the *Citizen*, had met to discuss the issue and appeared "greatly interested." The plan was to establish "nursery schools" where working mothers could send their children (ages two through six) while they themselves worked in the mill. The nurseries were funded primarily by federal money and by what the *Citizen* vaguely termed "the local community," but they were not quite free of charge. Working mothers paid a small fee for services rendered. The record remains silent as to whether low-cost nursery schools ever became a widespread feature of wartime Dalton, but their existence as a topic of corporate and public discussion signified the importance and high visibility of wage-earning mothers during the early 1940s.[26]

During the war, Dalton's textile workers—particularly those who worked for Crown or American Thread—enjoyed more respect from the local citizenry than ever before. In fact, this change in attitude was evident even before Pearl Harbor, as defense production quickened and the sacrifices of America's laborers became national news.[27] The wider community acceptance continued to show itself throughout the war in small but significant ways. In January 1942, the *Citizen* actually reported, on its front page, the names of the Hosiery Mill's newly elected union officers. Shortly thereafter it published a photograph—again on the front page—of children at a Boylston-Crown Valentine's Day party. A "Crown Mill News" column began to run intermittently. Written by millhands, it was a mill-village equivalent of the Dalton society page, listing visits made, visitors received, and parties thrown. The significance of these items is apparent only in light of their complete absence from Dalton's newspapers during the previous half-century.[28] Now, though they might run an occasional antilabor cartoon, editors of the *Citizen* found themselves printing stories favorable to working people—even union people. On Labor Day in 1942, the *Citizen* praised labor's efforts and emphasized that soldiers and factory hands were "working together" to win the war. The paper even went so far as to applaud the achievements of Detroit's unionized auto workers ("soldiers of production"). Dalton's working men won commendation from the *Citizen* by enlisting in the military at a steady clip, and the paper gave its stamp of approval to young mill women who joined the Women's Army Corps.[29]

Throughout the nation, workers rallied around the flag, assumed a position as America's patriotic leaders, and took responsibility for getting the job done. Similarly, the working people of Dalton simply refused to be ignored during World War II. Local unions sought to drive home their message: industrial workers were the heart of the war effort, both at home and abroad. In early 1943, American Thread's TWUA Local 134 placed a full-page advertisement in the *Citizen*, providing an "Honor Roll" of sixty-nine of its members who were presently serving in the armed services and noting that 98 percent of the workers in their mill were regularly buying war bonds. Several months later, Crown's union president, Otis M. Weaver, published a front-page announcement that clearly demonstrated Local 185's intention that Crown millhands take their proper place in Dalton's civic affairs. Weaver reminded readers that a local election was approaching and that all good citizens should vote and buy war bonds. He went further with a message directed to uptown Daltonians, one intended to reassure them about working-class patriotism but also to underscore the fundamental importance of labor power in the war effort. Weaver stated that he wanted "the public to know there will be no strikes called by this local for the next two years or till after the war is over regardless of how long it takes for America to win." This was a direct reference to the CIO's "no-strike" pledge, which had won raves from the Dalton press and which Weaver used effectively to enhance the image of local unions. He and other local labor officials sought to create what might be called the Union Patriot ideal.[30]

A remarkable event in July 1943 marked the high point of union respectability in Dalton. The previous month, workers at the American Thread plant had won a coveted Army-Navy "E" Award for excellence in war production. Local hoopla ensued. In mid-July the government descended on Dalton in the form of a band of dignitaries with movie cameras in tow. The "E" Award ceremony dominated the local press. The most stirring moment—reported fully by the *Citizen*—was an address by one of American Thread's union workers, Irene Bailey, who began her speech by proclaiming that "free labor will win [the war]" and pledging the workers' best efforts to "crush every vestige of Nazism and Fascism." Bailey successfully wove together the themes of patriotism, hard work, union solidarity, and freedom. "Ours is the only country in the world today," she said, "where working people enjoy the full and unrestricted rights of collective bargaining. It is through that process that we have worked out our problems with our company, and as a result friendly and harmonious relations exist today. The road to winning this honor has not been easy—you, my fellow workers, have toiled long and tirelessly, day in and day out—you have stuck to your job and you have done a good job." Although acknowledging that American Thread's management also played a role in winning the award, Bailey added, "But it is you, my fellow workers, who deserve the major part of this great honor." She concluded, "We are proud of our country—proud of our Company, and proud of our Union."[31]

Bailey's speech revealed the society-changing potential of the war. The entire scene was peculiar for a southern textile town. Ordinary workers—the very "lint-heads" whom middle-class townspeople had long scorned and derided—were being honored by the federal government. Moreover, in a society dominated by wealthy men, a wage-earning mother gave the keynote address with unquestionable eloquence and was quoted verbatim on the front page of the *Citizen*. And to top it all off, she made a powerful case that modern-day unionism was American-ism at its best. Bailey's words echoed the sentiments expressed in Otis Weaver's letter to the Dalton citizenry. In one sense, Bailey and Weaver merely reaffirmed what the workers had thought about themselves all along—that they were solid citizens, indispensable for the welfare of their town. But the two messages also pressed new claims: that Dalton's working people, long isolated on the fringes of civic affairs, were seeking center stage; and that unions would be the base of their prestige and power.

In many ways, then, the war opened new opportunities for Dalton's working people, but the costs were high. During the last two years of the war, the strains of emergency production became increasingly intense. In late 1943, industrial repre-sentatives from the Formica Insulation Company of Cincinnati, Ohio, paid Crown's millhands a visit. Formica used Crown's duck and sheeting to make "laminated plastics," which were then used in a variety of ways to outfit planes and ships. In a speech to the millhands, Formica's vice president stressed the impor-tance of their work. He then suggested that Crown's employees ought to be doing better. It is not difficult to imagine the workers, already weary, responding to this speech with something less than enthusiasm.[32]

By 1945 the pressure on workers to increase production intensified. "What's new on the duck production front at Crown Cotton Mills?" local editors asked. The *Citizen* outlined impressive production statistics—nearly a half-million yards of duck in December 1944 alone—but also quoted with approval the remarks of Lt. Rodman Lamorelle, the "Army's 'speed-up' man," who told Crown's workers that "absenteeism and job hopping, even though practiced by only a small percentage of workers, is, however, crippling capacity production in many vital war indus-tries." To inspire greater efforts, Lamorelle paraded two wounded vets through the mill. Several months later, in the spring of 1945, Crown won an army plaque for having the lowest level of absenteeism among Georgia's duck mills. Neil Hamilton was proud to announce that the mill had upped production "by 65 percent over its normal average." The workers were proud, too—but also exhausted. Half laugh-ingly, half seriously, Lucile Hall recalled, "The thing that irked me was that we had been working so hard, such long hours, you know, during the war, and they sent a little Yankee down here to tell us with a few fancy cuss words what a good job we were doing. We knew we were doing a good job, and we didn't appreciate him coming down and telling us about it."[33]

Crown's workers were not alone in being pushed to the limit. Government reports in the waning years of the war documented an ever more grueling and dangerous regimen for textile laborers. Machines ran at record speeds twenty-four hours a day and were often tended by exhausted or inexperienced millhands. Accident rates in Georgia's textile mills rose 48 percent between 1942 and 1944, prompting the state Department of Labor to establish a new set of factory safety regulations and to initiate regular safety inspections. In many mills, serious sanitation problems resulted from rapid overdevelopment and the steady deterioration of factory sewerage facilities. Work was steady, pay was good, and savings accumulated as never before, but on the underside of this situation were fatigue, injury, and disease.[34]

The double-edged sword represented by the war was evident in its impact on the Crown Mill community. On the one hand, war brought liberation for those who wanted out of the mill. On the other hand, it had an undeniably disruptive effect on the mill village. As young men from Crown enlisted or were drafted into the armed services, families and neighbors became separated. Young men died overseas. One woman interviewed still felt sorrow over "one of the boys that worked our end of the card room, Henry Smith. He went to the army and he was killed, and that made us all very sad. . . . We hated that." Anna Nell Garren and Sarah Bunch, sisters growing up on Jones Street, worried about four brothers who were overseas, as well as five neighbor boys. They recalled the constant fear of bad news. "There wasn't any telephone or anything, and messages had to be delivered by taxicab, you know, when they'd send a telegram. And there we was up there on that end of Jones Street with all these in service, and all of 'em overseas. Every time a taxi would come, it would scare you to death." Married couples not separated by the military sometimes lived and worked in separate cities. Parents shuttled their children among relatives. Young people left town seeking better opportunities and never returned to the mill village. During the late 1930s, labor turmoil had polarized a stable Crown community. Now World War II began to dismantle that community simply by scattering it across the nation and around the globe.[35]

Just as many small-town people were leaving home, the federal government came to town and established permanent residence. The power of the state to influence local economic affairs had never been stronger, and "state" power now emanated less from Atlanta than from Washington, D.C., home of "the Government." Like World War I, the Second World War spawned countless new agencies, but unlike the first war, this one created a permanent edifice of federal bureaucracy, one that dwarfed the visions of even the most ambitious New Dealers. During the war, labor received some good deals and some raw deals from Big Government. The National War Labor Board protected the rights of organized labor, but the national unions paid for that protection by agreeing to the "no-strike" clause that ostensibly prevented walkouts in defense industries. In addition, the Smith-Connally Act of 1943 placed federal limitations on wartime strikes. The Regional Labor Stabilization Act of 1943, enforced by the War Manpower Commission, made it difficult for workers to move from one job to another, even if they had better opportunities elsewhere.[36]

The ambiguity of government intervention became all too apparent in Dalton during the early months of 1945. Crown and American Thread flew into a productive frenzy when the quartermaster classified duck and yarn as "critical materials" for the military effort. But this edict also meant that yarn normally used by Dalton's spread plants had to be channeled to other industries. In effect, the government shut down every nonmilitary chenille plant in town. As a result, three thousand workers suddenly found themselves out of work, whereupon an army of state and federal agencies sprang into action. The Smaller War Plants Corporation helped some plants win military contracts for tents and parachutes. The U.S. Employment Service found "essential war jobs" for about one thousand workers, who rapidly signed on at American Thread in Dalton or at out-of-town plants such as the mill in Trion, Tubize Rayon in Rome, the naval ordnance plant in Macon, or the navy yard in Charleston, South Carolina. The Georgia Department of Labor, meanwhile, assisted more than one thousand Dalton workers with unemployment compensation payments of fourteen dollars per week to help keep workers and local merchants above water. The military's yarn and duck policy continued throughout the summer until the end of the war, thereby keeping Crown and American Thread awash with work while simultaneously crippling Dalton's chenille plants and creating problems that various government agencies were eager to address. By 1945 agencies in Washington had assumed a vast degree of control over the economy. The merits of this trend were debatable, but the trend itself seemed irreversible. The economic lives of Dalton's millhands and managers became increasingly entwined with the national bureaucracy. Not surprisingly, both capital and labor sought to gain leverage over federal policy.[37]

When it became clear in early 1945 that an Allied victory was only a matter of time, workers and industrialists turned their attention toward postwar challenges. Two months before the victory in Europe, the *Citizen* announced that the Dalton City Council, in an effort to "encourage the postwar expansion of the community," had voted to give a five-year tax exemption to all new industries.[38] Concern about the postwar economy only intensified after May 8, 1945, when Harry S Truman, who had become president following Franklin D. Roosevelt's death, proclaimed victory in Europe. Along with most of Dalton's businesses, Crown Mill and American Thread shut down in honor of V-E Day. But local journalists noted that the people remained quiet and somber; many voiced concern about the job yet to be done in the Far East.[39] People were also concerned about their jobs at home—perhaps about their unions as well. Some thought the victory in Europe would mean curtailed government orders and mass layoffs in the textile industry. Such concerns proved unwarranted. Although nearly 100,000 southern workers were soon laid off from the shipyards, airplane plants, and munitions factories that had sprung up in the wartime South, textiles continued to run strong through the end of the war. Particularly appealing to those at Crown Mill was the skyrocketing demand for the tents and storage supplies so critical for the Pacific theater. Southern cotton mills actually suffered an acute labor shortage during the final two

months of the war. Many industrialists hoped the layoffs in other military industries would help fill the gap, but the *Citizen* reported that "such workers do not
find 60 cents to 80 cents an hour [the pay in textile plants] very attractive where
they have been receiving $1.00 an hour in the strictly war-purpose plants."[40]

Despite fears of a postwar economic depression, the textile labor shortage of
mid-1945 signaled new and better job opportunities for the working people of
Dalton, not only for the duration of the war but also afterward. An advertisement
in the *Citizen* soliciting workers for Rome's Tubize Rayon plant provided a simple
reminder that labor market trends could have an immediate and tangible impact
on the lives of ordinary working people. "Have a steady peace-time job!" Tubize
promised in June 1945, even as the war in Asia continued unabated. "Pay above the
average with opportunity to make a bonus! Opportunity for promotion! First class
meals in Cafeteria! Group Insurance! Nursery for children ages 2–5 years! Swimming pool and other employee activities! Board and room available! Group or
Pooled Transportation can be arranged!" During the decades leading up to World
War II, this eye-popping advertisement would scarcely have been credited by
Dalton's cotton millers. The southern world of job possibilities had changed. Few
millhands from Dalton rushed to Rome, aside from some chenille workers whose
plants had been closed by government order. But even out-of-work spread workers who stayed home qualified for unemployment benefits, an economic safety net
unavailable to Georgia's textile families before the late 1930s.[41]

This corporate scramble to find textile workers alerted southern millhands to
their need to preserve war-won economic gains after Japan surrendered. The
TWUA constantly reminded Crown's workers that they must "win the peace" and
provided both encouragement and warnings about what lay ahead. The union's
national office kept an eye not only on the textile economy but also on political
trends that might affect southern workers. During the war, *Textile Labor* scru-
tinized Congress to monitor how southern representatives voted on labor legislation. Dalton's longtime congressman, Malcomb Tarver, who had spent his career
focusing on agriculture and who had no sympathy whatever for organized labor,
rated as one of Georgia's three worst representatives. According to the TWUA,
Tarver voted "wrong" more than 50 percent of the time. While looking toward
future battles with Tarver, the labor editors also noted with alarm in late 1944 that
city leaders in Newnan, Georgia, had passed a new ordinance requiring union
representatives to purchase a $5,000 license for the privilege of organizing within
the Newnan city limits. Winning the peace would require successful political
action against the likes of Tarver and the political elite of Georgia's textile towns.[42]

The postwar era arrived suddenly. On August 6, 1945, the United States dropped
an atomic bomb on Hiroshima, followed three days later by a second one on
Nagasaki, thereby forcing Japan's surrender and inaugurating the atomic age with
fearful power. At the Crown Mill, a less dramatic but nonetheless fundamental

turning point in the company's history was reached five days before the Hiroshima bombing, when Frank Springer died of a heart attack. Still at work on the day he died and apparently feeling fit at age seventy-one, Springer had been with the company for nearly its entire history. He had begun his career as a young boy in the spinning room in 1887, and he finished it as superintendent of the carding and spinning departments of the Old Mill and Mill No. 2, superintendent over the Boylston-Crown plant, and superintendent of all company housing. "Mr. Springer rose to his present position with Crown Mills through hard work," noted his obituary. "His rise to superintendent was the reward for diligence, ability to get along with people, and ambition."[43]

Springer's career at Crown was remarkable by any standards. His importance in shaping the company's history was undeniable. As a young man, he saw the chaotic living conditions of the early twentieth century gel into a cohesive mill-village community by World War I. As a superintendent during the 1920s, he promoted a kinship hiring policy, established and enforced rules for mill-village living, and emerged as the central power in Crown's paternalistic system. His arbitrary use of that power helped engender labor discontent during the early 1930s and inspired many workers to join the union. As a symbol of upward mobility, favoritism, and corporate power, Springer was a pivotal player in both the creation and the destruction of the old Crown Mill "family."

Frank Springer's death, like the end of the war itself, prompted questions about the future. What would become of the union, the mill village, the southern textile industry? Perhaps the workers' world could return to normal. But what was normal? Never before had so many southern workers been so secure economically. Would they be able to hold on to the relative improvements in their standard of living? What about the young people in the armed services, and what of those who were now entering high school? Would they follow the same paths as their parents? The unions faced their own set of troubling questions. During the war, Local 185 had grown stronger and had won impressive new benefits for its members; Irene Bailey had extolled the union to an applauding crowd; and the local press had begun to give Dalton's millhands their due. Would "normal" mean a return to weak unions and an antilabor press? Would unions maintain their involvement in Dalton's civic affairs? The future held promise but also the danger of a conservative backlash. In September 1945, *Textile Labor* put it succinctly: "With the end of the war, our union faces a crucial test. An era has ended—an era has begun."[44]

The TWUA went on the offensive as soon as the war ended. The International implored its members to face the uncertainty of the postwar era with determination, not timidity. "It must always be our union's task," the editors of *Textile Labor* wrote shortly after V-J Day, "to fight, by whatever means are at our disposal, for full employment, complete security, and an ever increasing standard of living."[45] Workers across the country took the initiative by going on strike to preserve or improve their existing contracts. During late 1945 and throughout 1946, an un-precedented wave of strikes swept America—North, West, and South—as weary, worried industrial workers sought to redress some of the hardships they had endured during the war and to secure a better way of life in the future. Battles between southern managers and millhands flared almost immediately. In Athens, Georgia, workers began a strike following V-J Day that lasted over four months. In October and November, *Textile Labor* reported numerous strikes in southern mills, many of them in Georgia. Some of these strikes were called in an effort to improve wages, but most erupted at mills where unions had been organized and protected during the war and where workers now claimed that their companies were engaging in union-busting activities and refusing to follow War Labor Board directives.[46]

In the aftermath of war, the TWUA stood as a symbol of both hope and anxiety for the CIO. Some 20 percent of the South's textile workers were union members at war's end. This figure was a marked improvement over the 1930s, but it ran far behind the national average for the CIO, whose membership had more than doubled during the war years. Most major industries in the North and West were solidly union by 1945, but a nonunion, low-wage region dragged down the earn-ings and political clout of unions everywhere. Southern textiles represented the weak link in the CIO's effort to forge a strong postwar labor front.

In June 1946, the CIO launched a major effort to organize southern workers, particularly those in textiles. The "Southern Organizing Drive"—or Operation Dixie, as it came to be called in the media—was, according to CIO president Philip Murray, "the most important drive of its kind ever undertaken by any labor organization in the history of the country." Seeking to strike a rapid blow for unionism in the postwar South, the CIO sent what it termed an "army of orga-nizers" to every southern state (plus parts of West Virginia), focusing on the major textile chains in the Carolinas, Georgia, and Alabama. If southern textiles could be organized, the reasoning went, the rest of southern industry would follow; and if the South were solidly organized, wage rates across the nation would uniformly rise and the political clout of organized labor would be enhanced. Murray spelled out his ideas on the crusade when he addressed a convention of union automobile workers in Atlantic City, New Jersey:

> We have been reading about things in the South for many years—poll tax, low wages and the inability of the average poor wage earner to vote on election day. . . . [T]here is only one way to cure that condition down there. . . . [T]he CIO has got to go into the South and carry the message of America to the people down there. . . . Lend all the support you can to this Southern drive, because the South, as you doubtless know, constitutes a type of economic millstone thrust around the necks of the people who are work-ing in the North.

This statement, filled with missionary and self-serving impulses, suggests one major problem with the drive—namely, that the CIO's national leaders viewed the South as a different country. The message also reflected Murray's goal of raising funds from northern workers, because he wanted all CIO unions to help finance the massive TWUA operation. All of the major textile mills in Dalton were already organized, so Operation Dixie had little direct impact on the town. But indirectly the TWUA drive stood to have an enormous impact on Local 185. The drive's success or failure would determine whether Dalton's union millhands would remain a minority within their region or whether their bargaining power would grow as they became part of a larger core of organized southern millhands.[47]

Union leaders everywhere understood that the battle to win the peace would be fought in the political arena. Big business and national unions were both aware that the Wagner Act and its mechanism of enforcement, the National Labor Relations Board (NLRB), had been central to the rapid rise of organized labor in the late 1930s and during the war. Big labor owed its existence partly to the successes of the New Deal political coalition that emerged during the 1930s, and vice versa, because New Dealers often relied on the labor vote. One reason for the federal protection offered to unions during World War II was that the Democrats needed the votes of organized workers. But if federal power had sustained big labor, federal power could also cripple it.

The CIO's leaders recognized this possibility, and in mid-1943 they organized the Political Action Committee (PAC) in response to Republican gains in congressional elections the previous year. Although coordinated by the national CIO office, PAC was actually an elaborate system of political clubs established in every town, congressional district, and state in the country. As such, PAC represented a new form of political activism by organized labor. The American Federation of Labor (the CIO's predecessor and rival) had normally eschewed politics, and the CIO's support for the Democrats in the late 1930s and early 1940s was merely an informal confirmation of the workers' own political inclinations. PAC marked a dramatic reversal of such political decentralization. As an innovative mechanism for coordinating and strengthening labor's political efforts and for educating workers about political trends and the processes of government, PAC won immediate notoriety. Republicans, conservative Democrats (most of whom were southerners), and business leaders condemned PAC as a strong-arm tactic that forced American workers to vote for candidates chosen by labor bureaucrats. Workers and liberal Democrats praised PAC as a long-overdue agent of true political equality and a means by which ordinary American workers could finally have a say in government.[48]

Although the CIO's PAC everywhere faced substantial barriers to political success, organized labor in Georgia and the South confronted an especially difficult task. Instead of operating within a liberal Democratic organization to battle against Republicans (as in the North and West), workers in Dixie had to struggle to make headway within a one-party system dominated by conservative Democrats. One way for southern workers to succeed, theoretically, was to create a new coalition that united working-class whites and blacks to combat the entrenched leadership. The odds of building this coalition were, however, very slim. The one-party South owed its very existence to the disfranchisement measures passed by Democrats during the late nineteenth and early twentieth centuries. The white primary and the poll tax had purged most blacks and many poor whites from the political process. Since the Populist crusade of the 1890s, there had been no serious attempt by disaffected whites to unite politically with African Americans, and even in the wake of World War II it was difficult to imagine that organized cotton-mill workers could overcome years of racial prejudice to advocate a biracial political alliance.[49]

But changes were in the wind. For one thing, African Americans were chipping away at the legal system that barred southern blacks from political participation. That effort bore some fruit in 1944, when the U.S. Supreme Court's *Smith* v. *Allwright* decision outlawed the white primary. Blacks throughout the nation emerged from the war years determined to win for themselves at home the democratic freedoms that they and other Americans had fought for overseas. Northern blacks were an increasingly important part of the Democratic party, and southern blacks were beginning to stir, albeit slowly, in the political arena. Equally important was the abolition of Georgia's poll tax law in 1945. Although the tax had never disfranchised all poor people, and certainly not all millhands, it did in fact keep many poor voters from the polls, which was one reason the CIO's PAC continued to assail Dixie's poll tax statutes. Georgia was the fourth southern state to erase such a law from its books, and the impact of that decision on state politics was felt immediately.[50]

With the abolition of the poll tax and the white primary, political participation increased dramatically in the state elections of 1946. Georgia voters turned out in uncharacteristically high numbers, and no doubt a large proportion of this surge was working-class whites who had embraced the notion of civic leadership during the war. More surprising, at least to white Georgians, was that black voters also comprised a significant part of the expanded electorate, especially in urban areas. The idea that African Americans could suddenly become a critical voting bloc in closely contested Democratic races was unbearable to many Caucasians, and a tidal wave of white-supremacist campaigning was not long in forming. Of course, race baiting had long been standard fare in Georgia politics, even when virtually no blacks could vote. But in the late 1940s, even though the language of white supremacy remained unchanged, the issue of race and politics took on a new complexity and a special urgency. In some scattered locales, white Democrats began to appeal to black voters, and the CIO, though still not a compelling presence in Georgia, was nonetheless making political waves in the state and, at the national level at least, publicly advocating biracial electoral strategies. In retro-spect, it seems obvious that working-class Georgians never had a chance to form a viable biracial alliance in the postwar decade, in part because the working people of the state were not tightly organized and also because white workers still saw blacks as problems, not allies. But to Dalton's cotton millers, the South of the late 1940s did not seem so unyielding. From their perspective, it seemed that if textile workers across the state could get organized and vote as a union, dramatic political change might well follow—even in the one-party South.[51]

In Dalton, ordinary workers had seldom been a major force in local politics, but during the late 1940s they sought to create a powerful labor coalition in northwest Georgia and in their own town. The CIO's PAC gave these workers a means of achieving local political goals while simultaneously broadening their view of labor problems and civic responsibility. The terse minutes from the meet-ings of Local 185's executive board note that the board attended the "Rome PAC Meeting" in the summer of 1946. That fall, as off-year state and national elections drew near, two Crown workers traveled to a state PAC meeting in Atlanta. The roads to Rome and Atlanta would become familiar to Crown's union hands as PAC activity expanded and continued into the next decade, but in 1946 the northwest Georgia PAC was a novel entity. Dominated by textile hands in Rome and Dalton, but also supported by CIO workers in other towns throughout the region, the northwest Georgia PAC worked to make Georgia's Seventh Congressional District a stronghold of labor power.[52]

The major goal of the Dalton-Rome PAC in 1946 was to oust Congressman Malcomb Tarver and replace him with a prolabor candidate. To the political elite in north Georgia, this goal must have seemed almost laughable. Tarver was firmly entrenched, a candidate who had not been defeated in forty years. Born in rural Whitfield County in 1885, Tarver attended local public schools and Mercer Law School in Rome before emerging as an up-and-coming Dalton lawyer in 1905. From 1908 to 1916 he served first as a representative and later as a senator in the Georgia legislature, after which he was elected for ten straight years as superior court judge for the Cherokee Circuit in northwest Georgia. In 1926 voters of the Seventh District sent Tarver to Congress, and there he remained, successfully winning reelection nine times. Tarver was the undisputed champion of north Georgia's courthouse crowd.[53]

PAC opposition to this powerful political figure first aroused the attention of the local press in April 1946, when one hundred delegates from unions in Dalton, Rome, Rockmart, Dallas, Lindale, Aragon, and Cedartown met in convention and resolved that Tarver was "anti-labor." Later, at a meeting of the Dalton PAC "unit," one worker apparently told a reporter that the PAC in northwest Georgia was "out to lick" Tarver. (This comment garnered much unfavorable press and inspired a resolution that only the PAC unit president could make authorized statements to reporters.) The *Citizen* apparently found it difficult to assess the CIO's political insurgency, for the tone in which it reported this story fluctuated between astonishment and incredulity. Tarver, the paper added, claimed to be sympathetic toward labor.[54]

If the northwest Georgia PAC initially rendered Tarver and the press almost speechless, the uptown crowd quickly recovered its capacity to heap abuse on all things CIO. Perhaps because Tarver was a longtime advocate of agricultural interests, the *Citizen* allowed Georgia Farm Bureau president H. L. Wingate the first shot. Wingate charged that "Sidney Hillman [the national leader of CIO-PAC] is an outright Communist. . . . The top ranking officials of the CIO are communistic in their beliefs. We are entirely too easy on these subversive elements that are entering our government and our communities." To workers who had viewed themselves as patriotic leaders during World War II, such remarks were sparks on dry tinder. Doubtless aware of the workers' sensitivity to insult, the *Citizen* quickly added, "The speaker declared that his remarks about Mr. Hillman and the CIO were not directed against those thousands of good Americans who were forced to become members of this organization in order to get and to hold their jobs." This anemic attempt to win the confidence of local union workers notwithstanding, mainstream Democrats were clearly alarmed about PAC and uncertain as to how they could deter the workers from voting as an anti-Tarver bloc.[55]

By early July, shortly before the election, the courthouse crowd viewed the situation with undisguised alarm. A large front-page editorial in the *Citizen* asked, "Will the CIO Succeed in Having Tarver Lose in Congress Race?" The editors blasted PAC as "the same old story of the Union big-wigs wanting to run things the way they want to see 'em run—regardless of the American people, the Government, or the average union member himself." Unwilling to admit that PAC involvement was voluntary for CIO members, the *Citizen* insisted that Dalton's cotton millers "know well enough that Mr. Tarver has been their friend—before they joined the unions and after they joined." Tarver himself claimed Sidney Hillman was "trying to mislead some of the textile workers in our district." The embattled congressman also charged that Hillman "writes books about how good Soviet Russia is. He is certainly tied up with a bunch of Communists in the PAC he heads. He is not a worker. The committee on un-American Activities says he never worked in an industrial plant a day in his life." Offering Dalton's workers a carrot along with the stick, Tarver added, "One hair of their heads is worth every bone in Sidney Hillman's body." He predicted that the workers in his district would not vote "like sheep" just because they had joined the CIO.[56]

Completely unmoved by Tarver's assertions, the union workers of the Seventh District trooped to the polls and gave the twenty-year incumbent a solid thumping. Tarver lost to Henderson Lanham, a resident of Rome who received absolutely no mention in the local press until the *Citizen* listed him as the victor in mid-July.

In Dalton, Tarver's home town, Lanham won an impressive 58 percent of the vote (2,448 to Tarver's 1,772). In the district as a whole, which elected its congressional leaders via a county unit system that undervalued urban votes and favored rural-oriented candidates like Tarver, Lanham won 21 unit votes to Tarver's 11. The CIO workers had won a stunning victory. How they did so remains largely a mystery; no union records from the campaign survived, and the Dalton papers carried virtually no news about the electoral activities of the PAC. But union workers in northwest Georgia were remarkably active in the postwar era. An arc of labor agitation ran southward through the Tennessee Valley region, across northwest Georgia and well into northeast Alabama toward Birmingham. The Dalton-Rome PAC lay at the heart of this labor crescent, creating a trouble spot for antiunion politicians. In 1946, for example, Whitfield County's PAC helped swing the county for gubernatorial candidate James C. Carmichael, who was anti–Ku Klux Klan and strongly prolabor. Carmichael lost the election, but Whitfield County's old politi-cal elite nonetheless could not have been completely pleased that their county voted in favor of a liberal gubernatorial candidate who promised that "discrimina-tion against organized labor would not be tolerated" in his administration.[57]

If organized labor had much to celebrate in northwest Georgia, however, the same was not true at the regional or national levels. Overall, PAC-supported candidates fared poorly in the 1946 elections, and a conservative trend was clearly in the making. Meanwhile Operation Dixie, after an early flurry of activity, quickly lost momentum and, for all practical purposes, was defeated by 1947. The southern textile organizing drive had floundered on poor strategy, postwar prosperity, worker skepticism, and intense employer resistance facilitated by a new federal law, the Taft-Hartley Act. Hotly debated during 1947, Taft-Hartley was a direct attack on the prolabor provisions of the Wagner Act. By curbing the power of the NLRB, the law won strong support from business groups and conservatives everywhere. The *Citizen* cheered the anti-Wagner movement and all efforts to derail the NLRB, which the paper called "that once haughty and arbitrary and dictatorial agency." Despite vigorous resistance from the CIO, Congress passed the Taft-Hartley Act over President Truman's veto. Even the *Citizen* admitted the new law was skewed too far toward the big business camp but glibly suggested that subsequent revision would render the law's provisions more moderate. Little did the editors know that the pendulum had swung permanently in the direction of conservative labor policies.[58]

Despite these setbacks, Dalton's union millhands moved quickly to reinforce their political clout, both at home and in the Georgia legislature. The minutes of Local 185's meetings reveal that in late January 1947 four members journeyed to Atlanta to attend the "announced Citizens Meeting," and several weeks later three members went to the "Atlanta Public Hearing on Labor Bills." Local 185 was beginning to connect itself to a larger world of labor activism and political conflict.

The union sent donations to workers who were on strike in nearby textile towns and voted to send a whopping $2,400 to the CIO's international emergency organizing fund in 1948. Union delegates traveled widely—most often to Rome, Atlanta, and Washington—to educate themselves about politics, to support their fellow union workers, to lobby for prolabor legislation, and to testify before both state and national legislative committees. Crown's workers sent more representatives to Atlanta to be on hand at the statehouse "when the Anti-Labor [bill] would be on the floor for Debate" in late February 1947. The workers' presence in Atlanta did not prevent state legislators from outlawing the closed shop by means of a "right to work" law, but both of Whitfield County's state representatives—Stafford Brooke and William ("Bill") Britton—voted against the bill.[59]

The political potential of PAC in northwest Georgia became evident in September 1947, when Congressman Lanham appointed all new members to the Democratic Executive Committee for the Seventh District. The list of Whitfield County's new Democratic leaders must have alarmed the north Georgia business community. Most of the ten board members were union workers at Crown Mill or had ties to the mill-worker community. One was Homer R. Craig, who had recently been elected president of TWUA Local 185. Otis M. Weaver, former president of the union and longtime millhand at Crown, also found a place on the committee. Luther Broom was an early union leader at Crown whose wife, Daisy H. Broom, worked at American Thread. By the late 1940s, Luther was working as a state oil inspector, although he still lived in the Crown Mill village. Hubert H. Coker, who had been raised at Crown and was active in the early union movement of the 1930s, was working for the state highway department in 1947. When he was appointed to the committee, he was still living in the mill village with his wife, Edith G. Coker, who worked at Crown. J. A. Cornelison lived near the village and had long run a small grocery and service station catering to Crown's mill families. R. Samuel White owned a home in the mill-village area and served as assistant chief of the Dalton fire department. Effie Bagby was a schoolteacher turned chenille worker who had relatives in the Crown Mill village. Her place on the Democratic committee was significant not only because women were rarely appointed to such political posts, but also because, as a spread-plant worker, she became an important symbol of labor power in an industry that had not yet been organized. In all, at least half of the Democratic Executive Committee of Whitfield County were (or had been) millhands, and at least four were well-known union leaders in Local 185.[60]

The direction of local politics depended largely on the cohesion of the labor vote, which in turn was integrally connected with the ward-based system of local elections. Dalton had four local political districts, called wards, each of which elected one representative (or alderman) to the city council. Any alderman could also serve as the mayor, who was chosen in an at-large election. The ward boundaries in Dalton resembled four wide rectangles stacked one on top of another; they were numbered consecutively, with the northernmost ward being Ward 1, the southernmost Ward 4. Ward 1, where the Crown Mill village and the Real Silk Hosiery Mill were located, was indisputably the most powerful labor district in the city. Ward 4, which encompassed both the Boylston plant and American Thread, was the other major labor area, but its returns never went so solidly for labor candidates. Wards 2 and 3 were sandwiched between the two labor districts. In these more affluent wards, referred to by the *Citizen* as the "downtown" districts, most whites could be expected to vote for well-to-do professionals and business leaders. But Dalton's black community lived in the eastern half of both these districts, and this arrangement created a measure of uncertainty as to what might happen when the African American community began to vote in earnest.

Lanham's prolabor committee represented a quiet transformation in local power, but the situation soon grew considerably less quiet. Dalton's uptown leaders and organized workers appeared headed toward a showdown. In mid-September 1947, the business contingent fired the first shot: apparently without warning, Wes Carter, foreman of the city's sanitation department, fired five "street and sanitary workers," all of whom had joined the newly organized CIO Local 731 of the United Public Workers union. Carter's action set off a firestorm of protest from Dalton's organized workers, who claimed the sanitation workers were fired simply because of their affiliation with Local 731. Carter had informed the employees in question that their discharge was ordered by the mayor and city council, "at the request of the city tax payers." Discontent came to a head at a clamorous city council meeting in early October. The working people of Dalton packed the city hall council room, and a CIO representative from Atlanta, William Stafford, was on hand. Raucous crowds at council meetings were not altogether unusual in Dalton. As the *Citizen* later pointed out, "This is not the first time an ugly mood has arisen during Council meetings, and it has not always been brought on by a labor situation. It has flared over taxes, and over street assessments, and over such a thing as the location of a skating rink." Nonetheless, editor Len Tracy knew an alarming situation when he saw one, and, for sheer political pandemonium, the council meeting of October 6 beat anything Daltonians had ever seen, roller rinks and all.[61]

The meeting offered a potent display of working-class bravado and a clear indication that organized labor in Dalton was intent on making its presence felt in the postwar political arena. Given the highly charged atmosphere, Mayor Gordon Kettles, a manager at the Prater Gin Company, sought to divert attention from the sanitation workers by offering the floor to Reverend C. T. Pratt, pastor of the Church of God of the Union Assembly. Although Pratt's prolabor views were well known, Kettles expected the minister to report on matters pertaining to the Dalton airport, which was run by the Union Assembly. But Pratt was not a popular Holiness preacher for nothing, and, once he had the floor, he took the opportunity to lambaste Wes Carter in what the *Citizen* called "an inflammatory speech" demanding the reinstatement of the sanitation workers. At this point, the mayor and council lost control of the meeting to angry workers who insisted that Carter's decision be reversed. Exactly what transpired next is not clear, but the mayor and council somehow found it within themselves to vote unanimously in favor of reinstating the five workers with back pay.

In a formal statement released after the meeting, the mayor and the city council claimed that "they were forced Monday night to vote for reinstatement *under threat of bodily harm*." Council member W. H. Bartenfeld, who owned the Dalton Tourist Court and represented Ward 1, the strongest center of labor power, claimed he overheard people saying that he "would not leave the City Hall alive" unless he voted for reinstatement. T. L. Shackleford, who owned an appliance store and represented Ward 4, said he was "invited two times to take off my glasses." Len Tracy later demanded "assault warrants" against workers in the "mob" who threatened the council with violence, and he insisted that council members "were *coerced* into reinstating the discharged men." But the editor's tone also revealed some disgust with the council itself for not standing firm and meeting the challenge and for not fully backing its appointed foreman. "Admittedly," Tracy noted, "after affairs reached a stage of threatened violence, the Council did well to retire as best it could." Actually, the council retired in more ways than one. On October 10, Mayor Kettles (who also served as alderman for Ward 3) and councilmen Bartenfeld and Shackleford, three of the city's four most powerful elected officials, resigned their posts.[62]

During the tumult of the meeting, a "special citizens committee" was "verbally appointed" (by whom remains unclear) to hold a public hearing on the dismissal of the sanitation workers. The citizens committee included Hubert Coker and Homer Craig, two of Lanham's recent appointees to the Whitfield Democratic Executive Committee and both dedicated CIO men. Besides these two, the committee included Ernest McDonald, owner of the North Dalton Grocery, and George Hanson, an employee of Chenille Machine Company. Alfred Jones, owner of Jones Motor Company and Burnette Truck and Tractor, was the only appointee who did not, by vocation, frequently associate with Dalton's working people. Although not solidly blue collar, the citizens designated to investigate the matter were clearly in favor of the discharged workers.[63]

The committee spent an evening taking testimony from the sanitation workers and Wes Carter. The proceedings revealed that the workers in question had served on the city payroll anywhere from two to ten years without incident. Carter admitted that the mayor and the city council had not ordered the firings and that he had acted alone. He defended himself by saying that the mayor had previously told him to fire anyone who did not put in a full eight-hour day, and he added that there had never been any attempt at union busting. Len Tracy's report on this testimony in the *Citizen* was surprisingly critical of Carter and offered unusual praise for the union workers, who apparently displayed considerable finesse in dealing with this touchy situation. "About 50 spectators, virtually all of them in workmen's clothing, were present and remained until the committee retired to write its report," Tracy wrote. "No union representatives from outside Dalton appeared before the meeting, which was conducted in entire orderliness."[64]

In the aftermath of the sanitation-worker incident, local government was in turmoil—or, as the *Citizen* described it, in a "legal maze." Because Gordon Kettles had been both mayor and councilman, once he, Bartenfeld, and Shackleford had resigned, only the alderman from Ward 2, Ed Long, still remained from the previously elected council. Long, who lived just south of the Crown Mill village and owned the Jitney Jungle Self Service Food Store, apparently did not feel threatened by the labor uprising. Guy Thomas, manager of the North Georgia Oil Company, became mayor pro tem. Beyond this, there was little coherence in the local power structure, and no one knew what might happen next. City Attorney Albert L. Hodge shrugged and admitted that numerous legal questions had to be settled before a new election could be set.[65]

Meanwhile conflicts continued to air in the local press. *Citizen* editor Len Tracy criticized the Reverend Pratt for his part in the controversial council meeting, and the prolabor minister lashed out in response. In a lengthy letter to the paper, he took Tracy to task for suggesting that the angry workers were anything other than law-abiding citizens. "I never said anything that would hurt the Mayor or the Council," Pratt insisted. "I just condemned their foreman and he stands condemned before God and man today." He continued at length, blending moral indignation and working-class sensibilities:

> Mr. Tracy could be fired and he wouldn't think he was treated right if he was fired without a cause given him. I wonder if Mr. Tracy would take a job cleaning up garbage. I stated in my speech that labor was here and if people didn't like it they had just as well leave town, for Jesus said, "The poor you have with you always." [Tracy] said I quoted Bible. I did quote Bible. I am a holiness preacher, the only kin God has. I am not seeking to please man. If you seek to please man you are an enemy to God. The difference in me and Mr. Tracy is he serves man and I am serving God. We find where truth and right has always caused an uproar among people who didn't want justice.[66]

It is easy to imagine uptown Daltonians ridiculing Pratt's letter. Indeed, Tracy seems to have published it only to reveal what he perceived to be the arrogant and confused rantings of an uneducated man. But the minister's sense of urgency and anger, along with his Old Testament visions of vindication, revealed a world of thought and emotion that was simply beyond the grasp of affluent Daltonians, with their schoolbred logic and steady, upscale Protestantism. Pratt spoke a language many southern millhands understood and appreciated, whether or not they ever supported his Holiness church. In any case, Tracy and Dalton's business leaders could not have found it reassuring that workers in Dalton had brought down the city government partly in response to a speech by the Reverend Pratt.

By early November, the date for an election to fill the vacancies in local government had been set. On December 10, 1947, Dalton's electorate would choose a mayor and a slate of councilmen to lead their city. The *Citizen* proved surprisingly reticent about the upcoming contest, remaining silent except to chastise the citizenry for its apathy. In a statement completely at odds with the politically tense situation, an editorial mourned that Daltonians exhibited "not the slightest excitement" about the election. This assessment could not have been more inaccurate, for citizens flocked to the polls in record numbers. On the day following the election, the *Citizen* reported that "the turn out of voters was the largest in any city election here in history." Fifty-six percent of the registered electorate (2,466 out of 4,400) cast votes for mayor. In the city's fourth ward, an area divided nearly equally into labor and business interests, the alderman's race drew ballots from a remarkable 91 percent of eligible voters (715 of 785).[67]

In the mayoral election, insurgent candidate P. D. Clark courted both the labor vote and the black vote. He was the political nightmare of Dalton's uptown leaders, a restaurant owner who openly stated, "I will stand for the right principles regardless of creed or color." Clark actually won handily in Ward 1 and ran a close race in Ward 4, but he received a thumping in the two downtown wards. As a result, Carlton McCamy, a local attorney who ran on no platform (his profession and place of residence were enough) won the at-large mayoral election with 55 percent of the vote. Van Kettles, father of the vanquished Gordon Kettles, won the alderman's race in Ward 3 by a slim margin. In Ward 1, Flint Williams, a machinist who worked for Crown, won a place on the council by a comfortable margin.[68]

Almost unmentioned but absolutely critical for the future of labor politics in Dalton was a slate of amendments to Dalton's city charter presented to voters for ratification. Amendment 1 called for "redistricting the city by wards," a well-worn strategy used by America's urban elite to divide and render ineffective any troublesome ethnic or working-class voting blocs. Amendment 2 called for a change to a "city manager" type of government. Reflecting a political strategy similar to that of redistricting, the city manager plan would mean that the city was run by a non-elected official appointed by the council members. Together, the two amendments could effectively shelter white business interests from political insurgencies such as the one that had emerged in Dalton's labor wards in 1947. Although it is not possible to determine the precise motivations behind these amendments, similar motions were made in a number of Georgia's towns and cities after blacks began voting again in 1946. As voiced by white elite political leaders, the justification for such electoral changes was to abolish the pernicious effects of "bloc voting," which translated as "black voting." In Dalton's case, the bloc vote also meant the labor vote. For wealthy whites in northwest Georgia, the most alarming aspect of the 1946 elections had been the emergence of labor politics, not the participation of black voters. P. D. Clark's campaign also made it clear that the black vote and the labor vote might possibly combine. Ward redistricting offered a useful local-level means to undercut any possibility of a biracial class coalition.

Dalton's PAC voters understood that the amendments threatened their interests. The redistricting measure called for splitting Wards 1 and 4 in half and lumping each new half with large chunks of Wards 2 and 3. Because the uptown wards were more densely populated, this arrangement would make it extremely difficult for a labor candidate to win a position on the city council in any ward. The council would then be strictly uptown in composition, and it could appoint a city manager in its own image. Ward 1, where the labor bloc was most powerful, was the only district to vote down the redistricting measure; in Ward 4, antiamendment voters lost a tight election. The two uptown wards favored the amendments by a handy majority. Both measures passed, and they spelled trouble for the workers' political ambitions. The chances of Flint Williams, or any other worker, running successfully in the future were slim at best. In the 1948 alderman's contest, for example, Crown millhand Walter W. James ran a distant fourth against Bill Bartenfeld, the very same councilman who had stepped down during the sanitation-worker crisis of 1947. Just when the workers' newfound political clout was beginning to reorient the patterns of local power, charter reforms saved the day for uptown business leaders.[69]

For PAC leaders in the South, matters of race presented extreme difficulties in the late 1940s. As long as mill-village life buffered Crown's white working families from anything more than casual involvement with local blacks, workers remained focused on organization and union consolidation. As long as blacks were excluded from local politics, Dalton's organized millhands could ignore the dilemmas of their Jim Crow society. But once their world of civic involvement and political activism began to expand, and once blacks began to reenter southern politics, the "race question" became central to the political world of Local 185.

Nothing revealed this new element more clearly than the city charter reforms of 1947, which effectively undermined the power of both the labor vote and the black vote in Dalton. The two were not one and the same, despite labor's support for openly biracial candidates such as P. D. Clark and despite the Reverend Pratt's racial liberalism. By no means did all of Dalton's PAC-supported politicians show an inclination to fight for black civil rights or to form a biracial voting alliance. Prolabor legislator Bill Britton, for example, voted against Georgia's "anti-Klan" bill in 1949, even as local editor Marc Pace condemned the postwar Klan and urged that the legislation be passed. When Pace pressed Britton on the issue, the friend of Dalton labor responded flippantly that the bill would make it illegal for children to wear Halloween masks or for nuns to wear habits. Similarly, prolabor Congressman Henderson Lanham continually opposed national civil rights legislation, even as he pushed for liberal economic measures for northwest Georgia's white workers. Local coalitions between white workers and blacks might have provided formidable opposition to uptown politicos. But as in the 1890s, poor whites and blacks in the 1940s could not manage to transcend race in order to form a class-based political alliance.[70]

The outlines of the new order were becoming clearer. Although organized labor had assumed a more active and influential role in shaping local and regional affairs, the power of union workers remained limited and tenuous. Dalton's TWUA Week in May 1949 reflected the gains organized labor had made—and, ultimately, the limitations of those gains. At the request of Local 185, the mayor and the city council agreed to proclaim May 8–14 "TWUA Week" in honor of the union's ten-year anniversary. The city officials, none of whom were workers or labor candidates, even went so far as to publish a resolution commending local unions for having "aided citizens of this community in securing decent wages, [and] better working conditions." They also praised the unions for fostering the "establishment of harmonious labor-management relations and [for having] participated in projects designed to result in the well-being of Dalton." Local political leaders even urged "the citizens of Dalton to participate in the public celebrations which have been arranged." For its part, the TWUA locals hung banners across Hamilton Street, put together a variety of textile exhibits for the public, sponsored lighthearted contests for the community, and donated books to the Dalton library and to Dalton High School. A national TWUA radio broadcast was aired on local station WBLJ. But the highlight of TWUA Week in Dalton was an open house held on Saturday night at the high school gymnasium. Mayor McCamy presided, and Kenneth Douty, director of the TWUA in Georgia, offered the keynote speech. Speeches soon gave way to entertainment, which included "both ballroom and square dancing." In all, TWUA Week in Dalton was a most impressive affair. Its very occurrence suggested the extent to which unions (and working people in general) had gained respect and power during the turbulent 1940s.[71]

"Congratulations TWUA on Your 10th Anniversary—May the Next 10 Be Even More Prosperous." So read a large notice in the *Citizen* during TWUA Week, compliments of Liles Drug Store. The decade celebrated by the city in May 1949 had been one of enormous change—the congratulatory bulletin was proof enough of that. Global conflict had done much to reshape the world, from the advent of the atomic age to the quiet celebration of organized labor in a southern textile town. What lay ahead in the next ten years was anybody's guess. The political tide had turned against the unions, both at home and in Washington. Yet Dalton's union workers received hospitable treatment during TWUA Week and were firmly connected to a stable network of CIO locals throughout north Georgia. By the late 1940s, Local 185 had become an accepted part of the Crown Mill community. Even

John Cronic, who had penned the bitter antiunion letters of 1939, now saw fit to file a grievance through the union for an "adjustment in work load." The effects of conflicts over the union—particularly the memories of the 1939 strike—never faded completely. But as the 1940s came to a close, the union no longer polarized the Crown Mill community as it once had. Indeed, as Dalton's millhands cele-brated TWUA Week in May 1949, it seemed—for a brief moment, at least—that the union was becoming an entrenched part of local tradition.[72]

But as TWUA Week drew to a close and Dalton moved toward the 1950s, it was clear that the late 1940s had been a time of lost opportunities for organized labor in the city and the South. TWUA Week, however important it might have been symbolically, was mere window dressing. The real power to shape local affairs had slipped away from the union—in the remapping of Dalton's political wards after 1947, in the failure of Operation Dixie to create a larger pool of union labor in the region, in the inability of national labor organizations to turn back the antiunion backlash in the U.S. Congress. Organized labor seemed to be holding its own in the America of the late 1940s. But the bottom line was that labor had "lost the peace," at least in the South. In the wake of TWUA Week, Crown's union workers probably did not sense this defeat, and they would not have abandoned the fight in any case. But growing beyond their present strength would be no small task. Looking toward the new decade, they could not possibly have foreseen the complexity of the future or the rapidity with which it would transform both their region and their own mill-village community.

12

DISAPPEARING MILL VILLAGES IN A CHANGING SOUTH

During the decade following Dalton's TWUA Week in 1949, the South underwent significant changes, not the least of which was the disappearance of its mill villages as company-owned entities. After having been the central institution of New South industry for half a century, mill villages vanished with surprising speed as textile firms throughout the region sold the mill houses to working people. By the late 1940s the trend was already apparent, and Crown Mill soon joined the procession, offering the old village houses for sale to Crown's millhands in 1953. Many southerners viewed "the passing of the mill village" as a startling departure from the past. Sociologist Harriet Herring, who carefully studied the phenomenon in the late 1940s, deemed it a "revolution in a southern institution."[1] So it was, in the sense that it reversed a long-standing textile tradition. Yet in another sense, the selling of the mill villages (or, from the workers' point of view, the buying of the mill villages) was less a sudden shift within a tradition-bound industry than it was a culmination of long-term trends that for two decades had been undermining mill-village paternalism and reshaping the southern labor market.

Most analyses of Dixie's textile workers in the post–World War II era have stressed the endurance of tradition in cotton-mill communities. The prevailing view is that mill villages were stuck in an economic and cultural time lock and that southern millhands remained inward-looking isolationists, suspicious of outsiders and seemingly impervious to the forces transforming the globe after 1945. One recent study, for example, speaks of "remarkable continuity between the workers in the mills of the 1930s and those of the 1980s, despite the modernization and change in culture in the intervening years." But this widely accepted view has been based more on sociological investigations and regional generalizations than on careful historical studies of mill-village communities.[2]

The war and postwar years altered the world of southern textiles in fundamentally important ways, and cotton-mill people and other ordinary southerners were caught up in those changes. Indeed, their occupational decisions helped restructure the regional labor market. The extent to which older millhands in the 1950s and 1960s continued to embrace traditional cultural norms was no greater than that of any group under which the economic landscape has begun to shift. The workers' economic behavior, in any case, demonstrated a willingness to explore new opportunities. "Opportunities" may be too sanguine a term, for the South was still the poorest region in the nation, and no one in the 1950s could foresee its transfiguration into the Sunbelt. The postwar South nonetheless offered ordinary white families new economic possibilities, and those possibilities had much to do with the disappearance of the mill villages. To explore the reasons for mill-village sales is to open a window on critical economic changes that were slowly undermining regional distinctions, slowly creating an increasingly "American" South.

Dalton emerged breathless from the turbulent 1940s, unaware that the pace of change would only quicken in the decade ahead. On the surface, many aspects of the small, upcountry city seemed unchanged from earlier decades. The population was still overwhelmingly southern-born, Anglo-Saxon, and Protestant. Blacks comprised only 8 percent of the population, and local developers continued to woo prospective industrialists, in a manner reminiscent of the 1880s, with the claim that Dalton had "no foreign element to contend with," a declaration that was both statistically accurate and culturally revealing. In 1950 the city was the kind of place in which large churches were still the most impressive buildings in town. Protestant to its core, Dalton had one church for every 550 residents, and nearly 60 percent of those churches were Baptist and Methodist, while another 21 percent were Holiness. Beneath this veneer of southern stasis, however, the structural underpinnings of Dalton were shifting.[3]

The city's population had increased 53 percent during the boom of the 1940s, making Dalton almost twice the size it had been in 1930 (see table A.1). As the wartime economic boom brought in new people, it also enlarged the chenille industry, which, in peacetime, expanded beyond the production of bedspreads to provide chenille rugs and robes for a burgeoning domestic market. This industrial expansion was led in part by a small but economically influential Jewish community, the members of which had migrated to Dalton from the northeast. The size of Dalton's Jewish population in 1950 is difficult to calculate, but their numbers were substantial enough to support a synagogue, the Temple Beth-El. This small cultural diversification paralleled a major economic shift in the town. To be sure, Dalton's economy was still based on textiles, but southern textiles underwent a drastic change after the war.[4]

In 1950 it was clear that the textile labor market had been altered since 1940, becoming predominantly female and residentially decentralized. Most of Dalton's factory workers in 1950 toiled in textiles, of course; 85 percent of all manufacturing laborers in Whitfield County were employed in some type of textile plant. Crown's millhands were still all white, and there is no evidence that other cotton mills or chenille plants employed blacks in any capacity. But changes could be seen in the gender ratio of the industry's work force. Women, whose numbers in southern cotton mills had declined between 1900 and 1940, now found themselves in greater demand. City leaders often acknowledged that women comprised a majority of workers in the chenille plants—in fact, they held 65 percent of the town's chenille jobs in 1950. It was not as widely known that female workers—not just single women, but wives and mothers—had also made a comeback in old-line cotton mills. At the outset of the 1950s, 52 percent of Whitfield County's cotton-mill workers were women.[5]

The change in hiring practices accompanied the decline of child labor, which had sustained Dalton's cotton mills in their formative decades but had now passed from the scene. The mill-village system itself was clearly waning. In 1930 almost all textile workers in the city lived in mill villages and were part of a family-centered labor system. Twenty years later, Dalton's textile work force was made up of adult men and women, most of whom lived in homes scattered across the county. Fifty-one percent of all cotton-mill workers in Whitfield County lived outside of Dalton in 1950. Among chenille workers, about 36 percent lived outside of the city limits. The size of the commuter work force was rapidly expanding, a development closely related to mill-village decline. It must have been difficult at the time to recognize these trends, much less comprehend their larger meaning. But Daltonians understood that fundamental changes were taking place when the town's mill villages began to disappear.

The passing of the mill village began in Dalton in May 1950, when American Thread announced the sale of its company-owned houses. "Employees of the local plant of American Thread Company are to be given an opportunity that every

American wants," stated the *Dalton Citizen*, "to own his own home." The Thread Mill village consisted of about 120 homes, virtually all of which were to be offered to the workers living in them. "In announcing the program," the paper noted, "American Thread Company stated that during the past few years a great number of its employees had indicated they would like to own their own home, and some have even bought or built homes outside the village." If a family chose not to accept the mill's offer, the house would "then be offered to some other employee who does not now occupy a house in the village." According to the paper, the houses could be had on easy terms. Only a small down payment was necessary, and twelve-year payment plans were available. Prices for the homes had yet to be determined. For that purpose, the company had hired the services of a South Carolina real-estate company, which had pledged to appraise the property fairly and consistently. As if to mollify the fears of readers who viewed such a plan as a wrenching departure from local custom, the paper added that the Thread Mill "is following pretty much a custom that other mills have successfully carried out." The *Citizen* heartily endorsed the plan and concluded, "We sincerely trust it works out to the best interest of the little working man who is the backbone of America."[6]

Two months later the *Citizen* continued the local saga with a follow-up story that may well have been written by American Thread's public relations department. The paper displayed eight photographs under the caption "Home Ownership Comes to Thread Mill Employees." The pictures showed workers adding extra rooms and screened-in porches, constructing garages, pouring better foundations, putting in driveways, leveling out their lawns, and giving the old homeplace a new coat of paint. "Home ownership," the *Citizen* pointed out, "reveals individual tastes." The paper intended to reveal the pride and initiative demonstrated in the millhands' efforts at home improvement. "Under this competitive spirit," the editors crowed, "Dalton's newest subdivision is rapidly losing its village uniformity. The new owners are quickly refitting the houses to their own needs and ideas. In the near future, it is expected that each house will have a distinctive appearance." In hindsight such remarks seem inappropriate and condescending, but the sincerity of the *Citizen*'s enthusiasm ought not be dismissed out of hand. In 1950 the cult of home ownership had never been stronger, as the paper's reference to the mill village as a "subdivision" bore witness. The suburban boom of the post–World War II era was not fueled entirely by the middle classes. The desire for home ownership was equally strong among America's working class, including cotton-mill workers in the nation's poorest region.[7]

The sale of the mill village nonetheless posed troubling questions that the *Citizen* never thought—or dared—to raise. If home ownership was such a worthwhile endeavor, should not American Thread and Crown Mill have offered the houses to their employees decades earlier? If home improvement projects were so rapidly undertaken by the new owners, did that not indicate that the workers' homes had long been inadequate to their needs? If the breakdown of village uniformity was such a positive change, why had companies always insisted on monotonous color schemes and housing arrangements? Because the houses had been built in the 1920s, would not workers in 1950 be paying much more for their homes than the mill had ever spent on them in the first place, even though the workers' rents had long since paid off the construction costs?

Such questions had worried labor groups since the early 1940s, when scattered sales of southern mill villages began to gain attention. In 1941 *Textile Labor*, the official newspaper of the TWUA, published a full-page article entitled "The Problem of the Mill Village: Employers Trying to Unload Worn-Out Houses on the Workers." The editors stated that "several mill owners are now attempting to force their employees to buy (on the good old installment plan) the shacks they have been renting for many years past." They ridiculed employers who chanted the new slogan, "The era of paternalism is dead in textiles." What these employers actually meant, the editors explained, was that "paternalism simply doesn't pay any longer!" Union leaders proposed a combined government-union intervention as a means of preventing workers from being forced to buy their homes. The paper intended this article to be the first in a series on the mill-village problem and asked southern millhands to send in their views on the subject. For reasons that were never stated, the anticipated series of articles did not materialize, probably because few workers vigorously opposed the home ownership scheme.[8]

There is little reason to suspect that workers were reluctant to purchase homes on the installment plan. For people who traditionally bought everything from automobiles to perms "on time," purchasing a home through an extended install-ment plan merely reflected the status quo of mill-family consumerism. Workers whose families had long since put down roots in a particular cotton-mill village, and who therefore had a stake in the community and a strong sense of place, must have felt particularly eager to assume ownership of their longtime residences—or at least anxious to avoid losing them. But America's entry into World War II brought a temporary hiatus in mill-village sales and concern over the issue.[9]

After the war, sales of the mill-village houses resumed at a more rapid pace than before, and concerns about the process reemerged. Harriet Herring viewed home ownership as an important step toward millhand independence and a more democratic society, but her work also hinted that mill managers sometimes left village residents with little choice but to buy their homes or find jobs elsewhere. Many workers, she said, were burdened by the "helpless feeling of compulsion to buy." Such concerns illuminated yet again the precarious economic position of southern cotton-mill workers. But the pace of sales continued to quicken, and everywhere a high percentage of workers accepted the option to buy.[10]

The central question was why southern mills would suddenly abandon their village housing. Even before the development of corporate paternalism, mills had built and maintained houses for their workers. In the South, the welfare capitalism that bloomed after 1900 was so tightly intertwined with company-owned mill villages that the two seemed virtually indistinguishable. The mill managers' abrupt decision to divest themselves of company housing—almost in unison—suggested that some fundamental restructuring of the southern textile world had taken place. Herring interviewed dozens of textile officials during the late 1940s to find the answer. Their responses were varied, but some were almost universal: subsidized housing was "no longer necessary in order to secure labor"; and "home ownership would make for more responsible citizens." Herring also found that some managers reacted to complaints by angry workers who could not get into inexpensive mill housing and had to live in higher-rent areas outside the village.[11]

Significantly, David D. Hamilton, the person most responsible for the selling of Crown's mill housing, gave almost identical responses when interviewed for this study. The grandson of "Mr. George," David became the fourth Hamilton to lead the company when his father, Cornelius Hamilton, died in 1951. David was part of a new generation of southern industrialists who, as Herring put it in 1949, "know they are operating in a different day from their predecessors . . . [and] are adapting their policies to the new day."[12]

Born in 1920, the year following Mr. George's death, David Hamilton experienced a pleasant childhood in Dalton during the 1920s and 1930s. He developed close relationships with both William K. Moore, who was president of Crown Mill when David came of age, and George Hamilton, Jr., David's "Uncle George." His was the boyhood of a small-town southern elite still rustic at the edges. Rock fights with boys in other uptown neighborhoods, quail hunts on bicycles (within the still-undeveloped city limits), and golf games on what he described as "a glorified cow pasture"—such activities filled the days of a textile manager in the making. Although he lived just several blocks south of the mill village on Thornton Avenue, David seldom visited the mill during his early years. His introduction to work at Crown Mill was gradual and undemanding, as he occasionally worked summers in the woodworking and machine shops. Like his father and uncle, he attended Dalton public schools. Graduating early from Dalton High, he attended a military academy before enrolling in Georgia Tech University, where he studied textile engineering. During World War II, David enlisted in the air force and rose to the rank of captain, but he never seriously considered a career in the military. In 1946, while he was still in the service, Crown's board of directors offered to make him an assistant vice president, and he accepted. His rise to company president occurred far more quickly than he or anyone else might have anticipated when both his uncle and his father died in rapid succession, leaving David, at age thirty-one, in charge of the corporation.[13]

David Hamilton's ascension to Crown's top position in 1951 marked the beginning of a new era for the mill. Despite his closeness to the men who headed Crown

before him, Hamilton viewed himself as part of a new generation of mill management. Upon assuming the position of assistant vice president, he had immediately
reinstated a cost-accounting system that he said had fallen into disuse. He wanted
"to get a better idea of what things cost." His attitudes about labor relations were
garnered not from Little George, Will Moore, or his father, but "from outside
sources, reading and so on." In fact, from his point of view, all of his predecessors,
however successful, "were all pretty much the old school." By old school he meant
they were not attentive enough to "interpersonal relationships" with their workers
and were largely unmindful of the problems that could arise from a system of
favoritism among frontline managers. Their methods of communication, he
suggested, were inadequate to the task. Hamilton's vocabulary bespoke a new
managerial order. He called millhands "employees" instead of "the help" or "his
people," as southern mill leaders had always done. His term for the mill village was
"subsidized housing." During the last two decades of its existence, Crown would be
run by a man who emphasized predictability, standardized employee relations,
and an increasingly precise attention to costs. The newest Hamilton in the big
office had few emotional ties to the policies of the past. He was not afraid of
change—a trait that became clear in 1953 when he and his fellow officials decided to
sell the Crown Mill village.[14]

In June 1953, after almost a year of careful deliberation, Crown's board of
directors resolved to "dispose of [the] mill village houses."[15] Explaining the decision to sell, Hamilton recalled, "I really had a gut feeling that the people would be
better off as homeowners than renters." He had more practical reasons as well. By
the early 1950s, the mill village had outlived its usefulness to the company. Indeed,
as Hamilton realized, it had become a distinct liability. When he became president,
only about a half to a third of the mill employees lived in company-owned
housing. "We were whittled down to the point," said Hamilton, "where we were
lucky if we had two employees in a four-room house." This was not simply bad
economy; it also proved to be a "bone of contention" within the mill workers'
community. As Hamilton pointed out, "When you only have available housing for
maybe a third of the people who work for you, and the other two-thirds didn't
have it available to them, then in effect you are subsidizing some of your employees
at the expense of others." It was this group of "others," who lived away from the
mill village and did not enjoy its low rents (which remained at one dollar per room
per month), who began to complain.[16]

Moreover, the demographics of mill-village life had changed. "At one time,"
recalled Hamilton, "you might have a mother and father [working in the mill] and
when the children were able to work, the children would be working in the plant.
Later on, people grew out of this kind of thing and the children went off in other
directions. Maybe even the wife went off in some different direction. We might
wind up with one employee in the house." One simple solution would have been to

require a certain number of workers per house, an old mill-village strategy in the South. But the new president doubtless recognized that the decline of child labor and the expansion of job opportunities prohibited any practical application of this strategy, and, as Hamilton himself noted, "there really wasn't any decent way you could tell people they couldn't live [in a mill-village house] because not enough of them worked in the plant." Company housing no longer paid. Given that mill-village rents had not been raised in over half a century and that the ever-aging dwellings were in constant need of repair, "the expense of the thing got to be a pretty major problem."[17]

Mill villages, of course, had always represented a major expense to southern textile corporations. But by helping to stabilize the work force, they had more than paid off in the long run. Ed Felker, who worked at Crown for more than forty years, lived in a mill house on Jones Street most of his life. He understood the system very well. "They lost money in taxes you know," he said. "They'd lose $50,000 a year more than they would take in rent. It was a losing proposition in one sense of the word, but in another sense it was a gain for them because they didn't have the labor turnover, because the people wouldn't move out of the house paying a dollar a room for a month. They would have to go somewhere else and pay three times that much, if they could find a house." Judging from scattered company records, Felker's financial calculations were close to the mark. In 1953 the company earned over $24,000 in rents from the mill village but spent over $60,000 for property taxes and village upkeep. By the early 1950s, the payoff simply was not there anymore.[18]

Without the media fanfare that accompanied the American Thread transactions, Crown quietly began to sell its 350 corporate-owned houses in the summer of 1953. By late October the process was complete, and stockholders at the annual meeting heard a report on "the successful sale to the employees of the mill village properties." Workers who lived in the houses at the time had the option to buy or leave. The union actually played an important, though indirect, role in the selling of the mill houses because it had established a standardized seniority system at Crown. If a family living in a company-owned home chose not to buy, the worker with highest seniority in the mill then had the option to purchase it. Many of the houses were actually duplexes but were sold as single family dwellings, and here again seniority made a key difference. "If they had a duplex where they had two families," explained Felker, "they would ask the family that had seniority in the mill. He had first preference. If he wanted it, he got it and the other person had to move out." One important clause in every contract involved resales. "Until the mill closed down," Sarah Bunch recalled, "it was stipulated in the sale of the houses that some member of the family kept the house, you know, they didn't just sell to everybody." Interest rates were only 4 percent, and weekly payments averaged from $4 to $6, depending on the price of the house. As one woman remembered, the house her family bought cost "$2,700 at the time, and they took out $4 a week." The mill took house payments right out of a worker's check, just as it had withheld rent. But for the millhands, there was a big difference between deductions for paying rent and deductions for paying off a note.[19]

By all accounts, most of Crown's homes were purchased by the families living in them. "There wasn't very many of the people that lived in the houses that didn't buy 'em," Sarah Bunch recalled. "Most of the people bought 'em because, you know, it was a pretty good deal." Like the millhands at American Thread, new homeowners at Crown went to work to improve their property. One resident described the changes to her own house: "I had a front porch added to it, nine feet wide by twenty-seven feet long. Had the inside done over completely and central heat and air conditioning put in. And I had Masonite put on the outside." Many millhands, then, believed their purchases were a good deal. Village sales also paid off for the corporation. In 1954, when the mill earned only $25,490 profit from its textile production, the company earned a quick $107,350 from down payments on houses. Ultimately Crown earned $522,701 from the sale of its 350 mill-village homes.[20]

The mill village disappeared from the South largely because changes in the regional labor market made it no longer a practical institution for either the managers or the millhands. The collapse of child labor—and with it the child-centered family labor system—lay at the heart of these changes. The demise of child labor occurred gradually. In the textile South, as throughout the nation, the use of child labor had been declining steadily since the turn of the century, as the market for capable adult labor stabilized and reformers pushed for child labor laws. High unemployment during the Great Depression further reduced the demand for teenage workers, and New Deal labor policies codified these trends, with the blessing of both industrialists and labor unions. Also during the 1930s, educational reformers in the South, including Governor Eurith D. Rivers of Georgia, successfully campaigned for free high school education. By the end of that decade, children under sixteen—who arguably had been the backbone of southern textiles during the industry's formative decades—could scarcely be found in American factories, North or South.

World War II consolidated previous labor market trends and created new barriers against child labor. Emergency war production soaked up adult labor from farms as well as towns, sent thousands of young adults into the armed services, brought married women into factories for full-time employment, and ensured that married couples could earn something approximating a family wage without relying on their children's wages. For young adults who had enlisted in the services or been drafted, and for those who had ventured far afield for better jobs, the war clearly had a broadening effect. "It's like the old song says," said David Hamilton, commenting on the postwar generation, "how you gonna keep 'em down on the farm after they've seen Paris?" Crown's workers also recalled such attitudes. Lifelong worker Sarah Bunch remembered, "After the war was over and they all came back, then people started going to school and branching out, doing different things." Anna Nell Garren agreed. When the "boys went overseas and got away from Dalton," she added, "they saw there was other things besides this. You know, something that was better." Educational opportunities and wartime experiences disrupted the familial cycle of cotton-mill labor, as Pat Lowrance's recollections illustrate. World War II, Lowrance recalled, "was the beginning of the change in the way that society thinks. . . . A lot of people from the mill towns or villages . . . saw more of the world because of the war than they had seen before, and that there was more there for them, or at least for their children, to have. And as they began to have more money, I think they wanted more things for their children." Parents no longer wanted their children "to live the way that they had lived. And I think that they just began to see that education was the key. . . . So it was important for them to see that their child was in school."[21]

The trend toward high school education in the mill village began even before World War II, but the war further encouraged the process. Public school tuition, the cost of school books, and traditions of child labor had always combined to keep mill children out of high school, and until the latter years of the 1930s few children advanced past the seventh grade. In the mid-thirties, the state of Georgia dropped textbook fees and soon eliminated tuition as well. "You know most people could afford to get their books," recalled Thelma Parker, "but they couldn't afford that tuition and books too. And that was a marvelous thing when they started issuing their books. Then just the very few things they had to buy were their supplies. And then that give everybody a chance for an education, whereas back when I was coming along, they didn't have a chance, unless their parents were wealthy." A major change for children at Crown Point School occurred in 1942, when Dalton extended its city limits, thereby annexing the mill village. "That," recalled longtime Crown Point principal Hazel Cruce, "put the school in the city, so we were a mill and city school [instead of a mill and county school]. So any child that I promoted from the seventh grade was eligible to go to Dalton High School. But before that line was extended, the children who wanted to go to high school went to one of the county high schools."[22]

By the end of the war, Crown Point children had begun to attend Dalton High almost as a matter of course. The change was striking, and mill people knew it. "I can tell you this," Pat Lowrance recalled. "Most of the young people that I knew in high school graduated from high school, you know, to get that diploma." Most children who got that diploma never returned to the mill. As Thelma Parker noted, they went on "to do other things. Not many ever did come back to the mill to do anything, other than the ones like, you know, . . . they come into a good [mill] job. But none of the others. They all went on and got better jobs."[23]

Crown Mill girls' softball team, city champs in 1947. Although these young women were still active in mill culture, their generation would soon abandon the mill village for alternative employment and a different way of life. (*Courtesy of Crown Gardens and Archives*)

Thus during the 1940s and 1950s most Crown Mill children moved beyond the mill, and in so doing they broke the long generational chain of family labor. Schooling and employment decisions were made by individuals or families, but taken together they had the effect of a collective walkout from the southern mills. It was not the first time a young cohort of millhands had abandoned the industry. A half-century earlier, some cotton millers had left the mill and returned to upcountry farms, thereby facilitating the creation of company paternalism. Now, in the post–World War II era, another group of young adults forsook the mill. They did so because a high school education had become attainable; because mill mothers, working for wages together with mill fathers, could earn a family income; and because the young people themselves were beginning to explore a larger world of possibilities. New opportunities consisted primarily of nontextile factory work but also some white-collar jobs. A few high school graduates from the village went on to college (some on the GI Bill) and into various professions. The irony was that textile outmigration before the First World War fostered mill-village paternalism, but the cotton-mill exodus after World War II had the opposite effect; it facilitated the demise of family-centered paternalism, because family labor was no longer central to textile labor recruitment.

Ordinary southern whites in two very different eras critically assessed the potential of mill-village life and turned away; in so doing, they shaped Dixie's industrial landscape in fundamental ways. To a degree often unappreciated, working people themselves were responsible for both the creation and the demise of mill-village paternalism in the South. But recognizing southern textile workers as agents of change in the post–World War II era runs against the grain of existing scholarship. According to standard interpretations, mill workers refused to alter their traditional way of life despite the changes reshaping the rest of Dixie. One recent synthesis claims that postwar millhands "preserved a historic relationship of regional hostility to unions" and maintained "fond memories of paternalistic proprietors." Post-1945 antiunionism, suggests another, reflected southern cotton-mill "traditions dating back to the 1880s." Historian James A. Hodges, reviewing the literature on the subject, accurately sums up the prevailing view that southern millhands remained "family centered, suspicious and distrustful of unions, relatively unskilled, poorly paid, minimally educated, low in self-esteem, and alienated, with a feeling of class only in the crudest sense of the market economy."[24]

Though seemingly powerful, this interpretation actually rests on a flimsy body of evidence. Perhaps it is widely accepted because it conveniently explains the South's persistently low rates of unionization. (Those low rates are, in fact, the most commonly used evidence in favor of the continuity argument.) The underlying assumption—one that should be questioned—is that Dixie's postwar union campaigns failed for the same reasons as earlier campaigns. Southern unions faced new difficulties after World War II, many of which stemmed more from national trends than from regional traditions.[25] Some historians seek not to portray changeless millhands within a changing South but to show that change itself was not what it seemed. In this view, southern manufacturing had always been and continued to be a conservative force in the region. Early developments in southern industry, as one historian contends, established a "philosophy of development" that engendered "a self-reinforcing pattern of slow growth wherein the potential for social and political disruption was minimal." According to this interpretation, a conservative southern elite took as its model of industry the slave plantation, entrapping workers—indeed, the entire region—in an economic system that stunted "normal" patterns of economic progress into the 1980s.[26]

Visions of continuity can be deceiving. They need to be evaluated at the community level and measured carefully against empirical indexes of socioeconomic change. In the Crown Mill community, life did change, in some ways dramatically, after the war. Old-timers in the 1960s knew full well that the traditional mill-village order had all but vanished. Change worked in both positive and negative ways, liberating children from the mills while severing traditional community bonds. Some new trends were disastrous for organized labor in Dixie, particularly the antilabor legislation (national and state) of the late 1940s and the national anticommunist crusade of the 1950s. Historians need not emphasize progress to argue that the lives of southern mill workers changed in clearly identifiable ways. Nor is it tantamount to a chamber of commerce speech to point out positive change. It is difficult to believe that southern cotton millers and southern society could remain essentially unchanged as mill villages vanished, educational and economic alternatives expanded, and child labor in the mills disappeared.

The demise of child labor was evident in the aging of Crown's work force after the 1930s. Statistics on the ages of newly hired workers can be calculated from the employment records Crown began to keep after the introduction of the Social Security system, which required the company to maintain an accurate account of each worker's tenure with the mill. These employee records list, among other things, the age at which workers were initially hired at Crown. A random sample of the cards reveals that, after 1940, newly hired workers were, on average, considerably older than their counterparts in earlier decades. The average worker hired before the war was about twenty-two years old (see table 12.1). In the 1940s the average hiring age rose to twenty-eight and continued to rise thereafter, reaching nearly thirty-two in the 1950s. These statistics confirm what every millhand and manager knew to be true: the child-centered family labor system was defunct, and the provision of mill-village housing was no longer an effective means of labor recruitment. Moreover, the figures suggest that the new employees had worked elsewhere before signing on with Crown and that, more than likely, they were not locals. Few trends would have a more profound impact on the community consciousness of Crown's longtime millhands.[27]

The aging of the textile work force was not unique to Dalton or the South. The national office of the TWUA discussed the issue forthrightly in a somber 1956 issue of *Textile Labor.* The cover of the issue, bathed in black, sent a clear warning: "Textiles: Crisis for America." The dearth of young people in the mills signaled a grim future for the industry. TWUA president William Pollock sounded the alarm: "Low wages, inferior working conditions and the lack of job security have in many areas dried up the flow of young workers into textile jobs. Where a reasonable alternative exists, young people will not go into the mills—and the alternatives are constantly becoming more numerous and more attractive. *This means a rapidly-aging work force, less adaptable to change and less able to meet the harsh pressures of modern, high-speed production.*" Pollock's words presaged long-term problems that would plague both textile producers and textile communities in the 1950s and 1960s, but for southern mills, the more immediate effect of the "dried-up flow" of workers was the selling of southern mill villages.[28]

To think of mill-village sales as "revolutionary" (in any sense of that nebulous term) is to grant the act of selling a transforming power that it did not possess. The larger system of corporate paternalism had infused mill housing with a special meaning and connected the workers' living space with the broader framework of welfare capitalism. Although it might be imagined that village sales marked the

TABLE 12.1. Average Age of Newly Hired Workers at Crown Mill, 1920–1969

	Average Age at Time Hired	Number of Workers in Sample
1920s	22.3	23
1930s	22.6	21
1940s	27.6	93
1950s	31.6	61
1960s	30.7	308

Source: Random sample of Crown Mill Employee Data Cards, CGA.

decline of paternalism, numerous socioeconomic and political undercurrents had already eroded the foundations of the family-centered system: New Deal labor legislation; unions that fought against favoritism; the impact of World War II; new educational and economic opportunities for southern youth; and, not to be underrated, the automobile boom. Mill-village paternalism disappeared, not with revolutionary suddenness, but gradually, in piecemeal fashion. As it happened, company housing was the last of its trappings to go. Corporate paternalism died out because labor market trends undermined its effectiveness. Those same trends made mill-village sales a foregone conclusion.

Two important developments shaped the postwar southern labor market: the rapid decline of family farms and the simultaneous expansion of nonagricultural jobs. The number of southerners employed in agriculture fell by nearly 60 percent between 1940 and 1960, with most of that precipitous decline coming after 1950 (see table 12.2). Georgia had 198,191 farms in 1950 but only 106,350 by decade's end—a reduction of 46 percent. Through mechanization and irrigation, American cotton production moved rapidly westward, causing a sharp drop in the number of labor-intensive cotton farms in the Southeast. The number of cotton bales produced in Georgia fell by nearly 80,000 (from 598,492 to 521,374) in the last five years of the 1950s. At the same time, soybeans took hold in the state, becoming the new cash crop of choice as production figures rose from 157,245 bushels in 1954 to a startling 1,028,050 bushels in 1959. An acre of soybeans required 95 percent less labor time to produce than an acre of cotton. The South's "green revolution" was partly a response to the increasing dearth of farm labor, but the trends were mutually reinforcing, because conversion to soybeans encouraged an even greater rural exodus. Coupled with the soybean boom was a noticeable rise in cattle and poultry production, both of which tended toward large-scale, capital-intensive operations that required few workers. These changes led historian David Goldfield to quip, "By the mid-1970s, Georgia was less appropriately the Peach State than the Chicken State." Southern sharecropping—the institution that had defined eco-

TABLE 12.2. Employment Trends in the South, 1940–1960:
Workers in Selected Occupations (in thousands)

	1940	1950	1960	Change, 1940–60 (percentage)
Agriculture[a]	4,235	3,178	1,714	−59.5
Manufacturing	1,864	2,622	3,501	87.8
Service-producing[b]	5,127	7,129	9,202	79.5
All occupations[c]	12,156	14,472	16,439	35.2

Source: Maddox et al., *The Advancing South*, pp. 240–41, app. table 6-1.
Note: "South" here includes the eleven former Confederate states, plus Arkansas and Oklahoma.
[a]Includes forestry and fisheries.
[b]Includes transportation, communications, public utilities, trade, finance, insurance, real estate, services, and government.
[c]Workers in mining, construction, and unspecified jobs are not included in the three separate categories listed above; therefore, the total number of workers shown here is greater than the sum of the three categories.

nomic and social relationships in the countryside for half a century and had pushed thousands of poor whites into Dixie's cotton mills—became increasingly rare. During the 1950s, the number of tenant farms (of all types) in Georgia fell from 85,664 to 26,467, a remarkable plunge of nearly 70 percent. Given such trends, the southern labor market—and hence the world of southern textiles—could not remain unchanged.[29]

The rapid decline in agricultural jobs did not create a regional labor glut because the manufacturing and service sectors expanded at an even greater rate. Between 1940 and 1960, employment in southern manufacturing increased 88 percent, and jobs in the service sector increased by 80 percent. These new wage-earning opportunities were available mostly to whites. In both manufacturing and service work, jobs for whites increased nearly three times faster than those for blacks. During the 1940s and 1950s, blacks abandoned Dixie at an unprecedented rate, in numbers that made the Great Migration of the World War I era appear a mere trickle. In contrast, during the 1950s the South experienced a net *increase* in white inmigration for the first time in the twentieth century, perhaps because the manufacturing jobs opening up in the region were not necessarily low-wage positions. The only southern industries that actually experienced a decline in employment during the 1950s were textiles and lumber processing—traditional low-wage industries that employed 36 percent of all southern factory hands in 1950 but only 23 percent by 1960. In the South, six industries boasted employment growth rates of 60 percent or more during the 1950s. Four of these were clearly high-wage industries: electrical machinery, transportation equipment, nonelectrical machinery, and metals. By 1960 these four industries combined accounted for 23 percent of all manufacturing jobs in the state.[30]

These new trends in agriculture and industry were manifest in Whitfield County. During the 1950s, production of cotton and orchard crops fell as that of soybeans and poultry rose. The total number of farms in the county declined by 39 percent, and tenant farms witnessed a sharp 62 percent drop. Meanwhile, non-agricultural jobs expanded noticeably. The number of industrial workers in Whitfield increased by 53 percent between the late 1940s and the late 1950s (5,875 in 1947 to 9,014 in 1958), reaching 11,071 in 1963. More than half of the county's labor force worked in manufacturing by 1960, while another 27 percent were employed in white-collar occupations. This new cadre of wage earners was overwhelmingly native-born and white. The population of Whitfield County in 1960 was only 4.5 percent black and less than 1 percent foreign-born. Curiously, though, it was not overwhelmingly urban. Many families who had quit agriculture still remained in the countryside or lived on the outskirts of Dalton. Automobiles, better roads, and less expensive rural housing encouraged thousands of workers to commute from outlying areas or from adjacent counties where industry was still undeveloped. A commuter work force meant that textile mills were no longer dependent on labor from within the mill village or even from within the city. This, in turn, meant that the next generation of cotton millers would be less community-minded.[31]

The industrial growth in Whitfield County during the 1950s was due largely to the invention of "wall-to-wall" carpeting in Dalton, which soon became known as the Carpet Capital of the World. By a symbolically appropriate coincidence, the passing of the Crown Mill village paralleled the meteoric rise of Dalton's carpet industry. Even during the town's years as the Bedspread Capital of the Universe, old-line textiles mills—particularly Crown and American Thread—had remained the backbone of the local economy. But during the 1950s, both cotton mills and spread plants were overwhelmed by the carpet boom. By the 1960s, Dalton's chamber of commerce could view Crown Mill and American Thread as relatively unimportant to the local economy.

The carpet crusade was led by the Tufted Textile Manufacturers' Association (TTMA). A cohesive and powerful industry force, the TTMA was a Dalton-based organization formed in the late 1930s to consolidate the efforts of bedspread manufacturers and to further the interests of the tufted textile industry. By the 1950s, the TTMA was the dominant manufacturing group in Dalton and boasted impressive financial and political connections. Unlike Dalton's earlier industrialists, many of the tufted textile leaders during the fifties were recently arrived Jews from northern cities. Uptown Daltonians responded with at best a reserved graciousness to the invasion of non-Protestant Yankees, but several newcomers made it big in carpets and became leaders in the TTMA. Most prominent of these was Ira Nochumson, a Jewish businessman from Chicago who was elected president of the

TTMA in 1953. Announcing Nochumson's new post, the *Citizen*, with some clum-siness, described the TTMA leader as "a member of the Jewish families of Dalton, [who] has done much not only for his nationality, but for all groups in the county." For his part, Nochumson quickly committed himself to the local culture, becom-ing a leading member of the Elks, the Masons, the Lions Club, and the Community Chest. He espoused a brand of booster rhetoric scarcely different from that of Thomas R. Jones in the 1880s or the Jaycees in the 1920s. Many chenille manufac-turers were still Dalton natives, but Nochumson and his fellow Jewish industrial-ists, such as Harry Saul and Arthur Richman, represented a new line of business leaders in Dalton, and their presence reflected the tentative beginnings of a more diverse and fluid southern society.[32]

Wherever they hailed from, chenille manufacturers were avidly antiunion. But unlike the hard-nosed antiunion industrialists who had dominated America and the South in the years before World War II, the TTMA used guarded rhetoric in speaking about unions and made frequent public displays of the fringe benefits and banquets they offered to local workers. Whereas old-style mill-village pater-nalism had maintained an inward, almost private community focus and had been defined by a complicated network of kinship ties, the TTMA's new brand of corporate welfare favored media-oriented public relations programs. The leaders of the organization publicized the carrot; less visible was the big stick. When the time came for them to resist unionization in the mid-1950s, they had cultivated strong allies—namely, the local press and the governor of Georgia—who were willing to assail organized labor on behalf of the TTMA.

The TTMA's fortunes expanded dramatically when the carpet industry took off in the early 1950s. From the beginnings of mechanized chenille production, the tufted textile industry had produced three main items: bedspreads, bathrobes, and rugs. Bedspreads had long been the dominant product, but in 1949 two tech-nological breakthroughs—rubber backing and broad-loom carpet machines—revolutionized the industry and laid the foundation for Dalton to become the Carpet Capital. A local invention, the new looms were from nine to twelve feet wide and contained up to twelve hundred needles each. In a single process, they could produce "broad loom" or "wall-to-wall" cotton carpets, which quickly found a huge national and international market. As early as the spring of 1951, the future was clear. As one TTMA spokesman reported, "This is the first time in history that floor coverings have gone ahead of spreads since the founding of the tufted textile industry. . . . Today tufted textile floor coverings have moved from the bathroom and bedroom into the living room and offices." During the previous year, rug and carpet production had increased 50 percent, compared to 12 percent for bedspreads and 6 percent for bathrobes. The total output of cotton floor coverings—only two million square yards in 1941—was an impressive fifty million square yards in 1953. Those carpet plants that could find enough workers were running twenty-four hours a day in three shifts. Dalton's carpet boom resulted from one of the few examples of southern technological innovation; it also created local spinoff industries of the type so common in the North and so rare in the South. "Because of the enlarged [carpet] operations," the *Citizen* proudly noted, "new industries, component parts necessary to the tufted business, have come to Dalton such as dye plants, laundries, yarn representatives, latex plants, machinery manufacturing plants, etc." This list of new enterprises—some of them indigenous to carpet production—signaled, albeit faintly, Dalton's liberation from the limitations of small-town southern industry, from its dependence on cotton mills and Yankee ingenuity.[33]

The carpet boom threw yet another new twist into the local labor market. It provided new opportunities for established workers, and it opened factory doors to thousands of rural whites from the north Georgia countryside. In effect, a new wave of people moved in from the country to fill the labor needs of Dalton's burgeoning carpet companies. The incentives for taking on factory employment for the first time—or for leaving cotton mills for carpet plants—were strong. In the wake of World War II, even before the carpet boom, Dalton's chenille plants aggressively recruited workers by offering attractive wages and working conditions. A typical postwar newspaper advertisement promised above-average earnings, generous benefits, air-conditioned factories, and even piped-in music during working hours. This last feature emphasized the quiet of the chenille plants and must have seemed nearly miraculous to those accustomed to the deafening roar of the cotton mills. As the carpet labor market stabilized, chenille wages dipped slightly below those in traditional textiles, but the work environment in the new plants was generally better.[34]

Whereas Dalton's chenille industry took off in the 1950s, Crown and other traditional textile plants suffered from erratic business cycles and increased foreign competition. The decade began with uncertainty. The Korean War spurred massive overproduction and wreaked havoc on the American textile industry for several years. The growing demand for synthetic fibers further complicated cotton-textile markets. Northern textiles suffered a stunning decline, and Yankee firms moved south in record numbers, a trend that augured well for Dixie's leading industry. But the same forces that undermined northern textiles also traveled south of the Mason-Dixon line. During the 1940s, the United States was the major producer of textiles in the world, and the South produced the lion's share. In the following decade, however, foreign competition—most of it from the Far East—hit an overly productive American textile industry hard. Figure 12.1 shows how quickly the American textile trade surplus shriveled in the 1950s. As late as 1952, American cotton-textile exports exceeded imports by more than 80 percent, but by 1960 the export differential had fallen to only 7 percent. By 1962 the United States was actually running a trade deficit of more than $40 million. It was

FIGURE 12.1.   The U.S. Textile Trade, 1945–1962

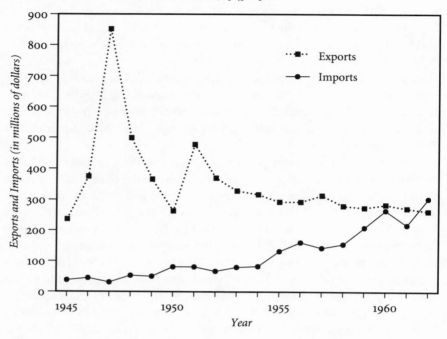

Source: U.S. Bureau of the Census, *Historical Statistics*, figures for "Cotton Manufactures," pp. 898, 900.

not simply that America's export market deteriorated; inexpensive imports also shrank the all-important domestic market. In Dalton the Real Silk Hosiery Mill shut down permanently in 1953, while Crown and American Thread struggled erratically. Crown confronted these depressing trends by opening a variety of subsidiary plants in north Georgia, all of which specialized in different textile lines than the parent plants in Dalton. At the same time, the company spent nearly $1 million to modernize the machinery at its Dalton plants, thereby slashing labor costs. Although neither the subsidiaries nor technological modernization achieved magical results, the company survived the decade.[35]

But if Crown remained in business, it was certainly not the same company it had been. To be sure, the community retained some of the old sensibilities. The family-purchase clause in Crown's housing contracts ensured that neighborhoods in the village area would be inhabited by traditional mill families for the next two decades. But despite this continuity, once Crown sold its mill village, little remained of the old order. The reverse was also true: because so little remained of the old system, Crown had no reason to maintain its village housing. The people who bought the mill houses were longtime Crown employees, but few of these families now had children working in the mill. "Old-timers" were not necessarily old, but they represented a community that was rapidly aging because going to work in the mill was no longer the natural thing for mill children to do. Crown no longer sponsored a company band, and the mill baseball teams gradually merged into new city leagues.

In the early 1950s, the Crown Mill whistle ceased to blow. There was no longer a Burial Association or a Crown Mill Savings Account. The Gold Dust Twins were long gone. Dalton High School had become as mundane among mill-village youth as Crown Point School once had been. Indeed, the mill's management sold Crown Point to the city in 1959. The city revamped the old school building and nearly eliminated Crown from the name. Some longtime cotton millers insisted that the new city school retain its identification with Crown, and for a time they were successful; but ultimately the school was completely remodeled and the name changed to Westwood. Baptisms could no longer be held in the old mill reservoir, which had been fenced in and had become overgrown with lily pads. In the mill itself, the settling of formal grievances by the union had become the status quo; the days of informality and favoritism symbolized by Frank Springer had long since passed. Crown View Baptist Church ultimately changed its name to the Second Baptist Church. The corner groceries no longer offered curbside service to mill-village homes. Indeed the old groceries were doomed, because widespread auto-mobile ownership made it possible for families in the village area to go further afield in search of bargains. Both inside the plant and in the surrounding neigh-borhoods, few remnants of the old Crown Mill culture remained.

By the mid-1950s, the union, of all things, represented one of the workers' strongest ties to tradition. Shortly after Crown sold its mill village, TWUA Local 185 saw its power and popularity reach unprecedented heights. At the same time, Dalton's booming tufted textile plants were completely nonunion. To local union workers, chenille plant employees represented an opportunity as much as they did a liability. The cotton millers had created a strong union town in the 1930s and 1940s; surely the unorganized chenille workers could be brought into the fold. Despite the failure of Operation Dixie, the possibility of greater labor unity in the emerging Carpet Capital still seemed plausible. But if the unions at Crown and American Thread hoped they could organize the chenille industry, those hopes were soon crushed. Dalton's isolated enclave of union power was extremely vulner-able to attack. Just how vulnerable was not fully understood by local union leaders until the Dalton Red Scare of 1955.

13

BOOMING UNIONS
AND UNION BUSTING

Despite the social and economic changes that transformed the South during and after World War II, Dixie's leading textile states remained predominantly nonunion. In 1953, when one-third of all the workers in the United States belonged to a union, only 15 percent of Georgia's work force was organized; in the Carolinas, fewer than one in ten carried a union card. But regional statistics obscured the fact that stable union enclaves did exist in the South. In a few towns and cities throughout the region, organized labor had taken root during the late 1930s and early 1940s and had survived—sometimes even thrived—during the postwar decade. Dalton, of course, was one such union enclave. With three large textile locals and a collection of smaller unions in other industries, the north Georgia city was part of a loose confederation of union towns in the southern Appalachian Valley. As Crown Mill's paternalism subsided noticeably in the early 1950s, TWUA Local 185 strengthened its position, increasing its membership dramatically and emerging as the nucleus of the postwar workers' community.[1]

But how much success could a strong TWUA local expect in a region largely devoid of textile unions, and, more important, how could a small-town local facilitate the growth of organized labor in the South? Local 185 responded vigorously to the challenges before it. It supported organization drives throughout Dixie and worked to create a prolabor political climate in Georgia. By the mid-1950s, however, a more immediate challenge for Dalton's unions had surfaced closer to home. Fueled by broadloom carpets, the chenille industry skyrocketed, swelling the city's work force by thousands of unorganized employees. In 1955, TWUA Locals 185 and 134 had never been stronger, but they recognized that chenilles would have to be organized if Dalton were to remain a bulwark of southern unionism. Considering that the town's old-line textile plants had all been organized for nearly a generation, it should have been a relatively simple task. To understand why it was not is to shed new light on the difficulties facing postwar organizers in Dixie, difficulties that stemmed as much from national trends as from regional peculiarities.

The early 1950s were heady years for TWUA Local 185. At that time, recalled John Bramblett, "the union was an established thing, it was a set thing, and it was not rough going like it was trying to form one, or get something in." The union had become the norm. In the 1930s, Crown's millhands had divided bitterly over the union, and tensions created by that split remained thereafter; but by the early 1950s, internal opposition to Local 185 had all but vanished, and almost every worker became a card-carrying member. Crown had never been a closed shop. Millhands had the choice of joining or not. Affiliating with the union did not affect a worker's wages and benefits, because nonunion hands were fully covered by the union contract. The proportion of Crown Mill employees who became dues-paying members of Local 185 therefore reflected the union's popularity.[2]

As table 13.1 shows, 1955 marked the high point of union support. In 1952 union membership in Local 185 stood at 630—a solid majority but still less than two-thirds of the mill's work force. By 1955 membership had skyrocketed to 917, a startling increase of 46 percent in only three years. To this day, some antiunion millhands in the Dalton area insist that the union won the support of only a slim majority of Crown's work force and that they themselves would have nothing to do with the union. Without underestimating the value of such testimony, the union's membership records (maintained by the Crown Mill office, due to the "check-off" system) demonstrate that millhands who refused to join Local 185 were part of a small minority in 1955. In that year, 94 percent of the workers were dues-paying union members. The overall rise in union membership in Dalton reflected national trends, but perhaps the surge in enrollment at Crown stemmed from the selling of the mill village, which may have convinced some older antiunion workers that Local 185 now offered the best hope of safeguarding their own interests.

TABLE 13.1. Union Membership at Crown Mill, 1952–1969

	Union Membership	Percentage Change	Percentage of Work Force[a]
1952	630	—	64.4
1953	752	+19.4	76.8
1954	776	+ 3.2	79.3
1955	917	+18.2	93.7
1956	894	− 2.5	91.3
1957	880	− 1.6	89.9
**	**	**	**
1967	550	−37.5	68.8
1968	497	− 9.6	66.3
1969	366	−26.4	52.3

Sources: TWUA Local 185, Dues Checkoff Records, 1952–57, 1967–69, and Seniority List, 1955, SLA; "Dalton, Georgia, for Release September 12, 1969," typed announcement from Crown Cotton Mill company files, CGA.
[a]Percentages for all years except 1955 and 1969 are best possible estimates only, due to lack of data on the exact size of the work force.
**Data for the years 1958–66 is missing from union records.

Perhaps, too, Crown's recent plant modernization and stretchouts convinced many alienated millhands to sign union cards.

The leaders of Local 185 in the 1950s were mostly longtime Crown Mill people. They were the Bunches, Brambletts, Craigs, Hustons, Kenemers, Travillians, and Weavers, sons and daughters of the old Crown Mill community of the 1920s and 1930s. When the union got organized in 1933, most of them were young and were already working in the mill. They and their families had been among the diehard holdouts in the strike of 1939; they had seen union gains and losses in the 1940s; they were politically active. They were not casual supporters of the union. Local 185 was central to their lives, central to their understanding of what it meant to be a mill worker in Dalton, Georgia, in America. Local 185 was virtually their career. They were the heart of the union, and they were relatively few in number, maybe two or three dozen millhands at any given time. These were the men and women who elected (and served as) officers of the local, voted on policies, attended conventions, testified before Congress, raised money for charities, decided whom their PAC should support in each election, and basically did all of the work of Local 185. They were the ones who worked closely with other unionists in Dalton, especially with the leaders of American Thread TWUA Local 134, to create a better environment for organized labor in north Georgia.

This core of leaders constantly sought greater participation from the union's growing general membership, but to no avail. Monthly business meetings were always poorly attended; door prizes and other enticements to bring in a crowd usually had no effect. All union members at Crown had dues deducted from their paychecks, and most looked to the union for help on the job, but few workers actually helped run the show. Perhaps the leadership blamed this lack of popular involvement on newly arrived workers who had no link with Crown's past, no identification with the union's history and struggles, and therefore no interest in the organization aside from the benefits they could gain from it. Perhaps, seen from the other direction, those newly arrived workers thought of the union core— rightly or not—as an unassailable clique. But such considerations do not explain why so many longtime Crown employees also remained detached. Perhaps most old-timers refrained from active involvement because they knew the organization was in capable hands and would function perfectly well without their own participation. After all, it was hard enough just to work full time in the mill without committing one's time to union administration during off hours. In any case, the union had a type of dual existence. Officially, Local 185 consisted of all card-carrying members, and as such it was a large organization. But because the vast majority of millhands took no active part in the governing of the local, the small group of leaders acted, in effect, as the union.[3]

The union's primary role in the lives of most millhands was to settle disputes that arose on the shop floor. Any rank-and-file worker—including nonunion mill-hands—could file a grievance through the union, and most workers did so at one time or another. The minutes of union meetings from the early 1950s were filled with concerns about stretchouts, speedups, and the "time-study man" and about issues relating to seniority and job security.[4]

But there was much more to Local 185 than on-the-job concerns. The union had originated and evolved in the 1930s as part of a larger process of community adjustment to extraordinary events, and thus it had always been closely inter-woven with the cultural and social infrastructure of the Crown Mill village. World War II and the CIO's postwar political campaigns had expanded the union's view beyond its own mill village, and as company paternalism faded, the union assumed responsibility for many traditional facets of community life. By the 1950s, Local 185 participated in a broad range of activities—from Crown Mill to Capitol Hill, from politics to philanthropy.

The local operated within a far-flung network of CIO unions throughout Dixie and the nation. Crown's union hands maintained a close relationship with Local 134 at American Thread. In 1949, for example, Local 185 distributed more than $700 in relief funds to Thread Mill workers who were on strike. Its motto, as expressed by one union leader, was that "one local's trouble was our trouble too and that we should help one another." The two Dalton unions worked closely together during the PAC campaigns of the late 1940s and early 1950s and formed the nucleus of the Whitfield County Labor Council, which superseded PAC in 1953 and cooperated with other county labor councils throughout northwest Georgia.[5] The Crown union continually sent money—hundreds of dollars each year—to other union locals in northwest Georgia that were on strike or trying to organize their plants. In 1950 Local 185 resolved to send "$50 to woodworkers Local 1721 in Chattanooga who are out on strike and are in need of help," and the following year it set up "an organizing committee for Calhoun Mills and new mills on the Cleveland Highway," adding that "the union is to furnish funds as needed."[6] Local 185 continued to send delegates to TWUA conferences and conventions throughout Georgia, the South, and the nation. These meetings usually focused on politics, union campaigns, and developments in the textile industry. Conferences were often explicitly educational, as was one—to which Local 185 sent representatives—that advertised itself as a special national "institute on labor and world affairs."[7]

As the union's support for other workers and its attention to education suggest, Local 185's involvement in these labor networks was closely related to its political interests. Crown's own Jack Gregg stated that the basic purpose of the Whitfield County Labor Council was to "elect people to office that will be friendly to labor." Despite the political setbacks of the late 1940s, Dalton's unions remained active in political campaigns at all levels of government. They monitored the voting records of state and national legislators and pushed for the repeal of the Taft-Hartley Act and Georgia's antilabor laws. Local 185 also fought to repeal the county unit electoral system, which worked against the political interests of organized labor. It pushed for "home rule" legislation in the Georgia statehouse and worked hard in support of bond issues to improve Dalton's public schools and sewer system. Occasionally Crown's workers rallied to support one of their own for a place on the city council, holding registration drives, driving voters to the polls, and donating several hundred dollars to various campaigns (all unsuccessful). These efforts dilated the workers' political outlook, a consequence explicitly sought by such union leaders as Dalton's John R. Bunch, who in 1952 asked "people to get literature on [the] First Amendment . . . [to] read it and give it to others to read."[8]

Local 185 also became a philanthropic organization. On the regional and national level, it contributed generously to the National Foundation for Infantile Paralysis and other service organizations and bought Christmas gifts for children in other southern mill villages. More important for its own community, Local 185 assisted Crown Mill workers who were sick and in need of financial help. Before World War II, the Crown Mill "family" took care of its own: workers passed the hat for injured or ailing millhands; the company sometimes provided support for needy families. But by the 1950s, the union local had shouldered the customary burden of community welfare among the millhands. Union records show that during the early 1950s, Local 185 routinely undertook such efforts on the workers' behalf, and Crown's millhands began to look to the union for support. On occasion it allowed modifications of the contract to help desperate workers. For example, when one worker was fired, the union helped get her job back, not because she was fired unjustly, but because "she is a widow woman with four children and really needs the work." More commonly the union sent money to needy families within the community. In late 1950, the executive board "recommended that the local union help members who are off from work on sick leaves and are in need (as Harley Pinson who has been sick almost a year and is really in need of help)." At another meeting, the union passed the hat and collected over fifty dollars for Mackie Palmer, who, one member reported, "is sick and needs help and asked that the union help him." Several months later, when millhand Cliff Smith took ill, Local 185 sent him the equivalent of his regular paycheck. In late 1957, a friend of George Howell sent a note to union president John Bunch saying that Howell "is in the Hospital seriously ill and won't be able to work for quite some time and he wanted me to ask you if you would please take up a donation for him at Sundays union meeting as his family is in desperate need of money, any that you can get will be greatly appreciated." So it went, as the older tradition of cooperative welfare among the cotton millers became a vital part of Local 185's role within the community.[9]

The union leadership also made certain that Local 185 played an active role in bringing better community services to Dalton and the mill neighborhoods. In 1950, for example, the union sent a delegate to Atlanta "to appear before the Public Service Commission to fight the increase in local phone rates." Local 185 also fought for better public schools in Dalton and Whitfield County and supported efforts to establish "the junior college we hope to get in Dalton." The local PAC campaigned for a bond issue to build a better sewer system. Continuing education programs for workers, which were a constant concern of Local 185, focused on services within the mill community. The union established leadership-training schools for elected officers, time-study schools for all members, and, most frequently, classes in "cotton-mill math." Less pragmatic—but symbolic of the union's expanding role in the workers' community—was the union-sponsored "singing program" held at the Whitfield County Courthouse in 1951.[10]

The leaders of Local 185 saw their organization as a partner in the running of Crown Mill, which may explain why they ran their union like a large business. They carefully monitored its finances and made sure its bills were paid at the beginning of each meeting. The union invested heavily in U.S. savings bonds—nearly $10,000 worth (with a maturity value of nearly $14,000) by early 1951. In early 1952, Local 185 purchased its own union hall, a spacious house on Underwood Street in northeast Dalton. Proudly identified with a new neon sign, the hall became the new community center for members of Local 185, which had its offices and held its meetings there. Some community traditions were still in evidence, as when the local's officers asked all members to come out "to the working," at which they would fix up the union hall and surrounding grounds. In the mill-village community, tradition and change had always walked arm in arm, so perhaps it was not surprising that in March 1952, union leaders called for the old-fashioned "working," and one month later they received a modern charter of incorporation from the state of Georgia. Local 185 was now a corporation in its own right. "Henceforth," the union resolved, "this organization is to be known as Local #185, Textile Workers Foundation, Inc." The union members had become stockholders in their own company.[11]

But these signs of union strength and maturity could not disguise the problems facing Dalton's TWUA locals. Operation Dixie, the much-ballyhooed postwar effort to organize southern workers, had floundered from the start and finally ground to a halt. Organized labor had been unable to force the repeal of the Taft-Hartley Act of 1947. Among other things, this law forbade mass picketing, sanctioned harsh injunctions against strikers, and made it possible for employers to sue unions for violation of "unfair labor practices." It also restructured the NLRB, labor's savior in the organizational campaigns of the late 1930s, so that now the board could be used by industrialists to attack unionization efforts. Moreover, the law changed the rules for union certification, making it harder for unions to schedule certification elections and granting employers a campaign period in which to convince workers (through persuasion or intimidation) not to vote for the union. Taken together, these provisions made it extremely difficult for unions to organize the unorganized, which was why Taft-Hartley was such a burden on southern labor. For existing unions, Taft-Hartley did not seem to have the deleterious effect predicted by many advocates of organized labor. But for the mass of nonunion workers in southern textiles, it created obstacles that organizers had not had to face during the late 1930s or early 1940s. The law also gave states the authority to outlaw certain forms of union security, namely the formation of a "union shop," in which workers had to join a union within a specified time period after obtaining employment there. These "right-to-work" laws in the South thus outlawed something that virtually no southern unions had in the first place. Their importance was symbolic; through them, legislators sent a signal to business leaders—and to workers—that unions in Georgia were too weak to wield any political clout and that unions were not welcome in the state. This situation was unlikely to change in the 1950s. As prolabor congressman Henderson Lanham reported to north Georgia's labor unions, national labor law was not likely to improve any time soon, and unions were going to have to learn to live with it. Older ones did usually live with it, but fledgling organizations often died from it.[12]

The TWUA's national organization was also struggling. Membership in the International had plummeted from more than 320,000 in 1950 to less than 200,000 in 1955. As northern textiles collapsed, the union was desperate for southern members. But the problems of the TWUA in Dixie were further aggravated in 1952 by a schism in the regional organization, caused when southern director George

Baldanzi bolted for the AFL after a conflict with national TWUA president Emil Rieve. Baldanzi's departure led about twenty thousand southern members out of the TWUA at a time when members in Dixie were already scarce. Dalton's unions remained with the TWUA, but Crown's Local 185 began to distance itself from the state TWUA office in Atlanta. The schism left Local 185 more isolated within the region, and events in Dalton only made matters worse. The rapid growth of the carpet industry was creating thousands of new nonunion jobs in the city. As if that were not enough, the Real Silk Hosiery Mill, which had a very strong union, shut down permanently in 1953. TWUA Locals 185 and 134 therefore had a keen interest in organizing the chenille workers.[13]

Prospects for unionizing the chenille industry had long been dim, but things looked brighter by the mid-1950s. Throughout the late 1930s and 1940s, employment in the spread plants had been erratic, almost seasonal, making unionization very difficult. In flush times the industry ran short of experienced workers, but booms always gave way to lulls and unemployment. Organized labor could gain no leverage in such a situation. As late as December 1951, the local office of the state employment service noted that "chenille plants have already started laying off workers . . . but that is the usual trend around Christmas time each year." But when carpet production took off, this pattern changed. A year later, the *Dalton Citizen* noted that the industry had broken all previous records for production and dollar volume, and that 1953 was expected to be an even better year. More significantly, the paper noted that tufted textile plants in Dalton were expected to run through the winter, thereby signaling an end to the seasonal employment patterns of earlier years. By late 1954, chenille production was running strong, and the labor market was tight. In February 1955, a staff member of the state employment office in Dalton announced that the job situation in the tufted textile plants was "better than I've ever seen it at this time of the year." Propelled by carpets, the chenille industry no longer relied on a seasonal work force but instead employed a permanent, well-trained group of tufted textile hands. Or, as one leader of the Tufted Textile Manufacturers' Association (TTMA) put it, chenille plants needed "experienced workers." From the perspective of labor organizers, the situation boded well for unionization.[14]

But the Dalton chenille campaign of 1955 proved from the start to be unusually troublesome. Neither the local unions nor the state TWUA office actually initiated the drive to form chenille unions. That campaign originated within the congregation of the Reverend Charlie T. Pratt's Church of God of the Union Assembly. The Holiness church had over five hundred members in Dalton and over ten thousand more in congregations scattered across the South—Georgia, Alabama, Tennessee, Kentucky, West Virginia, Texas, Arkansas—as well as in the midwestern manufacturing centers to which poor southern whites were migrating in search of work—especially urban areas in Ohio, Indiana, and Michigan. Brother Pratt's son, the

Reverend Jesse F. Pratt, had a church in Detroit. The Union Assembly's headquarters were in Dalton, where Charlie Pratt served as the church's "national moderator." After his explosive foray into local politics in the late 1940s, the Holiness minister continued to expand the Union Assembly and its church-owned businesses. By 1955 Pratt's congregation owned and operated a flour mill (the Whitfield Milling Company) and the Union Supermarket, which one observer called "a large modern and first-class food store." The church also ran a cannery that preserved vegetables raised on Church of God farms, a modernly equipped dairy that distributed free milk to poor families, the Union Slaughterhouse, and the Dalton Tourist Court and Restaurant. Brother Pratt's congregation in Dalton consisted primarily of chenille plant workers, along with some cotton millers and a smattering of poor farmers. As in the 1930s and 1940s, the Union Assembly remained a strong advocate of organized labor, and Pratt had an eye toward organizing the burgeoning carpet industry.[15]

The Holiness minister pushed his prolabor program a step further in 1954 when he recruited fellow southern radical Don West to publish a newspaper on behalf of the Union Assembly and the working people of the South. The result was *The Southerner: A Voice of the People*, which was published in Dalton and first hit the newsstands in March 1955. West was a native of the north Georgia countryside and a deeply religious man. He had spent his late teens doing church work in Appalachian communities and working his way through college, earning a bachelor of divinity degree in 1932 from Vanderbilt University, where he had studied under Alva W. Taylor, a southern theologian committed to social change. One year out of college, West joined fellow southern radical Myles Horton in establishing the Highlander Folk School in the mountains of east Tennessee, and the place ultimately became a leading center of southern dissent. West soon left Highlander, but he was hardly idle after his departure. He spent the remainder of the 1930s championing various liberal and radical causes—including organized labor and civil rights for southern blacks—throughout Georgia and the South. Whether West was a member of the Communist party is debatable; like many liberals of the 1930s, he supported Popular Front campaigns, working closely with Communist party members. During the 1940s, West held several pastorates in Congregational churches in Georgia, completed his doctoral degree, and secured a position in the English Department at Oglethorpe University in Atlanta. Under pressure from the *Atlanta Constitution*, Oglethorpe fired West from its faculty for his activism in the 1930s and for his support of Progressive party presidential candidate Henry Wallace in 1948. But the 1948 campaign put West in touch with Charlie Pratt, who served as cochair of the Progressive party in Georgia. The two became friends, and West was later ordained as a Church of God minister. Labor leaders in the TWUA state office may have seen the potential of a chenille organizing drive, but it was these two Holiness ministers, not the state office, who acted on that potential and sparked the chenille campaign of 1955.[16]

A casual glance at *The Southerner* left little doubt as to the church's ardently prolabor stance. West took every opportunity to boost unionization. The July 1955 edition carried the bold front-page headline, "Dalton Union Aids Carolina Workers." The accompanying story explained how Local 134 of American Thread had assisted workers at another American Thread mill in Clover, South Carolina, where the TWUA won a union certification election by nearly a two-to-one margin. West also enlivened the paper with stinging political cartoons aimed at anti-labor groups and at racism. Judging from letters to the editor—which came in from Michigan, Ohio, Missouri, New York, Oklahoma, West Virginia, North Carolina, and various towns in Georgia—the paper enjoyed a wide, though probably numerically limited, circulation.[17]

Wealthy whites in Dalton viewed *The Southerner* as Protestantism gone afoul, but Pratt and West saw it as Protestantism redeemed. They perceived the world as being engaged in a struggle between rich and poor, with God on the side of the oppressed. Their religion was one of deliverance in the here and now as well as in the by-and-by. They quoted scripture (often loosely phrased) that stressed the miseries that would come upon the rich and the blessings that would come to the poor. Their messages boiled down to this: Christ sides with poor workers; unions offer poor workers a better life; Christ, therefore, favors unionization as a form of godly retribution and justice. One minister writing for *The Southerner* voiced a common theme when he stated, "God was going to bring the proud and mighty low and lift up the weak and lowly." Often, too, the paper blended its advocacy of organized labor with the message of American liberty. One editorial, for example, concluded, "We believe in the principles of organized labor because we believe in the life and teaching of Jesus Christ; because we believe in the principles of our founding fathers; because we believe in genuine Americanism." In practice, these beliefs demanded avid support for unionism; as one minister wrote, "You can't be a Christian and a scab. The two just don't go together."[18]

In 1955 this sort of talk was likely to get one branded as a Communist, and the Union Assembly leaders knew it. Charlie Pratt wrote, "Anybody who ever stood up for the poor people has been called a communist. I've been called a communist. I'm not a communist, but I've always stood up for the laboring people." A minister from Tennessee put it more strongly: "If you are afraid of being called a communist, don't preach God's Bible." And he added, "If you don't want to be called a communist join up with the McCarthy gang and the Roman Catholic Hierarchy." This final barb was no passing addendum. The Union Assembly adherents were strongly anti-Catholic, in part because they associated Catholicism with McCarthyism. Hence, at a Union Assembly Labor Day rally in 1955, Jesse Pratt stated that he would rather be "called a communist than a Catholic." Don West even suggested a parallel between Catholic McCarthyites and Judas, both being "children of the devil" who accused the righteous. This was hardly the kind of talk likely to win support from the TWUA International office.[19]

Dalton's unions nonetheless applauded *The Southerner* and immediately aligned themselves with West and his paper. Crown's own TWUA Local 185 was particularly supportive, taking out full-page advertisements and writing editorials in support of organized labor. For the first few issues, Local 185 contributed its own "As We See It" column written by Jack Gregg and John R. Bunch, the local's president and secretary. Their column stressed the democratic system of union government and the community-mindedness of organized labor in Dalton. It also condemned the "shameful low wage level" in Dalton's chenille plants and pointed toward unionization as a remedy. TWUA Local 134 from American Thread was often featured in *The Southerner*, and Dalton's newest union, TWUA Local 1376 of the Dalton Textile Corporation, published a strong prounion letter in the paper, concluding, "If we all stick together I believe some day we will have all the plants organized in Dalton." "All the plants" meant, of course, the chenille plants.[20]

Far from being pleased about *The Southerner*, officials in the TWUA national office grew alarmed over the Dalton locals' association with Don West. By late April, business leaders from Dalton had spoken with Congressman Henderson Lanham about West and his newspaper, and they asked him to check into the situation. Lanham asked the House Un-American Activities Committee (HUAC) to look into West's background. HUAC sent Lanham a lengthy file detailing the minister's association with Communists and radical causes, whereupon the congressman immediately informed David S. Burgess of the Georgia State Industrial Union Council about the doings in Dalton. Lanham told Burgess that the "CIO will be damaged if the Textile locals continue their close collaboration with this publication" and added, "I do hope that you and Charlie Gillman [CIO Region 5 director] can disengage the labor unions of Whitfield County from their entanglement with West and his paper." After briefly meeting together and deciding not to confront the Dalton locals directly, Burgess and Gillman both wrote to William Pollock, then executive vice president of the TWUA, echoing Congressman Lanham's concerns and urging Pollock to act on the situation. In response Pollock contacted James O'Shea, the manager of TWUA's Northwest Georgia Joint Board, asking him to meet with the Dalton locals and to give them the HUAC information on West. A few days later, O'Shea met with the Dalton leaders, who, being on the bottom rung of this hierarchy, were apparently the last to learn of Don West's reputation as a Red.[21]

Dalton's union officials were upset by the news, because they realized West's past could mean trouble for the campaign (and because the TWUA's upper-level officials had been scheming behind their backs). The larger problem was not lost on local unionists. O'Shea put it clearly to Pollock in late May. "The people in Dalton knew nothing of [West's] background," he explained, and they recognized the need to distance themselves from him. He added that the locals had agreed to steer clear of *The Southerner*, at least in any official capacity. At the same time, though, O'Shea stressed that the Union Assembly was "a very influential and powerful Religious sect in this area, who urges its members to organize, [and] is greatly responsible for our organizing success in Dalton." Therein lay the dilemma. Any chenille campaign would need the Union Assembly's support, but at the same time West and his newspaper would be a heavy burden to the campaign.[22]

The TWUA's top officials had confronted the issue of labor radicalism and public image during the late 1940s and early 1950s by purging all Communists and radicals from the organization. Communist party members and fellow travelers had played critically important parts in the rapid rise of the CIO during the late 1930s and the World War II years, but the postwar era witnessed the advent of an increasingly centrist CIO. The CIO's own war on communism fueled the anticommunist flames that McCarthy and other Red-baiters subsequently used to bake their political opponents. An emerging group of avidly anticommunist union leaders sometimes even collaborated with HUAC in order to smear their radical rivals. The purges helped the CIO attain mainstream status but also narrowed the possible outlets for noncommunist radicals. In 1948 the CIO had attacked Henry Wallace, and it therefore did not please top officials in 1955 to see two former Wallace supporters—Pratt and West—spearheading a TWUA campaign.[23]

Dalton's union leaders, themselves in favor of the International's anticommunist stance, feared an assault on West from the International, and they urged national officials to exercise restraint in the matter. They argued that "to make an issue [of West] publicly would hurt us greatly in this area, with many members pulling out of the Union." O'Shea also urged Pollock "to take no drastic action that would hurt us in this area." Labor campaigns were still butting against the barriers of corporate America, but by the 1950s it had become increasingly difficult for local organizers to establish new areas of dissent acceptable to the International. As it turned out, Dalton's unions were right to fear the forces of anticommunism, but the attack on West did not come from the TWUA International.[24]

West's early efforts in Dalton brought both success and a severe backlash. Prounion chenille workers had begun to try to organize themselves by July 1955, and the TWUA sent in representatives to help. For concerned chenille manufacturers, there was little question where the trouble lay. Several plants distributed questionnaires asking workers to state their religious affiliation. By January 1956, dozens of employees who listed the Union Assembly as their church found themselves out of a job. West later reported that fifty-six chenille workers (which would have amounted to more than 10 percent of Pratt's congregation) had been fired because of their church membership. These workers appealed to the TWUA for help. The union did enter the fray, but by this time the situation was entirely too controversial for the International. The TWUA national office did ask for a Senate investigation into the firings, but top officials were openly apologetic for West's influence in Dalton's labor affairs. Some state and national TWUA leaders condemned the Reverend Pratt as a corrupt millionaire who pilfered money from his congregation and dodged taxes behind a facade of religion. They considered West a troublesome Red. Other potential allies of the Union Assembly and the chenille workers soon turned away as well. West contacted the Anti-Defamation League of B'nai B'rith, hoping the organization would defend Dalton's Holiness workers. But the league recoiled from the Union Assembly's avid anti-Catholicism and veiled anti-Semitism. "It is our opinion," they concluded, "that this is a good mess to stay away from at the present time."[25]

The chenille manufacturers and the local press were smart enough to downplay the issue of religion—even the issue of organized labor—and to hit the campaign in its most vulnerable spot: the alleged communism of Don West. Criticizing southern white Protestants was a delicate matter, and it was awkward to disparage organized labor in a town with strong, civic-minded unions. But in 1955 anything or anyone who smacked of communism was all but doomed in the public arena. When the Dalton press launched an all-out campaign to smear Don West as a Communist, a firestorm erupted in the city. An early issue of *The Southerner* declared, "You are not worth a dime to any church or union until you get to where you can stand the fire." But the conflagration that soon engulfed Dalton overwhelmed not only Don West and the Union Assembly but also the TWUA campaign to organize Dalton's chenille workers.[26]

Marc Pace, editor of both Dalton weeklies, was West's foremost opponent. Like West, Pace was young, dynamic, and a relative newcomer to the city. Unlike West, Pace had positioned himself squarely within the circle of Dalton's business leaders. One of a new breed of postwar southern journalists, Pace established a more professional format for his papers than had previous weeklies and sought an appropriate balance of local, national, and international news. Pace was a moderate (some white southerners might have said liberal) on the two most explosive southern issues of the day: organized labor and race. He derided the postwar Klan and published pictures and stories applauding the accomplishments of local blacks—something Dalton papers had never done before. Pace also accorded local unions (and working people in general) a level of respect. There were limits to his broad-mindedness, however. He opposed racial integration and scorned the CIO's national leaders. And when it came to communism, Pace left moderation at the editorial door. Fully in sympathy with the TTMA, he doubtless opposed unions in Dalton's chenille plants, but, as he understood very clearly, he did not have to oppose the TWUA outright so long as he could link Don West to communism.

The battle started with a bang. On August 21, 1955, the *Dalton News* published a full page of information on Don West taken (as boldly indicated) from "THE FILES OF THE COMMITTEE ON UN-AMERICAN ACTIVITIES, U.S. HOUSE OF REPRESENTATIVES." HUAC served as the principal collection agency for any material that might be used in an anticommunist smear campaign. The information published in the

News began with a government disclaimer that "it should be noted that the individual is not necessarily a Communist, a Communist sympathizer, or a fellow-traveler unless otherwise indicated." But "Communist" was written all over the report; that, of course, was Marc Pace's intent. "In answer to many questions . . . as to whether Don West . . . is really a Communist, we can merely say we don't know," the editor wrote. "However," he continued, "we can point you to the record, factual, uncolored, and absolutely untouched and non-edited, and you can arrive at your own conclusion." This was the tone and strategy followed by the local press throughout the anti-West campaign: write as if objectivity were the rule and publish an avalanche of material that could only be interpreted one way.[27]

The issue that carried the HUAC material also contained significant announcements from both the TTMA and the TWUA. The TTMA disclosed that chenille plants were raising wages 7 to 10 percent, effective immediately, and that "there undoubtedly will be another wage increase by late October or early November." The paper also revealed that the TTMA had voted to build a new national headquarters building in Dalton. These front-page stories sent clear messages: workers could expect wage increases without union intervention; and chenille manufacturing was indispensable to Dalton's economic growth. Workers themselves might have disputed the first point, seeing that the wage hikes were announced at the very time chenille organization was in the works. This new union movement was no mere rumor. In the same issue, a TWUA advertisement announced: "ATTENTION ALL CHENILLE WORKERS! You are invited to attend a special organizing meeting sponsored by the Textile Workers Union of America, CIO. . . . Learn the facts." Few readers could have missed the connections between the TWUA's chenille campaign, the TTMA's wage increase, and Marc Pace's attack on Don West.[28]

Pace had timed his release of the HUAC material carefully. When Don West had first arrived in town in late 1954, he stopped by Pace's office to talk about setting up *The Southerner*. Pace recognized West from the 1948 Wallace campaign and recalled West's alleged "Communistic background." Pace confronted West on this score, offending the minister, who denied any links to communism. Thus began a bitter relationship between two rival editors. At that time, Pace made no public comment about West's arrival; instead, he quietly asked Congressman Henderson Lanham to investigate West's record. Lanham sent Pace the information from HUAC's files in early May 1955, but Pace bided his time and revealed nothing. When the HUAC material finally appeared in the *News* that August, any perceptive reader could have noticed that it was dated May 3. It seemed no small coincidence that the initial attack on West appeared in the very same issue in which the TWUA publicly announced its chenille campaign. Rather than explain his delay in publishing the material, Pace simply denied he was acting on behalf of the TTMA and stated that "because of matters which are private and which cannot be disclosed, we could not release that data any earlier."[29]

Pace held nothing back once he had published the HUAC material. The follow-ing issue of the *Citizen* printed on the front page "a poem written some time ago by Don West" entitled "Listen, I'm a Communist," the opening lines of which read:

> I am a Communist
> > A Red
> > A Bolshevik!
> Do you, toilers of the South,
> > Know Me?
> Do you believe the lies,
> > Capitalists say
> > And print about me?
> > You sharecroppers
> > Renters,
> > Factory Workers,
> > Negroes, poor whites
> > Do you understand me,
> > Do you see
> > That I am you.
> > That I, the Communist,
> > Am you—?[30]

West countered immediately, claiming the "Communist" poem was an inaccurate and malicious revision of a poem published in his book *Clods of Southern Earth*, entitled "Listen, I'm an Agitator." West even gave Pace a copy of the "Agitator" poem, which Pace then published. But the "Agitator" poem was very similar to the "Communist" version and, in any case, clearly bespoke West's disdain of the status quo and his willingness to incite workers to fight against it. Those outraged by the "Communist" poem would hardly have been pacified by the "Agitator" version. To make matters worse for West, the *Citizen* soon branded him a liar by reprinting a section of a 1934 issue of the *Daily Worker*, a Communist newspaper, in which the "Communist" poem was presented under Don West's name.[31]

West sought to turn attention to the chenille campaign, but Pace skillfully deflected the spotlight back to the Communist issue. Pace always printed the embattled minister's rebuttals in his papers, apparently believing that, if given enough rope, West would hang himself. West insisted, "I am not the issue. The real issue is wages and working conditions and organization of the unorganized." But Pace responded with an editorial that argued, "West would like to align the tufted textile industry with these [HUAC] releases . . . [but] we checked into his back-ground for the sole purpose of letting our citizens know of it. At the time we hadn't even dreamed of any union connections." West wanted to know who paid for the full page of HUAC material. Pace countered, "It was presented by the newspapers as a public service. . . . Certainly, we wouldn't ask any one to pay for a page advertisement of that nature which is our duty to publish." In a subsequent editorial in the *Citizen,* Pace wrote: "As far as we are concerned, the only issue right now is Don West and his background. The fact that union organization movements are going on simultaneously with this series of West articles, editorials, etc, is something entirely out of our control." Even if Pace was being entirely honest, he sought to obscure the obvious point: that West and *The Southerner* were indispensable mobilizers for the chenille campaign, and that an attack on West amounted to an attack on the union.[32]

Local antagonism toward West quickly surfaced. The Veterans of Foreign Wars (VFW) launched the first assault from the community. In an open letter to the *News,* VFW commander Harry Campbell (a manager at Crown's Boylston plant) demanded that West account for the HUAC reports and state openly whether he had been or was presently a member of the Communist party. "If you are a person who believes in our way of life," wrote Campbell, "you will immediately respond to these questions." Other groups in Dalton apparently contemplated attacks of a more physical nature. Pace's weekly "Pipe Smoke" column warned against mob violence. He noted that "there were remarks about a group paying West a visit." The editor stated that "this newspaper condemns such action" and noted that West would have every right to defend himself; hence, "mob actions can be dangerous from either end—the attacked as well as the attackers." Pace then called forth a new and different assailant: "We say leave it to the law and to legal channels, including the Whitfield County grand jury if it is interested." The grand jury for the October term would be packed with leading business leaders who would indeed be interested.[33]

West answered the VFW charge with a long, carefully argued letter in the *Citizen.* Although his response echoed the classic replies to the blunt anticommunist interrogations of the late 1940s and 1950s, it doubtless won few converts to his point of view. West began by questioning whether "any man or group should set themselves up as an inquisitorial body, assuming the authority to call citizens in question relative to religious or political beliefs." He considered at length the multiple meanings given the word *Communist,* pointing out that the term had been used to slander reformers of all stripes, from noncommunist labor organizers to Franklin D. Roosevelt. Never one for modesty, West linked his own struggle for religious and political liberty to a long heritage of protest beginning with the Magna Carta and extending through Martin Luther, the American Constitution, and the Dalton chenille campaign.[34]

As a prelude to answering the VFW's questions, West attacked all McCarthy-style interrogations. Claiming he had often discussed his political views and would, under no duress, gladly and openly air them again, he argued that answering such questions on demand was another matter. "It would be nothing less than traitorous," he insisted, "for me to accede to the demands of any group in matters of conscience, whether it be president, Pope or even a little voluntary McCarthy Committee." Nonetheless, he understood the difficulty his reputation posed for the chenille campaign, and so he obliged the VFW "for the benefit of many honest citizens who may be confused by what they've heard or read." Voicing his concern for underpaid workers, he said, "I believe in a living wage and decent working conditions for all who labor. If they call that being a Communist, then I could be called one along with many millions of other Americans!" But then he stated explicitly, "I am NOT a Communist" and concluded by hammering home the points he most needed to convey: "I am not the issue. The real issue in the Dalton area is the rights of workers to organize and bargain collectively. The attack on me is only to confuse the issues. I do not believe the working people will allow this maneuver to succeed. In closing I want to say that I am an ordained minister in the Church of God of the Union Assembly and 100 percent American!"[35]

The battle of the press continued throughout the rest of 1955. The patterns of editorial combat remained the same: Pace would offer evidence to discredit West and Pratt and add stories demonstrating the sly tactics of Communists everywhere; the Union Assembly leaders would follow with rejoinders, which Pace published and held up to ridicule. Community groups continued to commend Pace for his efforts. The American Legion (Dalton Post 112), for example, praised the anticommunist campaign and condemned "those who in the name of religion and the church are undertaking to turn our people against each other and . . . are acting as a front for a foreign ideology seeking to destroy the very foundations of this Republic." After informally polling Daltonians about whether they felt communism presently posed a threat to the United States, the News offered the thoughts of "Hershel Eaker: chenille worker," who stated, "Communism is worse than a threat. It will ruin young people in the world today if they get mixed up in it. Communism is against the Bible and its teachings. I have always been taught that Jesus Christ is the Son of God and it is a disgrace to any nation in the world to believe Communism which is contrary to these teachings." Such innuendo was the mainstay of Pace's editorial assault. And the more West countered that unionism, not communism, was the real issue, the easier it was for Pace to smear the chenille campaign with indirect allegations.[36]

Outside the editorial room, the rough-and-tumble of the chenille campaign got rougher. The TWUA had focused its efforts on two mills, the General Latex and Chemical Corporation (Latex) and Belcraft Chenilles. Employees at both plants were attempting to organize, and during the period from August 31 to September 8, the companies laid off twenty-six workers (eighteen from Latex, eight from Belcraft). The TWUA charged that these workers were fired for trying to organize, and the union filed suit with the National Labor Relations Board.[37] At Belcraft the campaign remained under control to the extent that no strike occurred and physical violence at the plant was not in evidence. But all hell broke loose at Latex: the workers went on strike; the superior court imposed an injunction that limited picketing; the company called on the state to protect its strikebreakers; the governor of Georgia sent in state troopers to control the escalating situation; and violence began to rip both the community and the chenille campaign apart. Pace's crusade against West, Pratt, and communism in Dalton paralleled this conflict, helping to fuel local antagonisms and providing a powerful—and only vaguely indirect—force against chenille unionization.

For the TWUA, the chenille campaign was far from ordinary. Southern union drives had always presented challenges, but West's alleged communism created special dilemmas. The union based its campaign on the right to organize and on North-South wage differences. But the TWUA entered the scene after the Union Assembly had already generated support for the campaign, and that source of support proved problematic. Official union policies, which had led the CIO to purge Communist and Popular Front supporters (and generally to dissociate itself from all things radical), now posed problems for Dalton's chenille campaign, because both Pratt and West were viewed as radical by most southerners in 1955. The TWUA state office therefore faced a difficult—perhaps impossible—task. It had to capitalize on the prounion enthusiasm inspired by *The Southerner* while keeping its distance from West and Pratt. Partly because of the union's efforts to do this, and partly because of Pace's formidable editorial skills, the Don West controversy and the chenille campaign almost seemed like separate developments. But in reality no such separation was possible, as prounion workers soon discovered.

The strike at Latex began in mid-September and soon turned ugly. The plant employed only about fifty workers, but the conflict there assumed an importance out of proportion to the size of the work force. Almost all the hands banded together to form TWUA Local 10, which had the support of the national office when it voted to strike. The Whitfield County Superior Court quickly hit the pickets with a highly restrictive injunction, but the strike continued amid Pace's further denunciation of Union Assembly leaders. Widely publicized violence (known in mainstream papers as "the riot," even though no one was injured) erupted near the plant gate on September 29. The factory was not running, but a few nonunion employees went into the plant, as did company president G. B. Coit, an outsider from Massachusetts who came to investigate the labor situation. When Coit later drove away from the plant with a well-known strikebreaker riding by his side, a gang of union men intercepted and stopped the car not far from the factory, tilting it high into the air before letting it drop with a thud and pelting it with rocks. The following day, dynamite rocked the front yards of a Latex manager and a strikebreaker. Coit quickly called on the state for help. Georgia governor Marvin Griffin, aware of purported communism in Dalton, responded quickly by sending to Dalton a contingent of state troopers as well as several representatives of the

Georgia Bureau of Investigation. On October 11, a handful of regular antiunion workers and outside "scabs" entered the mill, escorted by the Georgia Highway Patrol.[38]

A group of union workers and some local supporters, calling themselves the Whitfield County Citizens' Committee, sought to change Griffin's course of action. (Dalton's anti-integration Citizens' Council frantically announced that it had "no connection at all" with this prolabor group.) The Citizens' Committee visited the governor, handed him petitions, and urged him to remove the troopers. Griffin informed the group that he would recall the troopers "as soon as the violence ceases." The committee argued that no violence had occurred for two weeks, but Griffin countered that "he had received a report of egg throwing" that morning. The union committee also asked Griffin to serve as an arbitrator in settling the strike, but the governor refused this request as well. In response to the workers' claim that Latex paid its Massachusetts workers seventy-seven cents per hour more than those in Dalton and that Coit was looking for "slave labor," the state's chief executive stated that he had never "held out cheap labor as an inducement" in his efforts to lure industry to Georgia. In a prepared statement to the press, Griffin announced, "State patrolmen were assigned to Dalton to preserve order after several breaches of the peace took place. They were sent to protect the lives and property of all citizens, both strikers and non-strikers alike, and will be kept there until all possibility of violence has subsided." The Citizens' Committee viewed the situation differently. The chairman of the committee, the Reverend J. B. Watters of the Olivia Baptist Church, termed Griffin's decision "an insult to our community" and claimed the governor was "giving a green light to scabs and strike-breakers all over the state." Violence continued—on whose part was a controversial issue—as a Latex truck was dynamited and the TWUA campaign headquarters was vandalized. The troopers stayed.[39]

Meanwhile, the local grand jury launched a powerful attack against both West and the Latex workers during the October term. In effect, the jury acted as a local-level HUAC. Superior court judge James H. Paschal chose the jurors with care, and Pace hailed them as "business men" who were working hard "in the interest of the community." Paschal charged the grand jury to investigate the press's allegations that "subversive organizations" were operating in Dalton. "You are free agents to investigate anything at any time in the county," he told the jury members, "and from recent reports there are some things that need investigating here in Dalton."[40]

The grand jury received added incentive to interrogate West after Edgar C. Bundy, an obscure anticommunist crusader from Illinois, came to town. Bundy, according to the *Citizen*, "held leading positions with the Illinois American Legion's Americanism Committee and its Anti-Subversive Commission." Traveling north along the Dixie Highway from Miami, where he had attended the legion's national convention, Bundy saw a Chattanooga, Tennessee, newspaper that reported Judge Paschal's concern over "Communist patterns" in Dalton. Doing a quick about-face, Bundy hurried to Dalton to warn the grand jury that he had heard Don West's name from undercover FBI agents who had infiltrated the Communist party. West, he said, was "a dangerous man." Furthermore, he added, "for every known Communist, there are 10 fellow travelers who are not known or identified [who] are equally dangerous." Received enthusiastically by both the grand jury and the business press, Bundy remained in town for several weeks, holding public meetings (sponsored by the local American Legion and VFW chapters) and making speeches (broadcast over local radio) on the dangers of communism and Don West. Infiltration, not direct and violent assault, Bundy said, was the Communist strategy for taking over America. "Under the guise of religion, education, and labor unions," he warned, "the infiltrators are trying to obtain their goal." The worst infiltrators were "those people who claim to be for the working people." Lest this statement be misinterpreted, the *Citizen* explained that Bundy meant "those people [who] get their money off the laboring class people"—by no subtle implication, West and Pratt. Shortly thereafter, the grand jury sent West a subpoena.[41]

Bundy was not the only outsider relied on to smear West and the chenille campaign. The *News* also advertised a series of radio broadcasts by Allston Calhoun, Jr., on the topic "Americanism Preferred." Calhoun was an anticommunist-for-hire who worked for the Foundation of Americanism Preferred, a privately sponsored group headquartered in Greenwood, South Carolina. Besides presenting his McCarthylike message to radio audiences, he wrote full-page advertisements for the *Citizen* and *News*. To the consternation of Dalton's TWUA locals, Calhoun drew explicit connections between communism and unionism. Referring to a United Auto Workers strike in Indiana, he spoke of the "CIO Communist-style dress parade revolution." Calhoun praised Governor Griffin for his "splendid and courageous action" and damned the "CIO-promoted insurrection" in Dalton. He further warned of the old "Reds" who had "announced themselves as 'reverends' and started up their own so-called church" as well as a "monthly sheet" (he never called it *The Southerner*) in which CIO representatives assailed his programs. Sometimes he signed his large ads "Calhoun, 'The Working Man's Friend.'" Americanism Preferred ads always carried the same message and tone. One version printed in both papers shrieked, "CIO CONVERTS NORMAL HUMAN BEINGS TO READY AGENTS FOR MOB VIOLENCE" and, in a slightly more graphic assault, "CIO MAN SPITS TOBACCO JUICE INTO FACE OF HIS OWN MOTHER."[42]

Latex workers, who were still on strike at the end of October despite court injunctions and state troopers, may not have spent much time pondering such comparisons, but they understood the need to restore their tarnished image. In a full-page ad in the *News*, thirty-three workers signed a lengthy statement that explained "our side of the story." The strikers insisted, "You have not been told the truth. It has been made to appear that we are a bunch of hoodlums and gangsters. We want you to know we are decent law-abiding citizens." The company, they said, had made no effort to settle. Strikebreakers "who have never worked at General Latex" were brought in from surrounding counties. The workers also pointed to antiunion violence apparently overlooked by Pace's reporters. "We have been cursed by these strike-breakers, they have used their cars to run some of us off the road." Moreover, said the workers, "the company has been before the Grand Jury and apparently told lies on us. The Grand Jury has indicted us without hearing our side of the story. . . . The only thing we have asked [the company] to do is to put back the five employees they have fired, to recognize our union and to treat us as human beings. . . . So far, all the company has been willing to do is have us arrested, disgrace our names, lie on us, [and] bring in strike breakers." In a poignant conclusion, the workers pleaded, "We are now and always have been law abiding citizens, we are hard working men who are trying to maintain a decent living for our family. We have lived here and around you most of our life."[43]

But the strike was doomed, and it left Latex workers bitter. By early November, the company was able to fill virtually every position in the small plant with strikebreakers, and the TWUA called off the strike on November 15, but very few of the strikers were actually given their jobs back.[44] In a resentful statement in the *News*, the former Latex workers lashed out at the treatment they had received. "Mr. Manufacturer," they complained, "when you joined the Manufacturers Association, how would you have felt if all the working people in Whitfield County would have started telling you that the Manufacturers Association was nothing but a bunch of Communists?" They went on to ask how the industrialists would have felt if their employees had hired someone like Allston Calhoun to smear the TTMA, if their companies had been taken from them due to their religious beliefs, if their freedom of speech had been destroyed when they sought to discuss the TTMA, if their workers had threatened them with starvation when they considered attending a TTMA meeting. The workers applauded the American government because it was "run by the people for the people" and voiced dismay that "some people in America who call themselves Americans don't like this form of Government." Such people "deny we working people the right of assembly, they deny us the freedom of speech, and they deny us the freedom of religion. They even try to deny us the privilege of calling ourselves American." If these rights had been taken away from the industrialists, "you would have said this is not America; this kind of crime can't go on in America. You would have said that's the way they do in China and Russia." But, they concluded, "Mr. Manufacturer, that has happened to us working people here in Whitfield County, who are trying to organize in the chenille industry."[45]

The TWUA locals at Crown and American Thread watched the campaign with dismay. For several months they had maintained a low profile but had worked behind the scenes to support the chenille effort. With the failure at Latex, they threw themselves into the fray and defended unions as bastions of democracy and community improvement. TWUA Locals 185 and 134 jointly issued their own lengthy public statement in the *News*, affirming that "unions, as a matter of public record, have fought an outstanding fight to rid themselves of Communist infiltration. There has never been and there is not now a single Communist in Local 185 or Local 134." Dalton's unions, the message continued, "stand for and work for . . . the things that make the community a better place in which to live," including higher standards of living for working people, which in turn meant better sales for local merchants. The statement explained union finances in order to demonstrate that no economic coercion was involved, and it outlined the impressive list of local and national charities to which the union contributed. Unions, the letter maintained, allowed workers at Crown and American Thread to "live and work as free people, free from the fear of unjust discharge or unjust treatment at the hands of their supervisors." The workers heaped on Allston Calhoun a particularly large serving of abuse. They derided him as a "paid parasite who produces nothing" except "hate and discord" and portrayed him as a cowardly stooge of antiunion chenille manufacturers. "What has Allston Calhoun done for Dalton?" the workers asked. "Has he lived and worked here for a better community?"[46]

The depths of angst among Dalton's established unions ought not be underestimated. As recently as 1949, the people of Dalton had helped local millhands celebrate TWUA Week. It must have seemed in 1955 that public opinion had turned against unionism with mind-numbing swiftness. The protestations of Locals 185 and 134 were accurate: local unions had been active and responsible organizations of community betterment, and they were proud of it. In their view, such behavior constituted good citizenship. They still believed, as they had professed during World War II, that unionism was Americanism. They saw themselves not as poor whites or radicals—and certainly not as Communist sympathizers—but as white middle-class homeowners, which, in the South of 1955, was exactly what they were. Dalton's union workers simply could not believe that Allston Calhoun's tirades were being given such huge amounts of space in their local newspapers. The insult had the effect of a rotten egg on an empty stomach, but the unions stood steady and refused to concede defeat.

After the Latex strike ended, the TWUA locals voiced strong support for pro-union chenille workers and urged them to organize. "Cheap labor is the base for the high profits [in the chenille industry], and you furnish the labor," Dalton's union millhands warned. "Pay heed to Allston Calhoun and you will continue to furnish the cheap labor." Locals 185 and 134 called on "the chenille workers in this area to join us in our unions to work for a better way of life." Union leaders tried to shake off the Latex defeat. When company officials announced that an NLRB election could be scheduled, TWUA representatives asserted, "We are confident and certain that when the election for the union is held the workers in the plant will vote union." This boast amounted to wishful thinking, because virtually all of the workers who now held jobs at Latex were antiunion strikebreakers, now eligible to vote down the union. But the TWUA soon received another chance, for at Belcraft Chenilles, a much larger plant, an election was on the horizon.[47]

The turmoil at Latex had obscured the numerically more important campaign proceeding simultaneously at Belcraft, which employed some two thousand workers (most of them in Dalton but some in Calhoun, a textile town thirty miles south). Belcraft workers had petitioned for a union election about the same time the Latex employees did, but no strike occurred at Belcraft to disrupt the normal process of the election. Two days after Locals 185 and 134 published their impassioned defense of unionization, the NLRB set the Belcraft election for December 15. Everyone knew this election would be critical. "TWUA spokesmen have indicated," the *Citizen* noted, "that the outcome of the Belcraft vote will determine to a great extent whether they continue the current unionization effort in other plants."[48]

Crown's union leaders threw themselves into a final frenzy of preparations to make the Belcraft election a success. Their hopes bloomed at an impressive labor rally held at the Whitfield County Courthouse on December 11. Locals 185 and 134 sponsored the meeting and urged the attendance of all organized workers in Dalton, including those from the "railroad brotherhood, electricians, painters, brick-masons, [and] plumbers." The goal of the rally, as advertised in the local papers, was to "work together as good honest people to make this area a better place in which to work and live." The timing of the meeting clearly indicated its dual purpose of redeeming the name of organized labor in Dalton and of encouraging chenille workers to vote for the union. "Our children and our friends," the millhands insisted, "deserve the best effort we can possibly give to this end."[49]

The meeting was an inspirational success for the city's union workers, who pledged support for the chenille campaign and condemned manufacturers and the local press for smearing Don West and the TWUA. If anyone suggested that Don West should leave Dalton for the good of the local unions and the good of the community, nothing appeared in the press about it. The city's union supporters once again blasted Allston Calhoun "as a man devoid of character, convictions or courage" and unanimously endorsed a strongly worded resolution that voiced "even greater scorn and contempt for the Dalton Chenille employers who have hired Allston Calhoun to aid them in their dirty work of stirring up deception, confusion and hatred." The workers also expressed their commitment to a unionized Dalton and their optimism for the future. Millhands from Crown and American Thread resolved to "reaffirm their spirit of solidarity and, in that spirit, take positive steps to unify our local and community action so that our efforts, as responsible citizens, may serve to make Dalton a better place to live in and work in for ourselves and our families as well as for all our neighbors." State and national labor leaders attended the meeting and made dramatic speeches, lending credibility to the resolutions and offering a show of national support for the chenille campaign. The rally had an energizing effect on longtime union hands. "This is the kind of meeting we've been needing for a long time," said Ralph Huston of Local 185. But it was anybody's guess whether such enthusiasm could counteract the deleterious effects of the anticommunist campaign, the state troopers, and the defeat at Latex.[50]

When the votes were counted on December 15, the chenille campaign had suffered a crippling blow. Belcraft workers cast 840 votes against the union (57 percent) and only 625 votes for it. Prounion workers and TWUA organizers tried to remain optimistic as they assembled in the American Thread union hall that evening. They unanimously resolved "to get the election set aside" as unfair. "We're going to keep right on till we get a union," said one leader. *The Southerner* insisted that "it's just the beginning. We'll win next time." In an editorial following the election, John Bunch contended, "We will have this better way of life in spite of the Allston Calhouns and those who pay them. This propaganda against unions and decent men will boomerang. When we all get organized there will be a better day for all." Courageous assessments aside, it was nonetheless apparent that union leaders harbored serious doubts in the wake of the Belcraft election. No subsequent unionization drives ever took place in Dalton. Belcraft was an ending, not a beginning.[51]

In a larger sense, the end of the chenille campaign also signaled the end of Dalton's established unions. The South remained largely nonunion, and industrial unions throughout America were on the verge of a long-term decline. Locals 185 and 134 could hardly expect to survive comfortably amid a sea of nonunion chenille workers. The cotton-mill workers no longer formed an indispensable core of purchasing power for Dalton's merchants. Equally important was the demise of the union's good reputation. The official civic recognition of TWUA Week in 1949 marked the high point of union acceptance in Dalton. After the smearing of Don West in 1955, in which local unions also were clearly indicted, it was not likely that a twentieth-anniversary celebration would be held. Dalton was growing, but the unions would not grow along with the Carpet Capital.

Once the chenille campaign had faltered, Marc Pace resumed his "West campaign" with a flurry of attacks in late December and early January. The grand jury for the fall term finally closed out its lengthy session with a report that strongly warned against Communist activity in Dalton, called for federal authorities to investigate the situation, requested the next grand jury to continue the effort to root out communism in the town, and condemned Don West for refusing to answer the jury's questions. The jury report also commended Marc Pace for his "alertness in this matter and [his] policy to expose such activity."[52] Noting a strong demand for back issues concerning Don West, Pace presented a special edition of the *Citizen* in mid-January that reprinted five full pages of "the more outstanding articles relative to Communism and the Don West campaign." Extra copies were available for a nickel. Conspicuously absent in the special edition were stories relating to the TWUA chenille campaign. The implication, one not at all conso- nant with the reality of the local labor situation, was that the West campaign was unconnected with the union effort.[53]

The special edition was the last straw for West, who tendered his resignation to Pratt. The Union Assembly actually voted West out of the church, but speculation ran wild as to whether West and Pratt had a falling out or were simply plotting a new strategy. Such speculation hardly mattered, for Pace had long since destroyed the public reputations of both men beyond redemption. In the process, he also discredited the union millhands of Crown Mill and helped ensure that unioniza- tion would slowly fade from Dalton.[54]

Local 185 suffered a steady decline in membership after 1955 (see table 13.1). This decline mirrored national trends, and numerous other factors were involved, but the chenille campaign disasters surely dampened union enthusiasm among younger millhands. The union workers at Crown and American Thread were getting older, and retirement began to thin the ranks of their locals. Dalton's newer millhands did not fill the void.[55]

Don West fled to anonymity on a north Georgia farm, while Marc Pace won the Whitfield County "Man of the Year" award. The divergent fates of these two men symbolized the new realities for organized labor in Dalton. The TTMA emerged as a dominant force in local affairs. The city's TWUA locals, which had seen so much promise at the beginning of 1955, were thrust suddenly into obscurity. Nothing in the modernizing economy was sacred. Just as the Great Depression and World War II had destroyed Dalton's mill-village paternalism, McCarthyism dealt a mortal blow to the town's labor unions. The workers of Local 185 found themselves isolated and embittered within their own city. The days of Dalton as a strong union town had passed. Before long the cotton mills themselves would be gone.

14

SHUTDOWN IN

THE SUNBELT

Novelist John Steinbeck once wrote that "communities, like people, have periods of health and times of sickness—even youth and age, hope and despondency."[1] Yes, and death. The people of Crown learned this the hard way during the 1960s, as their own community suffered a rapid and painful demise. Struggling to find a formula for economic stability in an increasingly chaotic textile industry, the mill management cut labor costs through speedups, stretchouts, and plant modernization. This strategy created work loads so arduous that even tried-and-true millhands became bitterly disillusioned with their jobs and their mill. Once the old family-labor system had collapsed, Crown hired scores of outsiders who commuted to work and had no ties to the older mill-village community. A generation gap further sundered the work force. The newly hired hands averaged about thirty years of age, but Crown's longtime employees, who were mostly in their fifties and sixties, considered them "youngsters." Older hands complained that the newcomers were shiftless, whereas younger workers viewed the old-timers as

The Crown Mill complex as it looked at the time of the shutdown. The original mill belfry is barely visible at the bottom left. Notice that the main road into town no longer cuts through the Crown Mill village. (*Courtesy of the Georgia Department of Archives and History*)

stooges of both the company and the union. In addition to the generation gap and the increasingly difficult work loads, the expansion of new industrial jobs in Dalton and the South created unprecedented labor turnover at Crown. Workers who had grown up in the mill stayed with it, but their ranks were thinning with age. The percentage of Crown's workers who were union members declined as younger employees refused to join. Unauthorized "wildcat" strikes broke out with increasing frequency, causing grief for both managers and union leaders. In the spring of 1969, Crown's managers closed down the Boylston plant. Then, on September 17, 1969, David Hamilton announced that the Crown Mill would soon discontinue production altogether. The shutdown destroyed an exhausted community.

There were ironies aplenty in Crown's collapse. Basic cotton textile mills began to fold in Dalton and the South at the very time the regional economy as a whole was experiencing a major upswing. Older industries as well as newer service and high-tech companies were abandoning the northern Rustbelt for the Sunbelt states of the South and Southwest. As the undisputed Carpet Capital of the World, Dalton stood as a prime example of small-city Sunbelt success. But the general economic expansion made cotton-mill jobs seem even less attractive, a situation that only made matters worse at the Crown Mill. Then, without their workers' even being aware of it, Crown's directors built carpet-yarn plants outside of Dalton and began to restructure the corporation. The success of these new enterprises made it easier for management to shut down the old Crown Mill. Many Daltonians blamed the union for the mill's demise, just as people in stagnating Rustbelt cities blamed organized labor for chasing industry to the Sunbelt. Labor problems actually did speed the closing of Crown, but those problems were not the union's doing. In fact, the only group that fought to save the Crown Cotton Mill in 1969 was the union—TWUA Local 185. That, in the end, was the ultimate irony.

For nearly a century the South had been the poorest region in the United States by any economic standard, but during the 1960s the region began a significant economic turnaround. The enthusiasm with which southern boosters embraced Sunbelt rhetoric was in itself good reason to doubt the good news. But Dixie's Sunbelt phenomenon was no illusion. Between 1957 and 1979, employment gains in Dixie exceeded those of other regions (including the West) in every branch of the economy. Regional growth statistics certainly obscured large pockets of poverty and economic stagnation, just as they always had in the "prosperous" North. But those Sunbelt statistics also offered undeniable evidence that the southern economy was undergoing important structural changes that further modified the region's distinctiveness. The South in 1970 offered a more diversified manufacturing base than ever before, as well as vastly expanded commercial, service, and government sectors.[2]

Much of the capital fueling the South's economic growth came from outside the region. Instead of colonizing the southern economy from afar, though, many northern corporations simply moved south altogether. But in the 1960s, the source of capital and control mattered less to Dixie's working families than it had during the old mill-village era. What did matter now were the expanding job opportunities created by that capital. Critics maintained, with some justification, that companies were fleeing the high-wage, prounion North for the low-wage, nonunion South, and that most factory jobs in Dixie remained at the low end of the industrial wage scale. In Georgia, it is true, most industrial wage earners did labor for low-wage companies, but during the 1960s high-wage factory jobs proliferated far more rapidly than low-paying ones (see table 14.1). From 1960 to 1970, employment increased by 76 percent in Georgia's high-wage industries, such as those that manufactured paper products and transportation equipment. Employment in traditional low-wage industries like food processing and textiles grew by only 19

TABLE 14.1. Wage Rankings and Employment Growth
in Georgia Industries, 1960–1970

Wage Ranking in 1970	Industry	Percentage Employment Growth, 1960–70	Percentage of Mfg. Jobs in Ga., 1970
1	Paper products	33.87	5.80
2	Transportation equipment	88.24	11.18
3	Primary metal industries	76.60	1.93
4	Electrical equipment	145.83	2.75
5	Fabricated metal products	143.48	3.91
6	Chemicals	32.35	3.15
7	Machinery	60.92	3.26
8	Stone, clay, glass	30.19	3.22
	All high-wage industries[a]	76.44	35.20
9	Food products	17.60	12.30
10	Textiles[b]	16.27	26.98
11	Lumber	−13.65	5.89
12	Furniture	18.99	2.19
13	Leather products	29.73	1.19
14	Apparel	47.06	16.31
	All low-wage industries[a]	19.33	64.86

Source: U.S. Department of Labor, Employment and Earnings.
[a]"High-wage" industries paid their production/nonsupervisory workers an average weekly wage above the state mean in 1970 ($106.27); "low-wage" industries paid below the state mean.
[b]Textile workers earned an average weekly wage that was 92 percent of the state mean in 1960 and 1970.

percent. By 1970 more than one of every three factory hands in Georgia worked in high-wage manufacturing.

In Dalton the carpet industry reigned supreme and became a powerful symbol of Sunbelt possibilities. The city's population actually stagnated during the 1960s (see table A.1), but that trend should not be misinterpreted as slow growth. The booming carpet industry and the added population that came with it simply spilled over the city limits and spread out north and west, as if Dalton and the surrounding area had become a miniature version of a large metropolitan district. This decentralized industrial sprawl pushed the total population of Whitfield County above 50,000 for the first time. Local growth was particularly conspicuous in the explosion of manufacturing jobs in the county, as shown in table 14.2. Between 1954, when carpets were first beginning to eclipse traditional chenille products (bedspreads and bathrobes), and 1963, by which time they clearly had become Dalton's central concern, the number of industrial jobs in the county

TABLE 14.2. Number of Production Workers in Manufacturing,
Whitfield County, Georgia, 1954–1972

Year	Whitfield County	Percentage Change	Georgia	Percentage Change
1954	8,077	—	1,635,700	—
1963	9,364	15.93	1,823,900	11.50
1972	15,700	67.66	2,317,000	27.03

Source: U.S. Bureau of the Census, County and City Data Book, 1956, 1967, 1977.
Note: No figures were available for Dalton separately.

increased nearly 16 percent, slightly more than the figure for the state as a whole. But during the next decade, local expansion was nothing less than remarkable. Between 1963 and 1972, industrial jobs in Whitfield jumped 68 percent, while the state figure for the same period was 27 percent—a healthy increase, but far below that of the Carpet Capital. According to Crown president David D. Hamilton, the carpet boom energized Dalton's industrialists as nothing else ever had. Broadloom carpets, an invention of the small-town South, awakened Dixie's textile leaders to regional entrepreneurial possibilities and made them painfully aware that they had been passively dependent on Yankee ingenuity for too long.[3]

But traditional textiles were not part of the Sunbelt phenomenon; they were, in fact, a casualty of it. Just as New England's cotton mills had gone into a precipitous and permanent decline during the 1920s, so Dixie's textile industry began a noticeable slide in the 1950s and continued to fall thereafter. The closing of Crown, far from being an isolated event, reflected the larger pattern of textile plant closures in Georgia and the South after World War II. Between 1946 and 1960, 202 textile mills were liquidated in the South, abolishing 54,290 jobs in the process.[4] Statistics on plant closings in the 1960s are not available, but an analysis of employment statistics for textiles suggests the extent of the industry's decline. The number of jobs available in Georgia's textile mills declined after the post–World War II boom subsided. Overall textile employment in the state fell by 6.5 percent during the 1950s, and during the following decade employment in cotton weaving mills such as Crown Mill (the core of Georgia's traditional textile industry) declined by 17 percent. As table 14.3 shows, the rapid expansion of the carpet industry in northwest Georgia during the 1960s masked the stagnation of basic textiles in the state. With the figures for floor-covering mills excluded, Georgia's overall textile employment in the 1960s—a period of rapid industrial expansion—remained virtually static.[5]

In Dalton no one needed statistics to recognize these trends, for during the 1960s the town experienced both the decline of traditional textiles and the growth

TABLE 14.3. Textile Workers in Georgia, 1960–1970 (in thousands)

Type of Mill[a]	1960	1970	Percentage Change
Cotton weaving mills	44.8	37.2	−16.96
Synthetic weaving mills	4.6	5.2	13.04
Knitting mills	9.1	9.9	8.79
Floor-covering mills[b]	12.0	26.7	122.50
Yarn and thread mills	15.0	21.9	46.00
All textile mills[c]	99.6	115.8	16.26
All mills excluding floor-covering mills	87.6	89.1	1.71

Source: U.S. Department of Labor, Employment and Earnings.
[a]Table includes only those manufacturing categories listed in Standard Industrial Category (SIC) 22, Textile Mill Products, as indicated in the above source. It does not include categories from SIC 23, Apparel and Other Textile Products.
[b]No figure for 1960 is available; the figure for 1961 is used here.
[c]These totals exceed the sum of the five categories above because the Department of Labor included in them some data from several subcategories of SIC 22 that were not reported.

of the carpet industry. Even before Crown shut down, the American Thread Mill had closed its doors. The number of workers employed at the Thread Mill had declined from nine hundred in 1950 to only three hundred by the time the mill closed in 1964. The deserted plant south of town stood as a silent reminder of textile vulnerability.[6]

Beginning in the 1950s, Crown confronted its own series of economic crises. In 1958, David Hamilton "presented the Board various plans to combat the present critical situation." After a successful year in 1960, the company warned stockholders, "The beginning of the new year finds us in a period of general poor business. Our order books are lower than they have been for some time. Textile operations in general will be hard pressed to duplicate results of the current year." This warning proved to be an understatement. In 1961 Crown lost over 10 percent on capital stock. The following year, the mill ran full tilt and sold a record amount of cloth yet suffered a net loss of $99,062, or a 7 percent loss on capital. Trying to explain this odd situation to stockholders, frustrated directors noted that, despite record-setting production, "paradoxically we are faced with a sagging price structure. Our ability to improve earnings will depend to a large degree on continuing to reduce our costs wherever possible and the fruition of industrial fabrics programs, now well out of the sampling stage, which promise improved profit margins over our previous styling." Between 1961 and 1963, the company lost an average of nearly $120,000 per year. This marked the worst three-year period at Crown since the early years of the Great Depression (see table A.2 and fig. A.1).[7]

It would nonetheless be wrong to suggest that the 1960s were a complete disaster for the Crown Mill. The overall trend was one of boom and bust, not simple economic devastation. For example, the decade's early losses were succeeded by three extremely good years for the company. From 1964 to 1966, Crown averaged a heady 19 percent return on capital (an average $329,126 per year net profit), the best years since the late 1940s and early 1950s. This mid-1960s boom did not, however, convince Crown's managers that prosperity had returned. Rather, they apparently viewed it as a temporary aberration in the industry that gave them more time to pursue alternatives.

The directors examined a variety of strategies for improving their situation, the most important of which involved diversified investments. In the mid-1950s, the company invested heavily in four subsidiaries, all of which were related to Crown's basic cotton textile production. The subsidiary companies reflected a growing tendency of Crown's directors to expand their investments beyond Dalton. These subsidiaries did not always prosper, but they first helped offset corporate losses sustained at the Crown Mill and ultimately mitigated those losses indirectly through their collective sale in 1962. Although investments in subsidiaries related to cotton textiles had proved only marginally helpful to the company, affiliates in other branches of the industry began to look appealing, particularly those in Dalton's own burgeoning carpet enterprises.[8]

Another classic managerial strategy for boosting profits or minimizing losses in textiles was to reduce labor costs through some combination of speedups, stretchouts, and plant modernization. Indeed, Crown had begun major efforts at modernization in the 1950s. In 1961, David Hamilton stated that during the previous decade the mill had been able "to double production with the same number of employees using approximately 20% fewer spinning spindles." He intended these figures as evidence of progress and emphasized that such improvements were necessary if cotton mills were to remain afloat. Workers and union officials, however, probably viewed such remarks with less enthusiasm than alarm. From their perspective, productivity gains usually meant greater work loads.[9]

The millhands' disdain for and difficulties with new machinery and new work loads led to the filing of many grievances and kept the union officials hopping.[10] The surviving minutes of union meetings during the early 1950s are filled with discussions about problems within the various departments of the mill.[11] As early as October 1949, the executive board moved to "turn in [a] grievance on the work load at the Boylston Crown." Similarly, in January 1951 the union moved that "spinners who were laid off at Boylston Crown Mill because they could not keep up [their] jobs be paid for time lost."[12] In this case, the grievance was not settled and the union filed for arbitration, stating that "some have been laid off because the work runs so bad it is impossible for them to keep it up." Problems continued to plague the union as stretchouts and speedups proceeded at Boylston. In May

1952, union officials announced that workers in the weave room at Mill No. 2 were in an uproar because "they have too many looms and cannot keep them up."[13] Closely related to the increased work loads was the union's concern with Crown's "time-study man," whose activities the executive board and shop stewards monitored closely and often opposed. At one general membership meeting, a state TWUA representative instructed the workers as to "the ways we should work during the check-up of our jobs." Local 185 also took the offensive by learning as much about the timing process as possible. The union held a regular school for workers to discuss the time-study system, purchased its own stopwatch, and even bought a tachometer "for checking [the] speed of machinery."[14]

Crown's managers continued down the path of modernization in the 1960s, and the results, so far as the workers were concerned, were brutal. At no time in the company's history were work loads so crushing as in the plant's final years. The stretchouts of earlier decades paled in comparison. Even loyal and normally content workers resented the stretchouts of the 1960s. Lucile Hall worked at Crown for over forty years and through all those years she truly enjoyed her work. "But toward the last," she recalled, "just before the mill closed down, it got so hard you just couldn't hardly make it. . . . Stretch, add more, add more." If older hands found the pace oppressive, new hands were overwhelmed, and few remained long with the company. John Bramblett, who worked twenty-four years for Crown and served as union president in the 1960s, remembered that many newcomers "just couldn't handle it, and they'd get disgusted with it and walk out." Sometimes, recalled another worker, newly hired hands "wouldn't even work a full shift. They'd walk out." Union vice president Bishop Caylor thought that working conditions at the plant were generally good when he began work in 1940, but, he added, "jobs all got so rough at the last, people lost interest."[15]

It was the same in cotton mills throughout the South, as Henry Wade's experience demonstrates. Wade, who came from a longtime Crown family and worked as a carder for Crown and several mills in Alabama from the 1930s through the 1960s, discovered that plant modernizations and stretchouts were widespread after World War II. During the 1950s, Wade and his wife found jobs at a plant in Alabama but worked there only four hours before quitting, because, he said, "the job was so hard, [we] just couldn't take it." Wade later worked steadily at another mill until the mid-1960s, when the managers drastically cut back the work force and increased the work loads. Although Wade was only in his forties at the time, his health began to fail from the strain. Confronting his boss for the last time, he said, "You've been a mighty good feller to work with, but it's a damn shame that a company put the kind of work load they did on these people here. This place ought to be blown up." Following that speech, Wade recalled, "I walked out. I quit. That was in 1965, and I said I hope to see the day, as I went out the door."[16]

If the hard work had paid well, it might have been worth it. But for workers on production quotas and bonus plans, stretchouts did not just made work unpleasant, they also undermined an individual's potential earning power. As one woman noted, "There was a while we made real good money, real good money for a while, just before the mill closed down. And then they got to add more where you couldn't make production [i.e., the piece-rate quota]." Moreover, as wages in most of Georgia's other industries rose steadily, textile wages did not remain competitive. In 1960 the average weekly wages for cotton-mill workers were 8 percent below the state average and more than 50 percent below those of workers in the top-paying transportation and paper industries. A decade later, textile earnings still measured only 92 percent of the state average, although the gap between cotton-mill work and the highest-paying factory jobs had narrowed slightly. Textile work was still the most common form of industrial work in the state, but during the 1960s, higher-paying factory jobs outpaced lower-paying ones (see table 14.1).[17]

In terms of luring labor away from Crown Mill, local opportunities were probably more attractive to Dalton's workers than developing industries elsewhere in the state. Most young people preferred work in the carpet plants, all other things being equal. By all accounts, even that of Crown's president, carpet work was easy compared to cotton-mill labor. David Hamilton averred that, "whereas people had to do a day's work in a textile mill if the mill was to survive, they didn't . . . in the carpet companies." On average, carpet plants paid as much or better than traditional textiles, and, more important, they offered pension plans and additional benefits that Crown and other mills seldom ever did. Carpet workers did not have union representation, and the 1955 campaign had squelched union enthusiasm. But in the early boom years of the industry, the carpet plants also piled on benefits and upped wages in an effort to undermine any desire on the workers' part to form a union. So although carpet-mill hands had no union—and a good portion of younger workers apparently wanted none at that time—the presence of strong unions at Crown and American Thread indirectly made the carpet plants better places to work than either of the two traditional textile mills. Given the more tempting choices in Dalton and the rest of the state, it proved difficult for Crown to recruit and retain enough well-trained workers during the 1960s.[18]

The labor supply problem was complicated by the exodus of almost an entire generation of young people from the mill-village area. The selling of the company housing in 1953 both reflected and facilitated this trend. Older members of the community were proud of those who moved beyond textile work, particularly those who attended college. Stories about upwardly mobile children are, to this day, passed around like cherished heirlooms among Dalton's aging cotton millers. Virginia Travillian became the owner of a jewelry store in Dalton. James Campbell, the last president of Local 185, had a son who became a judge. Donnie Felker became a dentist, William Floyd a cardiologist. Donald Broom worked for NASA. It is said that some young women left the village to train as nurses, and doubtless some succeeded at it. Aside from Virginia Travillian, however, the success stories are about men. For working-class women, opportunities for education and better jobs were still more restricted than for blue-collar men. Avenues for advancement were not equally available, and rising above the working class was by no means guaranteed or even universally desired. But for the generation coming of age in the 1960s, the decline of the old mill community offered a type of liberation. For many families, the sting of community deterioration was ameliorated by the salve of their children's upward mobility. Those with strong attachments to both the mill and the village, however, found growing old in a decaying community a painful experience. And the lack of new workers coming to the plant from the entrenched mill-village families created a vacuum in Crown's work force.[19]

A group of millhands from the outside—workers who had no relations in the old village, no sense of its history, no appreciation for its union—filled that void. As John Bramblett recalled, "Seemed like they hired these people who just come and go. . . . They was the people that come in, and we began having problems. People had lived together all their lives down there in the village . . . and everybody was friendly. But when those people began coming in from other towns and things, first thing you know, you had this person grumble at that one and you know, it just didn't work. They caused lots of friction really, because they didn't intend to stay." Lucile Hall had similar memories. "A few years before the mill closed down—I'd say four or five years before the mill closed down—they began to hire people that come from other places, as I say, drifters. Just come by and get a job—not the quality people that we had been used to working with, I'll say that. . . . Families raised up here, you knew 'em, but these newcomers had worked this place and that place and the other place, you know, just drifters."[20]

There is more reality and less romanticization in these views than one might suspect. Crown had to hire an outrageous number of operatives during the 1960s just to maintain a full work force. The employee cards maintained by the company beginning in the late 1930s offer a way to evaluate hiring trends. Using a sample of these cards and examining the date at which each worker was hired by the mill, one might expect to find that the need to recruit extra workers for emergency military production during World War II would have made the 1940s a peak decade for hiring. Compared to the fifties, it was, but compared to the sixties, it was not. During the mill's final decade, management had to hire more than three times the number of workers it had during the 1940s, and five times the number it had hired in the 1950s—even though the number of jobs in the mill actually decreased during the 1960s (see table 12.1). Such figures indicate an unprecedented labor turnover. No wonder the older millhands, whose working community had been very inclusive, were overwhelmed by the sheer volume of strangers moving in and out of their mill.[21]

The "drifters" also demonstrated a marked reluctance to join Local 185 or to abide by union contracts. During the early 1950s, most newcomers joined the organization, but the following decade witnessed a decline in Local 185's membership. The proportion of union members at Crown fell from 94 percent in the mid-1950s to about 70 percent in 1967 and tumbled to a mere 52 percent by mid-1969 (see table 13.1). Union records do not allow for a precise assessment of how age and seniority factors affected this decline. But because there is no evidence that old-timers were abandoning the union, and because the mill workers' own testimony suggests that newer millhands rejected union policies, the decline in union membership at Crown was probably a manifestation of the work-force generation gap. Conflict between young workers and old-timers—at the expense of union solidarity—was by no means unique to Crown Mill or the textile South in the 1960s. Throughout industrial America, particularly in towns and cities where unions had been formed during the torturous 1930s, young workers were often angry, eager for change, and frustrated with cumbersome union bureaucracies. Older workers (some of whom had been radicals and union trailblazers) seemed more conventional in contrast. They were well-settled, job-oriented, politically moderate union hands. Increasingly, as the 1960s wore on, the traditional leaders of TWUA Local 185 found themselves embattled by young, discontented workers, many of whom were not union members and some of whom were quick to organize unauthorized wildcat strikes.[22]

During the final three years of its operation, wildcat strikes rocked the Crown Mill, further exacerbating tensions within the plant. An unauthorized strike at the Boylston mill in March 1966 foreshadowed what would become a long and trying year for managers, workers, and union representatives at all levels. Walkouts and work stoppages clearly violated the union contract, which contained a no-strike clause. The March strike ended quickly. Crown sent word of it to the TWUA International, and TWUA president William Pollock responded with a telegram to Local 185 condemning the walkout. "No stoppage has been authorized by the General President," Pollock stated. "If such stoppage has occurred it is illegal and I urge all employees whom may be engaged therein to cease such action, return to work at once and take up any dispute pursuant to grievance and arbitration provisions of contract." This was to be a common refrain during the next three years. Crown's managers and the TWUA International office constantly tried to maintain control of the Crown Mill work force, but Local 185 itself was beset by internal conflict and by workers who openly condemned the union as an ineffective force in resolving shop floor grievances. The officers of Local 185 were caught in the middle: management blamed them for not controlling the rank-and-file and for secretly encouraging wildcat strikes; rank-and-file millhands suggested that the union leaders were in league with the company to impose more oppressive work loads and squeeze out more production.[23]

The company and the union signed a new contract on April 1, 1966, in which

Local 185 once again agreed "not to call, authorize, condone, or support any strike, slowdown, stay-in, sitdown, or sympathy strike at the Company's plants." The union also pledged to be vigilant in its efforts "to terminate any such interference with production," and the company reserved the right to "discipline or discharge" workers who violated the no-strike agreement. But before the month was over, disgruntled workers launched another wildcat at Boylston.[24]

On April 20, David Hamilton wired the following news to Pollock and to Paul Swaity, the TWUA's southern director: "Members of Local 185 involved in another unauthorized strike. . . . Your Local President [John] Bramblett . . . is unable to get people back on job. We demand immediate action." The issue was control of the workplace—prompted, in this case, by modernization and increased work loads. The company, which had recently begun to produce some rayon in addition to its cotton mainstays, had updated its rayon spinning frames and increased each frame tender's job from two frames to three. Frame tenders could not keep up the work and decided to fight it, not through normal grievance channels, but with a walk-out. The Boylston card room workers supported the frame tenders and walked out with them. One company supervisor expressed management's view quite well when he recalled that the angry workers "said they wanted the job to run better, and I said that the company wanted it to run better and that this wasn't anything but a mass demonstration. . . . I told them the company couldn't operate this way and it had to stop." At a special company-union meeting the following day, union leaders, along with some rank-and-file wildcatters, clarified their position. It was the old stretchout problem. A work load that included three new rayon frames made it impossible to keep up their work. They could not find time to take bathroom breaks or to eat lunch. They could not take advantage of their "fatigue allowance" because "if fatigue time were taken, [the] machines would get behind or messed up." Hamilton reluctantly agreed to let the frame tenders return to work on two frames until a work-load study could be made. Within a few days, he already regretted that decision.[25]

Trouble broke out almost immediately after the meeting when a rumor began to circulate that the work-load study would, as a predetermined conclusion, recommend three frames. Angry frame tenders and card tenders then boldly threatened to "shut this place down . . . at the snap of a finger." Crown's president informed Swaity that "we have no choice but to *insist* that the TWUA not sit back in this matter, but take immediate and positive steps to instill in the local leadership and the local membership some sense of responsibility to fulfill the terms of our agreement. . . . All we seem to have accomplished so far is, as I feared, to simply encourage such irresponsible conduct by our employees." By August the Boylston workers had begun yet another wildcat strike. Hamilton again insisted on the International's intervention. Paul Swaity responded that he was "equally disturbed" by the walkout and added, "I feel you personally have been very cooperative and am anxious to do all we can." But the truth was, Swaity did not have any solutions; he asked Hamilton for suggestions on how to handle the situation.[26]

Hamilton, who had the legal advantage, also had one important reason for settling with the union and the wildcat strikers: the Crown Mill labor shortage. As troubles continued throughout that year, disenchanted workers threatened to quit and take jobs at the Trion Mill, and those threats were taken seriously. Management repeatedly met with union representatives and rank-and-file workers to try to work out some compromise acceptable to all. Harmon Conner, the mill's personnel director, openly solicited the views of angry millhands on the principal problems facing the workers. The overriding complaint was of onerous work loads, and given the adverse reaction of Crown's most loyal millhands to the pace of labor in the late 1960s, such complaints cannot be passed off as the unwarranted protestations of a troublemaking few. The inordinately high turnover rate was evidence enough that something was wrong with work at Crown. The question was what to do about it. After the company employed an engineer to conduct a time study at Boylston, workers reacted sharply against the report, which basically sanctioned the increased work loads. Hamilton then agreed to let the union bring in its own time-study engineer to check the company's results.[27]

Remarkably, a representative of the TWUA International soon informed Local 185 that the company's time-study results were "pretty much in line with" the union's own study. This announcement sparked a season of discontent within the union and its workers. Some leaders of Local 185 argued heatedly and openly with International representatives, while others counseled moderation and adherence to standard grievance procedures. One Boylston worker actually assaulted John Bramblett, president of the local and a supporter of moderation. When asked by a mill supervisor if a worker named Smith had "slapped him," Bramblett answered no. But, he continued, if the supervisor had asked if Smith "hit him," he could have answered yes. Bramblett, at least, maintained his sense of humor, but the situation had turned very sour for everyone concerned—the company, the rank-and-file workers, the leaders of Local 185, and the state and national leaders of the TWUA. In December 1966, at yet another special meeting between company and union representatives, an exasperated David Hamilton suggested that the days of dialogue and compromise were at an end. The company's position, he said, was that management "will not talk to people anymore when they are off from work. [We] will only discuss matters through proper grievance procedures." The response by TWUA International representative Frederick W. Cory got to the heart of the matter: "People feel that [the] grievance procedure does not work, therefore they take matters into [their] own hands."[28]

As Crown's directors confronted an increasingly severe labor problem, they explored various options, but the ultimate solution was also the most obvious— carpets. Throughout the 1960s, management experimented with synthetic materials and considered plans for "various revised product and plant lines."[29] The most significant manifestation of their experiments was a new, "wholly owned subsidiary" called Texture-Tex, a synthetic carpet-yarn plant built just outside Dalton in Phelps, Georgia, about ten miles from the Crown Mill. Officially organized in mid-1966, Texture-Tex began operations the following year. Its success prompted plans for an expansion of the new plant, which the directors temporarily delayed. Instead they first built an entirely new plant in the undeveloped town of Valdosta in south Georgia. For the first time in Crown's history, the board of directors—still composed of virtually all local men—had decided to build a plant outside the Dalton area. In the late 1960s, the Texture-Tex carpet-yarn plants in Phelps and Valdosta assumed greater importance for the company as profits at the Crown Mills plunged once again. According to one company document, the Dalton plants lost $500,000 in 1969.[30]

As the Dalton enterprise declined, Crown's directors continued to diversify their corporate holdings. By August 1969 they had decided to expand the Phelps plant and to build a new knitting and finishing plant in Tifton, Georgia, called Knit-Tex. The company's transition from cotton textiles to carpet yarns reflected unique local circumstances, but in its broadest outlines, Crown's corporate strategy paralleled that of northern plants moving to the South. The idea was to cut losses—which included closing existing plants—and to avoid labor problems by reinvesting in other, safer enterprises. The Phelps plant neither retrained nor hired Crown's older, union millhands. Indeed, Crown's workers were not even informed that the company owned the new plant. Running away from labor problems in the Sunbelt did not necessitate a very long journey.[31]

The workers disagreed among themselves as to why management ultimately closed the Crown Mill. Rumors of a shutdown had circulated since the mid-1960s, and the American Thread Mill experience should have been a warning. Some of Crown's millhands simply believed that the mill's work regimen had become so difficult that the company could not recruit an adequate pool of steady workers. Others held that southern textiles could no longer compete with imports and that Crown's passing was part of an inevitable trend sweeping the region. Some workers believed that a thorough modernization program might have saved Crown Mill by cutting production costs and making it possible to tap new markets. The charge that management's failure to modernize led to Crown's demise echoes recent accusations by workers in the Rustbelt, but it is not entirely well grounded in Crown's case. The managers did, in fact, make several attempts to modernize their plant. None of these efforts alleviated the company's woes, and some only exacerbated the situation.[32]

In 1947 Crown's managers had purchased $800,000 of "badly needed equipment," and during the 1950s, the company spent about the same amount to overhaul Crown's carding and spinning operations. Overall, the company spent

$1,746,600 to improve the Crown Mill during the 1960s, making a partial shift to synthetics and purchasing over one hundred high-speed looms. But the new looms only compounded problems. They created turmoil among Crown's weavers, many of whom had worked for the mill for several decades and could not, according to one thirty-year veteran, stand the blistering pace of these machines. The looms also required extensive retraining and load adjustments, both of which grated against the workers' own notions of a proper work load. So if some millhands thought plant modernization was needed, it was equally true that many workers resisted the company's shift toward newer, faster machines. The view that management failed to upgrade Crown's productive facilities does contain a grain of truth, however. The company's brief boom in the mid-1960s suggests that Crown might have been salvageable. Moreover, the expenditures made to modernize the Dalton mill seem less impressive when compared with the startup costs of the Texture-Tex plants at Phelps ($1,389,255) and Valdosta ($1,427,000). During the 1960s, the company's expenditures for these two new plants exceeded the money spent on Crown by 61 percent. In the end, though, the real question was not whether modernization could have saved the mill but whether Crown could have survived under any circumstances, given the labor market realities of the late 1960s. The answer, most likely, was no.[33]

The corporation itself offered only terse explanations for the shutdowns. Boylston was the first to close in May 1969. As early as February, the company notified workers that it was cutting back on operations at Boylston "due to the lack of orders for the yarns which we are able to produce." In mid-May, a second announcement noted: "We have made every reasonable effort to obtain additional orders for the types of yarn that can be produced at Boylston, with little or no success. As a result of this, we have no alternative but to advise you that we are permanently discontinuing operations at the Boylston plant." The managers encouraged good workers from Boylston to accept jobs at the upper mills, where stable employees were badly needed. In effect, Hamilton was trying to save at least part of the old Crown Mill operation by consolidating the mill's best workers in Mills 1 and 2. The company's offer to transfer the Boylston hands had been tendered in February, but, as the May announcement noted, "some of you have refused this offer due to your having hopes of the resumption of operations at Boylston." The shutdown notice squelched any such hopes. "We regret that we had to make this decision to cease operations," the final memorandum read, "but we had no alternative in light of market conditions and our forecasts for the future." As it turned out, management's hope that Boylston's workers would move into Crown Mills 1 and 2 went unfulfilled. Newer workers did not care to stay around, and the older Boylston hands apparently saw little advantage in taking work at different plants. In one sense, the closing of Boylston was management's last effort to solve its labor problem. If all the Boylston old-timers had moved to the north

Dalton facilities, rapid labor turnover in the upper mills might have been curtailed, at least for a while.[34]

But problems in the two remaining mills would doubtless have continued even
if the Boylston workers had taken jobs there. In early June, even as the Boylston
machinery was being dismantled, weavers in the New Mill walked off their jobs in
another wildcat strike—as it turned out, the last. This walkout may have been the
final straw for the company. The TWUA national office, which also seemed to be
losing patience with Local 185, sent yet another frantic telegram to Dalton's union
leaders demanding that they get the wildcatters back to work. Meanwhile, it was
clear that Crown's cotton textile plants were going to lose big money in 1969,
whereas the new carpet-yarn plants were doing quite well.[35]

The mill's path now led inexorably toward closure. In early September, the
managers prepared a statement for the press that was posted for the workers on
September 12 and then released for publication. Without mentioning the Texture-
Tex plants by name, the notice announced that Crown "is realigning its manufacturing operations in a program which will involve phasing out its industrial fabric
and synthetic spinning operations." This was a roundabout way of declaring a
shutdown. Voicing his regret over this decision, Crown president David Hamilton
said, "We have tried over the past two years to come up with any reasonable
alternative that offered any hope of reestablishing these divisions as profitable
operations, but regrettably have not been able to do so." He also explained more
specifically what had led to this conclusion. "Depressed market conditions,
chronic worker shortages and absenteeism, and [the] continuing inability to pass
on increasing costs of production in the form of increased prices," he said, "was
responsible for the move." This explanation also avoided mentioning the company's new and booming carpet-yarn plants, and it made no attempt to offer any
explanation for the worker shortages, but from management's point of view,
Hamilton had offered an honest and accurate assessment. It was certainly better
than some of the rumors that began to circulate.[36]

The union was an easy target, and many people pinned the blame for the
shutdown squarely on Local 185. Many affluent townspeople and some former
millhands still claim that the union forced the company to fold. The evidence for
this argument is weak at best. By 1969 TWUA Local 185 had been the bargaining
agent for Crown's employees for more than thirty years, and there had been no
major shifts in management personnel or union leadership since the early 1950s. It
is difficult to believe the managers and union leaders at Crown suddenly found
themselves incapable of dealing with one another. Even though the union had
some strong disagreements with company policies during the late 1960s, Local 185
proved as eager as management to end labor unrest at the mill; but neither managers nor union officials could control the labor situation, which was due as much
to outside circumstances as to internal difficulties. Hearing rumors that the union

had closed the mill, stalwarts of Local 185 pointed to Dalton's carpet manufacturers as the source of this slander. "Well, a lot of people give the union credit for the mill closing down," recalled Sarah Bunch. "The Tufted Textile Manufacturing Association, you see, they wanted to keep their plants from organizing so they said, 'You see what the union done to the Crown Mill—the union closed it down.' That's what they would tell the people, you know, to try to keep the organization out of their plants." Whatever the carpet manufacturers said to their workers, the idea took root that the union had pushed the mill to the point of shutdown.[37]

In the end, though, it was the union that fought hardest to save the mill. The workers were interested in preserving not only their jobs but their community as well—at least what was left of it. It is not surprising that Crown's union hands fought the closing, given their history of activism. With millhands throughout Dalton they supported the General Textile Strike of 1934 and successfully organized their plant in the late 1930s. They struggled through the protracted strike of 1939 in their fight against wage cuts and stretchouts. Union membership boomed during and after World War II, as Dalton's locals successfully negotiated increasingly better contracts—sometimes amicably, sometimes through strikes. Along with their fellow union members in Rome and other northwest Georgia textile towns, Dalton's millhands became increasingly political in the late 1940s, sending to Congress and the Georgia statehouse some of the South's few elected prolabor liberals of that era. In 1947, organized millhands successfully ousted Dalton's antilabor administration and replaced it with a coalition of workers and prolabor politicians.[38] The union workers had, in short, a tradition of agitation in support of their causes. Moreover, they had a lot to lose, including decades of accumulated textile skills and all of their hard-won seniority. They stood to lose their union representation, their ability to shape the structure and pace of work in some small way. Union officers stood to lose status in the community, because the union had been their primary path for upward mobility. Due to a decision over which Crown's millhands had no control, Local 185 now stood to have its achievements decimated, even though it had been a partner in the running of Crown Mill since the late 1930s.

In contesting the shutdown, Local 185 sought the help of the government. The union openly questioned the company's contention that Crown was no longer an economically feasible enterprise. Shortly after Hamilton announced that the plant would close, James Campbell, president of the local, and Jimmy Walraven, an AFL-CIO International representative, voiced their concern to Senator Herman E. Talmadge and asked him for help (the irony being that the senator's father had helped break the General Textile Strike of 1934 and that neither Talmadge had been popular among Dalton millhands). Senator Talmadge offered polite sympathy but added, "I must respectfully advise you that Members of the United States Senate do not have jurisdiction over private business matters of this kind." He offered to contact Georgia's commissioner of labor so that "everything possible [can] be done to help secure new jobs for those who are being dislocated by the closing of the Crown Cotton Mills plant." This was not much help, as the labor commissioner's main function was to oversee the State Employment Service, which doubtless was aware of the Crown closure without Talmadge's notice.[39]

Ironically, state unemployment officers viewed the shutdown not as a problem but as a useful way to ease Dalton's labor shortage. In the carpet industry, they said, seven to eight hundred openings were now available, and because the shutdown involved only about seven hundred workers, there really was no problem for Crown's millhands. "There are already more jobs available in the community than there are people to fill them," said one official, who did not "foresee any difficulties in relocating the Crown workers." But Crown's union millhands, whose working careers and union local were at stake, did not see relocation possibilities as the proper standard by which to gauge the severity of the crisis. As it happened, the relocation of older hands would prove more difficult than the state employment office thought.[40]

The workers also turned to the TWUA International for help. As soon as the mill posted the closure announcement in September, Local 185 requested that the national office "investigate the truth of the claims of management as to the reasons for closing." But the International refused to investigate, and by the end of the year, the Crown plant stood silent and empty. Some months after the shutdown, the workers finally learned that the Crown Cotton Mills Corporation had built new plants in Valdosta, Phelps, and Tifton. How the workers learned of these plants—or, better yet, why they had not heard of them sooner—remains a mystery. The union workers received this news sometime in the spring of 1970 (they had continued to hold regular meetings to deal with issues relating to the shutdown) and were as outraged by the company's deception as they were by the International's timidity.[41]

In a sharply worded resolution, Local 185 denounced the TWUA national office. Stressing their long-term loyalty and commitment to the state and national aims of the TWUA, Crown's union hands nevertheless castigated the International for not carrying out a full investigation of management's claim that Crown was shut down "because of poor economic conditions which resulted in the company losing money." They angrily contended that "a diligent and reasonable investigation by the International would have disclosed the sham and deceit of the management and would have preserved the jobs of all members of Local 185." The local condemned this "irresponsible and inexcusable conduct" and resolved "that the International be censured for its gross dereliction of responsibility." The workers further demanded "that this resolution of censure be spread upon the official and permanent minutes of the convention and be distributed to all affiliates of the Textile Workers Union of America . . . in the same manner as are other officially adopted resolutions." Under pressure from the International, however, the executive board of Local 185 backed down and ultimately agreed not to present the resolution to the convention. In a final foray, the local did urge the International's executive council to "take the Resolution under advisement" and to "give a full report" explaining its failure to investigate the Crown Mill situation.[42]

The International revealed either its bureaucratic inefficiency or its lack of concern for the Crown Mill shutdown when, nearly four months after the mill had closed, TWUA General Secretary-Treasurer Sol Stetin sent Local 185 a curt form letter that stated, "A questionnaire was sent to you last month requesting information on the plant(s) in your local. . . . To date we have not received your reply." Another questionnaire was enclosed, along with an insistence that the local respond so the national office could have accurate records. James Campbell dutifully filled out the form—with some incredulity, no doubt—and entered in the column for number of employees a simple zero. "This plant has discontinued operations at this location," he wrote across the form. "There are no employees working in the plant at this time."[43]

It was a bitter end for Local 185, a southern union that had battled against the odds for longer than most. The TWUA's reluctance to investigate the Crown management's claims is difficult to understand. In the most fundamental sense, Crown *did* shut down for economic reasons, but there were labor matters involved, and surely the International should have tried to preserve a plant that boasted a strong southern local. To anyone with prounion leanings, this is a troubling tale. Southern industrialists had long insisted that Yankee union officials cared nothing for rank-and-file southern workers, a charge that was probably unfair. But in 1969 the TWUA national officials did remain aloof from a southern problem. Crown's workers were caught between two corporations—the Crown Mill and the TWUA International, neither of which demonstrated any real concern for Local 185.

For many of the old-timers from Crown, there was no place to go—or no place they wanted to go. Like the state employment office, Crown's management assured the public that "every effort will be made to assist the affected employees in locating other employment." David Hamilton "pointed out that other industries in the Dalton area are desperately short of needed employees." He was "both hopeful and confident that everyone would be relatively quickly relocated." Hamilton spoke honestly about the labor market, and he spoke sincerely. But rapid reemployment for seven hundred aging workers nonetheless proved difficult, and the Phelps plant would not hire workers laid off from the Crown Mill. Among workers hoping to find good jobs in Dalton's carpet mills, the advantages were clearly on the side of young people. Floor-covering plants were not particularly interested in older cotton-mill hands, especially those coming from a strong union mill. Textile skills perfected during long years at spinning frames and looms did not easily translate to carpet-mill technology.[44]

The old-time cotton-mill hands had lost the fruits of decades of familiarity and

Empty room in the Old Mill, 1985. (*Photo by author*)

seniority. Relocation meant becoming an outsider; it also meant the loss of their hard-won union, about which carpet workers seemed to care less. The worst hardships fell on workers who were somewhere between youth and retirement—millhands in their late fifties and early sixties. "The bad part about it," recalled one worker, "was when the mill closed down, so many people were caught too old to get a job and not old enough to draw Social Security. . . . I was one of the lucky ones. I got a job [after five months of looking for work], but others didn't, you know." Aging workers were often simply turned away by the carpet mills, or sometimes they were given low-paying, nonproduction jobs as security guards, warehouse workers, and carpet inspectors. This was relocation of a singularly painful sort, but no one, least of all the state employment office, seemed to give a damn. One of the most brutal characteristics of modernization—the degradation of older people—thus dealt the last devastating blow to a threadbare community. The actions of the Crown Corporation, the TWUA International, the state of Georgia, and Dalton's carpet plants all voiced the same idea: old workers were expendable.[45]

Like so many corporate communities that originated early in the twentieth century, the Crown Mill community collapsed when post–World War II developments changed the shape of the American economy. Some of the bonds that had held those corporate "families" together were cruel; the communities themselves had a coercive, exploitative side to them. But they gave ordinary workers a sense of place and purpose and, sometimes, economic security. As the welfare state re-placed welfare capitalism, and as World War II created new opportunities for many working-class children, the older communities underwent a gradual trans-formation. Beyond paternalism, family ties to corporations weakened and com-mitments to unions deepened. But then the unions themselves began to falter, and the changing economy swung a wrecking ball at the nation's blue-collar commu-nities. Those communities died hard, even ones that were well past their prime. Many veterans of the old Crown community had lived and worked there since the 1920s and found it difficult to recover from events of the 1960s—not just the mill's closing but also the utter devastation of their working lives and their community.

Cynics might say, perhaps rightly, that those jobs and that community were no longer worth keeping. But from the workers' point of view, at least the jobs and the community were theirs. The union may have been on the skids, but they had built it with their own sweat and sacrifice. Maybe by 1969 the community was only a pallid reflection of its former self, and perhaps it had never been much to speak of, but it was all they had. The "progress" of capitalism has never been kind to the past. Nothing is sacrosanct—not jobs, not unions, not communities. Such fluidity is only part of the price that southerners—indeed all Americans—have paid for creating a modern world. Maybe in 1969 the past was not worth holding on to at the Crown Cotton Mill. After all, children of the postwar era had abandoned the mill village as quickly as they could. But for those whose entire lives had been invested in the mill and the village, the Crown Mill community had offered some bit of security in an uncharitable world. For those people, and perhaps for them alone, the shutdown was an occasion for sadness.

ECHOES: THE CROWNAMERICA CENTENNIAL, 1984

In 1984 the old Crown Mill grounds came alive as the corporation celebrated its centennial. The motto of the day, "A Century of Textile Product Excellence," was emblazoned on large banners that hung at each end of a huge yellow-and-white-striped canopy. The tent towered over long lines of tables, offering shade to hundreds of Crown's current and former employees, who had gathered to enjoy an "old-fashioned bar-becue picnic" and the music of bluegrass legend Bill Monroe. A hundred years earlier, the land surround-ing Hamilton's Spring had been abuzz with con-struction crews building Dalton's first large-scale tex-tile factory. Now, in the Carpet Capital of the World, whose industrial output was nothing short of phe-nomenal, the old mill grounds were an appropriately quaint place to celebrate a century of "continuous operation."[1]

It was a curious centennial, given that the Crown Cotton Mills had been shut down for fifteen years. But the corporation had survived the closing of the cotton mills and, in 1972, had changed its name to CrownAmerica Incorporated. This new appellation reflected both the new direction taken by the corpo-ration and, in a larger sense, the integration of south-ern industry into the national economy. During the

1970s and early 1980s, CrownAmerica had dedicated itself more fully to carpet-yarn production; in 1981 the company went international, building its first over-seas facility—Texture-Tex Europe in Newport, South Wales—and establishing sales forces in both the United Kingdom and Australia. CrownAmerica had grown far beyond the tenuous textile enterprise launched in 1884.[2]

But a few significant traditions had endured. The Hamilton family remained dominant in the corporation, with G. Lane Hamilton serving as secretary-treasurer, H. Clay Hamilton as vice president, and David D. Hamilton as president. The old Crown Mill buildings were kept by the company as leasable space for warehousing and light manufacturing. The original company offices became the Crown Gardens and Archives, a community center and repository for historical materials, including Crown's company records. The Whitfield-Murray County Historical Society suc-ceeded in having the mill buildings and mill-village area designated as historical landmarks, and for the most part the old structures remained intact. Many of the former millhands continued to live in the houses they had bought from the company in 1953, and the former students of Crown Point School held annual reunions. The defunct mill village thus functioned as a kind of time capsule, blurring the boundaries of past and present. Pat Lowrance, who grew up on Jones Street, wrote of the centennial, "Crown Cotton Mill you have become CrownAmer-ica. . . . I could not be less than proud of your heritage for it is my own."[3]

Crown's directors had always demonstrated keen historical sensibilities, and it was not surprising that they made the most of their company's most important anniversary. They solicited the services of retired newspaper editor Marc Pace to write a brief centennial history of the company, which appeared as a special supplement in the local papers. They hired the Pulitzer Prize–winning photogra-pher Robin Hood to compose an artistic historical photograph to grace the front of the centennial publication. David Hamilton himself put considerable thought into the meaning of the centennial and the larger significance of Crown for Dalton. In an open letter to the local citizenry, he wrote:

> I regard this as a singular event, if for no other reason but that not too many United States corporations, or any others for that matter, have successfully reached such a period of continuous operation. More important, though, I regard it as singular because laying any modesty aside, I truly believe that Crown Cotton Mills/CrownAmerica has through this century earned and merited the title "Good Corporate Citizen." That a *corporation*, a bad word in some quarters, can accomplish this along with at least moderate financial success at the same time is, to say the least, quite gratifying to me.

Hamilton believed that "the credit for this dual accomplishment truly belongs to a century-long partnership of loyal and dedicated employees . . . and management that through the years has held before it these goals." He added, "It hasn't always

Crown Mill/CrownAmerica Centennial Celebration, 1984. (*Courtesy of Crown Gardens and Archives*)

been 'beer and skittles,' but I do believe that most everyone carries away from their association with the company pleasant and prideful memories of the relationship."[4]

Embedded in these words was the ethic of corporate community that had been an important part of Crown's history. But was there really a centennial community to celebrate? On one level, the celebration was an elaborate exercise in public relations and labor relations. As the company directors explained to stockholders in that year's annual report: "In the long journey from its beginnings in Dalton, Georgia, Crown has constantly strived to recognize the accomplishments of its employees. Appropriately during fiscal 1984, the focal point of the Company's anniversary celebrations was the employee workforce." Celebrations were also held in Valdosta and South Wales; clearly, though, the one-hundred-year mark had the greatest significance to the old Crown Mill community. The picnic near the Spring Lot was intended for Texture-Tex employees as well, but the focus of the event was the old mill; the location of the celebration and the large crowd of former Crown Mill workers in attendance was hardly an accident. On a deeper level, then, the centennial was an exercise in resurrection, an attempt to revive or at least pay tribute to the community that had expired with such bitterness fifteen years earlier.[5]

The workers' union—TWUA Local 185—though it had been a central part of the mill community for nearly four decades, was not part of the centennial celebration. In 1947, *Textile Labor* had christened Dalton a "real union town," and so it was at that time.[6] Less than two generations later, one might have been hard pressed to find carpet-mill workers who knew that strong, politically active unions had ever existed in their home town. At CrownAmerica in 1984, some memories were more eagerly resurrected than others. There were no unions in Dalton in 1984, and there are none today. The chamber of commerce proudly advertises this state of affairs to prospective industrialists. Listing Whitfield County's top ten employers (all carpet-related manufacturing plants except the Tappan microwave oven factory), one puff sheet offers information on union representation in each plant. The entry, ten times without variation, is "none." This less-than-subtle message is then repeated for seven other major employers in the Dalton area, including the schools, Hamilton Medical Center, and various manufacturing and financial enterprises. For almost thirty years, from the 1930s through the 1950s, textile unions played a critical role in the economic and political affairs of Dalton, despite the generally weak position of organized labor in the South. Today, an equally long time has passed since organized labor wielded any clout in the town.[7]

The continued growth of the nonunion carpet industry during the seventies further erased memories of Dalton's old-line textile mills, none of which had survived the sixties. During Crown Mill's final decade, local carpet production increased by a stunning 224 percent, and during the 1970s production rates ex-

David D. Hamilton, last president of Crown Mill, first president of CrownAmerica, in 1974. (*Courtesy of Crown Gardens and Archives*)

panded by another 76 percent. About the time CrownAmerica was preparing to celebrate its centennial in the shadow of a defunct cotton mill, Dalton's West Point–Pepperell Corporation (the leading carpet producer in 1980) sold $402 million in carpets. In 1984 Shaw Industries, a local enterprise that would soon become the industry leader and buy out West Point, had revenues of more than $400 million and annual earnings of more than $20 million. For its part, Crown-America had a net income of more than $580,000 in the first quarter of 1984; the amount of carpet yarn produced by the Texture-Tex plants had reached nearly one million pounds per week.[8]

Company president David Hamilton saw the transition from old-line cotton mills to cutting-edge carpet technology as one of fundamental significance for Dalton and the South. "What the cotton mills meant to the South primarily was to help pry the South loose from . . . a strictly agrarian economy to what we begin to see the South developing into today." And what was the South becoming? "I think the South is going to develop into the new smokestack belt of the country, for whatever that's worth. It may be good, it may be bad. But [America] certainly can't exist on high technology and services alone. I think the productivity of the country will be in the South." The dramatic ascendance of carpets in a small southern town helped inspire such optimism. "We used to think all the brains were somewhere else other than in the South, and I think we've . . . come to the realization that we can do the things that we used to think had to be done for us by someone else. I was probably as guilty of it as anybody. I used to think nobody could make any machinery except in New England. But if you look around here, all the machinery and equipment for the tufted carpet industry has really been developed here in Georgia." "People here," he quipped, "maybe they weren't smart enough to realize they weren't able to do this; they just went out and did it. I think they proved it to themselves, and I think they proved it to the world. And it has happened—not just in the carpet industry—it's happened in a lot of other ways in the South."[9]

The new carpet plants of the 1980s make the old textile mills seem archaic. Anyone accustomed to the New South's red-brick, heavyset mills would be surprised by the appearance of the carpet plants; inconspicuous, steel-sided buildings, they look more like warehouses than factories and are as likely to be tucked away in a semirural area as they are to be in town. On the inside, the larger carpet plants are generally spacious and well lighted. Compared to the old cotton mills, they are lint-free and quiet places to work. The workers who put rubber "backing" on carpets have the most unpleasant job, because the machines involved give off intense heat and use chemicals that stink of ammonia and burn the eyes. Overall, however, working conditions in carpet factories compare favorably with those in the old mills.

Whether better working conditions have created a better world for Dalton's millhands is a more difficult question. The evidence is not encouraging. Wages in the carpet plants are still low in relation to other industrial jobs. With no unions and little prospect for them, and with the generally sluggish state of the carpet industry at present, there is no pressure to increase wages. Some say that Dalton has no middle class, that people are either wealthy or not. As one day-care center director recently commented, "It's a town of haves and have-nots." A local physician explained that the carpet plants represent "a big, nonunionized industry that results in a stratification of society into either very rich or very poor." Although the local economic structure is not quite so simple, the notion of stratification has considerable validity. Looking back, of course, economic inequality was an ongoing phenomenon in the textile South; it was, indeed, central to the process of southern industrialization. But Dalton's union millhands of the 1940s and early 1950s reached a level of economic security and social respectability (which they subsequently lost) that offers a telling comparison to Dalton's present-day work force.[10]

In a recent study of Dalton's carpet workers, sociologist Joseph A. McDonald discovered a work force that was largely poor, dissatisfied, and without hope. He found no sense of community, either inside the mills or in the workers' own neighborhoods. Of the workers McDonald surveyed, most changed jobs frequently and did not know their fellow workers very well. Most startling of all, only one in ten knew who their neighbors were. Few statistics offer such a stark contrast with the past. It is impossible to imagine the people of Crown Mill—of any cotton-mill town—not knowing their neighbors. Some might argue that the new autonomy of the workers indicates not the demise of community but the rise of individual liberty—the creation of free spaces in which families may live unfettered by the constraints of company paternalism and union responsibilities. Perhaps, too, community bonds still exist beyond the workers' neighborhoods, in Dalton's working-class churches or bars. Perhaps. But it is difficult to escape the conclusion that what we are seeing here is the increasing fragmentation of Dalton's working people.[11]

For the old millhands who turned out for Crown's centennial celebration, though, "community" was both a thing of the past and an ongoing commitment. Families who had looked after one another through generations at Crown Mill continued to do so. They still made house calls, visited nursing homes, comforted the sick, mourned the dead. Many at the celebration were already quite ill. Some had byssinosis, or "brown lung," from breathing cotton dust in the mills all their lives; they were doomed to cough out their lungs and die, in the words of Erskine Caldwell, "with blood on their lips." Some older workers were accompanied by their children, many of whom moved out of the mill village after World War II but settled in the Dalton area. Mill families had continued to gather for the annual company reunion and their own Crown Point School reunions. The Old-Timers Baseball Club, consisting of anyone who had played for the Crown Mill nine, had its own yearly picnic to relive the camaraderie and swap a few stories. Such were the remnants of an industrial community long since expired. Without any sustaining force, without the mill or the union, the community of workers had no means of perpetuating itself. The Crown centennial was all the more poignant for that very reason.[12]

It is difficult to know what it all meant to them—the old millhands of Crown— as they sat beneath the anniversary tent in 1984. They were the inheritors of a community that their parents and kin before them had helped to create. They themselves transformed it during the 1930s and in the postwar decades, as they built and sustained a thriving union. Indirectly, they also had helped undermine it by encouraging their own children to move away from the mills. And in the end, their union sought unsuccessfully to save it, while catching most of the blame for destroying it. The modernization of the South was continuing apace, but the creation of new communities, of new industrial institutions, would fall to a new generation. Looking back, Crown's aging millhands knew more clearly than any historian ever could the odd blend of suffering and satisfaction that accompanied mill-village life. Their stories, their faces, their houses, their laughter, their hacking coughs—these offered fleeting glimpses of a past filled with the tragedy of poverty and the triumph of the human spirit. From 1884 to 1984, working people throughout the Western world learned the same basic story—a story of change and adaptation, of struggle and reconciliation, of bosses and corporate paternalism, of hardship and community. John Bramblett understood that story very well. He knew the farm and the factory, he lived his adult life within the Crown Mill community, and he served as a dedicated union leader. Thinking back, he summed up his life with words that somehow transcended the boundaries of the small-town South. "We lived a full life, no doubt about that," he recalled. "It was hard, and we had work, but we had a full life."[13]

APPENDIX A

SELECTED TABLES AND

CROWN MILL PROFIT CHART

TABLE A.1. Population of Dalton and Whitfield County, 1870–1970

	Dalton	Percentage Change	County[a]	Percentage Change	Dalton as Percentage of County
1870	1,809	—	8,308	—	17.9
1880	2,516	39.1	9,384	13.0	21.1
1890	3,046	21.1	9,870	5.2	23.6
1900	4,315	41.7	10,194	3.3	29.7
1910	5,324	23.4	10,610	4.1	33.4
1920	5,222	−1.9	11,675	10.0	30.9
1930	8,160	56.3	12,648	8.3	39.2
1940	10,448	28.0	15,657	23.8	40.0
1950	15,968	52.8	18,464	17.9	46.4
1960	17,868	11.9	24,241	31.3	42.4
1970[b]	18,872	5.6	36,236	49.5	34.2

Source: U.S. census returns.

[a]Excluding Dalton.

[b]Between 1960 and 1970, the city of Dalton annexed surrounding areas, thereby boosting its population by 1,027. The 1970 figures here reflect those annexations, without which the population of Dalton remained essentially unchanged from 1960 to 1970.

TABLE A.2. Crown Cotton Mill Profit Statements, 1884–1969

Fiscal Year Ending[a]	Net Profit (in $)	Capital Stock (in $1,000)	Percentage Return on Capital
1885[b]	−863	55	−2
1886	4,902	69	7
1887	19,123	71	27
1888	28,186	88	32
1889	11,082	101	11
1890	16,106	101	16
1891	22,553	101	22
1892	27,518	101	27
1893	26,343	101	26
1894	22,404	101	22
1895	50,785	123	41
1896	25,330	163	16
1897	26,068	163	16
1898	73,391	163	45
1899	69,116	163	42
1900	90,191	299	30
1901	21,200	299	7
1902	51,796	299	17
1903	103,437	299	35
1904	27,132	299	9
1905	106,602	299	36
1906	121,336	299	41
1907	132,961	299	45
1908	n.a.	n.a.	n.a.
1909	106,248	598	18
1910	50,945	598	9
1911	78,198	598	13
1912	156,321	598	26
1913	181,566	598	30
1914	104,660	598	18
1915	212,137	598	36
1916	268,768	598	45
1917	372,505	897	42
1918	166,748	897	19
1919	527,020	897	59
1920	580,462	897	65
1921	86,357	897	10
1922	270,290	897	30
1923	491,287	897	55
1924	274,157	897	31

TABLE A.2. (cont.)

Fiscal Year Ending[a]	Net Profit (in $)	Capital Stock (in $1,000)	Percentage Return on Capital
1925	490,736	897	55
1926	474,489	897	53
1927[c]	466,125	1,345	35
1928	292,247	1,345	22
1929	338,685	1,345	25
1930	−157,366	1,345	−12
1931	−279,764	1,345	−21
1932	−75,613	1,345	−6
1933	19,286	1,345	1
1934	63,568	1,345	5
1935	−32,786	1,345	−2
1936	22,457	1,345	2
1937	128,799	1,345	10
1938	−13,605	1,345	−1
1939	7,620	1,345	1
1940	131,896	1,345	10
1941	256,251	1,345	19
1942	355,536	1,345	26
1943	199,915	1,345	15
1944	159,256	1,345	12
1945	148,656	1,345	11
1946	487,433	1,345	36
1947	833,065	1,345	62
1948	1,039,888	1,345	77
1949	730,789	1,345	54
1950	417,472	1,345	31
1951	416,937	1,345	31
1952	200,425	1,345	15
1953	−26,061	1,345	−2
1954	123,046	1,345	9
1955	98,717	1,345	7
1956	325,647	1,345	24
1957	184,524	1,345	14
1958	31,387	1,345	2
1959	247,360	1,345	18
1960	254,625	1,345	19
1961[d]	−137,000	1,345	−10
1962	−99,062	1,345	−7
1963	−121,710	1,345	−9
1964	303,129	1,345	23

TABLE A.2. (cont.)

Fiscal Year Ending[a]	Net Profit (in $)	Capital Stock (in $1,000)	Percentage Return on Capital
1965	410,224	2,000	21
1966	274,026	2,000	14
1967	n.a.	2,000	n.a.
1968[e]	79,731	2,000	4
1969[e]	160,792	2,000	8

Source: Crown Cotton Mills Board of Directors Minutes, Books 1, 2, and 3; Ernst and Ernst Audit Reports, 1946–69, CGA.

[a]The company's fiscal year ran from September 1 to August 31.

[b]Only six months of production.

[c]Beginning with 1927, Crown's figures include the Boylston-Crown plant. In 1925 the Boylston mill lost 2 percent on capital; in 1926, it lost 4 percent. Boylston (apart from Crown) earned 7 percent on capital in 1927, its first profitable year.

[d]Estimates based on figures in Ann. Rpt. 1962, CGA.

[e]Texture-Tex profits are included. There are no separate figures for Crown Mill.

FIGURE A.1. Crown Mill Annual Profits, 1885–1969

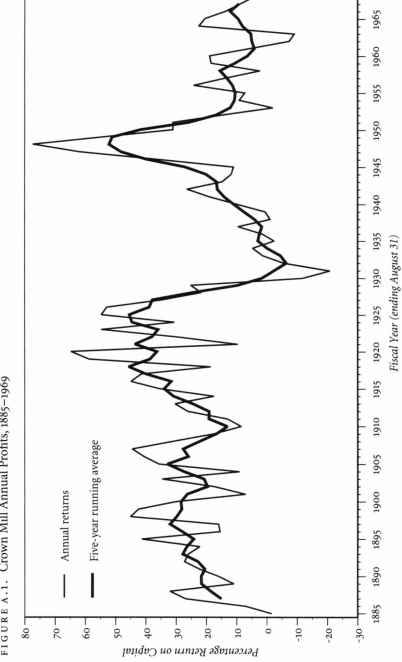

Source: Crown Cotton Mills Board of Directors Minutes, Books 1, 2, and 3; Ernst and Ernst Audit Reports, 1946–69, CGA.

TABLE A.3. Strike Support by Day and Mill, 1939

| Day of Strike | Day of Week | Date | Percentage of Workers on Strike | | |
			Old Mill	New Mill	Boylston
1	Tuesday	5/30	100	100	100
2	Wednesday	5/31	100	100	100
3	Thursday	6/1	100	100	100
4	Friday	6/2	100	100	100
5	Monday	6/5	100	100	100
6	Tuesday	6/6	100	100	100
7	Wednesday	6/7	100	100	100
8	Thursday	6/8	100	100	100
9	Friday	6/9	100	100	100
10	Monday	6/12	100	100	100
11	Tuesday	6/13	100	100	100
12	Wednesday	6/14	100	100	100
13	Thursday	6/15	100	100	100
14	Friday	6/16	100	100	100
15	Monday	6/19	100	100	100
16	Tuesday	6/20	100	100	100
17	Wednesday	6/21	100	100	100
18	Thursday	6/22	100	100	100
19	Friday	6/23	100	100	100
20	Monday	6/26	100	100	100
21	Tuesday	6/27	100	100	100
22	Wednesday	6/28	100	100	100
23	Thursday	6/29	100	100	100
24	Friday	6/30	100	100	100
25	Monday	7/3	100	100	100
26	Tuesday	7/4	100	100	100
27	Wednesday	7/5	100	100	100
28	Thursday	7/6	100	100	100
29	Friday	7/7	100	100	100
30	Monday	7/10	100	98	94
31	Tuesday	7/11	100	97	93
32	Wednesday	7/12	100	97	74
33	Thursday	7/13	100	97	51
34	Friday	7/14	98	94	49
35	Monday	7/17	97	81	47
36	Tuesday	7/18	88	73	46
37	Wednesday	7/19	85	69	45
38	Thursday	7/20	84	68	45
39	Friday	7/21	84	68	45

TABLE A.3. (cont.)

Day of Strike	Day of Week	Date	Percentage of Workers on Strike		
			Old Mill	New Mill	Boylston
40	Monday	7/24	80	66	47
41	Tuesday	7/25	79	64	46
42	Wednesday	7/26	76	63	46
43	Thursday	7/27	77	61	45
44	Friday	7/28	77	60	45
45	Monday	7/31	76	59	42
46	Tuesday	8/1	76	58	42
47	Wednesday	8/2	74	58	42
48	Thursday	8/3	74	58	42
49	Friday	8/4	75	59	41
50	Monday	8/7	75	56	43
51	Tuesday	8/8	74	56	41
52	Wednesday	8/9	74	56	40
53	Thursday	8/10	74	57	40
54	Friday	8/11	75	56	40
55	Monday	8/14	74	56	40
56	Tuesday	8/15	75	56	40
57	Wednesday	8/16	74	55	40
58	Thursday	8/17	74	55	40
59	Friday	8/18	74	55	40
60	Monday	8/21	74	55	40
61	Tuesday	8/22	74	56	41
62	Wednesday	8/23	73	55	40
63	Thursday	8/24	74	55	41
64	Friday	8/25	74	56	40
65	Monday	8/28	72	55	40
66	Tuesday	8/29	73	55	40
67	Wednesday	8/30	72	54	40
68	Thursday	8/31	72	54	40
69	Friday	9/1	72	54	40
70	Monday	9/4	72	55	39
71	Tuesday	9/5	73	54	38
72	Wednesday	9/6	73	54	40
73	Thursday	9/7	74	54	40
74	Friday	9/8	73	54	40
75	Monday	9/11	73	53	37
76	Tuesday	9/12	72	53	38
77	Wednesday	9/13	72	53	39
78	Thursday	9/14	73	53	40

TABLE A.3. (cont.)

| Day of Strike | Day of Week | Date | Percentage of Workers on Strike | | |
			Old Mill	New Mill	Boylston
79	Friday	9/15	74	53	38
80	Monday	9/18	73	54	39
81	Tuesday	9/19	73	54	39
82	Wednesday	9/20	72	54	40
83	Thursday	9/21	72	54	40
84	Friday	9/22	72	54	39
85	Monday	9/25	71	53	32
86	Tuesday	9/26	61	42	24
87	Wednesday	9/27	54	36	20
88	Thursday	9/28	50	32	17
89	Friday	9/29	48	32	20

Source: Crown Cotton Mills Payroll Records, 1939, CGA.

In trying to understand the Crown Mill workers, I sought to learn as much as possible about the individuals within their community. Only then was it possible to fathom the complex ways in which family relationships, gender, age, and income shaped their collective response to textile work and mill-village life. One reason local analyses are so valuable is that they make it possible to examine the interaction between individual and group behavior. They offer the statistical data necessary to intersect private circumstances with community action. Quantification is the art of using that data to re-create an accurate and detailed portrait of a community. Quantification need not turn complex historical actors into lifeless statistics. It can instead breathe life into a richly textured past that, lacking data and quantitative methods, would remain forever buried. There are a wide variety of ways to use statistics to study community. This appendix describes the data on individuals that was available to me as I sought to understand the Crown Mill community, and it discusses some of the ways I used the data to re-create the evolution of that community.

THE CENSUS SCHEDULES AND PAYROLL DATA

My understanding of Crown's millhands in the early twentieth century, especially as presented in chapter 5, is based largely on data collected from two different sources: the federal manuscript census schedules for the years 1900 and 1910 and the biweekly payroll records of the Crown Cotton Mill. Manuscript census data is a gold mine of information on the lives of ordinary people, but its usefulness is naturally circumscribed by the years under study. Crown was not operating in 1880, so the census from that year was useful only in tracing mill workers to their pre-Crown locations. Virtually all of the 1890 census records, including those for Georgia, were long ago destroyed by fire. The 1920 census was not open to the public at the time I conducted this study, although by the time this book is in print, it will be. As for the Crown Mill payroll records, there are substantial gaps in coverage, but the surviving volumes provided information for a variety of different analyses. For linking payroll data to the census data, I used the payrolls from 1900 and 1912 (the 1910 payroll was not available). For an investigation into the origins of the first Crown Mill workers, I used data from the 1888 and 1890 payrolls. To examine the evolution of wage rates and labor turnover, I used data from the following payroll years: 1890, 1896, 1902, 1908, 1915, 1922, and 1927. (For an explanation of the payroll book of 1939, with which I analyzed the Crown Mill strike of that year, see the section below on multiple regression and logit analysis.)

The decennial census manuscripts contain a wealth of information on every household and on every individual within each household. For both 1900 and 1910, I gathered data for every household in Whitfield County that included someone employed in a cotton mill. These families were considered "cotton-mill families" regardless of whether they lived in the mill village (the boundaries of which, at any rate, were impossible to determine in the census schedules). In 1900 Crown was the only textile plant in Whitfield County, so we can be reasonably certain anyone working in a cotton mill at that time was working for Crown. In 1910 the only other textile mill in Whitfield was the Elk Mill in south Dalton. The Elk Mill had a clearly demarcated mill village, so cotton millers there (about fifty in all) were not included in my data set. For each household, I extracted data concerning family size and property ownership. I also gathered information on all individuals within that household, including name, relation to household head, gender, age, marital status, state of birth, occupation, and ability to read and write.

A critical bit of information missing from the census manuscripts is wages earned by the household members, and for this reason it was important to link the census data to the Crown Mill payrolls. Analyzing the Crown Mill work force and how it changed from 1900 to the early 1910s required that data on workers listed in the census manuscripts be merged with data for those same workers found in the company payrolls for 1900 and 1912. Any individual found in both the census and the payroll was included in the analyses in chapter 5. Unless otherwise indicated, those found in one or the other, but not both, were excluded. Linking the names from payroll to census was sometimes made difficult by inconsistent spelling and the use of nicknames on the company payrolls. I leaned to the conservative side in record linkages, not matching a payroll entry to a census entry unless I could be comfortably certain the two individuals were indeed the same person.

During the late nineteenth and early twentieth centuries, Crown's payroll records retained basically the same format. They listed each worker's gross earnings per two-week pay period as well as the amount in deductions taken from those gross earnings. Hours or days worked were almost never listed in the payroll books that survive. Deductions were itemized in various ways, but the major deductions from workers' paychecks were always those for rent and for cash advances. This information was indispensable for analyzing rentals of company housing. The 1900 payroll grouped workers into four separate departments in the mill: carding, spinning, weaving, and engine room. Sometimes the same individual worker was listed as earning wages in two different departments during the same two-week pay period. In such cases, I merged the dual entries and coded those individuals as working in the department in which they earned the most money. The payroll records for 1912 omitted the engine room and included employees from the New Mill, which was built in 1908. The New Mill records were identical to the others, with the important exception that they did not separate employees by departments.

The Crown Mill payroll data for 1900 that I linked to the census data consisted of an eight-week sample. The workers were paid every two weeks, and so the sample consisted of four pay periods. My goal was to collect payroll data for an unexceptional, uninterrupted two-month period that would give the best indication of wages under "normal" conditions. To determine which four payrolls to analyze, I first calculated the average gross payroll for the entire year and then the average gross for every four contiguous payrolls to determine which eight-week period most closely approximated the yearly average. The pay periods from June 2 to July 14 met this criterion, having an average gross payroll of $2,752 compared to the $2,799 yearly average. For 1912, the pay periods between January 13 and February 24 proved to be the best choice.

There were some considerations worth noting concerning the linkage between the census data for 1910 and payroll records for 1912. In my regression analysis for 1912, the workers' ages were easily adjusted by adding two years to the census age. But there was no way to adjust for changes in a person's position within the household or for changes in marital status. Also, a number of workers listed in 1910 had left the mill by 1912, and others were listed on the payrolls who had not been among the cotton-mill families of 1910. Nevertheless, a sufficient number of workers was available for the 1912 regression analysis, and I encountered no problem of significance.

A few words on wage analyses are also in order. The wage rates for 1900 and 1912 used in tables 5.6 and 5.7 are based on average biweekly gross earnings. They were calculated by adding the gross earnings for each worker during the four consecutive pay periods and then dividing that sum by the number of pay periods for which each worker was actually listed on the payroll book (i.e., individual gross earnings/number of pay periods worked). Unless otherwise specified, my examinations of wage rates reflect gross earnings, because I was interested in the basic earning power of the millhands, apart from nonwage transactions such as rent. The analysis of real wages from 1890 to 1927 presented in table 5.5 is based on the mean earnings for the entire work force. For each year, I gathered information on every individual from four quarterly payrolls (when possible, I used the second payroll in January, April, July, and October). I then used these four payrolls to determine the average payroll size for the year. The wage analysis for each year was then based on the single payroll closest in size to that average. Calculating real wages over nearly a forty-year period requires the use of a consistent cost-of-living index.

In order to calculate "real" wages, it is necessary to have data on nominal wages for selected years and a set of consumer price indexes for those same years. Consumer price indexes reflect the relative amount of monetary inflation or deflation from one year to the next. There are a variety of such indexes; here I used the indexes produced by the Bureau of Labor Statistics (BLS) and cited in table 5.5. The BLS indexes used for this study reflect national not regional prices, and I used the indexes calculated for all consumer items. The consumer price index for any given year is a number that indicates a comparison between prices in that year and prices in a specified "base year." The base year always has an index equal to 100; the indexes to all other years are calculated in relation to that year: they can be above or below (or equal to) 100. If the base year is 1890, one may say that real-wage calculations for another year—for example, 1900—are "in 1890 dollars." For historical studies, it is naturally preferable to choose a base year in close proximity to the time period under study, which is why I used 1890 for that purpose. In the BLS figures that I used, the base year is actually 1967; I recalculated the indexes so that 1890 would be the base year. Such recalculations do not alter the way in which the indexes work; they simply make the real-wage calculations more meaningful in a historical context.[1]

To calculate average real wages for a population in a given year, divide the average wage of that population by the consumer price index for that year; then multiply by 100. That is, (average nominal wage/index number) × 100 = average real wage. For example, the average nominal wage of Crown's millhands in 1896 was $2.73, and my consumer price index figure was 92.6; hence, (2.73/92.6) × 100 = $2.95 average real wage (rounded off). The calculation of real cotton prices (as in table 5.4) is accomplished with the same formula, but my basic argument regarding staple prices warrants further explanation here. At various points throughout the book, especially in chapter 5, I suggest that cotton prices offered a rough but clearly recognizable indication of a farmer's economic prospects. This argument rests on the assumption that farmers maintained a "short-term" outlook, in which the quantity, quality, and production costs of their crops changed relatively little from year to year. Sharecroppers and tenants in the early twentieth-century South probably did labor under such conditions, and, as a consequence, the price of cotton would have been the principal factor in shaping their economic outlook. Because the potential benefits of farm prices, like the value of factory wages, depended on the overall cost of living, the calculation of real cotton prices was necessary for the analysis of the workers' labor market decisions.

The persistence rates and annual turnover rates for 1890, 1896, 1902, 1908, 1915, 1922, and 1927, presented in table 5.2, were calculated from the same payroll data with which I analyzed real wages. For annual turnover, I adopted an approach similar to that utilized by Jonathan Prude in his study of textile-mill labor turnover in rural Massachusetts.[2] In calculating the annual turnover, I used the four quarterly payrolls for each year. I took the number of newcomers who arrived during each year, added the number of workers who departed during that same year, and then divided that figure by the average payroll size for the year. (In this case, average payroll size was the mean of the four quarterly payrolls.) To calculate persistence rates from one payroll year to the next, I used only one payroll for each year—the one whose size was closest to the average payroll size for the year. Then I simply determined how many of the workers in any particular payroll year—say, 1902—were still listed in the next payroll year—in this instance, 1908. I spaced the intervals between payroll years as evenly as the surviving records permitted.

METHODS FOR MIGRATION ANALYSIS

The Soundex indexes to the federal manuscript census schedules provide a powerful, though sometimes cumbersome, tool for tracing individuals from one census year to another. At the time I researched this book, Soundex indexes were available for the years 1880, 1900, and 1910. No Soundex is available for census years earlier than 1880. The Soundex is an alphaphonetic indexing system based on the first letter of the household head's surname and a three-digit numerical code that represents the *sound* of that person's surname. This system helps eliminate the problems of inconsistent spelling from one census year to another. Unlike the manuscript census schedules, the Soundex indexes are not arranged by county but by codes within states. The Soundex provides a reference card for all households with children under ten years of age listed in the population schedules. Unlike the 1880 index, the Soundexes for 1900 and 1910 provide separate reference cards for individuals within households who were not immediately related to the household head. The coding system is easily understood and readily available in census guides.[3]

To trace an individual with this index, one must first code the last name and then find the set of cards with that particular code in the Soundex. For example, the name "Hamilton" is coded H-543. The first letter of the surname stands alone, followed by three numbers that reflect key letters in the name. Surnames that sound alike but were spelled differently by census enumerators will have the same code (e.g., "Upton" and "Uptine" are both coded U-135). Within each code series (e.g., H-543), the cards are arranged alphabetically by the household head's first name. Soundex cards provide some summary information about the household, such as the name, race, sex, age, and state of birth of each household member. More important, they give the exact reference one needs in order to locate that household in the census manuscripts for that year.

For this book, I used the Soundex indexes for Georgia (and, to a lesser extent, for the surrounding states) in four different migration analyses. First, I wanted to determine the locations from which Crown's earliest workers came. To do so, I collected the names of all workers listed on some of the earliest payrolls (randomly selected) from 1888 and 1890 and then tried to locate them in the 1880 Soundex for Georgia. The Soundexes are most useful when searching for household heads; otherwise one is compelled to search every name on every card within a certain code series. Because Crown's payrolls gave no information regarding the workers' personal characteristics, I had no choice but to search for them in this labor-intensive manner. By necessity, workers with very common surnames like Young or Smith had to be omitted from the analysis. Of the 138 individuals in the cohort of millhands from 1888 and 1890, I located 57 of them (41 percent of the total) in the Soundex for 1880 and subsequently gathered information about them and their households from the manuscript censuses.

The second analysis focused on the first decade of the twentieth century and utilized the Soundex index for 1910. My goal was to determine the destinations of people who left Crown Mill between 1900 an 1910 (as determined by an analysis of the manuscript censuses for Whitfield County in those years). Anyone in the county who was listed as a member of a cotton-mill household in 1900, and who was not listed in a mill family in 1910, was designated as an outmigrant. Because I gathered my original cohort of outmigrants from the census schedule of 1900, I knew the age and sex of each individual and could therefore narrow the cohort to those likely to be found as heads of households in 1910. Specifically, this meant I searched the 1910 Soundex for males who, in 1900, had been between the ages of six and sixty. Those with common surnames were excluded. Ultimately, I located 62 such individuals in the Soundex and traced them to the census schedules of 1910.

One shortcoming of this analysis was the methodological exclusion of female outmigrants. During the period under consideration, female millhands comprised nearly half of the southern textile work force, so obviously I needed to know something about their migration experiences if I were to gain a proper perspective on gender and community dynamics. But if locating male outmigrants is prob-lematic, tracing women from the 1900 to the 1910 census through the Soundex indexes is doubly difficult. The manner in which both the census manuscripts and Soundex indexes are structured—with most individuals listed under the names of household heads (usually men)—makes the odds very slim for tracing women independently of their families.

In trying to trace a cohort of females listed in 1900 as heads of households, I found none listed as such through the Soundex for 1910. Thereafter, I attempted to circumvent this problem by turning the patriarchal structure of the census to my advantage. Specifically, I tried to trace a group of female outmigrants indirectly, through their spouses. First, I compiled a list of all single female outmigrants from Crown Mill. Next, I narrowed this list to include only those who got married in Whitfield County between 1900 and 1910, as revealed in the county marriage records. Then, using the Soundex indexes for Georgia, Tennessee, and Alabama, I traced *their spouses* to the 1910 census. This analysis is also based on the assumption—a justifiable one, I think—that young women who married had a choice in whom they wedded and that they made that choice with some kind of future in mind. This method is not without its problems, though, especially in its bias toward women who married. Moreover, the results of the trace, numerically, were disappointing: of the seventy couples that were "traceable," I only found seventeen. But the effort enriched my understanding of the overall migration process (see chapter 5) and raised interesting questions regarding the place of young adult women in mill-village society.

Finally, I sought to determine the point of origin of workers who moved to Crown sometime between 1900 and 1910. As I had with the outmigrants, I obtained the original cohort of inmigrants by comparing the names of cotton-mill families listed in the Whitfield County manuscript censuses for 1900 and 1910 and then, again, reducing the original cohort. Only those males who were at least twenty-six years old in 1910—those who might have been household heads in 1900—seemed to be feasible candidates for tracing backward to the 1900 census. I also attempted to trace several widows from 1910 to 1900, but with no success. The limitations of census data for an analysis of individual migration are not easily overcome, even with the Soundex indexes. But these sources can greatly enhance our understanding of how ordinary Americans responded to and helped shape the labor market in the early twentieth century.

MULTIPLE REGRESSION AND LOGIT ANALYSIS

Multiple regression analysis is one of the most useful tools historians have at their disposal. It offers a means of resolving interpretive dilemmas that simple statistics (averages, ratios, percentages) cannot always settle. At the same time, it also raises new questions and leads our research in new directions. Many economists use regression to predict future trends, but historians use it to explain relationships that existed in the past. Although an increasing number of historians are now utilizing regression in their work, those who study American workers, with few exceptions, generally have not employed multivariate statistical methods, and some may be unfamiliar with their use. A brief, nontechnical discussion of regression is therefore in order here. For beginners to the subject, I strongly recommend Haskins and Jeffrey, *Understanding Quantitative History*, a lucid, user-friendly text. On a slightly more technical level, Lewis-Beck, *Applied Regression: An Introduction*, is very helpful.

Running a regression, like calculating an average or figuring a ratio, involves a mathematical procedure; most of us, however, need a computer to calculate multiple regression equations. For any given population, multiple regression measures how strongly a single *dependent* variable (e.g., *income*) is associated with a number of *independent* variables (e.g., *age, gender, race, level of education*). The outcome of the regression is reflected in a set of *coefficients*. (The coefficients are sometimes called *b* scores, because they function as the algebraic *b* in the regression equation.) Each independent variable receives a coefficient, and those coefficients are the central component of any multiple regression table. A coefficient measures two fundamental characteristics of the relationship between the dependent variable and the independent variable(s). First, it measures the strength of association— how strongly related an independent variable (e.g., *age*) is to the dependent variable (*income*). This measure of strength takes into consideration the extent to which all the other independent variables (*gender, race, level of education*) are also related to income. This statistical feat allows us to disentangle the various personal factors that were related to income in the population under study. In a standard "ordinary least squares" regression, the coefficient is equal to the amount of change that takes place, on average, in the dependent variable each time an independent variable is increased by one unit of measure. Coefficients also indicate the *direction* (negative or positive) of the observed relationship. Suppose, for example, income was positively related to education. The two variables would move in the same direction: the higher the level of education, the higher the income; the less education, the lower the income. If the relationship is negative, the variables will move in opposite directions (e.g., professorial satisfaction declines as committee assignments increase, and vice versa).

In a regression analysis, the coefficients are also tested for statistical significance. To greatly oversimplify, significance tests determine whether the observed relationship is an accurate reflection of reality. To be trustworthy, a coefficient must meet a minimum standard of reliability, traditionally the .05 level. For a coefficient to be significant at the .05 level means there is less than a 5 percent chance the coefficient is a statistical fluke; if the equation were run with one hundred different samples from the same population, we would be sure to get similar results at least ninety-five times. Variables whose coefficients do not achieve this level of reliability (or some other level set by the researcher) are deemed statistically insignificant. Such variables do not help explain the dependent variable.[4]

The most basic and frequently used form of regression is *ordinary least squares* regression, or OLS (the term *least squares* refers to the way in which the coefficients are estimated). When political historians analyze voting behavior by means of *ecological regression*, they are actually using OLS regression models. (The term *ecological* stems from the type of data and inference used, not from the type of regression.) I used an OLS regression model in chapter 5 to analyze "who earned what" at Crown Mill—what economists call a "wage-earnings functions" analysis. This was an effort to use individual data to help illuminate group behavior. As the patterns of outmigration became clearer, and as the trend toward an older, male-dominated work force became more evident, I sought to use data on individual earnings to better understand the dynamics of the southern textile labor market. My work with this data did not take place in an intellectual vacuum. Gavin Wright's economic history of the South helped to sharpen my understanding of the regional labor market and how it related to wages. Economic historians William H. Phillips and Cathy L. McHugh used multiple regression to explore wage determination among Dixie's mill workers.[5] My preliminary analyses of the Crown Mill wage data indicated that a variety of factors might help explain wages: age, gender, place within the household, experience, and literacy, among others. OLS regression offered a powerful means of determining which of these personal characteristics were associated with the millhands' earning power.

For my regression, the unit of analysis was each individual worker at the mill, but I limited my data in two ways. First, I included only full-time workers, defined as those who were listed in four consecutive biweekly payrolls. Crown had a group of "spare-hand" employees who lived with families near the mill and worked sporadically, but I wanted my regression to focus on the wages of "normal" full-time workers. Second, I excluded departmental supervisors from the data. Their wages were much higher than even the best-paid nonsupervisory employees, and my goal was to explain wage determination for ordinary rank-and-file millhands.

Most of the independent variables in my equation are so-called *dummy* variables. With a dummy variable, each case falls into one of two possible categories, represented numerically in the data by 1 or 0. The designations 1 and 0 do not represent values on an interval scale. No judgment of higher or lower, of superiority or inferiority, is implied. The numbers are simply tags that identify each case for the computer and tell it to which category the case should be assigned. Dummy variables, then, are always dichotomous (yes/no) propositions. To take three examples from table 5.7, each worker from Crown was labeled as being either male or female, literate or illiterate, born in Georgia or not born in Georgia. There is no rule as to which characteristic should receive the label 1 or 0; flipping a coin is as good a way as any to decide. Statistically speaking, it does not matter, but the coefficient is always interpreted in terms of the variable designated 1. For my regression, I gave *literacy* a 1; because the coefficient for *literacy* in table 5.7 is positive, we therefore know that literate workers commanded greater earning power. We would have come to the same conclusion had *illiteracy* been given a 1, because the relationship would then have been negative. Dummy variables are extremely useful because historians are often limited to dichotomous independent variables with which to address specific issues.

The basic results of my regression model are discussed in chapter 5, but some additional comments are worth making here. I did not think it unusual for age and gender to lose some of their explanatory power when other variables were added to the equation in model *ii*, but it was somewhat surprising that *both* variables lost their statistical significance in model *ii*. Interesting relationships appeared, the most enlightening of which was that between married household heads and earnings. The relationship in both years was positive and significant. We can be sure, then, that married household heads commanded greater earnings than non-household heads, regardless of age and gender. Naturally, most household heads were older males, so this result might be expected, but it does help clarify which older males were gaining an earnings advantage. Moreover, few millhands in 1900 were actually household heads; this finding therefore suggested an emerging managerial strategy to create a successful family labor system at Crown, a strategy that became more apparent as the decade progressed and the mill employed a larger number of household heads, especially males.

For newcomers to regression, a few more words of explanation might prove helpful. The strength of the coefficients in any regression run can only be directly compared if they operate on the same scale (e.g., years). If coefficients are on different scales (dollars, years, dummy variable) one must "standardize" the coefficients into numbers called *Betas* in order to make direct comparisons of strength (the computer easily transforms *b* scores into Betas), but even then such comparisons must be made with caution. Moreover, although I ran the 1912 data exactly as I had the 1900 data, using the same two models, it is not accurate to make comparisons between the coefficients for 1900 and 1912. Coefficients computed from distinctly different data sets—many different individuals and two different earnings scales—are not directly comparable. Arguably, though, one can create Betas and suggest comparisons, on average, across data sets, as I do in chapter 5, note 33. Unlike economists and policymakers, historians almost never use coefficients to calculate future trends. Often we are most interested in identifying those independent variables that were significantly related to our dependent variable, in which case significance scores are more important to us than the comparative strengths of the coefficients.

The dependent variable in my wage-earnings functions analyses is not simply earnings but a "log" of earnings. If the values of the dependent variable are tightly distributed, it is common to spread the distribution via a logarithmic transformation of that variable. Logging a variable in this way (the computer does it) helps enhance the clarity of the coefficients.

Finally, multiple regression analyses always include an R^2 statistic, technically called the "coefficient of multiple determination." The R^2 is calculated (by the computer) as being the sum of squared deviations explained by the regression, divided by the sum of squared deviations unexplained by the regression. It is always a number between 0 and 1. It indicates the extent to which all of the independent variables included in a regression model collectively "explain" the dependent variable. The higher the score, the better the model "fits" reality. Model 1900 *ii* earned an R^2 of .39. It may therefore be said that the model has explained 39 percent of the observed variance in the dependent variable. This lies within the very broad middle range of "acceptable" scores. Extremely low scores (e.g., .07) warn us that we have not put any meaningful variables in the equation; we would need to find other potential variables and see if they boost the score appreciably. But adding a new variable to the equation will always increase the R^2, and it is never permissible or necessary to add variables simply for that purpose. There is little agreement on what an adequate R^2 is. Regressions that use individuals as their unit of analysis (rather than aggregate data from countries, states, or regions) always tend to have a low R^2. Extremely high R^2 scores (e.g., .90) are very unlikely and may indicate a "multicollinearity" problem. Multicollinearity means that two or more of one's independent variables are strongly associated with one another, a problem that must be tested for and avoided in all regression analyses.

OLS regression as explained above, though by far the most flexible and powerful statistical tool historians have at their disposal, is not the only available method of regression analysis, nor is it always the most appropriate. One alternative form of regression is logit analysis. Statisticians developed logit in order to overcome an important limitation of OLS, namely, that it gives inaccurate coefficients if a dichotomous variable is used as the dependent variable. Sometimes, though, using a dichotomous (or dummy, or *discrete*) dependent variable is unavoidable. This was unexpectedly the case when I analyzed the Crown Mill strike of 1939, which is why I turned to logit.[6]

In chapter 10, I wanted to know which workers supported the strike and which workers broke it, or, more precisely, to determine what personal traits characterized diehard strikers as opposed to strikebreakers. From the point of view of multivariate statistical strategies, the problem was very similar to the wage-earnings functions analysis discussed above. Initially, I chose as my dependent variable *strike support*, which was defined as the number of days each worker remained on strike between mid-July and the end of September. This ten-week interval was the critical period when the millhands split over the union and the strike. A logical approach was to gather appropriate independent variables (about worker characteristics) and then to regress them against *strike support* in an OLS regression.

But I did not run an OLS regression, because the distribution of the dependent variable was decidedly polarized. Before analyzing the data, I had assumed that workers probably trickled back to the mill sporadically during the strike, in which case the dependent variable *strike support* would be a numeric variable with an interval scale similar to the dependent variable *earnings*. Dependent variables of this sort are standard in OLS equations. When I looked at the distribution of strike support, though, I found that the vast majority of workers fell into two groups: those who returned to work as soon as they could, and those who stayed out until the bitter end. As figure 10.1 revealed, nearly all strikebreakers returned to work as early as possible in July, and nearly all those who remained out after that time stayed out until the strike was settled. Few workers returned to work in the middle of the critical period. In effect, then, my interval-level dependent variable had the statistical qualities of a dichotomous dummy variable. OLS accepts dummy variables as independent variables, but using a dummy as a dependent variable will yield unreliable results.[7]

Logit gladly accepts dichotomous dependent variables. Only a decade ago, logit analysis was inaccessible to social scientists who could not write their own computer programs, but today most advanced statistical software packages offer logit capabilities. The estimated coefficients of a logit look like the regression coefficients in an OLS model. Technically, the logit coefficient is not the same as a b score, and the two types of coefficients cannot be directly compared. But as with OLS, coefficients for logit indicate the strength and direction of the observed relationship. And logit uses the same significance tests as OLS.

In analyzing the Crown Mill strike of 1939, I relied primarily on the payroll book for that year. By the late thirties, the process for hiring workers and keeping them on the payroll was far more sophisticated and bureaucratized than it was in earlier decades, especially before World War I. In 1939 each worker was assigned a particular number on the payroll page, and neither that number nor the person's name were omitted from the roll even if that person did not work during a payroll period. (If the worker quit or was fired, he or she was, of course, removed; but normal absences did not alter a person's place in the books.) The hours worked by each individual, even if none, were recorded every day. So for the duration of the Crown Mill strike of 1939, we have an exact record of how many days each individual worker remained on strike. Workers who crossed the picket lines and returned to the job had their hours duly recorded. The result is a singularly exceptional data set on individual strike behavior. In this case, modernization worked to the advantage of the historian.

The 1939 data is not without limitations, however. The payroll books list only the name and wages of each worker; other information on those millhands was scarce. There are no available census schedules to link with the payroll in 1939 (the 1940 manuscript census schedules will be opened to the public in the year 2012). City directories can sometimes offer useful information in the absence of census manuscripts, but the only surviving directory published around the time of the strike is the city directory for 1936, which offers only limited and unreliable data on mill-village residency and home ownership in 1939. Nonetheless, some important information on the workers' personal characteristics is available in scattered sources. Crown's 1927 payrolls provide a useful though somewhat crude index for classifying workers as "old-timers" or "newcomers." Federal income tax records retained by the company list each millhand's gross earnings for the fiscal quarter preceding the strike, thereby giving an accurate reading of "normal" earnings before the strike. Information on gender could often be gleaned from the worker's name or from other records. So, although the complete data set for 1939 was not as rich as I had hoped, it nonetheless included information on several important individual characteristics.

In the logit model presented in table 10.2, the dependent variable is not my initial variable for *strike support*. Instead, I used the values in that peculiarly distributed interval variable to create a proper dummy variable, *diehard*, which I then used as the dependent variable in the logit. The strike itself lasted eighty-nine work days. The critical period began on day 30, when the picket lines began to crack, and lasted sixty more work days until the strike ended. During that time, workers had to choose whether to stay out or return to work. *Diehard* equaled 1 for workers who remained on strike at least fifty-five of the sixty days that comprised the critical period; it was 0 for all others. Using fifty-five as a cutoff point was an arbitrary decision, but it was an obvious one to make. After the initial onslaught of strikebreakers returned to the mill, very few workers crossed the lines until day 84 of the strike (day 55 of the critical period), after which the picket lines fell apart quickly (see table A.3). Supervisors, who also were listed in the payroll book, were excluded from the analysis; because they were technically part of the "management," they were ineligible for union membership, and I was not using the logit to understand their behavior. I also excluded those for whom I had no data on "normal earnings." After these exclusions, 627 millhands were still left in the data set, a large number for any individual-level multivariate analysis. I also logged the variable *earnings* to improve the distribution. Independent variables may be logged, just as I logged the dependent variable in the wage-earnings functions analysis.

The dummy variables *worker in Old Mill* and *worker in Boylston* deserve further discussion. Some readers may notice that although there were three plants at Crown, only two dummy variables represent them in the logit table. There is no dummy variable for the New Mill (Mill No. 2). The secret to using dummy variables in regression analyses is to include one less dummy than there are possible categories. In most cases, where only two possibilities exist (0 and 1), only one dummy variable is entered into the equation. To represent three plants, I needed two dummies. The variable *Old Mill* codes every worker in that mill as 1, and everyone else as 0. *Boylston* codes every worker there as 1, and everyone else as 0. Workers in the New Mill had to be left out of the equation. If dummy variables for every category are included in the model, logit cannot calculate accurate coefficients. Workers from the New Mill—or whatever category is left out of the equation—are represented implicitly in the *constant*, and the coefficients for the dummies put into the model may be evaluated in relation to the *constant*. Both the variables *Old Mill* and *Boylston* were strongly related to *diehard*, but with a difference. Whereas *Old Mill* was positively related, *Boylston* was negatively related. Both coefficients were statistically significant. In both mills, there were diehard strikers and strikebreakers. But taken as a whole, Boylston's workers were much more likely to be strikebreakers than were the workers at the Old Mill. We can also infer from the *constant* that workers at Boylston were more likely to be strikebreakers than those at the New Mill.

Some readers may wish I had been able to determine more precisely why workers at the Old Mill were such diehard strikers and why millhands at Boylston were such eager strikebreakers. Of course, I share that wish. But a more thorough interpretation was not possible given the available information—or, more accurately, the lack thereof. Aside from some limited information on the stretchouts of the early 1930s and some documents concerning the wildcat strikes of the 1960s, the surviving Crown Mill records offered very limited insights into the actual operation of the mills. The workers I interviewed for this book did not indicate that the Old Mill was a worse place to work or a hotbed of unionism; nor did they give any indication that strike support was different at any of the three plants. Some records of Local 185 have survived, but there is almost nothing in them regarding the 1939 strike and nothing whatever on working conditions during the 1930s. So, in the end, one of the newest historical techniques brought me back to one of the profession's oldest problems—the lack of adequate information on issues of burning importance.

Such limitations do not strike me as cause for anguish. Historians who have not done any quantification may suppose that doing historical statistics involves plugging numbers into computers that spit out answers. But part of the beauty of quantitative analysis is that it almost always raises more questions than it answers. It has a way of leading our investigations in new and unanticipated directions. Quantification is not an effort to shut the book on historical issues. It is instead an ongoing process of discovery. Perhaps it is not too much to hope that the manner in which I used quantitative methods in *Creating the New South* will encourage others to join that process.

NOTES

Ann. Rpt.	Annual Reports of Crown Cotton Mills, CGA
BCPR	Boylston-Crown Cotton Mills Payroll Records, CGA
BDM	Crown Cotton Mills Board of Directors Minutes, Books 1 (1884–1919), 2 (1920–49), 3 (1950–63), and 4 (1964–70), CGA
Boyd v. *Crown*	*O. L. Boyd et al.* v. *Ben T. Huiet and Crown Cotton Mills*, Whitfield County Superior Court, case no. 8, July Term, 1940, Whitfield County Courthouse, Dalton, Ga.
CGA	Crown Gardens and Archives, Dalton, Ga.
CMHD	National Register of Historic Places, "Inventory and Nomination Form for the Crown Mill Historic District," CGA (typescript)
CPR	Crown Cotton Mills Payroll Records, CGA
EBM	Executive Board Meeting Minutes Book, 1946–53, TWUA Local 185 Records, SLA
GDAH	Georgia Department of Archives and History, Atlanta, Ga.
GM	Minutes of General Membership Meetings, June 1949–June 1953, TWUA Local 185 Records, SLA
History	Whitfield County History Commission, *Official History of Whitfield*
MDB	Miscellaneous Documents Box, CGA
Report	U.S. Bureau of the Census, *Tenth Census, 1880*, vol. 6, pt. 2, *Report on Cotton Production*
SHSW	State Historical Society of Wisconsin, Madison, Wis.
SLA	Southern Labor Archives, Atlanta, Ga.
SP	After Strike Papers File, CGA
TWUA	Textile Workers Union of America
UWS	Union–Work Stoppages–Strike File, CGA

INTRODUCTION

1. Older historical studies—published in the half-century before 1970—that deal with textile workers in the South include Mitchell, *Rise of Cotton Mills*; Evans, "Organized Labor Movement in Georgia"; Mitchell and Mitchell, *Industrial Revolution in the South*; Mitchell, *Textile Unionism and the South*; Tippett, *When Southern Labor Stirs*; Lahne, *Cotton Mill Worker*; and Marshall, *Labor in the South*. Often, these early historians relied on the work of sociologists and social workers, especially Potwin, *Cotton Mill People*; Herring, *Welfare Work in Mill Villages* and *Passing of the Mill Village*; Pope, *Millhands and Preachers*; Moreland, *Millways of Kent*.

During the 1970s, works about southern workers multiplied with Fink and Reed, *Essays in Southern Labor History*; Eller, *Miners, Millhands, and Mountaineers*; Flynt, *Dixie's Forgotten People*; McLaurin, *Knights of Labor*; Reed, Hough, and Fink, *Southern Workers*; Taft,

Organizing Dixie; and, specifically on textiles, McLaurin, *Paternalism and Protest*; Newman, "Work and Community Life"; Terrill, "Eager Hands"; Wright, "Cheap Labor and Southern Textiles before 1880."

2. In the 1980s, books on southern textiles and cotton-mill workers began to pour forth, including Billings, *Planters and the Making of a "New South"*; Byerly, *Hard Times Cotton Mill Girls*; Carlton, *Mill and Town*; Griffith, *Crisis of American Labor*; Hall et al., *Like a Family*; Hodges, *New Deal Labor Policy*; Janiewski, *Sisterhood Denied*; Leiter et al., *Hanging by a Thread*; McHugh, *Mill Family*; Newby, *Plain Folk*; Tullos, *Habits of Industry*. Articles and theses during the same period include Beatty, "Textile Labor"; DeNatale, "Bynum"; Frederickson, "Four Decades of Change"; Freeze, "Model Mill Men"; Hall, "Disorderly Women"; Irons, "Testing the New Deal"; Perry, "Middle-Class Townsmen"; Selby, " 'Better to Starve in the Shade' " and "Industrial Growth and Worker Protest"; Shirley, "From Congregation Town to Industrial City" and "Yeoman Culture and Millworker Protest"; Terrill, "Murder in Graniteville"; and Wright, "Cheap Labor and Southern Textiles, 1880–1930."

3. Hall et al., *Like a Family*; Newby, *Plain Folk*; and Tullos, *Habits of Industry*.

4. The exception has been economic historians interested in labor, notably Carlton, *Mill and Town*; McHugh, *Mill Family*; Phillips, "Labor Market" and "Southern Textile Mill Villages"; and Wright, *Old South, New South*.

5. See, in particular, Cash, *Mind of the South*; Billings, *Planters and the Making of a "New South"*; and, for a parallel but slightly different interpretation, Cobb, *Selling of the South*. This view stems from an influential body of literature that stresses "planter hegemony" from the Old South to the New, esp. in Moore, *Social Origins of Dictatorship and Democracy*, and Wiener, *Social Origins of the New South*. On Georgia, see Bartley, *Creation of Modern Georgia*; Wynne, *Continuity of Cotton*.

6. Woodward, *Origins of the New South*. On textiles, see Carlton, *Mill and Town*; Hall et al., *Like a Family*. For a broader context, see Doyle, *Nashville in the New South* and *New Men, New Cities, New South*; Eller, *Miners, Millhands, and Mountaineers*; Ford, "Rednecks and Merchants"; Waller, *Feud*; Wright, *Old South, New South*; Wallenstein, *From Slave South to New South*.

7. Mitchell, *Rise of Cotton Mills* and *William Gregg*. An implicit acceptance of this view recently reappeared in Andrews, *Men and the Mills*.

8. Melton McLaurin (*Paternalism and Protest*), David Carlton (*Mill and Town*), and I. A. Newby (*Plain Folk*) present interpretations along this line, but their arguments are more complex than this condensed version suggests. Their reasoning stems from a long-standing view that Dixie's poor white farmers were too individualistic to organize along economic class lines (see, e.g., Fite, *Cotton Fields No More*, p. 54; Range, *Century of Georgia Agriculture*, p. 149).

9. The most compelling version of this argument is offered in Hall et al., *Like a Family*. The notion that preindustrial rural Americans adhered to informal collectivist norms is put forth in much of the new rural history of both North and South. See, e.g., Eller, "Search for Community"; Faragher, *Sugar Creek*; Hahn, *Roots of Southern Populism*; Hahn and Prude, *Countryside*; Henretta, "Families and Farms"; Watson, "Conflict and Collaboration"; and Waller, *Feud*.

10. Unlike some historians, I see the difference between "company paternalism" and "welfare capitalism" as a matter of semantics, not substance; throughout the book I use the terms *company paternalism, corporate paternalism, industrial paternalism*, and *welfare capitalism* synonymously to mean institutionalized company policies intended to extend non-

wage benefits to workers, to create an identifiable corporate culture, or to regulate the living environment of the workers. I do not intend these expressions to mean notions of patriarchy, feelings of benevolence, or a highly personal style of management. Manifestations of patriarchy, noblesse oblige, and personalism were not so much the essence of paternalism as they were patterns of behavior that operated within and further complicated the system of paternalism.

11. See Newby, *Plain Folk*; Tullos, *Habits of Industry*.

12. Two examples of the master-slave model, both sensitive to the workers' plight, are Billings, *Planters and the Making of a "New South,"* and McLaurin, *Paternalism and Protest*. Alternative cultural explanations take several forms: Allen Tullos (*Habits of Industry*) and Gary Freeze ("Poor Girls Who Might Otherwise Be Wretched," in Leiter et al., *Hanging by a Thread*, chap. 2) attribute mill-village paternalism to upcountry traditions of Protestantism and patriarchy; Broadus Mitchell's *William Gregg* is an older study that finds the source of paternalism in southern (not necessarily planter) noblesse oblige; and I. A. Newby (*Plain Folk*) finds the roots of paternalism in traditional hierarchical socioeconomic relationships between rich and poor, which presumably transcended place and time.

13. On industrial paternalism and welfare capitalism in general, see Brandes, *American Welfare Capitalism*; Scranton, "Varieties of Paternalism." On particular industrial communities outside of the South in which company paternalism played an important role, see Dublin, *Women at Work*; Prude, *Coming of Industrial Order*; Wallace, *Rockdale*; Walkowitz, *Worker City, Company Town*; Lindsey, *Pullman Strike*; Hareven, *Family Time and Industrial Time*; Ozanne, *Century of Labor-Management Relations*; Cornford, *Workers and Dissent*; and Zahavi, *Workers, Managers, and Welfare Capitalism*. On industrial paternalism in Great Britain and Europe, see Joyce, *Work, Society, and Politics*; Accampo, *Industrialization*.

14. For the debate, see Brody, "Labor and the Great Depression," p. 242; Brandes, *American Welfare Capitalism*, chap. 14; and Zahavi, *Workers, Managers, and Welfare Capitalism*, pp. 102–4.

15. Zahavi, "Negotiated Loyalty" and *Workers, Managers, and Welfare Capitalism*.

16. This pattern is beginning to change, as exemplified in recent works such as Griffith, *Crisis of American Labor*; Hodges, "J. P. Stevens and the Union"; Conway, *Rise Gonna Rise*; and various chapters in Byerly, *Hard Times Cotton Mill Girls*; Tullos, *Habits of Industry*; and Leiter et al., *Hanging by a Thread*.

17. See Korstad and Lichtenstein, "Opportunities Found and Lost"; and Norrell, "Labor at the Ballot Box."

18. Roland, *Improbable Era*, pp. 17–18; Goldfield, *Promised Land*, p. 146; Botsch, *We Shall Not Overcome*; Griffith, *Crisis of American Labor* (which offers an instructive investigation of labor organizers themselves); and Hodges, *New Deal Labor Policy*, chap. 12 (which offers a concise review of the literature).

19. Recent studies on nontextile workers include Arnesen, *Waterfront Workers*; Rachleff, *Black Labor in Richmond*; Janiewski, *Sisterhood Denied*; Kelley, *Hammer and Hoe*; Korstad, "Daybreak of Freedom"; McKiven, "Class, Race, and Community"; Norrell, "Caste in Steel"; Shifflett, *Coal Towns*; Lewis, *Black Coal Miners*.

20. A pathbreaking study on blacks and race relations in the South Carolina upcountry is Burton, *In My Father's House*; Trotter, *Black Milwaukee*, demonstrates that studies of small black communities can be singularly instructive. On blacks in southern textiles, see Stokes, "Black and White Labor"; Frederickson, "Four Decades of Change"; Hall et al., *Like a Family*; and selections in Byerly, *Hard Times Cotton Mill Girls*.

BEGINNINGS

1. For information on the organizational meeting of 6 February 1884, early deliberations among the board of directors, and the process of incorporation, see BDM, Book 1, pp. 1–14 (quote on p. 11). At the organizational meeting, the fifteen men present decided to call their new enterprise "The Dalton Cotton Mills" (ibid., p. 3), but when the directors petitioned for a charter of incorporation on 20 February, they had changed the name, without explanation, to the Crown Cotton Mills.

2. John Hamilton Family File, CGA; *History*, chap. 3.

3. BDM, Book 1, quote on p. 29.

4. *Dalton Argus*, 24 Jan. 1885.

5. The population figure for 1885 is an estimate based on the federal census returns for 1880 and 1890. See table A.1 for population data for Dalton and Whitfield County.

6. *Dalton Citizen*, 23 Aug. 1934.

CHAPTER 1

1. *Manufacturers' Record*, 10 Apr. 1886, p. 293; *Atlanta Constitution*, 8 Apr. 1887.

2. The classic boosteristic history is Mitchell, *Rise of Cotton Mills*, which was published over seventy years ago; a recent and similarly upbeat effort is Andrews, *Men and the Mills*. Critics who contributed to the "industrial plantation" school include Frank Tannenbaum, "South Buries Its Anglo-Saxons" (which followed Mitchell's work by only two years); W. J. Cash, *Mind of the South*; and, more recently, Dwight B. Billings, Jr., *Planters and the Making of a "New South"*; Melton McLaurin, *Paternalism and Protest*; and Dale Newman, "Work and Community Life." Billings's work is part of a larger school of thought that stresses the continuity of planter control from the Old South to the New. See Moore, *Social Origins of Dictatorship*; Wiener, *Social Origins of the New South*; Bartley, *Creation of Modern Georgia*; Wynne, *Continuity of Cotton*; and, for an augmented version of the continuity school, Cobb, *Selling of the South*.

3. David L. Carlton (*Mill and Town*) contends that the rise of the mills was part of a larger regional transformation in the southern economy, an argument implicit in Hall et al., *Like a Family*; see also Wright, *Old South, New South*, chap. 5. None of these scholars, in arguing that the New South economy was in fact "new," accept the boosters' view of the happy, uplifted worker.

4. *History*, pp. viii, 36–39, 51.

5. For a good geographical description of north Georgia, see *Report*, pp. 285–90, 328; quote on p. 285.

6. Population figures are calculated from U.S. Bureau of the Census, *Compendium of the Tenth Census*, pt. 1, pp. 342–43. On the southern white yeomanry, see the old standard, Owsley, *Plain Folk of the Old South*; see also recent works by Lacy K. Ford (*Origins of Southern Radicalism*), Steven Hahn (*Roots of Southern Populism*), and Robert Kenzer (*Kinship and Neighborhood*).

7. *History*, pp. 44–45.

8. Sartain, *History of Walker County*, pp. 45–46, provides a list of the earliest settlers of that county (ca. 1835–1850). Within each militia district, the number of common surnames among the pioneers is striking. *History*, pp. 175–84, lists the names of all household heads in Murray County in 1850, and here again the many common surnames in close proximity suggest patterns of kin migration and settlement. Hahn (*Roots of Southern Populism*, pp. 52–

54) points to similar evidence; also see Kenzer, *Kinship and Neighborhood*. Kinship settlements in pioneer regions were not a peculiarly southern phenomenon. See Raitz and Ulack, *Appalachia*, pp. 115–22; Warren, *Community in America*, pp. 22–25; and Faragher, *Sugar Creek*.

9. Weiman, "Petty Commodity Production," pp. 83–84, 254–77, and "Economic Emancipation," pp. 76–78; Hahn, *Roots of Southern Populism*, pp. 47–49. Hahn considers the values and economic traditions of the plain folk a major barrier to market integration, while Weiman essentially sees upcountry farmers as nascent commercial farmers waiting for the advent of market opportunities. For the larger debate on the impact of the market economy on rural life, North and South, see Hahn and Prude, *Countryside*. On roads and trade connections in north Georgia before the railroad, see Ward, *Annals of Upper Georgia*, pp. 66, 79, 636 (quote on p. 1); Sartain, *History of Walker County*, pp. 43, 193, 216; and Adams and Coleman, *Atlas of American History*, p. 108. Edward L. Ayers (*Vengeance and Justice*, p. 108) provides a description of Cross Plains. General William T. Sherman paused during his Atlanta campaign in 1864 to complain that the roads in northwest Georgia "were only such as the country afforded, mere rough wagon ways" (Sherman, *Memoirs*, p. 35).

10. The best analysis of the W&A and its larger place in state politics is Wallenstein, *From Slave South to New South*. See also Phillips, *History of Transportation*, chap. 7; and Stone, "Dalton's Railroads."

11. *History*, pp. 39–40, 46–48, 50–51; White, *Statistics of the State of Georgia*, p. 440.

12. Wallenstein, *From Slave South to New South*, pt. 1 passim (quote on p. 37); *History*, pp. 50–51; *Dalton Argus*, 15 Aug. 1885; Hilliard, *Atlas*, pp. 57–63; Ward, *Annals of Upper Georgia*, pp. 15, 118–21; Hahn, *Roots of Southern Populism*, pp. 29–33, 46–47; Weiman, "Petty Commodity Production," pp. 6, 213–16, and "Economic Emancipation," p. 76; Phillips, *History of Transportation*, pp. 303–34, esp. 318, 327–29. The timing of the north Georgia wheat boom is difficult to pinpoint because the agricultural census figures for 1850 reflect an off year for wheat production, making it appear, correctly or not, that valley farmers did not shift immediately to commercial wheat production after the railroad came through in the late 1840s. For the record, census figures indicate that Whitfield County wheat production increased 242 percent between 1850 and 1860; Murray County production rose by 302 percent during the same period.

13. Duff Green and Edward White secured a charter for the Dalton and Gadsden Railroad (D&G) in 1854, and White tried to develop another line to North Carolina. See Green, "Duff Green," pp. 33–34; Green's obituary in *Atlanta Constitution*, 11 June 1875; *History*, p. 48; Phillips, *History of Transportation*, pp. 374–75; Stone, "Dalton's Railroads," p. 12. But the best efforts of these antebellum boosters failed to alter the situation. The D&G line was never built, and the North Carolina deal withered. Apparently, not all Daltonians were as growth-minded as White and Green; one observer recalled that many residents greeted the announcement of the proposed D&G railroad with "the hooting and mocking of an incredulous people" (*Dalton Argus*, 15 Aug. 1885). See also "Colonel Wrench Writes Some History," *Whitfield-Murray Historical Society Journal* 2 (Mar. 1986): 6. In 1860, statistics on manufactures in Floyd County, whose county seat was the growing city of Rome, were generally similar to those for Dalton, though somewhat larger. There was one substantial antebellum textile mill in northwest Georgia, the Trion Factory in Chattooga County, which in 1860 was capitalized at $80,000. It employed twenty men and fifty women. Other counties in northwest Georgia had very little manufacturing industry, large or small (U.S. Bureau of the Census, *Manufactures of the United States [1860]*, pp. 61–81).

14. Don Doyle (*New Men, New Cities, New South*, pp. 1–7) discusses antebellum restric-

tions on urban development; for a discussion of recent econometric analyses, see Fogel, *Without Consent or Contract*, chap. 4, esp. pp. 102−11.

15. *History*, pp. 53−71; Green, "Duff Green," pp. 37−38; Range, *Century of Georgia Agriculture*, p. 61. On the war's impact on the southern economy and Dixie's entrepreneurs, see DeCredico, *Patriotism for Profit*.

16. Phillips, *History of Transportation*, pp. 331−32; Wallenstein, *Slave South to New South*, p. 193; see also *History*, chap. 3. The war years brought other problems for north Georgia farmers, especially when a severe drought and corn crop failure in 1862 necessitated that emergency provisions be shipped in from other parts of the state to prevent starvation (Range, *Century of Georgia Agriculture*, p. 47).

17. Wallenstein, *Slave South to New South*, p. 171 and chap. 16 generally. Statistics on railroad mileage were calculated from U.S. Bureau of the Census, *Preliminary Report on the Eighth Census*, p. 230, and *Tenth Census, 1880: Report on the Agencies of Transportation*, 4:506. See also Eller, *Miners, Millhands, and Mountaineers*, chap. 2.

18. Weiher, "Cotton Industry," p. 123, table 1; Weiman, "Economic Emancipation," pp. 83−87. Dalton's population actually increased 39 percent during the depression-ridden 1870s (see population figures in table A.1). And despite the depression, Duff Green, Dalton's leading antebellum booster, continued to push for railroad development until his death in 1875 (see Green, "Duff Green," p. 41; *Atlanta Constitution*, 11 June 1875). Nonetheless, Dalton had its share of economic woes during the 1870s. "Business of all kinds is at a standstill," lamented Dalton's *North Georgia Citizen* in 1874. An influx of unemployed tramps added to the general disarray. "Little beggars and big beggars, white and black, literally swarm," despaired one local editor (quotes in Ayers, *Vengeance and Justice*, pp. 168−69).

19. *Report*, p. 326 (one reporter for the census from Murray County noted in 1880 that "No cotton is planted here without fertilizers of some kind" [p. 336]). See also Bode and Ginter, *Farm Tenancy*, chap. 7, esp. p. 171. During the 1870s, American farmers boosted their use of commercial fertilizers by 135 percent. Southerners accounted for a major part of this increase. Georgians, in fact, consumed 16 percent of the national total of commercial fertilizer in 1880. National figures calculated from U.S. Bureau of the Census, *Historical Statistics*, p. 469.

20. *Report*, p. 323. See also Weiman, "Economic Emancipation," pp. 76, 78, 81 (tables 3, 4, 6), and "Petty Commodity Production," chap. 4 and p. 380 (fig. 4.1). The cotton to corn ratio in 1880 was 2.3 in Whitfield, 4.3 in Murray, and 8.0 in the valley counties combined. Higher ratios could be found in the South Carolina upcountry (see Carlton, *Mill and Town*, p. 19).

21. *Report*, p. 438. On Blue Ridge developments, see *Dalton Argus*, 18 Oct. 1884; *North Georgia Citizen*, 9 Sept. 1897; and Stanley, *Little History of Gilmer County*. Peaches ultimately failed to bring prosperity to valley farmers, because they proved difficult to grow and market. By the turn of the century, urban markets were glutted and peach prices plummeted. See Pitts, *History of Gordon County*, pp. 346−49; and Fite, *Cotton Fields No More*, pp. 13−14.

22. *Report*, pp. 335−44 (quote on 336).

23. The *Atlanta Constitution*, 9 Mar. 1887, reported that "ten thousand bales were marketed from wagons" in Dalton during the fall of 1886. One Yankee observer wrote home that local cotton sales amounted to "three quarter million dollars annually" (see letter from "Major Blake," reprinted in *Dalton Argus*, 5 Apr. 1890). On the emergence of cotton-processing cities, see Weiher, "Cotton Industry," pp. 120−40; Goldfield, *Cotton Fields and Skyscrapers*, p. 88; *Dalton Argus*, 16 Apr. 1887; Carlton, *Mill and Town*, pp. 67−68.

24. Biographical information in *Cherokee Georgia*, pp. 107–10; examples of Oglesby's supply-business advertisements in *Dalton Argus*, 3 Mar. 1884, 27 Feb. 1886.

25. David Carlton (*Mill and Town*, pp. 64–68) discusses the importance of the cotton economy in providing the capital and rationale for building cotton mills. On the natural limits of cotton-servicing towns, see Weiher, "Cotton Industry."

26. *Dalton Argus*, 29 Aug. 1891.

27. Carlton, "Revolution from Above"; Blicksilver, *Cotton Manufacturing*; Beatty, "Lowells of the South."

28. For this and the following paragraph, see Wright, *Old South, New South*, chap. 5; Hall et al., *Like a Family*, chap. 1; McKiven, "Class, Race, and Community." On the New England experience, see Prude, *Coming of Industrial Order*; Johnson, "Modernization of Mayo Greenleaf Patch"; and esp. Goldin and Sokoloff, "Women, Children, and Industrialization."

29. *Dalton Argus*, 9 Apr. 1887; U.S. Bureau of the Census, *Tenth Census, 1880: Manufactures*, 2:207–10.

30. *History*, pp. 79–80; Wilson, *Today and Tomorrow*, p. 23. In Dalton and the South, Showalter was best known for composing the popular Protestant hymn, "Leaning on the Everlasting Arms," but the success of the A. J. Showalter Company demonstrated that he was a good businessman as well.

31. BDM, Book 1; obituary of Frank Hardwick, *North Georgia Citizen*, 6 Oct. 1921; misc. documents, Hamilton Family File, CGA; *Cherokee Georgia*, pp. 109–10. On the southern capitalization of southern mills, see also Carlton, *Mill and Town*, chaps. 1, 2; and Wright, *Old South, New South*, p. 131.

32. Cotton prices and average tenancy for the South in 1880 are found in U.S. Bureau of the Census, *Twelfth Census, 1900: Agriculture*, (2): 405, 409; county tenancy rates are in *Eleventh Census, 1890: Report on Farms and Homes*, 6:292–93. For a useful map of tenancy in Georgia counties in 1880, see Bode, *Farm Tenancy*, p. 149; *Report*, pp. 438, 440.

33. *Report*, pp. 440, 439.

34. *Jasper News*, 21 Feb. 1885; U.S. Bureau of the Census, *Eleventh Census, 1890: Report on Farms and Homes*, 6:292–93 and map section following p. 32; *Report*, p. 409; Range, *Century of Georgia Agriculture*, pt. 2; Hahn, *Roots of Southern Populism*, pp. 193–203. Conflicting assessments of fence laws can be found in Hahn, *Roots of Southern Populism*, chap. 7; Flynn, *White Land, Black Labor*, chap. 5; and Kantor and Kousser, "Common Sense or Commonwealth."

35. The Soundex index provides reference numbers to the federal manuscript census population schedules, which in turn provide a wealth of information on individual households. For a fuller description of the data and methods used in this migration analysis, see appendix B.

36. The "defeated lot" view stemmed from works such as de Graffenried, "Georgia Cracker"; Mitchell, *Rise of Cotton Mills*; and Newman, "Work and Community Life." Hall et al., *Like a Family*, and Newby, *Plain Folk*, offer diametrically opposed views of mill-worker culture, but both succeed in their efforts to take plain folk culture seriously and to point out ways in which millhands maintained their dignity within a very difficult environment.

37. The data on which this paragraph is based comes from the U.S. census manuscripts, Georgia, various counties, 1880 (see appendix B).

38. On the local origins of the early mill workers, see, for example, Mitchell, *Rise of Cotton Mills*, p. 186; Woodward, *Origins of the New South*, pp. 222–23; Wright, *Old South, New South*, pp. 136–37.

39. U.S. census manuscripts, Georgia, Whitfield County, 1880, enumeration district 195, pp. 46–49.

40. Ibid., pp. 46–47; CPR, 14 Apr. 1888. On Frank Hamilton's career, see *North Georgia Citizen*, 5 Nov. 1903; Pace, "CrownAmerica," p. 6.

41. U.S. census manuscripts, Georgia, Whitfield County, 1880, enumeration district 195, pp. 48–49; CPR, 14 Apr. 1888; U.S. census manuscripts, Georgia, Whitfield County, 1910.

42. U.S. census manuscripts, Georgia, Chattooga County, 1880, enumeration district 19, p. 16; CPR, 14 Apr. 1888; U.S. census manuscripts, Georgia, Whitfield County, 1900, enumeration district 106, p. 27.

43. U.S. census manuscripts, Georgia, Chattooga County, 1880, enumeration district 19, p. 19; CPR, 14 Apr. 1888.

44. U.S. census manuscripts, Georgia, Pickens County, 1880, enumeration district 162, p. 23; CPR, 14 Apr. 1888.

45. U.S. census manuscripts, Georgia, Pickens County, 1880, enumeration district 163, p. 12; CPR, 12 July 1890.

46. Newman, "Work and Community Life," p. 436.

CHAPTER 2

1. David Carlton notes that in South Carolina, "the triumphalism of the New South evangelists notwithstanding, the momentum of manufacturing development accelerated slowly and haltingly up to the great boom of the late 1890s" (*Mill and Town*, p. 82). In *Origins of the New South*, C. Vann Woodward appropriately entitled his chapter on post-bellum economic development "The Industrial Evolution" to counter the notion (put forth by Mitchell, *Rise of Cotton Mills*) of a sudden manufacturing boom in the early 1880s (see esp. Woodward, *Origins*, pp. 112–13, 131–33).

2. A good physical description of Crown Mill in its early years can be found in the *Atlanta Constitution*, 17 Apr. 1887; and see the Sanborn Fire Insurance Company map of Crown, 1885, copy at CGA.

3. J. H. Patton's family maintained its involvement with Crown as generations of his descendants subsequently served as directors (BDM, Book 1, p. 117; Pace, "CrownAmerica," pp. 6–7). Bass's brother later became mayor of Chattanooga, which attested to his family's prominence. During his tenure as president, Bass continued to fill the pulpit occasionally, even for non-Methodist churches (see Bass Family File, CGA; *Dalton Argus*, 1 May 1886).

4. *Dalton Argus*, 7 Mar. 1885; BDM, Book 1, pp. 20–21, 29, 37–38, 41. On the sources of Crown's capital, see table 1.1. The company's fiscal year ran from 1 September to 31 August (see table A.2 for Crown's profits).

5. *Dalton Argus*, 6 Sept., 4 Apr. 1884, 16, 28 Mar. 1885; see also 16 Jan. 1886.

6. Ibid., 6 June 1885. As late as 1889, a Georgia puff sheet hailed Dalton as "the healthiest portion of the North American Continent . . . which in twenty years will be the garden spot of the United States" (*State Town and Country*, Apr. 1889, p. 8). The Biltmore story is in Eller, *Miners, Millhands, and Mountaineers*, pp. 102–3.

7. *Dalton Argus*, 6 Sept. 1884; *North Georgia Citizen*, 15 July 1886.

8. *Dalton Argus*, 12 Mar., 10 Sept. 1887 (Wrench's advertisement, emphasis his). The *Argus*'s theme of industrial expansion and the need for a "boom" was maddeningly repetitive, as almost any issue from late 1886 and 1887 will demonstrate. For a few specific issues that give a good idea of the boosteristic mood, see 23 Oct. 1886, Jan. and Feb. 1887 (all issues), 5, 19 Mar., 2, 16, 30 Apr., 16 July, 3 Sept. 1887.

9. Crown's board of directors, elected by the stockholders, was from the beginning comprised of prominent men from Dalton, with a few men from Sweetwater included. This

pattern of leadership remained essentially unchanged throughout Crown's history, although in the company's first decade the turnover among directors was higher than it would be after the mid-1890s, by which time all of the original directors had been replaced—often by family members, which lent a clear sense of continuity among the company's leadership (BDM, Book 1, esp. pp. 53–54).

10. Ibid., pp. 72–73; *Dalton Argus*, 26 Mar., 9 Apr. 1887.

11. *Dalton Argus*, 4 Dec. 1886, 2 June 1888. On the dearth of capital in Dalton, see ibid., 14 Feb. 1885, 4 Dec. 1886. On the relationship between evangelical religion and industry in the North, see Wallace, *Rockdale*; Johnson, *A Shopkeeper's Millennium*.

12. *Dalton Argus*, 12 Mar., 9 Apr. 1887.

13. My account of the event described in these two paragraphs is based on the *Atlanta Constitution*, 8 Apr. 1887, and *Dalton Argus*, 9 Apr. 1887. The final two quotes are taken from *Atlanta Constitution*, 9 Apr. 1887.

14. *Dalton Argus*, 23 Apr. 1887, 14 Jan. 1888.

15. Cotton-mill campaigns in Dalton were frequent, if unsuccessful. See *Dalton Argus*, 21 May 1887, 2 June 1888, 12 Jan. 1889, 29 Mar. 1890, 29 Aug., 10 Oct. 1891 (both urging farmers to invest), 19 Mar., 2, 3 Apr., 11 June, 5 Aug. 1897. Similar campaigns took place in the nearby town of Calhoun, the seat of Gordon County (Reeve, *Climb the Hills*, p. 83).

16. See Hardwick's obituary in *North Georgia Citizen*, 6 Oct. 1921; see also *Dalton Argus*, 22 Oct. 1892; BDM, Book 1. On Jones, see *Cherokee Georgia*, p. 110. Even a casual glance at Dalton's newspapers during the 1880s and 1890s will demonstrate Jones's dominance in local affairs. For just a few issues in the *Dalton Argus* that suggest his economic and social roles, see 24 Jan. 1885, 1 May 1886, 2 June 1888, 29 Mar. 1890, 10 Sept. 1892. Jones was also extremely active at all levels of politics and was serving as a U.S. commissioner when he died in 1903. See his obituary in *Dalton Argus*, 17 Jan. 1903.

17. The John Hamilton Family File, CGA, contains an inventory of John Hamilton's estate in 1853, George Hamilton's Civil War record, and a copy of his obituary (which can also be found in *North Georgia Citizen*, 23 Jan. 1919). See also Boggess, "Crown Mill Historic District," CGA; Wilson, *Today and Tomorrow*, p. 53; Pace, "CrownAmerica," p. 7.

18. *Cherokee Georgia*, p. 110; Harben, *Georgians*, p. 38. Wayne Mixon offers an insightful overview of Harben's work (*Southern Writers*, pp. 51–57). New South themes are particularly prominent in Harben, *Abner Daniel*.

19. Shore, *Southern Capitalists*, p. 170. The following works point toward a distinct break in the economic leadership of the South after the Civil War (although this statement risks oversimplifying some more nuanced arguments): Woodward, *Origins of the New South*; Doyle, *New Men, New Cities, New South*; Carlton, *Mill and Town*; Hall et al., *Like a Family*; Ford, "Rednecks and Merchants"; and Wallenstein, *From Slave South to New South* (which focuses on public policy making). Among those who have stressed the continuity of either planter ideology or planter-family ties in southern business circles throughout the nineteenth century and beyond are Wiener, *Social Origins of the New South* and "Class Structure and Economic Development"; Billings, *Planters and the Making of a "New South"*; Beck, "Building the New South"; and Shore, *Southern Capitalists*.

20. On a larger scale, they also believed the economic advancement of towns like Dalton would help uplift their downtrodden region. Although New South boosters bowed toward sectional reconciliation and eagerly sought northern capital, they occasionally gave vent to southern nationalism. "There is no sectional feeling from a Confederate standpoint at the South," wrote Henry Wrench in the mid-1880s, "but commercially, every man, woman and child is looking to the day when our general progress, in every detail, shall outstrip New

England and the balance of mankind, and don't you forget it" (*Dalton Argus*, 29 Nov. 1884). See also Hearden, *Independence and Empire*.

21. See Ross, *Workers on the Edge*; Doyle, *Social Order of a Frontier Community*.

22. *Dalton Argus*, 3 May 1890.

23. *North Georgia Citizen*, 25 June 1874, quoted in Ayers, *Vengeance and Justice*, p. 251; *Dalton Argus*, 2 Oct. 1886.

24. *Dalton Argus*, 1 Sept. 1888. Local boosterism was not simply the domain of business-men but included their families as well. Wives and children of manufacturers sometimes reacted strongly to the economic changes taking place around them and attempted to place their stamps upon the emerging industrial order (e.g., see Wallace, *Rockdale*). In Dalton, leading women were not actively engaged in the business end of industrial development until the early twentieth century, but during the Dalton boom of the 1880s, they sometimes expressed their own boosteristic values through poems published in the local papers. For a revealing (and rhetorically racist) booster poem by Gertrude Manly Jones, spouse of the Crown Mill president, see *Dalton Argus*, 5 Mar. 1887; another example of female booster poetry is in ibid., 3 Sept. 1887.

25. *Atlanta Constitution*, 17 Apr. 1887. My thanks to Mary DeCredico for this reference.

26. Ibid.

27. Ibid. (emphasis mine in last quote).

28. *History*, pp. 88–93. These trends in Dalton reflected the broader patterns of develop-ment in southern and American Protestantism. See Farish, *Circuit Rider Dismounts*; Spain, *At Ease in Zion*; Ahlstrom, *Religious History*, pp. 715–29, chap. 7.

29. *History*, pp. 144–45. See also the display of art work, the photograph of Gertrude Jones, and a brief history of the Lesche Club in the Lesche Memorial Room, CGA. For typical Lesche programs reported in the local press, see *Dalton Argus*, 12 Dec. 1896 and 9 Jan. 1897 (in which Gertrude Jones read a paper on "Athens in the Age of Pericles").

30. *History*, p. 80; Harben, *Georgians*, p. 79.

31. *Dalton Argus*, 19 Apr., 19 July 1884, 6 June, 1 Aug. 1885, 1 May 1886, 1 Dec. 1887, 5 Apr. 1890, 10 Sept. 1892; *History*, p. 79. See also the prohibition campaign reported in both the *Dalton Argus* and *North Georgia Citizen* in spring 1892.

32. *Dalton Argus*, 5 Apr. 1890.

33. The *North Georgia Citizen* countered that "A Tax Payer" was "a pig seller . . . studying the small interest of his own, more than the general welfare of the town" (2 June 1888; other quotes in ibid., 4 Aug. 1888).

34. *Dalton Argus*, 22 May, 16 Aug., 9 Oct., 6 Nov. 1886, 29 Jan. 1887; BDM, Book 1, pp. 76–78.

35. *Dalton Argus*, 30 Oct., 20, 27 Nov. 1886. Harben, *Georgians*, p. 37. The spring flowed from a low-lying area rather than from the side of a hill, but the rest of Harben's description was accurate. The *State Town and Country* gives a description and illustration of the water-works after completion (Apr. 1889, p. 8).

36. *Dalton Argus*, 4 Aug. 1888.

CHAPTER 3

1. *Manufacturers' Record*, 10 Apr. 1886, p. 293. Hamilton seemed to have a skewed view of who Crown's workers actually were. He suggested that most millhands were married women who had mostly "nursed their babies" before the war. In fact, very few mothers

worked regularly for Crown until World War II. The work force in 1886 was composed largely of young single women and children.

2. Kraut, *Huddled Masses*, pp. 20–21 (for statistics on immigration); Doyle, *New Men, New Cities, New South*, pp. 11–13; Wright, *Old South, New South*, p. 12; Carlton, *Mill and Town*, pp. 112–15.

3. BDM, Book 1, pp. 84–85.

4. *Dalton Argus*, 30 Jan. 1886, 3 May 1890; *Atlanta Constitution* story, reprinted in *Dalton Argus*, 3 Jan. 1891. Specifically, Jones had negotiated a contract with the Farmers' Alliance to produce cotton bagging and, owing to the unspecified labor dispute, could not fulfill the order without borrowing funds.

5. McLaurin, *Paternalism and Protest*, chap. 4, and *Knights of Labor*.

6. Woodward, *Origins of the New South*, pp. 229–34; *Dalton Argus*, 25 July, 14 Nov. 1891; *Dalton Citizen*, 16 Sept. 1897.

7. Thompson, *Cotton Field to the Cotton Mill*, p. 138.

8. Newby, *Plain Folk*, pp. 519, 524. Newby insists that the plain folk had no collective tendencies and suggests that organizers purposefully misinformed the individualistic southern workers about the meaning of unionism in order to recruit members (ibid., chaps. 18–19). Arguments for rural-bred individualism may also be found in Fite, *Cotton Fields No More*, p. 54; Range, *Century of Georgia Agriculture*, p. 149; McLaurin, *Paternalism and Protest*, pp. 53–55, 58–59, 205–6; Carlton, *Mill and Town*, p. 214; Thompson, *Cotton Field to the Cotton Mill*, pp. 180, 188–90. Arguments for rural-bred collectivism may be found in Eller, "Search for Community"; Hahn, *Roots of Southern Populism*; Hall et al., *Like a Family*; Watson, "Conflict and Collaboration." On cooperative traditions in rural areas outside the South, see Henretta, "Families and Farms"; Faragher, *Sugar Creek*.

9. Thompson, *Touching Home*, p. 143. See also Sartain, *History of Walker County*, pp. 191–92; Owsley, *Plain Folk of the Old South*, pp. 104–15; Hahn, *Roots of Southern Populism*, pp. 54–56; Weiman, "Petty Commodity Production," pp. 86–87; Ward, *Annals of Upper Georgia*, pp. 66–67; Watkins and Watkins, *Yesterday in the Hills*, pp. 95–96.

10. Ward, *Annals of Upper Georgia*, pp. 71–72, 135–36, 143; see also Rikoon, *Threshing in the Midwest*.

11. Holmes, "Moonshining and Collective Violence," pp. 591–92; Ayers, *Vengeance and Justice*, pp. 143–48, 150, 161, 164, 223; Sartain, *History of Walker County*, chap. 20; Ward, *Annals of Upper Georgia*, pp. 344–49.

12. For discussions of these developments in Georgia, see Hahn, *Roots of Southern Populism*, chaps. 4–7; Woodward, *Tom Watson*, pp. 110–15.

13. *Dalton Argus*, 3 Mar. 1884, 24 Jan., 7 Mar. 1885, 22 May 1886, 2 Apr. 1887, 21 Jan., 2 June 1888, 29 Mar., 3 May 1890, 17 Jan., 2 May 1891, 22 Oct. 1892 (taxable wealth list); *Cherokee Georgia*, pp. 105–10.

14. CPR, 7 Jan.–22 Dec. 1888. For average weeky earnings at Crown, 1890–1927, see table 5.5.

15. The average number of millhands in Georgia for the following years was: 6,349 (1880); 10,314 (1890; percent change from 1880 = 62.45); 18,348 (1900; percent change from 1890 = 77.89). Crown Mill's profitability was calculated from table A.2.

16. Holmes, "Moonshining and Collective Violence," pp. 590–91, 596–98; Ayers, *Vengeance and Justice*, pp. 223, 255–59.

17. Owl Hollow Brotherhood statements quoted in Ayers, *Vengeance and Justice*, p. 258 (quotes as I use them are not in order of original); *Dalton Argus*, 2 Mar. 1889; Reeve, *Climb*

the Hills, p. 75. Mormons received brutal treatment from mobs and newspaper editors alike (see, e.g., *Dalton Argus*, 16 Aug. 1884, 7 Mar., 24 Oct. 1885).

18. *History*, pp. 88–93; Robin Burn and Angi Buchanan, "Old Time Religion," in Thompson, *Touching Home*, pp. 146–54 (quote on p. 151); Stanley, *Rough Road*.

19. Harben, *Georgians*, pp. 79, 150–54; *History*, p. 80; *Cherokee Georgia*, pp. 105–6.

20. *Dalton Argus*, 7 Nov. 1885, 17 Sept. 1887, 2 Aug. 1890, 30 Jan. 1892.

21. Shriner, *History of Murray County*, pp. 21–23, 44 (quote on p. 23).

22. On support for lynching, see, e.g., *Dalton Argus*, 28 May 1892, 30 July 1892 (Lee McDaniel story).

23. Harper, *Development of Agriculture*, pp. 8–9; Thompson, *Touching Home*, pp. 188–99; Holmes, "Moonshining and Collective Violence," pp. 593–96; Ayers, *Vengeance and Justice*, pp. 261–63. Federal revenue districts consisted of several counties patrolled by a district officer and his agents, who were under the authority of a central chief in Atlanta (Stanley, *Rough Road*, p. 137).

24. *Dalton Argus*, 26 July 1884; Holmes, "Moonshining and Collective Violence," pp. 596–97, 601.

25. Holmes, "Moonshining and Collective Violence," p. 596; idem, "Whitecapping in Late Nineteenth Century Georgia," in Fraser and Moore, *From the Old South to the New*, pp. 123–24; Ayers, *Vengeance and Justice*, p. 23. Chapter 1 of Ayers's book offers a perceptive analysis of southern honor, which provides a useful framework for understanding the paradox of unity and division in upcountry farming settlements. Altina L. Waller's insightful reconstruction of the Hatfield-McCoy feud demonstrates that family honor was not always easily calculated. As economic connections became more complex, the meaning of "family" was sometimes redefined to coincide more with interest group affiliation rather than with blood lines (Waller, *Feud*, esp. pp. 77–85).

26. Newby, *Plain Folk*, p. 514.

27. McLaurin, *Knights of Labor*; Garlock, *Guide to the Local Assemblies*, pp. 52–59.

28. Information in this and the following paragraph taken from McMath, *Populist Vanguard*; Woodward, *Tom Watson*, chap. 10; Shaw, *Wool-Hat Boys*, chap. 2; Hahn, *Roots of Southern Populism*, pp. 271–77.

29. On populism in Georgia, see Hahn, *Roots of Southern Populism*, pp. 269–71, 276–89; Kousser, *Shaping of Southern Politics*, pp. 214–17; Shaw, *Wool-Hat Boys*; and Woodward's still remarkable *Tom Watson*. More generally, see Goodwyn, *Democratic Promise*; Palmer, "*Man Over Money.*"

30. Kousser, *Shaping of Southern Politics*, pp. 209–16; Shaw, *Wool-Hat Boys*, p. 21, chap. 2; Hahn, *Roots of Southern Populism*, pp. 226–37, 272–77. Kousser notes that "It is difficult to believe that many poor Georgians [in the early 1890s] could have paid their poll taxes, already $10–15 in arrears in many cases, or that politicians could have assumed the burden for them. Consequently, many registrars must have winked at the law" (*Shaping of Southern Politics*, p. 215, n. 48).

31. For examples of Crown Mill leaders active in Democratic politics during the 1880s, see *Dalton Argus*, 9, 16 Aug. 1884, 4 Aug. 1888. Jones is quoted in ibid., 1 Oct. 1892. Note the importance of Dalton's Democratic vote in ibid., 8 Oct. 1892 and 6 Oct. 1894.

32. *Dalton Argus*, 23 Apr. 1892; for other Populist rallies, see 13 Aug. (first page mistakenly reads 18 Aug.), 17 Sept. 1892. Election statistics in ibid., 8 Oct. 1892, 6 Oct. 1894; the wealth of Whitfield's election districts calculated from tax returns in ibid., 9 Aug. 1890; and see Goodwyn, *Democratic Promise*, p. 422. Barton Shaw offers general accounts of the two

elections in Georgia (*Wool-Hat Boys*, chaps. 4, 7); and J. Morgan Kousser calculates estimated voting patterns for the state (*Shaping of Southern Politics*, p. 215, table 7.12).

33. On the 1896 election, see Goodwyn, *Democratic Promise*, chaps. 15, 16; Woodward, *Tom Watson*, chaps. 16, 17.

34. *Dalton Argus*, 9 May, 6 June, 18 July, 29 Aug. 1891, 3 Sept. 1892; Woodward, *Tom Watson*, pp. 189–92.

35. Evidence on the Dalton raid is sketchy and incomplete. William F. Holmes provides evidence to suggest that the whitecappers were Democrats, his primary concern being to dissociate the Populists, who were engaged in a formal "political movement," from the whitecappers, who were fighting "prepolitical" battles ("Moonshining and Collective Violence," pp. 607–9). Barton Shaw, on the other hand, ascribes blame for the mob to the Populists, his major goal being to undermine the myth of interracial tolerance within the third party (*Wool-Hat Boys*, chap. 5, esp. pp. 84–88). On race and populism in Georgia, see also Kousser, *Shaping of Southern Politics*, pp. 215–16.

36. Shaw, *Wool-Hat Boys*, pp. 167–71.

37. On labor activism around the turn of the century, see Evans, "History of the Organized Labor Movement," pp. 82–100; McLaurin, *Paternalism and Protest*, chaps. 5–7, pp. 196–99; Woodward, *Origins of the New South*, pp. 421–23; Escott, *Many Excellent People*, pp. 261–62; Carlton, *Mill and Town*, chap. 4.

38. Carlton, *Mill and Town*, chap. 3, esp. pp. 112–28; Newby, *Plain Folk*, chap. 16; Whites, "De Graffenried Controversy."

CHAPTER 4

1. BDM, Book 1, pp. 105–6, 111. On mill growth, see *Dalton Argus*, 5 Sept. 1885 (front page inaccurately reads 5 Aug.), 12 Sept. 1885, 1 Oct. 1892; *State Town and Country*, Apr. 1889, p. 7. For rumors of expansion, see *Dalton Argus*, 14 June, 22 Mar. 1890, 10 Sept. 1892. As a matter of convenience, dates concerning profits and company expansion throughout this chapter refer to Crown's fiscal year (1 September to 31 August) rather than calendar years. For example, 1887 means the fiscal year running from September 1886 through August 1887. When a date concerning a director or manager is provided, the calendar year is used.

2. This process of growth, presented in more detail in the paragraphs that follow, may be traced in BDM, Book 1. A concise version is presented in Pace, "CrownAmerica."

3. BDM, Book 1, pp. 15, 53–54, 93, 115, 118, 125.

4. See Tompkins, *Cotton Mill*, pp. 52–53.

5. BDM, Book 1, p. 124.

6. Ibid., pp. 121, 127, 135–36; CMHD, Item 7, p. 2.

7. BDM, Book 1, p. 25; *Dalton Argus*, 24 Jan., 1 Aug. 1885.

8. *Dalton Argus*, 22 Mar., 31 May, 26 July 1890, 1 Oct. 1892; BDM, Book 1, pp. 96–97, 127, 171, 175, 199, 201. For other references to machinery considerations and cloth quality, see BDM, p. 49. Jones's claim that nothing more could be done to increase efficiency proved somewhat less than true, for later that same day, the directors voted to put electric lights in the mill (BDM, Book 1, p. 98).

9. Thompson, *Cotton Field to the Cotton Mill*, pp. 65, 78; Blicksilver, *Cotton Manufacturing*, p. 24.

10. Bess Beatty provides clear evidence of links between northern machine shops and

North Carolina's cotton mills throughout the nineteenth century ("Lowells of the South," esp. pp. 53–55).

11. In its early years Crown operated a company store, and Hamilton advertised cloth for sale to the public in the local press. He also sold cloth to local merchants. See *Dalton Argus*, 9 May 1885, 2, 30 Oct. 1886.

12. *North Georgia Citizen*, 15 July 1897; and see *Dalton Argus*, 24 Apr. 1886.

13. BDM, Book 1, p. 60; *State Town and Country*, Apr. 1889, p. 7; *Dalton Argus*, 7 Nov. 1885, 22 Mar. 1890 (which stated that Crown had a "large and growing business with the Pacific slope"); and see Tompkins, *Cotton Mill*, chap. 11.

14. Quote in BDM, Book 1, p. 132. Southern mills also faced the risk of commission houses that failed, as did one of Crown's agents from Philadelphia during the 1890s economic depression (ibid., p. 129; see also Tompkins, *Cotton Mill*, p. 130). Crown had four selling agents in the early 1910s, of whom Lane was one. By 1920, Lane was Crown's only agent (*Moody's Railroads and Securities*, 1912, Railroads, p. 3070; *Moody's Railroads and Securities*, 1920, Industrial Section, p. 437). See also Pace, "CrownAmerica," pp. 7–8.

15. Beatty, "Lowells of the South"; McMath et al., *Engineering the New South*, chap. 3, esp. pp. 81–88 (the Georgia School of Technology changed its name to the Georgia Institute of Technology in the late 1940s [p. 244]); Pace, "CrownAmerica," pp. 7–8. Apparently Cornelius Hamilton left school to take the place of his older brother, Seth, who worked in the Crown office for a time and then disappeared without a trace (Hamilton interview).

16. BDM, Book 1, pp. 153, 191; CMHD, Item 7, p. 3; David Hamilton, quoted in Pace, "CrownAmerica," p. 6.

17. CMHD, Item 7, pp. 3–4, Item 8, pp. 1–2 (quote on p. 1). The boiler and engine rooms, smokestack, and warehouse (added in 1923) of Mill No. 2 were actually poured reinforced-concrete structures, thereby representing advanced architectural technology for the early twentieth century.

18. Information on Crown's directors and managers was gathered from BDM, Book 1, and Pace, "CrownAmerica," p. 7.

19. *Dalton Argus*, 1 May 1886; *North Georgia Citizen*, 28 Apr. 1910 (the victim in this case was Frank Bunch, age twenty-three, who had migrated from Murray County, where his body was shipped for burial); McLaurin, *Paternalism and Protest*, p. 35. I. A. Newby offers a thorough discussion of mill-village health and disease (*Plain Folk*, chap. 12).

20. *North Georgia Citizen*, 19 Aug. 1897. No story elaborating on the incident followed. According to D. A. Tompkins, one of North Carolina's most successful textile manufacturers in the late nineteenth century, sewerage purification facilities could be installed at very little expense (*Cotton Mill*, pp. 169–70).

21. Davidson, *Child Labor Legislation*, chap. 4; Thompson, *Cotton Field to the Cotton Mill*, p. 246 and chap. 12 generally.

22. Murphy, *Problems of the Present South*, p. 166 and chaps. 4 and 5 generally.

23. Harben, *Georgians*, pp. 37, 98.

24. Ibid., chap. 8 (introduces Blaithwait), pp. 128–32 (for the above exchange).

25. Walter S. Bogle, "Bill Is Introduced," in Bogle Clipping File, CGA; *North Georgia Citizen*, 26 Oct. 1899.

26. BDM, Book 1, pp. 76–78 (1888 contract); *North Georgia Citizen*, 16 Jan., 30 Sept., 28 Oct. 1897 (quote); Pace, "CrownAmerica," p. 5.

27. BDM, Book 1, pp. 137–44; *North Georgia Citizen*, 2 Sept. 1897, 5, 12, 19 Nov. 1903. The editor in 1903 was Frank Reynolds, the same editor cited above as opposing a child labor law.

28. Thompson, *Cotton Field to the Cotton Mill*, pp. 86–88; Pace, "CrownAmerica," p. 6;

BDM, Book 1, p. 148. Another example of the taxation game occurred in 1909, when Crown's directors proposed to build a new company office (which they never did) outside the city limits. Expecting trouble from civic leaders, the directors authorized president Hamilton to "employ counsel in case of any litigation" (BDM, Book 1, p. 190). On New England textiles, see Prude, *Coming of Industrial Order*.

29. BDM, Book 1, pp. 193, 195, 197; Pace, "CrownAmerica," p. 6.

30. BDM, Book 1, pp. 202–4.

31. Ibid., p. 202; CMHD, Item 7, p. 3; Pace, "CrownAmerica," p. 7.

CHAPTER 5

1. Of the workers listed in selected payrolls in 1888 and 1890, only one in ten remained with the mill in 1900. These calculations are based on CPR, 14 Apr. 1888, 12 July 1890, 2 June–14 July 1900.

2. Unless otherwise specified, the statistics given for Crown's work force in 1900 throughout this chapter pertain only to those individuals or households found in both the federal census manuscripts and in Crown's payroll books, a total of 389 millhands in 131 families. See appendix B for a description of this data. On child labor, see also Kemp, *Lewis Hine*; Davidson, *Child Labor Legislation*; Grantham, *Southern Progressivism*, pp. 178–99.

3. Crown's payroll books for 1900 divided the workers into four departments: carding, spinning, weaving, and engine room. The last of these was comprised exclusively of male workers and actually contained only a handful of men, who were either highly paid mechanics or poorly paid yard workers who performed odd jobs and shoveled coal.

4. For the statistical analyses in this chapter, I have adopted a broad definition of "cotton-mill families" to include all households in which any member worked as a wage earner in the Crown Mill.

5. CPR, 2 June–14 July 1900; U.S. census manuscripts, Georgia, Whitfield County, 1900.

6. Thompson, *Cotton Field to the Cotton Mill*, pp. 238–39. Thompson's analysis of this phenomenon is more subtle than this statement suggests.

7. Breeden interview; *Atlanta Constitution*, 3 Dec. 1899, quoted in Newby, *Plain Folk*, p. 499. C. T. Ladson of the Georgia Federation of Labor was arguing not that mills attracted adult male sluggards but that they often created "drones" by relying so heavily on child labor.

8. Thompson, *Cotton Field to the Cotton Mill*, pp. 133–40; Wright, *Old South, New South*, pp. 142–45; Harben, *Georgians*, pp. 129–31.

9. U.S. census manuscripts, Georgia, Whitfield County, 1900. Any family in which a household member paid rent to the company was counted as being in mill-village housing (CPR, 2 June–14 July 1900).

10. U.S. census manuscripts, Georgia, Whitfield County, 1900, 1910; CPR, 2 June–14 July 1900, 13 Jan.–24 Feb. 1912. Payroll records for 1910 were not available; only millhands listed in both the 1910 manuscript census and the 1912 payrolls are included in this analysis of workers in 1912.

11. Quote in Thompson, *Cotton Field to the Cotton Mill*, p. 153; and see Wright, *Old South, New South*, pp. 126, 132–33.

12. During the early twentieth century, American industrialists and government agencies were increasingly concerned about labor turnover in manufacturing and often attempted to measure it. The definitions and calculations of turnover varied considerably, however, as they have among latter-day historians. Jonathan Prude offers a useful discussion of method-

ologies and an analysis of payroll data from rural cotton mills in Massachusetts (*Coming of Industrial Order*, pp. 227–29, 270, appendix 1). Prude's annual "voluntary departure rate" statistic, which most closely approximates my own figures on annual turnover, usually remained under 100 percent and rose to 120 percent or more only five times between 1814 and 1859 (ibid., p. 270). See also the discussion in Rodgers, *Work Ethic*, pp. 163–65.

13. McHugh, *Mill Family*, p. 96; see also Tullos, *Habits of Industry*, p. 19.

14. For a description of the methods employed in this outmigration study, see appendix B.

15. U.S. census manuscripts, Georgia, Whitfield County, 1900; ibid., Bartow County, 1910; CPR, 2 June–14 July 1900.

16. U.S. census manuscripts, Georgia, Whitfield County, 1900, enumeration district 107, p. 12; ibid., 1910, enumeration district 157, p. 2.

17. Ibid., 1900, enumeration district 107, p. 14; ibid., 1910, enumeration district 151, p. 10.

18. Ibid., Hall County, 1910, enumeration district 91, p. 15.

19. Ibid., Gordon County, 1910, enumeration district 89, p. 7.

20. Ibid., Whitfield County, 1910, enumeration district 156, p. 11; CPR, 2 June–14 July 1900.

21. Frank Tannenbaum, *Darker Phases of the South* (New York: G. P. Putnam's Sons, 1924), quoted in Wright, *Old South, New South*, p. 146.

22. My strategy was to use the male-structured enumeration system to learn about female choices and migration patterns. Taking the entire cohort of single female out-migrants (those who were living with a cotton-mill family in 1900 and who had moved on by 1910), I obtained a list of those who were married in Whitfield County before 1910. Then, using the Soundex indexes for Georgia, Alabama, and Tennessee, I traced their *husbands'* names in the 1910 census.

23. A similar argument about labor transiency and information networks is made by Jonathan Prude (*Coming of Industrial Order*, chap. 5, esp. pp. 144–57).

24. On Crown's work force, see table 5.2; regional statistics in U.S. Bureau of the Census, *Twelfth Census, 1900: Manufactures*, 9(3): 57.

25. Newby, *Plain Folk*, chap. 3, esp. pp. 96–105; Hall et al., *Like a Family*, pp. 105–13. Sanford M. Jacoby points to a similar labor shortage in the industrial North during the early twentieth century, and his study suggests that labor shortages and rapid turnover had profound influences on the American factory system (*Employing Bureaucracy*).

26. Newby, *Plain Folk*, chap. 16 (quote on p. 474); Carlton, *Mill and Town*, pp. 243–48; Stokes, "Black and White Labor"; Evans, "Organized Labor Movement in Georgia"; Wright, *Old South, New South*, chap. 7, esp. pp. 177–97 (figures on black employment calculated from table on p. 179).

27. Wright, *Old South, New South*, p. 12. Wage differentials were calculated from U.S. Department of Labor, *History of Wages*, pp. 394–95; the percentage of foreign-born mill-hands was calculated from U.S. Senate, *Woman and Child Wage-Earners*, 1:17.

28. Again, I utilized the Soundex indexes for this work. In all, I located thirty-eight males listed in Georgia's 1900 census who were working for Crown in 1910. See appendix B for an explanation of the methods of this analysis.

29. U.S. census manuscripts, Georgia, Walker County, 1900, enumeration district 95, p. 6. Anthony F. C. Wallace (*Rockdale*), John Bodnar (*The Transplanted*), and William Deverell ("To Loosen the Safety Valve") offer diverse examples of the desire among America's wage earners to return to the land, including the desire of immigrants to save money in order to purchase land in their home countries (the famous "birds of passage").

30. Systematic analyses of southern textile wages, particularly "real" wages, are strangely lacking. Gavin Wright offers the most sophisticated discussion and also presents useful data, much of which jibes with my own (*Old South, New South*, chap. 5); Holland Thompson lists wage rates for some North Carolina mills that were somewhat higher than wage rates at Crown Mill (*Cotton Field to the Cotton Mill*, pp. 279, 284). State-level data for both New England and the South can be found in U.S. Department of Labor, *History of Wages*, pp. 363–95, 560–63.

31. The regression model I employ here has been adapted from McHugh, *Mill Family*, pp. 27–36, and "Earnings"; Phillips, "Labor Market."

32. For those new to multiple regression analysis and unaccustomed to reading regression tables, I offer a brief, nontechnical explanation of the technique in appendix B. There are four regression models presented in table 5.7: model *i* and model *ii* for 1900 and two identical models for 1912. In model *i*, only age and gender are regressed against earnings; in model *ii*, age and gender remain in the equation, but seven other variables are added. The idea is to begin simply and then build more complex models. Take, for example, the two models for 1900. In equation *i*, both age and gender are positively and significantly related to earnings, meaning that older workers earned more regardless of gender and that, on average, males earned more than females, even taking age into account. Note, though, how the variables *age* and *gender* lose both strength and significance after the other variables are added to the equation, meaning that their observed explanatory power in model *i* stemmed from other characteristics possessed by older, male workers.

33. It is also suggestive that the standardized Beta score for the variable for married household heads increased from .138 in 1900 to .406 twelve years later, which indicates that, on average, being a household head gave a worker a greater claim on wages as the twentieth century progressed. (Betas are statistically standardized regression coefficients; they allow for [cautious] comparisons across samples and among variables based on different numerical scales.)

34. Economic historian Cathy McHugh, who has more complete data on experience, points to generally similar results in a North Carolina mill (*Mill Family*, pp. 27–32).

35. Ibid., pp. 29, 36.

36. Some historians of education suggest that the inculcation of discipline in preindustrial people was one reason industrial boosters and reformers pushed for public schools in the nineteenth century. For a suggestive analysis, see Katz, *Irony of Early School Reform*.

37. The equation was the same as in table 5.7. The variables that proved significant (all at the .01 level) and their coefficients were as follows: married household heads, .137; literacy, .124; boarders, .163; and payroll deductions, .091. The R^2 was .37.

38. For a good regional view of erratic work in southern mills during this period, see Newby, *Plain Folk*, chap. 5.

39. CPR, 2 June–14 July 1900, 13 Jan.–24 Feb. 1912; U.S. census manuscripts, Georgia, Whitfield County, 1900, 1910.

40. The monthly earnings here represent the eight-week total of each family, divided by two. The figures given represent *net* income, after deductions for company housing, coal, and cash advances. The census data do not adequately reveal which families lived in company housing; this was determined instead by whether a family member paid the company rent (as indicated in the payroll books) during the eight-week sample.

41. In calculating rent as a proportion of family earnings, I only had access to a household's *mill* income, which means that, for families whose members brought in income from other lines of work (and this was not uncommon), these figures are actually inflated. A

family that had several children working outside the mill as well as in Crown therefore had an even greater economic incentive to remain in company housing. My figures were derived by calculating each mill-village family's gross mill earnings, before deductions, for the full eight weeks and by calculating the family's total rent deductions for that same period, then figuring total rent as a percentage of total earnings for each family.

CHAPTER 6

1. A large part of the "paternalism" problem in New South labor historiography stems from the long-standing use of the term to describe master-slave relationships. Eugene Genovese, drawing on the ideas of Antonio Gramsci, offers a brilliant analysis of paternalism in the Slave South, yet he also muddies the waters of postbellum labor history by asserting that labor relations in the industrial capitalist world are not properly labeled paternalistic (*Roll, Jordan, Roll,* esp. appendix).

2. The literature on nonsouthern paternalism is extensive. See, e.g., Scranton, "Varieties of Paternalism"; Zahavi, *Workers, Managers, and Welfare Capitalism*; Hareven, *Family Time and Industrial Time*; Wallace, *Rockdale*; Prude, "Early New England Textile Mills," esp. pp. 4–10; Walkowitz, *Worker City, Company Town*, esp. chaps. 2, 4, 6; Brandes, *American Welfare Capitalism*; Jacoby, *Employing Bureaucracy*. For European trends, see Accampo, *Industrialization*; Joyce, *Work, Society, and Politics*.

3. Perhaps the earliest argument that southern culture inspired mill-village paternalism was put forth by historian Broadus Mitchell, who saw in textile paternalism the positive reflection of an enlightened regional elite. Of one early textile leader Mitchell wrote, "*Noblesse oblige* was his intuition. . . . The subjects over whom he ruled in his little kingdom were economically as weak as he was strong, and yet no hint of exploitation ever entered his consciousness." Dixie's industrial pioneers, Mitchell insisted, cared for their working "subjects" in a manner befitting their social status in the South. Mitchell actually maintained a dual view of paternalism. By the late 1920s, he said, "a later generation of managers has maintained welfare programs first for profit, and second for the happiness and progress of the workpeople," a trend he found repugnant and unrepresentative of paternalism's early practitioners (Mitchell, *William Gregg*, p. 76; see also idem, *Rise of Cotton Mills*). For a good analysis of Mitchell's views, see Singal, *War Within*, chap. 3.

4. Billings, *Planters and the Making of a "New South*," pp. 102–4; McLaurin, *Paternalism and Protest*, chaps. 2–3; Cash, *Mind of the South*, pp. 204–6.

5. Laurie, *Artisans into Workers*, p. 119.

6. Tullos, *Habits of Industry*, pp. 4, 76–77. I. A. Newby's *Plain Folk* (chap. 9) offers an analogous argument. His study offers one of the few detailed analyses of how textile paternalism actually operated in the New South, and it suggests the importance of early twentieth-century labor market trends in spurring the rise of welfare capitalism. Ultimately, though, Newby interprets industrial paternalism not as a reflection of modernization but as a culturally familiar relationship between the rich and poor in any underdeveloped region. "Paternalism was an integral feature of life in the New South," he writes, "pervading relations between classes, races, sexes, as well as employers and employees. Traditional notions of hierarchy and social place permeated the society, and it would have been remarkable if pronounced forms of paternalism had not appeared in the mills and villages" (p. 262).

7. Queen interview.

8. See the relevant deeds and papers in John Hamilton Family File, CGA.

9. On the Brown incident, see above, chap. 4; Wade interview.

10. BDM, Book 1, p. 36; CMHD, Item 7, p. 6.

11. BDM, Book 1, p. 36; CMHD, Item 7, pp. 6–8; Tompkins, *Cotton Mill*, pp. 116–21 (quote on p. 117).

12. BDM, Book 1, p. 36; CMHD, Item 7, p. 6.

13. On these trends, see Brandes, *American Welfare Capitalism*; Carlton, *Mill and Town*; Grantham, *Southern Progressivism*; and Jacoby, *Employing Bureaucracy*.

14. BDM, Book 1, p. 150; CMHD, Item 7, p. 9; Cohen, *Children of the Mill* (which offers an analysis of corporate education outside the South).

15. Pace, "CrownAmerica," p. 6.

16. Bunch and Garren interview; Herring, *Welfare Work in Mill Villages*, chaps. 3–4; McHugh, *Mill Family*, chap. 4. It is worth noting that Crown Point School reunions are still held annually.

17. *Dalton Argus*, 9 July 1887 (which gives an early example of a company picnic); pictures of Crown Mill concert band, CGA; Bramblett, Thompson, and Hall interviews. The figures for the Christmas sacks were calculated from Trotter Brothers and Co. [Chattanooga] to Crown Cotton Mills, 14 Dec. 1920, and Crown Cotton Mills to Trotter Brothers and Co., 15 Dec. 1920, MDB.

18. *North Georgia Citizen*, 17 May, 5 July, 2, 16 Aug. 1917; Pace, "CrownAmerica," pp. 6–7; Hamilton interview.

19. See the Crown Cotton Mills Burial Association certificate file, CGA. The earliest surviving certificate is dated June 1905 and was number 46. It was the certificate of Ida Springer, wife of Frank Springer.

20. The only surviving insurance policy in the company records is in the Burial Association file (see policy no. 350 for Clem Collins, 25 July 1917). See also Herring, *Welfare Work in Mill Villages*; Lahne, *Cotton Mill Worker*, pp. 51–53.

21. Crown Employee Savings Account Books, CGA; obituary of George W. Hamilton, John Hamilton Family File, CGA; Hill interview.

22. *Textile Labor*, 3 May 1947; J. C. Metcalf to Frank and George Hamilton, Crown Cotton Mills, 17 Jan. 1929, MDB; Ellis interview.

23. Lowrance, Hall, and Ellis interviews.

24. Crown Cotton Mills to Mr. F. S. Pruden, Agent, Dalton, Ga., 28 June 1915; Manager, Atlanta Claim Division [Maryland Casualty Company of Baltimore] to Crown Cotton Mills, 17 Mar. 1914; see also other employee accident reports from the late 1910s; all in MDB.

25. State of Georgia, *Annual Report of the Commissioner of Commerce and Labor*, 1917 and 1918, GDAH (quote in 1917, p. 10). Much of the concern over labor centered on the migration of blacks, who during World War I abandoned the South in startling numbers to take on wartime industrial work in northern cities. But the shortage of white labor in the South should not be overlooked. George Tindall (*Emergence of the New South*) offers a useful overview of the war's impact on Dixie.

26. [Crown Mill] to Hon. Gordon Lee, M.C., 5 July 1917, MDB.

27. *North Georgia Citizen*, 16, 30 Aug. 1917, 23 Jan. 1919.

28. I. A. Newby offers a useful analysis of this often neglected topic (*Plain Folk*, chap. 12). See also the essays in Savitt and Young, *Disease and Distinctiveness*.

29. See Tindall, *Emergence of the New South*, pp. 325–26. Nearly a decade earlier, as company officials sought to attract laborers and stave off criticism from some local businessmen, one director advocated that funds be allocated for village beautification and the cleaning of Crown's "sewerlands" (BDM, Book 1, p. 179). Apparently, no such action was then taken.

30. BDM, Book 2, 17 Sept. 1919; "Report of Hospital Committee to Directors" (loose

sheet in ibid., dated 18 Dec. 1919); BDM, Book 2, 15 Sept. 1920. In vintage George Hamilton style, Crown's hospital committee stated (in the 18 December report) that the hospital's charter and its organization should "be hedged about by such legal conditions as will amply protect the Crown Cotton Mills, to the end of the greatest good to the greatest number of people at the least outlay." The hospital was not completed until 1921; wards were furnished by local elite organizations (*North Georgia Citizen*, 19 May 1921; see also Pace, "Crown-America," p. 7).

31. See Draper's blueprints, CGA; CMHD, Item 8, p. 3.

32. Ibid.; see also 1934 photograph, CGA.

CHAPTER 7

1. Hall interview. The "family" metaphor is expressed in almost every interview conducted for this study. See, e.g., Bramblett, Bunch and Garren, Crow, Defore, Felker, Hardin, Hill, Queen, and Thompson interviews. Unless otherwise indicated, all interviews in this chapter were conducted by the author in Dalton, Georgia, and were tape-recorded. See also Hall et al., *Like a Family*.

2. This and the following paragraphs are from Hill interview.

3. Tindall, *Emergence of the New South*, pp. 33–37, 111–12, 121–23, and chap. 4 generally; Bartley, *Creation of Modern Georgia*, pp. 169–70. During the last years of the twenties, when the industrial economy began to stall, the number of farms in Whitfield, Murray, Gordon, and Gilmer counties increased nearly 13 percent from the 1925 figure, but by the end of the decade there were still fewer farms than in 1920 (U.S. Bureau of the Census, *Fourteenth Census: Agriculture* and *Fifteenth Census: Agriculture*, county tables, 1920, 1925, 1930).

4. Crown Cotton Mill, Statement of Labor Conditions [for] State of Georgia, Department of Commerce and Labor, 1921, MDB; Sam Tibbs to Mr. Hamilton, 30 Dec. 1921; [Job applicant from New Holland] to Crown Mills, 9 Dec. 1921; W. O. Hall to Supt. Cotton Mill, 24 Nov. 1921; Roy Helton to Spinning Room Overseer, 9 Oct. 1921; all letters in MDB.

5. Nettie and Sarah Stover to Mr. Hamilton, G. W., Dec. 1921; Mrs. Willie Collier to Supt. [Crown Mill], 26 Nov. 1921. See also W. F. Houston [East Thomastown, Pa.] to Supt. of the Crown Cotton Mill, 6 Oct. 1921; L. Simmons [Eli, Ky.] to Supt. of the Crown Mill, 14 Feb. 1921; Katie Stafford [Macon, Ga.] to Overseer, 1 Feb. 1921; W. F. Blankenship [Resaca, Ga.] to Mr. George Hamilton, 5 Dec. 1921; J. W. Smith [San Antonio, Tex.] to Crown Cotton Mills, 25 Apr. 1921. Scattered letters from other years can be found in the same company file. Most were from people seeking lower-management positions, and most were from New England (there is, by the way, no evidence that Crown ever hired anyone from New England). See Roscoe B. Bailey to Mr. C. L. Hamilton, 2 Sept. 1925; [Applicant from Damariscotta, Maine], 3 Mar. 1926; James W. Booth [Saugus, Mass.] to Crown Cotton Mills, 24 Nov. 1936; W. F. Hutcherson [Palmetto, Ga.] to Mr. Geo. W. Hamilton, Supt., 28 July 1936; and Owen E. Hamer [Columbus, Ga.] to Mr. G. W. Hamilton, Supt., 3 Mar. 1939 (handwritten note at bottom says "no opening"); all letters in MDB. See also Crown Cotton Mill, Statement of Labor Conditions for State of Georgia, Department of Commerce and Labor, 1923, MDB.

6. *Directory of Dalton, 1924*, p. 1; *History*, pp. 157–59 (quote on p. 157). On American Thread, see Gena Connally, "The Yarn of the Thread Mill," printed in *Dalton Citizen-News*, 4 Mar. 1983. Statistics on wage earners and value added by manufacturing are based on the information provided in several volumes of the U.S. census: 14th (1920) and 15th (1930), *Manufactures*, esp. pp. 265–66 and 124–25, respectively; 14th–16th (1920–40), *Population*. Value-added figures refer to 1919 and 1929. No figures are given for Dalton alone. See also Tindall, *Emergence of the New South*, pp. 57, 95, and chap. 3.

7. Tindall, *Emergence of the New South*, pp. 75, 96; *Directory of Dalton, 1924*, p. 1; Bartley, *Creation of Modern Georgia*, p. 170. See also Brownell, *Urban Ethos*. Also in 1925, the Civitan Club sparked a successful drive to pave the five major country roads that connected Dalton with the hinterland. The plan called for costs to be shared by the county, state, and federal governments, with Whitfield County assuming one-quarter of the burden by issuing $400,000 in bonds. These paved roads greatly facilitated commerce between Dalton and its hinterland and also marked a shift among the local business class toward a broader vision of urban growth through state and federal assistance, a vision that foreshadowed the local-federal cooperation of the New Deal and World War II era. Many women's clubs organized as well. They were primarily concerned with enhancing the cultural life of the city, as well as with organized philanthropy (*History*, pp. 142–44, 171).

8. *Directory of Dalton, 1924*, pp. 1–2.

9. Crow interview; BDM, Book 2, 17 Sept. 1919 (on Crown's profits, see table A.2 and fig. A.1); CPR, Feb. 1926; BCPR, Feb. 1926; *Moody's Investments: Industrial Securities*, 1933, p. 312. On the textile industry during the 1920s, see Wright, *Old South, New South*, chap. 5; Blicksilver, *Cotton Manufacturing*, pt. 3.

10. BDM, Books 1, 2; Pace, "CrownAmerica," p. 7; Young, *Textile Leaders of the South*, pp. 602, 606.

11. Pace, "CrownAmerica," pp. 7–8; CrownAmerica, Inc., Annual Report, 1984, cover foldout, CGA; BDM, Book 2. In 1932 Boylston was reorganized to produce tufting yarn for Dalton's bedspread industry.

12. Hamilton, Parker, Wade, Queen, and Crow interviews. The workers' failure to recollect Moore is particularly puzzling given that he was, by all accounts and correspondence, a generous and widely known person in Dalton and throughout southern textile circles. More revealing of Moore's character than his obituary (William K. Moore Family File, CGA) are J. A. Miller to W. K. Moore, 5 Dec. 1932, and Huntington Babcock to "My Friends at Crown," 2 Dec. 1935 (both in MDB); and Hamilton interview.

13. Frank Springer's obituary, MDB; U.S. census manuscripts, Georgia, Whitfield County, 1900, 1910; Ellis, Hamilton, Hardin, Felker, Queen, Crow, and Wade interviews.

14. Caylor, Bunch and Garren interviews.

15. Lowrance interview; see also Felker, Bunch and Garren, Hill, Crow, Bramblett, and Ellis interviews.

16. Lowrance, Hall interviews. See also Parker, Bunch and Garren, and Crow interviews. Good neighboring was by no means a uniquely southern trait, as John Mack Faragher (*Sugar Creek*) makes clear.

17. Defore, Hardin, Hill, Lowrance, Parker, Queen, Rogers, Wade interviews; Hughes interview. See also Pope, *Millhands and Preachers*, pp. 84–91; Thompson, *Cotton Field to the Cotton Mill*, pp. 174–78.

18. Nancy Rogers, telephone interview with Polly Boggess, director, CGA, 12 Oct. 1985 (handwritten notes).

19. Rogers, Lowrance interviews; Kenemer quoted in Lowrance, "Kenemer Reminisces." Bunch and Garren, Queen interviews also deal with revivals.

20. Felker, Thompson, Parker interviews; see also Crow, Rogers, Bramblett, and Hill interviews. Anna Nell Garren recalled, "Daddy would . . . load that T Model with kids and go up to Willowdale. . . . There's a place up there they called the trestle where the railroad crosses the creek. And the creek made a turn just as it came under the trestle and everybody went swimming up there. Well, Daddy'd take a bunch of kids up there 'cause nobody didn't go to the swimming pool, didn't have the money to pay for the swimming pool. But we'd go up there and go swimming" (Bunch and Garren interview).

21. Bunch and Garren, Wade interviews. See also Hughes, Ellis, Crow, and Queen interviews; Lowrance, "Kenemer."

22. Felker interview; see also Bramblett, Lowrance, Bunch and Garren, Crow, Thompson, and Cruce interviews.

23. Hill interview; see also Bramblett, Ellis, Felker, Hardin, Thompson, and Parker interviews.

24. Wade, Ellis, Lowrance, Bunch and Garren, Defore, Hall, and Hardin interviews. Kenemer is quoted in Lowrance, "Kenemer." Not all mill children were allowed to go to movies, but those who were not recalled an active, community-oriented social life, especially in the churches (see Rogers interview).

25. Bramblett interview; see also Bunch and Garren, Defore, and Parker interviews.

26. Ellis, Parker, Bramblett, Hardin, and Hill interviews.

27. S. A. East [Tubize Chatillon, Rome, Ga.] to Baseball Manager, Boylston-Crown Mills, 20 May 1932; B. L. "Crook" Smith to Neil Hamilton, 31 Mar. 1931; B. L. Smith to Basketball Manager, Boylston Crown Mills, 22 Nov. 1932. Other references to the business side of mill-village athletics appear in A. G. Spalding & Bros. [Atlanta, Ga.] to Crown Cotton Mill, 17 May 1919; ibid., 10 June 1919; ibid., 19 Aug. 1921; R. M. Gibbons [Lindale, Ga.] to C. L. Hamilton, 2 Apr. 1926; ibid., 31 Mar. 1926; and Martin-Thompson Company [Chattanooga, Tenn.] to C. L. Hamilton, 6 May 1932. All letters in MDB.

I learned a great deal about baseball from interviews with Earl Harden and Henry Wade, both of whom attended games as children, made the squad as young men, and played on the 1939 championship team. My afternoon at the annual Crown Mill Old Timers' Baseball Reunion in 1985 was also very enlightening. Interviews with nonplayers attested to the importance of baseball in the community; see, e.g., Bramblett, Bunch, Crow, Ellis, Felker, and Hill interviews.

28. Wade, Hardin interviews; picture of the 1939 championship team, CGA. The *North Georgia Citizen* reported Crown's games each week during the 1930s.

29. W. A. Britton, quoted in James A. Mackay and Calvin Kytle, ["An Investigation to Determine Whether the Corporations Control the State of Georgia"], ca. 1947, George S. Mitchell Papers, Box 4, Manuscripts Department, Perkins Library, Duke University, Durham, N.C. Britton was doubtless expressing uptown condescension rather than his own views, because at the time he made this statement in the late 1940s, he was serving as a prolabor representative from Whitfield County in the Georgia statehouse. He was trying to point out how the middle-class attitudes of mill workers had improved since the rise of local unions, but his words clearly captured the view of most affluent Daltonians in the 1920s concerning mill people. My thanks to Janet Irons for sharing this information with me.

30. Bramblett, Bunch and Garren, Wade, and Thompson interviews; see also Ellis and Lowrance interviews.

31. Crow interview; see also Thompson, Hamilton interviews; Evans, "Organized Labor Movement in Georgia," chap. 6; and Newby, *Plain Folk*, chap. 16.

32. Hall, Hardin, and Lowrance interviews.

33. Mead and Hill, *Handbook of Denominations*, pp. 83–89; Anderson, *Vision of the Disinherited*, pp. 114, 120–21. There are a variety of Church of God groups. Here I am referring to the "Cleveland, Tennessee" branch.

34. *History*, p. 98; *Dalton City Directory*, 1936, p. 76; Anderson, *Vision of the Disinherited*, chap. 7 (quote on p. 136).

35. Lowrance, Rogers, Queen, Hall, Hill, and Ellis interviews.

36. Thompson, *Touching Home*, p. 132; Queen and Lowrance interviews.

CHAPTER 8

1. For some insightful recollections about Crown's mill-village economy, see two articles by Pat W. Lowrance in the *Dalton Citizen-News*: "Makin' Do" (10 Jan. 1984) and "Money Only Worth Its Weight in Charity" (17 July 1984).

2. Wade, Hill, Queen, Hall, Bunch and Garren interviews. On the family economy in southern textiles, see McHugh, *Mill Family*; Rhyne, *Some Southern Cotton Mill Workers*, pp. 79–83; Newby, *Plain Folk*, pp. 218–22, chaps. 8, 17; Hall et al., *Like a Family*, chaps. 2, 3.

3. Davidson, *Child Labor Legislation*, pp. 209–14, chap. 10. Dalton's newspaper was not on the list, published in the *Congressional Record* (vol. 3, pt. 15, pp. 1806–11), of those who supported the Keating Child Labor Bill in 1916; but Georgia's *Gainesville Herald* wrote that "the purpose of the bill is to prevent capitalists from coining child blood and child flesh into dollars" (ibid., p. 1808), a telling demonstration that the child labor issue still called forth powerful emotional appeals, despite the cool economic calculations that both sanctioned and undermined its use.

4. Wright, *Old South, New South*, pp. 140–46, 150–53; Crown Cotton Mill Child Labor Certificates, 1926–34, CGA; Felker interview.

5. Bramblett, Felker interviews; see also Caylor interview.

6. Thompson, Hughes interviews; see also Hill, Bunch and Garren, and Bramblett interviews.

7. Felker, Caylor, and Thompson interviews.

8. U.S. census manuscripts, Georgia, Whitfield County, 1900, 1910; Hardin interview; pictures of Crown Mill Band, ca. 1915, CGA.

9. Felker interview; see also Bramblett, Caylor, and Ellis interviews.

10. Potwin, *Cotton Mill People*, p. 148; Bramblett interview.

11. Hughes, Lowrance, and Rogers interviews; see also Parker, Hall, and Defore interviews. Kenemer is quoted in Lowrance, "Kenemer."

12. Wade, Crow interviews; see also Thompson and Felker interviews.

13. Defore, Parker, and Rogers interviews. See also Hall, Hill, Queen, Bramblett, and Thompson interviews.

14. T. M. Forbes [secretary, Cotton Manufacturers Association of Georgia] to W. K. Moore, 14 Oct. 1930 (in which Forbes voiced his surprise that twenty-six mills in the state—24 percent—had recently switched to the check system). W. K. Moore replied with a positive assessment of the new system, which Crown Mill had been using "only a few months" (letter to T. M. Forbes, 15 Oct. 1930); both letters in MDB. Moore stated the workers had adjusted to checks without any trouble and that the stores in the vicinity cashed the checks without service charges (only about 20 percent of the workers cashed their checks at the bank). For workers' descriptions of payday, see Rogers, Defore, Lowrance, Wade, Hall, Hill, Ellis, and Felker interviews. Not a single worker whom I interviewed mentioned the switch from cash payment to the check system.

15. Lowrance, Wade, Bramblett, and Thompson interviews; see also Ellis and Rogers interviews. Statistics computed from CPR, 1927; U.S. Department of Labor, *History of Wages*, pp. 394–95; U.S. Bureau of the Census, *Historical Statistics*, p. 170. A study of wages in a Gaston County, North Carolina, mill in 1926–27 found an average weekly wage of $15.72, but with wide variations (Rhyne, *Some Southern Cotton Mill Workers*, chap. 10, esp. pp. 94–95). Gavin Wright offers an analysis of the larger pattern of textile wages in Dixie (*Old South, New South*, pp. 147–55).

16. Defore and Queen interviews. Gary Cross and Peter R. Shergold offer a good intro-

duction to the larger issues involved in parental control of children's earnings ("Family Economy").

17. Charles Kenemer quoted in Lowrance, "Kenemer." See also Ellis, Wade, Parker, and Hill interviews.

18. Hall, Lowrance, Wade, Parker, Hardin, Rogers, Bramblett, Ellis, and Queen interviews. Quote is from Lowrance, "Money Only Worth Its Weight."

19. The information on the tufted textile industry in this and the following paragraphs is from Young, *Textile Leaders of the South*, pp. 659–63; "Tufted Bedspreads," unpublished manuscript, CGA; Hamilton, "Bedspread Bonanza"; *Dalton Citizen*, "Progress Edition," 1940, CGA; Fleming, "Northwest Georgia Carpet Finishing Industry," pp. 4–6; Prather, "Woman Who Started Bedspread Boulevard"; and Jorges, "From Tough Times to Tufting," pp. 1–3. My thanks to Hilliard Jolly for this last reference.

20. Bramblett, Hall, and Parker interviews. See also Wykoff, "Tufted Bedspread Sampler," CGA.

21. Hall interview; see also Defore, Rogers, Bunch and Garren, Hill, Lowrance, Thompson, and Parker interviews.

22. Thompson, Defore, Hall, and Lowrance interviews; Lowrance, "Makin' Do."

23. Defore, Bunch and Garren, Queen, Lowrance, Ellis, Parker interviews.

24. Hall, Bunch and Garren interviews.

25. Pat W. Lowrance, "Hugh Cheek . . . a Special Kind of Gentleman," *Dalton Citizen-News*, 12 Mar. 1985, and "Money Only Worth Its Weight."

26. Thompson, Caylor, Defore, Ellis, Rogers interviews; *Directory of Dalton, 1924*; *Dalton City Directory*, 1936.

27. Bunch and Garren, Defore, Ellis, Rogers, and Thompson interviews.

28. Parker interview; see also Bunch and Garren interview.

29. Rogers and Ellis interviews; see also Cruce, Felker, Parker, Hall, Hill, and Thompson interviews.

30. Anderson quote is H. R. Fitzgerald's approving paraphrase of Anderson's speech. Fitzgerald was president of the ACMA; Anderson was on the ACMA's board of directors. See H. R. Fitzgerald to the Cotton Manufacturers of the South, 28 June 1928; T. M. Forbes to W. K. Moore, 5 Aug. 1929; "ACMA Committees for the Year 1931–32," typewritten list; all in MDB. Gavin Wright offers a useful analysis of the night work issue (*Old South, New South*, pp. 207–16).

31. H. R. Fitzgerald to the Cotton Manufacturers of the South, 28 June 1928, to which are attached the duplicates of the night-work survey as completed by Crown's managers, MDB.

32. Crown Cotton Mills to Munds, Rogers, and Stackpole, 23 Jan. 1922, MDB. The Crown payroll records first list "bonus" earnings in 1922. Pictures of Crown's Barber-Coleman machines can be seen in CrownAmerica, Inc., Annual Report, special centennial issue, 1984, "Century of Textile Product Excellence," CGA. Hall et al. (*Like a Family*, pp. 201–2) and Tullos (*Habits of Industry*, pp. 198–204) offer helpful discussions of the Barber-Coleman machines and their impact on the workers. The industrialists' quest for mechanical means to enhance efficiency was widespread and reached beyond the mill walls, as illustrated in Crown's investigation into "truck recorders," which allowed managers "to get more work out of motor trucks" by mechanically monitoring the truck drivers' activities (Service Recorder Company [reply] to Crown Cotton Mills, 30 Nov. 1921, MDB).

33. Felker interview; Wright, *Old South, New South*, p. 153.

34. CPR, 1926; BCPR, 1926.

CHAPTER 9

1. For an interesting theoretical discussion of decision-making processes within corporate settings, see Hirschman, *Exit, Voice, and Loyalty*.

2. J. S. Hall to Cornelius Lucky Hamilton, 8 Apr. 1939, MDB. All unemployment figures were calculated from U.S. Bureau of the Census, *Fifteenth Census, 1930: Unemployment*, 1:15–16, 19, 261–62, 276–78. The unemployment data was taken as part of the regular census enumeration for 1930, and the question asked was whether any person in the household had been unemployed the day before the enumerator's visit. In the figures I present here, I have combined the numbers from the two basic classifications of unemployment used by the census bureau: "class A," which included "persons out of a job, able to work, and looking for a job"; and "class B," which included "persons having jobs but on lay-off without pay, excluding those sick or voluntarily idle." The census gave no unemployment figure for Dalton, but it is safe to say the figure exceeded that of Whitfield County. Consider, for example, the figures for Rome, Georgia, the county seat of Floyd County, whose economy was roughly similar to that of Dalton. Unemployment in Floyd County was only 3.9 percent, but the rate in Rome was already 6.1 percent.

3. On business closings during the Great Depression, compare the 1924 list of main businesses in *History* (p. 158) with the businesses listed in the *Dalton City Directory*, 1936. This method does not provide the specific dates of business closings, but it offers a rough gauge for measuring the impact of economic stagnation. See also Felker interview.

4. Cruce, Ellis, and Felker interviews; see also Wade, Bunch and Garren, Parker, Hall, and Defore interviews.

5. Crown Cotton Mills Community Chest Records, 1932, MDB.

6. Robert Maddox [Atlanta, Ga.] to W. K. Moore, 29 Oct. 1932; W. K. M[oore] to Robert Maddox, 31 Oct. 1932; both in MDB.

7. BDM, Book 2, 31 Aug. 1931; H. R. Fitzgerald to G. W. Hamilton, 3 Apr. 1930, and G. W. Hamilton to H. R. Fitzgerald, 5 Apr. 1930, in MDB.

8. No payrolls survived from the early 1930s, so figures for Crown's average number of millhands were taken from *Moody's Investments: Industrial Securities*, 1928 (p. 746), 1930 (p. 189), 1933 (p. 312). According to the union, Crown laid off fifty workers between July and October 1933 (handwritten notes from Crown's initial Industrial Relations Committee meeting, 11 Oct. 1933). These notes are located, as is much of the information on which this chapter is based, in the After Strike Papers File, CGA (hereafter cited as SP). This small but rich collection of documents contains correspondence between the company and the local union written in the aftermath of the 1934 General Textile Strike, some revealing memos passed among mill supervisors and men in the big office before and after the strike, and copies of a few notices posted in the plant by mill officials. On the purging of married women from the 1930s payrolls, see Frank Springer, undated memo (ca. 1935) regarding female spinning-room workers, SP.

9. John A. Spurgeon to C. F. Springer, 17 Oct. 1934, in James Ratcliff Cases File, SP.

10. "In the Question of Discharge for Public Drunkenness," undated memorandum, ibid.; "Deep-South Dalton, Real Union Town," *Textile Labor*, 3 May 1947 (for Gregg's recollections of Crown Mill during the 1930s); Bunch and Garren interview.

11. Bunch and Garren interview; see also Wade and Hamilton interviews.

12. Bunch and Garren interview; see also Lowrance, Parker, and Queen interviews.

Various versions of the snuff and Springer episode were told at almost every workers' gathering I attended in 1984–85, although some millhands were opposed to the use of snuff.

13. General accounts of organized labor during the 1930s include Bernstein, *Turbulent Years*; Green, *World of the Worker*, chap. 5; and Zieger, *American Workers*, chaps. 1–2.

14. Bunch and Garren interview; see also Crow, Thompson, millhand (name withheld upon request) interviews.

15. This point speaks to an ongoing debate regarding welfare capitalism and organized labor in the United States. Nearly two decades ago David Brody challenged traditional labor historians by suggesting that American workers had made peace with the corporate paternalism of the early twentieth century and that the rapid rise of industrial unionism in the 1930s might not have occurred had not the Great Depression undermined the economic underpinnings of welfare capitalism ("Labor and the Great Depression," esp. p. 242). Some historians, including Stuart D. Brandes (*American Welfare Capitalism*) and Jacquelyn Dowd Hall et al. (*Like a Family*), have countered that workers saw through the sham of corporate welfare programs and were, in effect, waiting until the time was ripe for unionization. Several recent community studies, including this one, tend to substantiate Brody's hypothesis. See, for example, Tamara K. Hareven's work, which speaks of "the workers' sense of betrayal by the corporation" and their fear that "their faith in the paternalism of the Amoskeag was no longer justified" (*Family Time and Industrial Time*, p. 309). Hareven argues that the millhands' disenchantment was channeled into organized protest and unionization. That this occurred during the 1920s, when New England textiles suffered their own great depression, only underscores the point. See also Zahavi, *Workers, Managers, and Welfare Capitalism*, a subtle analysis of northern shoemakers and their acceptance, and use, of corporate paternalism.

16. Felker interview; see also Bunch and Garren, Wade interviews. Federal government intervention into mill business, as reflected in the NIRA, was a new development, but by 1930, state-level government intervention was an ordinary part of the mill business, as exemplified by the child labor law, factory safety inspections by the Department of Commerce and Labor, and the requirement that any mill accidents be reported to the Industrial Commission of Georgia ("Employer's . . . Report of Accident," W. E. Christie [Assistant Commissioner, Department of Commerce and Labor, Atlanta] to G. W. Hamilton, 14 Sept. 1929, and [Hamilton] to W. E. Christie, 17 Sept. 1929, all in MDB; Crown Cotton Mill Child Labor Certificates, 1926–34).

17. J. A. Fraser [Atlanta, Ga.] to W. K. Moore, 19, 23 May 1923, MDB.

18. Crown's managers were well aware of the labor problems that had arisen from the stretchout system, and their national and state manufacturing associations kept them well informed of new labor legislation and its potential impact on workers (T. M. Forbes [Cotton Manufacturers Association of Georgia, Atlanta] to Members of the [CMAG], 17 Apr. 1931; ibid., 3 Dec. 1932; "Minutes of Directors Meeting of the [CMAG], 11 Oct. 1932; all in MDB). On the 1929 strikes, see Hall et al., *Like a Family*, chap. 4, esp. pp. 212–36; Tindall, *Emergence of the New South*, pp. 342–53; Tippett, *When Southern Labor Stirs*.

19. Minutes of the Industrial Relations Committee meeting, 11 Oct. 1933, SP.

20. Ibid.

21. *Dalton Citizen*, 14 Aug. 1934.

22. On the General Textile Strike of 1934, see Irons, "Testing the New Deal"; Hodges, *New Deal Labor Policy*, chaps. 4–5; Hall et al., *Like a Family*, chap. 6.

23. *Dalton Citizen*, 30 Aug. 1934; *Atlanta Constitution*, 2, 3 Sept. 1934. Other mills in the

area also shut down. In nearby Lafayette, for instance, eight hundred textile workers went on strike, shutting down the two mills in that small town.

24. *Dalton Citizen*, 30 Aug., 6 Sept. 1934; *Atlanta Constitution*, 3 Mar. 1934.

25. *Dalton Citizen*, 13 Sept. 1934.

26. Ibid., 6 Sept. 1934.

27. Ibid.; Bunch and Garren interview.

28. *Dalton Citizen*, 6, 20 Sept. 1934; Hodges, *New Deal Labor Policy*, pp. 109–10; press release on Honea Path murders, n.d., US MSS 129A, Ser. 4, Box 1, "1934 General Textile Strike," TWUA Records, SHSW (italics mine).

29. Thompson interview. See also Hill and Wade interviews; Hodges, *New Deal Labor Policy*, pp. 105–6.

30. *Dalton Citizen*, 6, 20 Sept. 1934.

31. Memo dated 11 Sept. 1933, SP. For an overview of the UTW after the General Textile Strike, see Hodges, *New Deal Labor Policy*, chap. 8.

32. T. F. Lockridge to [Will Moore], 8 Jan. 1935, SP. See also cases concerning L. H. Lents and Oscar Smith, ibid. In some cases, both managers and millhands demonstrated much confusion as to which workers had actually joined the union; see, for example, R. L. Campbell to [Springer], Information on Irwin Cox, 13 Sept. 1934 and 10 Aug. 1934; Sam Hardin to Frank Springer, 1 Oct. 1934; Josie Hedgewood to Frank Springer, 1 Nov. 1934; all in ibid.

33. [Will Moore] to Crown Mill employees, undated memos, ibid.

34. John Spurgeon to [Will Moore], 15 Oct. 1934, ibid.

35. Edith Kyle and Tom Crow to W. K. Moore, 10 Oct. 1934, ibid.

36. Spurgeon to [Springer], 15, 16 Oct. 1934, ibid.

37. Tom Crow to Will Moore, letter with petition attached (names of petitioners not listed), 2 Oct. 1934; Spurgeon to [Springer], 16 Oct. 1934; Spurgeon and Ratcliff to Will Moore, 3 Oct. 1934; Petition in favor of Ratcliff, 4 Oct. 1934; Catherine Chaffin to [Will Moore], handwritten note on back of petition; ibid.

38. Ratcliff and Spurgeon to [Will Moore], 11 Oct. 1934, ibid.

39. John A. Spurgeon to C. F. Springer, 17 Oct. 1934, ibid.

40. W. A. Britton, Chief of Police, to Frank Springer, 24 Jan. 1935; J. M. Bunch to Will K. Moore, 28 Jan. 1934; Springer to [Will Moore], undated memo concerning Sim Craig's arrest; Springer to "Whom It May Concern," memo dated 30 Mar. 1935; all in ibid.

41. "In the Question of Discharge for Public Drunkenness," undated memorandum, ibid.

42. J. M. Bunch to Will Moore, 18 Feb. 1935; [Spurgeon] to Will Moore, memo on "public drunkenness," 26 Mar. 1935; Union to [Will Moore], memo on drunkards not discharged, 3 Apr. 1935; all in ibid.

43. Spurgeon to Springer, 30 Mar. 1935, ibid.

44. Hamilton to Will Moore, unsigned letter, 26 Mar. 1935; J. M. Bunch to Will Moore, 27 Mar. 1935; both in ibid.

45. Bunch and Garren, Hardin, Thompson, and millhand (name withheld upon request) interviews.

CHAPTER 10

1. Zieger, *American Workers*, pp. 35–41; Hodges, *New Deal Labor Policy*, p. 142.

2. MSS 396, Box 67, "UTW Absorbed Locals"; US MSS 129A, Ser. 7A, Box 1, "Resolutions

and Determinations of TWOC, Friday, Sept. 3rd, 1937"; *Textile Workers Song Sheet,* US MSS 129A, Ser. 14A, Box 1, "Inter-Office Forms"; all in TWUA Records, SHSW. See also Hodges, *New Deal Labor Policy,* chap. 9; Richards, "History of the Textile Workers Union," chap. 2.

3. Richards, "History of the Textile Workers Union," pp. 91–149, esp. 108; *Dalton Citizen,* 8 June 1939; *Textile Labor,* 3 May 1947.

4. Hamilton's account of these developments is in *Dalton Citizen,* 8 June 1939.

5. Hodges, *New Deal Labor Policy,* pp. 175–77; *Dalton Citizen,* 8 June 1939; press release, 15 May 1939, US MSS 129A, Ser. 14A, Box 1, "Southern Phase of TWOC Organization," TWUA Records, SHSW. This last reference stated that despite corporate resistance, intimidation, and violence against unions, TWOC had "27 contracts below the Mason-Dixon line, covering 27,000 workers. It has won 60 NLRB elections, covering 40,000 workers. It has the signatures of 85,000 southern textile workers on pledge cards."

6. *Dalton Citizen,* 8 June 1939.

7. Ibid., 1 June 1939.

8. Ibid.; Defore interview. The quote about men in the road is from transcribed testimony in *Boyd* v. *Crown.*

9. *Dalton Citizen,* 22 June 1939.

10. *Boyd* v. *Crown.*

11. *Dalton Citizen,* 8 June 1939.

12. Ibid., 15 June 1939.

13. Ibid., 8 June 1939.

14. Hardin, Wade interviews; *Hosiery Worker,* 6 Apr. 1934, in George S. Mitchell Papers, Box 2, "Labor, Georgia," Manuscripts Department, Perkins Library, Duke University, Durham, N.C. (thanks to Janet Irons for this reference).

15. *Dalton Citizen,* 29 June, 6, 13 July 1939. American Thread unionists charged the press with inflating the number of returning workers. Although the *Chattanooga Times* reported 150 hands back at work, the Dalton union claimed the number was a mere 110 and that 238 were necessary to run a full shift (see *Dalton Citizen,* 20 July 1939).

16. This information and all subsequent calculations of strike support are based on CPR and BCPR, 1939. See table A.3 for statistics on strike support and appendix B for further elaboration on the data.

17. *Dalton Citizen,* 13 July 1939.

18. Ibid., 20, 27 July 1939.

19. Ibid., 27 July, 17 Aug. 1939.

20. Queen, Rogers, and Hardin interviews.

21. Caylor, Bunch and Garren, Bramblett, and Wade interviews.

22. Hardin interview; interviews with two millhands (names withheld upon request).

23. Bramblett, Ellis interviews; see also Lowrance, Bunch and Garren, Rogers, Defore, Crow, Parker, Thompson, and Hall interviews.

24. Hall et al., *Like a Family,* pp. 340–49.

25. Briefly, logit analysis is an alternative to the standard form of multiple regression analysis (ordinary least squares regression, or simply OLS) used in chapter 5. I have used logit instead of OLS because the dependent variable in the regression equation is a dichotomous, categorical variable. A dichotomous dependent variable has the qualities of a "dummy" variable, that is, it has only two possible values, neither of which can be said to be "higher" or "lower" on an interval scale. If such a variable is used as the dependent variable in an OLS equation, then the estimated coefficients will be inaccurate.

26. This result is further substantiated by information disclosed in a court case related to

the strike, in which a group of 159 strikebreakers sued both the state of Georgia and Crown Mill after the struggle had ended. In effect, these people represent a sample of Crown's strikebreakers (65 percent of the total number). Court records give the addresses of the claimants, and those residences are instructive: fully 66 percent of the sample lived in Crown Mill housing at the time of the conflict. In short, these strikebreakers clearly were not newcomers. Moreover, those who lived in Dalton but outside the mill village (11 percent of the sample) generally had addresses near the village and can hardly be viewed as outsiders. And if the testimony given by workers in the court case is any indication, the 23 percent who lived outside of Dalton (in small towns or in the countryside) were not outsiders but longtime workers who commuted to the mill and viewed themselves as part of the Crown community (see *Boyd* v. *Crown*). The representativeness of this sample is hard to evaluate, but it is a large sample, and given the results of the logit, it is unlikely that the residential distribution of nonclaimant strikebreakers was decidedly different from that of the claimants.

27. Queen interview.

28. *Crown Cotton Mills* v. *Lewis Weaver et al.*, No. 18, Whitfield County Superior Court, October Term, 1939; Injunction, etc., by John C. Mitchell, Judge Superior Court, 19 Aug. 1939, copy in Whitfield Superior Court minutes, Book No. 22, p. 388, Whitfield County Courthouse, Dalton, Ga.; *Dalton Citizen*, 24 Aug. 1939.

29. *Dalton Citizen*, 28 Sept. 1939.

30. Wade interview; see also Bunch and Garren and millhand (name withheld on request) interviews.

31. Bunch and Garren, millhand (name withheld upon request) interviews.

32. *Boyd* v. *Crown*.

33. Ibid.

CHAPTER 11

1. F. H. Babcock to C. L. "Neil" Hamilton, 2 Oct. 1939, MDB.

2. When I refer to Crown company business, years mean fiscal years, which ran from 1 September to 31 August. Hence 1940 refers to the fiscal year ending 31 August 1940. For Crown profits, see table A.2.

3. Even before the fall of France and the passage of America's National Defense Act in June 1940, the quartermaster of the War Department had conducted a thorough investigation of Crown's productive capabilities. The quartermaster issued a survey in May 1940. The final contract, after a series of cordial adjustments between Crown and the War Department, was agreed to by George W. Hamilton, Jr., president of Crown, on 21 August 1940. The mill agreed, in the event of a national emergency, to produce a variety of yarns and woven cloth (including duck, bunting, drills, and osnaburgs, amounting to 622,000 yards of cloth per month) for military use. This work would employ at least a full shift and possibly more. Some of the War Department's "Schedule of Production" forms indicate that Crown and the quartermaster had drawn up previous schedules of military production in May and June 1938, but other information about these earlier government orders, if they were such, has not been found in the company records. See "Atlanta Quartermaster Procurement Planning District," MDB.

4. F. C. Denning to Crown Cotton Mills, 8 Aug. 1940, ibid.

5. Ibid.

6. [George W. Hamilton, Jr.,] to J. H. Lane and Co., 10 Aug. 1940, MDB.

7. "Surplus: Crown Cotton Mills, from August 31, 1928, to August 31, 1946," loose-leaf report, ibid.

8. F. C. Denning to Crown Cotton Mills, 8 Aug. 1940, ibid. As Denning's correspondence indicated, textile leaders were closely attuned to—and at the forefront of—industrial mobilization. Cotton mills had reaped enormous profits during World War I and knew which way the wind was blowing in 1940. That June the Council of National Defense tapped Robert T. Stevens of the J. P. Stevens Company as chair of the Textile Products Division. Stevens launched an immediate campaign to gather information from industry leaders and soon became an aggressive coordinator of national textile interests, playing a key role in settling the "duck situation" that August. In time he took charge of procuring all textile products for the quartermaster general.

Early on, Stevens announced his wartime concerns for the textile industry. The four major potential problems that the Textile Products Division had to combat, he said, were (1) the federal government might take over production decisions and even factories; (2) the government might take over prices; (3) the mills would lose their profits to wartime taxes; and (4) (lest anyone had missed the general thrust of points 1, 2, and 3) that the textile industry might experience an overall loss of control to the government. Thanks in part to Stevens's active involvement, textile mill managers averted an overabundance of government control and secured wartime contracts that virtually guaranteed hefty profits. Textile leaders made their presence very much felt in both the Office of Price Administration and the War Production Board. Mildred G. Andrews offers a laudatory account of Stevens's efforts (*Men and the Mills*, pp. 135–38).

9. Solomon Barkin, TWUA research director, in *Textile Labor*, 1 Dec. 1940.

10. *Dalton Citizen*, 25 Sept. 1941.

11. U.S. Department of Labor, *Employment and Earnings*, p. 188.

12. *Dalton Citizen*, 7 Mar., 20 June, 28 July 1940. James Cobb offers an overview of pre–World War II efforts by southern business leaders (the focus is on Mississippi) to attract industry (*Selling of the South*, chap. 1).

13. *Dalton Citizen*, 25 July, 17 Oct. 1940.

14. This saying was a regular weekly blurb in the *Dalton Citizen*. The 7 March 1940 edition also includes an editorial waxing eloquent about "bedspread Georgia" and a poem by "LWC," who, judging by what might be termed the poet's general lack of subtlety, was doubtless getting rich off the burgeoning industry: "At night when rain is on the roof / We sleep beneath the warp and woof / Of Dalton's famous spreads. / Whene're we wake to greet the sun / The feeling is a pleasant one / They're on a billion beds!"

15. For just a few references to chenille plant creations and expansions prior to Pearl Harbor, see *Dalton Citizen*, 5, 19 Oct. 1939, 1 Feb., 21 Mar., 11 July, 24 Oct. 1940, 9 Jan., 20 Mar., 1, 15 May 1941.

16. Ibid., 26 Oct. 1939.

17. Ibid., 24 Oct. 1940. In the summer of 1940, Dalton's workers actually experienced a rise in unemployment, but this situation eased rapidly in succeeding months.

18. Ibid., 3 Apr. 1941.

19. Ibid., 17 Apr. 1941.

20. From 1940, when Crown began to receive military contracts, through 1943, Hill's yearly earnings increased 69.6 percent, while inflation during the same period was only 9.8 percent. Most of this boost to Hill's earning power actually occurred before Pearl Harbor, but her annual earnings continued to rise until 1944, when she missed nearly a year's work in order to give birth to her first child. It must have amazed the Hills to discover that, after

missing a full seven-and-a-half months of work in 1944 to care for her new son, Cletus Hill, Jr., and having worked full-time for only fourteen weeks of the year, Lillie earned as much in 1944 as she had for an entire year of steady work in 1938 (even after controlling for inflation). These figures are calculated from Lillie Ann Goforth Hill, Social Security Record Book, 1937–70, copy in author's possession (courtesy of Lillie Hill, Dalton, Ga.); U.S. Bureau of the Census, *Historical Statistics*, p. 210.

21. Georgia Department of Labor, Annual Report, 1941, p. 7, GDAH; *Textile Labor*, 3 Dec. 1941.

22. *Textile Labor*, March, July 1942; more generally, see Zieger, *American Workers*, chap. 3.

23. *Textile Labor*, July 1943.

24. Felker, Caylor interviews.

25. *Dalton Citizen*, 27 Aug. 1942; Bramblett interview.

26. *Dalton Citizen*, 19 Oct. 1944. On married women's work at Crown, see Bunch and Garren, Hughes interviews. Married women's factory work during World War II in the South is a virtually unexplored topic. On the non-South, see Milkman, *Gender at Work*.

27. The local press maintained a singularly antiunion stance after the 1939 strike and throughout early 1940 (see, e.g., *Dalton Citizen*, 6, 13 June, 8 Aug., 12 Sept. 1940), but in late 1940 and 1941 the press began to publish more news about Dalton's working people and even to offer favorable stories about local unions (see ibid., 17 Oct., 28 Nov., 19 Dec. 1940, 1 Jan., 6 Feb., 24 Apr., 28 Aug. 1941).

28. Ibid., 15 Jan., 9, 19 Feb. 1942.

29. Ibid., 3 Sept., 17 Dec. 1942, 4 Feb., 27 May, 16 Sept. 1943.

30. Ibid., 4 Feb., 24 June 1943.

31. Ibid., 15 July 1943. Irene Bailey was listed in Dalton's city directory for 1936 as the spouse of Archie E. Bailey and as the mother of one child. The couple lived in the American Thread mill village. In 1936 Irene was not listed as a worker, so she may have returned to the mill during the war like many wives and mothers in the textile South. The couple was not listed in the next city directory, which was compiled in 1948.

32. *Dalton Citizen*, 25 Nov. 1943.

33. Ibid., 25 Jan., 15 Mar. 1945; Lucile Hall interview. When it became clear that American cotton mills were far surpassing British mills in production per person-hour, the British authorities launched an investigation. The result was the Platt Report, which, while attempting to show that American millhands were simply better workers, inadvertently painted a picture of grueling work regimens for textile workers in the United States. Virtually all mills ran three eight-hour shifts (without breaks) for six days a week, using high-speed machinery, implementing scientific management techniques, and forcing their workers to tend an ever greater number of machines. America's millhands, the report concluded, were not overworked; they were "indefatigable" (see Andrews, *Men and the Mills*, p. 146, which accepts both the spirit and the letter of the Platt Report).

34. In 1940 and 1941, when war production had already started, a total of 10,015 industrial accidents (excluding fatalities) was reported in Georgia's textile mills. During the next two years the accident rate rose to 14,813. Most of these were minor accidents (72 percent in 1940–41 and 74 percent in 1942–43) for which millhands received no compensation from the state. About one in four accidents in both time periods were classified as "temporary" and therefore compensable. Slightly more than 3 percent in both periods were "permanent," either "partial" or "total." There were twelve fatalities during 1940–41 and nine during 1942–43. No comparable figures are available for 1945. In 1940–41, textile mill accidents comprised 12.83 percent of the state's total reported industrial accidents; in 1942–43, textile

accidents increased to 16.53 percent of the state total. The Department of Labor report in 1945 also stressed the need for improved sanitation in Georgia's mills. It was not heartening that the new rules of factory sanitation had to specify "adequate screening and rat proofing . . . for such services as lunch, toilet, locker, wash and first aid rooms, and any place where people work." The September 1944 issue of *Textile Labor* discussed a cotton mill near Atlanta in which the drinking water was constantly polluted by sewage. Apparently such stories had some basis in fact, because the Department of Labor noted similar problems in Georgia's factories, adding, "This condition is not altogether infrequent." All figures in this note are computed from Georgia Department of Labor, Annual Report, 1942 (p. 44), 1944 (p. 38), 1945 (opening letter of Labor Commissioner Ben T. Huiet and pp. 3, 38–43, 41–42), all in GDAH.

35. Hall, Bunch and Garren interviews. See also Hardin interview; Zieger, *American Workers*, p. 97.

36. Robert Zieger offers a useful overview of organized labor's "no-strike" pledge and the workings of the National War Labor Board (*American Workers*, pp. 85–94). Not surprisingly, the labor stabilization law created an uproar. See the *Dalton Citizen*, 8 July 1943, in which the deputy regional director of the War Manpower Commission tried to clarify the new law, over which, he claimed, there was "almost universal misunderstanding."

37. *Dalton Citizen*, 11, 18 Jan., 5 Apr., 21 June 1945. By the end of the war, the editors of the *Dalton Citizen* had apparently already mastered the ability to cheer government's problem-solving agencies while simultaneously blaming America's socioeconomic problems on government bureaucracy. For example, editors praised President Truman and Congress for pushing through a much-needed national emergency housing act in early 1946 at a cost of $850 million. One week later, they argued that the housing shortage itself was the product of big government and its bureaucratic bungling (see ibid., 14, 21 Feb. 1946).

38. Ibid., 8 Mar. 1945. As early as fall 1944, local editors had voiced concern over Dalton's postwar economic prospects and the need to have jobs waiting for returning GIs. See ibid., 26 Oct. 1944, for one example, and ibid., 16 Nov. 1944, for a large front-page story headlined "Area Post-War Plans Ready."

39. Ibid., 10 May 1945.

40. *Textile Labor* noted, just before the Allied victory over Japan, that military demand for duck was up 100 percent in 1945 compared with government requirements in 1943–44 (Aug. 1945). On the textile labor shortage, see *Dalton Citizen*, 2 Aug. 1945, which cites a report from the Atlanta Federal Reserve Bank.

41. *Dalton Citizen*, 21 June 1945.

42. *Textile Labor*, Oct. 1943, Sept. 1944.

43. *Dalton Citizen*, 2 Aug. 1945.

44. *Textile Labor*, Sept. 1945.

45. Ibid.

46. See Zieger, *American Workers*, pp. 97–108; *Textile Labor*, Oct., Nov. 1945.

47. *Final Proceedings of the Eighth Constitutional Convention of the Congress of Industrial Organizations*, Nov. 1946 (Washington, D.C.: Allied Printing), pp. 52–53, 57, noted that TWUA had signed 436 new contracts nationwide between 1943 and 1946, covering 101,976 workers. The report on the southern campaign added that the CIO had won 86 percent of the 174 National Labor Relations Board (NLRB) elections (150 wins to 24 losses) since the drive began.

On Operation Dixie, see Griffith, *Crisis of American Labor*; Salmond, *Miss Lucy of the CIO*, chap. 7; Marshall, *Labor in the South*, chap. 15 (Murray's first quote on p. 254). Murray's speech to the auto workers is quoted from Walter P. Reuther to All Union Locals, 18 May 1946, UAW Local 216 Papers, Archives of Labor History and Urban Affairs, Wayne State University.

48. Zieger, *American Workers*, pp. 114–23.

49. On disfranchisement and the rise of the one-party South, see Kousser, *Shaping of Southern Politics*.

50. Key, *Southern Politics*, chaps. 6, 27–29 (esp. p. 578, n. 2); Bartley, *Creation of Modern Georgia*, pp. 185–90.

51. Key, *Southern Politics*, pp. 124–29, 606–8.

52. EBM, 13 June, 28 Sept. 1946.

53. *Dalton Citizen*, special centennial edition, 16 Oct. 1947.

54. Ibid., 4 Apr. 1946. The local PAC unit also emphasized that Tarver had voted "wrong" on both the Patman Housing Bill (against it) and on a price control bill (to weaken it), two issues about which the CIO International was particularly concerned.

55. *Dalton Citizen*, 11 Apr. 1946.

56. Ibid., 11 July 1946.

57. The Tarver campaign received sporadic coverage in the *Citizen* from mid-April through mid-July; the election results were reported on 18 July 1946. In that issue, the popular vote was listed as 36,678 for Lanham, 12,319 for Tarver; in the paper's special centennial issue (16 Oct. 1947), a story on Tarver inexplicably claimed that Tarver had amassed a 2,000-vote popular majority in the 1946 election but lost via the county unit electoral system. What I call here the "crescent of labor" is a largely understudied area in southern labor history. Surprisingly little work has been done on organized workers in Atlanta and Chattanooga, for example. The labor activism of this area in the immediate postwar period can be seen in a survey of *Textile Labor* for the late 1940s. There seems to have been a symbiotic relationship between the area's labor activism and the successes of the left-liberal Highlander Folk School in east Tennessee (see Glen, *Highlander*).

58. Griffith, *Crisis of American Labor*; Zieger, *American Workers*, pp. 108–23; *Dalton Citizen*, 27 Feb., 28 June 1947.

59. A casual perusal through the Local 185 executive board minutes during the late 1940s will clearly demonstrate the point about expanding connections to regional and national labor. For the trips to Atlanta specifically mentioned here, see EBM, 26 Jan., 24 Feb. 1947; *Dalton Citizen*, 6 Mar. 1947.

60. Lanham's committee is listed in *Dalton Citizen*, 4 Sept. 1947; further information about those listed was compiled from the Dalton city directories for 1936 and 1948; *Textile Labor*, 3 May 1947; informal conversations with former Crown workers.

61. *Dalton Citizen*, 9, 16 Oct. 1947. In ibid., 25 Mar. 1948, Stafford reappeared in the local press as Georgia secretary for Henry Wallace's Progressive party and as a target (ironically) of the CIO's purge of left-leaning unionists.

62. Ibid., 9, 16 Oct. 1947 (italics in original).

63. Ibid.; *Dalton City Directory*, 1948.

64. *Dalton Citizen*, 16 Oct. 1947.

65. Ibid.

66. Ibid., 9, 16 Oct. 1947.

67. Ibid., 8, 20 Nov., 4, 11 Dec. 1947.

68. Ibid., 4 (Clark's quote), 11 Dec. 1947.

69. Ibid., 4, 11 Dec. 1947, 23 Nov., 9 Dec. 1948.

70. See ibid., 6 Jan. 1948, 3 Feb. 1949 (Britton's remark), for examples of anti-Klan

editorials. The same editors were against national civil rights measures that would impinge on local control and local solutions (see, e.g., 23 Sept. 1948). Taking a typically confusing stand on race relations and civil rights, the 17 March 1949 issue supports civil rights legislation in one article and opposes it in another. The issue of southern labor and race in the 1940s is woefully understudied; for a pathbreaking study, see Korstad and Lichtenstein, "Opportunities Found and Lost."

71. *Dalton Citizen*, 21, 28 Apr., 5, 12, 19 May 1949. Early in 1949, Local 185 had received a letter from the state CIO office asking Crown's union to set up a "10th anniversary committee" in Dalton. Local 185 pledged $100 for the festivities and agreed to "absorb the additional expense of the 10th anniversary committee" (EBM, 13 Feb., 13 Mar. 1949).

72. *Dalton Citizen*, 12 May 1949; Cronic quoted in EBM, 29 Jan. 1949.

CHAPTER 12

1. Herring, *Passing of the Mill Village*.

2. See Moreland, *Millways of Kent* and "Kent Revisited" ("Kent" was York, South Carolina, and Moreland's sociological fieldwork was done in 1948 and 1958); Gilman, *Human Relations*; Cobb, *Selling of the South*, chap. 10, esp. pp. 265–68; Griffith, *Crisis of American Labor* (which sees the traditional cultural climate of the South and its mill villages as one of several factors in mitigating postwar unionization). Two books on earlier periods that point toward continuity in the postwar era are Carlton, *Mill and Town*, which notes, "The hostilities of the period before 1920 produced an antipathy toward the town that is still discernible in southern mill centers, and the grievances of the operatives of that age against reformers live on in the operatives' present-day distrust of unions and liberals" (p. 271); and Hodges, *New Deal Labor Policy*, pp. 192–98 (quote on p. 192). Two recent surveys that stress textile-worker continuity despite their overall themes of change are Roland, *Improbable Era* (see esp. pp. 17–18); and Goldfield, *Promised Land* (esp. pp. 146–47). Joseph A. McDonald offers a portrait of passive and alienated workers in Dalton's carpet industry in the 1970s ("Textile Workers and Unionization"). McDonald, a sociologist, provides a sophisticated quantitative analysis of recent employee questionnaires; his historical analysis of Dalton's industrial development is less impressive.

3. *Dalton City Directory*, 1948, pp. 429–34 (quote on p. 11).

4. Ibid., 1936, 1948; *Dalton Citizen*, 11 June, 19 Nov. 1953.

5. Population and labor statistics in this and the following paragraph were computed from U.S. Bureau of the Census, *Census of Population: 1950*, vol. 2, *Characteristics of the Population*, pt. 11, Georgia, pp. 11, 35, 38, 68, 72, 144.

6. *Dalton Citizen*, 11 May 1950.

7. Ibid., 13 July 1950.

8. *Textile Labor*, 1 Sept. 1941.

9. To suggest that most workers wanted to buy the homes in which they lived is not to say all workers were happy with what they bought. Rumblings of discontent rolled through American Thread in early 1951, when homeowners first confronted county tax assessors. In late February, some fifty workers from American Thread gathered before the city council to protest the recent tax assessments of their newly purchased homes. This was front-page news in the *Citizen*. The workers complained that the village homes were all assessed equally, even though they ranged in size from three to six rooms per house. The protesters, presumably those who owned the smaller, three-room homes, called for a reassessment. As one worker, Herman A. Scott, informed the *Citizen*, "Something is awful wrong when a

three-room house is valued at $1,750, and right along side it, a six-room dwelling for the same. They handed us a book to sign, and gave us no chance to file a fair tax return." Although this protest did not reflect labor solidarity, as presumably workers in six-room houses had little complaint about their assessment, it nonetheless bespoke an ongoing frustration festering in the ranks of Dalton's millhands. Many felt they were not being treated as equal citizens in local political and economic affairs (see *Dalton Citizen*, 22 Feb. 1951). According to Dalton city directories, Herman Scott was a longtime employee—an overseer, in fact—at the American Thread Mill. It is unclear whether the man referred to in the *Citizen* was the overseer or his son, Herman, Jr., who also worked at American Thread.

10. Herring, *Passing of the Mill Village*, p. 52.

11. Ibid., pp. 16–23.

12. Ibid., p. 113; BDM, Book 3, 12 Mar. 1946, 28 Sept. 1949 (David replaced Henry Hamilton, who died 29 August, as secretary and a director), 12 Dec. 1950 (Neil elected president upon the death of "Little George"), 26 Sept. 1951 (G. Lane Hamilton, David's cousin, filled George's place on the board of directors), 11 Dec. 1951 (upon Neil's death, David was elected president; also Joe K. Hamilton, son of longtime master mechanic Frank Hamilton, was elected to fill Neil's place on the board, in addition to his ongoing duties as Crown's general production manager).

13. Hamilton interview.

14. Ibid.

15. BDM, Book 3, 17 June 1952, 17 June, 28 Oct. 1953.

16. Hamilton interview.

17. Ibid.

18. Hamilton, Felker interviews; Crown Cotton Mills statement of profit and loss, year ending 31 August 1953, MDB.

19. BDM, Book 3, 31 Aug. 1954; Felker, Bunch and Garren interviews.

20. Bunch and Garren interview; BDM, Book 3, 31 Aug. 1954, 31 Aug. 1955.

21. Hamilton, Bunch and Garren, Lowrance interviews.

22. Parker, Cruce, interviews.

23. Lowrance, Parker interviews. By the mid-1960s, 89 percent of all Georgians between the ages of five and seventeen would be enrolled in school; the national average was only 84 percent (see Maddox et al., *Advancing South*, p. 236).

24. Roland, *Improbable Era*, pp. 17–18; Goldfield, *Promised Land*, p. 146; Hodges, *New Deal Labor Policy*, pp. 192–93.

25. Too often the argument for historical continuity is based on the works of sociologists, particularly John Kenneth Moreland (*Millways of Kent*), Joseph McDonald ("Textile Workers"), and Robert Botsch (*We Shall Not Overcome*)—all of which offer rich descriptions of contemporary realities but fail to demonstrate a thorough grasp of larger historical developments.

26. Cobb, *Selling of the South*, chap. 10 (quote on p. 267).

27. Crown Mill Employee Data Cards, CGA. There are an estimated ten thousand cards, of which I took an approximate 5 percent sample. The cards are 8-x-5-inch note cards, filed in alphabetical order. They have spaces reserved for the following information: name, social security number, date of birth, date employment began, date employment ended, reason employment ended, occupation at Crown, work record, male/female, married/single. Unfortunately, the cards were seldom filled out completely. Names, birth dates, and employment dates are universally noted. Reason for termination, "work record" notes, occupation, and even marital status are usually not indicated.

28. *Textile Labor,* Sept. 1956 (italics in original).

29. U.S. Bureau of the Census, *Census of Agriculture: 1959,* 1(28): county table 2 and pp. 182–94; Goldfield, *Promised Land,* pp. 22–27 (quote on p. 25); Dodd and Dodd, *Historical Statistics,* pp. 18–21. Two major works on larger agricultural trends (which offer differing assessments of southern change) are Daniel, *Breaking the Land,* and Fite, *Cotton Fields No More.*

30. Maddox et al., *Advancing South,* pp. 45 (table 3-5), 24 (table 2-3).

31. U.S. Bureau of the Census, *Census of Agriculture: 1959,* 1(28): pp. 182–94 and county table 2; idem, *County and City Data Book,* 1952, pp. 146–53; ibid., 1967, pp. 72–81.

32. *Dalton Citizen,* 11 June (quote), 19 Nov. 1953; Dalton city directories for 1936 and 1948.

33. *Dalton Citizen,* 22 Dec. 1949, 1 Mar. 1951 (an early reference to "wall-to-wall carpeting"), 21 Feb., 23 Oct. 1952, 15 Oct., 19 Nov. 1953.

34. As late as 1980, a survey of Dalton's carpet workers (who in 1980 were, on average, in their early forties) revealed that one-third had been the children of farmers (McDonald, "Textile Workers," p. 142, table 5-2). On postwar urbanization generally, see Goldfield, *Promised Land,* pp. 33–39.

35. Ann. Rpt., 1960, CGA; Andrews, *Men and the Mills,* p. 110.

CHAPTER 13

1. The union membership figures are for nonagricultural employees; see Troy, *Distribution of Union Membership,* pp. 18–19, table 4.

2. Bramblett interview.

3. The work of these deeply committed union members is apparent in GM and EBM. Minutes for the general membership meetings do not give attendance figures, but it is clear from those listed as participants and the recording of votes taken that those in attendance at the general meetings were essentially the executive officers, shop stewards, and their families.

4. For more on Local 185's concern with stretchouts, speedups, and textile modernization during the 1950s, see chapter 14 below.

5. GM, 27 Aug. (quote), 10 Sept. 1949; EBM, 20 Aug. 1949, 29 Sept. 1951; Minutes of the Whitfield County Labor Council, Oct. 1953–Aug. 1954, TWUA Local 185 Records, Box 9, SLA. In the Whitfield County organization, each union local had one delegate for each one hundred members. The labor council was organized, and had its first meeting, on 25 October 1953; the minutes for mid-1954 are the last ones available in the TWUA Local 185 Records, SLA.

6. GM, 26 Nov. 1949, 28 Jan. 1950, 14 Jan. (quote on Calhoun Mills), 24 Mar., 14 Apr., 9 June, 14 July, 25 Aug., 20 Oct., 15 Dec. 1951, 7, 19 June, 6 Sept., 18 Oct. 1952, 24 May 1953; EBM, 5 Nov. (quote on Local 1721), 31 Dec. 1950, 18 Mar. 1951.

7. See, e.g., GM, 23 July 1949, 28 Jan., 9 Aug., 26 Nov., 11 Dec. 1950, 11 Aug., 20 Oct. 1951, 5 Jan., 1 Mar., 16 Aug. (quote), 18 Oct. 1952; EBM, 3 Dec. 1950, 13 Oct. 1951.

8. First quote in Minutes of the Whitfield County Labor Council, 6 Feb. 1954, TWUA Local 185 Records, Box 9, SLA; for specific references to PAC activities, see GM, 9, 23 July, 10, 24 Aug., 22 Oct. 1949, 12 Apr., 28 July, 25 Aug., 6 Oct. 1953; EBM, 15 Oct. 1949, 26 Sept., 3 Dec. 1950, 28 Apr. 1951. For other local, regional, and national political activities, see GM, 11 June, 10 Dec. 1949, 22 July, 14 Oct. 1950, 17 Nov., 15 Dec. 1951, 15 Mar., 5 Apr., 4 Oct. (Bunch's quote) 1952; EBM, 25 Sept., 17 Nov., 29 Dec. 1951.

9. [Friend of Mr. George Howell] to J. R. Bunch, President, 27 Sept. 1957, TWUA Local 185 Records, Box 1, "Misc. Correspondence [to J. R. Bunch]," SLA. For national and regional

philanthropic efforts, see GM, 24 Aug. 1949, 12 Nov. 1950, 10 Mar., 17 Nov., 1 Dec. 1951, 15 Nov., 20 Dec. 1952, 25 Jan., 10 May 1953. On community concerns, see EBM, 5 Nov. 1950; GM, 22 July, 14 Oct., 26 Nov. 1950, 20 Oct. (Local 185 president, Jack Gregg, "talks about the charity drive to be conducted in Dalton and wants all the people to cooperate with it"), 15 Dec. 1951.

10. Quotes in EBM, 22 Apr. 1950; GM, 9 Sept. 1950, 5 Apr. 1952, 1 Dec. 1951. See also EBM, 26 Sept. 1950; GM, 26 Aug., 23 Sept., 14 Oct. 1950, 24 Mar., 12, 26 May 1951, 2 Jan. 1952.

11. EBM, 3 Sept., 31 Dec. 1949, 27 May 1952 (charter of incorporation); GM, 12 Nov., 10 Dec. 1949, 10 Mar., 14 Apr., 1 Dec. 1951, 2 Feb., 15 Mar., 19 June 1952, 12 Apr. 1953 (showing how the union became an employer in its own right, e.g., "Mr. Nelson has been employed to bring six loads of dirt [to the Union Hall yard] at $5.50 per load").

12. Griffith, *Crisis of American Labor*; Zieger, *American Workers*, pp. 108–21; Goldfield, *Decline of Organized Labor*, pp. 184–86; Lanham speech in *Congressional Record*, House of Representatives, 11 June 1957, p. 7823.

13. Troy, *Trade Union Membership*, p. A-27, table A-2; Fink, *Labor Unions*, p. 385, and *Biographical Dictionary*, p. 12.

14. *Dalton Citizen*, 22 Dec. 1949, 17 Aug. 1950, 17 May, 13 Dec. 1951, 23 Oct., 27 Nov. 1952, 18 June, 24 Sept. 1953, 21 Oct. 1954, 24 Feb. 1955.

15. *The Southerner*, July 1955; *Dalton Citizen*, 25 Mar. 1948; Dunbar, *Against the Grain*, p. 246.

16. On southern radicalism during the 1930s and beyond, see Glen, *Highlander* (on West, pp. 16–20, 26); Dunbar, *Against the Grain*, (on West, pp. 211–13, 228–29); and Kelley, *Hammer and Hoe*, which notes that in 1940 West contributed a column called "The Awakening Church" to the *Southern News Almanac*, a radical paper published in Birmingham, Alabama (pp. 196–97). The format of that paper, and the sentiments West voiced in it, were similar to what later emerged in West's own paper, *The Southerner*. Kelley states that West "joined the Communist Party in 1934" (p. 126); Dunbar suggests that West's party affiliation remains uncertain (p. 54).

17. Few issues of *The Southerner* have survived. I have been able to locate only three issues: May 1955, at SLA; July 1955, at CGA; and Jan. 1956, which is on microfilm at the University of Georgia Libraries. I determined the date of the first issue from the May and July 1955 issues, which are volume 1, issue numbers 3 and 5, respectively. The January 1956 issue was probably the last, as West left town permanently shortly thereafter.

18. Quotes from *The Southerner*, May 1955, but similar ideas and phrases can be found in the other issues of the paper and in Pratt's and West's statements in the local business press during 1955.

19. *The Southerner*, May 1955; John W. Edelman [TWUA Washington representative] to Very Reverend Msgr. George G. Higgins, 9 Sept. 1955, John Ramsey Papers, Box 1563, folder 99, SLA; Donald L. West to James O'Shea, 23 May 1955, ibid., Box 1559, folder 49.

20. *The Southerner*, May 1955. John R. Bunch eventually went into full-time work for the TWUA International. The son of Crown's second union president, Marion Bunch, John enlisted in the navy during World War II and later returned to work for Crown. Just before World War II he had married Sarah Travillian, who also came from a strong union family and herself became an influential person in the union. During the 1950s, John held several important posts in Local 185, including that of president. By the early 1960s, John left Local 185 to work for the International and was active in union campaigns in other Georgia towns. On the Bunch family, see Bunch and Garren interview; *Textile Labor*, Dec. 1962, Jan., Nov. 1963; TWUA Local 185 Records, SLA, generally.

21. "Statement of David Burgess, Executive Secretary, Georgia State CIO Council," 10

May 1955; C. H. Gillman to William Pollock, 10 May 1955; David S. Burgess to William Pollock, 11 May 1955 (this letter has attached the HUAC report on West requested by Congressman Lanham); William Pollock to James O'Shea, 13 May 1955; William Pollock to David S. Burgess, 16 May 1955; William Pollock to Charles H. Gillman, 16 May 1955; James O'Shea to William Pollock, 17 May 1955; all in John Ramsey Papers, Box 1559, folder 49, SLA.

22. James O'Shea to William Pollock, 17 May 1955, John Ramsey Papers, Box 1559, folder 49, SLA. In an apparent concession to the International's wishes, Local 185's "As We See It" column disappeared from *The Southerner*, but John Bunch continued to publish his own independent "As I See It" column in the paper.

23. For a useful overview of the CIO's anticommunist purges, see Zieger, *American Workers*, pp. 123–34.

24. James O'Shea to William Pollock, 17 May 1955; O'Shea to Donald L. West, 19 May 1955; West to O'Shea, 23 May 1955; O'Shea to Pollock, 31 May 1955; Pollock to O'Shea, 6 June 1955; all in John Ramsey Papers, Box 1559, folder 49, SLA.

25. John G. Ramsey to Victor Reuther et al., 12 Oct. 1955; John W. Edelman [TWUA Representative in Washington, D.C.,] to Very Reverend Msgr. George G. Higgins [National Catholic Welfare Conference], 9 Sept. 1955; Edelman to "Dear Mr. Senator" [for release], 8 Sept. 1955; Ramsey to Rev. S. Wilkes Dendy [Presbyterian Church, Dalton], 21 Oct. 1955; Milton Ellerin, Southeastern Office, Anti-Defamation League of B'nai B'rith, Atlanta, Ga., to [John Ramsey?], 14 Sept. 1955; news release for the *Atlanta Journal*, 9 Sept. 1955; all in John Ramsey Papers, Box 1563, folder 99, SLA; Dunbar, *Against the Grain*, p. 246.

26. *The Southerner*, Jan. 1956.

27. *Dalton News*, 21 Aug. 1955. The *Dalton Citizen* later offered a special "review of some of the more outstanding articles relative to Communism and the Don West campaign"; the review issue also reprinted the *News*'s HUAC report (12 Jan. 1956, pp. 17–22; hereafter cited as "West Edition").

28. *Dalton News*, 21 Aug. 1955.

29. Ibid., 28 Aug. 1955.

30. *Dalton Citizen*, 25 Aug. 1955.

31. For the poems and the controversy surrounding them, see ibid., 25 Aug., 1 Sept. 1955; *Dalton News*, 28 Aug. 1955. The *Daily Worker* reprint is in *Dalton Citizen*, 8 Sept. 1955.

32. *Dalton News*, 28 Aug. 1955; *Dalton Citizen*, 1 Sept. 1955.

33. Ibid.

34. *Dalton Citizen*, 1 Sept. 1955.

35. Ibid.

36. *Dalton News*, 11, 18 Sept. 1955 (quotes); *Dalton Citizen*, 15, 22 Sept. 1955; and see "West Edition" for a recap of the campaign that reflects the tone of the editorial battle.

37. *Dalton Citizen*, 8 Sept. 1955; *Dalton News*, 18 Sept. 1955. The correct spelling for Latex is strangely difficult to determine. Dalton's business press first used "Lawtex" in reporting the workers' complaints in the *Citizen*, 8 Sept. 1955. Thereafter, however, both the *Citizen* and the *News* referred only to "Latex." *The Southerner* usually used "Lawtex." The strikers themselves used "Latex" (*Dalton News*, 30 Oct. 1955).

38. The action can be followed in *Dalton Citizen*, 15, 22, 29 Sept., 6, 13, 20 Oct. 1955; *Dalton News*, 18, 25 Sept., 2, 16, 23 Oct. 1955.

39. *Dalton News*, 6 Nov. 1955; *Dalton Citizen*, 10 Nov. 1955. Little is known about Watters or Olivia Baptist Church. The 1948 city directory lists a W. P. Waters as an employee of the Crown Cotton Mills and a resident of the mill village; Olivia Baptist is not listed in the 1948 directory. As for the dynamite explosions in September and October, TWUA organizer

Robert Freeman strongly implied that they were the work of antiunionists trying to discredit the TWUA: "It's an insult to organized labor and the community for anyone to think that the union would dynamite anybody's place of business or throw explosives into somebody's yard. We are trying to get a contract and trying to build up an atmosphere of decency. We certainly couldn't get a contract with a company by such methods" (*Dalton Citizen,* 10 Nov. 1955).

40. *Dalton Citizen,* 6, 13 Oct. 1955.

41. Ibid., 6, 20 Oct. 1955; *Dalton News,* 16, 23 Oct. 1955. West feared a "frame up effort" and wrote some friends in New York to express his concerns. Pace got hold of an issue of the *National Guardian,* in which West's concerns were aired, and used it to smear West by linking him to northerners (that Bundy was from Illinois never seemed to matter) and by portraying him as disloyal to Dalton for trying to give the city and its leaders a bad name (see *Dalton News,* 3 Nov. 1955).

42. *Dalton News,* 18 Sept. 1955; *Dalton Citizen,* 17, 24 Nov., 11 Dec. 1955.

43. *Dalton News,* 30 Oct. 1955.

44. *Dalton Citizen,* 17 Nov. 1955; *Dalton News,* 20 Nov. 1955.

45. *Dalton News,* 4 Dec. 1955.

46. Ibid.

47. *Dalton Citizen,* 17 Nov. 1955; *Dalton News,* 20 Nov., 4 Dec. 1955.

48. *Dalton Citizen,* 8 Dec. 1955.

49. Ibid.

50. *The Southerner,* Jan. 1956.

51. *Dalton News,* 18 Dec. 1955; *The Southerner,* Jan. 1956.

52. *Dalton Citizen,* 29 Dec. 1955, 5 Jan. 1956. The grand jury also questioned the trustworthiness of the police department in connection with the Latex violence (see ibid., 22, 29 Dec. 1955). The Civil Service Commission, a three-person body appointed by the city council, was responsible for the operation of the police and fire departments in Dalton and had been, since the late 1940s, a group generally considered sympathetic to organized labor; indeed, the commission was often comprised of leaders of TWUA locals 185 and 134 (see *Textile Labor,* 3 May 1947).

53. *Dalton Citizen,* 5, 12 Jan. 1956.

54. Dunbar, *Against the Grain,* pp. 246–47; *Dalton Citizen,* 26 Jan. 1956.

55. Chenille rug workers at the Dixie Belle Mill in Calhoun, Georgia, won an unexpected victory for the TWUA in late 1962. Ironically, one of the key ingredients in the Calhoun campaign was the TWUA's efforts to hold a Calhoun election that excluded Dixie Belle workers in Dalton, which was apparently less open to unionization. Dixie Belle in Calhoun (with about 1,000 workers) was owned by Dalton's Belcraft Chenilles Company, which tried unsuccessfully to have the Dalton plants *included* in the election. The vote in favor of the union in Calhoun was two to one. The victory inspired talk of new campaigns in the Dalton area, but none ever occurred (see *Textile Labor,* Dec. 1962, Jan. 1963). On the national decline of organized labor since the mid-1950s, see Goldfield, *Decline of Organized Labor.*

CHAPTER 14

1. John Steinbeck, *The Winter of Our Discontent* (New York: Viking, 1961), p. 181.

2. Robert J. Newman provides the growth differential data (*Growth in the American South,* p. 11). Other views of the southern economy after World War II are found in Maddox et al., *Advancing South;* Wright, *Old South, New South,* chap. 8; Goldfield, *Promised Land;*

and Roland, *Improbable Era*, chap. 1, which expresses the conventional view that "despite the undeniable gains of the South [between World War II and the early 1970s], it remained a poor cousin of the affluent American society" (p. 26).

3. Population figures and the direction of growth beyond Dalton are calculated from U.S. Bureau of the Census, *Census of Population: 1970*, vol. 1, *Characteristics of the Population*, pt. A, Number of Inhabitants, sec. 1, pp. 12.15, 12.17, 12.20, 12.31–32; Hamilton interview.

4. During the same fifteen-year period, some six hundred textile plants closed in the North. Statistics for 1949–60 can be found in U.S. House, *Impact of Automation on Employment*, p. 176, tables 5, 6 (part of a larger report by Solomon Barkan, research director of the TWUA).

5. Statistics for textile mill shutdowns are virtually unattainable for the 1960s, not merely for the South but for the nation as a whole. But see *America's Textile Reporter*, 27 July 1961, sec. 2, pp. 73–74, which lists textile plant liquidations by state (no dates specified, but presumably during 1960–61). The data shows that 23 mills shut down in Georgia, 68 in the South as a whole; outside the South, 210 mills were liquidated, mostly in the New England states. The only other readily available figures on American plant closures and job losses for the 1970s (though these are not without problems) are in Bluestone and Harrison, *Deindustrialization of America*, esp. pp. 30, 266–69. Bluestone, citing an article entitled "Can Congress Control Runaways?" (*Dollars and Sense*, no. 51 [Nov. 1979]: 9), states that "during the 1970s, almost 60 percent of all the textile mill closings in the United States occurred in the South" (p. 33). Carla M. Weiss's recent bibliography on shutdowns demonstrates that research on the topic has increased markedly in recent years; there are several new studies on southern textiles but none as yet on Georgia's cotton mills (*Plant Closings*). Figures for Georgia textiles in the 1950s are from U.S. Department of Labor, *Employment and Earnings*, p. 190.

6. Gena Connally, "The Yarn of the Thread Mill," *Dalton Citizen-News*, 4 Mar. 1983.

7. Ann. Rpt. 1960, 1961, 1962, CGA.

8. BDM, Book 3, 20 June, 24 Oct. 1956, 20 June 1962. In 1956 Crown purchased 80 percent of the Cotton Goods Company, a New York textile agency; 54 percent of Joseph W. Woods Company, which was owned by Crown's longtime textile agent, J. H. Lane and Company; and, finally, all of J. H. Lane itself. These purchases signaled the massive shift in textile *administration* from northern textile centers to the South, a shift that had lagged behind the earlier regional transference in textile production. Crown also acquired, although records do not pinpoint when (probably the early 1950s), the Ft. Mountain Weavers plant in nearby Murray County. By 1959 the Ft. Mountain plant ceased to produce textiles on a regular basis and was reorganized as a selling agent and "research organization" (BDM, Book 3, 17 June 1959). The subsidiaries paid off to a limited extent in fiscal year 1961, when Crown Mill lost $117,620 while the subsidiaries generated a combined profit of $45,292, cutting corporate losses overall to $72,328 (BDM, Book 3, 22 Mar. 1961).

9. David D. Hamilton, untitled article on history of Crown Cotton Mills, CGA.

10. The workers who actually dealt with grievances and larger problems in the plant were part of a tightly organized system of union leadership. The top elected officials—president, vice president, recording secretary, and financial secretary—along with three additional elected "executives" formed the executive board of Local 185. Below the executive board were the shop stewards. The workers in every department elected a "steward" to serve as the union leader in their "shop." In 1953, for example, there were sixteen shop stewards from Crown's three plants—No. 1, No. 2, and Boylston. Each spinning and weaving room ran two shifts and therefore had two shop stewards. The No. 2 carding room ran three shifts and had

three shop stewards (occasionally the weave room and spinning room of Mill No. 2 also ran three shifts). Only the cloth room at Mill No. 2 ran a single shift and therefore had only a single shop steward. Every two weeks the executive board met with the shop stewards. Together they would examine the complex problems that the workers faced. Millhands with a problem went first to their shop steward, who sought to settle the issue with the immediate overseer and, if need be, the superintendent. If no agreement could be reached, troubled millhands could file a grievance that their shop steward presented at the biweekly meeting. The executive board and shop stewards then had to decide whether to go forward with the grievance. If they sent the grievance on to the mill management and no resolution could be reached, the union called for arbitration, in which unbiased mediators (approved by both union and management) would be empowered to pass down a ruling that was binding for both sides.

11. Workers analyzed their workplace concerns at length and in considerable detail, as the union minutes illustrate. At a special executive board meeting called for 29 September 1950, for example, union leaders discussed "whether or not spare hands can roll persons who are placed on jobs by jobs being cut out who have less seniority and are temporarily on spare floor." In this case the board decided "that a spare hand can replace a spare hand with less seniority on either shift (as Mildred Graham may replace George Smith who is on spare floor by temporary discontinuance of his job)" (EBM, Book 3, 29 Sept. 1950).

12. Ibid., 29 Oct. 1949, 14 Jan. 1951.

13. Ibid., 17 May, 15 Nov. 1952; GM, 14 Jan. 1951, 21 June 1952, 10 Jan. 1953.

14. GM, 28 Jan. 1950, 14 Jan. 1951 (quotes); ibid., 10 Sept. 1949, 23 Sept. 1950, Sept. 1951, 2 Jan. 1952.

15. Hall, Bramblett, Wade, and Caylor interviews. For more information on the stretchouts of the 1960s, see Defore, Hill, and Rogers interviews. Without making too much of a few statistical observations, it is nonetheless instructive that in a sample of thirty-five union grievances filed at Crown during the 1960s, slightly more than half concerned work loads or the relationship of work loads to wages (TWUA Local 185 Records, SLA).

16. Wade interview. *Textile Labor*, Nov. 1963, p. 4, noted that work loads in the cotton mills of Canton, Georgia, "had been sharply increased" and that "the Canton workers decided they had it" and had successfully organized a union.

17. Hall interview.

18. Hamilton interview. See also Defore, Felker, Hill, and Wade interviews.

19. Felker, Bramblett, Bunch and Garren, and Cruce interviews.

20. Bramblett, Hall interviews. For similar reactions, see Felker, Caylor, Hamilton, and Lowrance interviews.

21. On the Crown Mill employee cards, see chap. 12, n. 27 above.

22. Heather Thompson describes how the generation gap tore apart auto workers in Detroit in 1973, when one thousand leaders of the United Automobile Workers union—wielding baseball bats—stormed a "wildcat" picket line of young, left-leaning members of the UAW itself ("Lordstown and the Rank-and-File of the 1970s," paper presented at the Social Science History Association annual meeting, Washington, D.C., Nov. 1989). More generally, see Zieger, *American Workers*, chap. 6.

23. The surviving company records pertaining to the wildcat strikes (which may not be complete) identify walkouts (sometimes of individual departments, sometimes of entire plants) in March, April, August, and December 1966 and on 3 August 1967 and 2 June 1969. On the walkout in March 1966, see G. L. Hamilton, Crown Cotton Mills, to Textile Workers Union of America, Local 185, 28 Mar. 1966; William Pollock to Harmon Connor, Western

Union telegram, 24 Mar. 1966; in UWS. See also Caylor, Defore, Hamilton, and Hill interviews. An interesting parallel to Crown's experience took place in the North as textiles in that region began to collapse; Tamara Hareven notes that as the Amoskeag plant in Manchester, New Hampshire, neared shutdown in the early 1930s, "both management and the union had to admit their helplessness in the face of the workers' uncontrolled anger and despair" (*Family Time and Industrial Time*, p. 352).

24. "Text of Agreement between Crown Cotton Mills and Textile Workers Union of America," Dalton, Georgia, 1 Apr. 1966, pp. 50-51, MDB.

25. David D. Hamilton to Paul Swaity, Western Union telegram, 20 Apr. 1966; handwritten notes [probably taken by Harmon Conner, Crown Mill personnel director] of interviews with Boylston supervisors, 20 Apr. 1966, and minutes of union-company meeting, 21 Apr. 1966; all in UWS.

26. David Hamilton to Paul Swaity, 25 Apr. 1966; Hamilton to Swaity, 19 Aug. 1966; Swaity to Hamilton, 23 Aug. 1966; in ibid.

27. Harmon Conner, handwritten minutes of union-company meeting, 8 June 1966; handwritten notes (also by Conner) from employee interviews, 9, 10 June 1966; Frederick W. Cory [TWUA International representative] to Harmon Conner, 26 July 1966; Conner to Cory, 28 July 1966; unattributed notes from special union-company meeting, 5 Aug. 1966; all in ibid.

28. Frank A. Constangy to H. Eugene Kinney, 18 Aug. 1966; Harmon Conner, handwritten notes of meeting with union, 18 Aug. 1966; unattributed notes from union-company meetings, 7, 10, 24 Oct. 1966; Harmon Conner, handwritten notes of special union-company meeting, 13 Dec. 1966; in ibid. See also *Textile Union's Newsletter*, n.d. [probably late 1966], vol. 1, no. 3, MDB. This is the only issue I have seen of a newsletter that served the TWUA in north Georgia. In this issue, International representative Frederick W. Cory provides a story aimed at quelling the Crown Mill wildcats. He applauds Crown's use of a TWUA time-study engineer and adds: "This is the only way that such a problem can be solved. Workers on the job cannot settle these problems; for only engineers can find the facts needed. When the workers use pressures which violate union contracts, they only do harm to themselves and their fellow union members" (p. 1).

29. BDM, Book 3, 28 Mar. 1962. See also ibid., 16 Dec. 1959, 20 Mar., 19 June 1963; ibid., Book 4, 14 Feb. 1964, 16 June, 15 Dec. 1965.

30. Unfortunately Crown's profits for the crucial period 1967-69 are almost impossible to determine from surviving company records. No audit survived for 1967, and, beginning in 1968, the Texture-Tex profits were combined with the Crown figures in the company audits. Crown and Texture-Tex together netted a profit of $160,792 in 1969. But a separate note to stockholders states that the Crown plant lost $500,000 that same year. If both of these figures are correct, then the Texture-Tex plants would have earned a net profit of $760,792 in 1969.

31. BDM, Book 4, 1 Feb., 16 Mar. 1966, 25 Oct. 1967, 24 Sept. 1968, 18 Apr., 25 June, 22 Aug. 1969, 28 Jan., 18 Sept. 1970.

32. Bunch and Garren, Thompson, Wade, Bramblett, Hall, Crow, and Defore interviews.

33. On plant expenditures, see BDM, Book 2, 24 Sept. 1947; ibid., Book 3, 13 Mar., 26 Sept. 1951, 17 June 1952, 17 June, 16 Dec. 1959, 20 Apr. 1961, 20 June 1962; ibid., Book 4, 28 Oct., 16 Dec. 1964, 16 June, 27 Oct 1965, 16 Mar. 1966, 15 Mar., 21 June, 25 Oct. 1967, 24 Sept. 1968, 18 Apr. 1969. As the years of these citations suggest, the modernization urges of Crown's managers waxed and waned, with a most notable gap occurring in the 1950s. The figure for the Phelps plant includes the costs of poststart-up expansions in 1967 and 1969. On the labor problems associated with the power looms purchased in 1967, see Caylor interview.

34. "To: All Employees of the Boylston Plant of Crown Cotton Mills," typescript, n.d. [ca. 15 May 1969], MDB; Bramblett interview.

35. Harmon Conner to Scott Hoymon, Southern Director, TWUA, 2 June 1969; Scott Hoymon to TWUA Local 185, Western Union telegram, 2 June 1969; both in UWS.

36. [Crown Cotton Mills], "For Release September 12, 1969," typescript, MDB.

37. Bunch and Garren interview; see also Bramblett interview.

38. See chapter 11 above. Some basic information on these trends is found in *Dalton Citizen*, 1 Nov. 1945, 11 July 1946, 4 Sept., 9, 16 Oct. 1947, 22, 29 July 1948; *Textile Labor*, July 1943, 3 May 1947.

39. Herman E. Talmadge to Jimmy Walraven and James Campbell, 26 Sept. 1969, James Campbell File, CGA.

40. Undated newspaper article ("Crown Cotton Mill to Close in Dalton") by Tom Walker [possibly from the *Atlanta Constitution*], ibid.

41. Untitled officers list and roll call record for the Local 185 executive board meetings (the last meeting noted is 18 May, but the union continued to do business at least through August). Most of the postclosure dealings between Local 185 and Crown Cotton Mills had to do with how the phaseout affected the workers' pension plan, accrued vacation pay, insurance coverage, Christmas bonus, and severance pay (see esp. David D. Hamilton to Jimmy Walraven, 14 Oct. 1969; A. R. Marshall, "In the Matter of Arbitration between Crown Cotton Mills, Dalton, Georgia, and Textile Workers Union of America, Local Union Number 185, AFL-CIO: Awards and Opinion," 4 Aug. 1970). All of the above in ibid.

42. Original "Resolution" [otherwise untitled], n.d.; James Campbell to Sol Stetin, 1 June 1970; ibid.

43. Sol Stetin to Dear Brother or Sister, 18 Feb. 1970, ibid.

44. "Dalton, Georgia, for Release September 12, 1969," typescript, MDB; Hamilton interview.

45. Hall interview; see also Bunch and Garren, Caylor, Felker, Wade, and Rogers interviews.

ECHOES

1. Ann. Rpt., 1984, CGA.

2. Ibid.

3. Pat W. Lowrance, "A Salute to CrownAmerica," *Dalton Citizen-News*, 24 Apr. 1984.

4. Hamilton, quoted in Pace, "CrownAmerica," p. 2.

5. Ann. Rpt., 1984, CGA.

6. *Textile Labor*, 3 May 1947.

7. The union information cited here is in a flyer distributed by the Dalton Chamber of Commerce, copy in author's possession. This sheet also has information on the percentage of workers in each plant who were female, which appears to be industry shorthand meaning that women receive lower wages and, according to the chamber of commerce, have less inclination to unionize. The percentages of female employees ranged from a low of 25 to a high of 65, with the average being 43 percent.

8. *New York Times*, 27 May 1990; *Washington Post*, 27 Sept. 1987; Pace, "CrownAmerica," p. 3; *Wall Street Journal*, 12 June 1991.

9. Hamilton interview.

10. "Georgia Manufacturing Wage Survey by Market Area, June 1985," a publication of the Research Division, Georgia Department of Industry and Trade, copy in author's possession; quotes in *Washington Post*, 27 Sept. 1987.

11. McDonald, "Textile Workers and Unionization"; Botsch, *We Shall Not Overcome* (which provides a similar portrait of working-class malaise).

12. On brown lung, see Robert E. Botsch, "The Passing of the Brown Lung Association: An Evaluation of a Grassroots Interest Group," paper presented at the Southern Historical Association annual meeting, Lexington, Ky., Nov. 1989 (Caldwell quoted on p. 1); Charles Levenstein et al., "Labor and Byssinosis," in Rosner and Markowitz, *Dying for Work*, pp. 208–23. See also Pat W. Lowrance, "Reunion at Crown Mill a Good Day," *Dalton Citizen-News*, 18 June 1985.

13. Bramblett interview.

APPENDIX B

1. To recalculate base years, take the index number for the new base year of your choice (e.g., for the BLS figures used here [1967=100], the index number for my preferred base year of 1890 was 27). Divide all other index numbers by that base figure (in this case, 27). The original index number for 1896 was 25; with the base year set at 1890, the new index number for 1896 would be 92.6 (25/27). Obviously, the new index number for 1890 would then become 100.

2. Prude, *Coming of Industrial Order*, appendix 1.

3. An explanation of the Soundex and the coding system may be found in National Archives Trust Fund Board, *1900 Federal Population Census*, pp. v–vi, 83, and *1910 Federal Population Census*, pp. vii, 39.

4. What I am discussing here is the most common use of significance tests in historical research. Social scientists would rightly add that significance tests, as well as confidence intervals and standard errors, can be used to test a wide variety of statistical hypotheses. It is also worth noting that statistical tests were devised largely to deal with the problem of sampling error. Because I am analyzing the entire population of Crown Mill workers and not a sample of that population, it might well be asked whether statistical tests are appropriate. There is no definitive answer to this question. If, however, we assume that Crown serves as a selective sample of the larger population of southern millhands, then significance tests do seem in order.

5. Wright, *Old South, New South*; Phillips, "Labor Market"; McHugh, "Earnings" and *Mill Family*.

6. I offer a nontechnical discussion of logit in "Regression Options for Historians: Choosing among OLS, Tobit, Logit, and Probit Models," California Institute of Technology, Humanities Working Paper 152, July 1992. For a technical discussion of logit, see Hanushek and Jackson, *Statistical Methods*, chap. 7. Other forms of multivariate analysis include probit (which is an approach similar to logit) and tobit. See a lucid discussion of these in Hoffman, *Church and Community*, app. 1; and a technical account in G. S. Maddala, *Limited-Dependent and Qualitative Variables in Econometrics* (Cambridge: Cambridge University Press, 1983).

7. One of the important assumptions of OLS models is that the error term will have constant variance across all of the observations; this statistical quality is called homoskedasticity. If a dichotomous variable is used as the dependent variable in an OLS equation, the above assumption will be violated, and the coefficients cannot be trusted.

BIBLIOGRAPHY

CROWN COTTON MILLS COMPANY RECORDS

The Crown Mill records, open to the public at the Crown Gardens and Archives in Dalton, Georgia, offer a rich collection for the study of southern textiles from the 1880s through the 1960s. For the most part, however, the collection remains uncataloged. As a result, it has sometimes been difficult for me to give precise citations in my notes. Most bound volumes in the archives, such as payroll ledgers, can be found easily enough, and materials from clearly identifiable files (which are listed below with the manuscripts located at Crown Gardens) are readily accessible. In order to provide citations for the letters and documents that I found in scattered and unlabeled boxes, I placed either the originals or, in most cases, copies of the originals in a container labeled Miscellaneous Documents Box (MDB), which is available at Crown Gardens.

MANUSCRIPTS

Atlanta, Georgia
Georgia Department of Archives and History
   State of Georgia, Commissioner of Commerce and Labor, Annual Reports, 1912–30
   State of Georgia, Department of Industrial Relations, Annual Reports, 1932–33
   State of Georgia, Department of Labor, Annual Reports, 1938–56
Southern Labor Archives
   John Ramsey Papers
   Records of the Textile Workers Union of America, Local 185, Amalgamated Clothing and
     Textile Workers Union Collection, 82-19

Dalton, Georgia
Crown Gardens and Archives
   After Strike Papers File
   David P. Bass Family File
   Polly Boggess. "The Crown Mill Historic District" (typescript)
   Walter Bogle Newspaper Clipping File
   James Campbell File
   David D. Hamilton. Untitled article on history of Crown Cotton Mills (typescript)
   John Hamilton Family File
   William K. Moore Family File
   National Register of Historic Places. "Inventory and Nomination Form for the Crown
     Mill Historic District" (typescript)
   Union–Work Stoppages–Strike File
   Cheryl Wykoff, comp. "Tufted Bedspread Sampler" (typescript)
Dalton Regional Library
   City of Dalton Scrapbooks

Whitfield County Courthouse
   O. L. Boyd et al. v. *Ben T. Huiet and Crown Cotton Mills,* Whitfield County Superior
      Court, Case No. 8, July Term, 1940
   Crown Cotton Mills v. *Lewis Weaver et al.,* no. 18, Whitfield County Superior Court, Oc-
      tober Term, 1939 (Whitfield County Superior Court Minutes, Book No. 22, p. 388)
   Whitfield County Marriage Records, 1900–1910

Madison, Wisconsin
State Historical Society of Wisconsin
   Textile Workers Union of America Records

INTERVIEWS

All interviews were conducted by the author in Dalton, Georgia, or Whitfield County. Unless otherwise noted, they were tape-recorded. Copies of the tapes (some of which have
been transcribed) are housed at the Crown Gardens and Archives in Dalton, Georgia, and
the Center for Appalachian Studies, Virginia Polytechnic Institute and State University,
Blacksburg, Virginia.

John Bramblett, 29 June 1985
Jean Breeden, 18 July 1985 (handwritten notes of interview)
Sarah Bunch and Anna Nell Garren, 24 June 1985
Bishop Caylor, 17 July 1985
J. W. Crow, 1 July 1985
Hazel Cruce, 17 July 1985
Willie Mae Defore, 19 July 1985
Desmond Ellis, 12 June 1985
Ed Felker, 3 November 1984
Lucile Hall, 22 June 1985
David D. Hamilton, 30 July 1985
Earl Hardin, 25 June 1985
Lillie Ann Hill, 4 June 1985
Juanita Hughes, 18 July 1985 (handwritten notes of interview)
Patricia Lowrance, 30 July 1985
Thelma Parker, 11 June 1985
Sibyl Queen, 26 June 1985
Nancy Lowman Rogers, 12 October 1985
Marselle Thompson, 11 July 1985
Henry M. Wade, 12 July 1985

NEWSPAPERS, PERIODICALS, AND CITY DIRECTORIES

America's Textile Reporter
Atlanta Constitution
Cherokee Georgia (single issue, n.p., ca. 1889, copy in CGA)
Dalton Argus
Dalton Citizen

Dalton Citizen-News
Dalton City Directory, 1936, 1948 (copies in CGA)
Dalton News
Directory of Dalton, Georgia, and Suburbs, 1924 (Dalton, Ga.: A. J. Showalter Co., 1924, copy in CGA)
Jasper News
Manufacturers' Record (Baltimore, Md.)
Moody's Manual of Investments, American and Foreign: Industrial Securities (New York: Moody's Investors Services, 1928, 1930, 1933)
Moody's Manual of Railroads and Securities (New York: Moody's Investors Services, 1912, 1920)
North Georgia Citizen (Dalton, Ga.)
The Southerner: A Voice of the People (Dalton, Ga.)
State Town and Country, April 1889 (Atlanta, Ga., copy in CGA)
Textile Labor

FEDERAL GOVERNMENT DOCUMENTS

National Archives Trust Fund Board. *The 1900 Federal Population Census.* Washington, D.C., 1978.
———. *The 1910 Federal Population Census.* Washington, D.C., 1982.
U.S. Bureau of the Census. Census Manuscripts, Population Schedules, Georgia, 1880, 1900, 1910.
———. *Census of Agriculture: 1959.* Vol. 1, *Counties*, pt. 28, Georgia. Washington, D.C., 1961.
———. *Census of Population: 1950.* Vol. 2, *Characteristics of the Population*, pt. 11, Georgia. Washington, D.C., 1952.
———. *Census of Population: 1970.* Vol. 1, *Characteristics of the Population*, pt. A, Number of Inhabitants, sec. 1. Washington, D.C., 1972.
———. *Compendium of the Tenth Census*, pts. 1 and 2. Washington, D.C., 1883.
———. *County and City Data Book.* Washington, D.C., 1953, 1967, 1977.
———. *Eleventh Census of the United States, 1890.* Vol. 1, *Report on the Statistics of Agriculture.* Vol. 6, *Report on Farms and Homes.* Vol. 15, pt. 1, *Report on the Population of the United States.* Washington, D.C., 1895–96.
———. *Fifteenth Census of the United States, 1930.* Vol. 1, *Unemployment.* Vol. 2, pt. 2, *Agriculture.* Vol. 3, pt. 1, *Population.* Vol. 3, *Manufactures.* Washington, D.C., 1931–33.
———. *Fourteenth Census of the United States, 1920.* Vol. 3, *Population.* Vol. 4, pt. 2, *Agriculture.* Vols. 9–10, *Manufactures.* Washington, D.C., 1922–23.
———. *Historical Statistics of the United States: Colonial Times to 1970, Bicentennial Edition, Part 1.* Washington, D.C., 1975.
———. *Manufactures of the United States [1860].* Washington, D.C., 1864.
———. *Preliminary Report on the Eighth Census, 1860.* Washington, D.C., 1862.
———. *Sixteenth Census of the United States, 1940.* Vol. 1, pt. 3, *Agriculture.* Vol. 2, pt. 2, *Population.* Washington, D.C., 1942–43.
———. Soundex Indexes to Manuscript Census Schedules, Alabama, Georgia, South Carolina, Tennessee, 1880, 1900, 1910.
———. *Tenth Census of the United States, 1880.* Vol. 1, *Statistics of the Population of the United States.* Vol. 2, *Report on Manufactures.* Vol. 3, *Report on the Productions of Agri-*

culture. Vol. 4, *Report on the Agencies of Transportation in the United States: Statistics of Railroads.* Vol. 6, pt. 2, *Report on Cotton Production in the United States.* Washington, D.C., 1883–84.

———. *Thirteenth Census of the United States, 1910.* Vol. 2, *Population.* Washington, D.C., 1913.

———. *Twelfth Census of the United States, 1900.* Vol. 1, pt. 1, *Population.* Vol. 8, pt. 2, *Manufactures.* Vol. 9, pt. 3, *Manufactures,* Special Report on Selected Industries. Washington, D.C., 1901–2.

U.S. Congress. House. Committee on Education and Labor. *Impact of Automation on Employment: Hearings before the Subcommittee on Unemployment and the Impact of Automation.* 87th Cong., 1st sess. Washington, D.C., 1961.

———. Senate. *Report on Condition of Woman and Child Wage-Earners in the United States.* Vol. 1, *Cotton Textile Industry.* 61st Cong., 2d sess., S. Doc. 645. Washington, D.C., 1910.

U.S. Department of Labor. Bureau of Labor Statistics. *Employment and Earnings, States and Areas, 1939–75.* Washington, D.C., 1977.

———. *History of Wages in the United States from Colonial Times to 1928 [with supplement for 1929–33].* Washington, D.C., 1934.

BOOKS, ARTICLES, AND THESES

Accampo, Elinor. *Industrialization, Family Life, and Class Relations: Saint Chamond, 1815–1914.* Berkeley: University of California Press, 1989.

Adams, James Truslow, and R. L. Coleman, eds. *Atlas of American History.* New York: Charles Scribner's Sons, 1943.

Ahlstrom, Sydney E. *A Religious History of the American People.* New Haven, Conn.: Yale University Press, 1972.

Anderson, Robert Mapes. *Vision of the Disinherited: The Making of American Pentecostalism.* New York: Oxford University Press, 1979.

Andrews, Mildred G. *The Men and the Mills: A History of the Southern Textile Industry.* Macon, Ga.: Mercer University Press, 1987.

Arneson, Eric. *Waterfront Workers of New Orleans: Race, Class, and Politics, 1863–1923.* New York: Oxford University Press, 1991.

Ayers, Edward L. *Vengeance and Justice: Crime and Punishment in the 19th-Century American South.* New York: Oxford University Press, 1984.

Bartley, Numan V. *The Creation of Modern Georgia.* Athens: University of Georgia Press, 1985.

Beatty, Bess. "Lowells of the South: Northern Influence on the Nineteenth-Century North Carolina Textile Industry, 1830–1890." *Journal of Southern History* 53 (February 1987): 37–62.

———. "Textile Labor in the North Carolina Piedmont: Mill Owner Images and Mill Worker Responses, 1830–1900." *Labor History* 25 (Fall 1984): 485–503.

Beck, John J. "Building the New South: A Revolution from Above in a Piedmont County." *Journal of Southern History* 53 (August 1987): 441–70.

———. "Development in the Piedmont South: Rowan County, North Carolina, 1850–1900." Ph.D. diss., University of North Carolina, 1984.

Bensman, David, and Roberta Lynch. *Rusted Dreams: Hard Times in a Steel Community.* New York: McGraw-Hill, 1987.

Bernstein, Irving. *The Lean Years: A History of the American Worker, 1920–1933*. Boston: Houghton Mifflin, 1960.

———. *The Turbulent Years: A History of the American Worker, 1933–1941*. Boston: Houghton Mifflin, 1970.

Billings, Dwight B., Jr. *Planters and the Making of a "New South": Class, Politics, and Development in North Carolina, 1865–1900*. Chapel Hill: University of North Carolina Press, 1979.

Blicksilver, Jack. *Cotton Manufacturing in the Southeast: An Historical Analysis*. Atlanta, Ga.: Georgia State University, School of Business Administration, Bureau of Business and Economic Research, 1959.

Bluestone, Barry, and Bennett Harrison. *The Deindustrialization of America: Plant Closings, Community Abandonment, and the Dismantling of Basic Industry*. New York: Basic Books, 1982.

Bode, Frederick A., and Donald E. Ginter. *Farm Tenancy and the Census in Antebellum Georgia*. Athens: University of Georgia Press, 1986.

Bodnar, John. *The Transplanted: A History of Immigrants in Urban America*. Bloomington: Indiana University Press, 1985.

Botsch, Robert E. *We Shall Not Overcome: Populism and Southern Blue-Collar Workers*. Chapel Hill: University of North Carolina Press, 1980.

Brandes, Stuart D. *American Welfare Capitalism, 1880–1940*. Chicago: University of Chicago Press, 1976.

Brody, David. "Labor and the Great Depression: The Interpretive Prospects." *Labor History* 13 (Spring 1972): 231–44.

———. *Workers in Industrial America: Essays on the Twentieth-Century Struggle*. New York: Oxford University Press, 1981.

Brown, John M. *Yesteryears: Pictoral History of Calhoun and Gordon County, Georgia, 1830–1977*. Dalton, Ga.: Lee Printing Co., 1977.

Brownell, Blaine. *The Urban Ethos in the South, 1920–1930*. Baton Rouge: Louisiana State University Press, 1975.

Brownell, Blaine, and David Goldfield. *The City in Southern History: The Growth of Urban Civilization in the South*. Port Washington, N.Y.: Kennikat Press, 1977.

Burton, Orville Vernon. *In My Father's House Are Many Mansions: Family and Community in Edgefield, South Carolina*. Chapel Hill: University of North Carolina Press, 1985.

Burton, Orville Vernon, and Robert C. McMath, eds. *Towards a New South?: Studies in Post–Civil War Communities*. Westport, Conn.: Greenwood Press, 1982.

Byerly, Victoria. *Hard Times Cotton Mill Girls: Personal Histories of Womanhood and Poverty in the South*. Ithaca, N.Y.: ILR Press, 1986.

Carlton, David L. *Mill and Town in South Carolina, 1880–1920*. Baton Rouge: Louisiana State University Press, 1982.

———. "The Revolution from Above: The National Market and the Beginnings of Industrialization in North Carolina." *Journal of American History* 77 (September 1990): 445–75.

Cash, W. J. *The Mind of the South*. New York: Knopf, 1941.

Cobb, James C. *Industrialization and Southern Society, 1877–1984*. Lexington: University Press of Kentucky, 1984.

———. *The Selling of the South: The Southern Crusade for Industrial Development, 1936–1980*. Baton Rouge: Louisiana State University Press, 1982.

Cohen, Ronald D. *Children of the Mill: Schooling and Society in Gary, Indiana, 1906–1960*. Bloomington: Indiana University Press, 1990.

Coleman, Kenneth, ed. *A History of Georgia.* Athens: University of Georgia Press, 1977.

Conway, Mimi. *Rise Gonna Rise: A Portrait of Southern Textile Workers.* Garden City, N.Y.: Anchor Press/Doubleday, 1979.

Cooney, Robert. "The Modern South: Organized Labor's New Frontier." *American Federationist* 68 (May 1961): 15–19.

Cornford, Daniel A. *Workers and Dissent in the Redwood Empire.* Philadelphia, Pa.: Temple University Press, 1987.

Cross, Gary, and Peter R. Shergold. "The Family Economy and the Market: Wages and Residence of Pennsylvanian Women in the 1890s." *Journal of Family History* 11, no. 3 (1986): 245–65.

Daniel, Pete. *Breaking the Land: The Transformation of Cotton, Tobacco, and Rice Culture since 1880.* Urbana: University of Illinois Press, 1985.

———. *Standing at the Crossroads: Southern Life in the Twentieth Century.* New York: Hill and Wang, 1986.

Davidson, Elizabeth H. *Child Labor Legislation in the Southern Textile States.* Chapel Hill: University of North Carolina Press, 1939.

De Graffenried, Clare. "The Georgia Cracker in the Cotton Mills." *Century* 41 (February 1891): 483–98.

DeNatale, Douglas. "Bynum: The Coming of Mill Village Life to a North Carolina County." Ph.D. diss., University of Pennsylvania, 1985.

Deverell, William. "To Loosen the Safety Valve: Eastern Workers and Western Lands." *Western Historical Quarterly* 19 (August 1988): 269–85.

Dodd, Donald B., and Wynelle S. Dodd. *Historical Statistics of the South, 1790–1970.* Tuscaloosa: University of Alabama Press, 1973.

Doyle, Don H. *Nashville in the New South, 1880–1920.* Knoxville: University of Tennessee Press, 1985.

———. *Nashville since the 1920s.* Knoxville: University of Tennessee Press, 1985.

———. *New Men, New Cities, New South: Atlanta, Nashville, Charleston, Mobile, 1860–1910.* Chapel Hill: University of North Carolina Press, 1990.

———. *The Social Order of a Frontier Community: Jacksonville, Illinois, 1825–1870.* Urbana: University of Illinois Press, 1978.

Dublin, Thomas. *Women at Work: The Transformation of Work and Community in Lowell, Massachusetts, 1826–1860.* New York: Columbia University Press, 1979.

Dubofsky, Melvyn. "Not So 'Turbulent Years': Another Look at the American 1930s." *Amerikastudien* 24 (January 1979): 5–20.

Dunbar, Anthony P. *Against the Grain: Southern Radicals and Prophets, 1929–1959.* Charlottesville: University Press of Virginia, 1981.

Eller, Ronald D. *Miners, Millhands, and Mountaineers: Industrialization of the Appalachian South, 1880–1930.* Knoxville: University of Tennessee Press, 1982.

———. "The Search for Community in Appalachia." *Appalachian Heritage* 14 (Fall 1986): 45–51.

Escott, Paul D. *Many Excellent People: Power and Privilege in North Carolina, 1850–1900.* Chapel Hill: University of North Carolina Press, 1985.

Evans, Mercer G. "The History of the Organized Labor Movement in Georgia." Ph.D. diss., University of Chicago, 1929.

Faragher, John Mack. *Sugar Creek: Life on the Illinois Frontier.* New Haven, Conn.: Yale University Press, 1986.

Farish, Hunter D. *The Circuit Rider Dismounts: A Social History of Southern Methodism, 1865–1900.* Richmond: Dietz Press, 1938.

Fink, Gary M. *Biographical Dictionary of American Labor Leaders.* Westport, Conn.: Greenwood Press, 1974.

———. *Labor Unions.* Westport, Conn.: Greenwood Press, 1977.

Fink, Gary, and Merl E. Reed, eds. *Essays in Southern Labor History: Selected Papers, Southern Labor History Conference, 1976.* Westport, Conn.: Greenwood Press, 1977.

Fite, Gilbert C. *Cotton Fields No More: Southern Agriculture, 1865–1980.* Lexington: University Press of Kentucky, 1984.

Fleming, James B. "The Northwest Georgia Carpet Finishing Industry: Its Operations and Financing." M.A. thesis, Rutgers University, 1974.

Flynn, Charles L., Jr. *White Land, Black Labor: Caste and Class in Late Nineteenth-Century Georgia.* Baton Rouge: Louisiana State University Press, 1983.

Flynt, J. Wayne. *Dixie's Forgotten People: The South's Poor Whites.* Bloomington: Indiana University Press, 1979.

———. "The New Deal and Southern Labor." In *The New Deal and the South,* edited by James C. Cobb and Michael V. Namorato, pp. 63–96. Jackson: University Press of Mississippi, 1984.

Fogel, Robert William. *Without Consent or Contract: The Rise and Fall of American Slavery.* New York: W. W. Norton, 1989.

Ford, Lacy K., Jr. *Origins of Southern Radicalism: The South Carolina Upcountry, 1800–1860.* New York: Oxford University Press, 1988.

———. "Rednecks and Merchants: Economic Development and Social Tensions in the South Carolina Upcountry, 1865–1900." *Journal of American History* 71 (September 1984): 294–318.

Ford, Thomas R., ed. *The Southern Appalachian Region: A Survey.* Lexington: University Press of Kentucky, 1962.

Fraser, Walter J., and Winfred B. Moore, eds. *From the Old South to the New: Essays on the Transitional South.* Westport, Conn.: Greenwood Press, 1981.

Frederickson, Mary. "Four Decades of Change: Black Workers in Southern Textiles, 1941–1981." *Radical America* 16 (November–December 1982): 27–44.

Freeze, Gary Richard. "Model Mill Men of the New South: Paternalism and Methodism in the Odell Cotton Mills of North Carolina, 1877–1908." Ph.D. diss., University of North Carolina, 1988.

Garlock, Jonathan, comp. *Guide to the Local Assemblies of the Knights of Labor.* Westport, Conn.: Greenwood Press, 1982.

Genovese, Eugene D. *Roll, Jordan, Roll: The World the Slaves Made.* New York: Vintage Books, 1976.

Gilman, Glen. *Human Relations in the Industrial Southeast: A Study of the Textile Industry.* Chapel Hill: University of North Carolina Press, 1956.

Glen, John M. *Highlander: No Ordinary School.* Lexington: University Press of Kentucky, 1988.

Goldfield, David R. *Cotton Fields and Skyscrapers: Southern City and Region, 1607–1980.* Baton Rouge: Louisiana State University Press, 1982.

———. *Promised Land: The South since 1945.* Arlington Heights, Ill.: Harlan Davidson, 1987.

Goldfield, Michael. *The Decline of Organized Labor in the United States.* Chicago: University of Chicago Press, 1987.

Goldin, Claudia. *Understanding the Gender Gap: An Economic History of American Women.* New York: Oxford University Press, 1990.

Goldin, Claudia, and Kenneth Sokoloff. "Women, Children, and Industrialization in the

Early Republic: Evidence from the Manufacturing Censuses." *Journal of Economic History* 42 (December 1982): 741–74.

Goldscheider, Calvin. *Population, Modernization, and Social Structure.* Boston: Little, Brown, 1971.

Goodwyn, Lawrence. *Democratic Promise: The Populist Moment in America.* New York: Oxford University Press, 1976.

Grantham, Dewey W. *Southern Progressivism: The Reconciliation of Progress and Tradition.* Knoxville: University of Tennessee Press, 1983.

Green, Fletcher M. "Duff Green: Industrial Promoter." *Journal of Southern History* 2 (February 1936): 29–42.

Green, James R. *The World of the Worker: Labor in Twentieth-Century America.* New York: Hill and Wang, 1980.

Griffith, Barbara S. *The Crisis of American Labor: Operation Dixie and the Defeat of the CIO.* Philadelphia: Temple University Press, 1988.

Gutman, Herbert G. *Work, Culture, and Society in Industrializing America: Essays in American Working-Class and Social History.* New York: Knopf, 1976.

Gutman, Herbert G., and Donald H. Bell. *The New England Working Class and the New Labor History.* Urbana: University of Illinois Press, 1987.

Hahn, Steven. *The Roots of Southern Populism: Yeoman Farmers and the Transformation of the Georgia Upcountry, 1850–1890.* New York: Oxford University Press, 1983.

Hahn, Steven, and Jonathan Prude, eds. *The Countryside in the Age of Capitalist Transformation: Essays in the Social History of Rural America.* Chapel Hill: University of North Carolina Press, 1985.

Hall, Jacquelyn Dowd. "Disorderly Women: Gender and Labor Militancy in the Appalachian South." *Journal of American History* 73 (September 1986): 354–82.

Hall, Jacquelyn Dowd, James Leloudis, Robert Korstad, Mary Murphy, Lu Ann Jones, and Christopher B. Daly. "Cotton Mill People: Work, Community, and Protest in the Textile South, 1880–1940." *American Historical Review* 91 (April 1986): 245–86.

———. *Like a Family: The Making of a Southern Cotton Mill World.* Chapel Hill: University of North Carolina Press, 1987.

Hamilton, R. E. "Bedspread Bonanza." *Reader's Digest,* April 1941, pp. 41–44.

Hanushek, Eric A., and John E. Jackson. *Statistical Methods for Social Sciences.* New York: Academic Press, 1977.

Harben, Will N. *Abner Daniel.* New York: Harper and Bros., 1902.

———. *The Georgians.* New York: Harper and Bros., 1904.

Harper, Roland McMillan. *The Development of Agriculture in Georgia from 1850 to 1920: A Series of Four Articles, from the Georgia Historical Quarterly.* University, Ala.: privately published, 1923.

Hareven, Tamara K. *Family Time and Industrial Time: The Relationship between the Family and Work in a New England Industrial Community.* Cambridge: Cambridge University Press, 1982.

Hareven, Tamara K., and Randolph Langenbach. *Amoskeag: Life and Work in an American Factory-City.* New York: Pantheon Books, 1978.

Haskins, Loren, and Kirk Jeffrey. *Understanding Quantitative History.* Cambridge, Mass.: MIT Press, 1990.

Hearden, Patrick J. *Independence and Empire: The New South's Cotton Mill Campaign, 1865–1901.* DeKalb: Northern Illinois University Press, 1982.

Henretta, James A. "Families and Farms: *Mentalité* in Pre-Industrial America." *William and Mary Quarterly,* ser. III, vol. 35 (1978): 3–33.

Herring, Harriet L. *Passing of the Mill Village: Revolution in a Southern Institution.* Chapel Hill: University of North Carolina Press, 1949.

———. *Welfare Work in Mill Villages: The Story of Extra-Mill Activities in North Carolina.* Chapel Hill: University of North Carolina Press, 1929.

Hilliard, Sam Bowers. *Atlas of Antebellum Southern Agriculture.* Baton Rouge: Louisiana State University Press, 1984.

Hine, Robert V. *Community on the American Frontier: Separate but Not Alone.* Norman: University of Oklahoma Press, 1980.

Hirschman, Albert O. *Exit, Voice, and Loyalty: Response to Decline in Firms, Organizations, and States.* Cambridge, Mass.: Harvard University Press, 1970.

Hodges, James A. "J. P. Stevens and the Union: Struggle for the South." Paper presented at the Southern Labor Studies Conference, Atlanta, Ga., 1991.

———. *New Deal Labor Policy and the Southern Cotton Textile Industry, 1933–1941.* Knoxville: University of Tennessee Press, 1986.

Hoffman, Philip T. *Church and Community in the Diocese of Lyon, 1500–1789.* New Haven, Conn.: Yale University Press, 1984.

Holmes, William F. "Moonshining and Collective Violence: Georgia, 1889–1895." *Journal of American History* 67 (December 1980): 589–611.

Irons, Janet. "Testing the New Deal: The General Textile Strike of 1934." Ph.D. diss., Duke University, 1988.

Jacoby, Sanford M. *Employing Bureaucracy: Managers, Unions, and the Transformation of Work in American Industry, 1900–1945.* New York: Columbia University Press, 1985.

Janiewski, Dolores E. *Sisterhood Denied: Race, Gender, and Class in a New South Community.* Philadelphia, Pa.: Temple University Press, 1985.

Johnson, Paul E. "The Modernization of Mayo Greenleaf Patch: Land, Family, and Marginality in New England, 1766–1818." *New England Quarterly* 55 (December 1982): 488–516.

———. *A Shopkeeper's Millennium: Society and Revivals in Rochester, New York, 1815–1837.* New York: Hill and Wang, 1978.

Jones, Alton DuMar. "Progressivism in Georgia, 1898–1918." Ph.D. diss., Emory University, 1963.

Jorges, Janet. "From Tough Times to Tufting: A Study of the Growth and Development of the Carpet Industry in the North Georgia Area." Honors thesis, University of Tennessee at Chattanooga. Reprinted by the Carpet and Rug Institute, Dalton, Georgia, in CRI Reports, vol. 3, special issue.

Joyce, Patrick. *Work, Society, and Politics: The Culture of the Factory in Later Victorian England.* New Brunswick, N.J.: Rutgers University Press, 1980.

Kantor, Shawn E., and J. Morgan Kousser. "Common Sense or Commonwealth: The Fence Law and Institutional Change in the Postbellum South." *Journal of Southern History* (forthcoming, 1993).

Katz, Michael B. *The Irony of Early School Reform: Educational Innovation in Mid-Nineteenth-Century Massachusetts.* Cambridge, Mass.: Harvard University Press, 1968.

Kelley, Robin D. G. *Hammer and Hoe: Alabama Communists during the Great Depression.* Chapel Hill: University of North Carolina Press, 1990.

Kemp, John R. *Lewis Hine: Photographs of Child Labor in the New South.* Jackson: University Press of Mississippi, 1986.

Kenzer, Robert C. *Kinship and Neighborhood in a Southern Community: Orange County, North Carolina, 1849–1881.* Knoxville: University of Tennessee Press, 1987.

Kessler-Harris, Alice. *Out to Work: A History of Wage-Earning Women in the United States.* New York: Oxford University Press, 1982.

Korstad, Robert. "Daybreak of Freedom: Tobacco Workers and the C.I.O., Winston-Salem, North Carolina, 1943–1950." Ph.D. diss., University of North Carolina, 1987.

Korstad, Robert, and Nelson Lichtenstein. "Opportunities Found and Lost: Labor, Radicals, and the Early Civil Rights Movement." *Journal of American History* 75 (December 1988): 786–811.

Kousser, J. Morgan. *The Shaping of Southern Politics: Suffrage Restriction and the Establishment of the One-Party South, 1880–1910.* New Haven, Conn.: Yale University Press, 1974.

Kraut, Alan M. *The Huddled Masses: The Immigrant in American Society, 1880–1921.* Arlington Heights, Ill.: Harlan Davidson, 1982.

Lahne, Herbert J. *The Cotton Mill Worker.* New York: Farrar and Rinehart, 1944.

Laurie, Bruce. *Artisans into Workers: Labor in Nineteenth-Century America.* New York: Noonday Press, 1989.

Leiter, Jeffrey, Michael D. Schulman, and Rhonda Zingraff, eds. *Hanging by a Thread: Social Change in Southern Textiles.* Ithaca, N.Y.: ILR Press, 1991.

Lewis, Ronald L. *Black Coal Miners in America: Race, Class, and Community Conflict, 1780–1980.* Lexington: University Press of Kentucky, 1987.

Lewis-Beck, Michael S. *Applied Regression: An Introduction.* Beverly Hills, Calif.: Sage Publications, 1980.

Lindsey, Almont. *The Pullman Strike: The Story of a Unique Experiment and of a Great Labor Upheaval.* Chicago: University of Chicago Press, 1942.

Lowrance, Pat W. "Kenemer Reminisces 'The Way It Was.' " *Dalton Citizen-News,* 21 May 1985.

McDonald, Joseph A. "Textile Workers and Unionization: A Community Study." Ph.D. diss., University of Tennessee, 1981.

McHugh, Cathy L. "Earnings in the Post-bellum Southern Cotton Textile Industry: A Case Study." *Explorations in Economic History* 21 (January 1984): 28–39.

———. "The Family Labor System in the Southern Cotton Textile Industry, 1880–1915." Ph.D. diss., Stanford University, 1981.

———. *Mill Family: The Labor System in the Southern Cotton Textile Industry, 1880–1915.* New York: Oxford University Press, 1988.

McKiven, Henry M., Jr. "Class, Race, and Community: Iron and Steel Workers in Birmingham, Alabama, 1875–1920." Ph.D. diss., Vanderbilt University, 1990.

McLaurin, Melton Alonza. *The Knights of Labor in the South.* Westport, Conn.: Greenwood Press, 1978.

———. *Paternalism and Protest: Southern Cotton Mill Workers and Organized Labor, 1875–1905.* Westport, Conn.: Greenwood Press, 1971.

McMath, Robert C., Jr. *Populist Vanguard: A History of the Southern Farmers' Alliance.* New York: W. W. Norton, 1975.

McMath, Robert C., Jr., Ronald H. Bayor, James E. Brittain, Lawrence Foster, August W. Giebelhaus, and Germaine M. Reed. *Engineering the New South: Georgia Tech, 1885–1985.* Athens: University of Georgia Press, 1985.

Maddox, James G., with E. E. Liebhafsky, Vivian W. Henderson, and Herbert M. Hamlin. *The Advancing South: Manpower Prospects and Problems.* New York: Twentieth Century Fund, 1967.

Marshall, F. Ray. *Labor in the South.* Cambridge, Mass.: Harvard University Press, 1967.

Mason, Lucy Randolph. *To Win These Rights: A Personal Story of the CIO in the South.* 1952. Reprint. Westport, Conn.: Greenwood Press, 1970.

Mead, Frank S., and Samuel S. Hill, eds. *Handbook of Denominations in the United States*. New 8th ed. Nashville, Tenn.: Abingdon Press, 1985.

Meadows, John C., ed. *Contemporary Georgia*. Athens: University of Georgia Press, 1942.

Milkman, Ruth. *Gender at Work: The Dynamics of Job Segregation by Sex during World War II*. Urbana: University of Illinois Press, 1987.

Mitchell, Broadus. *The Rise of Cotton Mills in the South*. Baltimore, Md.: Johns Hopkins University Press, 1921.

———. *William Gregg: Factory Master of the Old South*. Chapel Hill: University of North Carolina Press, 1928.

Mitchell, Broadus, and George Sinclair Mitchell. *The Industrial Revolution in the South*. Baltimore, Md.: Johns Hopkins University Press, 1930.

Mitchell, George Sinclair. *Textile Unionism and the South*. Chapel Hill: University of North Carolina Press, 1931.

Mixon, Wayne. *Southern Writers and the New South Movement, 1865–1913*. Chapel Hill: University of North Carolina Press, 1980.

Montgomery, David. *The Fall of the House of Labor: The Workplace, the State, and American Labor Activism, 1865–1925*. Cambridge: Cambridge University Press, 1987.

Moore, Barrington, Jr. *Social Origins of Dictatorship and Democracy: Lord and Peasant in the Making of the Modern World*. Boston: Beacon Press, 1966.

Moreland, John Kenneth. "Kent Revisited: Blue-Collar Aspirations and Achievements." In *Blue-Collar World: Studies of the American Worker*, edited by Arthur B. Shostak and William Gomberg, pp. 134–43. Englewood Cliffs, N.J.: Prentice-Hall, 1964.

———. *Millways of Kent*. Chapel Hill: University of North Carolina Press, 1958.

Murphy, Edgar G. *Problems of the Present South*. New York: Longmans, Green, 1904.

Newby, I. A. *Plain Folk in the New South: Social Change and Cultural Persistence, 1880–1915*. Baton Rouge: Louisiana State University Press, 1989.

Newman, Dale. "Work and Community Life in a Southern Textile Town." *Labor History* 19 (Spring 1978): 204–25.

Newman, Robert J. *Growth in the American South: Changing Regional Employment and Wage Patterns in the 1960s and 1970s*. New York: New York University Press, 1984.

Norrell, Robert J. "Caste in Steel: Jim Crow Careers in Birmingham." *Journal of American History* 73 (December 1986): 669–94.

———. "Labor at the Ballot Box: Alabama Politics from the New Deal to the Dixiecrat Movement." *Journal of Southern History* 57 (May 1991): 201–34.

Owsley, Frank Lawrence. *Plain Folk of the Old South*. Baton Rouge: Louisiana State University Press, 1949.

Ozanne, Robert. *A Century of Labor-Management Relations at McCormick and International Harvester*. Madison: University of Wisconsin Press, 1967.

Pace, Marc. "CrownAmerica and Texture-Tex: A Century of Textile Product Excellence." *Daily Citizen-News* (Dalton), 18 April 1984 (CrownAmerica, Inc., Centennial Publication; copy at CGA).

Palmer, Bruce. *"Man Over Money": The Southern Populist Critique of American Capitalism*. Chapel Hill: University of North Carolina Press, 1980.

Perry, Robert Eugene. "Middle-Class Townsmen and Northern Capital: The Rise of the Alabama Cotton Textile Industry, 1865–1900." Ph.D. diss., Vanderbilt University, 1986.

Phillips, Ulrich Bonnell. *A History of Transportation in the Eastern Cotton Belt to 1860*. New York: Columbia University Press, 1908.

Phillips, William H. "The Labor Market of Southern Textile Mill Villages: Some Micro Evidence." *Explorations in Economic History* 23 (April 1986): 103–23.

——. "Southern Textile Mill Villages on the Eve of World War II: The Courtnay Mill of South Carolina." *Journal of Economic History* 45 (June 1985): 269–76.

Pitts, Lulie. *History of Gordon County, Georgia (Official)*. Calhoun, Ga.: Press of The Calhoun Times, 1933.

Pope, Liston. *Millhands and Preachers: A Study of Gastonia*. New Haven, Conn.: Yale University Press, 1942.

Potwin, Marjorie A. *Cotton Mill People of the Piedmont: A Study in Social Change*. New York: Columbia University Press, 1927.

Prather, James D. "Woman Who Started Bedspread Boulevard." *Atlanta Journal Magazine*, 11 April 1937, p. 6.

Prior, John P. "From Community to National Unionism: North Carolina Textile Labor Organizations, July 1932–September 1934." M.A. thesis, University of North Carolina, 1972.

Prude, Jonathan. *The Coming of Industrial Order: Town and Factory Life in Rural Massachusetts, 1810–1860*. New York: Cambridge University Press, 1983.

——. "The Social System of Early New England Textile Mills: A Case Study, 1812–40." In *Working-Class America: Essays on Labor, Community, and American Society*, edited by Michael H. Frisch and Daniel J. Walkowitz, pp. 1–36. Urbana: University of Illinois Press, 1983.

Rachleff, Peter. *Black Labor in Richmond, 1865–1890*. Urbana: University of Illinois Press, 1989.

Raitz, Karl B., and Richard Ulack. *Appalachia, a Regional Geography: Land, People, and Development*. Boulder, Colo.: Westview Press, 1984.

Range, Willard. *A Century of Georgia Agriculture, 1850–1950*. Athens: University of Georgia Press, 1954.

Ransom, Roger L., and Richard Sutch. *One Kind of Freedom: The Economic Consequences of Emancipation*. Cambridge: Cambridge University Press, 1977.

Reed, Merl E., Leslie S. Hough, and Gary M Fink. *Southern Workers and Their Unions, 1880–1975: Selected Papers, The Second Southern Labor History Conference, 1978*. Westport, Conn.: Greenwood Press, 1978.

Reeve, Jewell B. *Climb the Hills of Gordon*. Easley, S.C.: Southern Historical Press, 1979.

Rhyne, Jennings J. *Some Southern Cotton Mill Workers and Their Villages*. Chapel Hill: University of North Carolina Press, 1930.

Richards, Paul David. "The History of the Textile Workers Union of America, CIO, in the South, 1937 to 1945." Ph.D. diss., University of Wisconsin, 1978.

Rikoon, J. Sanford. *Threshing in the Midwest, 1820–1940: A Study of Traditional Culture and Technological Change*. Bloomington: Indiana University Press, 1988.

Rodgers, Daniel T. *The Work Ethic in Industrial America, 1850–1920*. Chicago: University of Chicago Press, 1978.

Roland, Charles P. *The Improbable Era: The South since World War II*. Rev. ed. Lexington: University Press of Kentucky, 1976.

Rosner, David, and Gerald Markowitz. *Dying for Work: Workers' Safety and Health in Twentieth-Century America*. Bloomington: Indiana University Press, 1989.

Ross, Steven J. *Workers on the Edge: Work, Leisure, and Politics in Industrializing Cincinnati, 1788–1890*. New York: Columbia University Press, 1985.

Salmond, John A. *Miss Lucy of the CIO: The Life and Times of Lucy Randolph Mason, 1882–1959*. Athens: University of Georgia Press, 1988.

Sartain, James Alfred. *History of Walker County, Georgia*. Dalton, Ga.: A. J. Showalter, 1932.

Savitt, Todd L., and James Harvey Young, eds. *Disease and Distinctiveness in the American South.* Knoxville: University of Tennessee Press, 1988.

Saxonhouse, Gary, and Gavin Wright, eds. *Technique, Spirit, and Form in the Making of Modern Economies: Essays in Honor of William N. Parker.* Greenwich, Conn.: JAI Press, 1984.

Scranton, Philip. *Proprietary Capitalism: The Textile Manufacture at Philadelphia, 1800–1885.* Cambridge: Cambridge University Press, 1983.

———. "Varieties of Paternalism: Industrial Structures and the Social Relations of Production in American Textiles." *American Quarterly* 36 (Summer 1984): 235–57.

Selby, John G. " 'Better to Starve in the Shade than in the Factory': Labor Protest in High Point, North Carolina, in the early 1930s." *North Carolina Historical Review* 65 (January 1987): 43–64.

———. "Industrial Growth and Worker Protest in a New South City: High Point, North Carolina, 1859–1959." Ph.D. diss., University of North Carolina, 1984.

Shaw, Barton C. *The Wool-Hat Boys: Georgia's Populist Party.* Baton Rouge: Louisiana State University Press 1984.

Sherman, William T. *Memoirs of General William T. Sherman.* Westport, Conn.: Greenwood Press, 1977.

Shifflett, Crandall A. *Coal Towns: Life, Work, and Culture in Company Towns.* Knoxville: University of Tennessee Press, 1991.

Shirley, James Michael. "From Congregation Town to Industrial City: Industrialization, Class, and Culture in Nineteenth-Century Winston and Salem, North Carolina." Ph.D. diss., Emory University, 1986.

———. "Yeoman Culture and Millworker Protest in Antebellum Salem, North Carolina." *Journal of Southern History* 57 (August 1991): 427–52.

Shore, Laurence. *Southern Capitalists: The Ideological Leadership of an Elite, 1832–1885.* Chapel Hill: University of North Carolina Press, 1986.

Shriner, Charles H. *History of Murray County.* N.p., 1911.

Singal, Daniel Joseph. *The War Within: From Victorian to Modernist Thought in the South, 1919–1945.* Chapel Hill: University of North Carolina Press, 1982.

Slayton, Robert A. *Back of the Yards: The Making of a Local Democracy.* Chicago: University of Chicago Press, 1986.

Spain, Rufus B. *At Ease in Zion: Social History of Southern Baptists, 1865–1900.* Nashville, Tenn.: Vanderbilt University Press, 1967.

Stanley, Lawrence L. *The Gilmer County Area of Georgia 200 Years Ago and Pages from Gilmer County History, 1832–1977.* N.p., 1977.

———. *A Little History of Gilmer County.* N.p., 1975.

———. *A Rough Road in a Good Land.* N.p., 1971.

Stokes, Allen Heath, Jr. "Black and White Labor in the Development of the Southern Textile Industry, 1880–1920." Ph.D. diss., University of South Carolina, 1977.

Stone, Larry C. "Dalton's Railroads." *Whitfield-Murray Historical Society Journal* 1 (January 1985): 11–13.

Taft, Philip. *Organizing Dixie: Alabama Workers in the Industrial Era.* Revised and edited by Gary M Fink. Westport, Conn.: Greenwood Press, 1981.

Tannenbaum, Frank. "The South Buries Its Anglo-Saxons." *Century* 106 (June 1923): 205–15.

Tentler, Leslie Woodcock. *Wage-Earning Women: Industrial Work and Family Life in the United States, 1900–1930.* New York: Oxford University Press, 1979.

Terrill, Tom E. "Eager Hands: Labor for Southern Textiles, 1850–1860." *Journal of Economic History* 36 (March 1976): 84–101.

——. "Murder in Graniteville." In *Towards a New South?: Studies in Post–Civil War Communities*, edited by Orville Vernon Burton and Robert C. McMath, pp. 193–222. Westport, Conn.: Greenwood Press, 1982.

Thompson, E. P. *The Making of the English Working Class*. New York: Vintage Books, 1966.

——. "Time, Work-Discipline, and Industrial Capitalism." *Past and Present* 38 (December 1967): 56–97.

Thompson, Holland. *From the Cotton Field to the Cotton Mill: A Study of the Industrial Transition in North Carolina*. New York: Macmillan, 1906.

Thompson, K., ed. *Touching Home: A Collection of History and Folklore from the Copper Basin, Fannin County Area*. Orlando, Fla.: Daniel Publishers, 1976.

Tindall, George B. *The Emergence of the New South, 1913–1945*. Baton Rouge: Louisiana State University Press, 1967.

Tippett, Tom. *When Southern Labor Stirs*. New York: Jonathan Cape and Harrison Smith, 1931.

Tompkins, D. A. *Cotton Mill, Commercial Features: A Text-book for the Use of Textile Schools and Investors*. Charlotte, N.C.: privately printed, 1899.

Trotter, Joe William, Jr. *Black Milwaukee: The Making of an Industrial Proletariat, 1915–1945*. Urbana: University of Illinois Press, 1988.

Troy, Leo. *Distribution of Union Membership among the States, 1939 and 1953*. New York: National Bureau of Economic Research, 1957.

——. *Trade Union Membership, 1897–1962*. New York: National Bureau of Economic Research, 1965.

Tullos, Allen. *Habits of Industry: White Culture and the Transformation of the Carolina Piedmont*. Chapel Hill: University of North Carolina Press, 1989.

Walkowitz, Daniel J. *Worker City, Company Town: Iron and Cotton-Worker Protest in Troy and Cohoes, New York, 1855–84*. Urbana: University of Illinois Press, 1978.

Wallace, Anthony F. C. *Rockdale: The Growth of an American Village in the Early Industrial Revolution*. New York: W. W. Norton, 1980.

Wallenstein, Peter. *From Slave South to New South: Public Policy in Nineteenth-Century Georgia*. Chapel Hill: University of North Carolina Press, 1987.

Waller, Altina L. *Feud: Hatfields, McCoys, and Social Change in Appalachia, 1860–1900*. Chapel Hill: University of North Carolina Press, 1988.

Ward, George Gordon. *The Annals of Upper Georgia, Centered in Gilmer County*. Carrollton, Ga.: Thomasson Printing and Office Equipment, 1965.

Warren, Roland I. *The Community in America*. 2d ed. Chicago: Rand McNally, 1972.

Watkins, Floyd C., and Charles H. Watkins. *Yesterday in the Hills*. 1963. Reprint. Athens: University of Georgia Press, 1973.

Watson, Harry L. "Conflict and Collaboration: Yeomen, Slaveholders, and Politics in the Antebellum South." *Social History* 10 (October 1985): 273–98.

Weiher, Kenneth. "The Cotton Industry and Southern Urbanization, 1880–1930." *Explorations in Economic History* 14 (April 1977): 120–40.

Weiman, David F. "The Economic Emancipation of the Non-Slaveholding Class: Upcountry Farmers in the Georgia Cotton Economy." *Journal of Economic History* 45 (March 1985): 71–93.

——. "Petty Commodity Production in the Cotton South: Upcountry Farmers in the Georgia Cotton Economy, 1840–80." Ph.D. diss., Stanford University, 1984.

Weiss, Carla M. *Plant Closings: A Selected Bibliography of Materials Published 1986 through 1990*. Ithaca, N.Y.: ILR Press, 1991.

White, George. *Historical Collections of Georgia*. New York: Pudney and Russell, 1854.

———. *Statistics of the State of Georgia*. Savannah, Ga.: W. Thorne Williams, 1849.

Whites, LeeAnn. "The De Graffenried Controversy: Class, Race, and Gender in the New South." *Journal of Southern History* 54 (August 1988): 449–78.

Whitfield County History Commission. *Official History of Whitfield County, Georgia*. Dalton, Ga.: A. J. Showalter, 1939.

Wiener, Jonathan M. "Class Structure and Economic Development in the American South, 1865–1955." *American Historical Review* 84 (October 1979): 970–92.

———. *Social Origins of the New South: Alabama, 1860–1885*. Baton Rouge: Louisiana State University Press, 1978.

Wilson, George O., ed. *Today and Tomorrow Become Yesterday*. Dalton, Ga: n.p., 1976 (Dalton bicentennial souvenir book; copy at CGA).

Woodman, Harold D. "Sequel to Slavery: The New History Views the Postbellum South." *Journal of Southern History* 43 (November 1977): 523–54.

Woodward, C. Vann. *Origins of the New South, 1877–1913*. Baton Rouge: Louisiana State University Press, 1951.

———. *Tom Watson: Agrarian Rebel*. Savannah, Ga.: Beehive Press, 1938.

Wright, Gavin. "Cheap Labor and Southern Textiles, 1880–1930." *Quarterly Journal of Economics* 96 (November 1981): 605–29.

———. "Cheap Labor and Southern Textiles before 1880." *Journal of Economic History* 39 (September 1979): 655–80.

———. *Old South, New South: Revolutions in the Southern Economy since the Civil War*. New York: Basic Books, 1986.

Wynne, Lewis Nicholas. *The Continuity of Cotton: Planter Politics in Georgia, 1865–1892*. Macon, Ga.: Mercer University Press, 1986.

Young, Marjorie W., ed. *Textile Leaders of the South*. Anderson, S.C.: J. R. Young, 1963.

Zahavi, Gerald. "Negotiated Loyalty: Welfare Capitalism and the Shoeworkers of Endicott Johnson, 1920–1940." *Journal of American History* 70 (December 1983): 602–20.

———. *Workers, Managers, and Welfare Capitalism: The Shoeworkers and Tanners of Endicott Johnson, 1890–1950*. Urbana: University of Illinois Press, 1988.

Zieger, Robert H. *American Workers, American Unions, 1920–1985*. Baltimore: Johns Hopkins University Press, 1986.